# BOXING

# BOXING

## A CULTURAL HISTORY

### KASIA BODDY

REAKTION BOOKS

*For David*

Published by Reaktion Books Ltd
33 Great Sutton Street
London EC1V ODX
www.reaktionbooks.co.uk

First published 2008

Printed and bound in China

British Library Cataloguing in Publication Data
Boddy, Kasia
Boxing : a cultural history
1. Boxing – Social aspects – History
2. Boxing – History
I. Title
796.8'3'09

ISBN 978 1 86189 369 7

# Contents

# Introduction

The symbolism of boxing does not allow for ambiguity; it is, as amateur middleweight Albert Camus put it, 'utterly Manichean'. The rites of boxing 'simplify everything. Good and evil, the winner and the loser.'[1] More than anything, the boxing match has served as a metaphor for opposition – the struggle between two bodies before an audience, usually for money, representing struggles between opposing qualities, ideas and values. In the modern works that this book considers, those struggles involve nationality, class, race, ethnicity, religion, politics, and different versions of masculinity. As light heavyweight Roy Jones, Jr. once said, 'if it made money, it made sense.'[2] But the conflicts dramatized in modern boxing also rework the fundamental oppositions set up in the very earliest texts: brawn versus brain; boastfulness versus modesty; youth versus experience. In literary and artistic terms, the clash is also often one of voices and styles. In the *Protagoras*, Plato even likens the moves and countermoves of Socratic debate to a boxing match.[3]

Boxing, it seems, has been around forever. The first evidence of the sport can be found in Mesopotamian stone reliefs from the end of the fourth millennium BC. Since then there has hardly been a time in which young men, and sometimes women, did not raise their gloved or ungloved fists to one other. William Roberts's 1914 watercolour *The Boxing Match, Novices* conveys the relentless succession of contenders, champions and palookas that makes up the history of boxing. Throughout this history, potters, painters, poets, novelists, cartoonists, song-writers, photographers and film-makers have been there to record and make sense of the bruising, bloody confrontation. 'For some reason,' sportswriter Gary Wills remarked, 'people don't want fighters just to be fighters.'[4]

Writing about boxing is often nostalgic, evoking a golden age long since departed. Today the period most keenly remembered is that of the late 1960s and early '70s, a time dominated by Muhammad Ali, a time, as a recent documentary would have it, 'when we were kings'.[5] Not long before, however, many were sure that the 1930s and '40s represented the peak of excellence, and lamented the arrival of televised sport as the end of a 'heroic cycle'.[6] Further

1
William Roberts,
*The Boxing Match,
Novices*, 1914.

7

back still, early twentieth-century commentators considered the Regency as the time when pugilism flourished as never since; while for Regency writers, true glory and prowess resided in the sport's original manifestations in classical Greece. In the third century AD, Philostratus looked back to the good old days before 'the energetic became sluggards, the hardened became weak, and Sicilian gluttony gained the upper hand'.[7]

Although this book is about boxing in its modern form, myths about the golden ages of classical and Regency boxing have had such a lasting impact on ways of thinking about the sport that I begin with them. The first two chapters chart the early history of boxing and the establishment of ideas about courage and honour, ritual and spectatorship, beauty and the grotesque that are still in use today. The third chapter explores what pugilistic style meant to Regency painters and writers.

The golden age of English boxing was over by 1830. Nevertheless, the sport continued to hold sway over the popular imagination throughout the nineteenth century. Chapter Four considers the divide between (dangerous, illegal) prize fighting and (honourable, muscular Christian) sparring in the Victorian era, and the appeal of each to writers as different as George Eliot and Arthur Conan Doyle. The *fin de siècle* rise of professional boxing (and its association with the development of mass media such as journalism and cinema in America) is the subject of Chapter Five. Women (welcome participants in the eighteenth century) now re-entered the arenas as spectators. Chapter Six shifts the focus to questions of race and ethnicity, investigating the ways in which boxing was associated with assimilation for young Jewish immigrants and the ways in which black American boxers struggled against the early twentieth-century colour line. The career and enormous cultural impact of Jack Johnson, the first of the twentieth-century's great black heavyweights, is explored in some detail. Another iconic presence, Jack Dempsey, dominates Chapter Seven. The chapter considers the sports-mad twenties and argues that many of modernism's styles were self-consciously pugilistic.

The final two chapters take us to the end of the twentieth century. Chapter Eight discusses mid-century representations of boxing and the ways in which the sport now featured largely as a metaphor for corruption and endurance – that is, until a young fighter called Joe Louis emerged on the scene. Finally, Chapter Nine examines the era of Muhammad Ali, television, Black Power, and further compensatory white hopes. The conclusion brings the story up to date, taking into account, among other matters, Mike Tyson and hip hop, conceptual art's glove fetishism and the enduring appeal of sweaty gyms.

# 1

# The Classical Golden Age

Looking back nostalgically from the third century AD to the glorious athletic past of Classical Greece, Philostratus claimed that the Spartans invented boxing.[1] In fact, activities resembling boxing and wrestling were recorded much earlier, in third millennium BC Egypt and Mesopotamia. By the late Bronze Age (1600–1200 BC) images of pugilists could be found across the Eastern Mediterranean – some, like the figures on a Mycenean pot from Cyprus, are fairly sketchy (illus. 2); others, like the fresco of the young *Boxing Boys* from Thera (illus. 43), are striking and detailed.[2] In both cases, the boxers adopt an attitude similar to that found in Greek vase paintings 1,000 years later. The earliest of Greek literary works, the *Iliad* and the *Odyssey*, written in the eighth century BC, describe athletic games held at the time of the Trojan war, traditionally dated around 1200 BC.

The funeral games for Patroclus in the *Iliad* (*c*. 750 BC) include the 'first report of a prize fight' in literature.[3] The games come late in the war, and in the penultimate book of the poem. Anthropologists and classical scholars have long debated the role of sports on such occasions. While some suggest that the funeral games simply served to celebrate the courage of the dead warrior, others argue that they were religious festivals and that sport was linked to ritual sacrifice.[4] Discussions of the symbolic role of boxing and other forms of violent combat sport often draw on Clifford Geertz's essay on Balinese cockfighting, and Réne Girard's *Violence and the Sacred*. Geertz argues that the cockfight should not be seen merely as a form of popular entertainment, but as a blood sacrifice to the forces threatening social order. 'Deep play', a term that Geertz adopts from Bentham, is a game whose stakes are so high that, from a utilitarian point of view, it is irrational to play; this does not make the game unplayable, however, but elevates it. Instead of merely demanding the calculation of odds, the game works symbolically to represent the uncertain gamble that is life itself.[5] The competitors involved in such contests are simultaneously derided and honoured, acting, as Girard put it, as 'substitutes for all the members of the community', while 'offered up by the community itself.'[6] 'The winner symbolically "lives" by winning the ritual contest, the losers "die"', and the spectators are vaccinated 'with the evil of violence against the evil of violence'.[7]

2
Two boxers on
a fragment of a
Mycenaean pot
from Cyprus,
*c.* 1300–1200 BC.

The games described in the penultimate book of the *Iliad* certainly do more than simply provide more entertaining fight scenes. Most commentators read the funeral games for Patroclus as one of the poem's 'representative moments'; that is, they encapsulate the issues of honour and reward that the poem usually dramatizes on the battlefield.[8] For some commentators, their function is to 'purify' combat – that is, to imitate it but conceal its true deadly character.[9] For others, though, the real point is that, to the watching gods, the horrors of war (involving such dramatic moments as Achilles' pursuit of Hector) is itself like an athletic spectacle.[10] Prize-giving – the nature and function of reward – forms the topic of much debate. The boxing contest is preceded by Achilles giving Nestor a two-handled bowl 'simply as a gift', for now 'old age has its cruel hold' upon him. He accepts it, acknowledging that 'now it is for younger men to face these trials'. The prizes for the boxing match are then set forth: the winner will receive 'a hard-working mule', signifying endurance, the loser a two-handled cup. Prefiguring the boasts of Muhammad Ali, Epeios claims the prize before any competitor has even stepped forward:

> I say I am the greatest . . . It will certainly be done as I say – I will smash right through the man's skin and shatter his bones. And his friends had better gather here ready for his funeral, to carry him away when my fists have broken him.[11]

Finally someone steps forward, Euryalos, another 'godlike man' of noble lineage, though we hear little about him. It seems to be an even match, but Homer presents it in very general terms – a 'flurry of heavy hands meeting', a 'fearful crunching of jaws', followed by a knockout blow to Euryalos's collarbone. All that matters is that Epeios's boasts are justified – he *is* the greatest (after all, he is also the man who designed the wooden horse). 'Godlike', he is also described as 'great-hearted' because, despite his threats, he does not kill his opponent, but lifts him to his feet. Symbolic conflict acts as the transition between combat with consequences and combat with none, between narrative complication and closure. It quarantines real violence (the crunching of jaws) by enfolding it between two layers of symbolic violence (the bloodthirsty boast, the raising of the vanquished). Boxing, here, is the ultimate deep play.

Justified boastfulness also features in the *Odyssey* (*c.* 725 BC). In book eight, the Phaeacians seek to impress the travel-weary Odysseus with a display of their athletic prowess. All goes well until Laodamas, son of the prince and a champion boxer, urges their guest to participate, telling him, 'there is no greater glory that can befall a man living than what he achieves by speed of his feet or strength of his hands'. When Odysseus declines, arguing that home is all he can think of, Laodamas rashly counters, 'You do not resemble an athlete.' Such a challenge does not go unanswered by the 'darkly resourceful Odysseus'. He grabs a heavy discus, and then offers to take on anyone at boxing, wrestling or running, 'except Laodamas / himself, for he is my host; who would fight with his friend?'[12] The crisis is averted when the prince intervenes with music and dancing. Odysseus is less successful in avoiding a fight when, ten books later, disguised again, he returns home to Ithaca. There, Iros, a large and greedy beggar, insults him gratuitously. Egged on by Penelope's suitors, Iros rejects Odysseus's claim of solidarity between beggars and demands a 'battle of hands'.[13] The suitors enjoy this tremendously and offer prizes. Here we find the first instance of spectators as villains in a boxing story: unwilling to fight themselves, but vicariously enjoying the risks someone else will run, and gambling on the outcome.[14] Although Odysseus is outweighed and does not fight at full capacity (he is still anxious to conceal his identity), he manages to break some bones in Iros's neck, and as a final humiliation drags his opponent's prostrate body to the foot of the courtyard wall. Survival is the issue here, not prize-winning. The contest is 'a street fight that happens to involve a very skilful athlete in disguise'.[15] If the *Iliad* reminds us of Ali's theatrical boasting, the *Odyssey* anticipates his resilience.

Such pragmatism was of no use to subsequent idealizations of pugilism's golden age. As Tom Winnifrith points out, 'there is not in Homer the belief that behaving well somehow wins matches and battles'.[16] However reluctant Odysseus is to fight, when persuaded he does not hold back. Honour and restraint, however, were central to the Virgilian ethos of the Roman Empire. It was Virgil, not Homer, who was evoked by the nineteenth-century muscular Christians, and the founding of the modern Olympics in 1896 was 'fired by Virgilian enthusiasm'.[17] Greater honour, paradoxically, was accompanied by even greater brutality. This is apparent if we compare the gloves used in Greek and Roman times.[18] Today, boxers tend to use eight- to ten-ounce gloves in competition and anything up to eighteen-ounce gloves for sparring. Heavier gloves give greater protection both to the hands of the person striking the blow, and to the face and body of the blow's recipient. Until around the end of the fifth century BC, strips of leather of between ten and twelve feet long were used as 'soft gloves' (*himantes*). These protected the knuckles rather than the opponent's face. They were replaced by *caestus*, 'sharp gloves', lined with metal, which could maim and even kill an opponent (illus. 3). Dryden translated Virgil's *caestus* as:

> The Gloves of Death, with sev'n distinguish'd folds,
> Of tough Bull Hides; the space within is spread
> With Iron, or with loads of heavy Lead.[19]

This sounds like the kind of excessive violence, much more than sufficient to its purpose, that Odysseus tried hard to avoid.

The fact that boxing gloves were made of bull hide may have been the reason that boxers and bulls were often compared with each other. In the *Argonautica*, Apollonius likens Amycus and Polydeuces to 'a pair of bulls angrily disputing for a grazing heifer', while Virgil, in the *Georgics*, describes a young heifer as he trains for a fight, 'learn[ing] to put / Fury into his horns' and 'sparring with the air'.[20] The link between boxers and bulls continued into the twentieth century with men fighting under names like 'El Toro' and 'Bronx Bull', and their opponents figured as matadors. Hemingway admired the way a particular animal used his left and right horn, 'just like a boxer', while for Mailer, it was George Foreman's ability to use his gloves 'like horns' that made him so dangerous.[21]

The funeral games for Anchises staged in the *Aeneid* (19 BC) recall, and to some extent imitate, those of the *Iliad*. But Virgil's structure is more intricate and his tone is quite different from Homer's easy exuberance.[22] The boat and foot races over, Aeneas sets out prizes for the boxing – a bullock for the victor, and a sword and helmet for the loser. As in the *Iliad*, one man comes forward immediately. Here is it Dares, the Trojan, 'who stood there with his head held high to begin the battle, flexing his shoulders, throwing lefts and rights and thrashing the air. They looked around for an opponent, but no one in all that company dared go near him or put on the gloves'. Thinking there is to be no contest, Dares goes to collect the bullock as his prize. Only then does Entellus, spurred on by Acestes, come forward.

Dares is obviously modelled on the brash and youthful Epeios, but while Homer simply confirms that Epeios is 'godlike' with a straightforward victory, Virgil makes both character and action more complicated. Entellus is not presented as just any opponent (as Euryalos had been in the *Iliad*); he is motivated less by a desire for prizes or boastfulness than by a complex mixture of emotions. Acestes' words have roused his sense of honour; he feels indebted to his teacher, the god Eryx; he does not want to be thought a liar, or a coward; he feels himself a representative of Sicily against Troy. In all things Entellus is the antithesis of Dares:

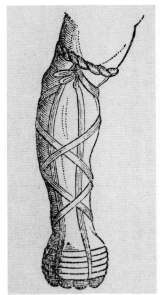
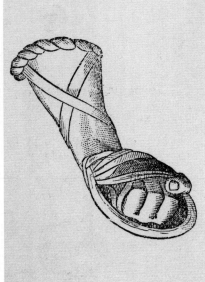
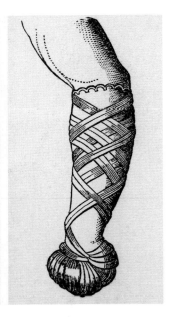

3
Three types of early
boxing glove.

Dares had youth on his side and speed of foot. Entellus had the reach
and the weight, but his knees were going. He was slow and shaky and his
whole huge body heaved with the agony of breathing. Blow upon blow
they threw at each other and missed. Blow upon blow drummed on the
hollow rib cage, boomed on the chest and showered round the head and
ears, and the cheekbones rattled with the weight of the punches.

Dares begins well, knocking Entellus down; the giant man falls 'as a hollow pine
tree falls, torn up by the roots on great Mount Ida' – a common simile in classical, and subsequent, depictions of fights. But, as we might expect, this only
spurs on Entellus:

> He returned to the fray with his ferocity renewed and anger rousing
> him to new heights of violence. His strength was kindled by shame at
> his fall and pride in his prowess, and in a white heat of fury he drove
> Dares before him all over the arena, hammering him with rights and
> lefts and allowing him no rest or respite. Like hailstones from a dark
> cloud rattling down on roofs, Entellus battered Dares with a shower of
> blows from both hands and sent him spinning.[23]

Dares may have the strength, youth and confidence of a young animal, but
Entellus, armed with psychological demons as well as mere muscles, is a true
force of nature – falling like a pine tree and retaliating with blows like hailstones.
Nature, or 'savage passion', must, however, be controlled, and so 'Father Aeneas'
intervenes and ends the fight. This is one of the first fight stories in which the
restraining referee is the hero.[24] Aeneas tells Dares to acknowledge that 'the

13

divine will has turned against you', while Entellus ritually slaughters the bull he has won in honour of Eryx, and retires from boxing. The two men play no further part in the poem: boxing itself seems like a relic from some long-gone mythic age. The values of Augustan Rome have been made clear: piety is the basis for power and success; temperance and restraint the mark of a military leader.[25]

In years to come, the fights described by Homer and Virgil would provide models for many writers. Both tell stories of drama and suspense, but each has a different emphasis. In Homer, fighting may come as a last resort but when it does, no punches are pulled, and there is no need to be modest about one's prowess. Virgil's fighters are equipped with lethal gloves, but checked by the need to govern their anger, and by vanity.


## BOXING BY ANALOGY

Homer and Virgil both compare conduct in games to that in war. It is not always the case that the same man is good at both activities, merely that they are analogous. In the *Iliad*, Epeios's boast begins, 'Is it not enough that I am less good in battle? . . . a man cannot be expert in all things'.[26] Less expert at boxing, but more so at battle, is Achilles, yet he shares with Epeios a firm belief in his own ability. He boasts that no one is a match for him, and we soon see that no one can challenge his 'invincible hands'.[27] And in the *Aeneid*, we are reminded of Dares and Enthellus when later we come to compare the behaviour of Turnus and Aeneas in a real fight to the death.[28] The relationship between pugilism and war is also at the forefront of many of Plato's references to boxing (three of his dialogues are set in the gymnasium and *palaestra*). In the *Laws*, he argues for the necessity of training soldiers to be prepared for war by comparing them with boxers training for fight ('if we were training boxers . . . would we go straight into the ring unprepared by a daily work-out against an opponent?'); in the *Republic* the analogy is extended further – as 'one boxer in perfect training is easily a match for two men who are not boxers, but rich and fat', so a well-prepared Athens could go to war against wealthier and more powerful enemies.[29]

Boxing similes were not only used in discussions of war and its attendant virtues and risks. They can also be found, for example, in debates about the qualities needed for successful political debating (Plutarch) and ways of dealing with the dishonest in everyday life (Marcus Aurelius).[30] Aristotle evokes boxing in the *Nicomachean Ethics* (*c.* 330 BC) when he wants to explain the nature of pain and pleasure in courage. Men who withstand painful things, he writes, are brave, while those spurred on by passions such as revenge are 'pugnacious but not brave'. Sometimes, however, there is a gap between the pleasant end 'which courage sets before itself' and the painful 'attending circumstances'. This is the case in athletic contests:

> the end at which boxers aim is pleasant – the crown and the honours –
> but the blows they take are distressing to flesh and blood, and painful,

and so is their whole exertion; and because the blows and the exertions are many the end, which is but small, appears to have nothing in it.[31]

Boxers are brave because, in the heat of the fight, it is not prizes but virtue (courage) that motivates them. Courage, like all Aristotelian virtues, operates as a mediating strategy between other qualities; here, confidence and fear. Too much confidence, or too little fear, and no courage is needed; too much fear or too little confidence, and one is paralyzed.

The use of boxing analogies to discuss virtue was not restricted to classical philosophy. The nature of courage required for religious struggle (and the importance of keeping your eyes on the prize) was one of the subjects of the First Letter to the Corinthians (c. 48 AD). There Paul insists that he is a genuine fighter rather than a shadow boxer ('one that beateth the air', in the King James version). Moreover, he goes on, in a phrase that would prove resonant for muscular Christianity, 'I keep under my own body, and bring it into subjection.'[32]

## AT THE GAMES

Boxing played an important part in the games of ancient Greece; both in the four great Panhellenic festivals – the Olympian, Pythian, Nemean and Isthmian – and in the numerous local games held in individual cities. The most prestigious Games, the Olympic, began in 776 BC, and boxing was introduced in 688 BC.[33] The festival spanned five days; the first and last were reserved for ceremonies and celebrations; boxing took place on the fourth day at midday so that neither competitor had the sun in his eyes. The sport was similar to modern boxing to the extent that each competitor attempted to injure or exhaust his opponent by punching him. There were, however, no rounds, rest periods, weight classes or points systems. There was no rule against hitting an opponent when down and no confined ring. Boxers were paired by lot; a single elimination format was used. A winner was declared when one boxer was no longer physically able to continue (illus. 4). Although the Olympic ideal has long been evoked as a model of fairness and sportsmanship, often in contrast to modern corruption, Pausanias's *Guide to Greece* (170 AD) reveals that fight fixing actually began at the 98th Olympics:

> Eulopos of Thessaly bribed the boxers who entered, Agetor of Arkadia and Prytanis of Kyzikos, and also Phormion of Halikarnassos, who won the boxing at the previous Olympics. This is said to have been the first crime ever committed in the games, and Eulopos and the men he bribed were the first to be fined . . .[34]

The Romans were generally disdainful of the Greek love of the gymnasium, but boxing also played a part in the Ludi Romani. According to Suetonius, 'none

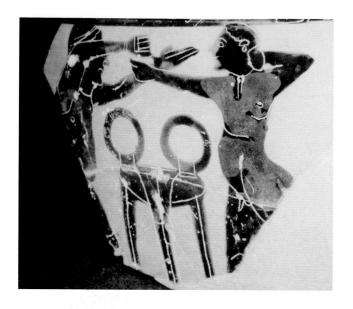

4
Boxers with prize
tripod in back-
ground, fragment
of Black-figure
vase, mid-sixth
century BC.

of Augustus's predecessors had ever provided so many, so different, or such splen-
did public shows'. He goes on to detail wild-beast hunts, mock sea-battles and
gladiatorial shows of all kinds, but says that Augustus's 'chief delight was to watch
boxing, particularly when the fighters were Italians – and not merely professional
bouts, in which he often used to pit Italians against Greeks or Africans against
each other, but slogging matches between untrained roughs in narrow city alleys'
(illus. 5).[35] The boxers in these contests used the oxhide *caestus*, and injuries were
severe. This perhaps accounts for Augustus's introduction of a series of regulations as to who could take part (a senatorial decree banned persons 'of good
family' from events such as boxing) and who could watch such contests.[36]
Suetonius notes that whereas 'men and women had hitherto always sat together,
Augustus confined women to the back rows even at gladiatorial shows':

> No women at all were allowed to witness the athletic contests; indeed,
> when the audience clamoured at the Games for a special boxing match
> to celebrate his appointment as Chief Pontiff, Augustus postponed this
> until early the next morning, and issued a proclamation to the effect
> that it was the Chief Pontiff's desire that women should not attend the
> Theatre before ten o'clock.[37]

In a reassessment of Plato's *Laws*, Cicero argued that the theatre should be kept
free from the bloody sport of the Games, but it is clear that some infiltration
took place.[38] Horace complained of crowds calling out for boxers or bears in
the middle of a play, while Terence attributed the failure of one his plays to the
rival attraction of boxing.[39] A couple of millennia later, Bertolt Brecht was to
make a new theatre out of such infiltrations. While Brecht felt that boxing fans
viewed the sport with cool objectivity and rationally judged the performance

16

of each participant, the more common view (exemplified in every Hollywood fight film and first expressed in another classic work of the late Roman Empire, St Augustine's *Confessions*) was that boxing degrades its audience as much as its participants. St Augustine tells the story of a reluctant visit to the gladiatorial arena by his pupil, Alypius. At first Alypius closes his eyes, but he cannot close his ears. When the crowd roars, he is unable to contain his curiosity and so opens his eyes. Immediately, and dramatically, he is corrupted by what he sees: 'he fell, and fell more pitifully than the man whose fall had drawn that roar of excitement from the crowd'.[40]

The funeral games of Homer's and Virgil's epics provide one enduring model for depicting sporting events. Another can be found in the odes, known as epinicians (epi-Niké-ans), written by the fifth-century BC poets Pindar and Bacchylides, in celebration of the victors in the athletic games.

> To the lyre the Muse granted tales of gods and children of gods, of the victor in boxing, of the horse first in the race, of the loves of swains, and of freedom over wine.[41]

> Pierian Muses, daughters
> of Zeus who rules
> on high, you are famed for your
> skill with the lyre: strum
> and weave for us then intricate
> songs for Argeius, the junior boxer,
> the Isthmian games' victor.[42]

If epic poetry memorialized battles that spanned decades and had national significance, the epinician celebrated the fleeting triumphs of sport, giving 'lasting form to the deed of the moment.'[43]

> I look for help to the Muses
> with their blue-black hair,
> to bless my song of how, in this life,
> contingent, ephemeral,
> a few things somehow endure.[44]

The victories of the athletes were often represented as imitative of the battle victories of epic heroes such as Achilles and Odysseus, whose triumphs in turn were compared to those of the gods.

> Let Hagesidamos
> Who has won in the boxing at Olympia,
> Thank Illas as Patroklos thanked Achilles.
> One born to prowess
> May be whetted and stirred
> To win huge glory
> If a God be his helper.[45]

Also located within this hierarchy of kinds of victory was the poet himself, without whom all heroes would be forgotten, and whose memorializing skill was itself worthy of praise (and medals).[46] A different notion of honour emerges, one less directly attached to the virtues necessary for combat and having more to do with those essential to art. According to Richmond Lattimore, it was the 'very uselessness of . . . [the athletic] triumphs which attracted Pindar': 'A victory meant that time, expense, and hard work had been lavished on an achievement that brought no calculable advantage, only honour and beauty.'[47]

> Father Zeus, ruler on Atabyrion's ridges,
> Honour the rite of Olympian victory,
>
> And a man who has found prowess in boxing.
> Grant him favour and joy
> From citizens and strangers.
> For he goes straight on a road that hates pride,
> And knows well what a true heart
> From noble fathers has revealed to him.[48]

The odes of Bacchylides and Pindar, which firmly connect the activities of the poet with those of the athlete, were echoed in Roman times by Horace and by neo-classical poets in the eighteenth century.[49] It might be argued that epinician tradition also lies behind some of the more extravagant claims made by sports-writers in modern times.

## THE BODY, BEAUTIFUL AND VULNERABLE

Today classical Greek athletics continues to fascinate us, not simply because of the sporting principles it initiated, but because of the language it provides for talking about the human body, and, particularly, its glories. Training, and the culture of the gymnasium, are treated widely in Greek literature, and much writing about that culture focuses on the beauties of the naked bodies displayed there. Disapproving of the violence of the Roman gladiatorial contests, Dio Chrysostom sets up an alternative in the gentler, more philosophical, world of the Greek gymnasium where his ideal boxer Melancomas 'did not consider it courage to strike his opponent or to receive an injury himself, but thought this indicated a lack of stamina and a desire to have done with the contest'. Melancomas's unblemished beauty is directly linked to his moral virtues – his discipline, courage, modesty and self-control. Dio compares Melancomas to his closest rival, Iatrocles, whom he remembers in training.

> He was a very tall and beautiful young man; and besides, the exercises he was taking made his body seem, quite naturally, still taller and more beautiful. He was giving a most brilliant performance, and in so spirited a way that he seemed more like a man in an actual contest. Then, when he stopped exercising and the crowd began to draw away, we studied him more closely. He was just like one of the most care-

fully wrought statues, and also he had a colour like well blended bronze.[50]

If Melancomas's beauty reveals his inner virtue, that of Iatrocles exists on the surface only.[51]

The comparison of (stationary) athletes with statues would prove enduring and later commentators were less inclined to worry about the gap between outer and inner beauty. Boxing's revival in the eighteenth century coincided with a revival of interest in the classics, and much writing about the male boxer, then and later, drew on notions of statuesque perfection as exemplified by Greek athletes. In 1755, for example, the German Hellenist, Winckelmann, famously argued that the excellence of Greek art was, in some part, due to the availability of fine models:

> The gymnasia, where, sheltered by public modesty, the youths exercised themselves naked, were the schools of art. These the philosopher frequented, as well as the artist. Socrates for the instruction of a Charmides, Autolycus, Lysis; Phidias for the improvement of his art by their beauty. Here he studied the elasticity of the muscles, the ever varying motions of the frame, the outlines of fair forms, or the contour left by the young wrestler in the sand. Here beautiful nakedness appeared with such liveliness of expression, such truth and variety of situations, such a noble air of the body, as it would be ridiculous to look for in any hired model of our academies.[52]

Gymnasia were, of course, also places of seduction and athletic statues often highly eroticized, but Winckelmann insisted that 'ideal beauty' was about establishing a connection to 'something superior to nature; ideal beauties, brainborn images' – what James Davidson defines as 'the sculptural complement to the idealism of Platonic philosophy'. 'The ideal body is not at all earthly or earthy: it provides an accurate material reflection of the heavenly, the insubstantial and the divine.'[53]

There was, however, one undeniable difference between artistic and real life bodies. Whereas art is long, the real bodies exemplifying physical perfection, were, of course, perishable. Pindar's odes capture the fleeting moments of an ideal physical state as well as those of victory. The very transience of the ideal body is made all the more poignant by the less than perfect bodies that surround it. This phenomenon is foregrounded in boxing – and not in other Olympic sports such as the discus or running – by the fact that while the processes of training are all about perfecting the body, and while at the moment of triumph, the body may move beautifully, the sport itself is all about damaging (and making ugly) the body.[54] Apollonian form could only temporarily contain Dionysian energy. The odd exception only serves to prove the rule. Dio Chrysostom praises Melancomas – 'although boxing was his speciality, he

remained as free from marks as any of the runners' – while, much later, the thought of 'pretty boy' Janiro's unmarked face fuels Jake La Motta's paranoia in Martin Scorsese's *Raging Bull*.[55]

The damaged body of the boxer appeared in literature and art as early as its beautiful counterpart. A popular model for later writers, Theocritus's version of the mythical fight between Polydeuces and Amycus in the *Idylls* (third century BC) was based on real fights he had seen in the stadium. His account is alert to technical detail and strategy, but perhaps even more memorable are his graphic descriptions of the wounds that fighters carry and inflict.[56] While searching for the legendary golden fleece, Castor and Polydeuces – sons of Leda and Zeus, and brothers of Helen of Troy – are shipwrecked on Bebrycia. There, in a grove, Polydeuces,

6
Etruscan engraved bronze; probably Polydeuces training with a punch bag, with Amycus to his right; late fourth century BC.

an Olympic champion, encounters Amycus, the King of the Bebryces, brother of the Cyclops and 'a giant of a man' (illus. 6):

> He was an awesome spectacle: His ears were thickened
> By blows from leather mitts, and his huge chest and broad back swelled
> Like the iron flesh of a hammered statue. Where his shoulders and hard arms
> Met, the muscles jutted out like rounded boulders, polished smooth
> By the whirling onrush of a winter torrent.

One thing leads to another and soon the 'son of Zeus' has challenged the aggressive and inhospitable 'son of Poseidon' to a fight, the loser agreeing to become the winner's slave. The description that follows relishes the damage done to 'this huge / Mound of a man':

> A loud cheer rose from the heroes, when they saw the ugly wounds
> Around Amycus' mouth and jaw, and his eyes narrowed to slits in his
> Swollen face. . .

Another punch and Amycus's nose is skinned; a few more and his face is 'smashed' into 'a dreadful pulp. / His sweating flesh collapsed, and his colossal form shrank in on itself'. Finally, Polydeuces finishes off the fight with a blow to his opponent's mouth, head and left temple ('The bone cracked open, and the dark blood spurted out'). With Amycus lying 'near to death', Polydeuces, clear-skinned and with 'limbs enlarged', walks away.[57] He lets his opponent live.[58]

The contest between modern Greek speed, skill and 'guile', and mythic bulk has proved unsatisfyingly one-sided.[59] The main purpose of Theocritus's description seems to be to dwell on the damage done, a purpose not unheard-of in subsequent representations of pugilism.

Not all depictions of a boxer's injuries are marked by such gruesome relish. Many are simply documentary; vase paintings often depict blood streaming from the boxer's nose as well as from cuts on his cheeks.[60] A more sophisticated realism can be found in the fourth-century statue of a battered boxer, sometimes known as 'The Pugilist at Rest' (illus. 7).[61] In a 1993 short story of that title, the American writer Thom Jones describes it:

> The statue depicts a muscular athlete approaching his middle age. He has a thick beard and a full head of curly hair. In addition to the telltale broken nose and cauliflower ears of a boxer, the pugilist has the slanted, drooping brows that bespeak broken nerves. Also, the forehead is piled with scar tissue . . .
>
> The pugilist is sitting on a rock with his forearms balanced on his thighs. That he is seated and not pacing implies that he has been through all this many times before. It appears that he is conserving his strength. His head is turned as if he were looking over his shoulder – as if someone had just whispered something to him. It is in this that the 'art' of the sculpture is conveyed to the viewer. Could it be that someone has just summoned him to the arena? There is a slight look of befuddlement on his face, but there is no trace of fear . . . Beside the deformities on his noble face, there is also the suggestion of weariness and philosophical resignation.[62]

The sculpture is notable for the acute detail in its rendering of wounds both long-accumulated and from the immediate fight. Scars are visible all over the body but especially on the face, the nose is broken, the right eye swollen. Moreover, the bronze statue has red copper inlaid in order to indicate fresh facial wounds and blood that has dripped down on to the right arm and thigh. Attention is also drawn to the athlete's tangled hair, his finger and toenails, weary face and sagging muscle. 'No other work of art from antiquity,' writes Harris 'takes us into the stadium with such intimacy as this statue.'[63]

The destruction of the boxer's body, and in particular his face, also provides the basis of much gruesome humour in Lucilius's debunking epigrams:

> Your head, Apollophanes, has become a sieve, or the lower edge of a worm-eaten book, all exactly like ant-holes, crooked and straight . . . But go on boxing without fear, for even if you are struck on the head you will have the marks you have – you can't have more.[64]

With loss of face comes loss of identity:

7
*The Pugilist at Rest*, also known as the *Terme Boxer*, bronze copy, 1st century AD, of a signed 4th-century sculpture by Apollonius.

When Ulysses after twenty years came safe to his home, Argos the dog recognized his appearance when he saw him, but you, Stratophon, after boxing for four hours, have become not only unrecognizable to dogs but to the city. If you will trouble to look at your face in a glass, you will say on your oath, 'I am not Stratophon.'[65]

Narcissus died because he fell in love his own reflected image. By this reckoning, however, the vanity of boxers is likely to prove short-lived:

> Having such a mug, Olympicus, go not to a fountain nor look in any transparent water, for you, like Narcissus, seeing your face clearly, will die, hating yourself to the death.[66]

While ancient literature and art have provided models for subsequent depictions of the boxer as an exemplar of either statuesque beauty or grotesque injury (often contrasted as the ideal and the real), it is worth remembering that the figure that most appealed to aficionados was neither. Philostratus notes that while the best fighters have small bellies, 'such people are light and have good respiration', a big-bellied boxer also has a certain advantage, 'for such a belly hinders blows at the face.'[67]

## BOXING AGAINST EROS

The body was never, of course, merely a sign of temporal vulnerability and metaphysical dissolution. The *palaestra* was also the setting for homoerotic admiration and seduction, where the vulnerable as well as the statuesque body proved attractive:

> When Menecharmus, Anticles's son, won the boxing match, I crowned him with ten soft fillets, and thrice I kissed him all dabbled with blood as he was, but the blood was sweeter to me than myrrh.[68]

Although most writing about exercise focuses on men, women also used gymnasia and, in Greece, participated in women's games.[69] This fuelled heterosexual fantasies, particularly among nostalgic Romans. One of Ovid's *Heroides*, a series of imaginary letters from mythical figures to their lovers, is a letter from Paris to Helen. In it he describes the power of her beauty and imagines Theseus coming upon her competing in the *palaestra*, 'a naked maiden with naked men'. 'I revere his act, I can only wonder / why he ever let you be returned.'[70] Another Augustan love poet, Propertius, also evokes Helen in recalling the glory days of Spartan athletics. Particularly commendable was the Spartan practice of having naked men and women competing together. Propertius waxes lyrical about naked women 'covered in dust' at the finishing-post, and with swords strapped to 'snow-white thighs'. Even the binding of 'arms with thongs for boxing' excites him, and he imagines two bare-breasted Amazons resembling Pollux and Castor '(One soon to be prize boxer, the other horseman)/ Between whom Helen with bare nipples took up arms.' Roman women, in contrast, pay 'boring attention to perfumed hair'.[71]

If pugilism had its erotic qualities, erotic love could also be seen as a potentially pugilistic activity:

Bring water, bring wine, O boy, and bring me the flowery
Crowns. Bring them, since I am indeed boxing against Eros!
(Anacreon)

Whoever challenges Eros to a match
Like a boxer fist-to-fist, he is out of his wits.
(Sophocles)[72]

Multiple contests are possible: the lover struggles against the conventional resistance of the beloved; rival lovers compete; the lover's desire struggles for expression. Boxing might even be easier than love. In another epigram by Lucilius,
sexual yielding is more devastating than any acknowledgment of defeat in the
stadium:

> Cleombrotos ceased to be a pugilist, but afterwards married and now
> has at home all the blows of the Isthmian and Nemean games, a pug-
> nacious old woman hitting as hard as in the Olympian fights, and he
> dreads his own house more than he ever dreaded the ring. Whenever
> he gets his wind, he is beaten with all the strokes known in every match
> to make him pay her his debt; and if he pays it, he is beaten again.[73]

But love and pugilism are not only comparable as amateur sports; in some ways
the analogy works better on the professional level. Thomas F. Scanlon notes
that athletes and courtesans are paired in many poems, and describes a fifth-
century BC column-krater which places on opposite sides, and in near-identical
poses, an athlete and a courtesan. 'The pun may be interpreted on several
levels,' he writes: 'she is "athletic"; he is a "courtesan" whose prizes are her
payment; both place a premium on the beauty of the body; both possess
erotic attraction.'[74]

In the classical era, then, boxing was the literal or metaphoric subject of a
great variety of representations, many of which will recur in the chapters which
follow. More often than not, whether it is Homer describing the contest between Epeios and Euryalos, or Aristotle defining courage, or Pindar the function
of poetry, or Lucilius marriage, the representations turn on a violence which is
at once actual and symbolic. It is the inextricable mixture in pugilism of high
decorum and low cunning, of beauty and damage, of rhetoric and bodily fluids,
which has made it for so long and so productively a way to imagine conflict.

# 2

# The English Golden Age

There is some evidence, from thirteenth-century legal records and fourteenth-century psalters, that sports resembling wrestling, cudgelling and boxing existed in Britain in the Middle Ages (illus. 8).[1] These references, however, are fleeting; fighting with hands and sticks was a plebeian rather than an aristocratic activity, and as such did not feature in medieval art and literature to the same extent as sports such as jousting, archery or hunting. By the sixteenth century, British boxing's Greek origins had been largely forgotten and if the sport was considered at all, it was grouped with other rowdy rural pastimes such as cock-fighting and bear-baiting; all were outlawed under the Puritan government of Cromwell.[2] When the Restoration brought a relaxation of public morality, many traditional rural sports became popular in the expanding cities, 'supported by city nobles, local squires migrating to the commercial centers, and growing numbers of working-class men.'[3] In the cities these sports began to change. Between 1500 and 1800, Peter Burke notes, 'there was a gradual shift taking place from the more spontaneous and participatory forms of entertainment towards the more formally-organised and commercialised spectator sports, a shift which was, of course, to go much further after 1800'.[4] Samuel Pepys's diary for 5 August 1660 notes (in one short paragraph) a trip to the doctor to fetch an ointment for his sick wife, dinner at Westminster, attending Common Prayer at St Margaret's church, and, undoubtedly the highlight of his day, 'a fray' at Westminster stairs between 'Mynheer Clinke, a Dutchman, that was at Hartlib's wedding, and a waterman, which made good sport'.[5]

The first boxing-match recorded in a newspaper, *The Protestant Mercury*, took place in 1681 in the presence of the Duke of Albemarle, with the winner, a butcher, already recognized 'the best at that exercise in England'.[6] The tradesmen who most depended on upper-body strength – watermen, butchers and blacksmiths – were the ones most frequently associated with pugilism in the days before the sport became 'scientific'.

In 1719, James Figg opened an indoor arena, or, as he called it, 'Amphitheatre', and school near Adam and Eve Court off London's Oxford Road (now Oxford Street), where he taught boxing along with quarterstaff, backsword and

8
Two men wrestling, flanked by spectators, one of whom holds a pole surmounted by a cockerel, a prize for the winner; Bas-de-page scene, detail from the Queen Mary Psalter, c. 1310–20

9
Anonymous printmaker, *Figg's Card*, c. 1794.

cudgelling. A promotional card (once attributed to Hogarth) was distributed at Figg's booth at Southwark Fair, and his advertisements promised that the booth was 'fitted up in a most commodious manner for the better reception of gentlemen' (illus. 9). Samuel Johnson's uncle, Andrew, ran a similar booth at Smithfield meat market.[7]

Although boxing matches were frequently advertised as 'trials of manhood', women as well as men could often be found fighting at the booths and bear-garden (illus. 10).[8] In August 1723, *The London Journal* noted that 'scarce a week passes but we have a Boxing-Match at the Bear-Garden between women'.[9] It would not have been unusual, while browsing the newspaper, to come upon a challenge and reply such as this (from 1722):

CHALLENGE
I, Elizabeth Wilkinson of Clerkenwell, having had some words with Hannah Hyfield, and requiring satisfaction, do invite her to meet me upon the stage, and box me for three guineas, each woman holding half a crown in each hand, and the first woman that drops the money to lose the battle.

ANSWER
I, Hannah Hyfield, of Newgate-market, hearing of the resoluteness of Elizabeth Wilkinson, will not fail, God willing, to give her more blows than words – desiring home blows, and from her no favour; she may expect a good thumping![10]

Most reports of women's fighting (all are written by men) focused on the scanty dress rather than the skill of the participants. Foreign visitors to London were particularly intrigued. Recalling his visit to London in 1710, von Uffenbach described a fight between two women 'without stays and in nothing but a shift', while Martin Nogüe's *Voyages et Aventures* (1728) reported matches between girls and women 'stripped to the waist'; William Hickey, meanwhile, described coming upon two women boxing near Drury Lane in 1749, 'their faces entirely covered in blood, bosoms bare, and the clothes nearly torn from their bodies'.[11] Pierre Jean Grosley was particularly outraged to see a fight between a man and a woman in Holborn: 'I was witness to five or six bouts of the combat; which surprised me the more, as the woman had, upon her left arm, an infant a year or two old, which was so far from crying out, as is natural for children to do even in circumstances of less danger, that it did not so much as seem to knit its brow, but appeared to attend to a lesson of what it was one day to practice itself.'[12]

The quality of English fighting women received patriotic endorsement in the anonymous *Sal Dab Giving Monsieur a Receipt in Full* of 1766 (illus. 11). Sal bloodies the nose of a dandyish Frenchman who, despite his general hopelessness, has managed to lay bare her bosoms; another woman, meanwhile, applies a lobster to his naked bottom. A pub-sign above advertises 'The Good Woman'.[13]

10
Butler Clowes (after John Collett), *The Female Bruisers*, 1770, mezzotint.

Boxing began to flourish in the early eighteenth century, at the expense of other sports such as quarterstaff and backsword, by attracting the support of the wealthy and powerful. In 1723 a ring was erected in Hyde Park 'by order of his Majesty' George I, and the next champion of note, a former Thames waterman called John Broughton, secured the patronage of the Duke of Cumberland. The early patrons supported their fighters in training and wagered huge sums on their fights; *The Gentleman's Magazine* reported in one instance that 'many thousands depended' on the outcome of a fight.[14] Without the eighteenth-century love of gambling, argues Dennis Brailsford, 'pugilism . . . would have been unthinkable', and with large bets came a need for rules to limit disputes.[15] The great Enlightenment project of systemization and law-making thus extended to pugilism, with the first written rules of prize-fighting published under Broughton's name in 1743.[16] Although the rules were intended simply to regulate his own establishment, they were soon widely adopted. 'No one sport', claims Brailsford, 'owed more for its beginnings to one man than boxing owed to him' (illus. 12).[17]

The rules specified how a round would begin and end; how the seconds and umpires should conduct themselves; how the money should be divided; and that a fight was over when one man could not be brought back to the scratch line in the centre of the ring. After 1746, English gamblers adapted the notion of

horse handicapping and began dividing boxers into light, middle, and heavyweight classes (there was, however, only one 'champion' who tended to be the heaviest). By 1838, these rules had developed into the 29 English Prize Ring Rules. Wrestling holds, such as the cross-buttocks, remained a part of boxing until the Queensberry rules abolished them in the 1860s.

Champion from 1734 to 1750, Broughton promoted bareknuckle bouts at his Amphitheatre near Marylebone Fields, including Battles Royal in which a champion took on up to seven challengers at a time. The fights took place on an unfenced stage with several rows of seating for gentlemen; these rows were separated from the platform by a gap where the other spectators stood, their eyes level with the pugilists' feet.

# RULES

### TO BE OBSERVED IN ALL BATTLES ON THE STAGE

I. THAT a fquare of a Yard be chalked in the middle of the Stage; and on every frefh fet-to after a fall, or being parted from the rails, each Second is to bring his Man to the fide of the fquare, and place him oppofite to the other, and till they are fairly fet-to at the Lines, it fhall not be lawful for one to ftrike at the other.

II. That, in order to prevent any Difputes, the time a Man lies after a fall, if the Second does not bring his Man to the fide of the fquare, within the fpace of half a minute, he fhall be deemed a beaten Man.

III. That in every main Battle, no perfon whatever fhall be upon the Stage, except the Principals and their Seconds; the fame rule to be obferved in bye-battles, except that in the latter, Mr. Broughton is allowed to be upon the Stage to keep decorum, and to affift Gentlemen in getting to their places, provided always he does not interfere in the Battle; and whoever pretends to infringe thefe Rules to be turned immediately out of the houfe. Every body is to quit the Stage as foon as the Champions are ftripped, before the fet-to.

IV. That no Champion be deemed beaten, unlefs he fails coming up to the line in the limited time, or that his own Second declares him beaten. No Second is to be allowed to afk his man's Adversary any queftions, or advife him to give out.

V. That in bye-battles, the winning man to have two-thirds of the Money given, which fhall be publicly divided upon the Stage, notwithftanding any private agreements to the contrary.

VI. That to prevent Difputes, in every main Battle the Principals fhall, on coming on the Stage, choofe from among the gentlemen prefent two Umpires, who fhall abfolutely decide all Difputes that may arife about the Battle; and if the two Umpires cannot agree, the faid Umpires to choofe a third, who is to determine it.

VII. That no perfon is to hit his Adverfary when he is down, or feize him by the ham, the breeches, or any part below the waift: a man on his knees to be reckoned down.

*As agreed by feveral Gentlemen at Broughton's Amphitheatre,*
*Tottenham Court Road, Auguft 16, 1743.*

Broughton capitalized on the popularity of prize-fighting with the upper classes by offering tuition for 'persons of quality and distinction' at his school in the Haymarket. What was offered differed from prize-fighting in many respects: the exclusion of women, the absence of gambling, and the lack of police intervention. The most important difference, however, was the style of fighting involved, and in particular the introduction of large padded gloves, or mufflers. Broughton's advertisement promised, in order that 'persons of quality and distinction may not be debarred from entering a course of those lectures':

they will be given the utmost tenderness, for which reason mufflers are provided that will effectively secure them for the inconveniency of black eyes, broken jaws and bloody noses.[18]

Sparring with mufflers was different enough from bareknuckle prize-fighting to be deemed a separate sport, albeit one that was parasitic on the rough glamour of its ancestor. The journalist Pierce Egan described sparring as 'a mock encounter; but, at the same time, a representation, and, in most cases an exact one, of real fighting' (which of course remained the Platonic Form).[19] Whether or not he attended prize-fights, a modern urban gentleman who exercised gently with his padded gloves could believe himself in touch with an older, and somehow more authentic, England.

## 'FISTS AND THE MAN I SING'[20]

Broughton advertised his academy with a quotation from the *Aeneid*, urging that Britons who 'boast themselves inheritors of the *Greek* and *Roman* virtues, should follow their example and [encourage] conflicts of this magnanimous kind'. James Faber's classically styled portrait of the fighter was accompanied by a verse comparing him to the 'athletic heroes' celebrated by Pindar.[21] Such connections were not unusual. For over a hundred years classical precedent had been used to describe, and justify, British pugilism. In 1612, Robert Dover reinvented the annual Cotswolds sports as 'Olimpick Games' in an anti-Puritan gesture and an attempt to marry English country and classical traditions.[22] In 1636 a group of Dover's friends, including Ben Jonson and Michael Drayton, produced the *Annalia Dubrensia*, a collection of poems celebrating the games as a revival of the 'Golden Age's Glories', and defending their 'harmlesse merriment' from Puritan censure. John Stratford's poem lists many classical sports including boxing (he alludes to Virgil's Eutellus, who 'at Caestus, had the best / In mighty strength surpassing all the rest') before noting that 'the old world's sports' are 'now transferred over / Into our Cotswold by thee, worthy Dover.'[23]

Poetry itself is understood as a kind of sport, and sport as a rival to poetry, in another poem of this period, John Suckling's 'A Session of the Poets' (1646). Apollo must decide which poet deserves to be Laureate. Each comes forward to compete until it is the turn of Suckling himself. Apollo is told that he is not present:

> That of all men living he cared not for't,
> He loved not the Muses as well as his sport;
>
> And prized black eyes, or a lucky hit
> At bowls, above all the Trophies of wit . . .[24]

Apollo is not amused, and issues a fine.

A desire to evoke classical boxing led Figg, and Broughton after him, to describe their schools as 'amphitheatres', and Jonathan Richardson to depict Figg in a 1714 portrait as 'the Gladiator ad Vivum'. Travellers on the Grand Tour began to collect classical and Renaissance sculptures of boxers, and these were carefully studied by modern artists.[25] But emulation soon led to (mock heroic) competition and to frequent claims that English sport was best. In Moses Browne's 'A Survey of the Amhitheatre' (1736), the mild English version comes out ahead of the 'dread' Roman. In Rome, fighters 'met to kill, or be killed, / But ours to have their pockets filled.'[26] John Byrom's 1725 'Extempore Verses Upon a Tryal of Skill between the Two Great Masters of the Noble Science of Defence, Messrs. Figg and Sutton' develops, at some length, the contention that modern English boxers (and books) have surpassed their ancient models:

> Now, after such Men, who can bear to be told
> Of your Roman and Greek puny Heroes of Old?
> To compare such poor Dogs as Alcides, and Theseus
> To Sutton and Figg would be very facetious.
> Were Hector himself, with Apollo to back him,
> To encounter with Sutton – zooks, how he would thwack him!
> Or Achilles, tho' old Mother Thetis had dipt him,
> With Figg – odds my Life, how he would have unript him!

By the mid-eighteenth century battles of boxers and books such as this had become commonplace (although sadly not all rhymed 'Theseus' with 'facetious', or asked whether Figg should 'be pair'd with a Cap-a pee Roman, / Who scorn'd any Fence but a jolly Abdomen?').[27]

Christopher Anstey's *The Patriot* (1767) – 'A Pindaric Address to Lord Buckhorse', the *nom de guerre* of Broughton's sparring partner, John Smith – burlesqued the tendency to describe prize-fighters in such elevated terms. Something of a classical hodge-podge, it intersperses quotations from Homer, Theocritus, Virgil, Lucian and others with calls for aid from the muses:

> Bid CLIO quit her blest Abode,
> And speed her Flight to Oxford-Road,
> Adore the Theatre of BROUGHTON,
> And kiss the Stage his Lordship fought on . . .

Buckhorse's 'Patriotic Virtues' are celebrated at a time when '*Alba*'s warlike Sons of Yore' have been displaced by 'Meek Cardinals' wielding undue influence upon the 'Tender Minds of Youth'. Buckhorse is called upon to found a Cambridge college, and thus 'form a Plan of Education / To mend the Morals of the Nation.'[28]

Eleven years previously, in 1756, Anstey had (anonymously) published a little-known work entitled *Memoirs of the Noted Buckhorse*, a picaresque satire of the metropolitan world of 'Bucks, Bloods and Jemmys' into which, he imagines, the boxer is initiated. 'He learned to swear very prettily, lie with a good Grace, flatter and deceive, promise any thing, and perform, – as great People generally do.'[29] Much of the humour here, as in *The Patriot*, comes from imagining the working-class prize-fighter as a Lord, a society figure who wields influence as well as his fists. After two volumes of adventures, the *Memoirs* end with Buckhorse, tired of waiting for his friends to secure him a position in the Army, resolving to 'turn PATRIOT'. This allows an extended joke on a version of patriotism that entails 'rail[ing] against the Ministry' and 'season[ing] his Discourses with Bribery, Corruption, and *Hanover*.'[30]

## 'NO WEAPONS BUT WHAT NATURE HAD FURNISHED HIM WITH'

Henry Fielding began *Tom Jones* in 1747, the year that Broughton opened his academy, and the novel reflects contemporary interest in the sport and its classical origins.[31] Broughton's advertisement is even quoted in a footnote.[32] Fielding's take on the subject is characteristically 'prosai-comi-epic'.[33] Chapter Eight of Book One, for example, is entitled 'A battle sung by the muses in the Homerican style, and which none but the classical reader can taste'. The battle sung features 'our Amazonian heroine', Molly Seagrim, against many opponents, most notably Goody Brown. Fielding's exploitation of the comic potential of women's boxing had begun in 1741, when, in *Shamela*, he has Henrietta Maria Honora Andrews end a letter to her daughter with the apology, 'You will excuse the shortness of this scroll; for I have sprained my right hand, with boxing three new made officers. – Tho' to my comfort, I beat them all.'[34]

In the case of Molly Seagrim and Goody Brown, we are treated to a full description of women at 'fisticuff-war'. The women begin, cautiously, by merely tearing at each other's hair, but soon move onto each other's clothes so that 'in a very few minutes they were both naked to the middle.'[35] Goody has the advantage of having no bosom; her breasts are 'an ancient parchment, upon which one might have drummed a considerable while without doing her any damage'. Molly is 'differently formed in those parts' and therefore susceptible to 'a fatal blow had not the lucky arrival of Tom Jones at this point put an immediate end to the bloody scene'. Tom now fights Goody (perhaps, Fielding suggests, he forgot she was a woman; perhaps he couldn't tell) and the surrounding mob.

For Fielding, the language of boxing was as open to mockery as the language of classical poetry. In *Joseph Andrews* (1742), we are momentarily anxious for Parson Adams when his opponent concludes '(to use the Language of fighting) *that he had done his Business*; or, in the Language of Poetry, *that he had sent him to the Shades below*; in plain *English, that he was dead*'.[36] Plain English is of course the language of the narrator, and the novel – Fielding's 'new province of writing'[37] – which may include, and absorb, the mock-heroic and the colloquial, but whose character is, above all, democratic, excluding no reader by resort to the language of the coterie. Plain, and reasonable, English would have prevented yet another altercation in *Tom Jones*: when the classically educated schoolteacher, Partridge, uses the phrase 'non sequitur', the sergeant mistakes it for an insult – 'None of your outlandish linguo . . . I will not sit still and hear the cloth abused' – and he formally challenges Partridge to fight.[38]

As the novel progresses, Tom has many opportunities to display his boxing skill, and employs all the latest techniques including 'one of those punches in the guts which, though the spectators at Broughton's Ampitheatre have such exquisite delight in seeing them, convey little pleasure in the feeling'.[39] One opponent is even convinced he must be a professional prize-fighter: 'I'll have nothing more to do with you; you have been upon the stage, or I'm d__nably mistaken', to which the narrator adds: 'such was the agility and strength of our hero that he was perhaps a match for one of the first-rate boxers, and could with great ease have beaten all the muffled graduates of Mr. Broughton's school'.[40]

Tom is superior to the 'muffled graduates' because of his willingness to fight bare-fisted; Bonnell Thornton and George Colman later mocked that 'most of our young fellows gave up the gauntlet for scented gloves; and loathing the mutton fists of vulgar carmen and porters, they rather chose to hang their hands in a sling, to make them white and delicate as a lady's'.[41] More fundamentally, fighting for Tom is a matter of 'appetite' rather than education. Tom has many appetites – for fighting, for food, for drink, but mainly for sex. These are seen to be equally natural, and often one appetite leads to another. Broughton promised that learning to box would bring his pupils success with women, evoking his exhibition sparring partner, the famously ugly Buckhorse, whose 'ruling passions' were said to be 'LOVE and BOXING, in both of which he was equally formidable; . . . neither nymph nor bruiser could withstand the violence of his attack, for it was generally allowed he conquered both by the strength of his members, and the rigour of his parts'.[42] Christopher Anstey's novel Memoirs of the Noted Buckhorse also gets much mileage out of its hero's reputation as a ladies' man. Many women praise his 'manly Beauties' and three marry him.[43] But Tom needs no lessons in either love or boxing. Consider, to take only one of many examples, the 'Battle of Upton', which takes place at the inn where Tom and a 'fair companion' are lodging. In this case, the key intervention is that of the chambermaid, Susan, 'as two-handed a wench (according to the phrase) as any in the country'.[44]

Fights in Fielding's novels are often the means by which moral worth is revealed. He disagreed strongly with Samuel Richardson's view that virtue is a state of mind, arguing that the 'Actions of Men seem to be the justest Interpreters of their Thoughts, and the truest Standards by which we may judge them'.[45] Many fights begin with the excuse of defending feminine honour. Parson Adams, in Joseph Andrews, for example, refutes an argument about the nature of courage in a single blow by instinctively leaping to the defence of a young woman in trouble. Adams, the first muscled if not muscular Christian, proceeds with 'no weapons but what Nature had furnished him with', and, it seems, some surreptitiously acquired technical knowledge.[46] But given that the women are often as adept as the men with their fists – Mr Partridge is certainly no match for Mrs Partridge – many of the situations presented seem primarily to furnish excuses for a good punch-up. Fighting (like sex) is ubiquitous in Fielding's novels; some-thing that English men and women just like to do. It is an activity natural to all classes and all professions – chambermaids, squires, landladies, schoolteachers, army officers and the aptly named Reverend Mr. Thwackum all pitch in.[47] The very ubiquity of fights throughout the novels is comically conservative, as if Field-ing is asking, 'what else can you expect from human nature?'[48] There may be lots of bleeding, and preferably some female nudity, but the conclusion of a boxing match, for Fielding, is also comic, and conservative in its effect (a jovial hand-shake with the balance of power unchanged), rather than tragic and radical (epit-omized by the deadly Jacobite duel).[49] After knocking out Blifil, for example, Jones immediately reaches over to see if he is alright, and soon Blifil is back on his feet. Fielding interrupts his narrative to talk about the significance of this incident with a seriousness that is evident from his plain English:

> Here we cannot suppress a pious wish that all quarrels were to be de-cided by those weapons only, with which Nature, knowing what is proper for us, hath supplied us; and that cold iron was to be used in digging no bowels, but those of the earth. Then would war, the pastime of monarchs, be almost inoffensive, and battles between great armies might be fought at the particular desire of several ladies of quality, who, together, with the kings themselves, might be actual spectators of the conflict. Then might the field be this moment well strewn with human carcasses, and the next, the dead men, or infinitely the greatest part of them, might get up . . .[50]

Some years later the prize-fighter Daniel Mendoza approvingly cited this pas-sage, and used it to justify his profession.[51]

Broughton advertised boxing as a 'truly *British* Art', claiming that its study would prove an antidote to '*foreign Effeminacy*', as well as, of course, enabling practitioners to be able 'to boast themselves Inheritors of the *Greek* and *Roman* Virtues'. Broughton, and his followers, seemed to find no contradiction in these two claims. 'Britishness' was, however, as Christopher Johnson notes, a 'highly contentious' notion in 1747, only a year after the bloody Battle of Culloden which had ended the Jacobite Rebellion; French troops had supported the Young Pre-tender, Bonnie Prince Charlie, against the Hanoverian King George II (for whom both Tom Jones, and Broughton's patron, the Duke of Cumberland, fought). Exactly contemporary with *Tom Jones*, William Hogarth's *The March to Finchley* (1749) memorializes the soldiers who had travelled north to meet the Jacobites three years earlier. The exuberant crowd that Hogarth depicts seems, as Jenny Uglow puts it, to be celebrating a public holiday rather than facing a national emergency. On the left of the scene, a crowd has gathered outside the boxing booth of Broughton's rival, George Taylor, to watch a fight. Uglow interprets this as representing either 'the murderous rivalry of Cain and Abel now trans-lated into civil war' or 'the natural fighting spirit of the people, cheered on by an excited crowd'.[52] To define Britishness, as Broughton did, in the pseudo-military vocabulary of 'championism' (a concoction of pugnacious Protestanism, egalitarianism, national pride and moral righteousness) would, presumably, not have found favour with many northern and Catholic Britons. Championism represented a quite particular form of Englishness.

Throughout the eighteenth century, French visitors to England had observed the 'well-known taste of the English for combats of men and animals, and for those horrible scenes of slaughter and blood, which other nations have banished from their theatres.' 'Any Thing that Looks like Fighting, is delicious to an *Englishman*,' concluded Misson in 1719.[53] After a visit to London in 1766, during which he seemed to trip over 'street-scufflers' at every corner, Pierre Jean Grosley recorded that boxing was a 'species of combat' not merely 'congenial to the character of the English' but 'inherent in English blood'.[54]

While Grosley was appalled by the ubiquity of street-fighting, and the casualness with which it was undertaken, James Boswell relished a scuffle. His diary entry for 13 June 1763 describes a trip to Vauxhall Gardens as 'quite delicious' not despite, but because of, a 'quarrel between a gentleman and a waiter':

> A great crowd gathered round and roared out, 'A ring-a ring,' which is the signal for making room for the parties to box it out. My spirits rose, and I was exerting myself with much vehemence. At last the constable came to quell the riot. I seized his baton in a good-humoured way which made him laugh, and I rapped upon the people's heads, bawling out, 'Who will resist the Peace? A ring, a ring.'[55]

Boswell's enthusiasm recalls that displayed by Samuel Pepys a hundred years earlier. He obviously had a fondness for critical, and social, pugilists as well. Boswell's portrait of Samuel Johnson depicts a man who, while hot-tempered, is quick to reconcile and apologize. Pierce Egan relates the tale of Johnson's having a 'regular set to with an athletic brewer's servant, who had insulted him in Fleet-street' – he 'gave the fellow a complete milling in a few minutes' – and concludes that Johnson was '*striking* proof of pugilism being a national trait'. Mrs Thrale describes him as 'very conversant in the art of attack and defense by boxing, which science he learned from his uncle Andrew'.[56] More importantly, Johnson included definitions (illustrated by literary quotations) of 'box' and 'boxer' and 'to box' in *The Dictionary of the English Language* (1755).[57]

In 1750, an ill-prepared Broughton was finally defeated and blinded by a Norfolk butcher, Jack Slack. His patron, the Duke of Cumberland, who lost a £10,000 bet, accused Broughton of throwing the fight and angrily withdrew his support. Within months, Broughton's Amphitheatre closed and prize-fighting was officially, if not effectively, outlawed. A more striking demonstration of the dependence of the sport on aristocratic patronage can hardly be imagined. Contests continued to be staged, but gradually moved away from the metropolitan centres.[58] Ten years earlier, as Paul Whitehead had observed in 'The Gymnasiad', anti-boxing legislation had been 'dormant'. Now bailiffs woke up to its existence and fighters were increasingly likely to be arrested.[59]

In 1754, 'Mr Town' (Bonnell Thornton and George Colman, members of the satirical Nonsense Club) joshed that Broughton's defeat was a 'public calamity'. They imagined the 'professors of the noble art of Boxing' forming a 'kind of disbanded army' and inevitably turning to crime. 'Some have been forced to exercise their art in knocking down passengers in dark alleys and corners; while others have learned to open their fists and ply their fingers in picking pockets.'[60] But not everyone was unhappy at the prospect of the boxing academies closing. An appreciation of boxing was, for some, less the classless mark of an honest man, as Fielding had suggested, than yet another empty indulgence practised by wealthy Londoners. In *The Vicar of Wakefield* (1766), for example, Oliver Goldsmith presents the rakish young squire Thornhill as a corrupting influence on the innocent country vicar and his family. Thornhill visits his tenants frequently and 'amuses them by describing the town, with every part of which he was particularly acquainted'. He even sets the vicar's two little boys to box, 'to make them *sharp*, as he called it'. Thornhill's cowardice is later revealed when he sends another brother to fight duels on his behalf, and he is finally declared 'as complete a villain as ever disgraced humanity'.[61] In 1751, Hogarth published a series of prints entitled *The Four Stages of Cruelty*, 'in the hopes of preventing in some degree the cruel treatment of poor Animals' on the streets of London. The Second Stage includes a man whipping a horse and a sheep being beaten, and, on the wall, notices advertise cock-fighting and an up-coming match between George Taylor and James Field at Broughton's Amphitheatre. Field is also named in the last print of the series, 'The Reward of Cruelty' – his name is engraved above a skeleton which overlooks the dissection of an executed criminal. Field had recently been hanged for robbery and his life-story was circulated in a pamphlet that ran to several editions, *The Bruiser knock'd down*.[62] Boxing had changed its meaning for Hogarth. Whereas previously he had presented the sport as one of many manifestations of exuberant Englishness, in 1751 he aligns it with the cruelties of cock-fighting, execution and dissection.

A NOBLE ART AND A SCIENCE

English pugilism's revival (and, for many, the beginning of its golden age) began in the 1780s, when once again the highest echelons of the aristocracy, including the Prince of Wales, became interested in the sport. As war with France loomed, this was due partly to boxing's reputed association with a particularly English form of courage, and partly to a highly publicized series of fights between Richard Humphries and Daniel Mendoza.

Daniel Mendoza's *Memoirs* (1816) may have been the first ghost-written sports autobiography. Whoever wrote it, the book provides a vivid picture not only of the prize-fighting world but of late eighteenth-century London life more generally. The story is of a man who tries to make a living in various respectable trades – as a greengrocer, tobacconist or glazier – but whom circumstance, usually involving the honour of women or Judaism, continually compels to resort to his fists.

The names of Mendoza's first opponents – Harry the Coal-heaver, and Sam Martin, 'The Bath Butcher' – suggest their weighty force. Relatively small at 5ft 7in and 160 pounds (he would now be classified as a middleweight), Mendoza, often known simply as 'the Jew', defeated them with a combination of speed, agility and technique. One of his 'prominent traits', noted Pierce Egan, was to exhaust the strength of an opponent who 'depended upon that particular circumstance to stamp him a formidable boxer', by 'acting on the defensive till the assault in turn could be practised with success'. Previously, pugilistic fighting was somewhat static as opponents stood toe to toe and exchanged blows. It was considered unmanly to move, so blows were blocked rather than avoided by footwork. John Godfrey, for example, described Broughton's style:

> BROUGHTON steps bold and firmly in, bids a Welcome to the coming Blow, receives it with the guardian Arm; then with a general Summons of his swelling Muscles and his firm Body, seconding his Arm, and supplying it with all its Weight, pours the Pile-driving Force upon his Man.[63]

Mendoza introduced a style of fighting which relied on footwork, jabs, and defence rather than simply pure brute force. Although most commentators (including the Prince of Wales) praised his style as elegant, sophisticated and, perhaps most important, wonderful to watch, some complained that 'there was something cowardly about a fighter who frequently retreated and relied on superior agility and speed to win rather than standing up in true British bulldog style and hammering away doggedly until he or his opponent dropped'.[64] 'The Jew', the anti-Semites said, was 'cunning'.[65]

In 1788, Mendoza embarked on a highly publicized series of contests with Richard Humphries, 'The Gentleman Fighter' (illus. 44). Tapping into late eighteenth-century English anxieties about its burgeoning Jewish population, the fights attracted large crowds. Mendoza and Humphries were the first boxers whose careers were successfully marketed in terms of ethnic hostility.[66] Mendoza lost the first fight and immediately wrote to a popular newspaper complaining about his opponent's deviousness and lack of courage. Thus began a prolonged battle of words between the two fighters, which boosted sales of *The World* considerably, and which is reprinted in full in the *Memoirs*. Letter followed letter like punch and counterpunch, with the result that the inevitable rematch between the two men was a guaranteed sell-out, with both men profiting. Mendoza decisively won the second and third fights and became a celebrity; his face was reproduced on commemorative coins and beer mugs and his name was incorporated into the texts of contemporary plays.[67] He claimed the title of champion when Big Ben Brain retired in 1791 and confirmed it with victories over Bill Ward in 1792 and 1794. The following year, he lost the championship (in dubious circumstances) to John Jackson.

One of the most interesting aspects of Mendoza's memoirs is the light it sheds on the commercial side of pugilism.[68] Like most prize-fighters then (and since), Mendoza used his high-profile victories as a springboard to other, more lucrative, enterprises – exhibitions at London's Lyceum theatre, tours of Britain and Ireland, and a successful boxing academy. He eventually became a publican.[69]

By 1795, according to G. M. Trevelyan, 'scientific pugilism' had become the 'chief national interest'.[70] This is overstating things, but, in certain quarters, boxing had become very fashionable. Spoken of as both a 'science' and a 'noble art of self-defence', pugilism could be studied from books such as Mendoza's 1787 *The Art of Boxing*, and numerous 'sixpenny teachers', as well as at the more expensive and exclusive academies in London, and beyond. Mendoza's school was in the City, Humphries catered particularly for the pupils of Westminster School, and, on gaining the title, John Jackson retired immediately to set up rooms in Bond Street. In 1807, the fictional narrator of Robert Southey's *Letters from England*, Don Manuel Alvarez Espriella, observed, in a letter on the 'Fashionables', that 'the Amateurs of Boxing . . . attend the academies of the two great professors Jackson and Mendoza, the Aristotle and Plato of pugilism'.[71]

A typical amateur was Joseph Moser's 1794 creation, Timothy Twig. Twig's adventures in modish London (related back to Wales in comic verse letters) include the study of 'matter and motion': 'I'm deep in philosophy at the Lyceum'. Twig praises Mendoza, Humphries and others 'for shewing the town, / The genteel method to knock a man down.'[72] A 1788 advertisement for Humphries's school promised that 'Such gentlemen as are prevented by weak constitution from taking a lesson may be qualified for polite Assemblies with artificial Bloody Noses and Black Eyes' (illus. 13). Another drawing, by Rowlandson, detailed the 'six stages of marring a face' (illus. 14).

13
*School for Boxing*, 1788.

14
Thomas Rowland-
son, *Six Stages of
Marring a Face*,
May 1792, etching.

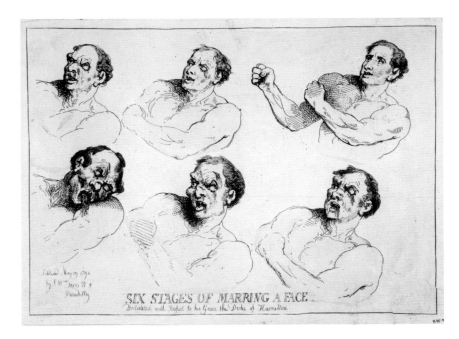

SIX STAGES OF MARRING A FACE.
*Dedicated with Respect to his Grace the Duke of Hamilton.*

The *ars pugnandi* had much to recommend it to the young gentleman about town. For a start it was an art that would 'promote health', 'give courage to the timid', and 'repress insolence'. But more importantly, Mendoza promised, it would enable 'men to stand in their own defence' (and that of their property) on the streets of the growing metropolis. It would provide them with the means to resist 'the assaults they are daily exposed to'.[73] Furthermore, it would enable them to defend their honour without resorting to the potentially more deadly practice of duelling which was, in any case, considered French. In one of the earliest published references to boxing in 1709, Richard Steele had advocated the use of 'wrathful Hands' as an alternative to 'that unchristian-like and bloody Custom of Duelling', and Fielding, as we have already seen, preferred the comic-conservative boxing match to the tragic and radical duel.[74] In the introduction to his 1816 *Memoirs*, Mendoza argued that if boxing were abolished, men would not forget their injuries but instead 'adopt other modes of revenging their wrongs, either by resorting to the dreadful practice of duelling, or by schemes of secret machinations against each other'.[75]

Finally, because it was based on natural strength and the mastery of technique rather than the ownership of weaponry, boxing, it was claimed, would allow men of all classes to fight on equal terms. 'Fair play' was much spoken of and admired, and again considered a particularly English and democratic virtue.[76] In 1698 a French visitor, Henri Misson, had noted, with some surprise, the sight of the Duke of Grafton and his coachman 'at Fisticuffs, in the open street', 'the very widest Part of the Strand'. The coachman, he reports, was 'lamb'd most horribly'.

In France, we punish such Rascals with our Cane, and sometimes with the flat of our sword: but in England this is never practis'd; they use neither Sword nor Stick against a Man that is unarm'd: and if an unfortunate stranger (for an Englishman would never take it into his head) should draw his Sword upon one that had none, he'd have a hundred People upon him in a Moment that would perhaps lay him so flat that he would hardly get up again until the Resurrection.[77]

Misson notes that, 'If the Coachman is soundly drubb'd, which happens almost always, that goes for Payment; but if he is the *Beator*, the *Beatée* must pay the Money about which they quarrel'd.' Should his readers worry about the implications of such seeming democracy, he adds, in a footnote, 'A Gentleman seldom exposes himself to such a Battel, without he is sure he's strongest.'

Fair play was also much admired in professional contests. In 1790, during their final fight, Mendoza had Humphries in such a helpless state that he could have injured him at will, but he famously 'laid down' his opponent on the ground. (Egan reports this 'truth' in the face of anti-Semitic 'prejudice' which allows 'good actions' to be 'passed over'.[78]) In an 1805 fight Hen Pearce (the Game Chicken) forced Jem Belcher against the ropes. At this stage of his career Belcher only had the use of one eye, and the crowd feared that Pearce would deliberately blind him. Instead, Pearce is supposed to have pulled back out of a punch, saying, 'I'll take no advantage of thee, Jem; I'll not hit thee, no, lest I hurt the other eye.' He repeated this behaviour in a later round, and the audience was 'lost in admiration'.[79]

## 'THE PUGILISTIC HONOUR OF THE COUNTRY WAS AT STAKE'

William Windham, a friend of Samuel Johnson and a protégé of Edmund Burke, was elected to Parliament in 1784 and by 1792 became one of the most ardent supporters of the government's fearful and repressive legislation against 'aliens' and 'seditious' meetings; in 1801, he opposed preliminary moves to peace with France; in 1806, his career peaked when he served as Secretary for War and Colonies. Windham was also a vocal supporter of pugilism, recording attendance at more than twenty fights in his diary, along with regret on one occasion at letting himself 'be drawn by Boswell to explore . . . Wapping, instead of going when everything was prepared, to see the battle between Ward and Stanyard, which turned out a very good one'.[80] That was in 1792. Six years earlier, 'Fighting Windham' (his Eton nickname) noted his first 'excursion' to a fight, between Sam Martin and Humphries, ('Richard I think'), after a journey on which the talk was much of 'foreign wars and foreign politics'.[81] By the end of the century, evangelical reformers increasingly condemned pugilism as a 'detestable traffic in human flesh', on par with the slave trade, but Windham retorted that it was only such 'cruel sports' that protected the 'Old English character' from the threat of Jacobinism.[82] By 1809 he was making the connection between war and sport explicit, writing indignantly to a friend:

A smart contest this between Maddox and Richmond! Why are we to boast so much of the native valour of our troops at Talavera, at Vimeira, and at Maida, yet to discourage all the practices and habits which tend to keep alive the same sentiments and feelings? The sentiments that filled the minds of the three thousand people who attended the two pugilists, were just the same in kind as those which inspired the higher combatants on the occasions before enumerated. It is the circumstances only in which they are displayed, that makes the difference . . . But when I get on these topics, I never know how to stop.[83]

If sparring was, in Egan's terms, 'a representation' of prize-fighting, prize-fighting in turn had become a representation of war.

'The cult of heroic endeavour and aggressive maleness that was so pronounced in patrician art and literature at this time', notes Linda Colley, 'was just as prominent in popular ballads and songs.'[84] Pierce Egan's *Boxiana* is certainly full of songs and poems about 'Boney' and what will be done to the 'little upstart King'. 'A Boxing We Will Go', for example, was often 'sung at the convivial meetings of the Fancy':

> Italians stab their friends behind,
> In darkest shades of night;
> But Britons they are bold and kind,
> And box their friends by light.
>
> The sons of France their pistols use,
>  Pop, pop, and they have done;
> But Britons with their hands will bruise,
>  And scorn away to run.
>  . . .
> Since boxing is a manly game,
>  And Briton's recreation;
> By boxing we will raise our fame,
>  'Bove any other nation.
>  . . .
> A fig for Boney – let's have done
>  With that ungracious name;
> We'll drink and pass our days in fun,
>  And box to raise our fame.[85]

'It seems probable,' writes Colley, 'that some Britons at least volunteered [for the army] not so much because they were anxious to fight for anything in particular, but simply because they wanted to fight – period.'[86]

Unfortunately for British fight fans, there was no possibility of a French fighter coming forward to allow a symbolic 'flooring' of Boney. Although matches were frequently organized to enact and illustrate anxieties about new immigrant populations (Jewish and Irish), no foreigner had challenged an English champion since 1733.[87] Since then, as Egan put it, the champion cap had passed from 'the nob of one native to another'.[88] By 1810, however, the desire was strong for a foreign opponent against whom British courage and valour could be expressed. If France was not willing, perhaps a surrogate battle could pitch Britain against another very recent enemy, the United States (illus. 45).

A peace treaty had been formally signed between Great Britain and the United States in 1783, but relations between the two countries remained strained in the years that followed. Finally the British policy of intercepting merchant ships on the high seas, in order to prevent neutral trade with France, provoked the United States into declaring war in 1812. Two years later, what some have termed the Second Revolutionary War ended after the British suffered substantial losses. It is in the context of these events that the championship fights between Tom Cribb and Tom Molineaux in 1810 and 1811 should be understood.[89] Rounds one and two of Britain versus the United States were complicated only by the fact that Molineaux was black, a former slave from Virginia.

Throughout the eighteenth century, young Virginians were frequently sent to England to complete their education. There, some witnessed prize-fights and attended boxing academies. In a 1785 letter Thomas Jefferson complained that in learning 'drinking, horse racing and boxing' ('the peculiarities of English education') young Americans might also acquire 'a fondness for European luxury and dissipation, and a contempt for the simplicity of [their] own country'.[90] Boxing may have been un-republican, but it was certainly popular among slave-owners, many of whom, in search of gambling opportunities, trained their slaves to compete with those from other plantations, sometimes rewarding those who earned them money with their freedom.[91]

Whether or not some slaves did obtain manumission, it is certainly true that the first professional boxers in America were free blacks. Some ended up in England. Before Molineaux, the most famous was Bill Richmond. Brought to England in 1777 at the age of fourteen as a servant to the Duke of Northumberland, Richmond first trained as a cabinet maker and, after a reasonably successful career as a pugilist, continued to promote fights and train fighters while managing a tavern next door to the Fives Court. In 1805 Richmond had been defeated by a young Tom Cribb and, according to legend, he wanted a protégé to exact revenge.

Thought to have been born a slave in Virginia, Tom Molineaux arrived in New York at the age of twenty as a freeman and began to fight at the Catherine Street market. Four years later, he set sail to England with the plan of challenging Cribb, by then champion of England (which at that time also meant champion of the world). The fight that took place between the two men on 18 December 1810, at Capthall Common, Sussex, is one of the most mythologized events of the Regency (illus. 15 and illus. 16). Pierce Egan recalled the feverish atmosphere of the day:

15
Staffordshire
portrait figure
of Tom Cribb,
c. 1810–15.

16
Staffordshire
portrait figure of
Tom Molineaux,
c. 1810–15.

The pugilistic honour of the country was at stake . . . the national laurels to be borne away by a foreigner – the mere idea to an English breast was afflicting, and the reality could not be endured – that it should seem, the spectators were ready to exclaim –

*Forbid it heaven, forbid it man!*[92]

After nineteen rounds in driving icy rain those spectators did more than exclaim; they rushed into the ring and broke one of Molineaux's fingers in the scrimmage. Nevertheless, the American continued to dominate and at the beginning of the 28th round, Cribb seemed unable to rise. At that point his second leapt up and accused Molineaux of hiding lead bullets in his fists. By the time this charge had been refuted, Cribb had recovered enough to continue. Molineaux's bad luck continued when he hit his head on one of the stakes at the corner of the ring, and in the 39th round he conceded the fight. Egan's report is equivocal. He is careful not to claim a breach of fair play, but concedes that it was Molineaux's 'colour alone' which 'prevented him from becoming the hero of that fight'.

A few days later Molineaux published an open letter to Cribb: 'Sir, – My friends think, that had the weather on last Tuesday, the day upon which I contended with you, not been so unfavourable, I should have won the battle'. He challenged

Cribb to a second meeting, 'expressing the confident hope, that the circumstance of my being a different colour to that of a people amongst whom I have sought protection will not in any way operate to my prejudice.'[93]

The following year (before a crowd estimated at 15–20,000) Cribb, who had spent eleven weeks with the noted trainer, Captain Barclay, defeated an ill-prepared Molineaux in what the *Times* described as a 'most obstinate and sanguinary combat'.[94] Once Cribb was safely champion, the fans could once more become magnanimous, and soon songs were sung about Molineaux's bravery – 'Tho' beat, he proved a man my boys, what more could a man do' – and he too was co-opted into imaginary contests with Boney.

The blurring of the language of war and the language of sport was not restricted to those who watched from the sidelines. Wellington himself famously described Waterloo as 'a pounding match' and said of its opposing armies, 'both were what the boxers call gluttons'.[95] The war ended in 1815, and Thomas Moore's 'Epistle from Tom Cribb to Big Ben, Concerning some Foul Play in a Late Transaction' (1818), satirically compares the conduct of the allies in exiling Napoleon to St Helena to kicking a man when he is down.

> 'Foul! Foul!' all the lads of the Fancy exclaim -
> Charley Shock is electrified – Belcher spits flame –
> And Molyneux – ay, even Blacky cries 'shame!'
> Time was, when John Bull little difference spied
> 'Twixt the foe at his feet, and the friend at his side;
> When he found (such his humour in fighting and eating)
> His foe, like his beefsteak, the sweeter for beating.[96]

In the years that followed, although Boney remained in St Helena, pugilistic jingoism showed no signs of abating. 'In the mythology of the Ring,' writes Peter Bailey, 'the fist was England's national weapon and the skilful and courageous wielding of it in public kept alive the spirit of Waterloo.'[97] Many found it useful to recall foreign enemies in the period of increased civil unrest that followed the war's end.

## 'HAVING THE LUCK TO BE BORN AN ENGLISHMAN'

A rhetoric of nationalist masculinity was not new to the Napoleonic period, but what was new, perhaps, was the anxiety, and urgency, with which it was deployed. The spectre of effeminacy was constantly evoked. Boxing was not merely British and democratic, but, in its direct physicality, a more masculine way of fighting than relatively at-a-distance foreign methods (the dagger and knife) mentioned in popular songs such as 'A Boxing We Will Go'.[98] Works such as 'Defence of Boxing' (a 'political view of the subject'), by Windham's friend, William Cobbett, make much of supposed links between effeminacy and tyranny. Boxing, Cobbett claimed, could stave off 'national degradation' and help prevent 'submission to a foreign yoke'. 'Commerce, Opulence, Luxury, Effeminacy, Cowardice, Slavery,' he maintained, 'are the stages of national degradation.' By threatening to replace 'hardy' sports by those 'requiring less strength, and exposing the persons engaged in them to less bodily suffering', Britain was already showing symptoms of effeminacy and edging dangerously towards 'national cowardice'.[99] And if the effeminate nation then turned to undemocratic weapons such as the knife or the dagger, a decline into slavery was practically inevitable.[100]

But while Cobbett saw in boxing an unambiguous solution to the threat of national effeminacy, others were less certain both about nation and about masculinity. In *Boxiana*, the Protestant Irish Pierce Egan sometimes claimed boxing for England and sometimes for Britain. In 'The Two Drovers' (1827), Walter Scott kept the distinction clear; boxing is an English sport. The story is set in the 1780s, and presents a conflict between two friends – a Highlander, Robin Oig, and an Englishman, Harry Wakefield – two different forms of combat – the sword and the fists – and two versions of masculinity.[101] The drovers are physically very different. Robin Oig was 'small of stature, as the epithet Oig implies, and not very strongly limbed'; on the other hand, he was 'as light and alert as one of the deer of his mountains'. Harry Wakefield was 'nearly six feet high, gallantly formed to keep the rounds at Smithfield, or maintain the ring at a wrestling match; and although he might have been overmatched, perhaps, among the regular professors of the Fancy, yet, as a yokel or a rustic, or a chance customer, he was able to give a bellyful to any amateur of the pugilistic art.'[102]

The men quarrel over who has the right to graze his sheep in a particular field, just on the English side of the Border. Harry wants a 'turn-up' and even offers to wear gloves. But Robin prefers the broadsword – 'I have no skill to fight like a jackanapes, with hands and nails'. Neither is a gentleman, but both are anxious to claim that status – Robin by evoking the Highland and European traditions of sword-fighting; Harry by boasting prowess in the fashionable English 'puglistic art'. They start with Harry's game, at which he beats Robin 'with as much ease as a boy bowls down a nine-pin'. In victory, Harry offers dubious consolation to his friend:

> 'Tis not thy fault, man, that not having the luck to be born an Englishman, thou canst not fight more than a school-girl.'
>
> 'I can fight,' answered Robin Oig sternly, but calmly, 'and you shall know it. You, Harry Waakfelt, shewed me today how the Saxon churls fight – I shew you now how the Highland Dunniewassal fights.'
>
> He seconded the word with the action, and plunged the dagger, which he suddenly displayed, into the broad breast of the English yeoman, with such fatal certainty and force, that the hilt made a hollow sound against the breast-bone, and the double-edged point split the very heart of his victim.

Both men are aware of the physical intimacy of fighting. Harry had hoped that the boxing match would end up with a clasping of hands and the two men 'better friends than ever'; it would be a 'tussle for love on the sod'. Although Robin suggests that boxing, a form of fighting 'with hands and nails', is unseemly, even animalistic, in its intimate physicality, his later plunge of the dirk into his friend's heart might be read as a more complete consummation of their uneasy relationship; it is certainly more suggestively phallic than the mere touch of hands.[103] Slurs of effeminacy (fighting like a schoolgirl, etc.) have given way to something else. 'The Two Drovers' ends with Robin Oig on trial, and with the judge reflecting on the cultural relativity of codes of honour. This has been, after all, a tale of the Borders.

A rather different interpretation of effeminacy, one with personal rather than political implications, is also introduced in Cobbett's essay when he refers to the prize-fighter Jem Belcher. Egan had described Belcher as having a 'prepossessing appearance, genteel and remarkably placid in his behaviour'.[104] He was generally thought to be a bit of a dandy, and wore 'immaculate dark clothes, set off by a vivid and extravagant neckcloth (usually blue with white spots)' which became known as a 'belcher' (illus. 17).[105] Cobbett, however, did not refer to Belcher's reputation for elegance (perhaps because he believed that 'women . . . *despise personal vanity in men*') and instead characterized him as 'a monster, a perfect ruffian'.[106] Nevertheless, there is 'scarcely a female Saint, perhaps, who would not, in her way to the conventicle, or even during the snuffling there to be heard, take a peep at him from beneath her hood. Can as much be said by any one of those noblemen and gentlemen who have been spending the best years of their lives in danc-ing by night and playing cricket by day?'

No wonder, Cobbett – the ex-soldier – added, women like soldiers. Effeminacy in this passage seems simply to mean sexual unattractiveness; war is forgotten in the face of more pressing issues. A little monstrous manliness would get you the girl.

Sometimes it would also get you the guy. References to boxers' groupies or 'macaronis' can be found in several eigh-teenth-century poems. 'Macaroni' was a derogatory label for young men who had travelled to France and Italy and came back with long hair and a taste for foreign food. In June 1770 the *Oxford Magazine* noted that 'a kind of animal, neither male not female, a thing of the neuter gender' had 'lately started up amongst us. It is called a Macaroni. It talks without mean-ing, it smiles without pleasantry, it eats without appetite, it rides without exercise, it wenches without passion.'[107] Three years later, in *Auld Reikie*, his poem of Edinburgh life, Robert Fergusson describes the drunken procession of the presumably beef-eating 'Bruiser' and the 'feckless Race o' Macaronies' who pursue him.[108] Christopher Anstey's burlesque *The Patriot* (1767) expressed the hope that Buckhorse's 'manly Strength' might 'greatly discompose':

> The Features of our modern Beaux,
>     And from their Macaroni Faces
> Send packing all the Loves and Graces;[109]

By the early nineteenth century, raucous descriptions of men pursuing boxers and women participating in fights (both, for eighteenth-century men, unfailing sources of comedy) had ceased; fighting was now a serious manly business and women largely featured as imaginary witnesses to this manliness. (Many historians have argued that from the 1770s onwards there was an increased cultural insistence on separate spheres for women and men.[110]) Sometimes descriptions of women spectators contain the frisson that Cobbett seems to experience in imagining the 'female Saint' peeping at the boxer from beneath her hood, but most often women are evoked precisely to show how alien their presence would be in the manly world of the Fancy. B. W. Proctor, for example, speculated in 1820 that 'if women were to attend the prize-fight how charming might it become':

> With what an air would our boxers strike, did they know that bright eyes were looking on them! How delicately would they '*peel!*' and with what elegant indifference would they come up to '*the scratch!*' The consciousness in question would generate the finest feeling amongst them: honour would ever be upper-most in their thoughts, even in a fall.[111]

Proctor clearly thought that any feminine involvement would ruin boxing. Not everyone agreed. After reluctantly attending a fight in 1818, Thomas Moore noted in his diary that it was not as 'horrid' as he had expected; indeed, 'had there been a proportionate mixture of women in the immense ring formed around, it would have been a very brilliant spectacle'.[112]

## GENTLEMAN JACK, PROFESSOR OF PUGILISM

John Jackson became Champion of the Prize Ring in 1795 when, in a clear breach of the rules – grabbing and pulling an opponent's hair was not permitted – he defeated Daniel Mendoza. A shrewd businessman, Jackson soon retired to join forces with fencing instructor Harry Angelo in his rooms at 13, New Bond Street. As one boxing historian put it, this initiated a new era in the 'gymnastic education of the aristocracy. Not to have had lessons of Jackson was a reproach. To attempt a list of his pupils would be to copy one-third of the then peerage.'[113] 'All the young nobility flock to his standard,' proclaimed Eaton Stannard Barrett in 1817, 'and, after a few months, find, with great delight, that they are matches for any drayman in town.'[114] Pupils included the Prince Regent, who had been a fan of Jackson's since watching him fight in Croydon in 1788. In 1821, the Prince turned to Jackson to provide eighteen prize-fighters as ushers at his coronation. Their presence had more than ceremonial purpose, for when George's estranged wife, the notorious Queen Caroline, arrived at Westminster Abbey to claim her position as Consort, the pugilists rushed to the door. William Cobbett was affronted, 'When she got to the door, and made an attempt to enter, she was actually thrust back *by the hands of a common prize-fighter*.'[115]

A less demanding, but no less devoted, pupil of Jackson's was George Gordon Byron, whose 1811 poem 'Hints from Horace' instructed that 'men unpractised in exchanging knocks / Must go to Jackson ere they dare to box.'[116] On leaving Cambridge in 1806, Byron took up boxing with great passion, initially as part of a rigorous regime of exercise and dieting; he quickly lost 3½ stone. When he moved to London in 1808, he spent a great deal of time in Jackson's company (Thomas Moore's *Life* features some of Byron's rather bossy letters to Jackson from that time) and later visits to the capital always included a trip to the New Bond Street rooms.[117] On 17 March 1814, for example, he noted that he had 'been sparring with Jackson for exercise this morning, and mean to continue and renew my acquaintance with my muffles'.

> My chest, and arms, and wind are in a very good plight, and I am not in flesh. I used to be a hard hitter, and my arms are very long for my height (5 feet 8½ inches); at any rate exercise is good, and this, the severest of all; fencing and the broad-sword never fatigued me so much.[118]

Some years later, in a note to the Eleventh Canto of *Don Juan*, he paid tribute to 'My friend and corporeal pastor and master, John Jackson, Esquire, professor of pugilism, who I trust still retains the strength and symmetry of his model of a form, together with his good humour, and athletic as well as mental accomplishments.'[119] Byron, whose Achilles tendons were so contracted he could only walk on the balls of his toes and who had been reviled as 'a lame brat' by his mother, remained, throughout his life, anxious about his own looks and an admirer of good looks in others.[120] Although this is never mentioned in his writings, boxing and swimming surely appealed to Byron as sports in which the impact of his lameness was minimal.[121]

Jackson's portrait was hung among the family pictures at Newstead Abbey, Byron's family home, and included in a collage of boxers on his dressing screen. The four-panel, six-foot high screen features theatrical portraits on one side and, on the other, coloured prints of prize-fighters and fights; some reports from *Boxiana* are included and some accounts of fights are handwritten. Both sequences are arranged chronologically; the boxing sequence begins with Figg and Broughton and ends with Jackson (illus. 18/19).[122]

18
Byron's screen: four
panels, *c.* 1811–14,
popular prints
collaged onto a
wooden frame.

19
Detail of Byron's
screen, featuring
Tom Molineaux.

John Jackson, one of whose nicknames was 'Commander-in-Chief', may also have been the model for John Johnson, the 'British friend' with whom Don Juan fights the Turks in canto eight of Byron's satire.[123] This is suggested by the description of their thrashing by 'Turkish batteries' as 'like a flail, / Or a good boxer' in stanza XLIII, and the ambiguous phrasing in stanza XCVII, where 'Jack' could refer to the first or surname:

> Up came John Johnson (I will not say Jack)
> For that were vulgar, cold, and commonplace,
> On great occasions such as an attack . . .

Johnson certainly inspires the sort of admiring devotion in Juan that Jackson did in Byron. While Juan is a 'mere novice' at war, Johnson is 'a noble fellow' who is frequently 'very busy without bustle'; in return, we are happy to learn, Johnson 'really loved him in his way'.[124]

Byron's interest in boxing did not stem wholly from its healthful benefits. The glamorous demi-monde of prize-fighting also appealed. An 1807 letter described London life as consisting of, among other diversions, 'routs, riots, balls and boxing matches', a lifestyle that would be duplicated by Don Juan, who passed his London afternoons 'in visits, luncheons, / Lounging and boxing'.[125]

At this time, the boxing world centred on a handful of London pubs in the back rooms of which boxers often trained, and where their managers might meet, and dine, with wealthy backers. On retiring, many boxers opened pubs attracting a sporting clientele with their trophies and their stories. Bob Gregson's Castle Tavern in High Holborn opened in 1810 and its snuggery soon became an inner sanctum for the Fancy. After Gregson was convicted for debt evasion, Tom Belcher took over, 'skimm[ing] the cream off the Fancy', as Egan put it, for another fourteen years.[126] After Tom Spring defeated Bill Neate, Egan noted that 'Belcher's house, the Castle Tavern, was like a fair; Randall's was crowded to suffocation; Holt's hadn't room for a pin; Eales' was overstocked; and Tom Cribb's was crammed with visitors.'[127] Byron was a regular customer at all these houses, especially Cribb's – 'Tom is an old friend of mine; I have seen some of his best battles in my nonage', Byron noted after an evening during which he 'drank more than I like'.[128]

Two of the most famous regulars at Jackson's Academy, Cribb's pub, and the London fights, were fictional – Corinthian Tom and his country cousin, Jerry Hawthorne, the rakish heroes of Pierce Egan's picaresque bestseller, *Life in London* (1821), a work lavishly illustrated by his friends, Robert and George Cruikshank (George, 'not averse from using his fists in an up-and-down tussle', was sometimes compared to the fighter Tom Spring).[129] The three men often worked together, and between them created a distinctive 'flash' style of commentary on Regency life (illus. 48). The next chapter will explore this style in some detail.

The appeal of *Life in London* lay largely in its promising to bring together high and low life. A trip to the Royal Academy, for example, is followed by, and juxtaposed with, one to the slums – cousin Jerry must enjoy the complete urban experience. When John Clare read *Don Juan* in 1824 he wrote in his journal that Byron's 'Hero seems a fit partner for [Egan's] Tom and Jerry'.[130] Byron himself boasted of 'eternal parties', featuring '*Jockies*, Gamblers, *Boxers*, *Authors, parsons,* and *poets* . . . a precious Mixture, but they go on well together.'[131] Boxing culture throve on the promise of social promiscuity. The readers of *Life in London* were largely neither upper nor working class, but they could, with Egan's help, imagine themselves mingling with members of both. At the Castle Tavern, Egan wrote, 'You may be seated next to an M.P. without being aware of that honour; or you may likewise rub against some noble lord without committing a breach of privilege. You may meet poets on the look-out for a hero, artists for subjects; and boxers for customers.'[132] Readers, whether 'fire-side heroes' or 'sprightly maidens', could, he promised, '"see Life" without receiving a *scratch*.'[133]

Some found this picture of social promiscuity more frightening than appealing. In *Tales of a Traveller* (1824), Washington Irving's Buckthorne described a boxing match as nothing more than 'an arena, where the noble and illustrious are jostled into familiarity with the infamous and the vulgar'. 'What, in fact, is The Fancy itself,' he continued, 'but a chain of easy communication, extending down form the peer to the pick-pocket, through the medium of which a man of rank may find he has shaken hands at three removes, with the murderer on the gibbet?'[134]

For Byron the effect of moving between high and low life had psychological as well as social consequences. In a journal entry for 23 November 1813, largely preoccupied with feeling 'wound up' after an unpleasant dream, he noted the therapeutic effects of such jaunts:

> I must not dream again; – it spoils even reality. I will go out of doors and see what the fog will do for me. Jackson has been here: the boxing world much as usual; – but the club increases. I shall dine at Crib's tomorrow. I like energy – even animal energy – of all kinds; and I have need of both mental and corporeal. I have not dined out, nor indeed, at all, lately: have heard no music – have seen nobody. Now for a plunge – high life and low life. Amant alterna Camænæ [The Muses love alternating verses.][135]

An insistence on the value of alternating between the mental and corporeal, or more, an insistence on the necessity of the physical for 'the ethereal', recurs throughout his notebooks. On 19 April 1814, he recorded having spent four days lovesick and alone, except, it emerges, for daily visits from Jackson:

> I have sparred for exercise (windows open) with Jackson an hour daily, to attenuate and keep up the ethereal part of me. The more violent the fatigue the better my spirits for the rest of the day . . . To-day I have

boxed an hour – written an ode to Napoleon Buonaparte – copied it – eaten six biscuits – drunk four bottles of soda water – redde away the rest of my time – besides giving poor [Webster?] a world of advice on this mistress of his . . .[136]

The detailed nature of Byron's accounting – including the perennial dieter's awareness of the precise number of biscuits he has consumed – suggests that he did not leave the balance of high and low, physical and emotional, to chance. On the day of his mother's funeral in 1811, Byron called for his page to bring his boxing gloves for his daily exercise rather than follow the coffin to the family vault. The sparring that day, the page recalled, was more violent than usual.[137] After his beloved brother Tom died in 1818, a distraught John Keats was taken to a prize-fight at Crawley Downs by well-meaning friends. Pugilism, the 'Regency answer to grief, stoical and worldly', did not seem to work in his case.[138]

# 3

# Pugilism and Style

All the great poets should have been fighters. Take Keats and Shelley,
for an example. They were pretty good poets, but they died young.
You know why? Because they didn't train.
Cassius Clay, 1964[1]

Byron consistently affected hauteur about those who took writing too seriously;
a gesture characteristic of what Christopher Ricks terms his 'flippant lordli-
ness'.[2] In an 1821 journal entry, he noted that his mother, Madame de Staël and
the *Edinburgh Review* had all, at various times, compared him to Rousseau. A
page then follows in which he explains why he cannot see 'any point of resemblance'. There are many points of contrast, and some interestingly odd
conjunctions. The first comes in Byron's initial distinction – 'he wrote prose, I
verse; he was of the people, I the Aristocracy'. Prose then is aligned with 'the
people'; poetry with the Aristocracy. The revelation that 'he liked Botany, I like
flowers, and herbs, and trees, but know nothing of their pedigrees' further
damns prose for its utilitarianism. Rousseau is little more than an Enlightenment taxonomist. From then on, it is a short step (a mere colon) from 'He wrote
with hesitation and care, I with rapidity and rarely with pains' to an account of
what 'better' things an aristocrat might find to do:

> *He* could never ride nor swim 'nor was cunning of the fence', *I* am an
> excellent swimmer, a decent though not at all dashing rider ... sufficient
> of fence ... not a bad boxer when I could keep my temper, which was
> difficult, but which I strove to do ever since I knocked down Mr Purling
> and put his knee-pad out (with the gloves on) in Angelo's and Jackson's
> rooms in 1806 during the sparring ...

In a journal entry of 1813, written before going to dinner at Tom Cribb's with
Jackson, Byron complained that 'the mighty stir made about scribbling and
scribes' was a 'sign of effeminacy, degeneracy and weakness. Who would write,
who had anything better to do?'[3]

Byron's concern with class is evident in the scorn he expressed five years later for Leigh Hunt's reference to poetry as a 'profession': 'I thought that Poetry was an *art*, or an *attribute*, and not a *profession*.'[4] There was one profession, however, which Byron admired unreservedly. Pugilism was an activity in which the boundaries between professional and amateur were clear. Nonchalance was not therefore required, and proper training was desirable. Byron could train as hard as he liked to box, without anyone suspecting that he was not a gentleman. And even he thought that there were literary activities which required a comparable professional attitude. In 'Hints from Horace' (1811), Byron lambasted the *Edinburgh Review* critic Francis Jeffrey as unqualified to discuss his poems, suggesting that no boxer would presume to enter the ring without proper training.[5]

In this chapter, I shall explore some of the ways in which, during the early decades of the nineteenth century, writers and artists found in pugilism not only a subject-matter, but the basis for a method.

## LITERARY FLASH

Writing about pugilism reached its zenith in the 1820s, at a time when the sport itself had begun to wane. At the forefront of the fad was undoubtedly Pierce Egan's *Boxiana; or Sketches of Ancient and Modern Pugilism*. The first volume appeared in 1812, followed by a second in 1818, a third in 1821, and a new series in two volumes in 1828 and 1829. His round-by-round accounts of fights between Mendoza and Humphries, or Cribb and Molineaux, are still the major sources quoted today. In 1824, he began editing a weekly paper, *Pierce Egan's Life in London and Sporting Guide*, which later developed into the famous sporting journal, *Bell's Life in London*. What distinguished Egan's work from other boxing histories of the period (such as William Oxberry's 1812 *Pancratia*) was its great verve and distinctive style. Dubbed 'the Great Lexicographer of the Fancy', Egan did not just reflect the language of the Fancy, he created it.[6] His 1822 edition of Francis Grose's *Classical Dictionary of the Vulgar Tongue* included many of his own coinings.

Egan's writing is characterized by a lively mixture of elaborate metaphors, dreadful puns and awful verse. In this passage from 'The Fancy on the Road to Moulsey Hurst', aided by a lavish supply of commas, italics and capitals, he describes a particular type of 'fancier':

> His heart is up to his mouth every moment for fear he should be *floored*, he is anxious to look like a SWELL, if 'tis only for a day: he has therefore *borrowed a prad* to *come it strong*, without recollecting, that to be a *top-of-the-tree buck* requires something more than the *furnishing* hand of a tailor, or the assistance of the groom. It should also be remembered, that although the CORINTHIAN at times descend hastily down a few steps, to take a peep into the lower regions of society, to mark their habits and customs, yet many of them can as hastily regain their

eminency, as the player throws off his dress, and appear in reality –
a GENTLEMAN.[7]

The horseman's flash style is an unsuccessful attempt at assuming a higher class
position – his gig is '*hired*', his horse ('*prad*') borrowed, and his clothes reflect the
taste of his tailor. The enterprise is doomed, Egan suggests; it is obvious to anyone really flash, really knowing, that he is an impostor, an 'EMPTY BOUNCE'. The
CORINTHIAN's 'mark[ing]' of 'the habits and customs' of a lower class is not,
however, subject to the same disparagement. He does not cling to his disguise,
but readily, 'hastily', throws it off to resume his status. Slumming is temporary
and permissible while social climbing, which strives for permanent change,
is not.

Class mobility was a key element in the spread of boxing and its idiom during this period. The early nineteenth century saw the establishment of numerous magazines, many of which catered for a growing 'army of bachelor clerks
and lawyer's apprentices' whose aspiration to gentility often manifested itself
as an interest in traditionally aristocratic pastimes.[8] Flash slang involved the
middle-class imitation of an upper-class imitation of lower-class idioms.[9]

The Tory *Blackwood's Edinburgh Magazine* was particularly keen on
traditional squirish activities such as pugilism and published numerous reports,
stories and articles on the sport. (In 1822 it declared itself 'a real Magazine of
mirth, misanthropy, wit, wisdom, folly, fiction, fun, festivity, theology, bruising
and thingumbob'.[10]) Most notable were the boxing writings of John Wilson,
Professor of Moral Philosophy at Edinburgh University, writing as *Blackwood's*
fictional editor, 'Christopher North'. Wilson had boxed while a student at
Oxford – his friend Thomas De Quincey recalled that 'not a man, who could
either 'give' or 'take', but boasted to have punished, or to have been punished by,
*Wilson of Mallens* [Magdalen]' – and often depicted himself in *Blackwood's* as a
kind of critical pugilist.[11] But while Hugh MacDiarmid later wrote scathingly of
Wilson as 'the most extraordinary exponent' of the kind of 'verbiage' which is
intended 'simply to batter the hearer into a pulpy state of vague acquiescence',
others relished both the verbiage and the battering.[12] 'I cannot express . . . the
heavenliness of associations connected with such articles as Professor Wilson's,'
wrote Branwell Brontë in 1835, 'read and re-read while a little child, with all their
poetry of language and divine flights into that visionary realm of imagination'.[13]

One of Wilson's finest flights of imagination can be found in the May 1820
issue of *Blackwood's* in the form of a '"Luctus" on the Death of Sir Daniel Donnelly, Late Champion of Ireland.' The prize-fighter had died after a particularly
heavy drinking session. Wilson included copiously footnoted tributes from
imagined scholars in Greek, Hebrew and Latin, along with poems in the style of
Byron and Wordsworth. While Byron is perhaps too obvious a target, and 'Child
Daniel' not particularly funny, the 'extract from my great auto-biographical
poem' contributed by W. W. is sharply attentive to both the Lake Poet's style and
his distance from the world (and slang) of the Fancy:

> . . . Yea, even I,
> Albeit, who never 'ruffian'd' in the ring,
> Nor know of 'challenge', save the echoing hills;
> Nor 'fibbing', save that poesy doth feign,
> Nor heard his fame, but as the mutterings
> Of clouds contentious on Helvellyn's side,
> Distant, yet deep, aguise a strange regret,
> And mourn Donnelly – Honourable Sir Daniel: – [14]

Wordsworth enjoyed a rare immunity to 'boximania'.[15] By the 1820s, it had become almost unthinkable in certain circles not to understand boxing slang or the 'flash'. The *OED* cites the first instance of 'flash' being used to mean 'dashing, ostentatious, swaggering, "swell"' in 1785: the slightly later meaning of 'belonging to, connected with, or resembling, the class of sporting men, *esp.* the patrons of the ring' dates from 1808. But the two meanings seem related. 'A flash man upon the town' is surely swaggering and dandyish, as well as knowledgeable about prize-fighting. A third, related, meaning is 'knowing, wide-awake, "smart", "fly"'. Egan opens *Boxiana* with a footnote explaining the Fancy 'as many of our readers may not be flash to the above term'. But it seems likely, as Egan must surely have realized, that if a reader was flash to 'flash', he would be flash to 'the Fancy'.[16]

Keats's description of Byron's *Don Juan* as 'a flash poem' seems to draw on all these meanings; few poems are so knowing, swaggering, and connected to practitioners and patrons of the ring.[17] Canto XI presents an encounter between Juan, newly arrived in London from Spain, and an assailant called Tom, 'full flash, all fancy', whom Juan shoots and kills. 'O Jack, I'm floor'd' are his final words. Byron then devotes a stanza to the memory of Tom, 'so prime, so swell, so nutty, and so knowing'. Tom would have understood such flash language, but Juan does not even understand standard English.[18] A note is supplied, which refuses to explain anything because, Byron says, 'the advance of science and of language has rendered it unnecessary to translate the above good and true English, spoken in its original purity by the select mobility and their patrons'. He directs any readers who 'require a traduction' to Gentleman Jackson.[19] In 1808, John Cam Hobhouse commented that his friend had been 'deeply admitted into the penetralia Jacksoniana'; some years later, in his *Life of Lord Byron*, Thomas Moore recalled his amusement at observing 'how perfectly familiar with the annals of "The Ring", and with all the most recondite phraseology of "the Fancy", was the sublime poet of Childe Harold'.[20] (Byron's attachment to boxing and its language was, Moore felt, one of his several 'boyish tastes'.)

Gary Dyer argues that Byron and his friends were attracted to the Fancy's dialect because it 'was fashioned to hide meanings from outsiders'.[21] Indeed as Thomas Moore put it in the preface to his satirical poem 'Tom Crib's Memorial to Congress', flash 'was invented, and is still used, like the cipher of the diplomatists, for purposes of secrecy'.[22] What that secrecy meant to upper-class 'fanciers' like Byron is a matter for speculation. Dyer reads Byron's secrets as always ultimately referring back to sodomy. Byron's biographer, Benita Eissler, maintains that Jackson and Angelo were 'rumoured' to be lovers as well as business partners, and that the Academy served as a cover for illicit meetings.[23] While there is no direct evidence for this, it is certainly true that Byron's London circle was interested in sodomy as well as in boxing.

But a secret language surely holds other attractions. One is exclusivity, or, in the age of the beginnings of commercial journalism, the pretence of exclusivity. In the course of a general denunciation of the Fives Court as a 'college of scoundrelism' in 1824, Washington Irving's Buckthorne asks, 'what is the slang language of "The Fancy" but a jargon by which fools and knaves commune and understand each other, and enjoy a kind of superiority over the uninitiated?'[24] Robert Southey's fictional Don Espriella, 'writing to the uninitiated' back in Spain in 1807, certainly takes great pleasure in explaining such terms as 'bottom', 'a pleasant fighter' and 'much punished'.[25] In 1818, however, phrases such as these remain untranslated by Byron, although he tells us that only what he calls 'the select mobility and their patrons' will understand; only they speak 'good and true English'. Byron's play on 'select nobility' does more than suggest that boxers are like noblemen. His footnote also mocks the widespread tendency to explain flash language in footnotes. By freely coining his own new phrase, 'select mobility', Byron is attacking jargon's claim to provide unique access to knowledge.

Many other poets made comparable play with boxing language. The narrator of Henry Luttrell's *Advice to Julia: A Letter in Rhyme* (1820) stops a perfectly adequate description of a fight to apologise for his lack of pugilistic vocabulary:

> But hold. – Such prowess to describe
> Asks all the jargon of the tribe;
> And though enough to serve my turn
> From 'Boxiana' I might learn,
> Or borrow from an ampler store
> In the bright page of Thomas Moore . . .[26]

Thomas Moore is an interesting choice of source, for he much disliked boxing. Nevertheless, Moore too sought out the company of Jackson, and once attended a fight (which was 'altogether not so horrid as I expected') for the sake of his verse; in order 'to pick up as much of the flash *from authority*, as possible'.[27] Although he 'got very little out of Jackson', he went on to write two popular poems on pugilistic themes.

John Hamilton Reynolds, on the other hand, loved boxing (he was the boxing correspondent, as well as theatre critic, for the *London Magazine*). As a young man he regularly attended fights and sparred, while writing poetry and working as a clerk in an insurance office. *The Fancy* (1820) is semi-autobiography disguised as the fictional biography of Peter Corcoran, boxing groupie and 'Student of Law' (the name was borrowed from an eighteenth-century fighter and had the advantage of sharing an acronym with the Pugilistic Club). Corcoran is also a poet, and much of *The Fancy* consists of his poems: 'pugilism', the editor notes, 'engrossed nearly all his thoughts, and coloured all his writings'. The writing is full of cringe-worthy pugilistic puns. Consider, for example, one of the 'Stanzas to Kate, On Appearing Before Her After a Casual "Turn Up"':

> You know I love sparring and poesy, Kate,
> And scarcely care whether I'm hit at, or kiss'd; –
> You know that Spring equally makes me elate,
> With the blow of a flower, and the blow of a fist.

'Spring' is asterisked, and the fictional editor writes, 'I am not sure whether Mr. Corcoran alluded here to the *season*, or the pugilist of this name.'[28]

Such pompous comments work to distance the reader from the editor as well as from Corcoran. In the preface, for example, he notes that 'this style of writing is not good – it is too broken, irresolute, and rugged; and it is too anxious in its search after smart expressions to be continuous or elevated in its substance'.[29] By the book's end, we become aware both of the compulsive appeal of such 'rugged' and punning language – particularly as a way of deflating the 'elevated' discourse of much poetry; again Wordsworth seems a target here – and of its repetitive limitations.

A wider look at the literature of the 1820s (in particular magazine literature) shows just how pervasive an addiction to flash really was. Thomas De Quincey, for example, savoured its use in a variety of contexts, some of which were more apposite than others. Boxing slang works particularly well in a July 1828 attack on 'The Pretensions of Phrenology', because both boxing and phrenology are interested in the human skull. Medical and sporting jargon are set against each other in a description of the phrenologists who, 'after receiving a few hard thumps on the *frontal sinus* and the *cerebellum*, . . . were fain to have recourse to shifting and shuffling; *bobbing aside their brain-boxes*'. In the debate De Quincey champions the philosopher Sir William Hamilton, who we soon learn is no '*shy fighter*', no '*flincher*', a '*tolerably hard hitter*' and 'rather an *ugly customer*': 'the *chanceried nobs* of his two antagonists exhibit indisputable proofs of his pugilistic prowess, and of the *punishment* he is capable of administering'. And this is only the opening paragraph.[30]

Later that same month, De Quincey became a co-editor of the Edinburgh *Evening Post*, contributing the latest news from London and writing many short editorial notices. One addressed a dispute between two Edinburgh intellectuals on the teaching of Greek at Scottish universities with the promise of organizing 'a *set-to* . . . in our Publishing Office, between three and four' on any day of their choosing.[31] De Quincey and his co-editor, the Reverend Andrew Crichton, did not get on, and Crichton's own articles often contained digs at De Quincey's 'addiction' to metaphors drawn from the 'vile' sport of boxing. The 'defence of

. . . pugilism' is 'very shallow', and 'monstrously inconsistent with Christian principles', he wrote in a review of *Blackwood's*; an author who resorts to 'the slang of the fancy' has 'a rough lump of the brute in him, which ought to be cut out by the scalpel'.[32] The surgical metaphor is itself an implicit rebuke to such authors.

## 'HARD WORDS AND HARD BLOWS' IN HAZLITT

In essays on topics ranging from parliamentary debate to sculpture to theatre to boxing, William Hazlitt talked about blows. The Reformation struck a 'death-blow' at 'scarlet vice and bloated hypocrisy'; William Godwin's *Enquiry concerning Political Justice* dealt a 'blow to the philosophical mind of the country'; Wordsworth's 'popular, inartificial style gets rid (at a blow) of . . . all the high places of poetry.'[33] 'On Shakespeare and Milton' (1818) reads like a comparison of the styles of two boxers rather than two writers. Shakespeare's blows are 'rapid and devious', 'the stroke like the lightning's, is sure as it is sudden'. Milton, on the other hand, 'always labours, and almost always succeeds'.[34] 'Milton has great gusto. He repeats his blow twice; grapples with and exhausts his subject.'[35]

And it is not only poems which deal blows. In an 1826 essay 'On the Prose-Style of Poets', Hazlitt asserts categorically that 'every word should be a blow: every thought should instantly grapple with its fellow'. 'Weight', 'precision' and 'contact' are needed to strike the best blow, and produce the best prose. Some writers display some of these virtues; few all. Byron's prose, for example, is 'heavy, laboured and coarse: he tries to knock some one down with the butt-end of every line'.[36]

Hazlitt foregrounds the relationship between fighting and writing styles in an 1821 essay on William Cobbett. The essay begins by comparing the radical politician to the boxer Tom Cribb. Initially the comparison seems to be based on the fact of Cobbett's devotion to pugilism and his self-representation as, like Cribb, a living embodiment of John Bull.[37] Hazlitt then moves on to matters of style:

> His blows are as hard, and he himself is impenetrable. One has no notion of him as making use of a fine pen, but a great mutton-fist; his style stuns his readers, and he 'fillips the ear of the public with a three-man beetle'.[38]

The last phrase is a quotation from *Henry IV* part 2, and its inclusion, alongside sporting analogy, is a favourite technique of Hazlitt's. In the pages that follow, the metaphor is developed more fully. Cobbett has a 'pugnacious disposition, that must have an antagonist power to contend with', but this is a 'bad propensity' since:

> If his blows were straightforward and steadily directed to the same object, no unpopular Minister could live before him; instead of which

he lays about right and left, impartially and remorselessly, makes a clear stage, has all the ring to himself, and then runs out of it when he should stand his ground.[39]

The essay concludes by shifting the comparison. Cobbett is now no longer England's hero, Tom Cribb, but 'Big Ben', Benjamin Brain, known to be 'bullying and cowardly'. Not so tall but very stocky, Brain had defeated the long-reigning champion Tom Johnson in 1791 in 'a most tremendous battle'.[40] Johnson had been a favourite of the fashionable Fancy, and was even reputed to have worn pink laces in his boxing boots.[41] Big Ben was less gentlemanly. He badly damaged Johnson's nose in the second round, and fought on regardless, even when, in his distress, Johnson soon after broke a finger on a ring post. For many commentators this victory marks the end of the first era of British boxing, when men stood toe-to-toe and punched away without much technique. For Hazlitt to compare Cobbett to Big Ben is to insult not just his bravery, but also his skill and intelligence. Cobbett, he concludes, is 'a Big Ben in politics, who will fall upon others and crush them by his weight, but is not prepared for resistance, and is soon staggered by a few smart blows'.[42]

Hazlitt's most sustained comparison of fighting and writing can be found in 'Jack Tars', an essay originally published in 1826 under the title 'English and Foreign Manners'. 'There are two things that an Englishman understands,' Hazlitt begins, 'hard words and hard blows,' and he goes on to define the English character in terms of a sort of aggressive empiricism. French audiences appreciate Racine and Molière, whose 'dramatic dialogue is frothy verbiage'; English audiences prefer to watch boxing, where 'every Englishman feels his power to give and take blows increased by sympathy', or, what is put forward as its equivalent, English plays whose dialogue 'constantly clings to the concrete and has a *purchase* upon matter'. Englishmen, in short, perceive the world through violent opposition. This makes them feel 'alive' and also manly. 'The English are not a nation of women . . . it cannot be denied they are a pugnacious set.'[43]

A complex alignment of qualities is being made. Some are familiar – pugnacity, masculinity and Englishness; new to the mix is empiricism, defined as the pugnacious, masculine, English way of perceiving the world. The English 'require the heavy, hard, and tangible only, something for them to grapple with and resist, to try their strength and their unimpressibility upon'.[44] English empiricism is, in Hazlitt's terms, less concerned with what John Locke called secondary qualities (colour, taste and smell are, Hazlitt maintained, of more interest to the French), than 'the heavy, hard and tangible' primary qualities.[45] The solid materialism of Englishness ('our lumpish clay') is a favourite theme of Hazlitt's, especially in opposition to light French liveliness. English criticism of French culture is difficult, he argued, because 'the strength of the blow is always defeated by the very insignificance and want of resistance in the object'.[46]

'The same images and trains of thought stick by me', Hazlitt wrote in his 'Farewell to Essay-Writing' (1828).[47] This is clearly true, but his use of boxing idiom and metaphor was not an unthinking tick. Indeed, it serves much more various and complex purposes in his work than it does in that of any other writer of the time. Contemporary discussions of Hazlitt's language, however, rarely went beyond politically motivated condemnation or praise. *Blackwood's* argued that prize-fighters were 'downright Tories' and therefore belonged in *Blackwood's*, but other journals were more interested in suggesting that neither Hazlitt or pugilists were suitable for their polite middle-class readers. The *New Edinburgh Review* was 'sorry to say' that some of Hazlitt's allusions were 'of the lowest and most shockingly indelicate description'. It joined the *Quarterly Review* in dismissing him as a 'Slang-Whanger':

> We utterly loathe him where he seems most at home, namely, among pugilists, and wagerers, and professional tennis-players, passing current their vain glorious slang. We protest against allusions to the very existence of the Bens and Bills and Jacks and Jems and Joes of 'the ring', in any printed page above the destination of the ale-bench; but to have their nauseous vocabulary defiling the language of a printed book, regularly entered at Stationers' Hall, and destined for the use of men and women of education, taste, and delicacy, is quite past endurance . . . we strenuously protest against this bang up style, this 'fancy diction', in a series of 'original essays'. Our conclusion, at least, is irresistible, – the author has not kept good company . . .[48]

The anti-Cockney snobbery of the Tory journals would not have surprised Hazlitt, nor would the qualified support of John Hamilton Reynolds, author of *The Fancy*, and boxing correspondent of the liberal *London Magazine*. Indeed Reynolds's only criticism of the second volume of *Table Talk* – that Hazlitt's points are put forward too directly – is itself made in '*fancy* diction':

> The style of this book is singularly nervous [i.e. sinewy, strong and vigorous] and direct, and seems to aim at mastering its subject by dint of mere hard hitting. There is no such thing as manoeuvring for a blow. The language strikes out, and if the intention is not fulfilled, the blow is repeated until the subject falls.[49]

Fascinated by boxing's metaphorical possibilities, Hazlitt wrote only one essay on the thing itself, 'The Fight' (1822). One of the most influential and frequently anthologized pieces on boxing, the essay encompasses many of the themes already discussed – style, Englishness, masculinity, the material world – and presents them in a manner at once casual and densely considered.

Consider the epigraph, which rewrites Hamlet's musings on what he hopes to accomplish by putting on a play for Claudius's benefit (or punishment):

— The *fight*, the *fight's* the thing,
Wherein I'll catch the conscience of the king.[50]

Hazlitt's substitution of 'fight' for 'play' has two implications: first, that a fight *is* a play, a kind of performance; secondly, that this particular fight/play is a performance from which something is to be learnt. Hamlet's play will catch the king's conscience. What about the fight Hazlitt witnesses? The contest is first of all a contest of performed styles; styles that we have come to think of as French and English. The champion, Bill Hickman, the Gasman, is 'light, vigorous, elastic', his skin glistening in the sun 'like a panther's hide'; his unfavoured challenger, Bill Neate, is 'great, heavy, clumsy', with long arms 'like two sledge-hammers'. At one point, 'Neate seemed like a lifeless lump of flesh and bone, round which the Gasman's blows played with the rapidity of electricity or lightning.' The two men also differ in personality. Hickman is a Homeric boaster, who arrives to fight 'like the cock-of-the-walk'. Hazlitt is more judgmental than Homer, however, and complains that Hickman 'strutted about more than became a hero'. Neate is modest and celebrates his eventual victory 'without any appearance of arrogance'.

In general, though, both men wonderfully exemplify courage and endurance. But of what kind? Classical comparison casts Neate as Ajax to Hickman's Diomed, Hector to his Achilles. The fight itself amply confirms the 'high and heroic state of man'. It reminds Hazlitt of the 'dark encounter' between clouds over the Caspian, in Milton's *Paradise Lost*, as Satan faces Sin and Death at hell's gates.[51] And yet the life actually lived during a fight is nasty, brutish, and (relatively) short. The fighter's triumph is not only transitory, but in essence banal ('The eyes were filled with blood, the nose streamed blood, the mouth gaped blood'), and invariably surreptitious (like a 1990s rave, the fight between Hickman and Neate took place, at the shortest possible notice, in a field near Newbury). Could it be that the literary form best suited to this brief battle was not epic poetry, but the essay?

Hazlitt's essay, like the preparations made for the fight by participants and spectators alike, is much ado, if not exactly about nothing, then about something as fleeting as it is pungent. He finds it difficult enough to get himself out of London. Missing the mail coach prompts a self-reproach that seems excessive, 'I had missed it as I missed everything else, by my own absurdity.' Finally, however, he is on his way, and as he puts on a great coat, his mood improves. Leaving London behind, he enters another world with its own distinctive rules and customs. Joe Toms walks up Chancery Lane 'with that quick jerk and impatient stride which distinguishes a lover of the FANCY'; in the coach to the fight Hazlitt meets a man 'whose costume bespoke him one of the FANCY'; on the way back he describes his friend, Pigott, as being 'dressed in character for the occasion, or like one of the FANCY; that is, with a double portion of great coats, clogs, and overhauls'. It is only on the journey home that Hazlitt himself is properly 'dressed in character'; Pigott supplies him with a 'genteel drab great coat and green silk handkerchief (which I must say became me exceedingly).' The costume gives him the confidence to deride a group of 'Goths and Vandals . . . not real flash-men, but interlopers, noisy pretenders, butchers from Tothillfields, brokers from Whitechapel' who brashly interrupt a discussion of the respective merits of roasted fowl and mutton-chops. The essay ends with him reluctantly returning these clothes. So far, so Pierce Egan.

Like Egan, Hazlitt relished flash language. 'The Fight' is littered with italicized idioms: *'turn-up'*, *'swells'*, *'the scratch'*, *'pluck'*. But the great literary virtue of an essay is that it does not have to stick to one kind of performance. Hazlitt rapidly expands his repertoire of allusion beyond Homer, Shakespeare, and Milton. His allusions politicize pugilism. They enhance its democratic credentials. Riding in the coach with Toms, he recites, 'in an involuntary fit of enthusiasm', some lines of Spenser on delight and liberty; Toms promptly translates these 'into the vulgate' as meaning *'Going to see a fight'*. The connection between boxing, sentiment and (political as well as psychological) liberty is reinforced on the return journey, when Pigott reads out passages from Rousseau's *New Eloise*. And if literature can enhance an appreciation of boxing, boxing also has literary potential. Hazlitt is enchanted by the conversation of a man he meets in the pub, and tells him that he talks as well as Cobbett writes. Perhaps in response to his critics, Hazlitt makes it clear that sporting interests are not the preserve of Tory squires; middle-class radicals can make them urban, modern and sophisticated.

Hazlitt's pleasure in joining this convivial, masculine world is palpable. This had been his first fight, he announces at the beginning of the essay, 'yet it more than answered my expectations'. But what were those expectations? In 'On Going A Journey', published four months earlier, Hazlitt had written of the desire to 'forget the town and all that is in it'. In the town was his landlady's daughter, Sarah Walker, whose charms and unfaithfulness form the subject of an autobiographical meditation, *Liber Amoris* (1823). She is never mentioned here, but Hazlitt does occasionally (and rather cryptically) evoke his misery. The essay begins by dedicating what follows to 'Ladies'. He compliments 'the fairest of the fair' and the 'loveliest of the lovely' and entreats them to 'notice the exploits of the brave'. But a rather sour note emerges when he urges ladies to consider 'how many more ye kill with poison baits than ever fell in the ring'. These words gain a poignant resonance when we consider that an early draft of the essay contained a passage about his lovelorn wretchedness. David Bromwich argues that an awareness of this passage reveals 'the under-plot' of the essay and explains its 'impetuous pace' and 'arbitrary high spirits'.[52]

'The Fight' tells the story of a man who is almost successful at escaping himself. If romance is a *'hysterica passio'*, the Fancy is 'the most practical of all things', and its emphasis on mundane facts – its thoroughly English empiricism – distracts him most of the time.[53] 'The FANCY are not men of imagination', he is pleased to note. Occasionally, though, he slips back into self-pity. After describing the pleasures of the training regime, he cannot help adding:

'Is this life not more sweet than mine?' I was going to say; but I will not libel any life by comparing it to mine, which is (at the date these presents) bitter as coloquintida and the dregs of aconitum!

But such passages of lovesick rhetoric (passages common in *Liber Amoris*) are infrequent. As long as he can talk of boxing and mutton-chops, love and London can be kept at bay:

> A stranger takes his hue and character from the time and place. He is a part of the furniture and costume of an inn . . . I associate nothing with my travelling companion but present objects and passing events. In his ignorance of me and my affairs, I in a manner forget myself.[54]

Hazlitt's language of the blow provided him with a means to compare poets and politicians to athletes and (democratically) to judge one against the other.[55] The 'blows' of John Cavanagh, the fives-player, for example, were 'not undecided and ineffectual', unlike Coleridge's 'wavering' prose.[56] Hazlitt also judged his own work by the standard of sport, and sometimes found it lacking. 'What is there that I can do as well as this?' he once asked on observing some Indian jugglers. 'Nothing', was his reply. 'I have always had this feeling of the inefficacy and slow progress of intellectual compared to mechanical excellence, and it has always made me somewhat dissatisfied.'[57] 'I have a much greater ambition to be the best racket-player, than the best prose-writer of the age.'[58] But most of the time, Hazlitt did believe that prose could eventually achieve its own excellence, comparable (among other things) to relation between parts in the Elgin marbles; 'one part being given, another cannot be otherwise than it.'[59] 'The Fight' ends with a 'P.S.', in which Hazlitt agrees with his friend Toms's description of the fight as 'a complete thing'. The last sentence – 'I hope he will relish my account of it' – suggests that the essay is consciously striving to be something equally 'complete', something in which all the parts harmoniously create a whole (however ephemeral).

## SCULPTING AND PAINTING THE BOXERS

In the same month that 'The Fight' appeared, Hazlitt published the first of three essays on the Elgin Marbles. His remarks there, and elsewhere, directly attack Sir Joshua Reynolds's *Discourses* (1769–1790), which argued that the beauty of a work of art was 'general and intellectual': 'the sight never beheld it, nor has the hand expressed it: it is an idea residing in the breast of the artist'.[60] On this view, the artist is completely divorced from the craftsman who works with his eyes, hands and materials. Hazlitt, on the other hand, emphasized the ways in which art resembled craft and sport – and in all these spheres genius could emerge. One of the pleasures of painting, he maintained, was that, unlike writing, it 'exercises the body' and requires 'a continued and steady exertion of muscular power'. The best paintings, and sculptures, were those in which the muscular power of both sitter and artist remain apparent. The Elgin Marbles 'do not seem to be the outer surface of a hard and immovable block of marble, but to be actuated by an internal machinery'; in Hogarth's pictures, 'every feature and muscle is put into full play.' Both are 'the reverse of still life'; both are comparable to the 'harmonious, flowing, varied prose' of the essayist.[61]

Hazlitt frequently included Hogarth in his pantheon of English geniuses, all of whom rejected notions of the ideal in order to grapple with matter as it is and who defined beauty in democratic and empirical terms. 'The eye alone must determine us in our choice of what is most pleasing to itself,' Hogarth wrote in *The Analysis of Beauty* (1753), and in that choice, sports fans have at least as good an eye as sculptors or anatomists:

> Almost everyone is farther advanced in the knowledge of this specula- tive part of proportion that he imagines; especially he hath been inter- ested in the success of them; and the better he is acquainted with the nature of the exercise itself, still the better the judge he becomes of the figure that is to perform it.

In terms that would be echoed in the twentieth century by Bertolt Brecht and Ezra Pound, Hogarth argued against aesthetic contemplation as a disinterested activity. The more interested the spectator is (by which he presumably means the more money he has wagered) the better his judgment is.

> For this reason, no sooner are two boxers stript to fight, but even a butcher, thus skill'd, shews himself a considerable critic in proportion; and on this sort of judgment often gives, or takes the odds, at bare sight only of the combatants. I have heard a blacksmith harangue like an anatomist, or sculptor, on the beauty of a boxer's figure, tho' not per- haps in the same terms . . .

Too many contemporary artists, Hogarth maintained, learn about the human body by looking at sculpture (particularly classical sculpture) rather than by looking at people.

> I firmly believe, that one of our common proficients in the athletic art, would be able to instruct and direct the best sculptor living, (who hath not seen, or is wholly ignorant of this exercise) in what would give the statue of an English-boxer, a much better proportion, as to character, than is to be seen, even in the famous group of antique boxers, (or as some call them, Roman wrestlers) so much admired to this day.[62]

Hogarth is referring to a sculpture, now knows as 'The Wrestlers', which was much praised and studied by the English Academicians, and formed the basis for an extensive discussion of muscles in both Joshua Reynolds's Tenth

Discourse (1780) and John Flaxman's *Lectures on Sculpture* (1829).[63] Small bronze copies were widely disseminated.[64] In order to understand and thus represent human movement, Flaxman argued, the sculptor must understand anatomy, geometry and mechanics:

> The forced action of the boxers renders the muscular configuration of their shoulders so different in appearance from moderate action and states of rest, that we derive a double advantage from the anatomical consideration of their forms: first, we shall learn the cause of each particular form, and, secondly, we shall be convinced how rationally and justly the ancients copied nature.[65]

Hogarth, meanwhile, had looked to Figg, Broughton and George Taylor as his models. Two years before writing the *Analysis*, he had produced a series of drawings of the dying Taylor (supposedly intended for his tombstone), including *Death giving George Taylor a Cross-Buttock* and *George Taylor Breaking the Ribs of Death* (illus. 20). But it was Figg ('more of a *slaughterer* than . . . a neat, finished pugilist') who especially appealed to Hogarth, not only as an exemplar of English vigour and honesty, but also as a fellow modern urban professional.[66] Figg appeared in several of Hogarth's satirical paintings and prints: in *Southwark Fair* (1732) he sits grimly upon a blind horse in the right-hand corner, in *A Midnight Modern Conversation* (1733) he is sprawled drunkenly in the foreground, and in plate two of *The Rake's Progress* (1735), 'Surrounded by Artists and Professors', he is pushed into the background by a dandyish French fencing master.[67]

20
William Hogarth, *George Taylor's Epitaph: George Taylor Breaking the Ribs of Death*, pen and ink over pencil and chalk, *c.* 1750.

Fifty years on, boxing was much more respectable than it had been in Hogarth's day, and Hazlitt noted approvingly that the actor Edmund Kean was not ashamed to admit to 'borrow[ing] . . . from the last efforts of Painter in his fight with Oliver' in his portrayal of Richard III's final moments.[68] Next door to the Fives Court, retired prize-fighter Bill Richmond ran the Horse and Dolphin, a pub where he was said to have initiated the fashion of sparring bare-chested in order that spectators could admire the muscular development of the fighters. Various members of the nearby Royal Academy, including Benjamin Haydon and the President, Joseph Farington, frequented the Fives Court and Horse and Dolphin, but more often the boxers posed at the Academy's life classes.[69] Farington's diary for 19 June 1808 records a visit to the home of his friend Dr Anthony Carlisle, soon to be elected Professor of Anatomy at the Royal Academy, where the company were presented with 'Gregson, the Pugilist, stripped naked to be exhibited to us on acct. of the fineness of *His form*'. Farington's approach is not that of Hogarth, or Hazlitt. The real is only interesting in its relation to the ideal. Gregson the pugilist quickly becomes Gregson the anatomical specimen, the classical approximation:

> All admired the beauty of His proportions from the Knee or rather from the waist upwards, including His arms, & small head. The Bone of His leg West Sd [side] is too short & His toes are not long enough & there is something of heaviness abt the thighs – Knees & legs, – but on the whole He was allowed to be the finest figure the persons present had seen. He was placed in many attitudes.[70]

While Hogarth was always concerned about proportion in relation to function ('fitness') – what 'dimensions of muscle are proper (according to the principle of the steelyard) to move such or such a length of arm with this or that degree of swiftness of force' – the Academicians had very little interest in the use of the bones and muscles they were contemplating.[71] Boxers were to be admired to the extent that their bodies approximated pre-determined ideals of beauty, not because they worked well. Ben Marshall's portrait of Jackson, copied as a mezzotint by Charles Turner in 1810, positions the clothed prize-fighter beside a classical sculpture. We cannot help comparing their legs (illus. 21).

Ten days after Farington first saw Gregson, the party reassembled at Lord Elgin's house to see him 'naked among the Antique figures', the newly arrived fragments of the Panthenon frieze now known as the Elgin Marbles. As soon as the fighters arrived, one recalled, 'ancient art and the works of Phidias were forgotten'.[72] At the end of July, four of the leading fighters of the day – Jackson, Belcher, Gulley and Dutch Sam – were brought to Elgin's for a 'Pugilistick Exhibition'. Farington noted that the sculptor John Rossi particularly admired Dutch Sam's figure 'on account of the *Symmetry* & the *parts being expressed*', and Sam is thought to be the model for Rossi's 1828 sculpture, *Athleta Britannicus* (illus. 22).[73] An attempt at pure classicism, we have no idea when looking at the

sculpture that the model was a nineteenth-century Jew from the East End of London.[74]

The pugilist's identity is also not apparent in Sir Thomas Lawrence's portraits of his childhood friend, John Jackson. The first, exhibited at the Royal Academy exhibition of 1797, featured him, twice-lifesize, as *Satan Summoning His Legions*, to illustrate Milton's line, 'Awake, arise, or be forever fallen.'[75] As Peter Radford notes, the painting makes an 'obvious boxing pun about having been knocked down and having to get up', but this was for private consumption. While the body was Jackson's – Egan had described him as 'one of the best made men in the kingdom'; others praised his 'small' joints, 'knit in the manner which is copied so inimitably in many of the statues and paintings of Michelangelo' – the face was that of the actor, John Kemble.[76] The same combination featured in an 1800 painting of Rolla, from Sheridan's *Pizarro*.[77] Jackson's

22
Charles Rossi,
*Athleta Britannica*,
1828.

muscular body was a useful starting point from which to paint grand subjects; his face, and profession, were not important.

Historical context returned, to be married with classical precedent, in the most widely known boxing image of the early nineteenth century, Théodore Géricault's lithograph *Les Boxeurs* (illus. 23). On the one hand, it makes reference to contemporary events and setting. The boxers, dressed in modern clothes, are usually taken to be Cribb and Molineaux, and we can pick out a few men in suits and one in a prominent top hat in the crowd. Two beer tankards are prominently placed in the bottom right-hand corner. The anglophile Géricault had not attended either fight between the two men – he first visited England in 1820 – but he would have witnessed boxing matches in the Paris studio of painter Horace Vernet, a rendezvous for Restoration liberals, and perhaps, more importantly, he was familiar with English sporting engravings. His decision to depict the scene in a lithograph also signalled a commitment to the contemporary. Lithography was then a new technique and was associated mainly with political satire and other forms of ephemera.[78]

Géricault differs from Hogarth, however, in that he fuses references to the modern scene with allusions to classical and Renaissance art; he had recently returned to Paris after some years in Italy. Michelangelo's influence, in particular, is apparent in the sharp contours, strained poses, bulging muscles and heroic stylization of the fighters.[79] Several spectators are also portrayed naked to the waist. Most striking is one in the left foreground – perhaps having just

been defeated himself? – who lies in a languid classical pose practically at the fighters' feet. The mixture of realist and classical conventions is disconcerting, but allows Géricault to present the fight as both sharply contemporary and grandly mythical.

*Les Boxeurs* positions its opponents very deliberately in the centre of the work, in identical monumental stances. They are static, unlike the fighters in Géricault's more naturalistic pencil and pen studies of the same year (illus. 24). The black man wears white trousers; the white man's trousers have black stripes. Géricault is obviously interested in tonal contrast, an interest that would be revived in George Bellows's depictions of interracial boxing a hundred years later. But Géricault's time, and his politics, were different from Bellows's. Black men also feature in Géricault's great paintings of 1819, *The African Slave* and *The Raft of the Medusa*, works that are often discussed in the context of liberal campaigns against France's complicity in the slave trade, and Toussaint L'Ouverture's heroic rebellion in Haiti.[80] In most images of the contest between Cribb and Molineaux, the American appeared as little more than a caricature, often barefooted, 'blackamoor' (illus. 47). In Géricault's lithograph, he is not only complementary but absolutely equal to his opponent; here, it seems possible that he might win.

## 'THE ERA OF BOXIMANIA'

Works of the early twenties, such as Hazlitt's 'The Fight' (1822), Egan's *Life in London* (1821) and John Hamilton Reynolds's *The Fancy* (1820) celebrated a cultural moment that was coming to an end. An elegiac air infects their exuberance. In 1818, Reynolds abandoned poetry (and boxing) to become a lawyer, and in 1820, about to marry, and with his good friend, Keats, very ill, he wrote *The Fancy* as a 'final parting with his youth, his poetry, and the forbidden delights of youth'.[81] But if Londoners were leaving the Fancy behind, out-of-towners were becoming increasingly interested. London's sporting pubs were fast becoming tourist attractions, and places like the Castle Tavern in Holborn assumed legendary status.

In Howarth in Yorkshire, the Brontë children were keen readers of *Blackwood's Magazine*, which was passed to them by a neighbour until 1831. One of their parodies, *The Young Men's Magazine*, included an 'Advertisement' by Charlotte and Branwell, issuing a challenge to 'a match at fisty-cuffs'.[82] Their juvenilia is populated by young noblemen, always 'masters of the art', who set at each other 'in slashing style'.[83] Charlotte eventually lost interest, but Branwell continued to read *Blackwood's* and *Bell's Life*. Numerous references to, and sketches of, his pugilistic heroes can also be found in his letters.[84]

Brontë could not decide whether he wanted to be a painter or a poet. The poems he submitted to *Blackwood's* were always rejected. In July 1835, he wrote a letter to the Royal Academy of Art asking for an interview. His biographers have debated whether he actually sent this letter, and whether, as a result, he visited London the following month. He claimed that he went. The uncertainty stems from the detailed account of London adventures he gave on his supposed return. Juliet Barker, who doubts the trip took place, maintains that Brontë's impressions of the Castle Tavern, and his account of conversations with its land-lord, Tom Spring, were lifted straight from the pages of Egan's *Boxiana* and *Book of Sports* (1832), which gives a particularly lively and detailed description of the tavern and its patrons.[85]

A country boy who really did visit the pilgrimage sights of the Fancy was the poet John Clare. On his third visit to London in 1824, Clare was taken by the painter Oliver Rippingille to the Castle Tavern, and to Jack Randall's Hole in the Wall in Chancery Lane – where Hazlitt's 'The Fight' begins – and to see some sparring at the Fives Court. Clare later recalled:

> I caught the mania so much from Rip for such things that I soon became far more eager for the fancy than himself and I watch'd the appearance of every new Hero on the stage with as eager curosity [sic] to see what sort of fellow he was as I had before done the Poets – and I left the place with one wish strongly in uppermost and that was that I was but a Lord to patronize Jones the Sailor Boy who took my fancy as being the finest fellow in the Ring.[86]

Iain McCalman and Maureen Perkins speculate that Clare may also have attended one of the numerous theatrical adaptations of Egan's *Life in London*, and argue that 'there can be little doubt that he modelled his own metropolitan tourist programmes on the "sprees and larks" of Egan's fictional heroes'.[87]

In the Northampton asylum in which he spent the last years of his life, Clare adopted many pseudonyms and alter egos, including those of some of the prize-fighters he had watched on that trip to London. Inventing new names was of course a speciality of prize-fighters, but Jonathan Bate speculates that 'the persona of the pugilist became Clare's stance of defiance' in the violent atmosphere of the asylum.[88] Clare was seen shadow-boxing in his cell, crying out 'I'm Jones the Sailor Boy', and 'I'm Tom Spring', or, as 'Jack Randall Champion of the Prize Ring', issuing a 'Challenge to All the World' for 'A Fair Stand Up Fight'.[89] On one occasion Clare (soon to write his own 'Child Harold' and 'Don Juan a Poem') even referred to himself as 'Boxer Byron / made of Iron, alias / Box-iron / At Spring-field.'[90] The personae of Box-iron and Boxer (Lord) Byron pull in different directions: Clare wanted to be both the self-made working-class prize-fighter and the kind of Lord who patronized such men. But his assumption of these roles brought no relief from his isolation and increasing alienation from both worlds. One letter (to an unidentified and possibly imaginary correspondent) laments that although 'It is well known that I am a prize-fighter by profession and a man that has never feared any body in my life either in the ring or out of it . . . there is none to accept my challenges which I have from time to time given to the public.'[91]

Two months before he died, an ailing Branwell Brontë wrote to Joseph Leyland, signing off with the remark that he was 'nearly worn out'. The letter was accompanied by a sketch of a man lying in bed and a skeleton standing over him. The skeleton is saying that 'the half minute time's up, so come to the scratch; won't you?' The prostrate man replies, 'Blast your eyes, it's no use, for I cannot come', and above is written – 'Jack Shaw, the Guardsman, and Jack Painter of Norfolk'. Painter had been defeated by Shaw in 1815 (just weeks before Shaw died heroically at Waterloo). The fight was largely memorable for Painter's courageous resilience: he 'received ten knock-down blows in succession; and, although requested to resign the battle, not the slightest chance appeared in his favour, he refused to quit the ring till nature was exhausted'.[92]

Branwell Brontë, a painter himself, died in 1848, and John Clare followed in 1864. Both men lasted longer than the Fives Court; built in 1802 at the start of pugilism's vogue, it was pulled down in 1826 as part of the development of Trafalgar Square (illus. 49). The golden age of boxing was over.

# 4

# 'Fighting, Rightly Understood'

'Modern legislation is chiefly remarkable for its oppressive interference with the elegant amusements of the mob,' complained *Punch*, tongue largely in cheek, in 1841.

> Bartholomew-fair is abolished; bull-baiting, cock-pits, and duck-hunts are put down by act of Parliament; prize-fighting, by the New Police . . . The 'masses' see no pleasure now.[1]

The establishment of Robert Peel's New Police in 1829 had gradually made it possible to enforce a series of legal judgments to outlaw the prize-ring. But these judgments did little more than confirm the shift in public attitudes to the sport. By the time of Victoria's accession in 1837, prize-fighting was firmly in decline. Pugilists had served as ushers at George IV's coronation in 1821, but the patronage of Queen Victoria or the presence of her Prince Consort at ringside was unthinkable. Respectable middle-class society saw no place for an unruly sport favoured by an alliance of the working and upper classes (the 'bawling, hustling, and smashing' Populace and the 'great broad-shouldered' Barbarians, as Matthew Arnold put it), while evangelical Christianity stressed its brutish nature.[2] Only 30 years earlier, newspapers had extolled the manly virtues of pugilism; now they stressed its physical and moral dangers. The *New Sporting Magazine*, founded by R. S. Surtees in 1834, announced in its prospectus that 'prize-fighting, Bull-baiting and Cock-fighting' were 'low and demoralizing pursuits' and would be excluded from its pages.[3] In their place Surtees substituted the 'jaunts and jollities' of riding and hunting.

A series of scandals ranging from thrown fights to murder was partly to blame. In 1824 fight-promoter John Thurtell was hanged for the murder of a gambling associate and the trial made sensational news; a few months later magistrates stopped a fight ('if it could be so termed', said Egan) at Moulsey Hurst and arrested both fighters.[4] The following year even Hazlitt admitted that 'the Fancy have lately lost something of their gloss in public estimation; and, after the last fight, few would go far to see a Neate or a Spring set-to'.[5] In the years that followed the pugilists themselves tried to improve matters – Spring, for example, set up the Fair Play Club in 1828 – but without aristocratic backing and finance, the boxers lacked the necessary authority to regulate their sport. 'When honour and fame cease to influence the combatants,' lamented Vincent Dowling, editor of *Bell's Life*, 'a system of low gambling is substituted.'[6]

Many also considered large gatherings of unruly fight fans to be threatening, as large-scale popular protest, from the Luddites to the Chartists, continued into the 1820s. William Cobbett had noted in 1805 that boxing matches do not merely 'give rise to assemblages of people; they tend to make the people bold'.[7] But without an obvious foreign enemy, such boldness was no longer welcome. Increasingly, reforming magistrates clamped down on those involved in staging fights. They even began to appear in this capacity in novels. In Dickens's *The Pickwick Papers* (1836–7), George Nupkins boasts of having 'rushed into a prize-ring . . . attended only by six special constables; and, at the hazard of falling a sacrifice to the angry passions of an infuriated multitude, prohibited a pugilistic contest between the Middlesex Dumpling, and the Suffolk Bantam'.[8] The magistrate in George Borrow's *Lavengro* (1851), meanwhile, confesses that although 'of course, I cannot patronize the thing very openly, yet I sometimes see a prize-fight'.[9] In Thomas Hardy's *The Mayor of Casterbridge* (1886), set in the 1840s, the town's Roman Amphitheatre is described as a popular venue for 'pugilistic encounters' because it is 'secluded' and 'entirely invisible to the outside world save by climbing to the top of the enclosure'.[10]

The era of the great boxers also seemed to be over. New champions such as Tom Spring continued to attract a following, but the tone of much journalism was resolutely elegiac. A newspaper account of Spring's defeat of the aging Tom Oliver on 20 February 1821 (a fight attended by the schoolboy William Gladstone, bunking off from Eton), described the pair as 'first-raters of the present day' but greatly inferior to their predecessors.[11] The great fighters, and commentators, of the Regency died soon afterwards: 'Gentleman John' Jackson in 1845; Tom Cribb in 1848; Pierce Egan in 1849; and Tom Spring in 1851, the year in which, in *Lavengro*, George Borrow lamented the passing of the great days of prize-fighting.

> I have known the time when a pugilistic encounter between two noted champions was almost considered in the light of a national affair; when tens of thousands of individuals, high and low, meditated and brooded upon it, the first thing in the morning and the last thing at night, until the great event was decided. But the time is passed, and people will say, thank God that it is; all I have to say is, that the French still live on the other side of the water, and are still casting their eyes hitherward – and that in the days of pugilism it was no vain boast to say, that one Englishman was a match for two of t'other race; at present it would be a vain boast to say so, for these are not the days of pugilism.[12]

Although the Molineaux–Cribb fights had generated much British excitement in 1810, for 'the first quarter of the nineteenth century most Americans were unaware that boxing matches even took place in their country'.[13] In the decades that followed, however, ever-increasing numbers of immigrants began to establish the sport. An Irishman vs. an Englishman was a reliable crowd-puller, but very few of the early immigrants made a living through prize-fighting.

During the 1830s, some British fighters, facing ever-more limited opportunities at home, decided to cross the Atlantic to capitalize on budding American interest in bare-knuckle bouts. The first to make the journey was James ('Deaf') Burke, who had been unable to find an opponent since a 98-round battle ended in his adversary's death. Burke arrived in New York in 1836, where he appeared on stage at Conklin's Hall 'as the Venetian statue' – poses included 'Hercules struggling with the Nemean lion, in five attitudes' and 'Samson slaying the Philistines with a jaw bone'.[14] The following year he had two fights against Irishmen; one in New Orleans, which degenerated into chaos (Irish supporters attacked Burke, accusing him of unfair play), and the other on Hart's Island, New York, which he easily won. The *New York Herald* reported the second match with showy reluctance; although we 'regret and detest' the kind of exhibition the British are so fond of, the paper declared, 'our duty as chroniclers compels us to make public what otherwise we should bury in oblivion'.[15]

While Burke had been in America, a quick-witted Nottingham fighter called William Thompson, or more usually Bendigo, had emerged as a real contender for the Championship. Burke fought Bendigo on his return to England in 1839, but was disqualified for head-butting; Bendigo lost the championship to Ben Caunt in 1842, and regained it from him in 1845 (both were bitterly contested fights). In 1850, he retired from the ring and, in a development considered to be a sign of the times, became a Methodist preacher.[16]

Burke and Bendigo are both mentioned in Herman Melville's 1851 novel, *Moby-Dick*. While there is no evidence that Melville attended any of their fights, these were widely reported in the American press. Certainly Melville felt that Bendigo was well enough known to refer to him in an 1847 letter to a sick cousin in Rio: 'come back to us again and send a challenge across the water to fight Bendigo for the Champion's Belt of all England'.[17]

Nationalist bravado also informs Chapter 37 of *Moby-Dick*, which ends with a famous passage in which Captain Ahab challenges the 'great gods' to 'swerve' him from his goal of taking revenge on the White Whale to whom he had lost a leg. In evoking his 'fixed purpose', Ahab compares himself to a train: 'Over unsounded gorges, through the rifled hearts of mountains, under torrents' beds, unerringly I rush! Naught's an obstacle, naught's an angle to the iron way!' Less often noted is Ahab's comparison of the unswerving nature of a train on its iron way to a boxer facing his opponent. Ahab begins his soliloquy by evoking his own 'steel skull . . . the sort that needs no helmet in the most brain-battering fight!' He then addresses 'ye great gods' directly:

> I laugh and hoot at ye, ye cricket-players, ye pugilists, ye deaf Burkes and blinded Bendigoes! I will not say as schoolboys do to bullies, – Take some one of your one size: don't pommel me! No, ye've knocked me down, and I am up again; but ye have run and hidden. Come forth from behind your cotton bags! I have no long gun to reach ye; come and see if ye can swerve me. Swerve me? Ye cannot swerve me, else ye swerve yourselves! Man has ye there.[18]

Ahab's claim that the English bruiser gods will not be able to stop his advance on the whale is pure (and characteristic) bluster. Only a few years later, however, an American boxer, with a more credible claim to be unswervable, appeared on the scene. In 1858, the Irish-American fighter John C. Heenan sent a real 'challenge across the water', not to Bendigo but to the then 'Champion of England', Tom Sayers.

In January 1860 Heenan set off for England carrying a considerable burden of expectation. He appealed to both ethnic and national loyalties – to Irish-Americans, he was fighting as 'a son of Erin', to American-born nativists (many of whom had supported his opponents at home), Heenan was now a representative of 'Uncle Sammy', a defender of 'dear Columbia's pride'.[19] (A similarly convenient move took place 100 years later when, by taking on the German Max Schmeling, Joe Louis became an 'American' as well as a 'Negro' fighter.)

In England, meanwhile, the Heenan-Sayers fight was greeted as the beginning of a 'Great Pugilistic Revival'; in truth, however, it represented old-style English pugilism's last stand.[20] This round of Britain vs. the United States differed in many ways from that which had taken place 50 years earlier. Steadily if slowly growing in the United States, prize-fighting had continued to decline in Britain, a shift in the balance of power reflected in the fact that it was now an English David (5ft 8in and 150 pounds) who was to face an American Goliath (4 inches taller and nearly 40 pounds heavier). Heenan, named for his home town as the 'Benicia Boy', was also nine years younger than Sayers.[21] While much of the American press looked forward to a test of national supremacy, the British press treated the event as a brutal anachronism and campaigned to stop it taking place. The Manchester *Guardian*, for example, argued against the association of healthy 'muscular art' with the 'unhealthy excitement' which surrounded prize-fighting:

> The fighters . . . perform their part for money; not to develop their manly energies; nor do they assist in developing the physical powers of those around them. Instead of going to witness a prize-fight, let men don the gloves and learn and practice the art of fighting for themselves.[22]

The rhetoric intensified, culminating in a parliamentary debate four days before the fight took place. One MP called for the Home Secretary and the Prime Minister to intervene and stop what was clearly a 'meditated breach of the peace'. Pursuing what he described as a 'moderate path', Palmerston argued that he could see no reason why a prize-fight should constitute a greater breach of the peace than a 'balloon ascent'.[23]

Heenan vs. Sayers went ahead on 17 April 1860, in Farnborough, Hampshire, the town having been chosen partly because of its excellent rail links.[24] Thousands of spectators attended. After 37 rounds, over two hours, and many injuries – Heenan was reduced to near-blindness in his right eye – the contest ended in chaos and a draw was declared.[25] Although *Bell's Life* cheerfully debated who had come off worse, concluding that 'Heenan's mug was decidedly the most disfigured', the extreme violence of the fight shocked many.[26] The *New York Herald*, meanwhile, complained that 'the Britons . . . stopped the fight in order to save their money':

> Let Mr. Bull, who seems to be growing old and shaky about his pins, keep his five-pound notes – we are rich enough to do without them. We do not really want his money, but simply desired to let him know that we could whip him in a matter of muscle as well as in yachts, clipper ships, steamboats, india-rubber shoes and other things, city railways, sewing machines, the electric telegraph, reading machines, pretty women, and unpickable bank locks.[27]

The following month, in an essay on his walks into 'shy neighbourhoods', Charles Dickens, as 'the uncommercial traveller', noted 'the fancy of a humble artist' in small shop windows, 'as exemplified in two portraits representing Mr Thomas Sayers, of Great Britain, and Mr John Heenan, of the United States of America':

> These illustrious men are highly coloured, in fighting trim and fighting attitude. To suggest the pastoral and meditative nature of their peaceful calling, Mr Heenan is represented by an emerald sward with primroses and other modest flowers springing up under the heels of his half-boots; while Mr Sayers is impelled to the administration of his favourite blow, the Auctioneer, by the silent eloquence of a village church. The humble homes of England, with their domestic virtues and honeysuckle porches, urge both heroes to go in and win; and the lark and other singing birds are observable in the upper air, ecstatically carolling their thanks to Heaven for a fight. On the whole, the associations entwined with the pugilistic art by this artist are much in the manner of Izaak Walton.[28]

Dickens's target is, as ever, hypocrisy and affectation: not boxing itself, but attempts to take the edge off a violent sport by wrapping it in a highly romanticized pastoralism.

THE GREAT FIGHT FOR THE CHAMPIONSHIP.
BETWEEN JOHN C. HEENAN "THE BENICIA BOY", & TOM SAYERS "CHAMPION OF ENGLAND".
*Which took place April 17th 1860, at Farnborough, England.*
THE BATTLE LASTED 2 HOURS 20 MINUTES 42 ROUNDS, WHEN THE MOB RUSHED IN & ENDED THE FIGHT.
HEENAN stands 6ft 1½ in, fighting weight 190 lbs. Born May 2nd 1835.     SAYERS stands 5ft 8 in, fighting wt 150 lbs. Born 1826.

25
Currier and Ives,
*The Great Fight for
the Championship:
Between John C.
Heenan 'The Benicia
Boy' and Tom Sayers
'Champion of
England'*, 1860,
lithograph.

In the months that followed, portraits of the fighters and depictions of the fight itself gained wide circulation. The *New York Illustrated News* even sent over an engraver to pick up ringside drawings so that he could prepare the blocks on the trans-Atlantic voyage for immediate printing.[29] Two of the most widely circulated prints were by J. B. Rowbotham and Currier and Ives; both are rather formal images of the boxers squaring off before the contest begins. Intended to commemorate an energetic and violent occasion, they are, ironically, static and peaceful (illus. 25). One of these prints catches the eye of Stephen Dedalus in James Joyce's *Ulysses* (1922), which is set on 16 June 1904, the day the *Times* reported the sale of the Sayers-Heenan championship belt.[30] Stephen is window-shopping when his eye is caught by 'a faded 1860 print of Heenan boxing Sayers'.

> Staring backers with square hats stood around the roped prizering. The heavyweights in light loincloths proposed gently each to the other his bulbous fists. And they are throbbing: heroes' hearts.[31]

The inappropriate gentleness of Victorian representations of boxing was something that Dickens, as we have seen, took comic advantage of. Disraeli, too, in his 1845 novel *Sybil*, brought pugilism and cosy domesticity together. After Sybil is arrested with her radical father at a Chartist gathering, a 'kind-hearted inspector' takes her home rather than leaving her to languish overnight in prison. There his wife puts her to bed in a comfortable room decorated with 'a piece of faded embroidery . . . and opposite it . . . portraits of [the pugilists] Dick Curtis and Dutch Sam, who had been the tutors of her husband, and now lived as heroes in his memory'. For them, there is no contradiction between the male (pugilistic) and female (domestic) arts.[32]

But if the inhabitants of 'humble homes' were untroubled about the compatibility of an interest in boxing and a devotion to larks and honeysuckle porches, those of less humble dwellings were not so sure. In the weeks following the fight, *Punch* ran a series of cartoons in which 'extremely proper-looking personages' went to great lengths to disguise their interest in Sayers vs. Heenan (illus. 26). Certainly the days of un-abashed flash appreciation were long gone; Victorian gentlemen, like Disraeli's Egremont, generally had the 'good taste not to let [their] predilection for sports degenerate into slang'.[33] The predilection itself, however, did not die out.

One proper-looking personage who retained a lively interest in boxing was the publisher John Blackwood who, a week after the fight, wrote to George Lewes, then in Rome with George Eliot:

INTERESTING INTELLIGENCE.

SMALL BOY (to respectable and extremely proper-looking personage). " *Here y' are, Guv'nor! Sportin' Telegraft a penny! 'as got hall the latest 'ticklars 'bout the Mill atween Tom Sayers and the Benicia Bo-oy!* "

I have not much news from London, the fight for the Championship monopolizing everyone's attention. It is quite comical and I cannot help feeling as keen as possible about gallant little Tom Sayers with his one arm maintaining such a fight. I am satisfied if he had not lost the use of his right arm he would have polished off the giant.

26 'Interesting Intelligence', *Punch*, 21 April 1860.

Although he begins by talking of 'everyone' as if that does not include himself, and describes the brouhaha as 'quite comical', Blackwood soon slips into a discussion of the details of the fight. His authoritative commentary is, however, quickly (dis)qualified by the un-Corinthian remark, 'I never saw a prize fight, and I daresay five minutes conversation with the worthy Tom would effectually cool my enthusiasm.'[34] He had no intention of degenerating into slang.

Three years later the poet William Allingham expressed a similarly tempered enthusiasm. His diary for 6 July 1863 excitedly records a glimpse of Sayers, 'a middle-sized but singularly well-knit figure of a man, strong, light, easy of movement, almost Greek in his poses but altogether natural and unconscious'. A few days later, having seen Sayers fight 'Young Brooks' in a Lymington cricket field, he expands on his reflections:

The high-shouldered pugilist such as Leech draws is not the genuine article. Sayers has rather falling shoulders though wide and muscular, so has Heenan, and Tom King. Ease and freedom of movement characterizes them all, especially Sayers. They doubtless enjoy life in their way, so long as they keep within tolerable bounds, and the fighting itself is a great animal pleasure.[35]

Yet even while praising Sayers, both Blackwood and Allingham felt it necessary to distance themselves from the boxer; Blackwood by suggesting the limits of his conversation, Allingham by alluding to the pugilistic lifestyle and the necessity of keeping it 'within tolerable bounds'. William Thackeray mocked such equivocation in his 1860 'roundabout' essay on the Heenan–Sayers fight for the *Cornhill Magazine* entitled 'On Some Late Great Victories'. 'Ought Mr. Sayers be honoured for being brave, or punished for being naughty?' What the Victorian public wanted, Thackeray complained, was to have it both ways: to say to 'naughty' Tom Sayers, 'we are moralists, and reprimand you; and you are hereby reprimanded accordingly', but, at the same time, to reserve the option of changing their minds. 'I mean that fighting, of course, is wrong; but that there are occasions when, &c. . .'[36]

Changing attitudes to boxing typified the gap between the Regency world that Thackeray had grown up in and the Victorian world of his adulthood. As a schoolboy he had loved the 'extraordinary slang' of Pierce Egan's rakish tales, but as an adult he recalled Tom and Jerry as 'a little vulgar'; 'brilliant but somewhat barbarous, it must be confessed'. 'There is enjoyment of life in these young bucks of 1823 which contrasts strangely with our feelings of 1860.'[37] Egan's tales of sporting gentlemen were now only to be found 'in the corner of some old country-house library' of a Corinthian 'grandpappa'.[38]

The vulgar energetic world of the Corinthians is immortalized in *Vanity Fair* (1845), set during the Napoleonic Wars. The novel contains many incidental references to the Fancy, most of which are associated with dissipated young men who hanker after the life of Tom and Jerry, but who don't, somehow, quite come up to scratch. After a drunken night at Vauxhall Gardens, for example, Jos Sedley tries to fight a hackney-coachman but instead is carried off to bed. The next day, his friends, knowing he can't remember a thing, tease Sedley that he 'hit him flat out, like Molyneux. The watchman says he never saw a fellow go down so straight.'[39]

The Crawley family is full of boxers. After being sent down from Cambridge, Rawdon Crawley becomes a 'celebrated "blood" or dandy about town': 'Boxing, rat-hunting, the fives-court, and four-in-hand driving were then the fashion of our British aristocracy; and he was adept in all these noble sciences.' When Becky Sharp (who will marry him) asks his sister whether he is clever, she is told that he has 'not an idea in the world beyond his horses, and his regiment, and his hunting, and his play'. Rawdon's uncle, the Reverend Bute Crawley, has similar tastes. While studying theology at Oxford, he 'had thrashed all the best bruisers of the "town"', and 'carried his taste for boxing and athletic exercises into life; there was not a fight within twenty miles at which he was not present' (illus. 51).[40]

The most fully developed portrait of an Egan-like young Buck is the Reverend's son, James Crawley, a good-looking 'young Oxonian' who has 'acquired the inestimable polish of living in a fast set at a small college'. Excited by a coach journey with 'the Tutbury Pet' and a night at Tom Cribb's Arms, where he was 'enchanted by the Pet's conversation', he proceeds to his aunt's house to ingratiate himself into her will. There, however, he gets increasingly drunk on her good port, and after describing 'the different pugilistic qualities' of his favourite fighters, offers to take on his cousin 'with or without gloves'. This then leads to a disquisition on his favourite theme, 'old blood':

> There's nothing like old blood; no, dammy, nothing like it. I'm none of your radicals. I know what it is to be a gentleman, dammy. . . look at the fellers in a fight; aye, look at a dawg killing rats, – which is it wins? the good blooded ones.

The more 'ruby fluid' James ingests, the stronger his devotion to good old blood becomes. The example of 'good blood' he provides, however, suggests that it is a fluid he himself lacks:

> Why, only last term, just before I was rusticated, that is, I mean just before I had the measles, ha, ha, – there was me and Ringwood of Christchurch, Bob Ringwood, Lord Cinqbar's son, having our beer at the 'Bell' at Blenheim, when the Banbury bargeman offered to fight either of us for a bowl of punch. I couldn't. My arm was in a sling . . . Well, sir, I couldn't finish him, but Bob had his coat off at once – he stood up to the Banbury man for three minutes, and polished him off in four rounds, easy. Gad, how he did drop, sire, and what was it? Blood, sir, all blood.[41]

His aunt sends him away in disgust.

All this pugilistic ambition, and interest, is presented as not only rather ridiculous, but as out of touch with modern life. For Thackeray, pugilism epitomizes the profligate world of the Regency, a world that appealed to villains but also to students and minor army officers who refuse to grow up.[42] Captain Mc-Murdo is a 49-year-old 'Waterloo man' whose barracks room is 'hung around with boxing, sporting, and dancing pictures, presented to him by comrades as they retired from the regiment, and married and settled into a quiet life'. He is pictured sitting up in bed 'reading in Bell's Life an account of . . . [a] fight between the Tutbury Pet and the Barking Butcher'.[43] In Robert Browning's 1858 poem 'A Likeness', prints of boxers are relegated to the 'spoils of youth' that adorn a bachelor's room, along with 'masks, gloves and foils' and 'the cast from a fist ("not, alas! Mine, / But my master's, the Tipton Slasher")'; in Thackeray's novel, such artifacts are the spoils of eternal bachelors.[44]

84

The suggestion that an interest in boxing is rather adolescent (and hence mildly deplorable) is also made in George Eliot's *Middlemarch*, written slightly later (1871), and set slightly later, just before the Reform Bill of 1832, in a small Midlands community. Fred Vincy, 'a young gentleman without capital' and, despite a university education, 'generally unskilled', finds it particularly difficult to find a place for himself in the modern world. But Vincy is saved from a life of fecklessness by the love of his childhood sweetheart, Mary Garth, and eventual employment in estate management with her father, Caleb. A key moment in his transformation comes when he chances upon six farm labourers attacking the agents employed to build the new railway. Vincy tries to take control from the safety of his horse until one of the men shouts 'a defiance which he did not know to be Homeric': 'Yo git off your horse, young measter, and I'll have a round wi' ye, I wull. You daredn't come on w'out your hoss an' whip. I'll soon knock the breath out on ye, I would.' Vincy, who 'felt confidence in his power of boxing', tells them, 'I'll come back presently, and have a round with you all in turn, if you like.' Both Vincy and the farm labourers have grown up in a now outmoded feudal world and, uncertain how to act in the modern era that the railway represents, they easily fall back on the old (pugilistic) methods of settling disputes. But when Caleb Garth hears of Vincy's pugnacious intentions – 'It would be a good lesson for him. I shall not be five minutes' – he quickly intervenes. Garth, 'a powerful man . . [who] knew little of any fear except the fear of hurting others and the fear of having to speechify', is a modern man and knows how to operate in the modern world. Instead of fighting and teaching 'lessons', he reasons with the farm workers and reassures them about the impact of the railway on their livelihood.[45] On the following page, Fred Vincy falls off his horse into the mud – his real education is beginning.

The idealized Adam Bede, the eponymous hero of Eliot's second book, needs no such education. Published in 1859, but set during the Napoleonic wars, the novel contrasts its protagonist's fighting style with that of his rival in love, Arthur Donnithorne. From the opening pages of the novel, we are meant to admire Adam as a particularly British physical specimen:

> a large-boned muscular man nearly six feet high, with a back so flat and a head so well poised that when he drew himself up to take a more distant survey of his work, he had the air of a soldier standing at ease.[46]

Adam Bede is 'a Saxon', but with 'a mixture of Celtic blood' – a complete Briton. 'We want such fellows as he to lick the French,' a bystander remarks. Young squire Arthur Donnithorne is, by contrast, 'well-washed, high-bred, white-handed, yet looking as if he could deliver well from the left shoulder, and floor his man'. A boxer at Oxford, Arthur nonetheless acknowledges that Adam would knock him 'into next week' if they were to 'have a battle'.[47]

As indeed happens, inevitably, when Arthur seduces Hetty Sorel, whom Adam loves, and then abandons her. 'If you get hold of a chap that's got no shame nor conscience to stop him,' Adam had once remarked, 'you must try what you can do by bunging his eyes up.'[48] When Adam shows himself to be such a chap, he and Arthur do battle.

> The delicate-handed gentleman was a match for the workman in everything but strength, and Arthur's skill in parrying enabled him to protract the struggle for some long moments. But between unarmed men, the battle is to the strong, where the strong is no blunderer, and Arthur must sink under a well-planted blow of Adam's, as a steel rod is broken by an iron bar. The blow soon came, and Arthur fell, his head lying concealed in a tuft of fern, so that Adam could only discern his darkly-clad body.[49]

Looked at from one perspective, this passage, published in the same year as *The Origin of Species*, presents a classic scene of what Darwin called 'the law of battle' – instinct drives the two men to fight, 'with the instinctive fierceness of panthers', over a possible mate.[50] The very blows are forces of nature, 'like lightning'. From another perspective (and I would suggest, more centrally) the scene encapsulates class struggle, labour (represented by the industrial image of the blacksmith's 'iron bar') defeating feudal aristocracy (a sword-like 'steel rod'). This kind of scene occurs many times in Victorian fiction, with interesting variations. Here, it is worth noting that, although Adam's deference, and Christian pity, have returned by the beginning of the following chapter, he refuses to shake hands with Arthur: 'I don't forget what's owing to you as a gentleman; but in this thing we're man and man.'[51]

A year later, in the month of the Heenan–Sayers fight – April 1860 – George Eliot's third book, *The Mill on the Floss*, was published. While Eliot used 'mill' in her title to refer to a building on a river, the word also had another meaning in boxing slang – the fight was a 'mill'.[52] These alternatives proved irresistible to *Punch*, a magazine which relished the most hackneyed of puns. The humour of the cartoon lies in the seemingly obvious incompatibility between the novels (and drawing rooms) of Victorian womanhood and the very thought of a prize-fight (illus. 27).[53] This was a sentiment which now was accepted even by readers of *Blackwood's Magazine*.[54] In this context, it was of course great fun to make jokes about women reading fight-reports and even, occasionally, fighting themselves. Thomas Ingoldby's 1840 poem 'The Ghost' describes a man who fears 'his spouse might knock his head off', for 'spite of all her piety, her arm / She'd sometimes exercise when in a passion'. The narrator concludes,

> Within a well-roped ring, or on a stage,
>     Boxing may be a very pretty Fancy,
> When Messrs. Burke or Bendigo engage;
>     —'Tis not so well in Susan, Jane, or Nancy:
> To get well mill'd by any one's an evil,
>     But by a lady - 'tis the very Devil.[55]

*Constance (literary).* "Have you read this Account of 'The Mill on the Floss,' dear?"
*Edith (literal).* "No, indeed, I have not; and I wonder that you can find anything to interest you in the Description of a Disgusting Prize-Fight!"

In 1860, the joke seemed never ending in *Punch* cartoons, which showed men 'initiating' women (readers of *Belle's Life*, sic), and mothers handing over their babies to a burly boxing tutor (illus. 28).

The association of *The Mill on the Floss* with 'milling' is actually not as absurd as *Punch* had implied. A novel of childhood and adolescence, it focuses on the relationship between a brother and sister, Tom and Maggie Tulliver. Tom Tulliver is consistently depicted as a 'lad of honour' and a keen fighter. He particularly likes to read, and relate, 'fighting stories', and so his fellow pupil, Philip Wakem, who is said to have been 'brought up like a girl' and whose deformity makes him 'unfit for active sports', tells him the story of Ulysses, 'a little fellow, but very wise and cunning', in his battle against the Cyclops, Polyphemus. 'O what fun!' says Tom, but his words have an ironic resonance later in the novel when, some years later, he accuses Philip Wakem of not 'acting the part of a man and a gentleman' with his sister, Maggie. Philip replies, 'It is manly of you to talk in this way to *me*. Giants have an immemorial right to stupidity and insolent abuse.' Wakem's response recalls the Homer of their youth, and Tom is now cast as Cyclops. Tom's pugnacity exemplifies what Eliot terms 'masculine philosophy', yet it is a masculinity of a particularly limited (schoolboy) type, one whose morality is based on strength. However many Greek verbs he learns, Tom is unable to be anything other than 'an excellent bovine lad' who believes in the 'boys' justice' of the fist.[56]

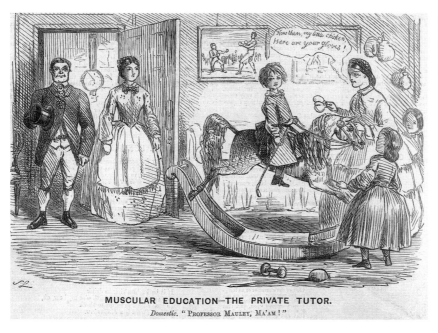

MUSCULAR EDUCATION—THE PRIVATE TUTOR.

*Domestic.* "Professor Mauley, Ma'am!"

The guilt-free pleasure of eighteenth-century fight scenes was no longer possible for Victorian writers or readers. Fighting could not be condoned, except, of course, in the service of a moral cause. Happily, moral causes were not hard to find; so much so that in 1901 George Bernard Shaw felt able to condemn what he described as the 'abominable vein of retaliatory violence all through the literature of the nineteenth century'.[57]

An exemplary case of morally justified retaliation occurs in Chapter Five of *Vanity Fair*. This is a very different occasion from the prize-fights mocked elsewhere in the novel. At 'Dr Swishtail's famous school', Dobbin, the son of a grocer, is consistently tormented by boys only slightly more secure in their status. Known to them by the name of 'Figs', he is neither a dandy nor a 'bruiser'. Although at his happiest when left alone to read the *Arabian Nights* while the rest of the school pursue sports, Dobbin cannot ignore the spectacle of 'the great chief and dandy' Cuff tormenting a smaller boy. The narrator speculates that Dobbin may be 'revolting' against the 'exercise of tyranny' or perhaps hankers after revenge. Whatever the reason, his coming forth is compared to that of 'little David' against 'brazen Goliath', and the North American colonies against George III.[58] The narrator, claiming that he has not 'the pen of a Napier or a *Bell's Life*', nonetheless describes the thirteenth, and final, round of the ensuing fight in the manner of that sporting journal:

> It was the last charge of the Guard (that is, it would have been, only Waterloo had not yet taken place) – it was Ney's column breasting the hills of La Haye Sainte, bristling with ten thousand bayonets, and crowned with twenty eagles – it was the shouts of the beef-eating

British, as leaping down the hill, they rushed to hug the enemy in the savage arms of battle – in other words, Cuff coming up full of pluck, but quite reeling and groggy, the Fig-merchant put in his left as usual on his adversary's nose, and sent him down for the last time.[59]

In this passage, which was to inspire similar parodies by James Joyce and Ralph Ellison in the twentieth century, Thackeray does more than simply show his familiarity both with the work of the military historian Sir William Napier and the popular magazine, *Bell's Life in London*. His target is the all too easy interchange between the discourses of prize-fighting and war (illus. 46).[60]

## SCHOOLBOY BOXERS: 'THE NATURAL AND THE ENGLISH WAY'

The 1850s and '60s saw the creation of many new public schools, in which 'representatives of old families [mixed] with the sons of the new middle classes'. These schools, claims Asa Briggs, instigated 'a gradual fusion of classes', by 'drawing upon a common store of values'.[61] Sport, placed at the heart of the curriculum, was one of the central ways in which those values were transmitted. Public school sporting stories became enormously popular, with Thomas Hughes's *Tom Brown's Schooldays* (1857) starting the trend and reinventing the schoolboy as a heroic character.[62]

Thomas Hughes's school was Rugby, whose headmaster, Thomas Arnold, epitomized the values of what became known as muscular Christianity.[63] Good character depended on a healthy mind in a healthy body – *mens sana in corpore sano*.[64] Although rugby and cricket are also considered, the delicate relationship between physical prowess and moral character finds its most vivid expression in the novel's depiction of boxing. Hughes begins a chapter entitled 'The Fight' with a warning:

> Let those young persons whose stomachs are not strong, or who think a good set-to with the weapons which God has given us all, an uncivilized, unchristian, or ungentlemanly affair, just skip this chapter at once, for it won't be to their taste.

The chapter chronicles Brown's initiation into muscular and manly Christian ways through a fight with, of course, a bigger boy. After the fight is over, Tom and 'the Slogger' shake hands 'with great satisfaction and mutual respect'. 'Fighting', Hughes concludes, 'is the natural and English way for English boys to settle their quarrels'(illus. 29).[65]

Throughout the next hundred years, in the pages of magazines at least, English boys continued to find quarrels which needed settling. In 1866 Edwin Brett's *Boys of England* was founded as 'A Magazine of Sport, Travel, Fun and Adventure', but it was not until 1879 and the launch of *The Boy's Own Paper* that sport became a staple of schoolboy stories. In 1948 E. S. Turner joked that

29
Arthur Hughes,
illustration for *Tom
Brown's Schooldays*
(1869 edition).

'any historian of the remote future relying exclusively on old volumes of boys' magazines for his knowledge of the British way of life in the early twentieth century . . . will record that the country was the battleground of an unending civil war between a small vigorous race known as Sportsmen and a large, sluggish and corrupt race known as Slackers'.[66] The battleground extended far beyond the school walls. After the First World War, *Marvel* ran a series of stories by Arthur S. Handy in which parsons, newspaper editors, farmers, dockers, millionaires, plumbers and taxi drivers all ended up as boxing heroes, while in the *Champion*, 'sport grew from a fetish to a frenzy' (illus. 57).[67]

In his advocacy of boxing, Thomas Hughes had higher ambitions than the mere settling of schoolboy quarrels and desires, or the exercising of 'the temper, and . . . the muscles of the back and legs'.

> Every one who is worth his salt has his enemies, who must be beaten, be they evil thoughts and habits in himself, or spiritual wickedness in high places, or Russians, or Border-ruffians, or Bill, Tom, or Harry, who will not let him live his life in quiet till he has thrashed them.[68]

On the one hand, fighting is 'natural', especially if you are English; on the other, 'rightly understood', it must always have a 'chivalrous' and Christian purpose behind it.[69] In *Tom Brown at Oxford* (1861), Hughes distinguished the self-indulgent 'muscleman' from the 'muscular Christian' who, like St Paul, brings his body into 'subjection'.[70]

Hughes's determination to avoid celebrating the mere 'muscleman' meant that for all his descriptions of sports and fighting, his works give very little sense of the bodies involved in them. The male body is present less as something concrete and material than as a sign of, or instrument for, chivalry. This was not the case in the work of Hughes's near contemporary, Walter Pater, whose essays, from 'Winckelmann' (1867) to 'The Age of Athletic Prizemen' (1894), marked yet another revival of interest in Greek sculpture and the 'Hellenic ideal' of the male body.[71] Published just two years before the modern Olympics began, 'The Age of Athletic Prizemen' celebrates 'peaceful combat as a fine art': an art manifested in sculptures of athletes and their poetic equivalents, Pindar's poems, 'sung in language suggestive of a sort of metallic beauty'.[72] For Pater the beauty of these works derived from their celebration of the fleeting moment: the athlete is poised 'just there for a moment, between the animal and spiritual worlds', between actions, and between youth and maturity. The emphasis on stillness ('repose' is Pater's word) suggests in turn what he calls 'sexless beauty': the white marble statues have been 'purged from the angry, bloodlike stains of action and passion'. The young athletes memorialized are curiously 'virginal yet virile'.[73] They represent the unity of unstained mind and unstained body.

St Paul's emphasis on subjugation appealed to both Hellenists and Muscular Christians. Pater stressed 'the religious significance of the Greek athletic service' and argued that 'the athletic life certainly breathes of abstinence, of rule, of *the keeping under* of oneself'.[74] But while Hughes promoted the moral consequences of such subjugation, Pater's emphasis was aesthetic.[75]

## QUEENSBERRY AND THE PROFESSIONALIZATION OF THE AMATEUR IDEAL

In many different contexts in nineteenth-century Britain, Asa Briggs wrote, there was 'an interplay between what happened nationally and what happened in the schools'.[76] Common to both was the codification of sports. The Football Association was founded in 1863, the cricketing yearbook *Wisden* was first produced in 1864, the Rugby Union rules (based on the Rugby School rules) were formulated in 1871, and in 1866 the Pugilists' Benevolent Association adopted a series of rules partly devised by the lightweight champion boxer, Arthur Chambers, but famously published, the following year, under the name of their 24-year-old endorser, the eighth Marquess of Queensberry, John Sholto Douglas.[77]

Boxing regulations had gradually become more rigorous during Victoria's reign: Broughton's 1743 rules were superseded in 1838 by the London Prize Rules (which were revised in 1853). These specified the size of a boxing ring, the use of turf, the role of seconds and umpires, and outlawed head-butting, kicking and

30
Mathew Brady,
two soldiers posed
as boxers at a
Federal camp
at Petersburg,
Virginia, April 1865.

biting. Most importantly, they also decreed that if the contest was undecided all bets were off.[78] The Queensberry Rules (essentially a modified version of those which had governed sparring for many years) went much further towards bridging the gap between the amateur and professional sport. All the grappling holds now associated with wrestling were disallowed, thus ensuring a more upright contest; weight categories for boxers were to be strictly observed, and gloves, which had been used mainly in training, were now to be compulsory in fights. Under the London Prize Rules, fights were to the finish, although exhausted fighters or their seconds might agree to a draw (as happened after 37 rounds in the case of Heenan vs. Sayers). Under the Queensberry rules, there would be a set number of rounds (usually no more than twenty), limited to three minutes each, with one minute between rounds; a man who was knocked down was allowed ten seconds to get to his feet or lose the fight by a knockout).

After the 1860s old-style prize-fights continued clandestinely, but they were no longer the national events that Sayers vs. Heenan had been. Endorsed by organizations such as the Amateur Athletic Club, the Queensberry rules were increasingly chosen over the London Prize Rules. Bare-knuckle boxing was giving way to boxing in its modern form.

Shortly after the end of the Civil War, the Marquess of Queensberry, accompanied by Arthur Chambers, visited the United States for, as his grandson notes, 'agreement with American supporters of the game was essential'.[79] Queensberry's rules came into effect slightly later in America than in Britain; John L. Sullivan's last contest under the London Prize Ring rules took place in 1889. In the United States, the dichotomy between attitudes towards professional and amateur boxing was particularly pronounced, perhaps because professional prize-fighting was even more violent and disorderly there. From the late 1840s until the Civil War, tension between 'natives' and the growing numbers of Irish immigrants found expression in a series of fiercely contested fights between various pairings of Tom Hyer, Yankee Sullivan, John Morrissey and John C. Heenan. The most colourful of these fighters was John Morrissey. Prize-fighting was only one element in what was effectively a wrong-side-of-the-tracks Benjamin Franklin career, ranging from street gangs to political 'shoulder-hitting' (persuading voters to make the 'right' choice) to the founding of the Saratoga race-track (with accompanying lucrative gambling opportunities) to serving two terms in Congress. Today, Morrissey is remembered for his involvement in the murder of William Poole – Bill the Butcher – the leader of a so-called Native American (anti-Irish) gang. Herbert Asbury told the story in *The Gangs of New York* (1927) and Martin Scorsese adapted it for the cinema in 2002.[80]

The passing of legislation to outlaw prize-fighting (in Massachusetts in 1849; in New York in 1859) coincided with a boom in sparring academies and cheap boxing manuals. Partly as a result of the Heenan–Sayers contest, boxing also became a popular form of camp recreation during the American Civil War; 'a poignant if fleeting alternative to the ghastliness of battle' (illus. 30).[81] From the antebellum period onwards, working-class prize-fighting was considered corrupt and deplorable, while genteel sparring was welcomed as a means of restoring 'vigour' (a popular word particularly by the end of the century) to middle-class men. Reformers such Thomas Wentworth Higginson argued that sports such as boxing counteracted what they saw as the inherently emasculating effects of city life.[82] 'I am satisfied', announced Oliver Wendell Holmes, Sr., the asthmatic 'Autocrat of the Breakfast Table', in 1858, 'that such a set of black-coated, stiff-jointed, soft-muscled, paste-complexioned youth as we can boast of in our Atlantic cities never before sprang from loins of Anglo-Saxon lineage.'[83] One of the delights of 'a manly self-hood' that Walt Whitman celebrated in his 1860 'Poem of Joys' was the 'joy of the strong-brawn'd fighter, towering in the arena, in perfect condition, conscious of power, thirsting to meet his opponent' (illus. 31).[84]

In the late 1870s and '80s, Henry James created American protagonists whose masculinity was directly shaped by the Civil War and its aftermath. Veterans of the war like Basil Ransom (in *The Bostonians*, 1886) and Christopher Newman (in *The American*, 1877) were 'national types' whose instinct for battle had been redirected into commercial and romantic ventures. To be 'a powerful specimen of an American', Newman must first of all be physically fit, strong and vigorous. A product of 'the elastic soil of the West', he was 'not a man to whom fatigue was familiar'; his rhetoric, too, involves delivering blows to his competitors and generally putting their noses 'out of joint'. It is not simply that Newman's 'physical capital' correlates with his financial and moral worth; rather, James suggests, it is his natural physical 'vigour' that allows his other accomplishments. 'What should I be afraid of?', he announces, 'I am too ridiculously tough'.[85] But Basil Ransom worries that men like Newman are becoming rare. The 'masculine tone', he complains, is under threat.[86] Perhaps America was growing 'old and soft'.[87]

31
George A. Hayes, *Bare Knuckles c.* 1870–85.

32
George Bellows, *Business-men's Class*, YMCA, lithograph, 1916.

Theodore Roosevelt wrote directly of the nationalistic (Anglo-Saxon American) imperative behind 'the strenuous life': 'There is no place in the world for nations who have become enervated by the soft and easy life, or who have lost their fibre of vigorous hardness and masculinity'.[88] Roosevelt also believed that boxing was also an ideal sport for city dwellers. 'When obliged to live in cities,' he wrote in his 1913 autobiography, 'I for a long time found that boxing and wrestling enabled me to get a good deal of exercise in condensed and attractive form.' But it was not only the possibility of a vigorous workout in a limited space that appealed. 'Powerful, vigorous men of strong animal development', he maintained, 'must have some way in which their animal spirits can find vent' (illus. 32).[89]

## 'BOX, DON'T FIGHT'

In Britain, finding vent for dangerous urban 'animal spirits' was one of the ambitions of the Christian socialist movement, which Thomas Hughes founded with F. D. Maurice and Charles Kingsley. One of their earliest initiatives was a night school and a series of Working Men's Associations. In 1854 the evening classes developed into the establishment of the Working Men's College. When Hughes proposed to teach boxing there, Maurice was alarmed, and indeed 'was afraid that the fighting in *Tom Brown's Schooldays* might be used to justify the brutalities of professional prize-fighting', in particular the notorious contest between Sayers and Heenan.[90]

Maurice need not have worried about associations of amateur sparring with the dying days of bare-knuckle prize-fighting for, even in the 1860s, and even in Britain, the two sports were coming to be seen as radically different.[91] Hughes loathed prize-fighting, writing in an 1864 letter that 'fighting in cold blood for money is under any conditions as brutal and degrading a custom as any nation can tolerate'.[92] But that was not to say that 'round shoulders, narrow chests, stiff limbs' were to be condoned; they were 'as bad as defective grammar and arithmetic'. Everybody at the college had to box with Hughes, and the sparring classes 'grew into informal social gatherings'.[93]

In 1880, the British Amateur Boxing Association was founded with the motto, 'Box, don't fight', and with this in mind, social and religious reformers encouraged the setting up of boxing clubs in working-class areas. The violence of the street, it was thought, could be redirected into the gym. In his 1899 study of East London, Walter Besant wrote of the importance of bringing the public school ideal into poor neighbourhoods:

> They work off their restlessness and get rid of the devil in the gymnasium with the boxing-gloves and with single stick; they contract habits of order and discipline; they become infected with some of the upper-class ideals, especially as regards honor and honesty, purity and temperance.

The language Besant uses here is suffused with, and indeed confuses, religious and medical imagery. Boxing would not only enact a kind of exorcism ('fifteen minutes with a stout adversary knock the devil out of a lad – the devil of restlessness and pugnacity'), but also, he suggests, become a kind of beneficial contagion.[94] This might also have other, more immediately practical, advantages. When, in Besant's novel *All Sorts and Conditions of Men* (1882), Angela Messenger worries about security in her utopian Palace of Delight (a model for the real People's Palace) her friend, the aristocrat-in-disguise Harry Le Breton, suggests engaging 'a professor of the noble art of self-defence'.[95]

In *East London*, Besant recalled the success of a church boxing club in Shoreditch, and urged readers who 'think that this is not the ideal amusement for a clergyman' to think again (illus. 33).[96] In fact many churches and later synagogues ran gyms and supported fighters.[97] The close involvement of organizations such as the Boy Scout Movement, the Jewish Lads' Brigade and Boys' Town in amateur boxing forms the basis of many fictional (as well as true) boxing stories well into the twentieth century.[98] The 'boxer-and-the priest' movie did particularly well during the thirties.[99]

Needless to say, Hollywood notwithstanding, boxing did not always succeed in ridding the streets of the devil. In his book on the Kray twins, John Pearson describes their early, highly successful, boxing careers in the London East End of the 1950s. Their father, he writes, 'thought that boxing would be the making of the twins, give them the discipline they needed, take them off the streets and give them something other than mischief to occupy their minds'. As amateurs, the twins won every bout they fought, and at the age of sixteen, they turned

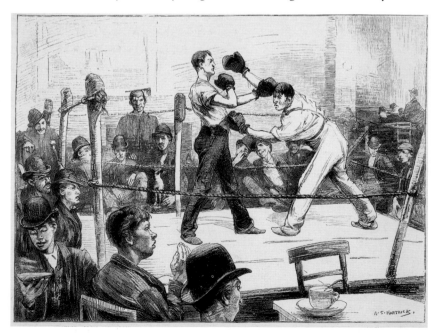

33
A. S. Hartnet, 'Men's Club in Connection with Holy Trinity Church, Shoreditch – A Boxing Match', *The Graphic*, 19 October 1889.

professional. But soon afterwards, Pearson notes, 'the street violence they were involved in mysteriously increased as well'.[100]

In the 'social problem' discourse of the late nineteenth century, reformers often talked about 'the way out' and here too boxing played a part.[101] In Arthur Morrison's 1896 novel of London's East End, *A Child of the Jago*, Father Sturt tries to 'wipe out the blackest spot in the Jago' by creating a lodging-house, a night-shelter, washhouses and a club where 'he gathered the men of the Jago indiscriminately, with sole condition of good behaviour on the premises'. 'And there they smoked, jumped, swung on horizontal bars, boxed, played at cards and bagatelle, free from interference save when interference became necessary.'[102] But despite the best efforts of Father Sturt, the violence of the streets is never channelled. A novel full of street battles, *A Child of the Jago* ends with a fight in which the protagonist, Dicky, is killed. With his dying breath, he says to Father Sturt that he's found another 'way out – better'.[103]

## THE FISTIC PHRASEOLOGY OF CHARLES DICKENS

George Orwell, claiming Dickens as a fellow pacifist in 1939, argued that he 'has no interest in pugilism':

> Considering the age in which he was writing, it is astonishing how little physical brutality there is in Dickens's novels . . . he sees the stupidity of violence, and also he belongs to a cautious urban class which does not deal in socks on the jaw, even in theory.[104]

Others have disagreed with this reading. John Carey, for example, notes that while Dickens 'saw himself as the great prophet of cosy, domestic virtue, purveyor of improving literature to the middle classes . . . violence and destruction were the most powerful stimulants to his imagination'.[105] This violence manifests itself in many ways; in murder, fire and cannibalism. 'Socks on the jaw' are also not uncommon. The shift in the cultural meanings of boxing in the Victorian era is nowhere better reflected than in a body of work which began in the 1830s and ended in the 1870s.

In an 1852 letter, Dickens wrote that 'Nobody can for a moment suppose that "sporting" amusements are the sports of the PEOPLE . . . they are the amusements of a peculiar and limited class', and boxers (and their supporters) often figure in his novels as hangovers from that peculiar class and a fading Regency world.[106] But while upper-class members of the Fancy, such as Sir Mulberry Hawk in *Nicholas Nickleby* (1838–9), are villains as well as fools, working-class or shabby-genteel sporting types, such Sam Weller, Pickwick's cheerfully cynical and pugilistic manservant, are usually treated with affection. In Dickens's first novel, *The Pickwick Papers* (1836–8), the joke on the nostalgic boxing fan is similar to that on the boxing prints in the 1860 'Uncommercial Traveller' piece. When Mr. Roker recalls the glory days of the butcher–pugilist with whom Pickwick is to share a room in the debtors' jail, he gazes 'abstractedly out of the grated window before him, as if he were fondly recalling some peaceful scene of his early youth':

> It seems but yesterday that he whopped the coal-heaver down Fox-under-the-Hill by the wharf there. I think I can see him now, a-coming up the Strand between the two street-keepers, a little sobered by the bruising, with a patch o' winegar and brown paper over his right eye-lid, and that 'ere lovely bull-dog, as pinned the little boy arterwards, a-following at his heels.[107]

Another recurrent joke features the pugilistic pretensions of clerks as a form of ersatz gentility. In *The Old Curiosity Shop* (1841) Dick Swiveller (bearer of a 'small limp' calling card and dandyish attire) attempts fisticuffs at the door of Daniel Quilp, where he 'hammer[ed] away with such good will and heartiness' that it takes Quilp a couple of minutes to dislodge him, and even then Swiveller 'perform[ed] a kind of dance round him and require[ed] to know "whether he wanted any more?"'.[108] Swiveller is not the only one of Dickens's characters to enjoy a little sparring dance or shadow boxing (which Addison had described as giving a man 'all the pleasure of boxing, without the blows').[109] Later in *The Old Curiosity Shop*, little Nell's gambling-addicted grandfather is tempted off the straight and narrow at a pub run by Jem Groves, a retired prize-fighter. Groves very much admires his own portrait upon the wall and is introduced 'sparring scientifically at a counterfeit Jem Groves, who was sparring at society in general from a black frame over the chimney-piece'.[110] Real and (safely) counterfeit violence, here and elsewhere in Dickens's work, exist side by side. Unable to take on his master directly ('I should have spoilt his features . . . if I could have afforded it', he later confesses), Newman Noggs, clerk to the odious Ralph Nickleby, shadow boxes outside his office door.

> He stood at a little distance from the door, with his face towards it; and with the sleeves of his coat turned back at the wrists, was occupied in bestowing the most vigorous, scientific, and straightforward blows upon the empty air.
>
> At first sight, this would have appeared merely a wise precaution in a man of sedentary habits, with the view of opening the chest and strengthening the muscles of the arms. But the intense eagerness and joy depicted in the face of Newman Noggs, which was suffused with perspiration; the surprising energy with which he directed a constant succession of blows towards a particular panel about five foot eight from the ground, and still worked away in the most untiring and persevering manner; would have sufficiently explained to the most attentive observer, that his imagination was thrashing to within an inch of his life, his body's most active employer, Mr. Ralph Nickleby.[111]

Dickens enjoyed the language of boxing as much as he did boxers, and nowhere more than in *Dombey and Son* (1846–8); indeed he stole the name (but little else) of a real prize-fighter, 'The Game Chicken' (Henry – 'Hen' – Pearce) for one of its characters. After coming into his inheritance, Mr Toots, a Corinthian past his sell-by-date, devotes himself to learning 'those gentle arts which refine and humanize existence, his chief instructor in which was an interesting character called the Game Chicken, who was always heard of at the bar of the Black Badger, wore a shaggy great-coat in the warmest weather, and knocked Mr. Toots about the head three times a week, for the small consideration of ten and six per visit'. We learn about the Game Chicken's past exploits, his glory against the Nobby Shropshire One, and his defeat ('he was severely fibbed . . . heavily grassed') by the Larkey Boy. When Mr Toots despairs of winning the love of Florence Dombey against the wishes of her father, the Chicken reassures him that 'it is within the resources of Science to double him up, with one blow in the waistcoat'.[112]

When, in *Bleak House* (1852–3), Mr Snagsby comments that 'when a time is named for tea, it's better to come up to it', his wife is appalled.

> 'To come up to it!' Mrs Snasgby repeats with severity. 'Up to it! As if
>     Mr Snagsby was a fighter!'
> 'Not at all, my dear,' says Mr. Snagsby.[113]

Mrs Snagsby views the use of boxing jargon as a sign of vulgarity, which must be avoided at all costs. Dickens, though, had no such qualms. A boxing pun may even be intended in the title of the opening chapter of *Bleak House*, 'In Chancery'. The *OED* gives as the slang meaning of the term, 'the position of the head when held under the opponent's left arm to be pommelled severely, the victim meanwhile being unable to retaliate effectively.'[114] The meaning derives, the Dictionary adds, 'from the tenacity and absolute control with which the Court of Chancery holds anything'. This legal metaphor was frequently used in boxing slang, and, with the new meaning attached, occasionally reapplied to law. In August 1841, *Punch* enjoyed a typical joke on 'legal pugilism':

> The Chancery bar has been lately occupied with a question relating to a patent for pins' heads . . . The lawyers are the best boxers, after all. Only let them get a head in chancery, even a pin's, and see how they make the proprietor bleed.[115]

Dickens used the phrase himself in *The Mystery of Edwin Drood* (1870) when the Revd Crisparkle affectionately takes on his mother and 'wound up by getting the old lady's head into Chancery, a technical term used in scientific circles, with a lightness of touch that hardly stirred the lightest lavender or cherry riband in it'.[116] In *Bleak House*, he may have wanted the phrase's additional meaning to reinforce the novel's emphasis on deadlock of various kinds.

Elsewhere, what Dickens terms 'fistic phraseology' proves remarkably versatile, and his relish in its use is palpable. Some metaphors have only fleeting comic potential, often to characterize a marriage: in the above example, the joke rests in the fact that Mrs rather than Mr Snagsby is clearly the pugilist in the family; in the opening chapter of *Nicholas Nickleby*, on the other hand, Mr. Godfrey Nickleby and his wife are described as 'two principles in a sparring match, who, when fortune is low and backers scarce, will chivalrously set to, for the mere pleasure of the buffeting.'[117] When Wemmick, in *Great Expectations* (1861), tries to put an arm around Miss Skiffins, she stops it with her green-gloved hands and 'the neatness of a placid boxer'.[118]

By putting pugilistic slang in the mouths of unlikely speakers in unlikely contexts, Dickens encourages his readers to think about the values such idioms conventionally entail. When the tender-hearted and literal-minded Mr Pickwick says 'Take that, Sir' to the wretched Job Trotter, Dickens intervenes with 'Take what?'

> In the ordinary acceptation of such language, it should have been a blow. As the world runs, it ought to have been a sound, hearty cuff; for Mr. Pickwick had been duped, deceived, and wronged by the destitute outcast who was now wholly in his power. Must we tell the truth? It was something from Mr. Pickwick's waistcoat, which chinked as it was given into Job's hand . . . [119]

Pickwick just does not do metaphors. However, it is not only in 'the Pickwickian sense' that words can be redefined.[120] In *David Copperfield* (1850), Mr Micawber repeatedly 'cull[s] a figure of speech from the vocabulary of our coarser national sports'. On several occasions Micawber describes himself as 'floored' by circumstances and at one point he tells David, 'I can show fight no more'. But the point about Mr Micawber is that he never gives up; however often he finds himself on the floor, he always does fight on. And the last time he tells David he is 'floored', it is by the friendliness of Mr Dick.[121]

Other metaphors are more fully developed. In Chapter Two of *Hard Times* (1854), the 'government officer' who accompanies Mr Gradgrind on his school inspection is given 'in his way (and in most other people's too)', the supplementary identity of 'professed pugilist; always in training'. This allows for considerable elaboration. Gradgrind came prepared

> always with a system to force down the general throat like a bolus, always to be heard of at the bar of his little Public-office, ready to fight all England. To continue in fistic phraseology, he had a genius for coming up to the scratch, wherever and whatever it was, and proving himself an ugly customer. He would go in and damage any subject whatever with his right, follow up with his left, stop, exchange, counter, bore his opponent (he always fought All England) to the ropes, and fall

upon him neatly. He was certain to knock the wind out of common-sense, and render that unlucky adversary deaf to the call of time.[122]

The pugilistic energies of the Regency have been diverted by utilitarian England, Dickens seems to be suggesting, and that is perhaps not wholly a good thing: in the classroom, the pugilist-turned-bureaucrat (once hero of 'the Fancy') is reduced to fighting 'fancy' in the form of flowered carpets, and pictures of horses on the walls.

While references to boxers and boxing slang remain incidental in Dickens's novels, fights in which boxing skills are employed occur remarkably frequently. Such fights, in particular those with a strong moral impetus behind them, were, of course, popular with readers. When Nicholas Nickleby asks Mr Crummles why he stages combats between mismatched opponents, Crummles replies, 'it's the essence of the combat that there should be a foot or two between them. How are you to get up the sympathies of the audience in a legitimate manner, if there isn't a little man contending against a big one'.[123] Such contests also serve a structural purpose, often marking turning points in the novels; in defending the honour of another (a sister or a mother or a small boy) the hero embarks on a new stage in his adventure. For example, after Noah Claypole insults his mother, Oliver Twist, 'crimson with fury', knocks him down with a blow that 'contains his whole force'; beaten in turn, he decides to run away from the workhouse – to London and into the clutches of Fagin (illus. 34).[124] Nicholas Nickleby experiences several such turning points, the most important occurring after his defeat of the cruel schoolmaster, Squeers. This fight is presented as the key incident of what can only be described as a kind of slave narrative. On Nickleby's arrival at the school, Squeers tells his wife that he now feels like 'a slave-driver in the West Indies [who] is allowed a man under him to see that his blacks don't run away, or get up a rebellion'; Nickleby is 'to do the same with *our* blacks'. On this analogy, the abject child, Smike, who runs away only to be recaptured, takes on the role of the beaten slave. But while in the classic American slave-narratives, he would fight either his master or overseer, here the overseer (Nickleby) intervenes on the slave's behalf and then the two run away together.[125]

Many of Dickens's fights combine a defence of vulnerable virtue with an awareness of class status and conflict, in a manner that recalls Adam Bede's battle. In Dickens, however, the fight is not usually between a decadent aristocrat and a humble peasant, but between various members of the middle class. John Carey argues that whenever 'virtuous muscles' are involved, Dickens's writing 'deteriorates'. 'Hopelessly dignified, the good characters brandish their sticks or fists, and the villains tumble. Dickens beams complacently. It is dutiful, perfunctory business.'[126] Although Carey's assessment rings true for some of the instances given above, there are other cases in which virtue and violence have a less easy relationship, and where the writing is far from perfunctory. Often considered as alternative versions of Dickens's own autobiography, *David*

34
George Cruikshank,
'Oliver plucks up
spirit', illustration
for *Oliver Twist*
(1837).

*Copperfield* and *Great Expectations* present their fisticuffs rather more anxiously and interestingly.

Aware of himself from an early age as a 'little gent', David Copperfield struggles to establish this fact in the world.[127] Chapter Eighteen presents some of the events that, in retrospect, he believes 'mark' the course of coming of age: these are falling in love, twice, and fighting the local butcher, twice.

'The terror of the youth of Canterbury', the butcher is reputed to have 'unnatural strength' because of 'the beef suet with which he anoints his hair'. He taunts David and punches some younger boys about the head, and so David decided to fight him. David loses the fight and goes home to tell Agnes (the girl he does not yet know he loves) all about it. Her response is perfect: 'she thinks I couldn't have done otherwise than fight the butcher, while she shrinks and trembles at my having fought him'. Following beef-steaks to the eyes, some bear's grease to the hair, another thwarted love, and 'new provocation', David fights the butcher again and this time wins, knocking his adversary's tooth out. Although David says of the first contest, 'I hardly know which is myself and which the butcher, we are always in such a tangle and tussle, knocking about the trodden grass', it is precisely to establish who he is, and particularly to make it clear to which class he belongs, that he fights.[128]

At the end of the chapter, the young David believes he is now prepared for life as a Regency gentleman manqué; indeed next time he sees the butcher he contemplates the gentlemanly act of throwing him 'five shillings to drink'. But David has not yet, his older self admits, fallen in love 'in earnest', nor has he yet fought in earnest. When, a few chapters later he takes sparring lessons with James Steerforth, he feels himself 'the greenest and most inexperienced of mortals'. (Mildly embarrassed about his lack of boxing skill in front of Steerforth, he could, however, 'never bear' to show it in front of a man he feels is his inferior, Steerforth's servant, Littimer.)[129]

The real fight in David's life is against Uriah Heep, a man whose social ambition is unsettlingly similar to his own (Heep calls David an 'upstart'; David calls Heep an over-reacher). Heep is described as creepy and fawning – a 'crawling impersonation of meanness'. He gives David 'damp fishy' handshakes, but he is not harmless. His hand may be damp but it is also revengeful, a 'cruel-looking hand'. It takes David a long time to realize this, and even longer to act on his feelings of disgust. When he first sees Heep admiring Agnes, he wishes he had 'leave to knock him down'; 30 pages later, he recalls another 'leer' and wonders 'that I did not collar him'; it takes another five pages before, 'enraged as I never was before and never have been since', he strikes the cheek that is 'invitingly' before him. 'I struck it with my open hand with that force that my fingers tingled as if I had burnt them'. By assuming a gentlemanly persona, David could break the butcher's tooth, but here there is not enough class distance for fists to be clenched. Fortunately for David, Mr. Micawber, who defines equality as being able to 'look my fellow man in the face, and punch his face if he offended me', has fewer class anxieties. He steps in and breaks Heep's wrist with a ruler wielded as a sword. David says he has never seen 'anything more ridiculous', but it is clear that he could not have done as much.[130]

David's uneasy sense of his own hands might be compared to his reading of the other pairs he encounters in the novel. Some are easily understood: Traddles, a clerk, has 'soft' hands; Ham Pegotty, a fisherman, has 'manly' hands. Others are more confusing. Heep's hands are both 'damp' and 'cruel'. Steerforth, the Byronic 'Oxford man', conceals his hands with gloves when he spars; he 'knew everything' about sports, says David, but this is a misreading. What he sees as Steerforth's harmless sporting 'skirmish with Miss Dartle', for example, is the gloved aftermath of an unsporting, ungloved, attack, for at the end of the novel we learn that it is Steerforth who has scarred her.[131]

An understanding of the social and moral weight carried by different kinds of hands features even more centrally in *Great Expectations*. When Pip first visits Satis House, he is overwhelmed by Estella's contempt for him; it is, he says, 'so strong, that it became infectious and I caught it'. 'I had never thought of being ashamed of my hands before; but I began to consider them a very indifferent pair.' Nevertheless, Estella instructs him to use his 'coarse hands' to play cards with her (she wins every game), and then feeds him outside on the courtyard stones. Pip's reaction to this is so powerful as to be inexpressible verbally – 'humiliated, hurt, spurned, offended, angry, sorry – I cannot hit upon the right name for the smart' – the only 'counteraction' he finds to 'the smart without a name' is to twist his hair, kick the wall and cry.[132]

A second visit to Satis House follows much the same pattern – cards followed by food in the yard 'in the former dog-like manner'. This time, however, Pip's wandering in the grounds leads not to self-flagellation, but the flagellation of the Pale Young Gentleman (Herbert Pocket). He has 'hit upon' something more than the right name. It is Pocket who initiates the bout by inviting Pip to 'come and fight'. As a young Regency gentleman, Pocket considers fighting a jolly game whose pleasure derives primarily from the following of 'laws', 'regular rules' and numerous 'preliminaries'. The first requirement is 'a reason for fighting' and so he pulls Pip's hair and charges his head into his stomach; next, proper ground must be found, along with 'a bottle of water and a sponge dipped in vinegar'; then one must 'denude for battle'. Pip finds this behaviour 'at once light-hearted, business-like, and blood-thirsty'. But of course Pip does not understand the nature of the game, or indeed that it is a game. He is 'morally and physically' offended by the attack on his hair and stomach ('particularly disagreeable after bread and meat') and just wants to hit his attacker and be done with it. Fighting, for him, in other words, should be a natural response to hurt, but instead he has to wait until the preparations are complete. When his first blow sends Pocket to the ground, he thinks that is the end of it, but Pocket keeps coming back for more – Pip floors him with every punch – stopping only for the pleasure of 'sponging himself or drinking out of the water-bottle, with the greatest satisfaction in seconding himself according to the form'. Finally Pocket throws his sponge in, and then has to explain to Pip that that means he has won.[133]

At first glance, the fight seems a perfect 'counteraction' to Estella's humiliating behaviour. The gentleman's spurious 'reason' – a butt to the stomach – has unwittingly hit Pip where it hurts, for his stomach is full of Estella's bread and meat. Now Pip no longer needs to hurt himself (by kicking at walls and twisting his hair), but can hurt someone else, someone who, like Estella, wants to play silly games with his hands. Pip even admits that 'the more I hit him, the harder I hit him'. But ultimately Pip finds only 'gloomy satisfaction' in his victory. Failing to understand that the fight was a game (the only game in which a blacksmith's apprentice could strike a gentleman), he is consumed by guilt and fear – 'I felt that the pale young gentleman's blood was on my head, and that the law would avenge it'. (That this is an extreme misinterpretation of events is confirmed later in the book when the two meet again, and Pocket asks Pip to forgive him 'for having knocked you about so.') Nor is his nameless smart (might 'nausea' be the word?) any better, despite the fact that he soon encounters Estella with 'a bright flush upon her face'. Aroused by what she sees as his instinctive vitality, she invites him to kiss her and he does. 'But I felt that the kiss was given to the coarse common boy as a piece of money might have been, and that it was worth nothing.' We might compare her response to that of the shrinking and trembling Agnes in *David Copperfield*.[134]

For all his considerable technical knowledge, Pocket is a poor physical specimen: 'pale', with 'red eyelids', 'pimples on his face and a breaking out in his mouth'. He is tall, but 'his elbows, knees, wrists, and heels' are the most developed parts. Pocket is also, Pip observes, 'inky', and 'has been at his books', although we do not learn if it is those that taught him about boxing. Pip knows nothing about the science of boxing, but fights with the 'coarse hands' that, at this point in the story, he feels are his only inheritance. His victory over a gentleman, and Estella's reaction, merely confirm that coarseness (while David's victory over a butcher briefly gave him gentlemanly airs). Like Joe, Pip is a blacksmith and blacksmiths, along with butchers, were famous as fighters. Joe strikes his horseshoes 'complete, in a single blow'; Pip has struck Pocket in the same way. Soon after, Mr Jaggers announces Pip's great expectations, and offers Joe financial compensation. Joe's reaction is remarkably like Pip's had been earlier: first, masochistic (he 'scooped his eyes with his disengaged wrist, as if he were bent on gouging himself') and then, pugilistic. Jaggers's patronizing words are finally stopped 'by Joe's suddenly working round him with every demonstration of pugilistic purpose'. The lawyer soon departs. It is only later (when he can 'see again' in writing his story) that Pip realizes that a 'muscular blacksmith's arm' is also the arm most likely to have a gentle and loving touch.[135]

One of the ideas that Dickens explored in *Great Expectations* was what it meant to be a gentleman. For much of the novel, Pip believes it is a matter of playing games, and Pocket soon proves a genial teacher of all manner of rules. Although David Copperfield had been happy to be treated 'like a plaything' by Steerforth, Pip will not assume that role for long.[136] Instead he learns the rules that govern the gentlemanly use of cutlery, domestic life, being an employer and financial management. It is only later, when he realizes the source of his wealth, that he comes to appreciate Mr. Pocket Senior's comment that 'no man who was not a true gentleman at heart, ever was . . . a true gentleman in manner'. In other words, Herbert Pocket is a gentleman not because he knows the many and complex rules of boxing, but because, when he plays that game (and when he does not), 'he bears all blows and buffets'.[137]

If Dickens's first novels explored the comic remnants of the Regency world, his last, *The Mystery of Edwin Drood* (unfinished at his death in 1870), presents one of the most appealing literary portraits of a Muscular Christian.[138] Minor Canon the Reverend Septimus Crisparkle is a man who is not ashamed to follow Hughes's advice and fight with 'the weapons which God has given us all'. Crisparkle is another of Dickens's shadow boxers, but in his case it is not a matter of imaginative thrashing. Rather he merely 'assist[s] his circulation by boxing at a looking glass with great science and prowess . . . while his radiant features teemed with innocence, and soft-hearted benevolence beamed from his boxing gloves'. As a prelude to breakfast he takes his mother's face between his boxing gloves and kisses it; 'Having done so with tenderness, the Reverend Septimus turned to again, countering with his left, and putting in his right, in a tremendous manner.'[139]

Later in the novel, Crisparkle uses his boxing knowledge to make an extended comparison of gentle pugilists and pugnacious philanthropists. When he arrives at the office of the Haven of Philanthropy, he finds it populated by 'Professors . . . ready for a turn-up with any Novice who might be on hand'.

> Preparations were in progress for a moral little Mill somewhere on the rural circuit, and other Professors were backing this or that Heavy-Weight as good for such or such speech-making hits, so very much after the manner of the sporting publicans, that the intended Resolutions might have been Rounds.

Although both pugilists and philanthropists have 'a propensity to "pitch into" [their] fellow-creatures', differences between the two 'professions' soon emerge. While the philanthropists cannot claim to be in good physical condition (they present a 'superabundance of what is known to Pugilistic Experts as Suet Pudding'), they easily top the prize-fighters in aggression, bad language, bad temper and foul play. Although much involved in charitable causes himself, Dickens objected strongly to what he called 'the cant of philanthropy' and its professionalization.[140] 'The Professors of the Noble Art,' Crisparkle concludes, are 'much nobler than the Professors of Philanthropy.'[141]

'IT WAS DIFFERENT IN THE DAYS OF WHICH I SPEAK . . .'[142]

As the nineteenth century drew to a close, English nostalgia for the golden age of Regency prize-fighting returned with fervour. There are various possible explanations for this. As the Queensberry rules took hold, it became clear that the new sport of gloved boxing was entirely different from the old bare-knuckle prize-fighting. That sense of loss was perhaps intensified by that fact that the golden age of pugilism had also been the time when British sporting and military superiority was clear. In 1884 Francis Galton observed the disturbing fact that the 'rising generation' simply couldn't hit straight. Describing a machine for measuring the swiftness and force of a person's blow, Galton noted, 'it was a matter of surprise to me, who was born in the days of pugilism, to find that the art of delivering a clean hit, straight from the shoulder, as required by this instrument, is nearly lost to the rising generation. Notwithstanding the simplicity of the test, a large proportion of persons bungled absurdly over it.'[143]

By the 1890s boxing was not simply a modern sport, but increasingly an American one. The last British heavyweight champion (until Lennox Lewis in 2002) was Robert Fitzsimmons, who won his title from 'Gentleman Jim' Corbett in 1897, and lost it two years later to Jim Jeffries.[144] The relinquishing of the heavyweight boxing crown was seen by some as symptomatic of the way in which America was forging ahead (economically and militarily) of a colonially overstretched Britain.

Angus Wilson described 'the naughty nineties' as a period in which the 'old unregenerate manliness of the Regency' resurfaced. His father is proposed as a representative figure: 'a middle class rentier', to whom 'being a man' meant 'paying a quid or two to a Covent Garden porter to fight him barefisted when he rolled home to the Tavistock Hotel after a night's card playing.'

> This was the old manliness that had united the ungodly upper class and the ungodly poor which had hidden its face from the blinding light of Queen Victoria's overwhelmingly pure home life; nothing to do with the manly thrashing which Tom Brown would administer to bullies after hearing the Doctor preach a heartening, noble and manly sermon in Rugby Chapel.[145]

This 'old manliness' reasserted itself against the watered-down Christian kind in a variety of different quarters. In his 1894 autobiography, novelist David Christie Murray confidently asserted that 'few greater blunders have been made by those who legislate for our well-being than by those moral people who abolished the Prize-Ring'. Many, he admits, will think him an 'irredeemable barbarian' for saying so, but he is keen to observe that a 'marked deterioration has been noticeable in the character of our people since the sport of the ring ceased to be a source of popular amusement'. Lost national pride is once again closely aligned with lost masculine 'virtue'. Looking back to his youth, Murray recalled the exploits of the Tipton Slasher (who 'trained my youthful hands to guard my youthful head') and the man who took his crown, Tom Sayers. Murray's emphasis is largely on the inevitability of champions (and men in general) succeeding each other, and the chapter, and indeed, the memoir, ends with Sayers's reflection that, 'It is my turn to-day and somebody else's tomorrow.'[146]

Among the many novels of the 1890s to evoke romantically the days of the great bare-knuckle champions is Arthur Conan Doyle's *Rodney Stone* (1896).[147] Like many of Doyle's historical novels, it is narrated by an old man looking back to his youth. Stone's Corinthian coming of age is interwoven with a Dickensian mystery story and a detailed account of the development of the sport, largely culled from *Boxiana*. In terms that recall Hazlitt's eulogy to male camaraderie in 'The Fight', Stone evokes the 'solid and virile' values of the past:

> The ale-drinking, the rude good-fellowship, the heartiness, the laughter at discomforts, the craving to see the fight – all these may be set down as vulgar and trivial by those to whom they are distasteful; but to me, listen-

35
Sidney Paget,
illustration for
Arthur Conan
Doyle, *Rodney Stone*
(1912).

I SAW HIM LOOK HARD AT HIS ANTAGONIST.

ing to the far-off and uncertain echoes of our distant past, they seem to
have been the very bones upon which much that is most solid and virile
in this ancient race was molded.[148]

Asked by his publisher George Newnes, 'Why that subject, of all subjects on
earth?', Doyle replied, 'Better that our sports should be a little too rough than
that we should run the risk of effeminacy' (illus. 35).[149]

    Conan Doyle was reputed to have been a fine boxer himself, and an interest
in the sport seeps into works in several different genres.[150] The French anti-hero

of his 1903 Napoleonic romp, *The Exploits of Brigadier Gerard*, for example, has several comically inept bouts against a 'solid and virile' Englishman.[151] It is from such Englishmen that Sherlock Holmes is descended. Although Holmes assures Watson that he is in large part 'a brain' and the rest of him 'mere appendix,' that appendix often proves quite useful. In *The Sign of Four* (1889), he encounters an ex-champion prize-fighter now working as a bodyguard.[152] Refused entrance, Holmes reminds the man of their acquaintance 'at Alison's rooms on the night of your benefit four years back'.

> 'Not Mr Sherlock Holmes!' roared the prize-fighter. 'God's truth! How could I have mistook you? If instead o' standin' there so quiet you had just stepped up and given me that cross-hit of yours under the jaw, I'd ha' known you without question. Ah, you're the one that has wasted your gifts, you have! You might have aimed high, if you had joined the fancy.'[153]

Holmes's jokey aside to Watson – 'if all else fails me, I have still one of the scientific professions open to me' – relies on the fact that both pugilism and detection were deemed 'scientific'. Yet this is no mere coincidence of terminology. Both prize-fighting and crime-solving, as depicted by Doyle, require the careful application of method and technique to an often elusive opponent. Furthermore both are solitary pursuits, shunning the support of team-members or a uniformed force. At the end of *Tom Brown's Schooldays* 'young master' tells his pupils that cricket 'ought to be such an unselfish game. It merges the individual in the eleven; he doesn't play that he may win but that his side may.' Tom agrees with this view, 'now one comes to think of it', but Holmes is a different case.[154] In the *Memoirs*, he confides in Watson about his college days. 'I was never a very sociable fellow, Watson, always rather fond of moping in my rooms and working out my own little methods of thought, so that I never mixed with the men of my year. Bar fencing and boxing I had few athletic traits'.[155] Boxing, as Holmes had known it, was the sport of loners and intellectuals, an amateur pursuit that depended on the cultivation of 'little methods of thought' as well as chivalric intentions. That, however, was no longer strictly the case by the 1890s. Boxing was becoming a business and a profession.

# 5

# 'Like Any Other Profession'

From the 1880s to the 1920s boxing was in a state of flux. One set of codes and regulations replaced another, British dominance collapsed in the face of new American prowess, and new audiences emerged through the development of popular mass media from magazines to film. By the mid-1920s, boxing had become a mainstream spectator sport in the United States, and its associations with an illegal subculture loosened, for a while at least.

These changes are epitomized in the career of the 'Boston strong boy', John L. Sullivan. In 1881, Sullivan was a bare-knuckle pugilist, scrapping on a barge on the Hudson River in order to evade the attention of police; less than a decade later he was boxing in gloves according to the Queensberry rules in an indoor arena, lit by electricity, in front of a crowd that included middle-class businessmen and their wives.

Described by his biographer as 'the first significant mass cultural hero in American life', Sullivan was one of the first sportsmen to become a celebrity through the services of the national popular press in general, and one magazine in particular.[1] Founded in 1846, the *Police Gazette* reached its heyday in the 1880s and '90s under the editorship of Richard Kyle Fox. Fox introduced a potent mix of celebrity gossip, racial stereotyping, and sport, all lavishly illustrated with woodcuts. The *Police Gazette*'s interest in sport, as Tom Wolfe points out, had 'nothing to do with the High Victorian ideal of "athletics", and everything to do with gambling'.[2] Readers, it seemed, would bet on absolutely anything, from cock-fighting, badger-baiting, rat-killing and butchery to wood-chopping, hairdressing, speedy water-drinking, weightlifting by the teeth, sleep deprivation, and fasting. The magazine awarded championship belts in all these 'events' and so challenges were regularly issued. But the *Police Gazette* was particularly interested in boxing. Gene Smith argues that, 'almost alone', Fox's magazine 'made boxing big business and so popular that [in 1882] the result of a Sullivan-Ryan fight was of immensely more interest to citizens than the result of a Garfield-Hancock Presidential election'.[3]

Sullivan had publicly humiliated Fox in 1881 by refusing to visit his table in a Boston saloon. 'If he wants to see John L. Sullivan,' the prize-fighter blustered,

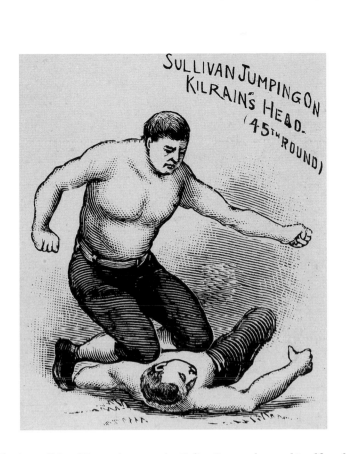

36
The 45th round of
Sullivan vs. Kilrain,
as illustrated in the
*Police Gazette* (1889).

'he can do the walking.' From then on, the *Police Gazette* devoted itself to slandering Sullivan, and Fox set about finding a fighter who could defeat him. English, Irish, American and New Zealand contenders were all featured in the magazine as they prepared to take him on. None succeeded. Finally, in 1889, Sullivan faced Jake Kilrain, whom Fox had dubbed champion of the world (although in fact he had only drawn with the British champion, Jem Smith).[4] Each side posted a $10,000 bet, winner to take all. Unfortunately for Fox, after 75 bloody rounds under the Mississippi sun, Sullivan also beat Kilrain (illus. 36). Fox finally gave up the feud and awarded him the *Police Gazette* championship belt.

Following his defeat of Kilrain, Sullivan did not simply become a celebrity; like Heenan and Sayers before him, he became a screen onto which a wide variety of feelings and attitudes could be projected. In the late nineteenth century, many of those feelings concerned doctrines of materialism, whether economic, aesthetic, physical, or national. The Cuban essayist, poet, and revolutionary leader, José Martí, for example, saw the 1882 Ryan–Sullivan fight as proof of the uncivilized, and outmoded, nature of North American life.[5] Robert Frost, on the contrary, used Sullivan's name to demonstrate 'the level of intelligence' in New Hampshire. 'The matter with the Mid-Victorians,' a farmer states in his poem, 'New Hampshire', 'Seems to have been a man named John L. Darwin.'[6] The farmer's conflation of the brute materialism of prize-fighting and that of Darwinism, Frost suggests, demonstrated high intelligence.

To young newspaperman Theodore Dreiser, 'raw, red-faced, big-fisted, broad-shouldered, drunken' Sullivan, 'with gaudy waistcoat and tie, and rings and pins set with enormous diamonds and rubies', embodied another kind of materialism, that of Gilded Age conspicuous consumption. Sullivan, Dreiser claimed, was 'the apotheosis of the humourously gross and vigorous and material . . . a sort of prize-fighting J. P. Morgan . . . I adored him'.[7] Dreiser drew on their 1893 meeting in his later fiction; most notably in a crucial scene in *Sister Carrie* (1900).[8] Having just helped Carrie take a step up in her inexorable rise, George Hurstwood goes to the 'gorgeous saloon' which he manages, and there encounters his rival for her affections, Charles Drouet.

> It was at five in the afternoon and the place was crowded with mer-chants, actors, managers, politicians – a goodly company of rotund, rosy figures, silk-hatted, starchy-bosomed, be-ringed and be-scarf-pinned to the queen's taste. John L. Sullivan, the pugilist, was at one end of the glittering bar, surrounded by a company of loudly dressed sports who were holding a most animated conversation. Drouet came across the floor with a festive stride, a new pair of tan shoes squeaking audibly his progress.

Sullivan's presence foreshadows the conflict between the two men for the prize of Carrie. It also suggests the terms in which the fight will be played out. If Sullivan is 'the apotheosis of the humourously gross and vigorous and material', Drouet, a travelling salesman in 'new tan shoes' is following, squeakily, in his footsteps. Saloon-manager Hurstwood has a solidity – 'composed in part of his fine clothes, his clean linen, his jewels, and, above all, his own sense of his importance' – which, in Carrie's eyes raises him above Drouet. By the end of the novel, however, he too will have met his match. The apotheosis of vigorous materialism, of course, turns out to be Carrie herself.[9]

Vachel Lindsay, meanwhile, considered Sullivan's materialism primarily in literary terms. His poem about the defeat of Kilrain describes the effect 'the Strong Boy of Boston' had on his nine-year-old self. Sullivan's example, Lindsay claimed, injected a much-needed infusion of red-blooded masculinity into his feminized late-Victorian life. Until hearing the 'battle trumpet sound' of John L., he had dressed like Little Lord Fauntleroy, and, when not under the sway of 'the cult of Tennyson's Elaine', had taken Louisa May Alcott as his 'gentle guide'.[10] After Sullivan's victory, it seems, being a Bostonian meant something differ-ent.[11] As a poem, 'The Strong Boy' is a good example of what Lindsay described as his deployment of 'the Higher Vaudeville imagination'. Like his more famous 'The Congo', it was meant to be chanted, and has a cheerful refrain:

'London Bridge is falling down.'
And . . .
John L. Sullivan

The strong boy
Of Boston
Broke every single rib of Jake Kilrain.[12]

But only three years after his defeat of Kilrain, Sullivan's great bare-knuckled strength had begun to seem old-fashioned; the future came in the form of James J. Corbett, 'Gentleman Jim', a bank clerk who taught sparring at San Francisco's Olympic Club. Corbett defeated Sullivan under the Queensberry rules in 1892, thus becoming the first gloved fighter to be recognized as heavyweight champion. The fight played out the classic antimonies of youth versus age, and science versus strength, but it also represented two different eras. Indeed some saw Sullivan's defeat as representing, once and for all, America's fall from grace (when hard-drinking men were hard-drinking men) into an age where even prize-fighters wore evening dress and sipped cocktails. Sullivan described Corbett as a 'damned dude'.

'Pompadour Jim', or more commonly 'Gentleman Jim', Corbett took his celebrity status and good looks seriously – 'why a fighter can't be careful about his appearance I don't understand' – and, with the help of his manager, William A. Brady, skilfully capitalized on them.[13] Not much had changed financially for boxers since Mendoza's day. They made little money from fighting itself. Any boxer with a well-known name took to the stage. All this would change with the introduction of film in the late 1890s, but until then Corbett toured the country, staging boxing exhibitions and appearing in a series of successful plays.[14] An example of his awareness of the tight control needed to maintain his celebrity can be found in his meeting with Mark Twain in 1894. When Twain jokingly challenged him to a contest, Corbett declined, 'so gravely', noted Twain, 'that one might easily have thought him in earnest'. Corbett, it seemed, was worried that Twain might knock him out 'by a purely accidental blow': 'then my reputation would be gone and you would have a double one. You have got fame enough already and you ought not to want to take mine away from me.'[15]

Fox's *Police Gazette* campaigned to make boxing legal as well as popular, but the sport continued to move in and out of legality until the 1920s, with different restrictions operating in different states at different times. Following their fight in Mississippi, for example, Sullivan and Kilrain were arrested and had to pay substantial fines to avoid imprisonment, while in 1895 legal obstructions meant that a planned fight between Jim Corbett and Bob Fitzsimmons had to move around the country several times before it finally took place two years later in Carson City, Nevada.[16] The desire to suppress prize-fighting during this period was not, as now, based on concerns about the health of the boxers. Rather, arguments about the legalization of boxing centred on its associations with crime and political corruption. In 1910 Corbett wrote that he hardly ever had a fight without a bribe being offered. 'The only objection I have to the prize ring', declared Theodore Roosevelt in 1913, 'is the crookedness that has attended its commercial development.'[17]

In the 1880s New York became one of the main centres of prize-fighting, despite frequent police disruption and calls from the press to end events 'which attract the worst ruffians and criminals in the city'.[18] Pushed out of the city, boxing clubs simply moved to nearby Long Island and Coney Island (popularly known as 'Sodom-by-the-Sea') where they continued to flourish. In order to try and control this spiralling illegal activity, New York became, in 1896, the first state to legalize a version of boxing by statute. Sparring with five-ounce gloves for a maximum of twenty rounds in buildings owned by incorporated athletic associations was now allowed, but 'disorderly gatherings' and police intervention continued, and, with the support of Governor Roosevelt, the law was repealed in 1900.

Outlawing professional boxing made little difference to the growth of its popularity, however, and in many places fights continued to be staged almost nightly. Those who were interested had no difficulty finding out where to go. One scam was to stage 'exhibitions' or, more commonly, to operate politically supported 'membership clubs'; anyone who paid a dollar could join the club and watch the fight. The status of athletic associations and saloon-based clubs shifted during the years that followed, until, in New York at least, boxing was finally legalized, and properly licensed, in 1920 (illus. 37).[19]

In his 1906 novel of the Chicago stockyards, *The Jungle*, Upton Sinclair described a club run by the Democratic Party's 'War-Whoop League', where cock fights, dog fights and boxing take place. 'The policemen in the district all belonged to the league, and instead of suppressing the fights, they sold tickets for them.' The clubhouse is a hotbed of 'agencies of corruption' including, among others, 'the prize-fighter and the professional slugger, the race-track

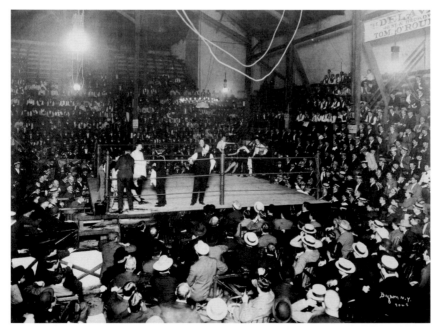

37
Kid McCoy at the Broadway Athletic Club, 1900.

"tout", the procurer, the white-slave agent, and the expert seducer of young girls', all of whom are, in turn, in 'blood brotherhood with the politician and the police'. 'More often than not', Sinclair wrote, 'they were one and the same person – the police captain would own the brothel he pretended to raid . . . On election day all those powers of vice and corruption were one power; they could tell within one per cent what the vote of their district would be, and they could change it at an hour's notice.'[20]

The boxing membership clubs were not merely magnets for criminals and corrupt politicians. As Jack London pointed out in his 1913 'alcoholic memoirs' of 'bouts' with John Barleycorn, the saloon was a place where men believed they could escape 'from the narrowness of women's influence into the wide free world of men'.[21] A steady stream of middle-class men, in pursuit of the strenuous life, passed though the doors of the boxing clubs, some more anxiously than others. In his *Life and Confessions*, the psychologist G. Stanley Hall admitted a compulsive interest in the 'raw side of human life', so much so that he 'never missed an opportunity to attend a prize fight if I could do so unknown and away from home'.[22] The artist Thomas Eakins was quite open about his interest in prize-fights, and, with his friend, sportswriter Clarence Cranmer, regularly attended the amphitheatre of the Philadelphia Arena, which was on the other side of Broad Street from the Pennsylvania Academy of Fine Arts.[23] His three major paintings of 1898 and 1899 feature fighters who appeared there during this time, and two of these were exhibited in the Academy's annual exhibitions. The illegal world of boxing had crossed the road. (Was Sylvester Stallone alluding to this when he has Rocky train on the steps of the Philadelphia Museum of Art?)

Eakins was uninterested in painting boxers exchanging blows. His paintings rather explore the moments within a fight when the action stops (*Taking the Count* and *Between Rounds*) and the moment when it is all over (*Salutat*). The professional activities surrounding the fight – involving the boxers' attendants, the referee, the press, and the police – interested him as much as the boxers themselves. In the first two paintings, large banners advertising a circus hang from the balcony. *Salutat* also alludes to gladiatorial combat (carved into the original frame of the painting were the words *dextra victrice conclamantes salutat*, 'the right hand of the victor salutes those acclaiming him'). Eakins wanted to show that the artist could find heroism and beauty in male semi-nudity without having recourse to Rome; modern America, he believed, provided ample material.[24] *Salutat* features Billy Smith, a local professional featherweight, known as 'Turkey Point'. While his chiselled white body evokes classical sculpture, his tanned face, neck and hands remind us that he is a working-class American boy (illus. 38).[25]

The victorious boxer's body, and in particular his musculature, is highlighted by bright electrical light, but the painting seems equally interested in celebrating his intimate involvement with the spectators (and indeed their intimate involvement with the artist, since all six men sitting along the railing are identifiable from Eakins's personal circle; his father is on the far right). Although a contemporary reviewer complained that these men are brought 'so

far forward as to give the impression that both victor and audience might shake hands', this seems to be one of the painting's great strengths.[26] The triumphantly raised right hand of Billy Smith is reflected in the raised right hand (with hat) of Eakins's friend, Clarence Cranmer; patches of blue (in Smith's sash and Cranmer's bow tie) also connect them. Without sportswriters such as Cranmer, Eakins may be suggesting, news of a boxer's victory would not travel far; more personally, without Cranmer's encouragement and support, Eakins might never have attended prize-fights or have gained access to boxers as models. And without such venues as the Philadelphia Arena, men could not gather together to gaze admiringly at other men. (As Michael Hutt points out, '*Salutat* reveals more of the male body than is strictly necessary'.[27]) The barrier that divides spectators and participants is less important than the links which connect them.

Several of Eakins's followers pursued his interest in boxing, finding in it a subject matter which would both challenge academic painting, and Americanize it in a properly 'manly' way. In the mid-1890s, Robert Henri, who had studied in Philadelphia with a pupil of Eakins, held regular gatherings where up-and-coming artists such as John Sloan and George Luks sometimes staged mock boxing matches. Luks invented numerous pugilistic personae for himself (Lusty Luks, Socko Sam, Curtain Conway, Monk-the-Morgue and Chicago Whitey). When he later became famous, he enjoyed telling journalists that, as Chicago Whitey, he fought some 150 fights, or that, as Lusty Luks, he was the former holder of the light heavyweight crown (illus. 39).[28]

In 1900 Henri moved to New York where, along with Sloan and Luks, he became successful as a member of the 'Immortal Eight', later dubbed the 'Ashcan school'. At the New York School of Art, he instructed his students to attend football games and boxing matches, in short to 'be a man first, an artist later'.[29] Nevertheless, art was the primary object of this manly activity. Henri believed that he could tell which students were 'fighters' and had 'guts' by looking at their work. Some ways of painting were, he maintained, more masculine than others and students were forbidden to use small brushes (which he considered effeminate) and urged to paint in 'the straightforward unfinicky manner of the

39
John Sloan's Philadelphia studio, December 1895. Sloan, second from the left, is watching a mock boxing match; George Luks is the boxer on the left.

male'.[30] The most prominent of Henri's students, and one who took this advice to heart, was George Bellows. Bellows frequently told journalists that his aim was to introduce 'manliness, frankness, love of the game' into his painting. 'Things that Henri only paid lip service to,' Edward Lucie-Smith argues, 'Bellows put into practice'.[31]

Bellows's studio was situated across the street from retired prize-fighter Tom Sharkey's saloon-cum-boxing club on Broadway, and, before he 'married and became semi-respectable' in 1910, he was a frequent visitor there.[32] The backroom at Tom Sharkey's, as depicted in Bellows's paintings, *Club Night* (1907) and *Stag at Sharkey's* (1909), is a rather hellish place (illus. 40). While Eakins depicted boxing spectators as decent sober middle-class men – many of whom are worthy of their own portraits – Bellows saw a mass of Goya-like grotesques. Those figures who can be distinguished, not so much by their faces as by their waistcoats and shirts, represent a mix of social classes and, as Marianna Doezema points out, 'a stereotypical range of reactions, from horror to fascination.'[33] ('The best part of a prize fight', wrote Charles Belmont Davis in 1906, 'is not the sight of two human brutes pounding each other into insensibility on a resined floor, but rather the yelling, crazy mob with its innate love of carnage that the two brutes have turned into the principal actors.'[34]) The claustrophobic atmosphere of *Stag at Sharkey's* is further intensified by the fact that the spectators encircle the boxers, and that they look up, rather than down, at the action. The viewer is situated among those spectators, virtually, but not quite, at ringside. The artist too may be included in the half-hidden portrait of a bald man whose eyes and raised eyebrows poke above the floor of the ring, 'as if he is here only to look. His head is inclined downward, perhaps toward a sketchbook, so he must glance sharply up to catch the action.' Bellows presents himself, Doezma argues, 'as a relatively detached observer, the professional artist in the act of gathering visual material'.[35]

Yet the painting is anything but detached. 'I didn't paint anatomy,' Bellows declared, 'I painted action'.[36] Some have read the immediacy and energy of this action, in which the limbs of nearly naked men are intertwined, as conflating a violent sexuality and a sexualized violence.[37] The club is so dark that little can be distinguished within it, except where a light from the left illuminates the white bodies of the boxers. The only colour present is the red of their faces (from exertion or blood?) which is reflected in the face of a bloodthirsty ringside spectator. Bellows is not interested in individual psychology or muscular precision. Instead he presents a thickly painted and almost abstract composition.

Bellows's early critics praised the 'manliness' of his style as well as his subject matter, but did not really explain what this meant. What was involved in translating manly subject matter, such as boxing, into style? Was it merely a matter of bold brush strokes and impasto? When James Huneker said that Bellows's 'muscular painting' hit the viewer 'between the eyes', he was suggesting that painting was itself a form of boxing.[38] Such claims recall Hazlitt's comments on Byron's masculine style some hundred years earlier, but a more relevant comparison might be with Hogarth's quarrel with academic painting.

40
George Bellows,
*Stag at Sharkey's*,
1909.

Both Hogarth and Bellows co-opted low-life activities such as boxing to epito-mize 'the real' in their propaganda battles against the artificiality of established conventions. Hogarth set low against high, down-to-earth Englishness against continental neo-classicism; Bellows set low against middle, American virility against Victorian sentimentality and the 'genteel tradition', John L. Sullivan against Louisa May Alcott.[39]

Frank Norris's advocacy of literary realism made similar connections. In a 1903 essay on the 'fakery' involved in most historical fiction, he proposed that novelists try harder to 'get at the life immediately around you'. Since 'we are all Anglo-Saxons enough to enjoy the sight of a fight', he argued, surely our litera-ture should strive to convey 'the essential vital, elemental, all-important true life within the spirit' evident at the best of these occasions; the novelist should strike to 'get at' 'Mr. Robert Fitzsimmons or Mr. James Jeffries'. The novelist's 'heavy' responsibility, he concluded, was not to make money but to write with 'sincerity'.[40] Realism was again proposed as the manly literary equivalent of pugilism, but this very move required romanticization. Norris did not consider the possibility that Fitzsimmons and Jeffries (both of Irish rather than Anglo-Saxon descent) might have been more interested in making money than in ex-pressing vitality, virility or sincerity.

Early nineteenth-century artists and writers had considered boxers wholly from the outside, as sub-cultural heroes or villains who, although their clothes, language or behaviour might be imitated, remained apart. In the 1880s, however, some artists and writers began to suggest that the fighter's life and experience might, in certain ways, resemble that of everyone else; it might even usefully be considered a representative life. This shift in attitude changed the way that boxers were represented in art. Increasingly boxers had more than satirical or metaphorical significance and the occasional walk-on part in a story. By the end of the nineteenth century, they began to feature in forms of representation, such as the novel and genre painting, that encouraged some degree of identification.

Thomas Eakins's boxing paintings, I have suggested, brought together policemen, sportswriters, sketch artists and boxers as men engaged in comparable professional activities. George Bernard Shaw made a similar claim in *Cashel Byron's Profession* (1886), which he intended as the first serious boxing novel. Instead of 'retaliatory violence' and 'romantic fisticuffs', it would deal with the challenges and injustices of the modern world. It would be about work and about sex, 'a hymn to skill and science over incoherent strength' and 'a daring anticipation of coming social developments'.[41] The book was a huge popular success. Running to many editions, it was pirated for the stage in the United States, prompting Shaw in 1901 to write a dramatic version (in blank verse), *The Admirable Bashville*.[42] But the novel's popularity, Shaw later lamented, did not stem from the pertinent social and political debates it addressed, but from its depiction of Cashel's 'professional performances'.[43] 'Here lay the whole schoolboy secret of the book's little vogue,' he complained. In 1902, P. G. Wodehouse praised Cashel Byron as 'the best drawn pugilist in fiction', and laughed at Shaw's dismissal of the English novel's 'gospel of pugilism'. 'And why not?' declared Wodehouse. 'All fights are good reading, and if the hero invariably wins, well, what does it matter?'[44]

Shaw had become interested in boxing in the late 1870s when his friend, Pakenham Beatty, an aspiring poet and keen amateur fighter, introduced him to Ned Donnelly, a 'Professor of Boxing' who ran a gymnasium near the Haymarket Theatre. In February 1883 Shaw completed *Cashel Byron's Profession* and a month later the two men entered for the Amateur Boxing Championship. (The first championship meeting of the Amateur Boxing Association had taken place in 1881.) Neither was chosen to compete. In a 1917 interview Shaw recalled this time, and in particular the 'brilliant boxer' Jack Burke. 'It was an exhibition spar of his that suggested the exploits of *Cashel Byron*.'[45]

After 1900 Shaw came to reject his boxing novel, and for twenty years largely stopped attending fights, primarily, he claimed, because the 'second-rate boxing' on offer 'reduced me to such a condition of deadly boredom that even disgust would have been a relief.'[46] In 1919, however, Shaw was persuaded to write an article for *The Nation* on Joe Beckett's European Heavyweight Championship fight against a man he considered a 'genius', Georges Carpentier (Arnold Bennett was *The New Statesman*'s correspondent), and in the 1920s, he became great friends with another scholarly fighter, Gene Tunney.[47] Tunney's reading was often commented upon by the press: on the eve of his first fight with Jack Dempsey in 1926, he was caught with Samuel Butler's *The Way of All Flesh*. Michael Holroyd reads Tunney's career as 'a Shavian romance' while Shaw himself praised Tunney for winning 'by mental and moral superiority . . . You might almost say that he wins because he has the good sense to win.'[48]

The main argument of *Cashel Byron's Profession* (and it is a very argumentative novel) is that 'the pugilistic profession is like any other profession'. 'The intelligent prize-fighter is not a knight-errant: he is a disillusioned man of business trying to make money at a certain weight and at certain risks, not of bodily injury (for a bruise is soon cured), but of pecuniary loss.'[49] What profession, the novel asks, might be open to Cashel Byron, son of an actress and pupil at a minor public school which promotes 'bodily exercises'? The school had encouraged Cashel to believe that the army was 'the only profession for a gentleman', but it is one that he cannot afford. He runs away as a sailor to Australia where he is taken in and trained by an ex-champion boxer (modelled on Ned Donnelly) who sagely tells him 'when you rise to be a regular professional, you wont care to spar with nobody without youre well paid for it'. This is confirmed later in the book when, like a Victorian hero, Cashel is forced to fight to defend the honour of a wealthy lady. But after the fight is over, he tells her, without Victorian chivalry, 'It's no pleasure to me to fight chance men in the streets for nothing; I don't get my living that way.' When he marries her, he gives up pugilism. 'He had gone through with it when it was his business; but he had no idea of doing it for pleasure.'[50]

Another man who turns to fighting purely to make some money is Robert Montgomery, the protagonist of Arthur Conan Doyle's 'The Croxley Master' (1905). Montgomery is a medical student who cannot afford the £60 needed to complete his degree. He is employed by a doctor who refuses to advance his wages and no other source of money seems forthcoming. 'His brains were fairly good, but brains of that quality were a drug in the market. He only excelled in his strength; and where was he to find a customer for that?' Fortunately, an opportunity arises for Montgomery to earn £60 if he beats the 'Croxley Master' ('twenty rounds, two-ounce gloves, Queensberry rules, and a decision on points if you fight to the finish'). Montgomery had excelled in university boxing, but had had 'no particular ambition' to enter amateur championships. Fighting for money is a different matter. 'He had thought bitterly that morning that there was no market for his strength, but here was one where his muscle might earn more in an hour than his brains in a year.' Montgomery is realistic about his chances: 'he knew enough to appreciate the difference which exists in boxing, as in every sport, between the amateur and the professional'. One of the Croxley Master's 'iron blows was worth three of his, and . . . without the gloves he could not have stood for three rounds against him. All the amateur work that he had done was the merest tapping and flapping when compared to those frightful blows, from arms toughed by the shovel and the crowbar.' However, he is in good physical shape, and can rely on 'that higher nerve energy which counts for nothing upon a measuring tape'. Furthermore, the Queensberry rules favour the scientific amateur over the old-style artisan pugilist. When Montgomery wins the fight, the Master urges him to a rematch, 'old style and bare knuckes'. But he refuses this offer, and one to become a professional fighter, in order to return to medical school.[51]

In 'The Croxley Master', Conan Doyle had come a long way from the Regency romance of *Rodney Stone* (published nine years earlier) to an almost Shavian position. 'It's not what a man would like to do that he must do in this world; it's what he *can* do,' declares Cashel Byron, 'and the only mortal thing I could do properly was fight.' Shaw reiterated this point in his own words nearly 40 years later: 'It was worth Carpentier's while to escape from the slavery of the coal pit and win £5,000 in 74 seconds with his fists. It would not have been worth his while if he had been Charles XII.'[52]

As work of last resort, Shaw further maintained, boxing had much in common with prostitution. His 1893 play *Mrs Warren's Profession* was originally subtitled 'A tragic variation on the theme of *Cashel Byron's Profession*', and he considered subtitling *Major Barbara* (1905) 'Andrew Undershaft's Profession'. Like Mrs Warren, arms dealer Andrew Undershaft and pugilist Cashel Byron 'do things for money that they would not do if they had other assured means of livelihood'.[53] If the word 'prostitution' is to be applied to one of these jobs, Shaw wrote, it should be applied 'impartially' to all. 'As long as society is so organized that the destitute athlete and the destitute beauty are forced to choose between underpaid drudgery as industrial producers, and comparative self-respect, plenty, and popularity as prize-fighters and mercenary brides, licit or illicit, it is idle to affect virtuous indignation at their expense.'[54] Although prostitution, arms-dealing and prize-fighting were professions which 'society officially repudiates', each of them, he maintained, could serve 'as a metaphor for the way in which that larger society is really conducted'. The 'prostitute class of men' did not only consist of prize-fighters: lawyers, doctors, clergymen, politicians, journalists and dramatists 'daily [use] their highest faculties to belie their real sentiments'.[55] On this reading, boxing was not merely 'a profession like any other', but expressive of the very nature of modern working life, its injustices and brutalities (illus. 41).

While Shaw and Conan Doyle maintained a clear distinction between the (degrading) professional and the (invigorating) amateur versions of boxing, their near contemporary, the American sociologist Thorstein Veblen, drew attention to a common element. Veblen's *The Theory of the Leisure Class* (1899) includes a chapter entitled 'Modern Survivals of Prowess', which considers the value of sport to the industrial and leisure classes. On the one hand, 'the leisure-class canon demands strict and comprehensive futility', which sport provides; on the other, the 'manly virtues' cultivated by sport 'do in fact further what may

broadly be called workmanship'. Sport, in short, cultivates 'two barbarian traits, ferocity and astuteness', both of which 'are highly serviceable for individual expediency in a life looking to invidious success . . . Both are fostered by the pecuniary culture. But both alike are of no use for the purposes of the collective life.'[56] Veblen's ideas recur in many subsequent accounts of sport. Theodor Adorno, for example, argued that while modern sports might seem 'to restore to the body some of the functions of which the machine has deprived it . . . they do so only to train men all the more inexorably to serve the machine'.[57]

## A MEATY BUSINESS

When the body was considered a machine, its workings were discussed in terms of 'fuel', 'efficiency' and 'waste'. The early twentieth century saw the development of nutrition as a field, led by Horace Fletcher, champion of mastication and 'rationally economic alimentation'. The body could, Fletcher promised, be run on the same principles as an efficiently managed factory.[58] These ideas quickly filtered through into popular fiction. The 'decivilization' of the dog Buck in Jack London's *The Call of the Wild* (1903) is, rather oddly, signalled by his adoption of Fletcherite principles. Buck is said to have 'achieved an internal as well as an external economy. He could eat anything, no matter how loathsome or indigestible and once eaten, the juices of his stomach extracted the least particle of nutriment; and his blood carried it to the farthest reaches of his body, building into the toughest and stoutest of tissues.'[59]

But while Buck might have been able to eat anything and still flourish as an efficient organism, human workers tended to have more particular nutritional needs. In the boxer's case, this invariably meant lots of meat. Discussions of meat in boxing stories (fictional and non-fictional) have traditionally assumed a rather magical aura: the boxer must eat meat in order to be meaty enough to fight against other slabs of men. It was easy for these activities to get confused. While Rocky, 'the Italian stallion', trains by punching sides of frozen beef, Jake La Motta (alternately described as a 'fucking gorilla', a 'fat pig' and a 'raging bull' in Martin Scorsese's film) hurls a steak across the room at his wife: 'You overcook it, it's no good. It defeats its own purpose.'[60] When Oliver Twist knocks out Noah Claypole in Dickens's 1838 novel, Mrs Sowerberry thinks the boy has gone mad. Mr Bumble soon puts her right: 'It's not Madness, ma'am . . . It's Meat.'[61]

Boxing became linked with meat partly because of the sport's early association with John Bull Englishness, and partly because many early boxers, including Tom Spring, Jem Belcher and Peter 'Young Rumpsteak' Crawley, were butchers; Moses Browne's 1736 poem, 'A Survey of the Amphitheatre', describes 'gentle butchers' engaged in 'that brotherhood's peculiar sport'.[62] Butchery was a trade that required considerable upper-body strength and provided a ready supply of prime steaks. The latter, rather than the former, was considered the significant factor, and early training manuals paid a great deal of attention to what should and should not be consumed. Francis Dowling, in *Fistiana* (1841), rejected 'young meat such as veal and lamb, [and] all white flesh, whether game or poultry' as 'good for nothing'. Only bloody beef contained sufficient 'nourishment for the muscle', and some maintained, the spirit.[63] Over a hundred years later, Norman Mailer was appalled at the thought of Ali eating fish and relieved to hear he had 'resumed the flesh of animals'.[64]

Sporting nutritionists were not invented in the twentieth century. An obsession with the boxer's diet first aroused public interest in the 1810 run-up to Tom Cribb's rematch with Tom Molineaux. Cribb's trainer, Captain Barclay, was determined that his boxer should lose two-and-a-half stone before the fight, and put him on a strict regime, even reputedly monitoring his excrement. *Blackwood's Magazine* ran a satirical article on the subject:

In the morning, at four of the clock, a serving-man doth enter my chamber, bringing me a cup containing half one quart of pig's urine, which I do drink . . . At breakfast I doe commonly eat 12 goose's eggs, dressed in whale's oil, wherefrom I experience much good effects. For dinner I doe chiefly prefer a roasted cat, whereof the hair has first been burned by the fire. If it be stuffed with salted herrings which are a good and pleasant fish, it will be better . . .[65]

And so on. But while popular mythology maintained that boxers are never short of meat – in *Sybil*, Disraeli's novel of 'the hungry forties', the only customers whom Mother Carey believes might be able to afford her 'butcher's meat' are prize-fighters or the mayor himself – the fighters themselves frequently told a different story.[66] The often-impoverished Daniel Mendoza concluded his reflections on training by stressing that 'above all, a man should be kept easy and comfortable in his situation, and therefore not be suffered to want a guinea in his pocket, or a good table to resort to'.[67]

Turn-of-the-century socialist fiction developed this theme at length. Meat is so important to Jack London's 1909 short story 'A Piece of Steak' and Arthur Morrison's 'Three Rounds' (1894) that it might almost be a character itself.

In 'Three Rounds', Neddy Milton arrives at the Regent Pub on the Bethnal Green Road in London's East End 'after a day's questing for an odd job'. He has put his name down to fight in an attempt to 'mend his fortunes' and provide an 'avenue of advancement', but the match turns out to be merely more casual labour. Neddy is 'weary in the feet' from having walked all day; rain has dampened his shoulders and seeped into what he fears is a hole in his boot. More worrying is the hole in his stomach. Breakfast was ten hours ago and since then he has had only 'a half-pint of four-ale'. Now it 'lay cold on the stomach for want of solid company'. At home 'less than half a loaf' remains, and he knows that if he goes there his mother will insist he have it. He has spent a shilling as his fee for the fight and he now contemplates all he could have bought with it: 'fried fish, for instance, whereof the aromas warm and rank, met him thrice in a hundred yards, and the frizzle, loud or faint, sang in his ears all along the Bethnal Green Road'. But he has invested, or gambled, the money in the fight and the promise it offers of something better than fish. For the time being, he must go hungry.[68]

Morrison continues the food theme in the pub. There, a potential backer asserts that 'it would be unsafe to back Neddy to fight anything but a beefsteak'; instead, unfortunately, his opponent is to be a butcher – 'red-faced, well-fed, fleshy, and confident', and a stone heavier. At the last minute, a friend gives Neddy a bite of his sausage roll – it is 'pallid', 'a heavy and a clammy thing' (processed rather than fresh meat) and, with the weight of a 'lump of cold lead', it sticks 'half-way', making breathing difficult.[69]

The situation is not promising and Morrison describes a fight that is hard labour for both men. Neddy, however, is 'a competent workman, with all his tools in order', and he gets down to work. By the second round, Patsy, the well-fed butcher, is still going strong, but hungry Neddy has 'a worn feeling in his arm-muscles' and notices his strength going 'earlier than in the last round'. He seems to be fading fast; aware of himself only as 'somebody with no control of his legs and no breath to spit away the blood from his nose as it ran and stuck over his lips.' He is knocked down but the bell saves him from being counted out. Behind on points and with 'little more than half a minute's boxing left in him' – the machine running on empty – his only chance to win in the third, and final, round, is by a knockout. Somehow or other – it is a mystery to him – this happens. 'Business' over, Neddy returns to the bar, but 'the stout red-faced men who smoked fourpenny cigars and drank special Scotch' ignore him. This hasn't been his big break after all, just another meaningless job. Perhaps next time, or the one after that, he thinks as he lays his head on the table and falls asleep.

At first glance, London's approach in 'A Piece of Steak' seems more romantic. He describes his has-been boxer-protagonist, Tom King, 'leaving to go out into the night', into the jungle: 'to get meat for his mate and cubs – not like the modern working-man going to his machine grind, but in the old, primitive, royal, animal way, by fighting for it'.[70]

London often brought up the distinction between the drudgeries and indignities of 'machine grind' and the 'old, primitive, royal, animal way'.[71] 'The Somnambulists', written in 1906 at the height of the intense concern about American meat production, imagines a meat manufacturer sitting down to a roast beef dinner. As the 'greasy juices of the meat' settle on his moustache, the manufacturer is 'fastidiously nauseated at the thought of two prize-fighters bruising each other with their fists'. And this is not the end of his hypocrisy: 'because it will cost him some money, he will refuse to protect the machines in his factory, though he is aware that the lack of such protection every year mangles, batters, and destroys out of all humanness thousands of working-men, women, and children'.[72] For traditional boxing butchers (sources of pure meat in two senses), the modern world has substituted factories in which machines 'batter' their operators as well as animal carcasses. 'Far better', London concluded, 'to have the front of one's face pushed in by the fist of an honest prize-fighter than to have the lining of one's stomach corroded by the embalmed beef of a dishonest manufacturer'.[73]

Discussing 'A Piece of Steak' in 1945, George Orwell expressed anxiety about the politics of London's 'instinctive tendency to accept *via victis* as a law of Nature': 'It is not so much an approval of the harshness of Nature, as a mystical belief that Nature *is* like that.'[74] But London's opposition between work and honest natural pugilism soon breaks down. The language that he uses to describe the fight continually confuses the primitive with the modern. If Tom King is presented as a 'fighting animal', he is also, like Neddy Milton, a modern urban worker, trying to scrape together a living. 'Sheer animal' that he is, fighting is nevertheless 'a plain business proposition' to King. In boxing terms at least, he

42
Jack London in boxing
pose in an undated
photograph.

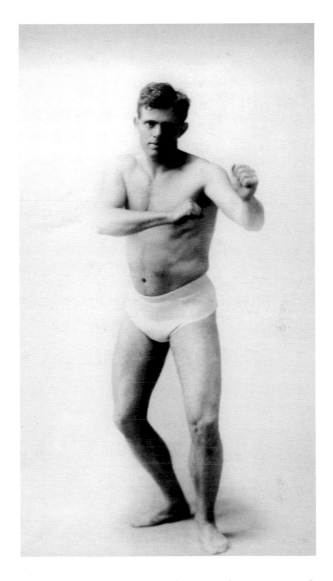

is 'old', and so he must fight with a 'policy of economy', in a manner that is 'parsimonious of effort', showing little 'expenditure of effort'. His experience is described as his 'chief asset'. The story revolves around another, missing, asset: the 'piece of steak' which he could not afford to have before the fight, and which, he thinks, would have enabled him to win.

> A great and terrible hatred rose up in him for the butchers who would not give him credit . . . A piece of steak was such a little thing, a few pennies at best; yet it meant thirty quid to him.

What Orwell terms London's 'natural urge towards the glorification of beauty' is thus checked by 'his knowledge, theoretical as well as practical, of what industrial capitalism means in terms of human suffering'.[75] While the meaty imagery that pervades this and other boxing stories evokes a world in which the 'old, primitive, royal, animal' ways still operate, it is clear that in the urban jungle, steak is simply what the modern worker requires to turn himself into the piece of meat that the capitalist 'machine' requires. The 'abysmal brute' is nothing more than a 'lean and hungry proletarian'.[76] The 'fight game', Midge Kelly tells his brother in the classic 1949 *noir* movie, *Champion*, is 'like any other business – only the blood shows'.[77]

London's only (human) alternative to capitalist boxing comes in his 1911 story, 'The Mexican', in which Felipe Rivera becomes a fighter to earn money to buy guns for the Mexican revolution.[78] Rivera's opponent, Danny Ward, is yet another casual worker who 'fought for money, and for the easy way of life that money would bring'. 'But the things Rivera fought for', London insists, 'burned in his brain.'[79]

## PLOTS OF EXHAUSTION: MUSCLE BANKRUPTCY

Both 'A Piece of Steak' and 'Three Rounds' are what Philip Fisher calls 'plots of exhaustion', plots concerned with strength and weakness rather than good and evil. 'Their essential matters are youth and age, freshness and exhaustion. Behind the plot of decline is the Darwinian description of struggle, survival, and extinction.'[80] The naturalist story tells not of an individual's gradually improving social position, Fisher argues, but rather of a rapid rise to the sexual reproductive peak, followed by a long, slow physical decline. Most of life then, on this model, is the story of decline. What Fisher terms the 'chronicle of subtraction' is exemplified in *Sister Carrie:*

> A man's fortune, or material progress, is very much the same as his bodily growth. Either he is growing stronger, healthier, wiser, as the youth approaching manhood; or he is growing weaker, older, less incisive mentally, as the man approaching old age. There are no other states.[81]

The boxing story provides an accelerated version of this phenomenon. If the arc of a man's life in general is short and sharp, that of a boxer's is considerably shorter and sharper. This was a theme in boxing literature from its very beginnings in Homer and Virgil, where the 'aged' (i.e. 35-year-old) boxer faced callow youth. 'No men are more subject to the caprice or changes of fortune than the pugilists', wrote Pierce Egan; 'victory brings them fame, riches, and patrons; . . . their lives pass on pleasantly, till defeat comes and reverses the scene.' Finally, 'a premature end puts a period to their misfortune'.[82] As Roland Barthes observed, the story of boxing is the story of 'the rise and fall of fortunes'.[83]

The naturalist emphasis, however, was less on ironic reversal than on thermodynamic expenditure. 'Vitality cannot be used over again,' wrote Jack

43
*The Boxing Boys*,
wall-painting from
Akrotiri, Thera, 17th
to 16th century BC.

45
*The Female Combatants, Or Who Shall*, 1776, etching.

44
*Humphreys vs Mendoza Jug*, 1788.

46
*The Prussian prize-fighter and his allies attempting to tame imperial Kate, or, the state of the European bruisers*, Cartoon shows Catherine II and Frederick William II as pugilists, stripped to the waist with fists raised. Published by William Dent, 14 February 1791.

47
*The Close of the Battle or the Champion Triumphant*, 1811.

48
Robert and George Cruikshank, 'Cribb's Parlour: Tom introducing Jerry and Logic to the Champion of England', coloured aquatint illustration from Pierce Egan, *Life in London* (1821).

49
Charles Turner after T. Blake, *The Interior of the Fives Court, with Randall and Turner Sparring*, 1825.

50
The Zoopraxiscope,
*Athletes Boxing,*
by Eadweard
Muybridge, *c.* 1893.

51
'Gown! Gown! Town!
Town! or, The Battle
of Peas Hill', illustra-
tion from *Gradus ad
Cantabrigiam* (1824).

52
Thomas Eakins, *Between Rounds*, 1898–9.

53
'If I Wuz the Man I Wuz, They Wouldn't Need Him', postcard, New York, 1912.

54
Cover of *The Coming Champion*, 1910, Blackface Minstrel Show, script for a sketch.

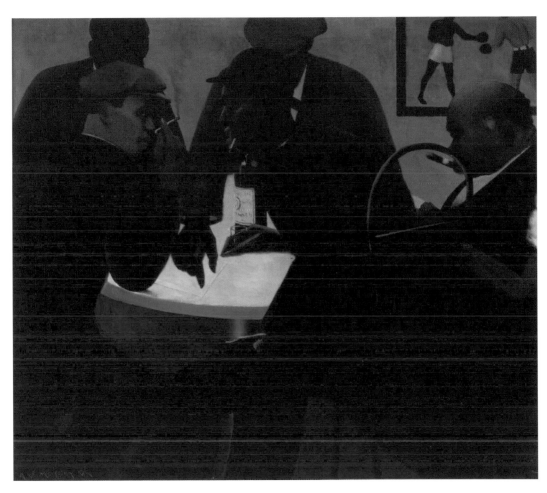

55
Archibald J. Motley Jr, *The Plotters*, 1933.

THE SYMPATHETIC SPECTATOR.

56
William Low, 'The Sympathetic Spectator', *Punch*, 15 October 1924.

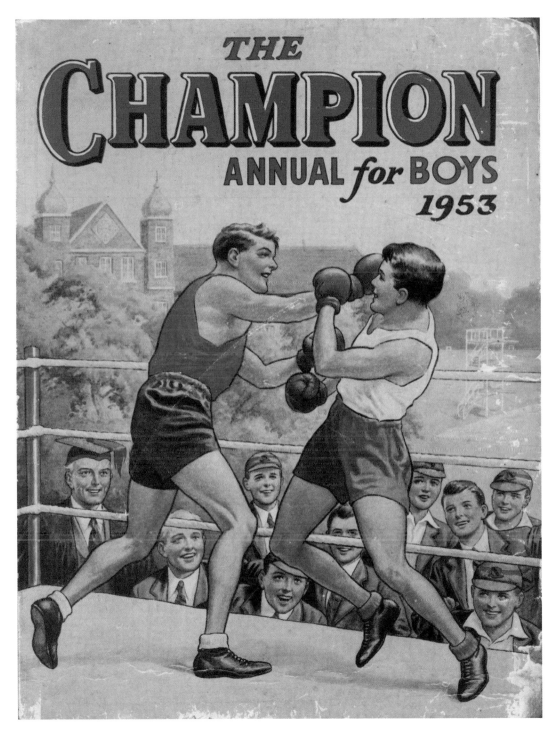

57
Cover of *The Champion* annual, 1953.

58
Cover of *The Fight* magazine, 13 February 1931.

59
Karl Arnold, Women Boxers, Berlin, from *Simplicissimus*, August 1923.

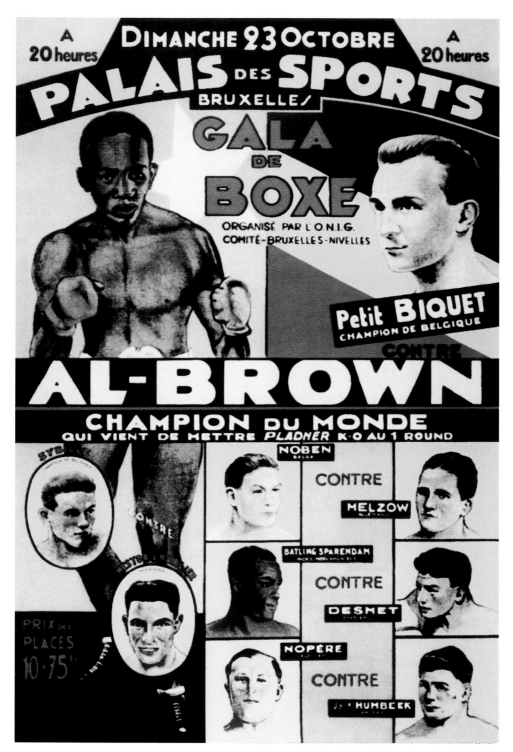

60
Poster advertising Panama Al Brown at the Palais des Sports, Brussels, 1938.

61
Aligi Sassu,
*Pugilatori*, 1929.

62
Max Pechstein, *Boxer in the Ring*, postcard to Erich Heckel, 4 November 1910.

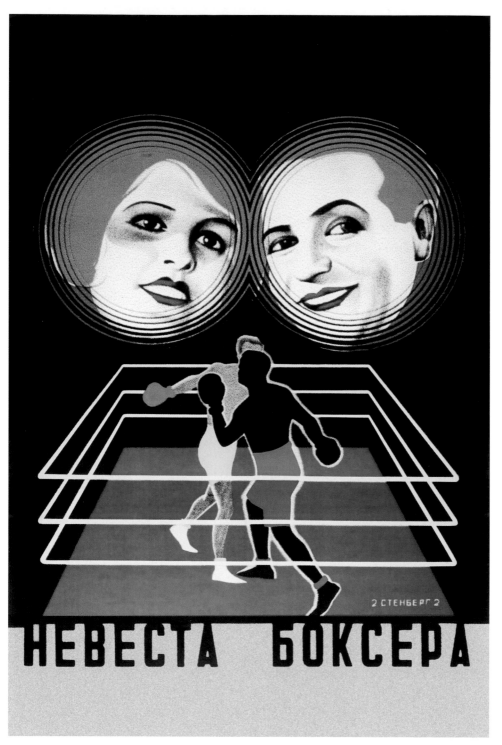

63
The Stenberg Brothers, poster for *The Boxer's Bride*, 1926.

London, in the popular terms of the late nineteenth century. 'If it be expended on one thing, there is none left for the other thing.'[84] London believed that the amount of vitality or energy available to an individual could be calculated quite precisely. In 1910, two days before Jack Johnson beat Jim Jeffries, he published an article applying 'a little science called histology', which, he claimed, 'has a lot of bearing on Jeff's case'. 'Each creature,' London wrote, 'is born with so many potential cell generations. When these generations are used up the creature dies . . . Each man has only so many cell generations, which means each man has only so much work in him.' From this, he deduced, 'each fighter is born with so many fights in him. When he has made those fights he is finished.' Predicting the outcome of a fight is no longer, then, a question of comparing the training methods of the fighters or noting who has recently had steak for dinner. Rather, commentators (and gamblers) should devise a formula to calculate how many cells have been lost by asking how many fights the boxer had fought, and how gruelling those fights were. Jeffries, London concluded, has plenty of cells left 'alive in his muscles'. But 'can he whip Johnson? This is another story.'[85]

In a 1906 essay, on 'what life means to me', London explained his decision to give up manual work for writing in similar terms. Muscle-power, the labourer's sole form of capital, did not renew itself. Determined not to die a 'muscle bankrupt', the nineteen-year-old London made up his mind to sell brain-power instead.[86] Authorship was not a matter of inspiration, but of rigorous work habits, and a watchful eye on market demand. Writing, like boxing, was supposed to be a way of escaping the factory, but somehow the logic of the factory remained.[87] Byron may have had to tussle with metaphors and hostile critics, but London faced more serious opponents. He frequently described the effort of writing and publishing as physical, especially when dealing with the machines of literary production. In *John Barleycorn*, an encounter with a particularly uncomfortable typewriter is described as a 'bout', but that is nothing compared to *Martin Eden* (1909), where the eponymous hero must tussle with 'the editorial machine', a 'cunning arrangement of cogs that changed the manuscript from one envelope to another and stuck on the stamps'. Although he is 'a good fighter', Martin is soon 'bleeding to death, and not years, but weeks would determine the fight'.[88] However much 'brain-power' the business of writing involved, no one could deny that it also was a vigorous, manly activity (illus. 42).

## TIME!

Under the old prize-fighting rules, the precise amount of energy a boxer had in him was measured not in terms of the weight of his blows but of how long he lasted. Many of the classic fights of the nineteenth century ran to 80 or 90 rounds. A round, however, had no fixed duration, and was usually, as Bernard Shaw noted, 'terminated by the fall of one of the combatants (in practice usually both of them), and was followed by an interval of half a minute for recuperation'. This meant that whenever a boxer needed a rest he could pretend to be knocked down. Under the Queensberry rules, the number of rounds was predetermined, as was their duration (usually three or four minutes) and 'a combatant who did not stand up to his opponent continuously during that time (ten seconds being allowed for rising in the event of a knock-down) lost the battle'. 'That unobtrusively slipped-on ten seconds limit', argued Shaw, 'has produced the modern glove fight.'[89] Under the old rules, it would not have mattered if a man stayed down for twelve or fifteen seconds, and 30-second knockout blows were fairly rare. Indeed, without gloves, a big blow was as likely to break a fighter's hands as knock down his opponent. Exhaustion was the usual reason for a man to lose.

But under the Queensberry rules, after 10 seconds, the fighter must either concede defeat or else 'stagger to his feet in a helpless condition and be eagerly battered into insensibility before he can recover his powers of self-defence'.[90] It was not until 1927 that a rule was introduced forbidding a boxer to hover over his downed opponent. Following its introduction, Gene Tunney benefited from a fourteen-second rest while the referee tried to persuade Jack Dempsey to go to a neutral corner. The fight is remembered as the 'Battle of the Long Count', but charges of a long count were not uncommon. After Jim Corbett was defeated by Bob Fitzsimmons in 1897, his manager insisted that the film of the fight be shown so that the length of time Fitzsimmons spent on the floor in the sixth round could be checked. Several stopwatches confirmed thirteen seconds until it was discovered that the projectionist had slowed down the hand-cranked machine.[91] Crafty boxers, and their managers, always did what they could to extend their rest and cut short that of their opponents. Some fighters were renowned for 'accidentally' stepping on the bell to cut a round short. The new rules made knockout blows much more likely. This development had serious medical consequences, greatly increasing 'the likelihood that fighters would become brain-damaged over a long career, for the trauma of repeated concussions had a cumulative effect, producing lesions that resulted in the "punch-drunk" syndrome', argues Eliott Gorn. In other words, 'boxing might look a bit less brutal, but became more dangerous'.[92]

The increased frequency of the knockout blow, combined with a limitation on the number of rounds that could be fought, also meant that boxing matches now lasted, at most, little more than an hour. Faster-paced, more offensive, and always with the potential for high drama, boxing was now much more marketable as a spectator sport; particularly so when film entered into the equation. The 'most important result of the Queensberry rules', Gorn writes, 'was not too make the ring less violent but to make it more assimilable to the entertainment industry and to mass commercial spectacles'.[93]

In 1847 Karl Marx wrote that since the 'pendulum of the clock has become as accurate a measure of the relative activity of two workers as it is of the speed of two locomotives', men have been 'effaced by their labour'. 'Time is everything, man is nothing; he is, at most, time's carcase.'[94] Certainly, as the nineteenth

century (and the industrial revolution) progressed, the clock assumed an ever-increasing importance in determining the pace of working lives, and gradually both worker and employer internalized its regular rhythms of work and rest. Under the Queensberry rules, the sound of the gong and the ten-count become boxing's equivalents of the factory whistle.[95]

Once the precise measurement of time became paramount, and before automatic devices took over, the timekeeper assumed a key role in the story of the fight, intervening as a *deus ex machina* to determine the course of its action.[96] Conan Doyle's Robert Montgomery is saved because the end of the round is announced ('Time!') before he can be counted out, while Neddy Milton wins because his opponent fails to rise while 'the time-keeper watched the seconds-hands pass its ten points' (illus. 64).

It did not take long for writers to find metaphorical potential in the call of time. In Arthur Morrison's novel *Cunning Murrell* (1900), set during the Crimean War, Roboshobery Dove is happily watching a boxing match on Canvey Island when he catches sight of a newspaper headline, 'The Baltic Fleet'. 'And then of a sudden, just at the cry of "Time", the paper went grey and blue before Roboshobery Dove's eyes, and the tumult of shouts died in his ears.' The paper had announced the death of a man he knew.[97]

The conjunction between calls of time in boxing and in life is further developed in John Masefield's 1911 poem, 'The Everlasting Mercy'. The poem features a fight over poaching rights between Saul Kane and his best friend. They box according to the Queensberry rules and Masefield ends each stanza with the call of 'Time!' Timing proves significant to the outcome of the fight; the 'clink, clink, clink' of brandy flasks that mark time save Kane from defeat in one round, and he wins by a knockout in another. But Masefield also suggests that Kane's life can be divided into rounds. The first few stanzas measure its progress in decades, 'from '41 to '51', 'from '51 to '61', 'from '61 to '67'. But the fight marks a change of pace. The night following his victory, Kane lies drunkenly awake listening to the village church clock 'ticking the time out' and ponders how it 'ticks to different men'. After several pages of soul-searching, he ends up in a pub where he is confronted by a Quaker woman, preaching temperance. As the clock chimes and closing time is announced, 'something broke inside my brain'. 'Miss Bourne stood still and I stood still, / And "Tick. Slow. Tick. Slow" went the clock.' Christ, it seems, has dealt his sin a knock-down blow.[98]

Referees and timekeepers also became the subjects of paintings, most notably Eakins's *Taking the Count* (1898) and *Between Rounds* (1898–9).[99] The tension of concentrated immobility is the most striking thing about these works, uniting all the participants in moments out of time.[100] *Taking the Count* was Eakins's first prize-fighting painting and was never exhibited during his lifetime. A huge work, it depicts, almost lifesize, the boxer Charlie McKeever standing waiting while the referee, a portrait of sportswriter Henry Walter Schlichter, counts to ten. McKeever's opponent, Joe Mack, crouches in the right-hand corner, seemingly waiting until the last moment to rise. His second can be seen offering advice between the legs of McKeever and Schlichter. A spectator sitting underneath one of the circus banners is looking at his watch, perhaps to confirm the accuracy of the count. *Between Rounds* depicts Billy Smith being attended to by his seconds (illus. 52). A poster advertising the fight between Smith and Tim Callahan hangs in the upper left corner of the painting. Smith's outstretched arms are reflected in those of his manager, Billy McCarney, who fans him; on a lower level, those of the timekeeper, and on a higher level, those of spectators leaning over the balcony. But, unlike *Salutat*, which wholeheartedly brings participants and spectators together, *Between Rounds* suggests the limits of knowledge for both ringside spectators and viewers of the painting. For one thing, as Michael Fried notes, we can 'only barely glimpse the watchface being studied by the timekeeper'.[101] The painting seems to distinguish those who, in various capacities, are engaged in some professional capacity from those who merely look on. The viewer is outside of, and slightly below, the ring. The timekeeper, the seconds, and the boxer are the central protagonists, but the policeman standing on the left, and the men in the press box (including perhaps an artist) are also active participants. The presence of each of these professional men is necessary for the fight to proceed. If this is a kind of circus, as the balcony banners suggest, it is also a keenly run business.[102]

In 1878 Eadweard Muybridge produced his first sequential photographs of moving horses. In the 1880s his experiments (with Thomas Eakins) at the University of Pennsylvania resulted in over 100,000 negatives of animal and human bodies in motion, including photographs of men boxing and shadow-boxing (illus 50). By looking at these sequences, viewers could learn more about both the way that bodies moved and the way the brain constructed an image of that movement out of many still components. Muybridge's photographs were said to support various contemporary theories about human nature. On the one hand, they drew attention to the similarities between human and animal movement, and refused to discriminate between methods of viewing humans and traditionally 'lower' forms of life, and so were regarded as evidence for evolutionary theory. On the other hand, they supported the popular metaphor of the human machine whose every movement could be timed and quantified.

Staging, and looking at, these images in the name of disinterested scientific curiosity, had, of course, nothing to do with the shocking and sensational world of prize-fighting. It was in the name of science that men (some from the university, others from local gyms) and women (most of whom were artists' models) allowed themselves to be photographed nude. Eakins conducted similarly stark and decontextualized motion studies, but many of his photographs from this period contain enough contextual setting and enough drama to complicate the scientific interest of his 'naked series'.[103] The sparring figures in *Two Male Students Posing as Boxers* (1886), for example, are carefully positioned within an artist's studio in which a cast of a man's torso sits next to a closed easel from which boxing gloves hang; between the men we glimpse a painting of an invertebrate skeleton upon another easel. The aesthetic study of anatomy, in various forms, is carefully signalled (illus. 65). In its woodland setting and careful arrangement of spectators' limbs, *Seven Males, Nude, Two Boxing at Centre* (1883) is rather different (illus. 66); another genre scene, it evokes both pastoral classicism and Manet's *Déjeuner sur l'herbe* (1863). Both Manet's painting and Eakins's photograph prominently position a reclining figure with knee bent in the bottom left-hand corner; in both cases a figure in the bottom left-hand corner observes activity in the centre of the image. Like Manet, Eakins wanted to make the nude 'modern'; for the American artist, however, the essence of modern nudity (like that of classical Greece on which it modelled itself) was communal and male.[104] Eakins's 1890s paintings depict the enclosed all-male world of professional boxing; his 1880s photographs explore a parallel community made up of his students at the Pennsylvania Academy and the Arts Students' League. It is the easy intimacy of that community that is most apparent in these photographs.

A desire to consider humanity scientifically also inspired literary work, but here too other interests tended to compromise a properly scientific methodology. In his classic 1880 exposition of naturalist technique, Emile Zola compared

writing a novel to performing a laboratory experiment; an experiment in which the effects of a specific heredity and environment on a character or group of characters was to be observed. One of the most frequently performed naturalist experiments was to test (once again) the thesis that 'living bodies . . . [can be] brought and reduced to the general mechanism of matter . . . that man's body is a machine'.[105] For the experiment to be successful, however, it had to be performed in a carefully controlled environment. The setting was to be both closely restricted and extreme enough to reveal what were thought of as the essentials of human nature. Characters 'must be twisted from the ordinary, wrenched out of the quiet, uneventful round of life, and flung into the throes of a vast and terrible drama that works itself out in unleashed passions, in blood and in sudden death'.[106] Examples of this type of extreme and restricted experiment include 'The Open Boat' (1897), in which Stephen Crane considers the effect of four shipwrecked men unable to land their boat, and *McTeague* (1899) where Frank Norris ends his antagonists' struggle for gold in an inescapable Death Valley.

Jack London's experimental settings range from the frozen snows of Alaska to ships in the violent seas of the Pacific, and to the socially brutal world of the boxing ring. In such environments, as this fight scene from *Martin Eden* suggests, sophisticated men swiftly revert (or devolve) to what Zola calls 'the animal machine':

> Then they fell upon each other, like young bulls, in all the glory of youth, with naked fists, with hatred, with desire to hurt, to maim, to destroy. All the painful, thousand years' gains of man in his upward climb through creation were lost. Only the electric light remained, a milestone on the path of the great human adventure. Martin and Cheese-Face were two savages, of the stone age, of the squatting place and the tree refuge. They sank lower and lower into the muddy abyss, back to the dregs of the raw beginnings of life, striving blindly and chemically, as atoms strive, as the star-dust of the heavens strives, colliding, recoiling and colliding again and eternally again.

In this scene, Barthes's story of the 'rise and fall of fortunes' seems to be straightforwardly reduced to the colliding of atoms and star-dust, but reading on, the issues are complicated considerably, as London introduces Martin's own perspective on the scene. He is described as being 'both onlooker and participant':

> It was to him, with his splendid power of vision, like staring into a kinetoscope. . . His long months of culture and refinement shuddered at the sight; then the present was blotted out of his consciousness, and the ghosts of the past possessed him . . .[107]

If the boxing ring is only one of many settings in which the validity of naturalist ideas can be tested and observed, it is one of the few in which the act of observation itself is emphasized. In boxing narratives – where the protagonist performs his rite in front of an audience – there are several levels of spectatorship operating. The fighters survey each other and the crowd watches them, while the writer or painter or filmmaker observes, and interprets, both fighters and crowd. The scientific observation of atoms colliding or muscles moving always exists in tension with multiple and often conflicting (financial, erotic, even aesthetic) viewing interests.

Martin Eden compares his sense of being both participant and observer in the fight to 'staring into a kinetoscope'. Thomas Edison's kinetoscope was the first commercially produced device for viewing film, and according to Terry Ramsaye, the opening of the first Kinetoscope Parlor on Broadway in 1894 marks the birth of the film industry. Initially there were only ten machines and, Ramsaye noted, 'long queues of patrons stood waiting to look into the peep hole machines': 'the spectator paid his twenty-five cents admission, and passed down the line to peer into the peep holes, while an attendant switched on the machines one after another. Presently Edison supplied a nickel-in-the-slot attachment which eliminated the man at the switches.'[108]

London evokes two aspects of the kinetoscope experience. Unlike later cinema-going, hunching over the peephole machine was an essentially private experience – the viewer did not know whether those around him were watching what he was, and, because the world around had been blocked out, what he saw could seem to come from his own consciousness. The intimacy and powerfully engaging nature of kinetoscope films is also apparent. At the height of the fight, Eden is somehow detached enough from his own actions to imagine watching them, but, ironically, that very act of observation so involves him that he re-engages and feels himself a participant again.[109]

It is unsurprising that Eden (and London) associated film with boxing. The very earliest films featured boxing matches, staged and choreographed in Edison's 'Black Maria' studio.[110] The first boxing film was made in August 1894 and consisted of six rounds of a minute each between minor prize-fighters, Mike Leonard and Jack Cushing. There was a seven-minute interval between rounds as the film was changed. Viewers paid 10c and, through the kinetoscope peephole, saw a round; paid another 10c, and saw the next. The result of the contest was kept secret, but 'some thrifty people went straight to the sixth Kinetoscope, to see only the end of the fight'. Since that portion of the film wore out, the secret remains.[111] The film was so popular that the following month another was made, this time featuring Peter Courtney against then champion Jim Corbett, who was repeatedly instructed to turn his face to the camera.[112]

The technology was developing fast, and the following year the Kinetoscope Exhibition Company developed a method (known as the 'Latham loop' and used in most cameras and projectors ever since) of filming continuously for eight minutes (a seven-minute increase). They used this to make a four-minute film of 'Young Griffo' vs. 'Battling Charles Barnett' on the roof of Madison Square Gardens, and, by shining an arc lamp behind a kinetoscope, projected the film on 20 May 1895; only a small, indistinct image was produced, but this was 'the world's first commercial presentation of projected film'.[113]

From 1895 to 1897, attempts were made to stage, and film, the heavyweight championship fight between Corbett and Robert Fitzsimmons. Fight promoter Dan Stuart had great difficulties in securing a location that would be free from legal interference, and would also suit Enoch Rector, who had an exclusive contract to film the contest. Stuart was the first promoter to recognize that he could earn more in film distribution rights than in gate receipts. The fight (or in Stuart's words, the 'fistic carnival') finally took place in Carson City, Nevada on 17

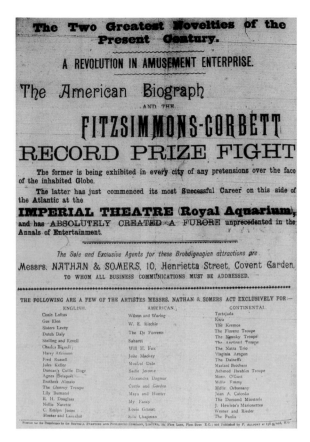

The Two Greatest Novelties of the Present Century.

A REVOLUTION IN AMUSEMENT ENTERPRISE.

The American Biograph

AND THE

FITZSIMMONS-CORBETT RECORD PRIZE FIGHT

The former is being exhibited in every city of any pretensions over the face of the inhabited Globe.

The latter has just commenced its most Successful Career on this side of the Atlantic at the

IMPERIAL THEATRE (Royal Aquarium),

and has ABSOLUTELY CREATED A FURORE unprecedented in the Annals of Entertainment.

The Sole and Exclusive Agents for these Brobdignagian attractions are

Messrs. NATHAN & SOMERS, 10, Henrietta Street, Covent Garden,

TO WHOM ALL BUSINESS COMMUNICATIONS MUST BE ADDRESSED.

THE FOLLOWING ARE A FEW OF THE ARTISTES MESSRS. NATHAN & SOMERS ACT EXCLUSIVELY FOR—

67
Poster advertising film of the Corbett–Fitzsimmons Record Prize Fight, London, 1897.

March (St Patrick's Day) 1897; Fitzsimmons won in the fourteenth round with his famous 'solar plexus punch'.[114] 'I consider that I have witnessed today the greatest fight with gloves that was ever held in this or any other country,' wrote gun-fighter Wyatt Earp for the *New York World*.[115]

Enoch Rector was at ringside with three cameras and 48,000 feet of film – he ended up using 11,000 (in other words, about two miles) which was finally edited to 2,880 feet, a figure whose significance becomes clear if we note that most films at this time used about 50 feet of film. The ring platform was painted with 'COPYRIGHT THE VERISCOPE COMPANY' so that spectators would know they were watching the real thing and not a re-enactment. (Rector was right to worry, for fake fight films were common, and Sigmund Lubin's 'Reproduction of the Corbett and Fitzsimmons Fight', played by two freight handlers from the Pennsylvania terminal, came out a week before the Veriscope film and did good business in Philadelphia. 'What do you expect for 10 cents, anyhow?' asked Lubin.[116]) Rector's four-reel Nevada fight film was the longest film yet seen, and it was shown as a prize exhibit at such up-market venues as New York's Academy of Music ('the first film invasion of the famous old Academy') and London's Imperial Theatre. A poster announcing its showing at the Imperial Theatre advertised 'a revolution in amusement enterprise' and 'Brobdignagian attractions' (sic) in the form of the 'two greatest novelties of the present century' (illus. 67). Henry James attended a showing, and 'quite revelled' in it.[117] Another writer who may have seen the film was James Joyce. In *Ulysses* (1922), young Patrick Dignam catches sight of a poster advertising a recent local boxing match, which sets him off reminiscing about other good 'puckers'. 'Fitzsimons', he thinks, is 'the best pucker going for strength', 'Jem Corbet' 'the best pucker for science'. Fitzsimmons, only a middleweight, as Patrick recalls, 'knocked the stuffings out of him, dodging and all'.[118] *Ulysses* is set in 1904, just seven years after the fight took place, and it is quite likely that Patrick's knowledge of it, and Joyce's, came from the Rector film.

Corbett's manager, William A. Brady, complained that while the film had made between $600,000 and $700,000, each fighter received only $80,000.[119] It didn't take long, however, before fighters, and their managers, negotiated a fairer share of the profits. 'Poor scrapper,' Bernard Shaw noted in 1901, 'is hardly the word for a modern fashionable pugilist', for the contests in which he engaged now took place 'in huge halls before enormous audiences, with cinematographs hard at work recording the scene for reproduction'.[120]

While the impact of film on the development of boxing was huge – opening up new and lucrative markets – it is fair to say that boxing also had an impact on the development of film. Claims for the relationship between the two vary from the circumspect – 'the evolution of the modern form of . . . [boxing] closely paralleled the development of the motion pictures' – to the bold – 'boxing created cinema'.[121] Early filmmakers were interested in filming boxing matches for a variety of reasons – personal, commercial and technical. Personally, it just happened that the Latham brothers and Enoch Rector (collectively the Kinetoscope Exhibition Company) were interested in boxing. Commercially, fight films were good business because they appealed to the male working-class audiences most likely to frequent kinetoscope parlours. Technically, although early cinema was obsessed with 'movement for movement's sake', early cameras were heavy and had a restricted viewpoint; it was, however, quite simple to set cameras to cover the relatively small space of the boxing ring within which lots of movement took place.[122] 'The cameraman could then grind away, secure in the certainty that the picture was not getting away from him, unless indeed the combatants jumped the ropes and ran away'.[123]

While boxing films were seen as a way of making boxing more palatable to middle-class tastes – spectators would be 'Without any of the Demoralizing Surroundings Unavoidable at the Actual Fight' – the association of film with the 'odium of pugilism' damaged attempts to gentrify the new art.[124] In *The Art of the Moving Picture* (1915), Vachel Lindsay wrote of 'trying to convert a talented and noble friend to the films. The first time we went there was a prize-fight between a black and a white man, not advertised, used as a filler. I said it was queer, and would not happen again. The next time my noble friend was persuaded to go, there was a cock-fight . . . The convert was not made.'[125] Lindsay's example is complicated by the fact that the film featured interracial boxing (something I'll consider in more detail in the next chapter), but there was also a broader sense among the middle-classes that a film show almost inevitably involved boxing. 'It is not very creditable to our civilization', complained the *New York Times* in 1897, 'that an achievement of what is now called the veriscope that has attracted and will attract the widest attention should be the representation of the prizefight'.[126] By 1912, an English critic, Frederick Talbot, noted the 'considerable opposition' which prize-fight films met. This, he said, 'should be welcomed as a healthy sign even by the film-producers themselves. The cinematograph can surely do more elevating, profitable and entertaining work than the recording of a prize-fight.'[127]

Before the first dedicated cinemas (the nickelodeons) opened in 1905, boxing films were often shown as part of an evening's entertainment at a music hall or in a burlesque or vaudeville show, where they often drew upon the conventions of the acts that surrounded them.[128] This generally meant matching tall, thin men against short, stout ones.[129] One of the great subjects for turn of the century British film-makers was the Boer War, and, although most films were topical, a few comic dramas were made. In 1900, for example, a film entitled 'Prize fight or Glove Contest between John Bull and President Kruger' was promoted as a comedy, while in the previous year, the Warwick Trade Co. (Ltd) produced a three-round, three-reel 'Comic Boxing Match' in which three foot six inches defeated six foot three inches on the deck of a ship bound for Africa.[130]

Charlie Chaplin's career began in the English music hall and several of his very early films feature similar slapstick pantomime. In Mack Sennett's *The Knockout* (1914), he has a bit-part as a referee who gets hit quite frequently and provides no help to cowardly heavyweight Fatty Arbuckle in his fight against a real boxer, Edgar Kennedy. When he loses the match, Fatty grabs a revolver from the attending sheriff, and the film ends with a spirited chase involving the Keystone Cops (illus. 68). A few days later Chaplin made another film with a pugilistic theme, *Mabel's Married Life*. There he plays a husband who is jealous of his wife's flirtation with a burly man.[131] He retreats to a saloon and gets very drunk, while Mabel, angry because Charlie did not defend himself, goes out and buys a boxing dummy. He comes home and, thinking he is taking on his

68
Charlie Chaplin and Fatty Arbuckle in a poster advertising *Counted Out* (1914), also known as *The Knockout*.

rival, fights the dummy. The dummy wins.[132] By the following year Chaplin had become both director and 'the tramp', and so in *The Champion* (1915), some pathos is injected to counter the comedy of balletic violence. With his faithful and hungry bulldog, the tramp find a lucky horseshoe just as he passes a training camp advertising for a sparring partner 'who can take a beating'. After watching several fighters being carried out on a stretcher, he puts the horseshoe into his glove. He wins. Suddenly favourite for the championship, Charlie, billed as the 'Jersey Mosquito', now has to fight without his horseshoe. His dog watches the fight, smiles when he lands a punch, and becomes fierce and then gloomy when he is knocked down. Finally the dog enters the ring and distracts Charlie's opponent so that he can land a knockout punch. Size, strength, and even Anglo-Saxon fair play emerge as no match for immigrant cleverness, cunning and luck.

Chaplin revisited these vaudeville boxing balletics in *City Lights* (1931), a defiantly silent film at the start of the sound era. As in *The Champion*, the tramp only resorts to boxing because he needs to feed another. This time it is a blind flower girl. He happily agrees to take part in a fixed fight, but unfortunately his opponent disappears after finding out the police are after him. Instead he is faced with Hank Mann, who is not only much bigger but refuses to take part in the fix. As his anxiety rises, Charlie begins to mince and flirt with the giant. His opponent is so unnerved by this that he hides behind a curtain to change into his shorts. The tramp has once more gained a (temporary) advantage over a physically superior opponent, one who finds sitting next to a supposed homosexual more frightening than being hit.[133] (Subsequently, however, Charlie is knocked out twice – once in the ring, and once by a falling glove in the dressing room.) Mark Winokur argues that these later films are not slapstick but what he calls transformative comedy. While 'slapstick insists on perpetuating into the realm of fantasy the insult to the body that occurs in the world', 'transformative comedy', he argues, 'insists on the intelligence of the body in *avoiding* insult (successfully or otherwise)'.[134] Although Chaplin was a fan of boxing and a friend of boxers, his films debunk much of the masculine and nativist posturing that surrounded it.[135]

Such debunking was not, of course, the ambition of D. W. Griffith in his 1915 film of the Civil War and its aftermath, *The Birth of a Nation*; the film most often credited with making movie-going respectable in America. Accompanied by an orchestral score, it was shown in large legitimate theatres at high prices and was an enormous (if hugely controversial) success. *The Birth of a Nation* aspired to the status of serious history as well as entertainment; Griffith's next film, *Intolerance* (1916), was a philosophical meditation on the development of a 'universal theme' through the ages. Only twenty years had passed since *Corbett vs Fitzsimmons* had first wowed audiences, but the aspirations of filmmakers had changed enormously. It might seem odd then that in 1919 Griffith decided to film Thomas Burke's story of a London prize-fighter and his daughter.[136] *Broken Blossoms* is about the destruction of a young girl (Lillian Gish) who is trapped between two competing versions of masculinity – one passive, oriental and threatening miscegenation (represented by her suitor, the Yellow Man, played by Richard Barthelmess), the other active, Anglo-Saxon and hyper-masculine (represented by her father, a prize-fighter called Battling Burrows, played by Donald Crisp and described in an inter-title as an 'abysmal brute, a gorilla of the jungles of East London').[137] The Yellow Man leans languidly against walls and on couches; Burrows pummels both his opponent (the 'Limehouse Tiger', played by real boxer, Kid McCoy) and his daughter (his 'punching bag').

The dialectic between these modes of conduct can also be mapped onto the formal conflict between the stasis of painting and the constant motion of narrative film. Dudley Andrew notes that while the Yellow Man is seen 'in gently curved poses which concentrate the dramatic energy within the frame', Battling Burrows's thrashing movements thrust 'our attention out of the frame and to the object of his aggression'.[138] Brigitte Peucker suggests that Griffith's decision to represent Burrows as a boxer was a way of alluding to 'proto- and early cinematic films'; both boxers and boxing movies were crude and primitive.[139] No one gets out of *Broken Blossoms* alive: Burrows kills Lucy, the Yellow Man shoots Burrows and then goes home to kill himself with a knife. A reference to the latest casualty figures from the Western Front suggests that the whole world might have battled itself to a halt.

### THE PRIZE-FIGHTER AND THE LADY

While maintaining that it was natural for women to admire fighters, John L. Sullivan was adamant that fights themselves should be seen only by men. The next generation was not so fastidious. Women made up a substantial part of the audience at the premiere of Rector's movie in 1897.[140] Miriam Hansen argues that this film, 'the cinematic mediation' of the prize-fight, as she calls it, opened up a previously forbidden spectacle to a large number of women who relished the sight of a little male flesh.[141] Indeed it seems that Corbett 'calculatedly played on his awareness of his "ladies' man" image' by dressing for his fight films in trunks that prominently display his bottom, 'not often found on other fighters' and rather similar to those worn by Billy Smith in Eakins's *Salutat*. But 'the Adonis of the Fistic arena', who also had a huge following as a stage actor, was clearly an exception. Dan Streible notes that 'subsequent fight films, even those showing Jim Corbett, never again attracted female patrons in significant numbers'.[142]

Even before the cinematic mediation of 1897, it was not unheard of for women to attend fights and to be seen to express an interest in prize-fighters. And again novelty was largely the point. In 1889, Nellie Bly, feature writer for the *New York World*, interviewed John L. Sullivan as he prepared for his fight with Jake Kilrain. Bly begins by announcing that she 'was surprised' by her visit, and the article goes on to explain why. She arrives at the house, which is 'in the prettiest part of town' and 'one would never imagine from the surroundings that a prize-fighter was being trained there'. When Sullivan enters the room, she finds him 'half-bashful', 'very boyish' and 'not ungraceful'. Next she admires his 'straight and shapely' fingers, and finds 'the closely trimmed nails . . . a lovely oval and pink'. Finally, they eat breakfast, and 'the daintiness of everything' from 'the white table linen and beautiful dishes, down to the large bunch of fragrant lilacs and another of beautifully shaped and coloured wild flowers, separated by a slipper filled with velvety pansies – was all entirely foreign to any idea I had ever conceived of prize-fighters and their surroundings'.[143] But while some women may have been attracted to prize-fighting by reassurances of clean nails and dainty dishes, others, it seems, went because they wanted to see blood and half-naked men (or at least that is what male readers liked to think). Steible points out that 'the figure of the lone, disguised woman at ringside became a recurring one in tabloid stories of the 1890s'; the *San Francisco Examiner*, for example, sent Annie Laurie (touted as 'the first woman to report a prize fight') who watched 'from behind a curtained booth' and reported back that 'men have a world into which women cannot enter'.[144] This was not strictly true. In Carson City in 1897, a special section was designated for women spectators, and Rose Fitzsimmons acted as one of her husband's seconds. 'As the battle went on,' reported the *Chicago Tribune*, 'she became more and more demonstrative, sometimes breaking out with exclamations which bordered on the profane.'[145] From the ring itself, meanwhile, James Corbett noticed in the crowd, 'a big, blonde, and very excited woman, her hair loose, hat jammed down over one ear, the blood from Fitz spattering her own face, and she, meanwhile, yelling at me things that were not at all flattering either to my skill as a fighter or my conduct as a gentleman'.[146] In 1905 the *San Francisco Examiner* reported the attendance of 'a few misplaced women' at the Nelson-Britt fight. 'A few of them looked like decent women, but the most gave token of being jaded, jades in search of some new torment for the sagging nerves' (illus. 69).[147]

These stories largely appealed to men who enjoying being a little shocked at the prospect of an occasional narrowing of the gap between manly boxing and their ideas of femininity. There is nothing like an exception to prove the rule. But some men – fight promoters and film-makers – actively encouraged the presence of women spectators, believing that their attendance would confer respectability on movie-going and provide a strong argument in favour of the legalization of prize-fighting. Streible notes that fight film advertisements often included 'such exaggerated inducements as "witnessed by hundreds of ladies"'.[148] In 1915, the Broadway Sporting Club advertised that women would be charged a reduced rate of 50 cents to attend the next fight. Over 1,000 men showed up, but only one woman. The club then offered triple trading stamps as an inducement to 'flee pink tea and sewing circles'.[149] Two women came.

It has become commonplace to suggest that when a male writer or artist depicts a woman looking at a man, the female point of view is really a mask for the male artist's own, usually erotic, interest. This is undoubtedly true in some cases, but there are other reasons (perhaps even conflicting reasons) why a man might explore a female point of view. We should not, for example, rule out the possibility of vanity. As the influence of Darwinian ideas spread, men (and later

69
George Bellows,
*Preliminaries to the
Big Bout*, 1916.

women) also became interested in boxing as a subject matter within which to explore the mechanisms of sexual selection, the 'struggle between the males for possession of the females'.[150]

*Cashel Byron's Profession* tells the story of the eponymous hero's romance with an independent, aristocratic 'New Woman', Lydia Carew. At first the attraction is aesthetic. Lydia, who is described as having 'a taste for . . . the fine arts', first encounters the boxer while walking, appropriately with a copy of *Faust*, in the woods of her home:

> The trees seem never ending: she began to think she must possess a forest as well as a park. At last she saw an opening. Hastening towards it, she came again into the sunlight, and stopped, dazzled by an apparition which she at first took to be a beautiful statue, but presently recognized, with a strange glow of delight, as a living man . . . the man was clad in a jersey and knee-breeches of white material, and his bare arms shone like those of a gladiator. His broad pectoral muscles, in their white covering, were like slabs of marble. Even his hair, short, crisp, and curly, seemed like burnished bronze in the evening light.[151]

When James Corbett played Cashel Byron in one of the early pirated stage versions, Shaw noted that 'American ladies were seized with a desire to go on the stage and be Lydia Carew for two thrilling hours'.[152] In the novel, too, it does not take Lydia long to recognize that Cashel's value is more than sculptural. Not that anyone would 'dare to suspect her . . . of anything so vulgarly human as sexual interest in Cashel'. 'A utilitarian before everything', Lydia assesses his animal vitality as a necessary complement to her own intellectualism and 'fine breeding', and decides to marry him in order to produce healthy children. 'I believe in the doctrine of heredity; and as my body is frail and my mind morbidly active, I think my impulse towards a man strong in body and untroubled in mind a trustworthy one.' He becomes, in other words, her stud. It is 'a plain proposition in eugenics', but it does not quite work. The boys turn out like her, and the girls like him, and she 'soon came to regard him as one of the children'.[153]

The female assessment of a potential mate was central to many of Jack London's fight scenes, and more often than not his emphasis is on male excitement in realizing that this is the case. While in *Great Expectations*, Pip had been appalled at Estella's flushed checks, London's men like to see their women aroused by a good fight. Expecting 'to find a shocked and frightened maiden countenance', they are often pleasantly surprised by a 'flushed and deeply interested face'. In the midst of a fierce exchange of blows, Martin Eden finds time to watch Lizzie Connolly watching him. 'Usually the girls screamed when the fellows got to scrapping, but. . . . she was looking on with bated breath, leaning slightly forward, so keen was her interest, one hand pressed to her breast, her cheek flushed, and in her eyes a great and amazed admiration.' Martin was 'thrilling all over'.[154]

London's interest in the female perspective is most fully explored in *The Game* (1905), a novella which grew out of his local club fight reports for the Oakland *Herald*; it remained one of his favourite works.[155] Chapter One begins with the protagonists Joe and Genevieve choosing a carpet. They are to be married the next day, but first Joe will fight one last time and he wants her to watch – 'I'll fight as never before with you lookin' at me'. Genevieve's response to this is ambiguous. On the one hand, she responds with appropriate feminine revulsion; on the other, 'the masculinity of the fighting male . . . [made] its inevitable appeal to her, a female, moulded by all heredity to seek out the strong man for mate'. Joe too experiences a conflict of desires:

> He saw only the antagonism between the concrete, flesh-and-blood Genevieve and the great, abstract, living Game. Each resented the other, each claimed him; he was torn with the strife, and yet drifted helpless on the current of their contention.[156]

Before any boxing has taken place, then, we see that the central fight of the story is to be between the values of the 'abstract' and 'the concrete'. Contrary to what we might expect, abstraction is allied with 'the Game' while romantic love concerns the physical.

Chapter Two goes back to consider Joe and Genevieve's courtship, and to emphasize the importance of what they *see* of each other in forming their relationship. As they walk in the park the eyes of passers-by are 'continually drawn to them,' and each observes the admiring glances the other attracts.[157] This emphasis on seeing and being seen sets the tone for the fight scene itself. As women were not allowed into the arena Genevieve disguises herself as a boy and watches the fight through a peephole in the wall.[158] As a boy, indeed wearing Joe's shoes, she is, for the first time in her life, unnoticed by the men in the hall, 'this haunt of men where women came not'. This, London suggests, is her first moment of liberation from what he calls 'the bounds laid down by that harshest of tyrants, the Mrs. Grundy of the working class'.[159] The next such moment comes when she sees Joe's 'beautiful nakedness'. She feels guilty 'in beholding what she knew must be sinful to behold', but London informs us that 'the pagan in her, original sin, and all nature urged her on'. The terms in which Genevieve perceives Joe are, however, far from straight-forwardly erotic. Rather, her appreciation curiously shifts between the religious and the aesthetic, and much of it is feminizing. Joe is 'godlike', and she feels 'sac-rilege' in looking at him, but his face is also 'like a cameo', a thing of 'Dresden china', and London tells us that 'her chromo-trained aesthetic sense exceeded its education'. Joe's delicacy, fragility, smoothness and fairness are also continually emphasized. His opponent, on the other hand, is the classic 'beast with a streak for a forehead', 'a thing savage, primordial, ferocious'.[160] Looking connects the concreteness of romantic love to the fight's abstraction.

During the central fight scenes, London seems to forget that we are seeing the fight from Genevieve's perspective, and there are several pages of detailed blow-by-blow description. Moreover, when Genevieve's perspective does return it seems confused, as if London was not really sure what do with it. On the one hand, he describes her attraction to what he calls the pagan values of pain, sex and death: 'She, too, was out of herself; softness and tenderness had vanished; she exulted in each crushing blow her lover delivered.' Yet, only moments later, her responses seem quite distinct from those of the crowd; she feels sick, faint, both 'overwrought with horror at what she had seen and was seeing' and baffled at the whole process. The fight in the ring ends when Joe slips and is caught on the chin with a lucky punch. Chance seems initially to be working for Genevieve, for believing that 'the Game had played him false', she concludes that 'he was more surely hers'. When she realizes that he is dead, however, it is with the acknowledgment that she had already lost him to 'the awful facts of this Game she did not understand'.[161] *The Game* is finally ambiguous about the status of both the boxer's body (it is a source not simply of violence, but of economic power, and self-expression) and the spectator's interpretation of the body (bio-logically, erotically, religiously and aesthetically). It is not only Joe's death that makes the conclusion bleak. He was also gambling on his ability to communi-cate the meaning of the Game to Genevieve, and that gamble failed as well. Women might look but they do not really understand men; London, however, understands that female lack of understanding.[162]

While Genevieve in *The Game* and Lydia in *Cashel Byron's Profession* achieve a certain power simply by watching men fight, other works of the period (again usually by men) imagine female power more directly as the women themselves don gloves (illus. 70). William H. Bishop's 1895 novel, *The Garden of Eden, usa*, for example, presents a utopia of sexual and economic equality in which cooking and housework are done by centralized machinery. This was perhaps the first novel to discuss rape as a social problem and certainly the first to suggest, as a possible form of resistance, boxing.[163] In the world outside utopia, Bishop argues, 'the power of self-defense or of indignant protest is more necessary to women than to men'. In the Garden of Eden, however, women box 'more in bravado of conventional prejudices than anything else'.[164]

Although Bishop's is not the only work in which a feminist agenda is present, many references to women boxing in this period seem to involve little more than a return to the scantily clad heroines of Fielding's day. In 1880 the *Police Gazette* announced that a Miss Libbie Ross was 'champion female boxer of America', and in 1884, Hattie Stewart was declared world female champion, but no one seemed to take these titles very seriously. More popular were stories in which women (ignoring Darwin) fought over men and against 'mashers', usually 'according to pugilistic rules' (illus. 71).[165] Athletic new women also featured in the new visual technologies, where great attention was paid to their costumes and what they revealed. A form of photography that was very popular between the 1850s and 1930s was stereoscopy. When two almost identical photographs, placed side by side, were seen though a stereoscope, a sense of depth and solidity was created. The technique was most often used to view images of landscape and women in their underwear. No. 95 in a late nineteenth-century 'Beauty Series' featured a Hallowe'en party boxing match entitled 'England's Advantage' (illus. 72). We cannot see either of the girl's faces, but that is hardly the point. The American 'beauty' has her opponent's glove in her face, and we

71
'The Girls Biffed
Each Other', from
*Police Gazette* (1890).

72
Stereoscopic photo
of a Hallowe'en
party boxing
match, 'England's
Advantage'.

THE GIRLS BIFFED EACH OTHER.

MAMIE HERBETT AND MABEL BROWN FIGHT FOR GEORGE
WOODWARD IN PLEASANTVILLE, N.J.

get a fine view (especially through a stereoscope) of the English girl's bloomers. Thomas Edison's 1898 film, *Comedy Set-To* was one of many early films in which women box for laughs. Starring the *Police Gazette* 'Champion Lady Bag Puncher', Belle Gordon, against Billy Curtis, it was, according to one magazine, 'refined, scientific, and a genuine comedy'. 'Belle Gordon is as frisky a little lady as ever donned a boxing outfit, and her abbreviated skirt, short sleeves and low necked waist make a very jaunty costume.'[166]

Women's arm muscles had suddenly become a new erogenous zone. The ethereal hero of Joris-Karl Huysmans's *A Rebours* (1884) falls briefly in love with a female acrobat, 'an American girl', largely because of her 'muscles of steel and arms of iron', while Everard in George Gissing's *The Odd Women* (1893) is very impressed by Rhoda Nunn's 'strong wrists, with exquisite vein-tracings on the pure white'.[167] In 1897 Frank Norris interviewed Alcide Capitaine, hailed as 'the female Sandow'. The resulting essay begins with sound feminist intentions. Norris addresses male readers who might be tempted to call her 'a "little woman" . . . and . . . might even . . . assume the certain condescension of man- ner that men – some men – display when talking to the "weaker" sex.' Such condescension would immediately vanish, however, when attempting to grasp her upper arm 'at first with one hand, then, failing in this, with two . . . A man must have large hands to do the thing, for the bicep measurement is fifteen and a half inches.' Norris, we now realize, is not primarily interested in Capitaine as a living refutation of sexism or a feminist role model. It is the fact that her body is so different when 'at ease' and when 'muscled up' that excites him so much. Muscles relaxed, she is a 'quiet, retiring sort of little body'; a little flexing, however, and 'Tom Sharkey himself would be proud of that arm.' 'Really it took one's breath away.' While many New Women cultivated athleticism as an alter- native to Victorian restrictions on their bodies and behaviour, the fantasies of their often rather prurient supporters rested on the conjunction, or rather disjunction, of the new and the old, the 'frame of a pugilist in the person of a girl not yet out of her teens'.[168]

Although descriptions such as this carry more than a touch of the freak show, they also represent a broader cultural tendency to define both male and female sexuality (often referred to as biological health or fitness) in masculine terms. Biceps, rather than breasts or hips, were considered indicators of fitness for both men and women. When Norris compares Capitaine to Tom Sharkey he is not saying that he would prefer to sleep with Sharkey (even vicariously). In social and psychological terms, Capitaine remains womanly, but (by being a little bit manly around the arms) she also reveals herself to be sexually active and biologically fit.

Early on in Jack London's first novel, *A Daughter of the Snows* (1902), Frona Welse offers her arm to an old family friend. '"'Tis muscle," he admitted, passing his hand admiringly over the swelling bunch; "just as though ye'd een workin' hard for yer livin'"'.

> 'Oh, I can swing clubs, and box, and fence,' she cried, successively strik-
> ing the typical postures; 'and swim, and make high dives, chin a bar
> twenty times, and – walk on my hands. There!'[169]

Like Genevieve, Frona is engaged in the task of sexual selection, but unlike
Genevieve, she is highly educated in Social Darwinian terminology and so can
recognize quite precisely what she is feeling. The novel is structured around
Frona's choice between two suitors, the rather brutish Gregory St Vincent, and
Vance Corliss, whose 'muscular development was more qualitative than quanti-
tative', and whom she eventually picks. Fortunately, Vance likes her too, and for
very similar reasons – 'the strength of her slenderness' and 'the joy of life', which
'romped through her blood, abstemiously filling out and rounding off each
shapely muscle . . . Especially he liked the swell of her forearm, which rose firm and
strong and tantalizing'.[170] Genevieve could only look at Joe uncomprehendingly;
Frona and Vance look at each other and rationally assess what they see. Theirs is
to be a marriage of biological equals, 'mate man' and 'mate woman' boxing together, just as London did with his second wife, Charmian (illus. 73).

As the nineteenth century drew to a close, writers lost interest in the distinctive sub-culture and language of boxing; instead, the sport became a focus for
many competing, and often oddly intermingling, discourses. In their rhetorical
battles, often with each other, eugenics, professionalism, strenuousness, realism
and feminism all drew upon pugilism to make their points. Missing from this
list, and this chapter, however, are two fiercely debated topics in early twentieth-
century America: nation, and race. It is these that the next chapter will consider.

# 6

# Fresh Hopes

'We are all Anglo-Saxons enough to enjoy the sight of a fight,' Frank Norris declared in 1903, before, unblushingly, going on to praise the talents of a New Zealander of Cornish descent, Bob Fitzsimmons.[1] A rather loose approach to matters of race, ethnicity and nationality had long been a feature in boxing, even when those affiliations were supposedly the point. Such leniency allowed a former American slave, Tom Molineaux, to be co-opted into the English battle against Napoleon in 1812, the Irish-born and California-bred John Heenan to be fêted as a symbol of both American and Irish anti-British sentiment in 1860, and Joe Louis to become a symbol of Jim Crow America's fight against foreign fascism in 1938.

The rapid development of sports in the United States in the late nineteenth and early twentieth century was closely linked to questions of national identity – what it meant to be an American, and more critically for the new immigrants, what was needed to become one.[2] 'To be an American, dress like an American, look like an American, and even, if only in fantasy, talk like an American' was the goal of the young immigrant.[3] Sports such as boxing provided a readily available subject-matter, and vocabulary, for recognizably American talk.

In Abraham Cahan's 1896 novella, *Yekl: A Tale of the New York Ghetto*, Yekl Podkovnik's metamorphosis into Jake, 'an American feller, a Yankee', is represented by his enthusiasm for dance halls and boxing. The story opens with Jake giving his fellow Lower East Side sweatshop workers a detailed account of the exploits of Sullivan, Corbett and others, proudly displaying his grasp of the correct idiom:

> '*Say*, Dzake,' the presser broke in, 'John Sullivan is *tzampion* no longer, is he?
>
> 'Oh no! Not always is it holiday!' Jake responded, with what he considered a Yankee jerk of his head. 'Why don't you know? Jimmie Corbett *leaked* him, and Jimmie *leaked* Cholly Meetchel, too. *You can betch you' bootsh!* Johnnie could not leak Chollie, *becaush* he is a big *bluffer*, Chollie is,' he pursued, his clean-shaven florid face beaming with enthu-

siasm for his subject, and with pride in the diminutive proper nouns he flaunted. 'But Jimmie *pundished* him. *Oh, didn't he knock him out off shight*! He came near making a meat-ball of him' – with a chuckle. 'He *tzettled* him in three *roynds*. I knew a feller who had seen the fight.'

'What is a *rawnd*, Dzake?' the presser inquired.[4]

Reading this slang-laden fight description (which then goes on into 'a minute exposition of "right-handers", "left-handers", "sending to sleep", "first blood", and other commodities of the fistic business') we might almost be back in Regency England. But there are important differences. The first thing to notice is a footnote that tells us that 'English words incorporated in the Yiddish of the characters of this narrative are given in italics'. Fluent standard English, in other words, represents fluent standard Yiddish. The English that appears in italics is the same kind of English that Pierce Egan italicized in the 1800s, and like Egan, Jake is putting on a costume when he uses 'diminutive proper nouns' and talks of 'tzampions' and 'roynds'. Sabinne Haenni suggests that this speech could 'qualify for the vaudeville stage'.[5] But Jake's language is further complicated by the fact that he has recently moved to New York from Boston, and so even his Yiddish is different from that of his co-workers and 'his r's could do credit to the thickest Irish brogue'. In Boston, Jake says, 'every Jew speaks English like a stream', but what kind of English is it that flows so freely? It is hardly standardized – one man says '*roynd*'; another '*rawnd*'. Cahan describes the English his characters speak as 'mutilated' and 'gibberish'.[6]

When his friends dismiss boxing as mere fighting, Jake evokes its rules. One of the men, a scholar called Bernstein, makes a joke: 'America is an educated country, so they won't even break each other's bones without grammar. They tear each other's sides according to "right and left", you know.' Cahan explains that 'this was a thrust at Jake's right-handers and left-handers, which had interfered with Jake's reading', and adds, in a footnote, that 'right and left' is 'a term relating to the Hebrew equivalent of the letter *s*, whose pronunciation depends on the right or left position of a mark over it'. The rules of Hebrew are thus juxtaposed with those of American boxing. Jake may 'speak quicker' than his friends, his American slang flowing 'like a stream', but he is illiterate; Bernstein has little standard English and less slang, but he is a Hebrew scholar.[7]

Cahan himself sat somewhere between his two characters.[8] Before *Yekl*, Cahan had published several stories in Yiddish and had enthusiastically welcomed the American publication of stories by I. L. Peretz and Shalom Aleichem. But Yiddish was generally regarded by Jewish intellectuals as non-literary. The languages of the literature were Hebrew, Russian, Polish, German, and, if a broad American audience was to be reached, English.[9] 'A Tale of the Ghetto' written specifically for those outside the ghetto, *Yekl* followed in the tradition of what was then known as 'local color' fiction and positioned its characters and their environment with anthropological exactness. The narrator is a key figure in this process, our tour guide around the ghetto, and our translator of its speech. His

English is self-consciously literary and genteel. The opening paragraph, for example, tells us that the boss was on Broadway 'where he had betaken himself two or three hours before', and that 'the little sweltering assemblage . . . beguiled their suspense variously'. Jules Chametzsky maintains that the extreme contrast between this language and that of Cahan's characters entails 'an arch and condescending attitude' towards them. 'Their fractured English is comic when it is not grotesque.'[10] But something more interesting seems to be going on. While the English the characters speak is, in Cahan's word, 'mutilated', as we have seen, their Yiddish (written *as English)* is fluent and in many ways, much more expressive than the narrator's English. Yiddish, Cahan notes, is 'omnivorous'. Several jokes in the text emerge from phrases or words that sound similar in Yiddish and English ('left and right' above; 'dinner' in Yiddish is 'thinner' in English). The language of the ghetto, like the ghetto itself, remains a complicated, and not wholly translatable, 'hodgepodge'. English may be the official language of the story but within its embrace are found several varieties of Yiddish (one of which is spoken with an Irish lilt), Russian and Hebrew (when Jake takes a Hebrew letter to be translated, Cahan jokes that it 'was Greek to Jake').[11]

For Jake, however, following boxing is not only about finding an excuse to show off his new mastery of American colloquialisms. It is also a 'trying on of roles . . . [a] delight in assuming new identities'; in particular new versions of masculinity.[12] Becoming an American man was not a matter of simply gaining something additional (a style on top); it also meant giving something up. The shifting balance between gains and losses is what the story is all about, and at times the debate slips into verbal sparring. When one of Jake's co-workers dismisses the fight talk, Jake is immediately 'on the defensive'.

> 'Don't you like it? I do,' Jake declared tartly. 'Once I live in America,' he pursued, on the defensive, 'I want to know that I live in America. *Dot'sh a kin' a man I am*! One must not be a *greenhorn*. Here a Jew is as good as a Gentile. How, then, would you have it? The way it is in Russia, where a Jew is afraid to stand within four ells of a Christian?'[13]

In the 1890s Zionists in Germany, England and the Unites States had begun to speak of a modern muscular Judaism, and often evoked the name of the early nineteenth-century Jewish boxers, Daniel Mendoza and Dutch Sam.[14] In the 'Proem' to *The Children of the Ghetto* (1914), Israel Zangwill told the story of an old peddler called Sleepy Sol who is defended from the brutality of a local hostler by his son-in-law, who turns out to be Dutch Sam. 'The young Jew paralysed him by putting his left hand negligently into his pocket. With his remaining hand he closed the hostler's right eye, and sent the flesh about it into mourning.' Zangwill included the story to make the point that 'Judæa has always a cosmos in little, and its prize-fighters and scientists, its philosophers and "fences" [etc] . . . have always been in the first rank.'[15] When Yekl defends his interest in prize-fighting by evoking Russian persecution of Jews, he seems to be aligning himself with muscular Judaism. To his friends, and indeed to most Orthodox Russian and Polish immigrants at this time, however, the idea of the tough Jew (the *muskeljuden*) was not merely an anathema but a contradiction in terms, and its adoption signalled the beginning of the end of traditional values.[16] In *The Spirit of the Ghetto* (1902), Hutchins Hapgood observed that many of those who talked of the 'crimes of which they read in the newspapers, of prize-fights, of budding business propositions . . . gradually quit going to synagogue, give up *heder* promptly when they are thirteen years old, avoid the Yiddish theatres, seek the up-town places of amusement, dress in the latest American fashion, and have a keen eye for the right thing in neckties'.[17]

When Bernstein asks Yekl, 'Are there no other Christians than *fighters* in America?' he might have added, are no other Americans than Irish-Americans? But neither man seems aware that Yekl's American icons were both first-generation Irish immigrants: Sullivan's parents came from Tralee and Athlone, Corbett's from Galway.[18] If you wanted to become an American in late nineteenth-century Boston it made sense to adopt an Irish brogue and talk about Sullivan and Corbett. At the time, Irishness was almost synonymous with pugnacity, and pugnacity was almost synonymous with Americanness; ergo the Irish were the 'real' Americans, the immigrants who best performed the accepted version of national identity.[19] Assimilation simply meant adopting the ways of the previous generation of immigrants.

The complexities of ethnic identification form the basis of O. Henry's 1906 story, 'The Coming-out of Maggie', in which an Irish girl sneaks her Italian boyfriend Tony Spinelli into the Clover Leaf Social Club under the name of Terry O'Sullivan. 'Terry' falls out with the leader of the Give and Take Athletic Association, Dempsey Donovan, who challenges him to a fight. Faced with Donovan, 'dancing, light-footed, with the wary grace of a modern pugilist', Terry reverts to his essential Tony-ness and, with 'a murderous look in his dark eyes', pulls a stiletto from his jacket. Maggie apologizes for bringing a 'Guinea' into the club and Donovan walks her home.[20] Tony Spinelli was not the only immigrant to adopt an Irish name; many turn-of-the-century Italian and Jewish fighters followed suit. Mushy Callahan was Jewish; Hugo Kelly was Italian.[21] In James T. Farrell's 1932 novel *Young Lonigan*, set in 1916, Old Man O'Brien remembers the good old days, 'when most of them [the boxers] were real Irish, lads who'd bless themselves before they fought: they weren't fake Irish like most of the present-day dagoes and wops and sheenies who took Hibernian names'. Meanwhile Davey Cohen, a Jewish boy, sees 'all the Irish race personified in the face of Studs Lonigan' and imagines himself 'punching that face, cutting it, bloodying the nose, blackening the eyes, mashing it'.[22]

Soon Jews were participating in, as well as watching and imagining, such fights. Along with Sullivan and Corbett, Yekl might have celebrated the San Francisco Jewish boxer, Joe Choynski, who fought Corbett, Fitzsimmons, Sharkey and Jack Johnson and whose father published *Public Opinion*, a muckraking newspaper that exposed anti-Semitism.[23] Corbett recalls that their 1889 fight was partly promoted as 'Jew versus Gentile'.[24] In 1905, the *Police Gazette* noted that a generation of 'peaceable and inoffensive' Russian Jewish immigrants had been succeeded by 'turbulent young men from whose ranks have been graduated a number of professional pugilists and boxers'.[25] The first Jewish-American champions were bantamweight Harry Harris, who won his crown in 1901, and featherweight Abe Attell, who held the title from 1904 to 1912. In New York's Lower East Side, the first popular Jewish fighter was Leach Cross (Louis Wallach) who, from 1906 to 1915, fought as 'The Fighting Dentist', while London's East End produced 1915 world welterweight champion Ted 'Kid' Lewis (Gershon Mendeloff), and lightweight and junior welterweight champion Jackie 'Kid' Berg (Judah Bergman), the 'Whitechapel Windmill', who famously hung his *tzitzis* on the ringpost at the start of each fight.[26] In 1920 the Italian Samuel Mandella began fighting under the Jewish-sounding name of Sammy Mandell, and by the early 1930s, Jews dominated boxing on both sides of the Atlantic, not simply as fighters and fans, but as promoters, trainers, managers, referees, journalists and sporting goods manufacturers.

It wasn't long before the story of the Jewish boy who broke his father's heart by becoming a boxer became a bit of a cliché. *His People*, a 1925 film about Jewish life on the Lower East Side, tells the story of Sammy and Morris Cominsky, both of whom stray from the ways of their Orthodox parents. Morris becomes a lawyer and Sammy a prize-fighter. As the father expels Sammy from the house, his words are presented in an inter-title:

> A box-fyteh!? So that's what you've become? For this we came to America? So that you should become a box-fyteh? Better you should be a gangster or even a murderer. The shame of it. A box-fyteh![27]

In *Nineteen Nineteen* (1932), John Dos Passos introduced the character of Benny Compton: 'The old people were Jews but at school Benny always said he no he wasn't a Jew he was an American'. The Compton children assimilate in different ways. Ben becomes a political activist, his sister Gladys a secretary, and their brother, Izzy 'palled around with an Irishman who was going to get him into the ring.' Although it is Benny and Gladys who eventually come to bad ends, it is Izzy's career choice that most upsets his parents. 'Momma cried and Pop forbade any of the kids to mention his name'.[28]

Boxing promoters capitalized on ethnic animosities and often matched a Jewish fighter against an Irishman or an Italian against either (illus. 74). Prompted by the gift of *The Jewish Boxers' Hall of Fame*, Herman Roth recalled many of the early Jewish champions (and in particular those from New Jersey) in a 1988 conversation with his son Philip, whom he had taken as a child to the Thursday night fights at Newark's Laurel Garden. 'They fought two battles', Herman said.

> They fought because they were fighters, and they fought because they were Jews. They'd put two guys in the ring, an Italian and a Jew, and

THE RING ·
Blackfriars Road — S.E.

Sunday — Oct. 27th. 1930

Welterweight
Eliminating Championship
Contest

Fifteen 3 minute Rounds

ALF
MANCINI
NOTTING HILL

V

HARRY
MASON
WHITECHAPEL

Reserved Seats.... 5/9 to £1/4/0
Unreserved.......... 1/10 to 4/6

ALF MANCINI

HARRY MASON

Irishman and a Jew, and they fought like they meant it, they fought to hurt. There was always a certain amount of hatred in it. Trying to show who was superior.[29]

As a teenager, Philip Roth 'could recite the names and weights of all the champions and contenders', and was particularly keen on Slapsie Maxie Rosenbloom, light heavyweight champion from 1932 to 1934. 'Jewish boxers and boxing aficionados,' he later noted, were a 'strange deviation from the norm' of Jewish culture and 'interesting largely for that reason'.

> In the world whose values first formed me, unrestrained physical violence was considered contemptible everywhere else. I could no more smash a nose with a fist than fire a pistol into someone's heart. And what imposed this restraint, if not on Slapsie Maxie Rosenbloom, then on me, was my being Jewish. In my scheme of things, Slapsie Maxie was a more miraculous Jewish phenomena by far than Dr. Albert Einstein.[30]

Although less strikingly named than Slapsie Maxie, the most famous Jewish boxer of the early twentieth century was undoubtedly Benny Leonard; Farrell's Davey Cohen describes him as 'one smart hebe that could beat the Irish at their own game' (illus. 75).[31] Benny's real surname was Leiner, but he fought under the name of Leonard, supposedly in case his mother read about his fights in the

*Jewish Daily Forward*. One day, returning home with a black eye, he was unable to conceal the truth from parents:

> My mother looked at my black eye and wept. My father, who had to work all week for $20, said, 'All right Benny, keep on fighting. It's worth getting a black eye for $20; I am getting verschwartzt [blackened] for $20 a week.[32]

75
Benny Leonard, cigarette card given away with *The Champion*, 3 June 1922.

Leonard became world lightweight champion in 1917 and retired undefeated in 1925.[33] Like many boxers, he then dabbled in vaudeville, including a 1921 appearance in one of the Marx Brothers' most successful stage shows, a fast-paced revue called *On the Mezzanine Floor*. The brothers were keen fight fans, and Harpo had known Leonard for some time (illus. 76).[34] Leonard was in love with Hattie Darling, the dancing violinist star of the show, and, as Groucho recalled, 'she was able to talk him into putting money into our act'. 'A few times he joined the act and would come on stage, and the four of us would try to box with him. The audience loved that. They loved to see a world champion kidding around on stage.'[35] After the Wall Street crash of 1929, Leonard briefly returned to boxing; 'The Great Bennah' died, while refereeing a fight, in 1947.

In 1980, Budd Schulberg recalled Leonard's importance to the children of Jewish immigrants; children who had 'tasted the fists and felt the shoe-leather of righteous Irish and Italian Christian children'. Benny Leonard was their 'superhero'. Schulberg, who was born in 1914, was luckier than most because his father, a Hollywood mogul, knew Leonard personally.

> To see him climb in the ring sporting the six-pointed Jewish star on his fighting trunks was to anticipate sweet revenge for all the bloody noses, split lips, and mocking laughter at pale little Jewish boys who had run the neighbourhood gauntlet.[36]

'More than any other group of athletes', Jewish boxers provided a 'vivid counterpoint to popular anti-Semitic stereotypes'.[37]

But the stereotypes were remarkably persistent. 'No Business' (1915), by Charles E. Van Loan, is the story of a boxer called Isidore Mandelbaum. Two Irish fight fans discuss his career, and while conceding that he can 'hit with both hands – hit hard too', they lament his lack of 'the heart and the stomach'.

Mandelbaum, they conclude, is 'a gladiator for revenue only'. 'The only part of the fight game that he likes is the split-up in the box office . . . He'll never fight for the pure love of fightin', understand me? Put an Irish heart in him . . . an' you'd have a champion – no less'. The men construct an elaborate set-up to encourage Mandelbaum to be a little more 'game' in the ring. It works and they're happy, but we never learn what Mandelbaum thought.[38]

Perhaps the most famous portrait from this period of a Jew who boxes is Robert Cohn in Ernest Hemingway's *The Sun Also Rises* (1926).[39] Cohn is not just any Jew, fresh off the boat, but 'a member, through his father, of one of the richest Jewish families in New York, and through his mother, one of the oldest'. He has many privileges that the novel's narrator, Jake Barnes, lacks. The first, a Princeton education, is mentioned in the novel's opening sentence: 'Robert Cohn was once middleweight boxing champion of Princeton.' 'Do not think that I am very much impressed by that as a boxing title', Jake quickly adds, 'but it meant a lot to Cohn.' The paragraph continues as a virtuoso exercise in deflation. We next learn that Cohn 'cared nothing for boxing, in fact he disliked it', and then that 'he never fought except in the gym'. In other words, Cohn is no sportsman. Princeton may have given him a 'flattened nose', but after he left, no one remembered him or his title.[40] The insinuation is that Cohn boxed in order to remove the obvious mark of his Jewishness, hoping to assume in its place the flat-nosed pugilistic style that Jake feels is his own birthright. Throughout the novel, Jake goes to great lengths to demonstrate that it takes more than a little outmoded Ivy League undergraduate 'spirit' to turn a Jew into a proper sporting strenuous American.[41]

The problem with Cohn, as Jake sees it, is that his responses to life, literature and sport are not genuine – they are, like Yekl's speech, merely a costume that he

76
The Marx Brothers
with their fists
raised.

dons. Cohn likes the idea of a mistress more than any actual mistress; the idea of 'a lady of title' more than Lady Brett Ashley; the idea of chivalrous battle more than a real fight. He thinks boxing is something that takes place in gyms, and worries that he'll be 'bored' at the corrida. His 'undergraduate quality' is constantly noted. At 34 he still wears polo shirts and reads novels full of fights and handshakes, novels like W. H. Hudson's romantic potboiler, *The Purple Land* (1885), which Jake claims he took 'literally'. When he stands up 'ready to do battle for his lady love', Jake mocks the 'childish, drunken heroic of it'. In his first fight outside the gym, Cohn ends up taking on everybody he can, all in the same spirit and in his polo shirt. He first knocks down Mike, who is 'not a fighter', and Jake, 'the human punching-bag', who then obliges him by shaking hands. But things are different with the toreador, Romero, who 'kept getting up and getting knocked down again'. When Cohn tries to shake hands with him, Romero punches him in the face. Mike dismisses both 'Jews and bullfighters' as 'those sorts of people'; Jake, however, knows that Brett's substitution of Romero for Robert, and himself, is a definite upgrade.[42]

Walter Benn Michaels remarks that 'Hemingway's obsessive commitment to distinguishing between Cohn and Jake only makes sense in the light of their being in some sense indistinguishable.'[43] For all their differences, Robert Cohn and Jake Barnes are both 'taken in hand' by Brett, 'manipulated' in a way that recalls the boxer dolls that Jake nearly trips over on the Boulevard des Capucines. There, a 'girl assistant' lackadaisically pulls the threads that make the dolls dance on stands, while she stands with 'folded hands', 'looking away'.[44]

## 'THE PECULIAR GIFT OF THE WHITE MAN'

The narrator of Herman Melville's 1846 novel, *Typee*, is surprised to find that the inhabitants of the South Sea island on which he is marooned don't understand boxing: 'not one of the natives', he complains, 'had soul enough in him to stand up like a man, and allow me to hammer away at him':

> The noble art of self-defence appeared to be regarded by them as the peculiar gift of the white man; and I make little doubt but that they supposed armies of Europeans were drawn up provided with nothing else but bony fists and stout hearts, with which they set to in column, and pummelled one another at the word of command.[45]

Despite the success of early nineteenth-century black boxers such as Tom Molineaux and Bill Richmond, by Melville's time it had become a commonplace that 'the noble art of self-defence' – an art no less – was 'the peculiar gift of the white man'. In 1908, this confidence would be shattered when a black American became heavyweight champion of the world and the country plunged into a feverish, and futile, search for a 'great white hope' with a sufficiently stout heart and bony fists to defeat him. After 1908, many whites played down 'art' and began to talk of nature.

Although black Americans had boxed before the Civil War, it was really only in the last quarter of the nineteenth century that they began to make any headway in the sport. This was partly to do with the development and professionalization of sport in general, and partly to do with the growth of a significant black urban population. James Weldon Johnson's *Black Manhattan* (1930) tells the story of the origins of black urban culture, and of the ways in which 'the Negro . . . effectively impressed himself upon the city and the country'. 'Within this period,' he noted, 'roughly speaking, the Negro in the North emerged and gained national notice in three great professional sports: horse-racing, baseball, and prize-fighting.' Johnson devotes most of his attention to boxing, the sport which, he maintained, had the advantage of depending (at least more than the others) on 'individual skill and stamina'.[46]

The growth of an urban black sporting and theatrical community was accompanied by the development of what Johnson calls a 'black Bohemia' of sporting and gambling clubs. The walls of a typical club 'were literally covered with photographs or lithographs of every colored man in America who had ever "done anything"'.

> There were pictures of Frederick Douglass and of Peter Jackson, of all the lesser lights of the prize-ring, of all the famous jockeys and the stage celebrities, down to the newest song and dance team . . . It was, in short, a centre of coloured Bohemians and sports.[47]

From the myriad of photographs and lithographs that cover the club walls, Johnson picks out two portraits – those of Frederick Douglass and Peter Jackson. Jackson was a great late nineteenth-century heavyweight (and I'll consider his career in a moment), but it is worth remembering that Frederick Douglass also had a reputation as a pugilist.

## 'A SLAVE BECOMES A MAN': DOUGLASS VS. COVEY

Before the Civil War, slaves in Southern states were often set to fight for the entertainment of their masters, who made money gambling on the outcome. Frederick Douglass, a runaway slave who became a prominent anti-slavery orator and author of the best-selling *Narrative of the Life of Frederick Douglass, an American Slave* (1845), noted with horror the way in which slave owners encouraged slaves to participate in boxing and wrestling matches, designed also to serve as 'safety-valves, to carry off the rebellious spirit of enslaved humanity'. As an alternative Sabbath activity, Douglass set up a school to teach his fellow slaves to read, but this had to be kept secret, 'for they had much rather see us engaged in those degrading sports, than to see us behaving like intellectual, moral, and accountable beings'.[48] For Douglass, reading, writing and speaking offered the ultimate resistance to slavery's dehumanization. Nevertheless, verbal self-expression is directly connected to violent, physical self-expression in the

*Narrative*. A 'turning-point' in the book, and in Douglass's 'career as a slave', is a fight, in which, as a sixteen-year-old boy, he takes on the brutal 'nigger-breaker' Edward Covey. Covey has broken Douglass's spirit – 'the disposition to read departed . . . behold a man transformed into a brute' – and it is only by fighting that he can again become a man who reads.

In some ways the shape of the book follows the form of a conversion narrative, and the depiction of the fight, which is dense in biblical allusion, refigures religious conversion. Covey is a 'professor of religion' – 'a pious soul', the *Narrative* ironically notes – but it is Douglass who is preaching a sermon.[49] In fighting Covey, Douglass becomes a combination of Daniel escaped from the Lions' Den, Jacob wrestling with the Angel, and the suffering Christ; the outcome of the fight is likened to 'a glorious resurrection from the tomb of slavery'.[50] Usually such a rebellion would have been rewarded with further whipping, but for reasons that Douglass does not fully convey, he remains unpunished. Neither man is really a loser here: Covey's 'unbounded reputation' as an overseer remained intact; Douglass gained the 'self-confidence' necessary to take the next steps in his progression towards freedom, and leadership. The conversion from bondage to freedom enacted here is not, therefore, actual – he would remain a slave for four more years – but psychological. Douglass's formulation, 'You have seen how a man was made a slave; you shall see how a slave was made a man', indicates that 'slave' and 'man' are to be understood as opposing and contradictory concepts (as indeed, Douglass believed, were 'slave' and 'American'). The events leading up to the fight show Covey whipping Douglass, and by this stage of the *Narrative*, we realize that to accept such whippings is to be in some way feminine.[51] In resisting (and in turn feminizing) Covey – a fierce tiger before, a trembling leaf afterwards – Douglass says he has 'revived within me a sense of my own manhood'. Only when this psychological transformation has taken place can the truly liberating activities – reading, writing and running away – develop a proper momentum.

It might be argued that this fight is very different from a boxing match. It did not have an audience, it was not undertaken for money or show; it was an authentic struggle. Yet in the context of the *Narrative*, as in all literary, or autobiographical descriptions of fights, the scene takes on some characteristics of a performance. In addition, it is important to remember that the *Narrative* was written primarily for an abolitionist readership, and that Douglass was consciously fashioning an acceptable image of the male slave. This put him in a difficult position. On the one hand, as Richard Yarborough observes, blacks were viewed as 'unmanly and otherwise inferior because they were enslaved'; on the other hand, they were seen as 'beasts and otherwise inferior if they rebelled violently'.[52] In presenting his fight with Covey, Douglass treads a fine line between appropriate manliness and frightening bestiality. Douglass wants to present himself to his readers as manly and assertive, yet not as too manly or too assertive. 'I held him uneasy causing the blood to run where I touched him with the ends of my fingers,' he wrote; an awkward description that seems to reflect his own uneasiness about what he had done.[53]

The problematic nature of this encounter is made evident if the later revisions of the *Narrative* are considered. In 1855, by now famous, Douglass expanded and revised his account as *My Bondage and My Freedom*; in 1881, a final version, *The Life and Times of Frederick Douglass*, was published. In these two later versions, he is not merely relating his escape from slavery; he is recounting the exemplary story of his life as a self-made man, Benjamin Franklin style. The fight remains central to the story, but its depiction is very different. Covey is transformed into the stock villain of the melodramatic novel, the 'scoundrel' and 'cowardly tormentor' against whom he must reluctantly defend himself. Douglass ends by apologizing to readers who might find his narration of the 'skirmish' as 'undignified' as the event itself.[54] This seems to be a move toward what David Leverentz calls 'genteel chumminess': 'at any rate,' wrote Douglass, '*I was resolved to fight*, and, what was better still, I was actually hard at it'.[55] Yet the very expansion of a single long paragraph to several pages of detailed description might be read as itself an act of politically motivated aggression.

Douglass's political views had changed significantly since 1845. Then, he opposed the idea of violent slave resistance, which he believed would delay abolition; instead he called for the peaceful conversion of slaveholders. After the introduction of the Fugitive Slave Act of 1850, he became frustrated with the ineffectiveness of non-violent persuasion and began to speak out in favour of active, violent, slave resistance as both morally defensible and more likely to end slavery.[56] Douglass may also have thought it necessary to develop the fight scene as counter-propaganda to Harriet Beecher Stowe's best-selling 1852 novel, *Uncle Tom's Cabin*, a work which certainly did not advocate slave rebellion. In a pivotal scene, Uncle Tom capitulates, with Christian stoicism, to the whip of Simon Legree.[57] Dramatizations of the novel were popular well into the twentieth century, and, in one of the ironies of segregated America, many black boxers, some of whom, like Peter Jackson and Jack Johnson, had recently defeated white opponents, found ready employment playing the mild, emasculated Tom.[58] *My Bondage* uses every means possible, including italics and capitals, to emphasize both Douglass's manliness – 'I was *nothing* before; I was A MAN NOW' – and the role that the fight played in developing it – 'A man, without force, is without the essential dignity of humanity.'[59]

As a free man, Douglass retained his faith in pugilistic metaphor and example. In 1862 he made a speech to a largely black audience in which he complained that 'we are striking the guilty rebels with our soft white hand, when we should be striking with the iron hand of the black man'.[60] The following year, he intensified his call of 'Men of Color, To Arms', arguing that the 'imperiled nation' must 'unchain against her foes her powerful black hand . . . Words are useful only as they stimulate blows . . . "Who would be free, must themselves strike the blow."'[61] At the height of the war, in 1864, Douglass declared that the conflict had 'swept away' many 'delusions' about black men. 'One was . . . that the Negro would not fight; that he . . . was a perfect lamb, or an "Uncle Tom"; disposed to take off his coat whenever required, fold his hands, and be whipped by anybody who wanted to whip him'. The war, Douglass noted, 'has proved that there is a great deal of human nature in the Negro, and that he will fight, as Mr. Quincy, our President, said, in earlier days than these, "when there is a reasonable probability of his whipping anybody"'.[62]

I have discussed Douglass vs. Covey in some detail partly because of its own interest as a fight story, but also because of its continued importance for black American writers, artists and political leaders throughout the twentieth century.[63] After his death in 1897, Douglass was frequently presented as a model of 'the New Negro Man', exemplary to some in his 'manly courage', and, to others, in his self-restraint and patience.[64] Paul Lawrence Dunbar's elegy, for example, celebrates him as 'no soft-tongued apologist' but a warrior: 'He died in action, with his armor on.'[65] A rather less forceful figure emerges in Booker T. Washington's 1906 biography, in which he both sought to establish himself as Douglass's rightful heir and to distance himself from his defiant tone. That Washington had some trouble with the Covey fight is indicated by the brevity of his account of it, and by his frequent use of words such as 'reckless' and 'rash'. The fight over, both men behave suspiciously well. Covey admits himself 'fairly outdone', while, Washington concludes, 'it speaks well for the natural dignity and good sense of young Douglass that he neither boasted of his triumph nor did anything rash as a consequence of it'.[66] A few years later, Washington would express concern at both the rash behaviour and boastfulness of the first black heavyweight champion, Jack Johnson.

Throughout the twentieth century, explorations of the nature of black leadership often allude to Douglass and his portrait crops up in many places, often aligned, or contrasted with, that of a prize-fighter. Douglass himself kept a picture of Peter Jackson in his study and, according to James Weldon Johnson, 'used to point to it and say, "Peter is doing a great deal with his fists to solve the Negro question"'.[67] For many, Frederick Douglass's battle with Covey remained the model of what an authentic black vs. white fight should be (illus. 77).

Following Emancipation and Reconstruction, increasing anxiety about policing the boundaries between blacks and whites led to the introduction of widespread segregation (institutionalized with the infamous Supreme Court Pessy vs. Ferguson decision of 1896 which guaranteed 'separate but equal' status for blacks). In 1903, W.E.B. Du Bois declared that 'the problem of the twentieth century' would be 'the problem of the color line', and the colour line was firmly asserted in most competitive sports.[68] Initially, boxing was less segregated than team sports such as baseball and football. George Dixon held the American bantamweight title from 1890 to 1892, and the featherweight title from 1892 to 1900; Joe Walcott was welterweight champion from 1901 to 1906, and Joe Gans was lightweight champion from 1902 to 1908. Although many white fans, particularly in the South, 'winced' every time a black boxer hit a white boxer, these fights continued.[69] But the heavyweight title carried heavier symbolism.

Today Peter Jackson is often described as the finest boxer never to have fought for a world title. He wanted to, but no champion would take him on.

Having won Australia's heavyweight championship in 1886, Jackson travelled to the United States looking for a match with John L. Sullivan. While he received an ecstatic reception from black Americans – 'in every city the local black community went wild with excitement over his presence and would honor him with a testimonial dinner' – Sullivan refused to meet him.[70] In 1891, in the face of a great deal of adverse publicity, Jim Corbett agreed to a contest. Corbett presented his decision to fight Jackson as a kind of experiment: 'There may be something in a dark opponent that is not found in a light one and, if so, it behooves me to find out.'[71] An unprecedented purse of $10,000 may also have helped. A classic of endurance, Jackson vs. Corbett was finally stopped in the 61st round, by which time the fighters were struggling to keep upright, and many spectators had fallen asleep.[72] As the fight had been declared a draw either man could justifiably have challenged Sullivan's title. Both did, but Sullivan ignored Jackson. A few months later Corbett won the title and immediately capitalized on his sex-symbol reputation by taking to the stage. He was not frightened of Jackson, he said, just too busy for a rematch. With no alternatives, Jackson also resorted to the theatre, where he toured as Uncle Tom. When he tried to introduce a little sparring into the role (and thus maintain his credibility as a championship contender) the press complained that he had 'degraded the character'.[73]

Peter Jackson's rather limited moment of glory came in 1892 at London's National Sporting Club. The Club had opened just six months earlier, and offered as the climax to its inaugural season a keenly fought contest between Jackson and Frank Slavin. The fight lived up to its billing. Soon everyone who was anyone claimed to have been there. Young Winston Churchill bunked off from Harrow to attend. He drew a rather ugly caricature of Jackson and reputedly used it to settle his tuckshop bill.[74] The fight may have inspired another artist, too: in his 1898 volume of woodcuts, *Almanac of Sports*, Sir William Nicholson chose to represent boxing with an image of a white and a black fighter, poised for action (illus. 78). The night itself was a study in contrasts. Jackson, celebrated as the Black Prince, dressed in white; Slavin, who was white, wore dark blue. Jackson was slim and 'beautifully proportioned'. But it was Slavin, 'with his beetle brows and smouldering, deep-sunken eyes, leonine mane, fierce moustache, hairy chest and arms', who was London's idol. He was also an unabashed

78
Sir William Nicholson, 'November' from *An Almanac of Twelve Sports*, 1898.

racist, and had loudly declared that 'to be beaten by a black fellow, however good a fellow, is a pill I shall never swallow'. Slavin had to swallow the pill, but it was administered with care. Jackson steadily demolished his outclassed opponent for nine rounds, then looked to the referee to stop the fight. Urged to box on, he brought Slavin to his knees with 'five mercifully gentle blows'. Someone heard him say, 'Sorry, Frank.'[75] Born in the Virgin Islands and raised in Australia, Jackson knew the gestures that were required of the Empire's subjects.[76] In 1930 James Weldon Johnson described Jackson as the first prize-fighter who was also a 'cultured gentleman'. 'His chivalry in the ring was so great that sports-writers down to today apply to him the doubtful compliment "a white colored man".'[77] The next black contender, Jack Johnson, would not be so chivalrous.

## THE GOLDEN GRIN

Writing in 1936 on the 'ethics of living Jim Crow', novelist Richard Wright noted many subjects that were 'taboo from the white man's point of view':

> American white women; the Ku Klux Klan; France, and how Negro soldiers fared while there; French women; Jack Johnson; the entire northern part of the United States; the Civil War; Abraham Lincoln; U. S. Grant; General Sherman; Catholics; the Pope; Jews; the Republican Party; slavery; social equality; Communism; Socialism; the 13th and 14th Amendments to the Constitution; or any topic calling for positive knowledge or manly self-assertion on the part of the Negro.[78]

Among a range of general topics such as 'slavery' and 'social equality', only four individuals are named: three are the liberators of the Civil War — General Sherman, Ulysses S. Grant, and Abraham Lincoln; the fourth, an early twentieth-century black boxer, Jack Johnson. How did Johnson end up in such illustrious company, and why his name was still taboo to whites in 1936?

Born in the port of Galveston, Texas in 1878, Arthur John Johnson was of the first generation of free black Americans. At thirteen he began working on the docks where he soon developed a reputation as a fighter, and, at seventeen, he took up boxing professionally. After beating all the other good black heavyweights, including Joe Jeanette and Sam Langford, he secured a title fight in Australia, then one of the world's boxing centres. The promoter's guarantee of $30,000 supposedly overcame the reluctance of then champion Tommy Burns (whose real name was Noah Brusso) to fight a black man. 'Shame on the money-mad Champion!' John L. Sullivan is said to have exclaimed, 'Shame on the man who upsets good American precedents because there are Dollars, Dollars, Dollars in it.'[79] On 26 December 1908, after fourteen rounds, during which Johnson casually taunted the out-matched Burns, the referee stopped the match.[80] Jack London was there, and his fight report established the terms in which Johnson would most often be subsequently described:

A golden smile tells the story, and that golden smile was Johnson's . . . At times . . . Johnson would deliberately assume the fierce, vicious, intent expression, only apparently for the purpose of suddenly relaxing and letting his teeth flash forth like the rise of a harvest moon, while his face beamed with all the happy care-free innocence of a little child . . . [Johnson's] part was the clown.[81]

London's view of Johnson as a clown or a minstrel drew upon the myth of black shiftless gaiety peddled by 'coon songs' popular since before the Civil War (characteristic numbers included 'A Nigger's Life is Always Gay' and 'Happy Are We, Darkies So Gay'). When Johnson entered the ring to fight Jim Jeffries in Reno in 1910, the band played 'All Coons Look Alike to Me'.[82] The popular press represented Johnson's victory with a flurry of Sambo cartoons, all emphasizing his smile.[83] Johnson's 'golden grin' (he had several gold teeth) quickly became his trademark, a symbol of laughing defiance that infuriated and obsessed white America. But what many critics described as Johnson's 'laziness' was in fact a carefully thought out defensive style. He fought with his hands low, at only chest height, and 'looked like an artist leaning back from a canvas to evaluate the picture from a distance'. This defensive style, Randy Roberts points out, was cultivated by all the great black heavyweights of the time; in order to secure fights they needed 'to just barely defeat' their white opponents.[84]

Within moments of Johnson's gaining the title, the search for an Anglo-Saxon challenger began. Former champion Jim Jeffries was the popular choice to come out of retirement and 'remove the golden smile from Jack Johnson's face'.[85] Jeffries was 'the great white hope'. Now ubiquitous, the phrase seems to have been coined by London, perhaps trying to evoke Roosevelt's reputation as the 'Great White Father' or Rudyard Kipling's 'White Man's Burden'. Written in response to the Roosevelt-led American takeover of the Philippines after the Spanish-American War in 1899, Kipling's poem instructs readers to 'Take up the White Man's Burden – / Send forth the best ye breed'.[86] The expectations of white America were a heavy burden indeed.

In the run-up to the Johnson-Jeffries fight, the Social Darwinian 'scientific' racist rhetoric of the day intensified. Promoter Tex Rickard foolishly advertised the fight as the 'ultimate test of racial superiority', and newspapers published articles predicting that Jeffries, who 'had Runnymede and Agincourt behind him', was bound to beat Johnson who 'had nothing but the jungle'.[87] The same result was also predicted, in song, by Groucho Marx, as an inadvisable part of his act at the Pekin, an all-black theatre in Chicago. Unfortunately for Groucho, 'Johnson was in the audience'; he 'barely survived the evening'.[88] 'Heart', the quality that Jews also seemed to lack, and a possible 'yellow streak' were much discussed. 'Is Johnson a typical example of his race in the lack of that intangible "something" that we call "heart"?' asked a typical newspaper columnist.[89] In the weird world of racial attribution, blacks did, it seemed, have some advantages. Would Johnson benefit from what some saw as an 'insensibility to pain which distinguishes the African and gives him a peculiar advantage in the sports of the ring'? Would Jeffries, 'a thinker' who 'undoubtedly possesses the worrying qualities of the white race' lose out to the 'care free and cool' Johnson? 'The art of relaxing', London claimed, was 'one of Johnson's great assets' since the 'tensing of muscle consumes energy'.[90]

What was announced as the 'fight of the century' finally took place in Reno, Nevada, on 4 July 1910, and ended in the fifteenth round when Jeffries's seconds threw in the towel. Assertions of white supremacy suddenly seemed a lot less certain.

News of the result spread quickly by telegraph; crowds gathered in front of the 'automatic bulletin' at the *New York Times* building, and the paper later reported Johnson's mother and sisters listening to its click on the stage of the Pekin Theatre in Chicago and sharing 'in the big crowd's happiness'.[91] But for blacks in less congenial surroundings, the result was not such good news. Louis Armstrong recalled being told to hurry home from his paper round in New Orleans, while Henry Crowder remembered thousands of whites gathering in Washington's Pennsylvania Avenue: 'no Negro dared show his face on that street'.[92] As the news spread by telegraph across America, lynchings, fights and full-scale riots were reported. Allen Guttman summarizes:

> In Houston, Charles Williams openly celebrated Johnson's triumph and a white man 'slashed his throat from ear to ear'; in Little Rock, two blacks were killed by a group of whites after an argument about the fight in a streetcar; in Roanoke, Virginia, a gang of white sailors injured several blacks; in Wilmington, Delaware, a group of blacks attacked a white and whites retaliated with a 'lynching bee'; in Atlanta a black ran amok with a knife; in Washington . . . two whites were fatally stabbed by blacks; in New York, one black was beaten to death and scores were injured; in Pueblo, Colorado, thirty people were injured in a race riot; in Shreveport, Louisiana, three blacks were killed by white assailants. Other murders or injuries were reported in New Orleans, Baltimore, Cincinnati, St Joseph, Los Angeles, Chattanooga, and many other small cities and towns.[93]

For some, the dead became martyrs in the struggle for equality. William Pickens, later field secretary of the NAACP, wrote in the *Chicago Defender* that 'it was a good deal better for Johnson to win, and a few Negroes to be killed in body for it, than for Johnson to have lost and all Negroes to have been killed in spirit by the preachments of inferiority from the combined white press'.[94] A 1910 postcard presented Johnson alongside Abraham Lincoln as 'Our Champions' (illus. 79).

In the months and years that followed, the search for a suitable white challenger continued. Johnson had refused to fight any black contenders, recognizing that in such contests he had nothing to gain and everything to lose. 'I am

champion of the world', he reputedly said, 'I have had a hard time to get a chance and I really think I am the only colored fellow who ever was given a chance to win the title . . . I'll retire the only colored heavyweight champion.'[95] Soon, as John Lardner put it, 'well-muscled white boys more than six feet two inches tall were not safe out of their mother's sight', but nothing seemed to work.[96] Seeing Johnson humble successive white hopes, many whites lost hope about the best that they could breed. Some took comfort in the belief that it was merely generational problem. 'Honestly', asked William A. Phelon, 'is there one single, genuine, solitary Hope, now rampant and challenging, that you believe could have gone five rounds with Bob Fitzsimmons?' Fitzsimmons, Sullivan, or Corbett 'could have plowed though the present staff of hopes like an axe through cheese'.[97] In a 1912 cartoon, a red-faced reveller looks at a poster advertising the latest challenger and reflects, 'If I wuz the man I wuz, they wouldn't need him' (illus. 53).

Some decided simply to ignore Johnson and staged all-white champion-ships. Georges Carpentier's London fight against Gunboat Smith in 1914, for instance, was billed the 'White World Heavy-Weight Championship'; Carpentier noted that this was 'certainly good publicity if perhaps a trifle unorthodox'.[98] Others relied on fiction for consolatory stories of white triumph. Just a few months after Jeffries's defeat, Jack London began work on *The Abysmal Brute*, the story of a white boy, Pat Glendon, who only fights other white boys. Nevertheless, Johnson's existence as the real champion was hard for London to forget. Glendon is described as 'the hope of the white race' and there is a passing reference to Jeffries who could have 'worried' him 'a bit, but only a bit'.[99] Jeffries and the Reno fight are also mentioned in Edgar Rice Burroughs's 1914 serial *The Mucker* and W.R.H. Trowbridge's *The White Hope* (1913), but there too, fictional compensation is provided. After defeating a series of 'white hopes', Burroughs's Chicago-Irish 'mucker', Billy Byrne, emerges as 'the most likely heavy since

Jeffries'. The story ends with a deal to fight 'the black champion', although Byrne's manager complains that the terms are 'as usual, rather one-sided'.[100] More ambitious in its fantasy, the finale of *The White Hope* sees the middle-weight crown wrested away from a 'grinning' black champion.

> The negro's knees sagged and he lurched forward . . . Sam Crowfoot, face down on the boards, with the sand of the ring showing in patches on his black skin, was out to the world.[101]

Much of the public agitation about Johnson's continuing success centred around its representation, and circulation, on film. In 1910, many states acted quickly to ban showings of the Reno film, arguing that riots would necessarily follow. The film was not shown in the South or in most American cities. When news spread that Johnson was due to defend his title against Jim Flynn on 4 July 1912, the '"white hopes" of Congress' got to work.[102] Just weeks after Johnson's knockout of Flynn, the Sims Act was passed, forbidding the interstate transportation of any film showing 'any prize fight or encounter of pugilists' for 'purposes of public exhibition' (illus. 80). In 1915, when D. W. Griffith's Klan-celebrating *The Birth of a Nation* was released, James Weldon Johnson wondered if 'some of the moral fervour' expended against prize-fight films might be extended to Griffith's movie.[103]

80
Advertisement for Jeffries–Johnson Fight Pictures, 1910.

Jeffries-Johnson Fight Pictures
(COPYRIGHTED.)
Taken at the Ring-side, Reno, Nevada, July 4, 1910, by the
NEW YORK HERALD
America's Greatest and Foremost Newspaper

Every Vital Moment of the
World's Greatest Heavy-weight Championship Battle

Together with an expert's description of the titanic struggle, now is offered to showmen for the first time at the ridiculously low figure of

$50.00--ROYALTY FOR EACH WEEK'S USE--$50.00

With an additional deposit of $50.00 or a guarantee from your local bank for the safe return of the pictures.

This is the Golden Opportunity for the Live, Up-to-the-minute Showman

HERE ARE POSITIVELY THE BEST PICTURES ON THE MARKET

and at a figure which allows the individual manager to secure for himself the profits which accrue from their exhibition. They are ready for immediate delivery, and all orders accompanied by certified check, postoffice or express money order will receive prompt attention and instantaneous delivery.

BIDS FOR STATE RIGHTS WILL BE CONSIDERED IF ACCOMPANIED BY CERTIFIED CHECK FOR TEN PER CENT. (10%) OF THE AMOUNT BID.

These are the Only Genuine Jeffries-Johnson Fight Pictures
(Copyrighted by the New York Herald.)

Numerous "fakes" and "doctored" imitations are being offered for sale or lease. Beware of them, and secure none but the originals and best.

Address All Communications to
LOUIS J. BERGER, Secretary,
1386 Broadway, Long Distance 'Phone, Murray Hill 6442. NEW YORK CITY.
REFERENCE: THE GREENWICH BANK, HERALD SQUARE BRANCH, NEW YORK CITY.

SPECIAL NOTICE: Any firm, corporation, or individual, infringing upon our rights in the matter of the Jeffries-Johnson Fight Pictures above mentioned and described, will be proceeded against forthwith for the violation of the United States Copyright Act.

Whites who had previously celebrated boxing as the sport of manly self-assertion, now remarked brutality. Theodore Roosevelt, longtime champion of the strenuous art, announced that he was forsaking boxing after Jeffries's defeat. 'I sincerely trust,' Roosevelt declared piously, 'that public sentiment will be so aroused, and will make itself felt so effectively, as to guarantee that this is the last prize fight to take place in the United States.'[104] How curious, W.E.B. Du Bois pointed, that it was only when the world champion was black that commentators felt the urge to object to boxing *per se*. 'Neither he nor his race invented prize fighting or particularly like it. Why then this thrill of national disgust? Because Johnson is black.'[105] In the years that followed Johnson's 1915 defeat, Du Bois remained unsure about the significance of boxers as cultural heroes. On the one hand, he worried that an interest in sport might distract black Americans from the importance of education, noting, for example, that the receipts from Harry Willis's fight with Luis Firpo were 'enough to endow a Negro University'.[106] On the other hand, the continuing success of black boxers in the 1920s was a repeated blow to white supremacy, and their continuing bad treatment a reminder that whites were 'afraid to meet black boxers in competition wherever equality and fairness in the contest are necessary'.[107]

As a folk hero Jack Johnson's reputation rested on much more than simply his boxing skill. In and out of the ring, he flamboyantly broke taboos. Urged by civil rights activist Ida B. Wells to invest in a gymnasium for black boys in Chicago's South Side, Johnson instead opened the Café de Champion, serving black and white customers together. Wells complained that he was catering to the 'worst passions of both races'.[108] By his own admission, Johnson was 'a dandy'; shaving his head and sporting everything Booker T. Washington had promised whites that accommodating blacks would refrain from wearing: 'a high hat, imitation gold eye-glasses, a showy walking-stick, kid gloves, fancy boots, and what not'.[109] In 1909 Washington's personal secretary argued that Johnson needed to 'refrain from anything resembling boastfulness'.[110] He also liked fast cars and famously hired a white chauffeur to drive him around.[111] Worse of all, Johnson spent his money on white prostitutes and had three wives, all white.[112] Just months after legislating against the interstate transportation of Johnson's films, the American legal system took another shot at the champion. In 1912 Johnson was charged with having violated the 1910 'White Slave Traffic Act', also known by the name of its sponsor, Mann. The Act was designed to target commercial vice rings and it was rare that individuals were taken to court. But, 'for Jack Johnson the government was willing to make an exception'. When charges concerning Lucille Cameron (a 'sporting woman' whom he later married) fell through, the government latched onto Belle Schreiber. Resentful at having been rejected by Johnson, she testified to receiving money and crossing state lines with the boxer.[113] Booker T. Washington issued a statement deploring Johnson's behaviour and claiming that it would injure the 'whole race'. 'I do not believe it is necessary for me to say that the honest, sober element of the Negro people of the United States is as severe in condemnation of this kind of immorality . . . as any other portion of the community.'[114] The whole case was, as Johnson later said, 'a rank frame-up'.[115] But that made no odds. Convicted by a white jury and sentenced to a year and a day in prison and a $1000 fine, he jumped bail and fled the country with Lucille in 1913. He spent the next two years in giving exhibition fights and performing as the 'agreeable gentleman with the settled smile and the shining white teeth' in vaudeville in Europe, Canada, and Mexico.[116] In 1915 Johnson agreed to defend his title against the white American Jess Willard in Havana. Willard knocked Johnson out in the 26th round according, Johnson later claimed, to a deal he had made with the FBI in order to be allowed to return to the States. Most boxing historians, having studied the film footage, believe that it was a fair fight.[117] On becoming champion, Willard immediately reinstated the colour line. It was upheld until 1937 when Joe Louis finally broke it for good.

In the years that followed his defeat, Johnson's star showed no signs of waning. When he arrived in Harlem in 1921, after finally serving his jail sentence in Kansas, he was welcomed by thousands as a returning hero. The explosion of 1920s black urban culture, now known as the Harlem Renaissance, established him as an iconic figure. Claude McKay's 1928 novel *Home to Harlem* is full of references to Johnson; every time someone gets hit his name is evoked. As well as pugnacity, the boxer represented the possibility of black celebrity. One little boy shows off to another that he 'done met mos'n all our big niggers', including Johnson, but both are upstaged by a Miss Curdy who claims to know 'all that upstage race gang that wouldn't touch Jack Johnson with a ten-foot pole'. The greatest compliment the protagonist Jake receives is when someone tells him, 'If I was as famous as Jack Johnson and rich as Madame Walker I'd prefer to have you as my friend than – President Wilson.'[118]

The eventful, and inspirational, life of Johnson appealed to writers, and even more to publishers. In 1930, following the success of the reissued *The Autobiography of an Ex-Colored Man*, publisher Blanche Knopf urged James Weldon Johnson to write a novel based on Johnson. When he refused, she turned to Walter White. Although he contemplated including Johnson in a planned series of biographical essays and wrote 152 pages of a novel about a boxer, neither project was completed.[119] Instead Johnson's story was told in minstrel show sketches such as *The Coming Champion* (illus. 54) and in a Broadway play by two white writers, Jim Tully and Frank Dazey, called *Black Boy*.[120] *Black Boy* opened in 1926, with Paul Robeson taking the lead (illus. 81). The fact that 'Black Boy' became involved with a white woman on stage prompted great controversy. Robert Coleman wrote in the New York *Daily Mirror* that 'the authors have cheapened their portrait of the pugilist by introducing the problem of race antagonism. In our opinion it is always in bad taste to introduce this unpleasant element.'[121]

### 'ASCERTAINING THE PROGRESS OF THE AMERICAN NEGRO'

The Harlem Renaissance of the 1920s was not simply a flowering of black art, but part of a much larger process of political and social change. Postwar political radicalism was largely diverted into a cultural patriotism which asked what 'gift' blacks could contribute to the American melting pot.[122] Works such as Alain Locke's *The New Negro* (1925) and V. F. Calverton's *An Anthology of American Negro Literature* (1929) sought to demonstrate 'the existence of the black tradition as a political defense of the racial self against racism'.[123] In a 1916 essay called 'Inside Measurement', James Weldon Johnson considered what he thought were the 'various methods of measurement for ascertaining the progress of the American Negro'. What he termed 'outside measurements' recorded growth in population and increase in wealth. An 'inner measurement' could be made by keeping 'a record of the number of intelligently written books bought and read each year by

the colored people'.[124] Johnson developed this idea further in *The Book of American Negro Poetry* (1922), where he argued that the artistic achievement of black Americans could go a long way in improving their social status in the United States.[125] In 1903 Du Bois had argued that an overemphasis on industrial education would not produce black leaders: instead a 'talented tenth' must be encouraged to achieve as cultured individuals in order to 'inspire the masses'.[126]

Johnson was a problematic figure for the Harlem intellectuals. On the one hand, it was widely believed that art and literature were the correct ways to demonstrate 'intellectual parity'. On the other, in 1915, Weldon Johnson conceded that 'there is not, perhaps, a spot on the globe where Jack Johnson's name is not familiar'.

Johnson's bad personal breaks deprived him of the sympathy and approval of most of his own race; yet it must be admitted that with these breaks left out of the question, his record as a pugilist has been something of a racial asset. The white race, in spite of its vaunted civilization, pays more attention to the argument of force than any other race in the world.[127]

Some years later, Weldon Johnson wrote of his meeting with Jack Johnson, and, alluding to Douglass's comment that Peter Jackson had done 'a great deal with his fists to solve the Negro question', concluded that 'after the reckoning of his big and little failings has been made, [Johnson] may be said to have done his share'.[128] If the celebration of a sports hero was difficult to square with a belief in artistic and intellectual achievement, one way to reconcile them was to consider boxing itself as an art or as analogous to art. In his 1916 essay, 'The Negro in American Art', Weldon Johnson had argued that 'there is nothing of artistic value belonging to America which has not been originated by the Negro'. As 'partial corroboration' he quoted the white avant-garde artist and editor Robert Coady, describing Jack Johnson's 'shadow dancing', as 'the most beautiful dancing of modern times'. 'When he strikes a fighting pose', Coady rhapsodized, 'we are carried back to the days of Greek bronzes.'[129] Perhaps it was not so far-fetched then to imagine Johnson as a member of the Talented Tenth.[130]

But not everyone agreed with such analogies. In 1926 George Schuyler denounced what he called 'The Negro-Art Hokum'. There was, he claimed, no unique 'Aframerican art': 'the literature, painting and sculpture of Aframericans – such as there is – is identical in kind with the literature, painting and sculpture of white Americans'. To say otherwise, he implied, was just another form of racist thinking:

> The mere mention of the word 'Negro' conjures up in the average white American's mind a composite stereotype of Bert Williams, Aunt Jemima, Uncle Tom, Jack Johnson, Florian Slappy, and the various monstrosities scrawled by cartoonists. Your average Aframerican no more resembles this stereotype than the average American resembles a composite of Andy Gump, Jim Jeffries, and a cartoon by Rube Goldberg.[131]

For Schuyler, Johnson's influence was of no more use than that of Uncle Tom; indeed, in some ways, it might be seen as worse. 'It must be tragic for a sensitive Negro to be a poet', George Bernard Shaw remarked to Claude McKay in 1920. 'Why didn't you choose pugilism instead of poetry for a profession?'[132]

### 'THE NEW NEGRO. WHEN HE'S HIT, HE HITS BACK!'

For the most part, Jack Johnson was celebrated less for his statuesque appearance than for his defiant qualities – however stereotypal those might be. During the First World War, for example, heavy black shells were nicknamed 'Jack Johnsons'.[133] Numerous songs celebrated his victory over Jeffries. One blues reworked

'Amazing Grace' so that the 'sweet' and saving sound was no longer God's word, but the thud of Jeffries hitting the canvas.

> Amaze an' Grace, how sweet it sounds,
> Jack Johnson knocked Jim Jeffries down.
> Jim Jeffries jumped up an' hit Jack on the chin,
> An' then Jack knocked him down agin.

> The Yankees hold the play,
> The white man pulls the trigger;
> But it makes no difference what the white man say,
> The world champion's still a nigger.[134]

However assertive the 'but' might be, it only serves highlight the limits of Johnson's victory in a world in which the white man 'holds the play' and 'pulls the trigger'. Other popular songs were less equivocal. 'The Black Gladiator: Veni, Vidi, Vici – Jack Johnson' celebrated his victory over Burns as 'proof that all men are the same / in muscle, sinew, and in brain / No blood flows through our veins / but that of Negro Ham's own strain / Master of all the world – your claim.'[135] 'Titanic', a 1912 song by Huddie Ledbetter (Leadbelly), is equally forthright. The flooring of Jeffries is matched as a blow to white supremacists only by the sinking of the *Titanic* (which wouldn't allow blacks as passengers).

> It was midnight on the sea,
> The band was playin' 'Nearer, My God, to Thee.'
> Cryin', 'Fare thee, Titanic, fare thee well!'
> . . .
> Jack Johnson wanted to get on boa'd;
> Captain Smith hollered, 'I ain't haulin' no coal.'
> Crying 'Fare thee, Titanic, fare thee well!'
> . . .
> Black man oughta shout for joy,
> Never lost a girl or either a boy.
> Crying, 'Fare thee, Titanic, fare thee well!'[136]

At the end of the First World War, the black soldiers who returned to America were unwilling to put up with escalating white racism. The summer of 1919 saw unprecedented race riots, and in their wake, the *Liberator* published Claude McKay's sonnet, 'If We Must Die', now often considered the 'inaugural address' of the Harlem Renaissance.[137] The poem depicted blacks as 'hogs', 'hunted and penned in an inglorious spot', and whites as 'mad and hungry dogs / Making their mock at our accursed lot'. It ends with the plea that 'though far outnumbered let us show brave, / And for their thousand blows deal one death-blow!'

Like men we'll face the murderous, cowardly pack,
Pressed to the wall, dying, but fighting back![138]

What was supposedly 'new' about the much discussed New Negro was not aggression but retaliation; not a desire to fight, but a renewed willingness to fight *back*.[139] In 1921, Rollin Lynde Hartt, a white Congregational minister and journalist, described 'a negro magazine' bearing the legend (an adaptation of Frederick Douglass's *Childe Harold* allusion), 'They who would be free must themselves strike the blow.' When hit, Hartt concluded, the New Negro, unlike 'the timorous, docile negro of the past', does not hesitate to 'hit back'.[140] The political radicalism of the New Negro was often linked to his 'dauntless manhood'. 'The Old Negro,' wrote J. A. Rogers in 1927, 'protests that he does not want social equality; the New . . . demands it.' While 'the Old . . . acts as if he were always in the way', 'the New is erect, manly, bold; if necessary, defiant'.[141]

For many, the New Negro was epitomized in the figure of Jack Johnson, and his name became a shorthand for many different kinds of 'erect, manly; if necessary, defiant' behaviour. Zora Neale Hurston noted that in the folk tales she grew up with, the trickster who 'outsmarted the devil' was always called 'Jack' or 'High John de Conquer'; he was 'our hope-bringer'.[142] After 1910, black men who challenged, and beat, white authority were commonly dubbed, or dubbed themselves, 'Jack Johnson'.[143] In 1934 Henry Crowder published a series of eight autobiographical vignettes about segregation, racial abuse, and 'hitting back' in *Negro*, an anthology edited by Nancy Cunard. In the first, he walks away after being refused service in a Georgia café, but by the second, he is not afraid to 'wade in'. The final vignette tells of Johnson's defeat of Jeffries and the fights that broke out in its wake in Washington. While the police search for 'a giant Negro armed with brass knuckles', 'we Negroes remained where we were, drinking and laughing'.[144]

One of the books reviewed in *Negro* was Sterling Brown's *Southern Road* (1932); Alain Locke designated Brown 'the New Negro Folk-Poet'.[145] In one of the strongest poems in the collection, 'Strange Legacies', Brown places Johnson alongside John Henry and 'a nameless couple' of sharecroppers as symbols of folk resilience; all endured their troubles, 'taking punishment'. The poem ends, 'guess we'll give it one mo' try'.

One thing you left with us, Jack Johnson.
One thing before they got you.

You used to stand there like a man,
Taking punishment
With a golden, spacious grin;
Confident.
Inviting big Jim Jeffries, who was boring in:
"Heah ah is, big boy; yuh sees whah Ise at.

Come on in . . ."

Thanks, Jack, for that.[146]

Some linked Johnson's 'hitting back' to Frederick Douglass's resistance to Covey, and Johnson himself lined up with Douglass against Booker T. Washington, who had condemned his behaviour on several occasions. Washington, Johnson wrote in 1927, ' has to my mind not been altogether frank in the statement of the problem or courageous in his solutions'. Douglass's 'honest and straightforward program has had more of an appeal to me, because he faced issues without compromising.'[147] In 1919, Johnson had taken out an advertisement in an Industrial Workers of the World magazine, *Gale's*, urging 'colored people' to leave 'the "boasted" land of the liberty' and move to Mexico where they would no longer be 'lynched, tortured, mobbed, persecuted and discriminated against'.[148]

In 1922 Claude McKay travelled to the Soviet Union, one of the first black Americans to be invited by the Bolshevik government. While in Moscow he was commissioned to write a short book to inform the Soviets about the condition of *Negry v Amerike* (*The Negroes in America*). Although McKay was keen to argue that race should be considered primarily 'from a class point of view', his analysis focuses as much on culture as on economics.[149] In a chapter titled 'Negroes in Sports', McKay provides a complex and astute reading of Jack Johnson and the ideological status of black boxers more generally.[150] The prize-fighter only has limited value as a symbol for defiance. Although the boxing ring can seem to be a site of struggle against white dominance (one where African-American workers 'exert all their efforts to gain the victory' and one where victory is possible), it nevertheless remains a 'large business . . . managed by corporations', white corporations that set the terms of black entrance and success. For McKay, it was foolish to believe that 'racial differences' could be resolved by 'fist fights arranged for a commercial purpose'.[151] Langston Hughes made a similar point in 'Prize Fighter' (1927):

> Only dumb guys fight
> If I wasn't dumb
> I wouldn't be fightin'.
> I could make six dollars a day.
> On the docks
> And I'd save more than I do now.
> Only dumb guys fight.[152]

But while Marxists such as Hughes and McKay pointed out the economic reality, the symbolism of Johnson's career, and interracial fighting more generally, continued to have resonance for many artists and writers. In Archibald J. Motley's 1933 painting, *The Plotters*, a fight between a black and a white boxer is used to represent not simply defiance and resilience, but conspiracy (illus. 55). The painting depicts a group of black men sitting at a table, and the title tells us what they are doing. Two men at the table look intently at one another while a partially obscured standing figure points at a piece of paper. On the wall behind the table we see part of a painting, featuring a black and a white boxer. The men at the table, like the boxers in the painting, seem too large for the confines of the framed space. A boxing match may be nothing more than a degrading, commercially motivated performance, nevertheless, as Motley suggests, it can symbolically represent a real fight.

A similar thought seems to lie behind 'Box Seat', a story in Jean Toomer's *Cane* (1923), in which a boxing match between dwarfs is performed as a grotesque spectacle. Dan Moore, angry and frustrated with the 'sick' world, has followed the respectable Muriel into the theatre. At first he is appalled by the freak show and thinks Muriel, who is trying to pass as white, a 'she-slave' for watching. But all of a sudden, play-acting breaks out into something else when one of the men 'lands a stiff blow'. 'This makes the other sore. He commences slugging. A real scrap is on.'

> The gong rings. No fooling this time. The dwarfs set to. They clinch. The referee parts them. One swings a cruel upper-cut and knocks the other down. A huge head hits the floor. Pop! The house roars. The fighter, groggy, scrambles up. The referee whispers to the contenders not to fight so hard. They ignore him. They charge. Their heads jab like boxing gloves. They kick and spit and bite. They pound each other furiously. Muriel pounds. The house pounds. Cut lips. Bloody noses. The referee asks for the gong. Time! The house roars. The dwarfs bow, are made to bow. The house wants more. The dwarfs are led from the stage.[153]

But the crowd is not satisfied until the violence of the contest is defused by the winner of the fight, Mr. Barry, singing 'a sentimental love song' to various girls in the audience. Finally Mr. Barry turns to Muriel, and offers her a white rose, which he has kissed with his blood-stained lips. She 'shrinks away', 'flinches back', 'tight in revulsion', but this only provokes him further. Dan reads the dwarf's eyes as a reproach and an acknowledgment of their shared identity as Christ-like freaks. He leaps up, shouts, JESUS WAS ONCE A LEPER!', and 'hooks' the jaw of the complaining man sitting next to him. The story ends with the man taking off his jacket to fight in earnest in an alley behind the theatre, but Dan, 'having forgotten him', walks away.[154]

## MATTERS OF COLOUR

Jack Johnson's career had a significant resonance for white, as well as black, artists and writers. While black artists saw Johnson as an inspirational figure (whether representing the possibility of celebrity, progress or defiance) and paid no attention either to his white opponents or to his white wives, whites were almost obsessively drawn to representations of a black and a white man fighting together. The only time that Johnson (or a Johnson-like figure) is mentioned without reference to a white opponent, or girlfriend, he functions as a minstrel figure.[155] In Conan Doyle's 1926 story, 'The Adventure of the Three Gables', a black boxer bursts into Sherlock Holmes's rooms at Baker Street and offends Dr Watson and the detective with his 'hideous mouth' and 'smell'. Watson's first impression is that 'he would have been a comic figure if he had not been terrific, for he was dressed in a very loud gray check suit with a flowing salmon-coloured tie. His broad face and flattened nose were thrust forward, as his sullen dark eyes, with a smouldering gleam of malice in them, turned from one of us to the other.' After he has left Holmes tells Watson that he is 'glad you were not forced to break his woolly head': 'he is really rather a harmless fellow, a great muscular, foolish, blustering baby, and easily cowed, as you have seen.'[156] Johnson is also 'easily cowed' in a story that William Carlos Williams included in his *Autobiography*. One day there was 'a near riot' in a café in Paris. 'They began tearing the chairs apart for clubs. When it was all over and the lights went on again they found the World's Champion under a table scared stiff. "That's not the kind of fight I'm interested in," he said frankly.'[157]

The image which perhaps best encapsulates the white response to Johnson is George Bellows's *Both Members of this Club* (1909), originally entitled *A Nigger and A White Man* (illus. 82). Bellows began work on the painting in October

82
George Bellows,
*Both Members of
This Club*, 1909.

1909, the month in which the terms for Johnson's fight against Jeffries were finally agreed. The setting is dark and the figures are elongated smears of white, brown and red paint; the faces in the crowd are grotesques. The painting re-works the geometrical design and impasto of earlier works such as *Stag at Sharkey's*, but is considerably larger and more claustrophobically 'dreamlike' in its atmosphere.[158] The title refers to the fact that, because of the legal restric-tions on prize-fights, boxers as well as spectators needed to take out a nominal club 'membership'. This practice meant that Jim Crow America found itself sanctioning organizations in which blacks and whites could both be members. In his choice of title, Bellows seems to be making a joke about the fact that a law designed to stop one undesirable practice (boxing) should lead to another (what Claude McKay described as the 'strange un-American' coming together of blacks and whites under equal terms).[159] The painting's perspective suggests that the viewer too has joined the club. After finishing *Both Members*, Bellows abandoned boxing as a subject for paintings until the mid-1920s. His litho-graphs, however, continue to explore America's obsession with interracial boxing.[160] *The White Hope* did not appear until 1921, by which time the colour line had been firmly re-established (illus. 83). It was now safe to imagine white defeat and black compassion.

'A Matter of Color' was the title of the first boxing story written by Ernest Hemingway, as a high school student in 1916. A Ring Lardner-style vernacular yarn with an O. Henry twist at the end, it presents a retired trainer telling the story of how he had once fixed a fight by hiring a 'big Swede' to clobber the black opponent, the young Joe Gans no less, with a baseball bat through a curtain.

But the Swede hit the white boxer by mistake. Back in the dressing room, the trainer asks him, 'Why in the name of the Prophet did you hit the white man instead of the black man?' The Swede replies, 'I bane color blind.'[161] The story ends there. (Joe Gans went on to become world lightweight champion.)

It is not surprising that in 1916 a young boxing fan such as Hemingway would have thought to write of a set-up against a black boxer. The previous year, Jack Johnson had finally been defeated by Willard, and soon afterwards he began to claim it was a set-up. Hemingway never commented directly on this fight, or indeed on Johnson's career, but his subsequent fiction repeatedly drew on interracial boxing for more than simply a snappy punch line. In *The Sun Also Rises* (1925), Bill Gorton returns to Paris after a trip to Vienna where he witnesses a fixed fight between a bribed black American and an unskilled local.

> Wonderful nigger. Looked like Tiger Flowers, only four times as big. All of a sudden everybody started to throw things. Not me. Nigger'd just knocked local boy down. Nigger put up his glove. Wanted to make a speech. Awful noble-looking nigger. Started to make a speech. Then local white boy hit him. Then he knocked white boy cold. Then everybody commenced to throw chairs . . . Big sporting evening.

For all his casually racist speech, Gorton is the good guy in the story, and he helps the fighter, who never gets the money owed to him, flee the enraged crowd. 'Injustice everywhere', he concludes.[162] Later in the same chapter, the two friends go off to have dinner with Jake's ex-lover, Brett (whom he notices is not wearing stockings), and her new fiancé, the 'very fit' Mike Campbell. When Mike asks, 'Isn't she a lovely piece? Don't you think so, Jake?', Bill replies, 'There's a fight tonight . . . Like to go?' The implication is that Jake, who has 'a rotten habit of picturing the bedroom scenes of my friends', wants to fight Mike.[163] Bill understands this impossible-to-realize ambition and provides an alternative outlet for his friend. Although he has to change the date to suit the novel's chronology, Hemingway makes a particular point of mentioning the names of the fighters they see in action, Charles Ledoux and Kid Francis. Once a great fighter, Ledoux was past his prime in 1925, and that night he lost 'a twelve-round decision in a furious brawl with his younger opponent'. Michael Reynolds notes that the evening confirmed Hemingway's view that 'champions never come back'; a view, which it seems, Jake was also entertaining.[164] Injustice (whether racial, economic or romantic) is indeed everywhere.

The White Hope era also informs Hemingway's 'The Light of the World' (1933), in which the teenage narrator and his friend, Tom, encounter a motley crew of late-night travellers at a railway station: 'five whores . . ., and six white men and four Indians'.[165] Among the prostitutes are two 'big' women, Alice and Peroxide, who argue about who really knew 'Steve' or 'Stanley' Ketchel (they also can't agree on the first name).[166] The cook remembers Stanley Ketchel's 1909 fight with Jack Johnson, in particular how Ketchel had floored Johnson in the twelfth round just before Johnson knocked him out.[167] Peroxide attributes Ketchel's defeat to a punch by Johnson ('the big black bastard') when Ketchel, 'the only man she ever loved', smiled at her in the audience. Alice remembers Steve Ketchel telling her she was 'a lovely piece'. They both refer continuously to Ketchel's 'whiteness' – 'I never saw a man as clean and as white and as beautiful', says Peroxide. 'White', as Walter Benn Michaels notes, 'becomes an adjective describing character instead of skin' and so Ketchel is figured as a kind of Christ-like figure, while Johnson, 'that black son of a bitch from hell', is the devil.[168] Ketchel's pseudo-divinity is suggested by such statements as 'I loved him like you love God'; 'His own father shot and killed him. Yes, by Christ, his own father'; and, of course, the title. Philip Young points out that Hemingway placed this story after 'the most pessimistic of all his stories', 'A Clean, Well-Lighted Place', in *Winner Take Nothing* 'as if the point of the story is really that the light of the world has gone out.'[169]

But there seems to be more going on under the surface of this particular iceberg. First of all, the confusion of names and facts is important, and once again, some knowledge of boxing history helps. Stanley Ketchel was not killed by his father – that was Steve Ketchel, a lightweight boxer, who never got near Johnson. Stanley was shot in 1910, by the husband of a woman with whom he was having an affair. Secondly, of all boxers, Stanley Ketchel was perhaps the most unlikely possible candidate for Redeemer. His nickname was the 'Michigan Assassin', and, according to one reporter, 'he couldn't get *enough* blood.'[170] While the prostitutes may be seeking salvation, the story that they tell is absurd. So what is going on? Howard Hannum argues that much of the dialogue between the two women 'has the quality of counterpunching', as if they are restaging Ketchel's contest against Johnson: here, the (bleached) blonde versus the heavyweight.[171] But the cook's role also needs to be considered. The discussion of whiteness begins when the narrator notices a 'white man' speaking; 'his face was white and his hands were white and thin'. The other men tease the cook about the whiteness of his hands ('he puts lemon juice on his hands') and hint that he is gay. Are these two things connected? And, if they are, what does that suggest about clean, white, beautiful Ketchel? When asked his age, Tom joins in the sexual bantering with hints at 'inversion' – 'I'm ninety-six and he's sixty-nine' – but throughout the boys remain uneasy and confused. By the end of the story, the narrator seems quite smitten with Alice ('she had the prettiest face I ever saw'). Tom notices this and says it is time to leave. The supposedly natural order of whites beating blacks, men having sex with women, and 'huge whores' being unappealing has been unsettled. When the cook asks where the boys are going, Tom replies, 'the other way from you'.

Racial and sexual ambiguities also trouble 'The Battler', one of the Nick Adams initiation stories in *In Our Time* (1922).[172] The story begins with Nick himself having just survived a battle with a brakeman on a freight train. He has been thrown off the train and lands with a scuffed knee and bruise on the face, of which he is rather proud – 'He wished he could see it' – but he is still standing. 'He was all right.' Nick then ventures into another battling arena – a firelit camp which seems to be a refuge but which also turns out to be a kind of boxing ring.[173] There he encounters Ad Francis, an ex-champion prize-fighter whose bruises are more impressive, and much more disgusting, than his own.

> In the firelight Nick saw that his face was misshapen. His nose was sunken, his eyes were like slits, he had queer-shaped lips. Nick did not perceive all this at once, he only saw the man's face was queerly formed and mutilated. It was like putty in color. Dead looking in the firelight.[174]

That 'Nick did not perceive all this at once' suggests that he kept looking away. 'Don't you like my pan?' the fighter asks, revealing even worse: 'He had only one ear. It was thickened and tight against the side of his head. Where the other one should have been there was a stump.' Although Nick is 'a little sick', he counters Ad's pugnacious assertions with gusto:

> 'It must have made him [the brakeman] feel good to bust you,' the man
>     said seriously.
> 'I'll bust him.' . . .
> All you kids are tough.'
> 'You got to be tough,' Nick said.
> 'That's what I said.'

Nick's pleasure at establishing a rapport with a fellow battler is short-lived, however. Ad, he discovers, is unstable ('crazy'), and depends on his companion Bugs to stop him battling. When Ad tries to start a fight with Nick, in 'an ugly parody of a boxing match', Bugs intervenes by knocking him out with a stick from behind in a manner that recalls 'A Matter of Color'.[175] Colour is also important here as Nick is obviously startled by the fact that Bugs is black, and makes a great deal of his 'negro's voice', the 'negro way' he walks, and his 'long nigger's legs'. Although it has been argued that the story reveals Hemingway's racism, these almost compulsively repeated epithets (like those describing whiteness in 'The Light of the World') seem to be Nick's as he struggles to understand the relationship between the two men. White prize-fighters, after all, were not supposed to have black friends. Bugs tells Nick a story about Ad which adds to his confusion. Ad had a woman manager, and it was always being 'written up in the papers all about brothers and sisters and how she loved her brother and how he loved his sister, and then they got married in New York and that made a lot of unpleasantness'. Nick vaguely remembers this, but then Bugs adds, 'of course they wasn't really brother and sister no more than a rabbit, but there was a lot of people didn't like it either way'. Bugs repeatedly stresses how 'awful good looking' the woman was, and how she 'looked enough like him to be twins'. Some have read this admiring comment (along with the description of Ad's face as 'queerly formed' and his lips as 'queer shaped') as a suggestion that

the two men may be lovers.[176] Less directly, like 'The Light of the World', the story slides anxiously between taboos – incest becomes homosexuality becomes miscegenation.

Interracial fighting provided a dramatic subject for many popular novels during this period, including Louis Hémon's *Battling Malone, Pugiliste* (1925), Alin Laubreaux's *Mulatto Johnny* (1931), and Joseph Moncure March's *The Set-Up* (1928). Starkly contrasting woodcuts depicting white and black fighters – whether expressionist in style (*The Set-Up)* or vaguely cubist (*Battling Malone*) – provided vivid illustrations (illus. 84 and illus. 85).[177] Joseph Moncure March's novels translated the exciting underbelly of twenties America into verse: *The Wild Party* deals with prohibition and *The Set-Up* with prize-fighting and the Jack Johnson story. *The Set-Up*'s protagonist Pansy is a middleweight who 'had the stuff, but his skin was brown; / And he never got a chance at the middleweight crown.' Finally, it seems, he will get a shot at the title, but then 'the brass-knuckled hand of the law / Hung a hot one

84
Woodcut from Joseph Moncure March, *The Set-Up* (1931 edition).

on Pansy's jaw.' Pansy is charged with bigamy and serves five years in prison. When he gets out he gradually rebuilds his career and finally gets a fight with a white boxer called Sailor. It is a set-up (Pansy's meant to take a fall) but no one has told him, thinking he'll lose anyway.

85
Clément Serveau, woodcut from Louis Hémon, *Battling Malone, Pugiliste* (1931).

His face was blank;
Grim in repose:
And what he was thinking
God only knows.
Those lynx-like eyes,
That skull without hair
Gave him a savage,
Menacing air.
He made you think
Of the missing link.
He looked like something
To catch and cage:
Like something that belonged
In a Jungle Age.[178]

After winning the fight, Pansy learns about the set-up. He tries to escape the gangsters but running away finds himself in the subway where he is hit by a train. In 1949 March's book was, loosely, to form the basis of a powerful film noir of the same title. The film changes many things, including the race of its protagonist. In 1928, however, stories of the Jungle Age were still popular.

Another popular work which drew on the Johnson myth was Mae West's 1930 novel, *The Constant Sinner*. It tells the story of a ruthless (yet not unappealing) 'lady of pleasure', Babe Gordon, and her adventures in the New York of the 1920s. One of the first things we learn about Babe is that, 'Every man she looked at she sized up as a fighter would an opponent.'[179] Her opponents are, first a white prizefighter, the Bearcat, then a black gangster, Money Johnson, and finally, an upper class white businessman, Baldwin. Babe's fighting talk seems to come easily to West, whose father was a boxer and who herself had affairs with numerous white and black fighters.[180]

What makes *The Constant Sinner* revealing of its time is not simply its boxing figuration of the battle between the sexes but, more specifically, the way it uses boxing to talk about interracial sexual relations. Bearcat, dubbed 'the salvation of our race' by one female admirer, does not hold the colour line and is described fighting Harlem Joe who 'moved like a panther and endeared himself to coloured worship by a famous watermelon grin'.

> The two contrasting bodies came to the ring centre, clasped gloves and received final instructions. The human throng pulled up taut and tense, to feast upon this supreme battle of black and white. The gong rang!
>
> The two bodies rushed at each other and became a whirlpool of stabbing, slashing arms, swirling like angry foam in boiling rapids, now white, now muddy black – a gush of red blood in the foam – the white form of Bearcat sank to the canvas.

Babe, who has already 'ruined more than one promising white hope', eventually leaves Bearcat for Money Johnson and a Harlem which West describes as 'the pool of sex, where all colours are blended, all bloods mingled'. Johnson, whose 'magnificent body, lynx-eyes, and pearly-white grin had brought the women of Harlem crawling to him', has eyes only for white Babe. Like his namesake Jack, 'he craved white women. He wanted the whitest and most beautiful, and so he fell for Babe Gordon'. The novel ends with Johnson being shot by the jealous Baldwin and a gullible Bearcat agreeing to take the blame. He of course gets off (in what some have seen as a parody of D. W. Griffith's *Birth of a Nation*) as the prosecutor argues that he was a hero for defending his wife against 'the low, lustful, black beast'. Baldwin's attraction to Babe is presented as entirely dependent on her association with Johnson. At the novel's end, when he finally has Babe (at least temporarily) he 'cannot avoid thinking of Babe's white body and Johnson's black body, darkness mating with dawn . . . He has Babe now to himself. He is happy. But the black and white pattern is indelibly woven into the tapestry of his memory.'[181]

The sex appeal of Jack Johnson, and black men like him, is just one of many targets in Wallace Thurman's bitterly funny satire of the Harlem Renaissance, *Infants of the Spring* (1932). Lucille tells the protagonist, Ray, 'one of the black hopes of Negro literature', that she will 'never go to bed with any white man . . . because I'd never be sure that I wasn't doing it just because he was white'. In fact Lucille feels almost white herself, as she justifies her infatuation for a painter called Bull, 'the personification of what the newspaper headlines are pleased to call a burly Negro'. The women in his paintings have 'pugilistic biceps'. 'I suppose I find the same thing in Bull that white women claim to find in a man like Jack Johnson,' concedes Lucille, 'That's the price I pay, evidently, for becoming civilized.'[182] Ray is in love with Lucille and later 'snaps' that Bull 'is so afraid of the white man that his only recourse is to floor one at every opportunity and on any pretext'. Indeed when Bull finds out that Lucille is pregnant, his response is to 'sock her in the jaw, and stalk away'. Ray helps her to get an abortion and she promises to lay off 'virile men . . . at least . . . for the purpose of procreation'. Bull, she concedes, was simply 'an experiment I had to make'.[183]

Interracial fighting is again linked to interracial sex in William Faulkner's *Absalom, Absalom!* (1936), which explores the history and legacy of American slavery from 1807 until 1910, the year in which Johnson defeated Jeffries. The novel opens with the narrative of a survivor of the Civil War, Rosa Coldfield. Rosa's sister Ellen married Thomas Sutpen, a man of poor origins and great social ambition, who has built a house in the woods with a group of 'wild Negroes'. Another of the novel's narrators, Mr. Compson, compares Sutpen's social awkwardness to that of John L. Sullivan 'having taught himself painfully and tediously to do the schottische, having drilled himself and drilled himself in secret until he now believed it no longer necessary to count the music's beat, say'. But having gone to great lengths to become the perfect Mississippi gentleman, ensconced in 'baronial splendor', Sutpen tends to slip back into his old ways, 'some opposite of respectability' in which strict racial segregation does not play a part. Rosa tells the story of Ellen watching a fight in Sutpen's stables:

> Yes, Ellen and those two children alone in that house twelve miles from town, and down there in the stable a hollow square of faces in the lantern light, the white faces on three sides, the black ones on the fourth, and in the centre two of the wild Negroes fighting, naked, not as white men fight, with rules and weapons, but as Negroes fight to hurt one another quick bad . . .

Ellen, Rosa says, 'accepted' this – 'this', she thinks, 'is all'. But it is not all. One night she enters and sees 'not the two black beasts she had expected to see but instead a white one and a black one' – the 'grande finale'. What frightens her is not the fight but the fact that men are indistinguishable. 'Her husband and father of her children', a slave owner, cannot be told apart from the slaves, the 'wild negroes' who 'belonged to him body and soul'. Rosa uses a kind of demonic Darwinian imagery to describe the fight scene that she has not witnessed. It becomes a primeval scene, as Rosa imagines Ellen witnessing the men with their 'teeth showing': 'both naked to the waist and gouging at one another's eyes as of they should not only have been the same color, but should have been covered in fur too'. And still that is not all. First, Ellen sees that her son Henry is watching, and then, what's much worse, that her daughter, Judith is also there. A final horror comes in the observation that the pattern of 'nigger and white' is repeated in 'Judith and . . . the negro girl beside her', Clytie (Sutpen's other daughter, by a slave mother) – 'two Sutpen faces'. Ellen's terror (certainly Rosa's) – that one cannot tell black from white, or sister from brother – becomes the novel's. The doubling of Sutpen and 'the wild niggers' ('his face exactly like the Negro's') is repeated in the doubling of Judith in Clytie; the intermingling of white and black bodies in a fight once again prefigures their sexual intermingling. *There is something in the touch of flesh with flesh which abrogates, cuts sharp and straight across the devious intricate channels of decorous ordering, which enemies, as well as lovers know because it makes them both . . . let flesh touch with flesh, and watch the fall of all the eggshell shibboleth of caste and color too.*[184]

## JAMES JOYCE AND 'THAT EPOCK-MARKING EVENT'

If Jack Johnson's victories over white opponents exercised white America in various ways, they also provoked those further afield. James Joyce, it is frequently asserted, didn't like sports, and especially not violent ones. Nevertheless, in 1910, according to his brother, Stanislaus, he read the plethora of newspaper articles building up to the Johnson-Jeffries fight. Stanislaus suggests that Joyce's 'ironical comments' on nationalism in 'that epock-marking event' formed 'a rough draft' of the Keogh-Bennett fight described in the 'Cyclops' section of *Ulysses* (1922).[185] Another source was a fight between a British soldier and a

Dubliner that he saw advertised in the *Freeman's Journal*.[186] American racist ideology is thus echoed and refigured in British and Irish nationalist terms. The debts of the Harlem Renaissance to the Irish Renaissance are well documented; this incident reveals that Irish literature also owes something to black America.[187]

The Keogh-Bennett fight is first alluded to in 'Lestrygonians', when Blazes Boylan is mentioned as the trainer of Keogh and a fight promoter.[188] It gets a proper airing, however, in 'Cyclops', when, at Barney Kiernan's pub in Little Britain Street, we learn that Boylan has made a hundred pounds by spreading the rumour that Keogh was 'on the beer'. 'Cyclops' is narrated by a nameless barfly, whose opinionated commentary is interrupted periodically by a series of extravagant parodies. One of the most exuberant parodies adopts the inflated language of early nineteenth-century fight reports, and from it we learn that the 'redcoat' has had his 'right eye nearly closed' by 'Dublin's pet lamb'. We immediately think of Ulysses and Polyphemus, and indeed, Heenan and Sayers, whose commemorative print Stephen Dedalus had seen earlier in the novel. Ignoring the attempts of Leopold Bloom to change the subject, another barfly, Alf Bergan notes, in a more up-to-date pugilistic jargon, that 'Myler dusted the floor with him . . . Heenan and Sayers was only a bloody fool to it. Handed him the mother and father of a beating.'[189]

Bloom's voice in 'Cyclops' is usually heard as one at war with the 'blindness' and aggressive masculine violence of racism and nationalism. Later in the scene, he famously rejects 'force, hatred, history, all that' in favour of 'love', 'the opposite of hatred'. This is generally taken to be Joyce's view as well. According to his brother, he wrote the scene 'not to express personal bias but to associate violence and brutality with patriotism'. While I do not wish to claim that Joyce is advocating violence, I suggest that the novel's repeated allusions to boxing do more than simply update Homer. A certain latent aggression is also expressed. Just before he speaks out against force, Bloom tells the pub denizens that he too belongs to a race, 'that is hated and persecuted. Also now. This very moment. This very instant', and while he speaks he nearly burns his fingers on his cigar. Unlike Ulysses, armed with his fiery club, Bloom does not get near the eye of his Cyclops. Nevertheless, he 'put[s] up his fist'. 'Talking about injustice' like this, the force of Bloom's feeling is expressed in staccato (punchy?) phrases and even single words, quite unlike his usual eloquent and loquacious speech:

> Robbed, says he. Plundered. Insulted. Persecuted. Taking what belongs to us by right. At this very moment, says he, putting up his fist, sold by auction off in Morocco like slaves or cattle.

Before talking about the 'opposite of hatred', the narrator tells us that Bloom 'collapses all of a sudden, twisting around all the opposite, as limp as a wet rag'. But this second Bloom does not completely displace the first. Bloom may be finally seem a 'wet rag', advocating love as he runs away from a flying biscuit tin, but something remains of the man who raises his fist in angry defiance.[190] How does one choose between two rather absurd clichés?

As the day goes on, Bloom himself seems uncertain about what role in which to cast himself.[191] On the beach, at little later, he ponders the incident: 'Got my own back there. Drunken ranters what I said about his God made him wince. Mistake to hit back. Or? No. Ought to go home and laugh at themselves . . . Suppose he hit me. Look at it other way round. Not so bad then. Perhaps not to hurt he meant.' In his conversations with Stephen in the cabshelter that night, Bloom continues to vacillate between self-congratulation on his cool and rational response, and anxiety about his lack of physicality. He tells the story of his encounter with the Citizen twice. In his first version he presents himself as 'much injured but on the whole eventempered' and assures Stephen that 'A soft answer turns away wrath'.

> I resent violence or intolerance in any shape or form . . . It's a patent absurdity to hate people because they live around the corner and speak another vernacular, so to speak . . . All those wretched quarrels, in his humble opinion, stirring up bad blood – bump of combativeness or gland of some kind, erroneously supposed to be about a punctilio of honour and a flag – were very largely a question of the money question . . .

This is partly said to reassure Stephen who has just survived a fight in 'Circe', but it is also serves as self-reassurance. Twenty pages later, the narrator returns to the subject, and gives it a rather different gloss:

> He, though often considerably misunderstood and the least pugnacious of mortals, be it repeated, departed from his customary habit to give him (metaphorically) one in the gizzard though so far as politics themselves were concerned, he was only too conscious of the casualties inevitably resulting from propaganda and displays of mutual animosity and the misery and suffering it entailed as a foregone conclusion on fine young fellows, chiefly, destruction of the fittest, in a word.[192]

At the start of this retelling at least, Bloom is associated with linguistic pugnacity and the hard 'vernacular' of his enemy. As the sentence proceeds, the narrative voice reconnects Bloom to his customary pacifism and its accompanying verbosity. If the clichés of pugnacity give readers (metaphorically) 'one in the gizzard', the clichés of pacifism put them (metaphorically) to sleep.[193]

Bloom's equivocal interpretation of the events in the pub is revealed again in 'Ithaca'. As tension mounted in the pub that afternoon, Bloom had started listing Jews: 'Mendelssohn was a jew and Karl Marx and Mercadante and Spinoza. And the Saviour was a jew and his father was a jew. Your God.' In his third list of 'anapocryphal illustrious sons of the law and children of a selected or rejected race' in 'Ithaca', Bloom again includes Mendelssohn and Spinoza, informing us of their professions (composer and philosopher respectively), but now he adds to their company Daniel Mendoza, the London pugilist credited with having introduced boxing into Ireland, and Ferdinand Lassalle, who, we are told, managed to combine the professions of 'reformer' and 'duellist'.[194] Fighters, it now seems, can be good Jews too. But this is not the last word on the subject. At the end of the chapter, when Bloom relates his day to Molly in bed, he does not mention the 'altercation' in the pub at all. He has not, despite all these rehearsals, been able to settle on a version of events that pleases him, or, more to the point, that he thinks will please Molly.[195]

Bloom's aspirations to get bigger and stronger are largely informed by Eugen Sandow's *Strength and How to Obtain It* (1897).[196] Sandow was a music hall muscleman rather than a sports hero, and his books were aimed at commercial travellers and other city workers like Bloom.[197] They offered a modern metropolitan kind of manliness distinct from the archaic nationalist version touted by the Citizen. Yet Sandow's presence is not unrelated to themes of injustice, revenge, or, indeed, the Cyclops. While the first part of Sandow's book is a conventional manual of exercises and measurement charts, part two – 'Incidents of My Professional Career' – reads at times like a Horatio Alger novel, for each 'incident' is most importantly a step onward and upward. One step involves the 'defeat' of two bodybuilding rivals, Samson and Cyclops. Sandow is at pains to stress that he is a small man and that 'in evening dress there was nothing . . . specially remarkable about my appearance. But when I took off my coat [to fight Cyclops] and the people could see my muscular development, the tone of indifference changed immediately to surprise and curiosity.' Sandow lets it be known that instead of exhibiting himself, he could have been a boxer. But although it would have been the 'shorter road to wealth', he was not tempted. 'No man', he concludes, 'can be a prize fighter and remain a gentleman'.[198]

Boxing, or at least street-fighting with pretensions to boxing, finally connects Stephen and Bloom in 'Circe', where Homer's underworld is refigured as a phantasmagoric vaudeville show. 'Nighttown' is a grotesque place where sex and violence come together, where a bawd sells 'maidenhead' for ten shillings and armless 'loiterers' in 'paintspeckled hats' can be found 'flop[ped] wrestling, growling in maimed sodden playfight.'[199] Earlier in the day, the romantic Stephen had briefly identified with Heenan and Sayers performing before a staring audience in a print he saw in a shop window. In 'Nighttown', when a drunken British soldier hits him square in the face, he is suddenly forced to become a participant rather than a spectator. Could there be a more definite victory for what Joyce, elsewhere, praised as the solid materialism of 'sudden reality' over 'romanticism'?[200]

An important difference between the two encounters is that the heroic and popular mid-nineteenth century pugilism that the Heenan vs. Sayers fight represented has been replaced by Queensberry-rules sparring, associated particularly with the army and with public schools – English violence disguised as

English honour. According to Stanislaus Joyce, his brother 'detested rugby, boxing and wrestling,' which he had to take part in at school, and 'which he considered a training not in self-control, as the English pretend, but in violence and brutality.'[201] In *Stephen Hero*, Joyce had described the 'system of hardy brutality' with which 'Anglo-Saxon educators' tried to 'cure' the 'fantastic ideal[ism]' of youth and had bemoaned the ugly 'Saxon slang' that accompanied such cures.[202] In 'Circe', the Saxon slang of 'biffing' and 'blighters', the basis of what Bernard Shaw had described as 'the vast propaganda of pugnacity in modern fiction', is as much the subject of mockery as the brutality itself.[203]

Like a good Homeric hero, Stephen drunkenly extends his hospitality to Privates Compton and Carr, the two red-coated British soldiers that he runs into on the street, stating that, although 'uninvited', they are his 'guests'. Nevertheless, that's not their fault. 'History is to blame'. Thinking that Stephen is insulting both Carr's girl, Cissy Caffrey ('faithful . . . although only a shilling whore') and Edward VII, Private Compton tells his friend to 'biff him one' – 'Go it, Harry. Do him one in the eye . . . he doesn't half want a thick ear, the blighter.'[204] Stephen, meanwhile, 'a bit sprung' and so especially facetious, mocks 'the noble art of self-pretence', misquotes Swift, and rather effetely complains about his hand, which 'hurts me slightly'. 'Personally,' he says, 'I detest action.' That may be so, but, as his friend Lynch points out, 'he likes dialectic'. In the sequence that follows, Edward VII appears as the referee – 'We have come here to witness a clean straight fight and we heartily wish both men the best of good luck.' As the fight begins, Stephen imaginatively transforms it, using the traditional imagery of both cataclysm and crucifixion, into a grand and heroic battle. But Private Carr brings the battle to a swift and bathetic end. Carr *'rushes Stephen, fists outstretched, and strikes him in the face. Stephen totters, collapses, falls stunned. He lies prone, his face to the sky, his hat rolling to the wall. Bloom follows and picks it up.'* As in the Heenan-Sayers and the Keogh-Bennett fights, the crowd breaks through, and chaos descends, but there are no firm allegiances. The 'hag' and 'bawd' switch sides repeatedly; the 'quarrelling knot' of the Irish, it seems, are too busy fighting among themselves to be concerned with the slapstick main event.[205]

By the time we reach this scene in 'Circe', it becomes clear that a pattern is being presented. All things pass and, 'being humus the same roturns', wrote Joyce in *Finnegans Wake* (1939).[206] In 'Wandering Rocks', Stephen sees an image of Heenan vs. Sayers in Farnborough in 1860; a few pages later, Patrick Dignam sees a poster advertising Bennett vs. Keogh, and thinks about the 1897 Carson City contest between Corbett and Fitzsimmons. In 'Cyclops', the connection between Farnborough in 1860 and Dublin in 1904 is reinforced (and, if we read Stanislaus Joyce, we can also make a connection to Reno in 1910). These discrete boxing matches all feature a small man taking on a big man, and an Irishman (broadly defined) taking on a British man.[207] They also recall the battles faced repeatedly by Ulysses on his journey home to Ithaca. Joyce's critics have, I would suggest, rather overplayed his rejection of such battles. Stanislaus Joyce recalled that his brother first encountered Homer through Lamb's *Adventures of Ulysses* and when 'asked to say which of the heroes they admired most', chose Ulysses 'in reaction against the general admiration of the heftier, muscle-bound dealers of Homeric blows'. Richard Ellmann, meanwhile, rather romantically maintained that 'Joyce makes his Ulysses a man who is not physically a fighter, but whose mind is unsubduable.' Ulysses, while certainly peace-loving, and neither 'hefty' nor 'muscle-bound', hardly avoided adept and well-placed 'Homeric blows'.[208] Bloom, and indeed Stephen, are certainly less willing or able fighters, but this is not to say that thoughts of fighting do not preoccupy them and that their fists are never clenched or raised. While parodying its posturing and patois, Joyce relished the dramatic possibilities of boxing. In all the many ways it unfolds, *Ulysses* is also, some of the time, a boxing novel.

Boxing images come less directly in *Finnegans Wake* (as does everything else), yet one of Joyce's many allusive patterns there links back to Johnson. The opening chapter of the novel introduces the comic strip characters of Mutt and Jute, representing the battle of 1014 between the Irish and Danes on the field of Clontarf. Mutt is the Irishman; Jute, the invader. Communication between the two is impossible – Mutt is 'jeffmute', Jute is 'haudibble'. The duo reappear in many guises throughout the novel – Butt and Taff; Bett and Tipp; Muta and Juva - as variants on the quarrelling brothers, Shem and Shaun, whose endless battles and reconciliations propel it forward. As Muta puts it, 'when we shall have acquired unification we shall pass on to diversity and when we shall have passed on to diversity we shall have acquired the instinct to combat and when we shall have acquired the instinct of combat we shall pass back to the spirit of appeasement'.[209]

Mutt and Jeff originate in a cartoon strip by H. C. (Bud) Fisher which first appeared under the title 'A. Mutt' on the racing page of the *San Francisco Chronicle* in 1907. Mutt first encountered Jeff on 27 March 1908, a 'sacred moment in our cultural development' remarked Gilbert Seldes. The encounter took place 'during the days before one of Jim Jeffries' fights'.

> It was as Mr Mutt passed the asylum walls that a strange creature confided to the air the notable remark that he himself was Jeffries. Mutt rescued the little gentleman and named him Jeff. In gratitude Jeff daily submits to indignities which might otherwise seem intolerable.[210]

Jeff's allegiance to Jeffries reached fruition in 1910 when he and Mutt resolve to see him fight Jack Johnson. Fisher devoted weeks of the strip to stories of the friends' mishaps as they travel to Reno, try to get seats, and then, with difficulty, try to get home again (illus. 86).

Dan Schiff suggests that the pair may have appealed to James Augustine Joyce because their names, Augustus Mutt and James Jeffries, represent a struggle within his own name and between two sides of his personality.[211] But Joyce may also have enjoyed the comical contrast the couple made – beanpole Mutt

86
Bud Fisher, 'A. Mutt',
1910: ' Mutt secures
a ticket to the
Jeffries–Johnson
fight'.

and stocky little Jeff – and the physical violence of their encounters. The last panel
was often reserved for a knockout. Jeff, having driven Mutt to distraction, is
usually the recipient; he is depicted conked or punched in the head, sometimes
accompanied by the word 'Pow!' A similar resolution can be found in the 'Night-
lessons' chapter of *Finnegans Wake*. In this 'drame' of 'caricatures', Shaun (the
Mutt of the two) becomes fed up with the boastful Shem, and 'floors' him.[212] The
'countinghands' of a referee suggest that a knockout has been accomplished, and
then go on to conduct Wagner. Shem forgives his 'bloater', and the chapter ends
with a catalogue of topics for the brothers' lessons, which range from 'When is a
Pun not a Pun?' to 'Do you approve of our Existing Parliamentary System?' to
'Compare the fistic styles of Jimmy Wilde and Jack Sharkey.'[213]

    The chapter takes the form of a central text, with marginal comments (from
the two brothers) on either side, and footnotes (from their sister, Izzy).[214] In the
final section, Shem (on the Right) is silent, but Shaun provides classical and
biblical parallels to the lesson themes. Flyweight Jimmy Wilde and heavyweight
Jack Sharkey are matched with Castor and Pollux, the brothers who encounter
Amycus in Theocritus' *Idylls*.[215] The names of the fighters may change, but
the schoolboy sport of light vs. large, and the philosophical sport of thesis vs.
antithesis, continue. 'Is a game over? The game goes on.'[216]

# 7

# Sport of the Future

Although he had fulfilled the stated brief by defeating Jack Johnson, Jess Willard was not the Great White Hope that so many had longed for.[1] Willard was large, slow and uncharismatic, and the public did not warm to their new white champion. It would be another four years before the White Hope of fantasy would emerge, realized in the tanned wiry body of Jack Dempsey. The Golden Grin would be laid to rest by a scowl.

Born into a poor Irish-American family in Manassa, Colorado, Dempsey was initially a fairly mediocre boxer, fighting for $100 a time in Western bars and living sporadically as a hobo. He struck lucky when he met up with manager Jack Kearns, who carefully groomed him for a shot at the championship. Kearns ensured that Dempsey only encountered opponents whom he could easily knock out, and that 'he spent nearly as much time making the rounds of newspaper offices as he did fighting'. Between them Kearns and promoter Tex Rickard carefully cultivated the image of the 'Manassa Mauler' as 'America's perfect fighting man'.[2] They knew that in the post-Johnson era (and even more so in the Klan-dominated twenties), there would be no money to be made in matching Dempsey against black opponents such as Harry Wills who might actually beat him. It made financial sense to maintain the colour line.[3]

By 1918 Damon Runyon, a syndicated columnist for the Hearst newspapers, was urging Willard to meet the new challenger. On 4 July 1919 (nine years after Johnson beat Jeffries), Dempsey fought Willard before 'a shirt-sleeved frontier mob' in Toledo, Ohio.[4] Willard was 6 foot 7 inches tall and weighed 245 pounds. Dempsey, 6 inches shorter and 55 pounds lighter, was definitely the underdog, and many thought the fight likely to be a poor affair. A sceptical Ring Lardner quipped: 'I guess I got those there Toledo Blues, / About this fight I simply can't enthuse.'[5]

Nevertheless, Dempsey defeated Willard in three rounds, with what boxing historians agree was an extraordinary excess of violence. Peter Heller describes the fight as 'one of the most savage in boxing history', and Joyce Carol Oates argues that Dempsey's ring style, 'swift, pitiless, always direct and percussive . . . changed American boxing forever'.[6] According to Paul Gallico, Dempsey was 'never a good boxer and had little or no defense. His protection was aggression.'[7]

That aggression was fêted and fetishized from the start.[8] This is Damon Runyon's gory account of the fallen Willard:

> At the feet of the gargantuan pugilist was a dark spot which was slowly widening on the brown canvas as it was replaced by the drip-drip-drip-drip of blood from the man's wounds. He was flecked with red from head to foot. The flesh on his enormous limbs shook like custard. He was like a man who had just been pulled from the wreck of an automobile, or railroad train.[9]

In his 1950 teach-yourself guide to 'explosive punching and aggressive defence', *Championship Fighting*, Dempsey himself recalled the fight, preferring to describe Willard as the victim of 'a premature mine blast' rather than of a car or rail accident:

> I won the ring's most coveted title by stopping a man much larger and stronger than I was . . . I blasted him into helplessness by exploding my body-weight against him . . . My body-weight was moving like lightning, and I was exploding that weight terrifically against the giant.[10]

Dempsey's persona was complicated. First of all, he was Jack the Giant Killer, an image that Kearns and Rickard were keen to exploit, matching him with another sluggish giant, Luis Angel Firpo, 'the Wild Bull of the Pampas', in 1923. But it was not merely success against all odds that Dempsey represented; it was the instant success of the knockout blow. The step-by-step rise of a Horatio Alger was old-fashioned; the impatient Twenties favoured the 'cocainizing punch'.[11] And there was still more to the Dempsey image. In the passage above, he litters his description with metaphors drawn from his days working in the Colorado mines, and he was often promoted as a rugged Westerner. Kearns ensured he tanned his face and upper body before the Willard fight, to give him the appearance, according to Runyon, of a 'saddle-colored demon'.[12] In the years that followed this ruggedness was carefully cultivated. Runyon coined the name 'Manassa Mauler', and ghost-wrote Dempsey's biography, 'A Tale of Two Fists', for serialization in the Hearst papers in 1919. Runyon, who had also grown up in Colorado, made much of Dempsey's early days free-riding the railroads.[13] When, in 1921, Dempsey knocked out the European light heavyweight champion, Georges Carpentier, the press described the victory as one for the frontier spirit (and old bare-knuckle days) against decadent European modernity (Carpentier, who liked to talk of the 'psychology of boxing', was dubbed the 'Orchid Man'[14]). Gallico's characterization of Dempsey as someone who had been schooled in 'the hobo jungles, bar-rooms, and mining camps of the West' was typical:

> Where Dempsey learned to fight, there were no rounds, rest intervals, gloves, referees, or attending seconds. There are no draws and no

decisions in rough and tough fighting. You had to win. If you lost you went to the hospital or to the undertaking parlor.[15]

Dempsey's supposed affinities with the spirit of the old frontier appealed to 1920s urban America precisely because, as Roderick Nash puts it, at that time 'the self-reliant rugged individual . . . seemed on the verge of becoming as irrelevant as the covered wagon'.[16]

The major difference between American boxing before 1920 and afterwards, was that it was now legal, and once legal it became big business. At the heart of that business was Madison Square Garden, which in 1925 assumed its third incarnation on the corner of 49th and 50th Street on Eighth Avenue.[17] When Max Schmeling arrived in the United States in 1929, he noted that 'the Garden and the Hearst Corporation took turns calling the shots'.[18] The Garden, as it quickly became known, was huge and intimidating. According to Jerry Doyle, the narrator of Hemingway's 1927 'Fifty Grand', the walk from the entrance to the ring 'looked like a half a mile'.[19]

This difference between small club illegal boxing and the new legal sport is strikingly apparent if we compare George Bellows's *Stag at Sharkey's* (1909) and his 1920s paintings of legitimate, high-profile boxing, *Ringside Seats* (1924) and *Dempsey and Firpo* (1924). Gone is the grotesque male intimacy of spectators and fighters, and with it, a dark, expressionist claustrophobia. In their place, Bellows depicts a brightly lit space, vibrant with colour but rather flat. The paintings have more in common with contemporary magazine illustrations of well-dressed men and women than with his earlier paintings. *Dempsey and Firpo* presents the famous moment in their 1923 fight when Firpo sent Dempsey flying into the ringside typewriters (illus. 87).[20]

The 1920s are often recalled as a golden age of sport, but it was an age of mass consumption rather than mass participation. Some thought that this was a very bad thing. In their 1929 sociological case study of Middletown, the Lynds noted that modern leisure was now 'mainly spent sitting down'.[21] 'A few play,' elaborated Stuart Chase, 'while the rest of us shout, clap hands . . . crush in our neighbours' hats, and get what thrill we may from passive rather than active participation.' For Chase, this was sport 'at one remove'.[22]

Worse still was listening to the radio ('sport at two removes'). While Jack Johnson's fights had been available to national audiences only by way of reports telegraphed to the newspapers, and illegal films, radio brought sport to all. Radio broadcasts of fights began in 1920 and the first title fight to be broadcast live on the radio was the 1921 Dempsey–Carpentier match. In Buenos Aires in 1923 crowds gathered in the home of nine-year-old Julio Cortázar to listen to the radio describe Firpo's defeat in New York (afterwards, he later wrote, 'there was weeping and brutal indignation, followed by humiliated melancholy that was almost colonial'.) In anticipation of Dempsey's 1926 fight against Tunney, Halperin's Department Store acquired the first radio in Fitzgerald, Georgia; Lois Garrison recalls that 'the whole town' gathered to listen to speakers rigged up in the

neighbouring streets.[23] Joe Louis grew up listening to Dempsey's fights on the radio, and the radio would bring Louis's fights to many more during the 1930s.[24]

    The sports pages of national newspapers (first introduced by Hearst in 1895) also played an important part in promoting and popularizing sport. Research by the American Society of Newspaper Editors in 1929 revealed that one out of four readers bought a paper primarily because of its sports page. The editors voted Jack Dempsey the 'greatest stimulation to circulation in 20 years'.[25] The press, and in particular the Hearst newspapers, saw to it that 'you knew Dempsey better than a member of your own family'.[26] During his seven-year reign as champion, Dempsey entertained readers with a divorce and remarriage to a Hollywood starlet, and a trial for draft evasion (he was acquitted on the grounds that he needed to provide financial support to his mother and wife). Boxing itself played a relatively small part in the story; in seven years, Dempsey only defended his title six times.[27]

    The flourishing of the sports pages is also associated with a golden age of American sports writing. In 1922, Nat Fleischer founded *The Ring*, still regarded as the leading boxing magazine, while the sports pages of the daily papers featured writers such as Damon Runyon, Ring Lardner and Paul Gallico, all of whom eventually moved successfully from (rather literary) sports reporting to

87
George Bellows,
*Dempsey and Firpo*,
1924.

212

(rather sporty) fiction. Although they detailed the minutiae of contemporary sports events, these writers never took sport entirely seriously, and certainly not solemnly. This is Heywood Broun, on Dempsey vs. Carpentier:

> [Carpentier's] head was back and his eyes and his smile flamed as he crawled through the ropes. And he gave some curious flick to his bathrobe as he turned to meet the applause. Until that very moment we had been for Dempsey, but suddenly we found ourselves up on our feet making silly noises. We shouted 'Carpentier! Carpentier! Carpentier!' and forgot even to be ashamed of our pronunciation.[28]

Broun's report exemplifies what sociologist Leo Lowenthal identified as a distinctive 1920s 'language of directness'. At the very moment when 'modern institutions of mass communication' were promising 'total coverage', he argued, journalists increased their use of 'you' or 'we' to create a compensatory sense of intimacy between writer and reader.[29] Boxing, perhaps, lent itself more readily then most sports to the language of directness. In 1924, *Punch* cartoonist William Low suggested a comparable intimacy between fighter and spectator (illus. 56). Low's spectator takes 'sympathy' to absurd lengths and eventually knocks himself out. Broun's article, more of which is quoted below, goes on to compare the Dempsey–Carpentier fight to Greek tragedy. Lowenthal claimed that such allusions were designed to confer 'pseudo-sanctity and pseudo-safety on the futile affairs of mass culture', and complained that they were mixed up with 'slang and colloquial speech'.[30] But this seems to miss the tone and the point. There is no 'linguistic confusion'. Like flash language in the 1820s, prose such as Broun's (and Lardner's, Gallico's and Runyon's) confidently celebrates its ability to embrace both high and low and to make a joke of either or both. Knowing cheerfulness was the tone of the 'boxing scribes'.[31]

It was also, largely, the tone of the cinema. 'Suddenly the mid-1920's movie theater became a very happy place', notes William Everson. 'Comedy was everywhere, and in all forms.'[32] Boxing movies were no exception and numerous comedies debunked the masculine posturing of the ring. Hal Roach wrote and produced many of them, including *The Champeen* (1923), Laurel and Hardy's *The Battle of the Century* (1927), and Joe and Chubby's *Boxing Gloves* (1929); others include Mack Sennett's *Scarum Much* (1924). One of the most successful boxing comedies was an independently made series *The Leather Pushers* (1922–4), starring Reginald Denny, a former Royal Flying Corps heavyweight champion. Now largely forgotten, in the mid-twenties Denny was 'Universal's most important star, and next to Chaplin, the highest-paid Englishman in pictures'. Denny was also responsible for introducing 'some comedy ideas' into what he called 'the hokum' of an adaptation of Jack London's boxing story, *The Abysmal Brute* (1923).[33]

For Paul Gallico, sports editor and columnist for the *Daily News*, the 1920s were a time of 'great, innocent ballyhoo', but for many others, particularly those on the left, the cocktail of sport, movies and the tabloid press made for a dangerous mass opiate.[34] Newspapers in the twenties, Robert K. Murray argued, moved away from the Progressive agenda of the pre-war years and 'began to view American life not so much as a political and economic struggle but as a hilarious merry-go-round of sport, crime, and sex'. A growing obsession with 'the antics . . . of Dempsey and Babe Ruth' may, he suggested, have 'helped take the nation's mind off bolshevism', both at home and abroad.[35] 'It was characteristic of the Jazz Age that it had no interest in politics at all', declared Scott Fitzgerald in 1931. That same year (one of the worst of the Depression) Frederick Allen Lewis published a history of 'the Coolidge Prosperity' and argued that one of its most 'striking characteristics . . . was the unparalleled rapidity and unanimity with which millions of men and women turned their attention, their talk, and their emotional interest upon a series of tremendous trifles – a heavyweight boxing-match, a murder trial, a new automobile, a transatlantic flight'. Lewis dubbed this era 'the Ballyhoo Years'.[36]

The changing nature of American newspapers and the celebrity cult of sportsmen and movie stars are recurring preoccupations in John Dos Passos's trilogy of novels, *USA* (1930–36). Each novel breaks up its narrative with a series of 'Newsreel' sections, collages of undated newspaper headlines, juxtaposed for connection and contrast. One such juxtaposition, in *Nineteen Nineteen*, involves Dempsey. There is something appalling, Dos Passos suggests, about the ease with which readers can slip from 'EARTHQUAKE IN ITALY DEVESTATES LIKE WAR' to 'DEMPSEY KNOCKS OUT WILLARD IN THIRD ROUND'.[37] Dempsey himself, as we have already seen, was only too willing to compare the effects of his pugnacity to catastrophe on a grand scale.

If the media attention given to Dempsey's 1919 fight against Willard was lavish, it was nothing compared to that generated two years later, when he took on 'gorgeous' Georges Carpentier. The 4 July Jersey City fight attracted 80,000 spectators and is remembered as the first million-dollar gate. The stark contrast between the two protagonists, arranged with great care once again by Rickard, succeeded in creating a journalistic frenzy. Carpentier agreed to the mis-match (he was considerably lighter than Dempsey) knowing that he could earn a lot in America – in Hollywood as well as in the ring.[38] Carpentier's fan base included European intellectuals such as George Bernard Shaw, Arnold Bennett and François Mauriac. Shaw and Bennett had fulsomely described his 1919 victory over Englishman Joe Beckett, while Mauriac thought Carpentier both as 'one of those graceful Apollos slightly grazed by the pick in the process of their ex-humation' and 'the type of honest man dear to Pascal'.[39] Sophisticated New Yorkers were also enchanted by the Frenchman. Heywood Broun described the fight as 'the finest tragic performance in the lives of ninety thousand persons'. It was, he joshed, 'sport for art's sake', comparable even to the work of Eugene O'Neill, 'the white hope of the American drama'. 'None of the crowds in Greece who went to somewhat more beautiful stadia in search of Euripides ever saw the spirit of tragedy more truly presented.'[40] Ring Lardner was less sentimental. He believed that the fight should never have taken place and satirized it ruthlessly in a short story called 'The Battle of the Century'. The Dempsey character, Jim Dugan, complains about his training: 'I've got to show the boys I'm working so they won't think it's a farce. Like it wasn't a farce already!' The real winner, the narrator notes, was Dugan's manager Charley Riggs (based on Tex Rickard), who not only 'came out with a profit for himself and his backer of something like half a million . . . but the way he handled it put him in a class by himself as a promoter. The big fights to come will be staged by Charley or they won't be big fights.'[41]

After the 1923 Firpo contest, Dempsey did not fight for three years. Instead he went to Hollywood, travelled in Europe, and retained a high profile through the gossip columns and product endorsements. By 1926, however, it was time to make some more money, and Rickard's next 'big fight' matched Dempsey against Gene Tunney as part of Philadelphia's sesquicentennial celebration. Marketing was again a crucial factor, and in choosing Dempsey's opponent, Rickard repeated the formula that had proved so profitable in the Carpentier fight. Dempsey was once again portrayed as the Western 'brute' and 'a slacker', while Tunney, a former us marine and aspiring Greenwich Village intellectual, was clean-living patriotism personified. The Associated Press made a great deal of the fact that Samuel Butler's *The Way of All Flesh* had been spotted on Tunney's bedside table.[42] The public personae of the two men were reinforced in their ring styles. Dempsey was an aggressive slugger, famous for his knockout blows; Tunney, a defensive counterpuncher, who gradually wore his opponents down. Dempsey was instinctual, a 'natural', a born 'killer'; Tunney a 'synthetic' boxer, a student of 'ring science'.[43] While this was a perennial opposition, its extraordinary success in 1926 suggests that it tapped into particular contemporary anxieties. While Tunney represented the middle-class ideal of self-improving and self-controlling masculinity (like Scott Fitzgerald's 'advertisement of the man'), Dempsey appealed to a persistent fantasy of untameable virility and independence.[44]

Dempsey was unfit and unprepared, but Rickard and his associates concealed this well from the public, who 'bet on the champion at preposterous odds'.[45] Tunney won the ten-round fight clearly on points, his defensive skills keeping Dempsey safely at a distance. Afterwards, Grantland Rice argued that the fight had not been a sporting contest but a 'Golden Fleece', and indeed the largest fight crowd in history (a crowd that included Chaplin, Hearst and various Astors, Mellons and Rockefellers) paid a record-breaking $1,895,733 for the privilege.[46] A rematch was inevitable, and in 1927, 145,000 spectators gathered at Soldier Fields, Chicago, in what would prove to be the culmination of Tex Rickard's career.[47]

When Dempsey fought Firpo in 1923, commentators were appalled by the way in which he stood over his prone opponent, ready to strike again as soon as Firpo rose to his feet. Although this was not allowed, the referee failed to intervene. New York boxing authorities then introduced a rule requiring the boxer who delivered the knockdown blow to go to a neutral corner prior to the referee beginning his ten-count. Many think this rule cost Dempsey his chance

at regaining the championship in his 1927 fight with Tunney, a fight which became known as the 'Long Count' (illus. 88). In the seventh round, Dempsey knocked Tunney down and stood over him ready to do the same again. The referee refused to begin the count until Dempsey retired to the farthest neutral corner, and by the time he reached nine, Tunney had recovered. 'Enough running. Come on and fight,' the frustrated Dempsey shouted, but Tunney managed to hold him off and win again, by a clear decision.[48]

Tunney was not a popular champion, partly because his defensive style was rather dull and partly because he was represented by the press as a snob who despised the average boxing fan. According to Sherwood Anderson, 'he was always a bit too patronizing about his trade'.[49] Tunney married a Connecticut socialite, delivered a course of lectures on Shakespeare at Yale, became a personal friend of Bernard Shaw and Thornton Wilder and, worst of all, dropped into conversation words such as 'ineffectual', 'hitherto' and 'cosmeticize'.[50] 'His fastidious and abstracted air suggested that he had won the world championship on his way to acquiring a good library.'[51] In 1928, after suffering from amnesia following a blow to the head, he decided to retire from boxing. His decision was praised by the *Journal of the American Medical Association* in an influential article on the effects of repeated cerebral injury, or 'punch drunkenness'.[52]

Tunney famously took a trip to the Alps with Shaw, and Sherwood Anderson (a Dempsey fan) imagined them walking 'along the road together':

> One was thinking, 'Here am I, a man of the mind. I have a close friend who is a prize fighter. How wonderful!' And there was the other thinking, 'I am a prize fighter, but I am no brute. I am a man of the mind. My being with this writer proves it.'

Anderson was eager to mock the mutual attraction of author and prize-fighter because he believed it originated in a false dichotomy. For Anderson, 'real' fighters, such as Dempsey and Jack Johnson, have 'better minds' than Tunney, and 'real' artists and writers are themselves men 'of action'.

> I have watched painters at work who were like fighters about to enter the prize ring . . . Thoughts and feelings elude like a fast opponent in the ring. You rush at your opponent – the mood. 'Oh, if I could only hit it squarely, send it sprawling!'

If Anderson's account of painting recalls Hazlitt, his model of writing, or rather the more energetic activity of manual typing, develops that proposed by Jack London. Anderson recalls visiting 'a writer friend' for dinner. When he arrives, the man is lying on his bed, exhausted. 'He was as a prize fighter might have been after a marvelous fight.' Anderson reports that this 'bout' had taken place after the man 'had been working for two years trying to get just the feeling he wanted in a certain piece of work.' That morning, he had sat down at his typewriter and produced 12,000 words. While London had focused merely on the production of quantities of writing, Anderson wants to relate the nature of production ('hitting and hitting' at the typewriter) to the flawless quality of the product, the 'timing' of the sentences and the 'feeling' expressed in them. In appearance, very different activities, fighting and writing end up looking exactly the same. 'Marvelous' writers don't need to hang out with 'marvelous' fighters; they *are* 'marvelous' fighters.[53]

Ernest Hemingway draws a similar conclusion in his 1926 'Banal Story' (although, unlike Anderson, he did not like Dempsey and believed Tunney, whose nose he once bloodied, to be 'one of the greatest of heavyweight champions'.[54]) Hemingway's satire is directed against popular 'intellectual' magazines such as the *Forum* and the story parodies many articles that actually appeared in the magazine. 'Do we want big men – or do we want them cultured?' is one of the many 'banal' questions that the writer-protagonist encounters in its pages. 'What star must our college students aim at? There is Jack Britton [a welterweight]. There is Doctor Henry Van Dyke [the clergyman author of inspirational stories]. Can we reconcile the two? Take the case of Young Stribling [a heavyweight].' The story ends with an account of the death and funeral of a bullfighter. In its attention to detail, and its lack of abstraction and posturing, this embedded story is not banal; in fact, it is a vignette that could easily have appeared in *In Our Time*. It is also a story that could only have been written by a man for whom there is no gulf between sophistication and size, a man like the protagonist (and the author) who is as confident in his knowledge of boxing as he is in his ability to write colloquial, immediate prose. 'Far away in Paris,' the narrator thinks, as he spits seeds from an orange, 'Mascart had knocked Danny Frush cuckoo in the second round . . . *There* was Romance.'[55]

## 'NOW THAT LADIES GO TO THE FIGHTS'

After 1920, it became increasingly fashionable for women to attend boxing matches; Rickard actively encouraged their presence in his efforts to make boxing mainstream entertainment. In 1889 Nellie Bly had reassured women readers about the 'daintiness' of John L. Sullivan's table linen and the cleanliness of his nails. But twenties readers were more interested in the boxer's face and figure. Cartoons depicted fighters receiving flowers and advertising hair cream (illus. 58, 92). Boxers were sex symbols and women were no longer coy about admitting it. 'How women love – / The rituals of Dempsey and Carpentier,' noted Mina Loy in a poem, 'Perlun', published the month after 2,000 women were estimated to have attended the 1921 New Jersey fight. (H. L. Mencken complained that he had missed the preliminary bouts because he had been distracted by a woman in a low-cut pink dress.[56]) Gösta Adrian-Nilsson's 1926 collage *Bloody Boxing Debut* juxtaposes images of Dempsey and Tunney with the words, 'Bloody', 'boxing debut', 'body' and 'a happy woman'.[57]

Women also began to write about boxers (if not boxing) for the daily papers. In 1914 Djuna Barnes reported on the phenomenon of women prize-fight spectators for the *New York World* magazine. At that time, she said that the main difference between male and female audiences was that when men looked at a boxer they noticed 'the muscles of his back', while women 'softly' praise his 'fine eyes': 'the woman's interest lies not in strength but in beauty'.[58] Five years later, she interviewed Jess Willard and described him with a suitably aesthetic vocabulary: 'His head, having been overlooked by Sargent, is reproduced in every forest that cutters have been – that gravely solemn thing, the stump of some huge tree staring in blunt Rodinesque mutilation from the ground.'[59] By 1921, when Barnes interviewed Jack Dempsey, it was no longer quite such a novelty to see women at boxing matches (illus. 89). She quotes Dempsey as saying, 'It's no longer enough to have speed and a good right arm to be the favorite. You have to be good-looking, too, now that ladies go to the fights.'[60] Katharine

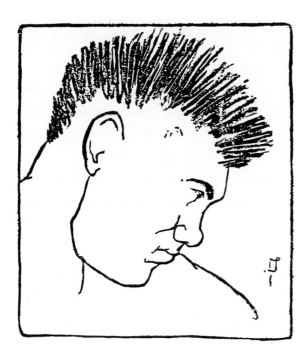

89
Djuna Barnes, *Jack Dempsey*, 1921.

Fullerton Gerould came to the same conclusion. Her reactions to Dempsey's 1926 fight with Tunney, she admitted, were 'only aesthetic and psychological'. 'I do not know what "happened"; or why Gene Tunney was able to beat Jack Dempsey. I keep unperturbed, my own deep sense of the spectacle'. Aesthetically Tunney did not appeal at all. His 'tall ugliness (as Henry James would have put it)' reminded her of a 'gasoline salesman'; fortunately, the 'ferocious face and beautiful body' of Dempsey 'suggested nothing but the great gladiator'.[61] Aesthetic contemplation of the statuesque male boxer often tipped over into (not always acknowledged) erotic excitement. Magazine illustrator Neysa McMein, for example, swooningly wrote of Carpentier that 'Michel Angelo would have fainted for joy with the beauty of his profile.'[62] All this emphasis on the boxer's head, profile, and 'fine eyes' conceals the fact that the men these women were looking at were standing before them bare-chested in shorts. Only Mae West was candid enough to write of the desire of 'soft' female bodies for the 'touch' of 'raw, irritated flesh which had been scraped on the ring ropes'.[63]

Colette's 1920 novel, *Chéri*, is the story of a pre-war love affair between a middle-aged woman and a boy half her age. After observing Chéri's hand while he's asleep – 'a hand not strictly feminine, yet a trifle prettier than one could have wished' – and noticing how pale and exhausted he seems, Léa resolves to feed him up (on strawberries, cream, and corn-fed chicken), and to hire him a boxing coach, Patron. Patron, she tells the jealous Chéri, has 'nothing of the dissipated schoolboy' about him: 'He has other attractions, and a good deal more to recommend him than a perky little face and two black rings round his eyes.'[64] Shortly afterwards, Léa watches Patron instructing Chéri in a little woodland alcove (a pastoral setting that recalls *Cashel Byron's Profession*):

> Léa smiled, and revelled in the warm sun, sitting still and watching the bouts between these two men, both young and both stripped. In her mind she kept comparing them. 'How handsome Patron is – as solid as a house! And the boy's shaping well. You don't find knees like his running about the streets every day of the week, or I'm no judge. His back, too, is . . . will be . . . marvellous . . . And the set of his head! quite a statue!'

Later in the day, Léa discusses Chéri's progress with Patron. Patron praises the boy's physique: 'There's muscles on him now such as you don't see on our French lads; his are more like a coloured boy's – though he couldn't look any whiter, I must say. Nice little muscles they are, and not too showy. He'll never have muscles like melons.' She then embarrasses him by replying, 'I should hope not, Patron! But then, you know, I didn't take him on for his boxing!'[65] Pugilistic sexual potency – often, as here, analogous to 'coloured' sexual potency – crops up in a variety of women's writing of the period. In Paris in 1930, the writer and publisher Nancy Cunard saw off (or possibly exacerbated) rumours about her close friendship with the black fighter Bob Scanlon by claiming he was giving her boxing lessons.[66]

Boxers crop up as sex objects in the work of writers as diverse as Rosamund Lehmann, Jane Bowles and Zelda Fitzgerald. Lehmann's heroine in *The Weather in the Streets* (1936), recovering from a failed love affair, takes up with a 'very handsome' boxer, Ed, whose powerful hands suggest 'magnetism' rather than 'comradeship' (and remind her of her ex).[67] In Jane Bowles's story, 'Going to Massachusetts', Janet tries to woo the feisty Sis, but Sis, 'full of fighting spirit', likes 'men who are champions. Like champion boxers' (especially when they're not in training). 'Whiskey,' she demanded. 'The world loves drunks, but it despises perverts. Athletes and boxers drink when they're not in training. All the time.'[68] In *Save Me the Waltz* (1936), Zelda Fitzgerald detailed 'the post-war extravagance which sent . . . some sixty thousand . . . Americans wandering over the face of Europe'. When her protagonists, David and Alabama, arrive at the Hôtel George-v in Paris, the bartender points out a Miss Dickie Axton, telling them, 'She'd been drinking in this bar the night she shot her lover in the Gare de l'Est.' We don't learn much more about Miss Axton, merely that 'her long legs struck forcefully forward as if she pressed her toes watchfully on the accelerator of the universe' and that 'people said she had slept with a Negro.' The bartender doesn't believe this. 'He didn't see where Miss Axton would have found the time between white gentlemen – pugilists, too, sometimes.'[69]

In his *Autobiography*, William Carlos Williams recalled a 1924 visit with his wife Floss to see the Hemingways' new baby. After supper, they go to a prize-fight.

> In the row in front of us . . . was Ogden Nash, upon whose back, when one of the fighters got bloodiest, Floss pounded as she screamed, "Kill him! Kill him!" to my horror and astonishment. Home by taxi early.

Only a few pages earlier, Williams had distinguished men, 'the technical morons of the tribe', from women who 'remain sound even in debauchery'. No wonder the taxi came early.[70]

Numerous films from the 1920s and '30s draw on the sexual lure of the champion boxer for respectable girls. Most, however, rather moralistically demonstrate how pugilistic sex drive, as well as sex appeal, could break careers as well as hearts. Usually there is a clear distinction between good and bad women. In *Love in the Ring* (1930), Max Schmeling stars as a boxer who falls under the influence of a society woman and nearly loses an important fight. His childhood sweetheart sets him right.[71] In *The Prizefighter and the Lady* (1933), Steve Morgan (Max Baer) wins the heart of Belle Mercer (Myrna Loy), a hard-working, sensible woman who is good for his career. She has 'a lot of mother' in her, but, she adds, 'a lot of woman too'. Belle and Steve marry but his roving eye and legions of fans soon lead to trouble. While Belle stays at home and listens to his fights on the radio, brassy blondes ogle the 'Adonis of the Ring' from the front row. 'I wouldn't mind having him on a pedestal in my front yard', one whispers. 'I bet you're a good dancer,' she says later when she manages to get closer. Corrupted by such women, Steve seems destined to lose an important fight – until Belle intervenes in his corner. He says he wants to quit ('I'm tired of being a big shot. I just want you') but she forbids it. She's doing her 'job' as his wife; he must finish his and become champion.[72]

The prevalence of prize-fighters as sex symbols put pressure on men to act the part, and many comedies of the period exploit the gap between the boxer and the average guy. The bobbed heroine of the 1926 German film *The Boxer's Bride* becomes so obsessed with boxers that her fiancé decides to pose as a fighter to win her affections.[73] A similar performance is undertaken by Alfred Butler, the hero of Buster Keaton's most successful silent film, *Battling Butler* (1926).[74] (Martin Scorsese later claimed that Keaton was 'the only person who had the right attitude about boxing in movies'.[75]) *Battling Butler* is about a wealthy fop whose father sends him to the mountains to 'rough it' and 'be a man'. Accompanied by his valet, Martin, Alfred Butler has no intention of roughing it. His camping equipment consists of a brass bed, full silver service dinnerware, and three changes of clothes a day. Masculinity, we realize early on, is an elaborate masquerade. Alfred falls in love with a local Mountain Girl (Sally O'Neil), but her brother and father reject his proposal of marriage until Martin tells them that Alfred is actually 'Battling Butler', a champion boxer. Unfortunately the real Battling hears of this fraud and decides to humiliate the impostor by having him fight the 'Alabama Murderer'. Alfred is taken for training, and locks up his wife to keep her from seeing his disgrace. After much nervous pacing in the changing room, however, he finds that the real Battling Butler has already fought and won the bout. The play on which the film was based ended here, but Keaton realized that a movie audience would not put up with this: 'we couldn't promise 'em for seven reels that I was goin' to fight in the ring and then not fight. So we staged a fight in the dressing room with the guy . . . and myself. And it worked out swell.'[76] While the early sparring sessions consisted of familiar choreographed slapstick, in the final fight, Walter Kerr notes, Keaton 'suddenly seems no comedian at all':

> Without warning, he can take no more. He turns on his assailant . . .
> pounding him bloody against the walls of the small room, picking him
> up off the floor to batter him senseless again.[77]

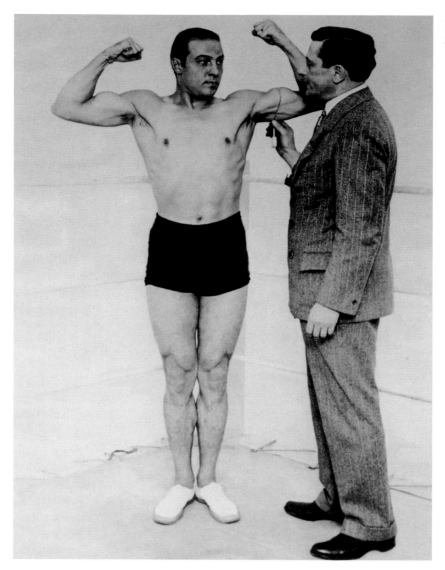

If Keaton provided an unexpected Dempsey, an even less likely contender
was Hollywood idol and 'catnip to women', Rudolph Valentino (illus. 90).[78] In
1921 Valentino became friendly with Dempsey who was living in Hollywood,
promoting the career of his actress wife, Estelle Taylor, and acting in a few films
himself. Although Valentino was a keen sportsman and often sparred with
Dempsey and other Hollywood friends, his image, forged by films such as *The
Four Horsemen of the Apocalypse* (1921) and *The Sheik* (1921), was that of dancer
and lover, roles, it seemed, that were neither properly manly nor properly American. 'While we try to assure ourselves in this country', wrote Vera Caspary in
1926, 'that dancing is as masculine as boxing and the dancer the physical peer
of the fighter, we don't honestly believe it.'[79]

Valentino's later films are often more concerned with exploring and exploiting his star persona than in creating parts for him to act. For example, in *Cobra* (1925) he played an Italian count who had gone to America to escape women-trouble, but found himself accused of being an 'indoor sheik'. Dempsey helped him prepare for the knockdown punch with which he decisively answered the charge. The scene was to prove tragically prescient. The following year Valentino was deeply offended when a *Chicago Tribune* journalist dubbed him a 'pink powder puff' and claimed he represented a threat to 'Homo Americanus'. 'Hollywood', the editorial stated, 'is a national school of masculinity. Rudy, the beautiful gardener's boy, is the prototype of the American male. Hell's bells. Oh, sugar.' Valentino responded with an open letter in a rival paper, challenging the journalist 'to meet me in the boxing . . . arena to prove in typical American fashion . . . which of us is more a man. I do not know how big you are but this challenge stands if you are as big as Jack Dempsey.'[80] The journalist never responded, but Valentino would not let the matter drop. With Dempsey's help, he staged a 'fight' with the sportswriter on the roof of a New York hotel. Valentino's opponent duly went down and the *Evening Journal* ran a headline, 'POWDER PUFF? WHAM!' The following month, Valentino was rushed to hospital with acute appendicitis and perforated gastric ulcers, the result, some claim, of all the boxing. Waking after surgery, his first words were reputedly, 'Did I behave like a pink powder puff or like a man?' After two weeks Valentino died, at the age of 31. Later that year, the annual *Everlast Record Book* published an advertisement for training bags with the text, 'Many a "Powder Puff" boxer developed a "kick like a mule's" that changed him to a "knockout artist"' (illus. 91). According to John Dos Passos, Valentino's tragedy resulted from trying 'to make good in he-man, two-fisted, bronco-busting, poker-playing, stock-juggling America'. After the actor's death, he noted, 'the champion himself [Dempsey] allowed himself to be quoted that the boy was fond of boxing and a great admirer of the champion.'[81]

The gap between movie star and pugilist was not, in fact, so big. While Valentino struggled to present himself a properly masculine American boxer – 'the Dempsey of the Nile', as Dorothy Parker quipped – the Manassa Mauler was told to get a Hollywood nose job.[82] After all, as

91
'Many a "Powder Puff"', advertisement for training bags, *Everlast Boxing Record*, 1926.

# MANY A "POWDER PUFF"

boxer developed a "kick like a mule's" that changed him to a "knockout artist"; many a logical contender gained a "sock" that brought him the championship, through the use of the Everlast Training Bag.

Almost every gymnasium in the U. S. has one or more Everlast Bags swinging from the ceiling. The gym director knows that Everlast Bags are not like ordinary "sand bags"; that Everlast Bags are filled with a special soft stuffing that minimizes the possibilities of injury to the user's hands.

No. C3 is 10 oz. canvas, machine sewed ..........$20.00

No. C2 is 12 oz. canvas, hand sewed .............. 30.00

No. L1 is the leather bag used in most
gymnasiums ................................................ 60.60

**EVERLAST SPORTING GOODS MANUFACTURING CO.**

275 Bowery               New York City

92
'Go easy this round, Basher; The Hair Cream Company is takin' 'is pitcher', cartoon in *Punch*, October 1935.

John R. Turnis noted in 1929, both sportsmen and actors were primarily sales-men in a rapidly expanding entertainment commodity market (illus. 92).

> The modern pugilist is last of all a fighter. A lecturer, and endorser of belts, underwear, shaving cream and storage batteries he must be. An apt speaker on the radio, a handy man with his pen when con-tracts are being flourished, knowing in the art of publicity – these are the gifts which must be cultivated by the pugilist of today. As he will need to contest on average but one bout a year, his ability is of far less importance.[83]

## 'AMERICA! THE FUTURE!': BOXING AND AMERICANISM

In Germany in 1916, the painter George Grosz was certain that America represented 'the future'.[84] It was not, however, the country itself that excited him so much as 'Americanism', which he later defined as 'a much used and much discussed word for an advancement in technical civilization that was permeating the world under American leadership.'[85] By the time of the First World War, 'American' had become almost synonymous for 'urban' and 'modern' throughout Europe. Wanda M. Corn describes how early twentieth-century European travellers to the United States, while dismissing its high culture as 'a pale imitation of their own . . . were fascinated by vaudeville, jazz, popular dances, comic books, movies, boxing, football and baseball, forms for which Europeans had few equivalents . . . they found them exotic and described them in great detail, often as if they were tribal rituals practiced by a strange barbarian race'.[86]

If 'American' translated into 'the urban', and 'the modern', 'boxing' increasingly featured as a synecdoche for all of these. This would have seemed absurd in, for example, the mid-nineteenth century, when prize-fighting was viewed as a lingering anachronism. But in the early twentieth century, boxers are frequently found in lists, assemblages, collages and films that claimed to represent cities, Americanism or modernity. Apollinaire's summing up of the urban modernity of Montparnasse in a series of twelve calligrammes included 'un terrible boxeur' (illus. 93); William Ruttman's film, *Berlin – The Symphony of a Great City* (1927) cut between scenes of nightclub dancing and boxing matches as alternative forms of evening entertainment; murals such as Anatol Shulkin's *American Life* (1934) and Thomas Hart Benton's *City Activities* (1930) included boxing matches in their encapsulations of 'the city' or 'America'.[87] Shulkin places a clinch between a black and a white fighter at the centre of a mural of crowded figures and scenes, including gangsters, strikers, acrobats, the trombone section of a jazz band, a roller-coaster and collapsing skyscrapers (illus. 94). Benton's mural focuses on the exaggerated, grotesque body in the city, and juxtaposes images of solitude in crowds – on the subway, watching dancers – with images of connection – kissing on a park bench and fighting in the spotlight of the boxing ring. 'How easy it is to slip / into the old mode, how hard to / cling firmly to the advance,' declared William Carlos Williams in *Spring and All* (1923). The advance could come in many forms,

93
Guillaume Apollinaire, 'Un terrible boxeur' from *Montparnasse* (1914).

94
Anatol Shulkin,
*American Life*, 1934.

but it must find itself 'freed from the handcuffs of "art"'. 'That is why', Williams maintained, 'boxing matches and / Chinese poems are the same'.[88]

America and Americanism were particularly on the minds of Germans in the Weimar republic (1919–32). While economists sought to emulate the successes of Henry Ford's production methods, the avant-garde embraced jazz, movies and sport, everything that had been denied them during the war years.[89] But if Americans indulged in the trivialities of popular culture as a way of shrugging off serious matters, Germans took it all very seriously. To champion American movies and sports stars was a way for many to assert their allegiance to modernity and to reject the nostalgic mode of much traditional German culture, which seemed mired in nature, nation and sentimental idealism.[90] 'The stadium vanquishes the art museum,' declared Hannes Meyer in 1926, 'and bodily reality replaces beautiful illusion. Sport unifies the individual with the masses.'[91] The following year Herbert Jhering argued that 'the penetration of the English-American jargon of the sports dialect' would do a 'proper service to the German language', and through the language, the German people. 'High German, intellectualized and burdened with culture, has gained in imagery and activity from the speech of engineering and the inroads of sports. A different kind of person, a different way of expressing himself.'[92] In modern boxing's promise of 'a different kind of person' lay the reason why both the Left and the Right, both Brecht and Hitler, admired the sport.[93]

Boxing was also the favourite sport of *Der Querschnitt*, a journal founded by art dealer Alfred Flechtheim and edited by Hermann von Wedderkop. 'We consider it our duty', a 1921 editorial declared, 'to promote boxing in German artistic circles as has long been the case elsewhere. In Paris Braque, Derain, Dufy, Matisse, Picasso, and Rodin are all enthusiastic boxing fans.'[94] In 1926, Flechtheim noted contentedly that, 'the Sportpalast doesn't recruit its public from beer-deliverymen and drivers alone; – all of Berlin's fine society is there, princes and princesses, painters and sculptors, literati . . . and all the actors who aren't working this evening.'[95] Flechtheim held regular soirées where members of the intelligentsia, including Heinrich Mann, Alfred Döblin, George Grosz, Rudolf Grossman, Willi Baumeister and Josef von Sternberg, could mingle with boxers such as Hans Breitensträter, Paul Samson-Körner and Max Schmeling. These meetings were

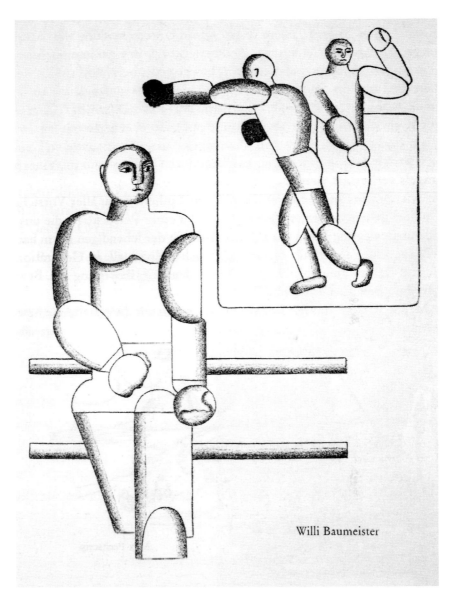

Willi Baumeister

often productive. Baumeister's paintings of 'impersonal' athletes were frequently reproduced in *Querschnitt* (illus. 95), while Grossman's series of lithographs, 'The Boxer', was distributed together with Breitensträter's autobiography.[96] Schmeling posed for numerous paintings and sculptures, including Rudolf Belling's bronze, which took pride of place at the Sport in Culture Exhibition in Berlin in May 1930. Ernst Krenek wrote an opera about him, *Heavyweight: The Nation's Honour*.[97] George Grosz painted Schmeling's portrait, and the two men exchanged thoughts on their respective professions. Grosz concluded that 'the painter and the boxer have at least one characteristic in common: both have to see through someone who at first glance is a complete stranger to them. What sort of man is that, what does his life look like, what kind of character does he have. I have to provide a picture, you must anticipate a mode of fighting.'[98]

Max Schmeling had taken up boxing after seeing the film of Dempsey's fight against Carpentier ('I saw it practically every evening for a week', he recalled). He turned professional in 1924 and in 1928 became European light heavyweight champion after knocking out Mussolini's favourite, Michele Bonaglia, in what was heralded as 'a triumph of the democratic principle over fascist Italy', and in 1930, the first modern non-American world champion, after fighting Jack Sharkey for Gene Tunney's vacant crown. Schmeling quickly realized that if he was going to get fights in the States, he needed an American manager and signed on with Joe Jacobs, a Hungarian Jew from New York. Their relationship was to cause Schmeling problems when Hitler came to power. He was none the less summoned to the Chancellory on several occasions and when he got married in 1933, Hitler sent him a Japanese maple tree as a wedding present.[99]

By the late twenties, what Schmeling termed 'boxing fever' was widespread and his gym became a fashionable place for film people like Carola Neher and Leni Riefenstahl to exercise. Marlene Dietrich, it was reported, preferred to use her punching ball at home.[100] But of all those infected with a passion for the United States, and with prize-fighting, the most persistent was undoubtedly Bertolt Brecht. In 1920 he complained in his diary, 'how boring Germany is! It's a good average country, its pale colours and surfaces are beautiful, but what inhabitants!' 'What's left?', he asked. 'America!' This sentiment was given a more melodramatic spin in a poem of the same year, 'Germany, You Blond Pale Creature':

Oh! carrion land, misery hole!
Shame strangles the remembrance of you
And in the young men whom
You have not ruined
America awakens.[101]

According to Grosz, even Brecht's suits were American, 'with padded shoulders and wedge-shaped trousers, a style no longer worn in America (but in Germany it made you look American).'[102]

A preoccupation with American city life informs much of Brecht's mid-1920s writing, and boxing was both a tantalizing part of that life, one of the 'great mythical diversions of the giant cities on the other side of the herring pond', and a symbol of its decadent, dynamic, jungle-like struggles.[103] *Man Equals Man* (1925) was the first of his Berlin plays to be infused with both the ethos of sports and what was known as the '*Neue Sachlichkeit*' or New Matter-of-Factness. The term has been applied to a diverse group of writers and artists who wanted to record the modern Germany in a detached and direct way (illus. 96). For Brecht, sportsmen epitomized the matter-of-fact, and no one more so than Jack Dempsey. As someone who eschewed science for knockout punches, Dempsey ('Tiger Jack, the Manassa Mauler') was Brecht's archetypal fighter, and indeed archetypal

American. The 'further boxing distances itself from the K.O.,' Brecht wrote, 'the less it has anything to do with real sport. A fighter who cannot beat his opponent into the ground hasn't, of course, really beaten him at all.'[104] *Man Equals Man* tells the story of a porter, Galy Gay, who is persuaded to take the place of Jeraiah Jip, a soldier and 'human fighting-machine'. Brecht used the phrase 'human fighting-machine' on several occasions, and in his poem, 'Tablet to the Memory of 12 World Champions', noted that it originated in connection with Billy Papke, middleweight champion from 1908 to 1913.[105] The play was accompanied by an interlude, 'The Elephant Calf,' which was to be performed in the theatre foyer during the intermission and which ends with Gay offering to fight one of the soldiers 'straight away for eight rounds with the four-ounce gloves'. The final stage direction is 'All off to the fight'. As Franco Ruffini notes, this could be read as a description of where the play itself is headed.[106]

The 'objective' boxing match also provided a model for *In the Jungle of Cities*, which Brecht worked on between 1921 and 1924, when he moved to

Berlin. Further boxing and American allusions were introduced before the play was published in 1927. Set in a mythical 1912 Chicago, strongly influenced by Upton Sinclair's *The Jungle*, the play presents a battle between Shlink, a rich merchant, and George Garga, a poor library employee (Brecht's note describes him as 'like A. Rimbaud in appearance. He is essentially a German translation into American from the French'.) Garga permits himself to have opinions on the books he deals with; Schlink wants to buy that right; Garga refuses. Chicago is the 'ring' in which the fight takes place, and when, in scene 9, Garga thinks he has won 'a technical knockout', he concludes that 'Chicago has thrown in the towel' for Shlink. But there are still two more rounds to go. In scene ten, Garga dies; in scene eleven, Shlink heads off to take on New York.[107] In 1924 Brecht began writing about a mythical American Sodom and Gomorrah which he called Mahagonny. He started with songs about whisky, poker and Jack Dempsey, and eventually wrote a full-length opera, *The Rise and Fall of the City of Mahagonny* (1930), which includes a boxing scene in which Trinity Moses and Joe box 'in time to the music'.[108] In 1927 the preparatory *Mahagonny-Songspiel* was staged in a boxing ring in front of projections by Caspar Neher at the Baden-Baden music festival.

During this time Brecht became a good friend of the middleweight boxer Paul Samson-Körner and wrote several works about him.[109] Samson-Körner was famous for his 'no-nonsense and effective' boxing technique. Schmeling praised it as an 'American style', reliant on 'concentration, mercilessness and toughness'.[110] More importantly, for Brecht, Samson-Körner was 'un-German'. If Germans could learn to box with unfussy efficiency like Americans, perhaps, as Samson-Körner himself suggested, they could become more like Americans in other ways. Individual physical productivity might spark national economic productivity.[111]

By the mid-1920s the cabaret revue had become the most popular form of entertainment in Berlin. Consisting of a large variety of fast-paced acts (including songs, dances and comedy), revues were thought to express the random juxtapositions and speed of modernity, its 'multiple interweaving of surfaces'.[112] Once again boxing was frequently included. Brecht's list of topics for a planned revue on Americanism in 1926 read: 'Record Girl, Smiling, Advertising, Boxing match, Revue, Tarzan, Sisday races, Slow Motion film, Business, radio.'[113] In 1922, the epitome of Americanism himself, Jack Dempsey, visited a Berlin revue where what the *New York Times* dubbed 'pugilettes' fought 'in décolleté fancy tights' (illus. 59).[114] Damon Runyon, who was also there, described one bout between 'a pretty sixteen-year-old girl and her older opponent.' He was amazed at 'the boxing skill and punching power displayed.'

> The young girl was outclassed for the first five rounds and was bleeding from the nose and mouth. The Americans thought it was a shame

that the bout was continued, when Jack Kearns sent Louie Meyer, one of our group here who speaks German, to the young girl's corner and told her to try a left hand body punch.

When the last round started the young girl staggered into her corner and let fly, according to Kearns's instructions. She knocked her opponent cold.

Dempsey thought the rounds were too long for girls, that their bodies were insufficiently protected and really disliked the entire business.[115]

Altogether the idol of Weimar Berlin found its excesses a little shocking. 'The people were friendly and gave me a fine reception, but as for the vice there, I wouldn't have believed there was anything like it in the world.'[116]

Those pursuing Americanism in Berlin always felt themselves a step behind what was going on in Paris, and there were other important differences between the two cities. Berliners looked to America to save them from economic and spiritual crisis, but, as Gramsci noted, Parisians treated Americanism merely as 'a form of make-up, a superficial foreign fashion'.[117] Indeed, for many Americans, 'cosmopolitan Paris was what America ought to be.'[118]

Boxing had been introduced to French culture in the early nineteenth century through an Anglophile sporting society (that included Géricault), and until the late nineteenth century, it was always advertised as *la boxe anglaise* to distinguish it from the French version (also known as *la savate*). In George Du Maurier's 1894 novel, *Trilby*, a group of young English artists devote part of each day to boxing in their Paris studio. Particularly adept at the sport is a large Yorkshireman called Taffy who has a 'mighty forearm' with muscles 'strong as iron bands' and biceps that 'equalled Mr Sandow's', and who only missed the charge at Balaklava because he had sprained his ankle playing leap-frog in the trenches. Taffy constitutes a kind of benchmark of traditional Anglo-Saxon masculinity against which the novel's other men are measured. A visitor from Oxford, for example, initially seems impressive because he has longer whiskers than Taffy, but then we learn that 'the mere sight of a boxing glove made him feel sick'. Taffy's biceps are no mere ornaments. Du Maurier builds them up for the specific purpose of slapping the evil Jewish interloper Svengali and swinging him by his nose. Afterwards, 'he had, for hours, the feel of that long, thick, shapely Hebrew nose being kneaded between his gloved fingers'. In bohemian Paris, where sexual and racial confusion reign, Taffy is the epitome of blue-eyed Englishness.[119]

Boxing is also an English sport for Marcel Proust, for whom one of the meanings of Englishness was sex. Boxers are sexual predators, but more often sexual objects, offering aristocrats what Claude Menieur describes as the charm of 'amours déclassés'.[120] In *In the Shadow of Young Girls in Flower*, the Marquis de Saint-Loup encounters some young girls by the beach whom he takes 'for the mistresses of racing cyclists or prize-fighters'; in *Sodom and Gomorrah*, the Baron de Charlus admires a man whose face expresses 'a delicacy which touches our hearts, a grace, a natural gentleness such as men do not possess' but is 'dismayed to learn that this young man runs after boxers'. In *The Captive*, we learn that the Baron 'confused his ruling passion with friendship, which does not resemble it in the least, and the athletes of Praxiteles with obliging boxers'.[121]

In the early years of the twentieth century, the United States took over from England as the centre of international boxing. In 1907, French dandies still 'strove to turn themselves into Englishmen', but by 1909, due to 'the advent of the Yankee boxers', 'everyone' was American. Paris, 'to make use of a cliché, went berserk', observed amateur pugilist and proto-Dadaist Arthur Cravan.[122] 'We had heard a good deal of American boxers, long before we had even set eyes on one,' recalled Georges Carpentier, 'The reverence in which we held them was next to sacrilegious, for they appeared as gods on the fistic firmament.' By 1912, the gods were walking the streets of Paris, and 'the American invasion' was 'in full swing'. 'Boxing tournaments were attracting bigger and bigger audiences,' Carpentier wrote, 'and even the most famous American boxing champions did not hesitate to pack their trunks and set off for Paris'.[123] (Later, Carpentier was to characterize his own new 'French style of boxing' as 'English science blended with American ruggedness.'[124]) The First World War brought more Americans to Europe, and in its aftermath, 'the old continent began to resound with the mis-pronounced names of American boxers'.[125]

An interest in boxing extended into many unlikely quarters. Colette wrote fight reports for *Le Matin*, Jean Cocteau managed middleweight Al Brown and rhapsodized about his 'active poetry' and its 'mysterious syntax', while artists as diverse as Picasso, Man Ray, Miró, Masson, Bonnard and Braque attended fights and sparred in their studios.[126] In Vladimir Nabokov's *Lolita*, Humbert Humbert recalls his Parisian marriage to Valeria: 'We had quite a few cozy evenings together, she deep in her *Paris-Soir*, I working at a rickety table. We went to movies, bicycle races and boxing matches.'[127]

For some Parisians, the appeal of boxing lay in its association with primitivism and black culture. By the outbreak of war in 1914, what some called 'negrophilia', and Apollinaire dubbed 'melanophilia', was well established; after 1920, it blossomed into 'melanomania'.[128] The black aesthetic was encapsulated in two figures, the male boxer and the female dancer, and one or other tended to be evoked in most discussions of African or black American art. Sometimes the two figures became interchangeable. Josephine Baker opened at the *Revue Nègre* in 1925 and immediately captivated the city. One critic praised the revue as 'rousing the tired public . . . to thrills and madness as otherwise only a boxing match can do', while Paul Colin, whose lithographs of Baker were published in 1927 as *Le tumulte noir*, described his first impressions of her as 'part rubber woman, part female tarzan' and 'part boxing kangaroo'. In 1931 Baker was filmed singing her hit *J'ai deux amours, mon Pays et Paris* as she crouched in the corner of a boxing ring.[129]

Black boxers also played a part in evocations of modernist primitivism. When, for example, Apollinaire lectured on African art at Paul Guillaume's gallery, Max Jacob described the event as the art dealer's 'Boxing School'.[130] While pre-war fighters such as Sam McVea, Joe Jeanette and, of course, Jack Johnson were much admired, the 'male Josephine Baker' was 'Panama' Al Brown (illus. 122).[131] Brown tried to establish a career as a bantamweight in Harlem in the early 1920s but finding few lucrative matches in the strictly segregated post-Jack-Johnson era, he moved to Paris in 1926. There he established himself as a successful fighter and man about town (illus. 60). Sponsored by Jean Cocteau (who briefly acted as his manager) he was a glamorous figure, often seen driving fast cars and drinking champagne in the city's most fashionable cafés. Brown's most controversial contest took place in 1931, when he agreed to participate in a gala with French champion Roger Simendé in order to raise funds for the Dakar-Djibouti mission, an expedition to Farica to document African civilization and collect artefacts for Paris's newly remodelled museum of ethnography and anthropology. Held in the Cirque d'Hiver before an audience which included Cocteau, Georges Bataille, Raymond Roussel and Michel Leiris, the boxing exhibition was a great success, raising over 100,000 francs. The mission finally resulted 'in the collection of approximately 3,500 objects at Trocadéro, the annotation and transcription of 30 African dialects, and the assembly of 6,000 photographs, 1,600 metres of film, and scores of documents for the remodelled museum.'[132] The new museum (in 1937 it became the Musée de l'Homme) was intended to move anthropology away from an emphasis on race and biology and toward the comparative study of different cultures. For some, the boxing gala indicates the incomplete nature of this shift. Many who attended viewed the fight not simply as a fund-raiser but as a primitive ritual itself worthy of anthropological study. 'The black man who fought that night', argues Jean Jamin 'prefigured the "*objets nègres*" that, two years later, the exhibition would bring back from the land of his ancestors'.[133]

Many black American boxers followed Brown across the Atlantic in search of work. The experience of one is the subject of Gwendolyn Bennett's short story 'Wedding Day', published in the Harlem journal *Fire!* in 1926. The story was loosely based on the life of Georgia-born Eugene Bullard, who travelled around the world working as a boxer before settling in Paris in 1913 at the age of nineteen. Along with Bob Scanlon, Bullard joined the French Foreign Legion when war broke out. After the Armistice he married Marcelle de Straumann, the daughter of a French countess. The wedding guests included 'outstanding people in all walks of life and colours and religions'. 'I felt as if I were back in the Foreign Legion,' said Bullard, 'where there is no prejudice and everybody appreciates everybody else just for himself as a human being'.[134] The boxer in Bennett's story does not fall in love with a French countess but with a white American prostitute. On the day they are due to marry, she sends him a letter saying that she '"just couldn't go through with it", white women just don't marry colored men.'[135] Bennett's substitution of an American for a Frenchwoman seems intended to show up the difference in the treatment of blacks in the two countries. That 'the separate, individual black-skinned man' received better treatment in France than anywhere else in Europe or America was widely held as axiomatic, as Claude McKay reported to the Soviet Congress in 1922.

> The black intelligensia of America looks upon France as the most cultured nation in the world; the single great country where all citizens enjoy equal rights before the law, without respect to race or skin color.

McKay's scepticism about such beliefs becomes clear in the following sentence where he notes that this individual 'good treatment' is 'valued so highly by Negroes that they are beginning to forget about the vile exploitation of Africans by the French'. For McKay, the limits of French justice were revealed by what he called 'the scandalous story of Siki and Carpentier'.[136]

Born in 1897 in the port of St Louis, Senegal (then called French West Africa), Baye Phal moved to France as a teenager. There he began to fight professionally as Battling Siki, and in 1914, he enlisted in the French army, where he earned both the Croix de Guerre and the Médaille Militaire.[137] When Siki fought Georges Carpentier for the light heavyweight championship on 24 September 1922 – the first million franc gate – he was the first black fighter to contest a championship for seven years.[138] After the first round, a relaxed Carpentier told his manager, 'I'll get him when I want to', but the script was disrupted by 'tough slowthinker' Siki and 'his mauling style'; in the sixth round, after a series of 'fearful, fast, hammering blows', Siki knocked the Frenchman out.[139] At this point, as Lincoln Steffens reported in the *New York Evening Journal*, sport ended, and 'as usual, business butted in'.[140] Claiming that Siki had tripped Carpentier, the referee disqualified him, but the crowd was furious, and so the judges, fearing a riot, reversed the decision. The 'applause of the crowd', recalled Bob Scanlon, 'was like a dozen machine-guns rattling'.[141] A few days later, Carpentier's manager appealed unsuccessfully. The French and American press revived the racism of the Johnson era with gusto. Newspapers dubbed Siki 'Championzee' and Siki's manager told the *New York Times* that 'Siki has something in him which is not human. A long time ago I used to think that if one could find an intelligent Gorilla and teach him to box, one would have the world's champion. Well, that's what I found in Siki.'[142] 'This kind of thing hurts me,' the boxer responded, 'I was never anywhere but a big city in all my life. I've never even seen a jungle.' After his victory, Siki became a Parisian celebrity, walking the streets dressed in spats, a frock coat and a monocle, with a lion on a leash, and drinking absinthe in the best cafés. Fashionable women had his silhouette painted on their arms. But Siki's moment of glory was short. His boxing career floundered, and in 1925, he was found shot dead on the street in Hell's Kitchen, New York; seemingly because of a bad debt. Until the body was identified, the police reported another 'nigger corpse'.[143]

'The Carpentier-Siki fight was a story, a good play,' wrote Lincoln Steffens, and for him, it was a story about Carpentier's defeat rather than Siki's victory.

'Man put to the test, and almost always failing' was, for Steffens, the constant story of 'business, reform, and politics'. In particular, it reminded him of the peace conferences. In 1922, the terms of the 1919 Versailles Treaty, 'a treaty of peace that was full of war', were still being discussed in conferences in Genoa, The Hague and Lausanne.[144] For Claude McKay, the Siki-Carpentier fight told a rather different political story. Among those present at ringside was Blaise Diagne, representing Senegal as the first black deputy in the French National Assembly. The previous year he had attended Paris's second All-African Congress, chaired by W.E.B. Du Bois. At the first Congress in 1919, Diagne (who co-chaired the event with Du Bois) had spoken against the Pan Africanism of Du Bois and Marcus Garvey, arguing that French Africans were treated equally to French citizens of European origin. In 1921, he walked out of the Congress rejecting its separatist agenda. But the events surrounding the Siki-Carpentier fight, were, McKay noted gleefully, a 'slap' to the 'black conservative deputy'. 'It is inconceivable', Diagne said after the fight, 'that Siki could be deprived of his victory simply because he is black.' 'The white man refused to accept the idea that the black man can be equal to him physically or spiritually.'[145]

AMATEURS AND PROFESSIONALS

Throughout the 1920s Parisian boxing was supported by the presence of a large white American expatriate community, and as David Trotter argues, they were as much a community of 'Americanists as Americans, living an image' that was already well-established.[146] Most famous of the expatriate fight-goers was undoubtedly Ernest Hemingway. who, it seemed sparred with everyone and anyone, and even occasionally with professional fighters for ten francs a round. In 1922, one of his regular partners, Henry Strater, painted him in a grey sweatshirt and dubbed the work the 'boxer portrait'.[147] In 1929, another expatriate, Morley Callaghan, knocked him down and the two men fell out for good. According to Callaghan, after the event, Hemingway sadly confessed, 'my writing is nothing. My boxing is everything.'[148]

Hemingway's habit of discussing the writers he would like to 'beat' to become 'champ' has become notorious, and, as will become apparent in future chapters, every writer who wants to acknowledge his influence, does so in similar terms.[149] Those he wrote about in his 1949 letter to Charles Scribner (Turgenev, Maupassant, and Tolstoy, who he was still 'squaring up to') were dead, but during his time in Paris, Hemingway was not averse to a real or rhetorical punch up with the living, with Pound, Miró and indeed pretty much anyone else willing to raise their fists in his presence.[150] Hemingway was obsessed with the way that champions succeeded one another, and strongly believed that once a great champ had lost his crown, there was no reclaiming it. When he was young and promising, this provided a useful metaphor for literary succession. The great writers of yesterday, he constantly maintained, like the great fighters, must give way to the new. In 1924 he complained to Pound that the authors

Ford Madox Ford was selecting for *transatlantic review* were the literary equivalents of Jim Jeffries, dragged out of retirement for one last fight. 'The thing to do with Ford is to kill him . . . I am fond of Ford. This ain't personal. It's literary.'[151]

Hemingway's teachers, Gertrude Stein and Sherwood Anderson, were also literary equivalents of Jeffries, ripe for the symbolic kill. They had done their work and could be admired as former champions, as long, of course, as they admitted their day was over. If they continued to want to compete, some drastic Oedipal action was needed. In 1926, before publishing *The Torrents of Spring*, a ruthless Anderson satire, he wrote to his friend justifying the book (his 'attempt to sock on the jaw'). If the letter opens with pugilistic brio, it soon becomes anxiously convoluted: 'You see I feel that if among ourselves we have to pull our punches, if when a man like yourself who can write very great things writes something that seems to me, (who have never written anything great but am anyway a fellow craftsman) rotten, I ought to tell you so.'[152] Anderson's reply continued the metaphor. 'Come out of it, man. I pack a little wallop myself. I've been middleweight champion myself. You seem to forget that . . . Did you ever hear of Kid McAllister – the nonpareil – that was me'.[153] Judy Jo Small and Michael Reynolds argue that this exchange of letters (which did not stop there) 'played a crucial role in shaping Hemingway's "The Killers" where a doomed heavyweight fighter named Ole Andreson resignedly faces the inevitable.'[154] Hemingway's break with Gertrude Stein came a little later, when in their memoirs of the twenties, each accused the other of stealing ideas. Hemingway said that Stein 'only gave real loyalty to people who were inferior to her'. Of course, he added, 'I always loved her very much and . . . never counter-punched when she left herself wide open.'[155]

In 1937 Wyndham Lewis recalled meeting Hemingway at his first visit to Ezra Pound's studio in Paris, 'a great change from the dark Kensington quarters':

> Having found his abode, I rang the bell. A great deal of noise was to be heard but no one answered: therefore I pushed open the door, which opened practically into the studio. A spendidly built young man, stripped to the waist, and with a torso of dazzling white, was standing not far from me. He was tall, handsome, and serene, and was repelling with his boxing gloves a hectic assault of Ezra's. After a final swing at the dazzling solar plexus Pound fell back upon his settee. The young man was Hemingway.[156]

To Lewis, Hemingway is a statue – 'dazzling white' and 'serene', and lacking in mobility. This is fairly inoffensive, but three years earlier, Lewis had depicted Hemingway as the quintessential 'dumb ox', an 'enthusiastic amateur of rude, crude, naked force in men and women'.[157] To Hemingway, such an attack could only be read (as indeed it was intended) as an attempt at a knockout blow, and, 30 years later, he responded in suitably pugilistic style with a rival account of the scene in Pound's studio. Chapter Twelve of *A Moveable Feast* is about Ezra

Pound, 'always a good friend'. Two of its four-and-a-half-pages, however, are devoted to an attack on Lewis. Hemingway begins with an account of teaching Pound to box and how he 'tried to make him look as good as possible'. Then Lewis enters and the insults begin to fly. First of all, Lewis's appearance gets a thorough battering: he looks 'like a character in the quarter', wears 'the uniform of the pre-war artist', and has a face like a frog; 'not a bullfrog' even, but 'just any frog'. A heavier punch follows – Lewis was 'hoping to see Ezra hurt' – and then Hemingway finishes off the assault by highlighting his metaphor. 'I watched Lewis carefully without seeming to look at him, as you do when you are boxing'. The sentence then concludes with its knockout blow, 'and I do not think I had ever seen a nastier-looking man'.[158]

It was Pound, however, who was the primary target of Lewis's satire in 1937. By boxing a man who looks like a statue in his own studio, Pound, Lewis suggests, was trying to be both aesthete and man of action, that is, 'violently American'. Lewis goes on:

> The 'tough guy' that has made Hemingway famous, and the 'strenuousness' of him of the Big Stick, are modes of the American ethos with which Pound is perfectly in tune . . . He exercises a sort of tribal attraction for his fellow-countrymen, over and above the effect of the glamour of the poetic genius.

Both 'the glamour of poetic genius' and the masculine posturing of boxing are merely forms of performance, and that is why, Lewis concludes, Pound is 'in his element' when performing.[159] In 'Patria Mia' (1913), Pound had been equally scathing of the '"school of virility"' which 'seems to imagine that man is differentiated from the lower animals by possession of the phallus' and whose work 'reads like a Sandow booklet', and the Swinburnean 'gorgeous school', whose aim is 'to name as many constellations and to encumber them with as many polysyllabic adjectives as possible'.[160] Lewis, of course, wants to associate Pound with both these clichéd schools – swooning Kensington aestheticism, *and* vulgar American-in-Paris virility – and to imply that he's not much good at either.

Lewis had first associated Americanism with pugilistic ambition in his 1917 short story, 'A Soldier of Humour', collected in *The Wild Body* (1927). There the narrator, Ker-Orr, 'a large blond clown, ever so vaguely reminiscent (in person) of William Blake, and some great American boxer whose name I forget', confronts a Frenchman who is trying to pass as an American in a railway dining car.

> I fully expected to be forced to fight my way out of the salle à manger, and was wondering whether his pugilistic methods would be those of Chicago or Toulouse . . . But I had laid him out quite flat. My answer to his final apostrophe was a blow below the belt: I was following it up by vanishing from the ring altogether . . .[161]

The manifestations of boxing metaphors in this passage are symptomatic. For Ker-Orr – whose presence as protagonist and narrator links the stories gathered in *The Wild Body* – is, in the relentless efficiency of his wildness, the closest Lewis came to describing himself as a thoroughly modern pugilist-aesthete. What is at issue in these stories is the protagonist-narrator's professional identity.[162] In *Blasting and Bombardiering*, Lewis's description of Pound's studio comes at the end of a passage reflecting on amateurism and professionalism in writing, and these issues feed into the later scene. In moving from London to Paris, Lewis suggested, Pound was not only trying to be American and masculine like Hemingway, he was also emulating Hemingway's air of professionalism.[163] But such issues had preoccupied Pound for many years. In 'A Retrospect' (1918), he rejected the opposition of amateur and professional in favour of one between amateur and expert. 'It is certain that the present chaos will endure,' he wrote, 'until the Art of poetry has been punched down the amateur gullet, until there is a general understanding that poetry is an art and not a pastime; such a knowledge of technique; of technique of surface and technique of content, that the amateurs will cease to try to drown out the masters.'[164]

'Punching' also featured in a 1912 letter that Pound wrote to Harriet Monroe, editor of *Poetry*, urging her to persevere with the magazine: 'we're in such a beautiful position to save the public's soul by punching its face that it seems a crime not to do so'.[165] What distinguished the expert (poet or boxer) from the amateur was not simply a willingness to throw punches, but the dedicated study of technique. Pound had developed this point in 'On Technique' (1911). The essay begins by bemoaning the absence of an interest in technique among modern poets and contrasts this with the keen technical knowledge and interest displayed by a boxing audience. Pound imagines 'a contest between Jack Johnson and the surviving "White Hope"', a contest with a great deal of money staked on it. The sporting crowd, Pound notes, would not want impressionistic 'character studies', but 'details' using precise technical terms such as 'left-lead' and 'counter'.[166] In later years, Pound was less inclined to suggest that poetry should be 'punched' in the face or down the gullet of the public, but he did retain a sufficient interest in boxers to be able to refer to them freely in a variety of contexts. Jack Dempsey is mentioned a couple of times: his comments on reading are included in a discussion of 'tastes' in *ABC of Reading*, and a G.I. song which rhymes 'Dempsey's mitts' with 'great big tits' is alluded to in *The Pisan Cantos*.[167] In 1941, Pound wrote to a colleague about the phrase 'the water-bug's mittens', which he was eventually to use in a late Canto. 'If I were 30 years younger,' he said, 'I would call 'em his boxing gloves.'[168]

In 1911, the same year that Pound was pondering technique, his protégé-to-be, T. S. Eliot, returned to Harvard after a year in Paris, bringing with him all sorts of European affectations. He carried a cane, hung a Gauguin *Crucifixion* on his wall, embraced the *élan vital* of Henri Bergson and began taking boxing lessons. Conrad Aiken recalled that these lessons took place 'at a toughish gymnasium in Boston's South End, where, under the tutelage of an ex-pugilist with some such moniker as Steve O'Donnell, he learned the rudiments of boxing, but also, as he put it, "how to swarm with passion up a rope" – his delight in this attainment was manifest.'[169] Steve O'Donnell had fought Peter Jackson in the 1880s, and performed exhibition bouts with James Corbett in 1890s, before taking on the job as Harvard University's 'Physical Culture and Boxing Instructor'.[170] Aiken plays down the institutional affiliation to imply that Eliot is dangerously slumming, but for worthwhile aesthetic effects. Aiken recalled Eliot arriving late one day for their regular post-boxing meal bearing 'a magnificent black eye, a shiner that did Steve great credit; it was really iridescent'. 'You will see me any morning in the park / Reading the comics and the sporting page,' remarks the 'self-possessed' speaker of the second section of Eliot's 1910 poem, 'Portrait of a Lady'.[171] That reading bore fruit in many ways.[172] Eliot thought of Sweeney, for example, as a 'man who in younger days was perhaps a professional pugilist, mildly successful; who then grew older and retired to keep a pub.'[173]

After the war, such Ivy League dandyish pugilism came in for much mockery, and not only from Pound and Lewis. In John Dos Passos's *Nineteen Nineteen* (1932), Blake Wigglesworth (known as Ned) is a Harvard aesthete who burns incense in front of his Buddha and finds everything except drinking boring; 'whenever politics or the war or anything like that came up he had a way of closing his eyes and throwing back his head and saying Blahblahblahblah.' The only time he comes to life is when he tells the story of an evening out with Barney, 'a boxing instructor, if he didn't have a weak heart he'd be welter-weight champion of New England'. Hearing of all this, Ned's roommate, the politicized Dick Savage, 'felt like smashing him in the face'.[174] The most fervent attacks on Ivy League sportsmen were, however, reserved, for those who did more than dabble in athleticism. The most damning of these would be Scott Fitzgerald's portrait in *The Great Gatsby* of Yale football star, Tom Buchanan, whose 'cruel body' and dodgy politics result in tragedy.[175]

Technique, and professionalism, as Lewis had noted, were also a central preoccupation of Hemingway. *The Sun Also Rises* (1926) begins with a description of Robert Cohn's amateur boxing skills (developed at Princeton and now exercised in the gymnasiums of Paris) and we soon learn to equate this with his dilettante dabbling in literature. Cohn has published a novel with 'a fairly good publisher' and Jake notes that 'it was not really such a bad novel as the critics later called it, although it was a very poor novel'. Now he is stuck on his second novel. Cohn is contrasted first with Jake himself, a journalist who is at his happiest after 'a good morning's work', and then with Bill Gorton, who has 'made a lot of money on his last book and was going to make a lot more'. Gorton arrives in Paris from New York where he has seen 'a whole crop of great light heavyweights. Any one of them was a good prospect to grow up, put on weight and trim Dempsey'. The suggestion is that Gorton is himself a literary contender, although his experience of crooked prize-fighting in Vienna reminds us that how impure the profession of boxing (and perhaps the profession of writing) really is. Much 'cleaner', from Jake's point of view, is bullfighting. Bullfighting is aligned to boxing – Jake describes a bull having 'a left and a right just like a boxer' – but, at its best, it is free from the corruption that has tainted the more modern sport. Pedro Romero, the only completely admirable character is the novel, represents the true artist. His 'work' (neither he nor Jake call it 'sport' or 'art' or 'craft') is characterized by its 'sincerity' (he does not 'simulate') and its 'absolute purity of line'. 'It was not brilliant bull-fighting', Jake says, 'it was only perfect bull-fighting.' But true art can only exist in what Jake characterizes as the primitive culture of Spain; elsewhere, all that fighters or writers can do is try to work 'hard' and 'clean'.[176]

A debate between amateurism and professionalism – in sport and in art – is enacted again in Scott Fitzgerald's *Tender is the Night* (1934), the story of Dick Diver, a young psychiatrist who abandons his professional codes of behaviour when he marries a young and beautiful patient.[177] The book is full of fights; fights for honour, and fights for nothing. Dick is contemptuous of a young Englishman who tells him 'a preposterous story about a boxing match with his best friend, in which they loved and bruised each other for an hour, always with great reserve.'[178] Suffering from what he only partly humorously diagnoses as 'non-combatant's shell-shock', Dick sees pointless conflict everywhere. It is impossible even to cash a cheque without running into the 'heavyweight champion of the world'. After failing to escape Europe and his fate, Dick finds himself in Rome, drunk and in a 'mock fight' of 'padded, glancing blows' with a taxi driver and then, unfortunately, a policeman. When he returns home, his colleagues discuss his bruises, speculating on his 'debauch' and his alibi of 'boxing on the trans-Atlantic trip. The American passengers box a lot on those transatlantic ships.'[179] But the fight that the crossing of the ocean represents is no sport. Dick's surname, Diver, as many have noted, evokes his deeper and deeper plunges into despair. It might also evoke what he has done in leaving America and marrying the wealthy Nicole. The marriage, he believes, has meant the end of his professional life. In order to save her, he has thrown his own fight; in boxing jargon, he has taken the money and taken a dive.[180]

## PUGILISTIC AESTHETICS

In the early twentieth century, the language of boxing provided experimental artists with metaphors for talking about a range of issues from forceful assertion to formal control, from the status of the individual character to the stance of an audience or reader. Boxing represented dialectic; the primitive; controlled and released energy; the moving body; and the body-as-machine. Just as importantly, it was not feminine and not sentimental and not refined. Best of all, the boxing match, increasingly epitomized by the knockout blow, was instantly destructive. In all these different ways, boxing was modern.

A good place to start is with Futurism, which, as Marinetti proclaimed, was an 'aesthetic of violence and blood' – an aesthetic, as many have pointed out, drawn from a mish-mash of Social Darwinian and Nietzschean ideas. This is point three of the 'Initial Manifesto of Futurism' (1909):

Literature has hitherto glorified thoughtful immobility, ecstasy and sleep; we shall extol aggressive movement, feverish insomnia, the double quick step, the somersault, the box on the ear, the fisticuff.[181]

In the years that followed, Marinetti and others presented 'the box on the ear' in a wide variety of settings. The 1917 film *Vita Futurista*, for example, included a scene of Marinetti and Ungari boxing before breakfast, while one of Marinetti and Masnata's 1933 'radio syntheses', 'Drama of Distance', juxtaposed eleven seconds of a variety of sounds including a military march, a tango, road noise and a boxing match.[182] Futurism was the latest in a long line of movements which evoked the language of boxing in an attempt to be modern and to overthrow academicism; what was new was an emphasis on dynamism and a vision of the body as a fusion of the organic and technological. In its celebration of the efficient machine and rejection of the 'maternal ditch', futurism also embraced Nietzsche's anti-feminism.

Before long, the pugnacious tone of Marinetti's statements infected the language of Futurism's admirers throughout Europe, from the Russian Cubo-Futurists who proposed a 'Slap in the Face of Public Taste', to D. H. Lawrence, who welcomed the 'revolt against beastly sentiment', to Mussolini, who reputedly described punching as 'an exquisitely fascist means of self-expression'.[183] Less portentous, but significant at the time, was a 1914 London brouhaha in which T. E. Hulme came to the defence of the sculptor, Jacob Epstein, against an attack by the Nietzschean art critic, Anthony Ludovici. 'The most appropriate means of dealing with [Ludovici]', Hulme wrote, 'would be a little personal violence.'[184] The letters pages of *The New Age* were soon filled with suggestions on how this might be enacted. A defender of Ludovici suggested that he might employ 'a pugilist of Jack Johnson's size' to present his case, then Hulme could take him on. Wyndham Lewis then entered the fray, arguing that Johnson would prefer to fight for Hulme and Epstein's 'secular gods'.[185]

But there was more to the Futurist (and Vorticist) evocation of boxing than simply the assertion of masculine aggression against convention and sentiment. Much of their language was drawn from Nietzsche's pronouncements about the importance of opposition for progress and the need for self-assertion through action rather than contemplation, and his quasi-thermodynamic theories about discharging energy. For Nietzsche and his diverse followers, art derived from 'a compulsion and urge to get rid of the exuberance of inner tension through muscular activity and movements of all kinds'.[186]

Movement of all kinds attracted the Futurists. 'We have lost the ability to understand the life of the motionless statue,' declared the Russian poet Vadim Shersheevich in the foreword to his 1916 collection of poems, *Automobile Gait*, 'but the movement of cholera bacilli at the time of an epidemic is comprehensible and fascinating to us.'[187] In 1928, the Italian painter Aligi Sassu, responding to the call for 'dynamism and muscular reform' in painting, declared that 'the dynamic body is a fantastic creation of the artistic spirit'. And if painting needed dynamized musculature, where better to find it than sports?[188] Sassu's early paintings feature the mechanized dynamism of cycle and motor races, and the human equivalent in boxing matches. (Not much earlier, George Bellows, a painter coming from a very different tradition, declared, 'I didn't paint anatomy; I painted action.'[189]) What 'dinamismo' entails in paintings such as Sassu's *Pugilatori* (1929) is the breaking up of form into parts (not dissimilar to cubist representations of the body), but then an attempt to suggest that those parts move at such high speeds as to make their boundaries indistinguishable (illus. 61). Total dynamism, a 1928 Italian manifesto suggested, would lead to the 'annihilation' of the body itself. Since human bodies (unlike automobiles) could not reach the speeds required for total dynamism, the form of the body remains in (a suitably Nietzschean) tension with its movement. Futurist paintings of boxers and cyclists recall Muybridge's photographic sequences.

Primitivist notions of ritualized fighting and ego-less selves are among the topics explored in the work of the Austrian novelist, and a rather different reader of Nietzsche, Robert Musil. The eponymous Man without Qualities, who we later learn is called Ulrich, is first described gazing out of his window with the air of 'a sick man who shrinks from every strong physical need'. Yet, immediately afterwards Ulrich crosses the room and hits a punch bag 'with a hard, sudden blow that seemed not exactly in keeping with moods of resignation or conditions of weakness'. Throughout the novel, Ulrich's actions suggest various habits, manners or characteristics, but none serve to define him. A few chapters later, Ulrich attempts to fight 'three louts' in the streets. 'He resisted the idea that the three faces suddenly glaring at him out of the night with rage and scorn were simply after his money, but chose to see them as a spontaneous materialization of free-floating hostility.' In a cinematic confusion of knees, skulls and 'fists growing larger all the time', he is knocked out. The next day he is found by a woman who offers to take him somewhere for help. In the taxi, he offers her 'a lively defense of his experience'. Aware that 'the doings of the body . . . were really too much in fashion', the meditative Ulrich first proposes that:

> The fascination of such a fight . . . was the rare chance it offered in civilian life to perform so many varied, vigorous, yet precisely coordinated movements in response to barely perceptible signals at a speed that made conscious thought impossible . . . at the moment of action . . . muscles and nerves leap and fence with the 'I'; but this 'I' – the whole body, the soul, the will, the central and entire person as legally distinguished from all others – is swept along by his muscles and nerves like Europa riding the Bull.

Ulrich moves from a notion of 'the fight' as one in which two men confront each other to one in which the conscious self, the 'I', is pitted in a losing battle against the instinctual body (a mere collection of nerves and muscles). He goes on:

> Basically . . . this experience of almost total ecstasy or transcendence of the conscious mind is akin to experiences now lost but known in the past to the mystics of all religions, which makes it a kind of contemporary substitute for an eternal human need. Even if it is not a very good substitute it is better than nothing, and boxing or similar kinds of sports that organize this principle into a rational system are therefore a species of theology, although one cannot expect this to be generally understood as yet.[190]

The mystical transcendence of the body described here recalls the paintings of Musil's near-contemporary, Egon Schiele. Schiele's 1913 portrait of a fighter presents his awkward contorted body in a manner that evokes religious or perhaps erotic martyrdom (illus. 97). In the 1913 Vienna of Musil's novel, however, a Vienna charged with 'vague atmospheric hostility', Ulrich soon moves on to other versions of theology.[191]

The interest of Futurist boxing images did not lie only in the permanence, or otherwise, of the self, but in the self's relation to another. What are the boundaries between one self and another? What happens when one body almost merges with another? For Wyndham Lewis, Futurism, which entailed a 'dispersal' of energy, could not answer this question; in its place, he proposed the idea of the Vortex, which compressed and retained energy. In his satirical 1930s description of Hemingway and Pound quoted above, Hemingway is a statue and the action between the two men is slow and stagey. In 1914, in the first issue of the Vorticist journal, *Blast*, Lewis describes boxing rather differently. This is 'The New Egos', one of twelve 'Vortices and Notes': 'According to the most approved contemporary methods in boxing, two men burrow into each other, and after an infinitude of little intimate pommels, one collapses.'[192] Here Lewis contrasts the contemporary method with the 'old style' of boxing, one in which 'two distinct, heroic figures were confronted, and one ninepin tried to knock the other ninepin over', an image which recalls his definition of the 'comic type' as 'a failure of a considerable energy, an imitation and standardizing of the self, suggesting the existence of a uniform humanity, – creating, that is, a little host as alike as ninepins; instead of one synthetic and various ego'.[193] The modern style of boxing – which involved the protagonists 'burrowing into each other' – was not comic and 'static', but rather grotesque, dynamic and symptomatic of a wider modern phenomenon. 'We all today,' Lewis wrote, '(possibly with a coldness reminiscent of the insect world) are in each other's vitals – overlap, intersect, and are Siamese to any extent.' A 'uniform humanity' of comic ninepins gives way to 'dehumanization' ('the chief Diagnostic of the Modern World'): 'the isolated figure of most ancient Art is an anachronism'. The body becomes instead something that exists in multiple and fluid forms, 'overlapping, intersecting' in the perpetual dynamism of insect-like dances, fights and sex.[194] Lewis's 1914 painting *Combat No. 3*, in which a pair of insect-like antagonists is transformed through combat into a Vorticist machine, might almost be an illustration for this passage (illus 98).[195]

In 1927, Lewis returned to boxing imagery and 'the religion of merging' in his meditations on the 'history of the ego', or rather 'the extinction of the "thinking subject"', and the rise, in its place, of the modern 'romance of action'. In both narratives, Lewis evokes Jack Dempsey. First Dempsey appears as one of the beneficiaries, and victims, of Schopenhauer's 'aimless' Will. It is the 'nonsensical' Will, says Lewis, that has produced 'Charlie Chaplin, the League of Nations, wireless, feminism, Rockefeller'.

> It causes, daily, millions of women to drift in front of, and swarm inside, gigantic clothes-shops in every great capital, buying silk-underclothing, cloche-hats, perfumes, vanishing cream, vanity-bags and furs; it causes the Prince of Wales to become one day a Druid, and the next a Boy-Scout; it enables Dempsey to hit Firpo on the nose, or Gene Tunney to strike Dempsey in the eye, and the sun to be eclipsed.[196]

The endless and random nature of such events makes what Lewis elsewhere calls the 'gospel of action' seem particularly ridiculous. Men of action, like Dempsey, live only 'in the moment, in moods of undiluted sensationalism'. How can their behaviour be applicable to any other field of human behaviour?

If you applied the conditions and standards required for the flowering

245

of a Jack Dempsey to a Beethoven, say, you would be doing what is done in a more general and less defined sense on all hands at this moment, as a thousand different activities mystically coalesce in response to the religion of merging, or mesmeric engulfing.[197]

While passages like this seem to warn against the coming of fascism and its body culture, when Lewis talks of the threat of 'mystical mass-doctrines', his target is rather mass democracy's 'religion of merging', and its attendant consumer and entertainment culture; the world as a 'gigantic clothes-shop' in which the 'gentlemanly Robot' Tunney arbitrarily succeeds Dempsey as the hero of the day.[198]

## THE BOXING MACHINE

In 1925 Adrienne Monnier, who ran an avant-garde bookshop in Paris, attended a concert in which the American composer George Antheil played his *Ballet Mécanique* for the first time. In imagery that drew on her trips to the fights with her partner, Sylvia Beach, and their friend, Ernest Hemingway, she described his performance:

> When he plays his music he is terrible, he boxes with the piano; he riddles it with blows and perseveres furiously until the instrument, the public, and he himself are knocked out. When he is finished he is red, he sponges his forehead; he comes down from the ring with his forehead lowered, his shoulders rocking, his brows knitted, his fists still clenched tight.[199]

'Boxing with the piano', which Monnier describes as an intense physical engagement, was a way of making the instrument sound less lyrical and more percussive and mechanical. There is an antagonism, and we are to believe, productive exchange of energy, between pianist and piano, just as there may be between poet and typewriter. Sounding more mechanical, in this sense, also seemed to be a way of sounding more modern.[200] According to Antheil himself, the very words 'Ballet Mécanique' were meant to evoke 'the spiritual exhaustion, the superathletic, non-sentimental period commencing "The Long Armistice"'.[201]

The 'superathleticism' of boxing also represented a 'non-sentimental' mechanical operation for Marcel Duchamp, who, incidentally, bore a striking resemblance to Georges Carpentier. (In 1924 Francis Picabia used a portrait of Carpentier for the cover of the Dada journal *391*, claiming it was a portrait of Duchamp.[202]) One of Duchamp's early studies for the nine-foot-high *The Large Glass*, or *The Bride Stripped Bare by Her Bachelors, Even* (1915–23) was entitled 'The Boxing Match'.[203] While the construction keeps the bride (on top) and her bachelors (below) apart, the notes, which Duchamp intended to be an integral part of the work, shows how they might come together. Sketched out in 1913, reworked as a photomontage in 1919, and included in a 1965 etching of *The Large Glass*

*Completed*, 'The Boxing Match' was never included in the construction, which was finally left 'definitely unfinished'.[204]

One of the most abstractly geometrical parts of the *Large Glass*, and one of its more complex mechanical operations, 'The Boxing Match' consisted of arcs and circles, 'presumably matching punches and swings'.[205] As Calvin Tompkins notes, 'it shows a clockwork mechanism that causes two battering rams to move up and down, loosening as they do the bride's clothes and causing them to fall. All this does not take place smoothly but jerkily'.[206] Jean Suquet describes these 'rams' as being held by the bachelors above their heads 'like musclemen, to hold up the horizon-garment of the Bride. The rams fall. The dress slips off – or at least begins to.' Suquet goes on to discuss Duchamp's speedy repudiation of 'these sideshow musclemen and their rigged *boxing match*' in favour of a fire (ignited gas will 'burn with desire'), but it is interesting to consider what the boxing analogy added to his original story.[207] In various interviews, Duchamp described the drawing as part of an attempt to 'get away' from 'personal style' and 'retinal painting': 'that was the period when I changed completely from splashing the paint on the canvas to an absolutely precise co-ordinated drawing; and with no relation to artistic handiwork'.[208] As a style, 'mechanical drawing' signalled the impersonal; as a subject matter, boxing, it seems, was intended to do the same. But can a machine designed to strip the clothes from a woman ever really be thought of as impersonal? André Breton described the *Large Glass* as 'a mechanistic, cynical interpretation of love: the passage of woman from the state of virginity to the state of non-virginity taken as the theme of an asentimental speculation'.[209] The role of 'musclemen' and 'a boxing match' in this passage certainly confirms the 'asentimental' nature of Duchamp's view of 'love', but such asentimentalism is hardly impersonal or even merely cynical. The exchange of energy between bride and bachelors is propelled by an inherent erotic aggression.

Aggressive anti-sentimentalism is also at work in Djuna Barnes's 1936 Paris novel, *Nightwood*, a novel that presents gender and sexual identities as roles to be performed mechanically, and love as a violent and 'bloodthirsty' business.[210] Jenny fights off her lover Robin by striking her repeatedly with powerful 'blows', while the transvestite Dr O'Connor ('heavily rouged and his lashes painted') lives in a room that is 'a cross between a *chambre à coucher* and a boxer's training camp'; he describes himself as 'an old worn out lioness, a coward in my corner'. Dr O'Connor tells the lovelorn Nora Flood that when a woman loves 'a Sodomite', she often finds her lover 'has committed the unpardonable error of not being able to exist' and ends up 'with a dummy' in her arms. That is, he says, 'God's last round, shadow-boxing, that the heart may be murdered'.[211]

## DADA AND THE CRITICAL INSTINCT OF 'KNOCK-OUT'

'Every man must shout' and use his 'fists', announced Tristan Tzara in 1918; 'there is great destructive, negative work to be done'.[212] Although developed largely in reaction to Futurism, Dadaism retained much of its language and gestures. In

247

the manifestos which followed, fists are continually evoked as essential Dadaist tools against establishment culture. That of 'Monsieur Aa The Antiphilosopher' in February 1920 begins 'without the pursuit of I worship you / which is a French boxer', and three months later, 'Monsieur Aa The Antiphilosopher Sends Us Another Manifesto' ends with the words 'Punch yourself in the face and drop dead.' Tzara later described one of his plays as 'a boxing match with words'.[213]

One of the things that the Dadaists adopted from Futurism was a fondness for soirées, what would now be called happenings or performance art; occasions in which, as Tzara put it, the 'vitality of every instant' could be affirmed. In 1916 the Cabaret Voltaire in Zurich staged a series of *soirées nègres*. Tzara recalled a typical evening:

> Boxing resumed: Cubist dance, costumes by Janco, each man his own bug drum on his head, noise, Negro music/ trabatgea bonoooooo oo ooooo/5 literary experiments: Tzara in tails stands before the curtain, stone sober for the animals, and explains the new aesthetic.[214]

Dada's interest in boxing drew partly on a familiar primitivist ideology that championed ritual over realism, and partly on a cabaret tradition in which boxing had long played a part, mingling with trapeze acts, jugglers and animal acts. Both these elements are also present in German Expressionism, one of Dada's targets. Max Pechstein's *Boxer in the Ring* (1910), for example, was one of a number of postcards by the *Brücke* artists recording cabaret acts ranging from can-can dancers, jugglers, and trapeze artists to boxers (illus. 62).[215] While Pechstein celebrated the popular and the primitive, he did not suggest that cabaret or the circus would change the world. Dada, however, like Futurism before it, hoped that the confrontational 'body events' on stage would spill out into the streets, that the city would become the arena and life itself a revolutionary performance.[216] When, in 1923, Malcolm Cowley punched a Parisian café proprietor on the jaw, he was surprised how impressed his Dadaist friends were.[217]

As Dada spread across Europe, and evolved into Surrealism, boxing imagery continued to be used to express bold repudiation of convention. Paul Dermée presented 'Boxing without Tears' at the 1920 Paris Dada Festival and Jacques Rigaut's 1929 surrealist autobiography includes the employment of his 'American right hook'. 'What a peal of laughter at my mistress's terrified face when, as she waited to receive a caress, I slugged her with my American right hook and her body fell several feet away'.[218] From the early days of Dada, an allusion to boxing was also intended to suggest an interest in dialectics. Picabia and René Clair's film, *Entr'Acte* (1924) opens with fifteen seconds of white boxing gloves punching each other against a black background, before moving on to present a seemingly random series of scenes and images. It is tempting to read André Breton's 'poem-objets' in the same way. One includes a series of handwritten phrases, such as 'these vague landscapes' and 'crouching in the house of my heart', among an assemblage of a bust of a man, an oil lantern, a framed photograph and toy boxing gloves. But while *Entr'Acte* deliberately frustrated attempts to provide a coherent reading, Breton struggled to create a surreal unity out of these 'contradictory conditions or phenomena'.[219]

The Dadaist who intermingled the discourses of boxing and poetry most fully and self-consciously was Arthur Cravan. Born Fabien Avenarius Lloyd in 1887, Cravan was the nephew of Oscar Wilde's wife, Constance, and wrote of his affinity with his uncle, 'although our chest measurement differs'.[220] In the tradition of his heroes Whitman and Rimbaud, Cravan ('the world's shortest-haired poet') used boxing as a means to *épater le bourgeois*. From 1912 to 1915, he published six issues of a polemical journal called *Maintenant*, which became a model for all subsequent Dada magazines. Mainly written by Cravan himself, *Maintenant* featured articles attacking modern writers and painters, insulting them about their physical as well as artistic shortcomings.[221] According to Gabrielle Buffet-Picabia, it was his review of the 1914 Independents Exhibition in Paris that 'made him famous'. The article offered 'a bit of good advice: take a few pills and purge your mind; do a lot of fucking or better still go into rigorous training: when the girth of your arms measures nineteen inches, you'll at least be a brute, if you're gifted'. Cravan justified this kind of criticism by claiming in Nietzschean terms that 'genius is nothing but an extraordinary manifestation of the body', but insulting individual bodies was a risky business. He so offended Marie Laurencin ('Now there's one who needs to have her skirts lifted up') that her lover Guillaume Apollinaire had him arrested for defamation of character.[222] 'In its systematic provocation,' Roger Shattuck suggested, Cravan's writing 'resembles a literary transposition of boxing techniques'.[223] But Cravan's

99
'Johnson and Cravan – and their wives', *The Soil*, April 1917.

were not just any boxing techniques; more precisely, as Mina Loy noted, 'the instinct of "knock-out" dominated his critique'.[224] But more was needed to be a true 'boxer-poet'.

In fact, Cravan's boxing had preceded his poetry. He took up the sport at sixteen and in 1910 won the French Amateur Light Heavyweight Championship. His hero, Jack Johnson, was, however, in a different league entirely. ('Ah! let me laugh, laugh, but truly laugh, like Jack Johnson!', he once wrote).[225] Cravan, who frequently asserted that he was 'ashamed of being white', befriended Johnson in Paris in 1916. Nina Hamnett recalled that he was often to be found 'sparring with negro boxers at Van Dongen's studio on Thursday afternoons'; one of those boxers was probably Johnson, who was posing for a portrait.[226] Soon the two men came up with a scheme to make both some money (illus. 99). They staged a fight in the Plaza de Toros in Barcelona, which only continued until the sixth round because, as part of the deal, they needed to put on a good show for the film cameras. The French poet Blaise Cendrars gave a lively, if inaccurate account of the contest.[227] Cravan used his earnings to pay for a transatlantic steamer on which he impressed fellow passenger Leon Trotsky.[228] At the end of 1918, he disappeared in bizarre circumstances off the coast of Mexico and was never seen again. That mystery, and Mina Loy's enduring love for her boxer-poet-husband soon became the stuff of legend.[229]

## 'COMRADES, DISCUSS RED SPORT'

In the late nineteenth century English boxing established itself in Moscow, and while never popular there to the extent that it was in Berlin or Paris, the sport had a certain following among the military. After 1917, however, boxing became rather controversial. Immediately after the Revolution, there was support for sports that would promote hard work and a strong defence. In November 1918, the first Soviet boxing championship was held in Moscow, and despite 'starvation, the cold, a typhoid outbreak and the Civil War', it attracted a large crowd.[230] By the mid-1920s, however, it was widely maintained that sports such as wrestling and boxing encouraged dangerous competitive and individualistic values. Although boxing was very popular at the time, with active gyms from Moscow to Odessa, and foreign films such as *The Boxer's Bride* doing well at the cinema, the first Trade-Union Games in 1925 excluded the sport, and the Leningrad Physical Culture Council banned it.[231] In 1928, Vladimir Mayakovsky wrote a poem called 'Comrades, discuss Red Sport!', in which he complained that 'sport has not changed much as yet'. The poem ends with an exhortation to sporting lads to pay attention to their political education as well as their biceps, for 'we need sportsmen who enlighten the masses'.[232]

The 'hygienists' argued that sports depended on an instrumental view of the body as a series of parts designed to perform specific function (bend, duck, punch) while physical culture promoted a more harmonious and holistic development. Whether boxing had a place in the new regimes was much debated.

In 1929 the Minister of Education and Arts, Anatoly Lunacharsky wrote an open letter to the press supporting the sport. Not only did boxing involve 'the whole nervous system, heart, blood circulation, the respiratory system and, in every way, the muscles of the upper part of the body and the legs; it develops inventiveness and accuracy . . . stamina, self-control, fearlessness, and courage more than any other sport'. It was inaccurate, Lunacharsky maintained, to dub boxing an essentially bourgeois enterprise for 'even the fiercest bout teaches one to regard one's opponent as a comrade with whom one has common cause'.[233] There was some sympathy for this view; Jack London was, after all, an extremely popular writer in the Soviet Union.[234] In the place of competitive sports, however, the Proletkultists proposed collective exercise and lavish sports spectacles (some parades mounted boxing rings on floats).[235] One of these spectacles, the Moscow Spartakiada athletic competition of 1928 (named for the Roman slave rebel Spartacus), was commemorated in a series of dynamic collage-based posters and postcards by Gustav Klucis. By designing posters for films and sports events, Constructivist artists such as Klucis and the Stenberg brothers signalled their intention to bridge the gap between avant-garde art and proletarian culture (illus. 63).

In general, the 1920s were 'years of physical culture or fitness . . . rather than sport', a trend that inspired derision from the Cambridge-educated and Berlin-based émigré, Vladimir Nabokov.[236] Nabokov was scathing about physical culture, 'in which everyone is condemned to do everything as one . . . not allowing that anyone might be better made than his neighbour'. These words were written in Berlin, where he lived from 1922 to 1937, and, according to his wife Véra, 'taught many subjects . . . languages, tennis, boxing. And prosody, prosody.'[237] For Nabokov, in 1925, play had an 'enticing, disturbing' quality entirely absent from both Communist gymnastics and the German 'goose step'. 'What we feel in our muscles is the essence of play', he wrote, but watching sports was also play. His essay ends with an account of Hans Breitensträter's defeat by the Spanish heavyweight Paulino Uzcudan and a lyrical vision of the spectators leaving the stadium after the fight:

> When we all emptied out on to the street in the frosty blue of a snowy night, I was certain that in the flabbiest father of a family, in the most modest youth, in the souls and muscles of all this crowd, which tomorrow early in the morning will disperse to offices, to shops, to factories, there was one and the same beautiful feeling, for the sake of which it was worthwhile to bring together two boxers, a feeling of confident sparkling strength, of cheerfulness, of manliness in the play of the inspiring boxers. And this playful feeling, perhaps, is more important and purer than many so-called 'elevated pleasures'.[238]

## 'ONLY VIA THE SPORTS ARENA CAN WE APPROACH THE THEATRICAL ARENA'

Post-war European interest in American culture was accompanied, if not driven, by a fascination with American economic practices and, in particular, with the successes of Frederick Taylor's time-and-motion studies and their application to factory production by Henry Ford. By the early twenties, Taylorism and Fordism had become bywords for efficiency and rationalization in many different spheres.

While the application of Taylorism to sport is often discussed, the importance of sport for Taylorism is less well known. *The Principles of Scientific Management* (1911) begins by asking how 'greater efficiency' can be achieved in the workplace and, in particular, how workers can be encouraged to work at a faster pace. Taylor notes that 'the English and American peoples are the greatest sportsmen in the world', and when playing sport (baseball and cricket are his examples) a typical workman 'strains every nerve to secure victory for his side.' But 'when the same workman returns to work on the following day, instead of using every effort to turn out the largest possible amount of work, in a majority of cases this man deliberately plans to do as little as he safely can'.[239] How can the worker be motivated to strive for productivity at work as well as in sports? Taylor's answer drew on many of the rationalizing regulations that such measures as the Queensberry rules had already introduced; specifying the 'task' to be done; learning to use 'strength to the very best advantage'; 'having proper scientifically determined periods of rest in close sequence to periods of work'; in short applying 'rigid rules of each motion of every man'.[240] These principles were applied to many aspects of Soviet, as well as American and European, life in the 1920s. 'Production gymnastics' were performed in factories, and the Taylorized performance of work movements was itself seen as a kind of sport. In the unalienated labour of socialism, it was argued, work and leisure should fuse.

Taylorism also had an impact on the theatre. In 1905 Vsevolod Meyerhold, previously known as an actor in Chekhov's plays at the Moscow Art Theatre, had opened an acting laboratory. There, and later in St Petersburg, he developed a series of exercises for his students to perform as a way of revolutionizing stage drama, moving it away from a psychological emphasis and breaking down the gap between actor and spectator. The studio was closed by the revolution in 1917, but reopened in Moscow in 1921. Meyerhold reintroduced his St Petersburg exercises and renamed them 'bio-mechanics'. Meyerhold's newly Taylorized exercises, 'by which each movement of the body' was to be 'differentiated and made fully expressive', included a 'blow to the nose', and were taught alongside gymnastics, juggling, fencing, ballet, tap dancing and boxing.[241] If during this period, sport was increasingly presented as a form of theatre, theorists like Meyerhold maintained that theatre should in turn learn from sport. 'Only via the sports arena can we approach the theatrical arena', he declared in 1922. Replacing psychological theories, Meyerhold's methods sought to establish a more objective basis for acting, based on an understanding of biology and mechanics.

The muscles and tendons of the actors were to be considered as comparable to piston rods and cylinders.

One of Meyerhold's students was Sergei Eisenstein who, in 1921, drew heavily on his principles for an 'agit-poster' of Jack London's short story, 'The Mexican', the story of a young revolutionary who boxes in order to get money for guns. Eisenstein was appointed by the First Workers' Theatre of the Proletkult to produce scenery and costumes, and for both drew heavily on Cubism and the circus. The climax of the agit-poster was the fight scene. The play's director, Valeri Smishlayev, wanted to portray this through the reaction of the characters who were observing an event that was supposedly taking place off-stage. Eisenstein, however, suggested that the fight be performed in front of the audience, in fact in the middle of the auditorium, as if it were taking place in a boxing ring. Although the theatre's firemen soon dismissed this suggestion, Eisenstein later recalled the scene as important to the development of his ideas about film. 'Here, my participation brought into the theatre "events" themselves – a purely cinematographic element, as distinguished from "reactions to events" – which is a purely theatrical element.'

> We dared the concreteness of factual events. The fight was to be carefully planned in advance but was to be utterly realistic. The playing of our young worker-actors in the fight scene differed radically from the acting elsewhere in the production . . . While the other scenes influenced the audience through intonation, gestures and mimicry, [this] scene employed realistic, even textual means – real fighting, bodies crashing to the ring floor, panting, the shine of sweat on the torso, and finally, the unforgettable smacking of gloves against taunt skin and strained muscles.[242]

In the years that followed Eisenstein moved from theatre into film, and developed the theory of montage with which he is now identified. Montage was also the method of Dziga Vertov, but Vertov remained interested in 'reactions to events'. He argued that the new cinema should replace the multiplicity of subjective reactions with an objective, collective response determined in advance by the artist or 'Cine-Eye'. In order to explain how this revolutionary approach might work, Vertov used the example of a crowd watching a boxing match. Each spectator at the fight itself came away with different impression of what had taken place, what Vertov dismissed as '*a series of incoherent impressions*'. In place of this, he wanted to subject 'the eye to the will of the camera'. The camera would film 'the consecutive movements of those fighting' and present them in such a way (montage 'in the most profitable order') that 'the relevant materials' would be presented before the spectators and their eyes would be 'forced' to witness 'the consecutive details that they must see'.[243] The movement of the Cine-Eye thus supersedes that of the fighters themselves; the actual conflict in the ring is replaced by a cinematic assault on the audience.

A more sophisticated approach informed Eisenstein's third film, *October* (1927), which told the story of the 1917 revolution, and included both actors and documentary footage, a combination that Eisenstein called the 'played and non-played'. In an essay on the film he used a boxing metaphor to describe the often-discussed 'opposition' between these two modes of film-making, only to dismiss it as a false contest.

> When there are two contestants it is usually the third who is right.
>> In the ring now:
>> Played and non-played.
>> That means that justice lies with the third.
>> *With the extra-played*.
>> With cinema that places itself *beyond* the played and the non-played.[244]

In 1921, boxing had appealed to Eisenstein as a sign of the real (the 'raw material' and 'fact' of the non-played rather than the falsity of the played), but by 1928, he rejected opposition itself (what he called the '*agitational theatre of attractions*') in favour of dialectics.[245] The model of the boxing match, in which one contestant is always victorious, had been superseded by one that maintained that both contestants could be accommodated in a productive synthesis.

Of course Meyerhold and his followers were not the only early twentieth-century figures who challenged the verbal and psychological emphasis of film and theatre by incorporating elements from the cabaret, the circus and the sports stadium. Throughout the twentieth century, sport continued to provide a model for theatrical performance, with the boxing ring providing an ideal space within which dramatic conflict could be staged. The theatricality of boxing is apparent, and much has been made, not least in this book, of the ease in which a boxing match (the ultimate two-hander) can be made to express conflict. The tropes of boxing have appealed to a wide range of playwrights and directors who reject the verbal and psychological in favour of a theatre that is at least one of the following – physical, ritualistic, popular, scientific and impersonal, or violent.[246] The French mime Etienne Decroux, for example, took Georges Carpentier as 'the motivating image' for his study of 'physical mime (tragedy section)', praising the boxer's 'vigor and grace; strength; elegance; dazzle and thought; a taste for danger and a smile'.[247] Antonin Artaud, meanwhile, posited a connection between the ritualistic purging of violence in a boxing match and in what he called the Theatre of Cruelty. According to Artaud, the actor and athlete are doubles, the only difference being that while the athlete makes 'muscular movements of physical exertion', the actor's efforts require 'affective musculature'. The actor must 'use his emotions in the same way a boxer uses his muscles.'[248]

Bertolt Brecht was less interested in making actors like sportsmen than in turning theatre audiences (as Pound, in 1911, had wanted to turn readers of poetry) into sports spectators. His 1926 essay, 'More Good Sports', begins by declaring, 'We pin our hopes on the sporting public'.

254

Make no bones about it, we have our eye on those huge pans of concrete filled with 15,000 men and women of every variety of class and physiognomy, the fairest and shrewdest audience in the world . . . The demoralization of our theatre audiences springs from the fact that neither theatre nor audience has any idea what is supposed to go on there. When people in sporting establishments buy their tickets they know exactly what is going to take place and that is exactly what does take place once they are in their seats: viz. highly trained persons developing their peculiar powers in the way most suited to them with the greatest sense of responsibility yet in such a way as to make one feel that they are doing it primarily for their own fun. Against that the traditional theatre nowadays is quite lacking in character.[249]

The boxing fan, sitting smoking in a brightly lit hall, represented Brecht's ideal spectator. Although the programme note for the 1928 Heidelberg production of *In the Jungle of Cities* described the fight as a microcosm of class struggle, Brecht originally conceived it as 'a fight for fighting's sake' to find out who was 'the best man' – in other words, sport. The prologue informs the audience that it is about to witness 'an inexplicable boxing match': 'Don't worry your heads about the motives for the fight, concentrate on the stakes. Judge impartially the techniques of the contenders, and keep your eyes fixed on the finish.'[250] Brecht hoped that by behaving like a fight audience, the theatre audience would abandon its traditional Aristotelian concerns with character and motive. The boxing match, in other words, exemplified what he termed 'epic theatre', a theatre which encourages the spectator to 'judge' the contents of the play objectively, and avoid emotional identification with its protagonists or events. 'Instead of sharing an experience the spectator must come to grips with things.'[251] Brecht maintained, as Pound had done, that the financial interest the boxing audience has in the outcome of the fight makes it more astute to its workings. If only, both hoped, something could similarly inspire poets and theatre audiences to pay attention to technique. Brecht's solution was to remove all attempts at concealment and mystification. Audiences should be encouraged to smoke as 'it is hopeless to "carry away" any man who is smoking and accordingly pretty well occupied with himself'. In addition, 'the theatre must acquire *qua* theatre the same fascinating reality as a sporting arena during a boxing match. The best thing is to show the machinery, the ropes and the flies.' Theatrical lighting should be bright and 'within the spectator's field of vision'. The spectator should see that 'arrangements have been made to show him something . . . No one would expect the lighting to be hidden at . . . a boxing match.' 'By these means,' Brecht concluded, 'one would soon have a theatre full of experts, just as one has sporting arenas full of experts.'[252] In the meantime, he would have been glad to note that in 1928, a Berlin theatre postponed a premiere because it coincided with the heavyweight title fight between Max Schmeling and Franz Diener.[253]

A connection between boxing and modernity dominated rhetoric in the 1920s, as it had in the 1820s. Both decades saw a flourishing of sport and of artistic experimentation in the wake of a major war. The language of boxing allowed for the assertion of both masculine and national invulnerability. But important changes in the nature of the sport had taken place in the hundred years that separated Byron from Hemingway. While the Fancy had created a distinctive and class-based male subculture, the 1920s saw sports stars become international celebrities for both men and women. Class was less an issue than race, and money was bigger than both. The nature of the contest had also changed. In the early nineteenth century, the hero of the ring was the man who could endure a beating for up to six hours; in the early twentieth century, it was the man who could knock out his opponent in less than 60 seconds. But one thing that does link the 1820s and 1920s is the short duration of the glory years. After Dempsey's defeat and Tunney's retirement, many noted the end of an era. Nostalgia returned to the language of commentators on both sport and art, and in 1949, Jean Arp declared that the golden age of heavyweight modernism was over. All that remained of its legacy were publicists and courtiers. It was now an 'era of flyweight glory'.[254]

# 8

# Save Me, Jack Dempsey;
# Save Me, Joe Louis

Boxing fans always like to imagine hypothetical contests: could John L. Sullivan have beaten Mike Tyson? How would Amir Khan have fared against Roberto Durán? In the 1930s imaginary contests between Joe Louis and Jack Dempsey were all the rage, and one forms the basis of Irwin Shaw's 1939 story, 'I Stand By Dempsey'. Two boxing fans leave a Madison Square Garden disgusted with the show. 'Not a bloody nose,' Flanagan said, 'Not a single drop of blood. Heavyweights! Heavyweight pansies!' The conversation switches to Joe Louis and whether Dempsey 'in his prime' would have beaten him. Gurske thinks he would, but Flanagan dismisses his fervour as the over-excitement of 'a little guy' – 'a guy is under five foot six, every time he gets in a argument he gets excited'. Finally Gurske snaps and throws a bottle at Flanagan, who lifts his friend into the air by the collar and declares him a 'hundred-and-thirty-pound Napoleon'. The story ends bizarrely with Flanagan laying Gurske over his knee and spanking him. It takes 32 strokes before Gurske will say 'I stand by Louis' and concedes that Louis would have beaten Dempsey in the second round.[1]

Louis and Dempsey were talismanic figures for many Americans during the Depression. In different ways, each man provided a focus for discussions of failure and success, endurance and survival, for a sense that one might be lucky or unlucky. The question of allegiance for one or other boxer was more complicated than simply white and black, although that discourse was often relevant. Dempsey was a figure from the past, the champion of the affluent twenties, struggling to adapt to new circumstance; Louis, meanwhile, emerged from the heart of the Depression and for many, seemed to suggest the promise of a new kind of future.

Jack Dempsey remained a popular figure long after he lost the title to Gene Tunney in 1927. This was partly due to the fact that, after Tunney's retirement the following year, the heavyweight title changed hands rapidly (from Max Schmeling to Jack Sharkey to Primo Carnera to Max Baer to James J. Braddock) with no enduring champion emerging until Joe Louis in 1937. (A. J. Liebling dubbed this period 'the Dark Age' of boxing.[2]) Dempsey, meanwhile, maintained and developed his public profile. After losing money in the 1929 crash and through an expensive divorce settlement in 1930, he began fighting exhibitions and refereeing, and in 1935 opened Jack Dempsey's 'gaudily meatish' Restaurant, near Madison Square Garden, which, after moving to Broadway, stayed in business until 1974.[3] During the economic boom of the twenties, Dempsey's youthful experiences of poverty had made him seem exotic to many Americans. He represented a rough-hewn relic of the frontier days, and was all the more modern for his seeming primitivism. At the height of the Depression, however, Dempsey's appeal shifted, as many more people felt that they were living in a world where conventional rules no longer applied; novelist Jo Sinclair, for example, described the Depression itself as 'getting slugged below the belt'.[4] No longer an intriguing anachronism, the Manassa Mauler became a representative man.

Dempsey's final defeats form the basis of Horace Gregory's poem, 'Dempsey, Dempsey', included in the influential 1935 anthology *Proletarian Literature in the United States*. The poem begins by addressing the ex-champion as the 'failure king of the USA', a model for all those who are down, but not yet out:

> there's a million boys that want to come back
> with hell in their eyes and a terrible sock
> that almost connects.
> They've got to come back, out of the street,
> out of some lowdown, lousy job
> or take a count with Dempsey.

But Dempsey cannot stop the 'big boss' who cuts their pay checks, Gregory suggests; he cannot even earn his own. As the poem's desperation intensifies, the final stanza recasts the enemy; the problem is not just 'the big boss' but those who 'quit' the fight.

> I can't get up, I'm dead, my legs
> are dead, see, I'm no good,
> they got me and I'm out,
> down for the count.
> I've quit, quit again,
> only God save Dempsey, make him get up again,
> Dempsey, Dempsey.[5]

Throughout the thirties and beyond, Dempsey served as an iconic figure both to those who identified with his losses and failures, and those who felt that they too could one day be champion of the world, if only they worked hard enough. Two photographs exemplify the conflicting aspects of his appeal. In the first, a touched-up studio print from 1937, he is pictured with an eight-year-old in Philadelphia supporting the United Studios campaign for boys' clubs – inspiring hope for the future (illus. 100). In the second, from 1939, he appears at the State Penitentiary in

100
Jack Dempsey meets eight-year-old John Panulla at the Germantown Boys Club, Philadelphia, 1937.

101
Jack Dempsey addresses prisoners at the State Penitentiary, Raleigh, North Carolina, 1939. The caption reads 'Many of the men whom he talked to have been in prison since he won his title.'

North Carolina; the ropes on the ring separating the boxer from the prisoners, but also suggesting that the ring itself might be a kind of prison (illus. 101).

## 'I COULD'VE BEEN A CONTENDER. I COULD'VE BEEN SOMEBODY.'[6]

In a 1933 sociological study of 'Americans at play', Jesse Frederick Steiner noted a 'growing interest in amateur boxing'; an interest, he argued, which had been stimulated by 'the Golden Gloves Amateur boxing contest sponsored by the Chicago *Daily Tribune* and the New York *Daily News*'. Such events, he maintained, 'demonstrated that the sport can draw large crowds when conducted as a boxing match and not as a prize fight'.[7] Steiner's comments suggest that the increased appeal of amateur boxing was due to a sudden revival in sporting spirit, but mass unemployment was probably a more significant factor. In 1933, 50 per cent of Americans between the age of fifteen and nineteen were unemployed. Otis L. Graham notes that, on average, young Americans waited two years to find work after finishing school and 'about 25 percent never found employment until the war'.[8] Considerable sums of public and charitable money were spent on creating sports facilities for a population that suddenly 'had more leisure and less money'.[9] Most contestants in boxing competitions did not view amateur success as an end in itself. At the very least, as Barney Ross recalled, amateurs won 'medals and trophies and watches which they could pawn for a few bucks':

> Sometimes you'd get a box of shirts, sometimes, ties or socks, some-times a pair of shoes. Whenever I won, I'd take my merchandise around to the ghetto neighbourhood and sell it as a bargain. I used to get a dollar for $2.95 shirts, a dollar for a box of ties and about two dollars for eight- or nine-dollar shoes.[10]

'Pawnshop fighting' was all very well, but the real goal was to turn professional and earn some serious money. Steven Riess notes that during the thirties, around 8,000 men boxed professionally, many more than ever before.[11] Only a handful made a living at the sport.

Neighbourhood gyms and small boxing clubs often had fierce ethnic affili-ations. Beryl Rosofsky, who, renamed Barney Ross, won the world lightweight championship in 1932, and the welterweight title in 1934, began fighting ama-teur bouts at Kid Howard's gym in Chicago's West Side. As his reputation began to spread, Ross recalled, his 'pals and neighbours from the old neighbourhood were all loyal to me and I was able to get a good crowd out for each fight'. When he became the first Golden Glover to win a professional title, the whole of Chicago seemed to adopt him. In his autobiography Ross presents his decision to take up boxing as a rational career choice: a steady job at Sears Roebuck would not satisfy his 'feverish desire to make a lot of money in a hurry', and Al Capone and the other 'big gangsters' had turned him down. Ross justified his choice of profession by saying that he needed to support his family after his orthodox Jewish father was murdered in his shop. 'If Pa had lived,' he wrote, 'I think he would have killed me before he ever would have permitted me to put on a pair of gloves and climb into a ring.'[12] According to legend, Ross's mother came to accept his boxing, sewed the Star of David onto his trunks, and on Friday nights prayed for him at the synagogue before walking five miles to the stadium to watch him fight. Ross retired in 1938, and after Pearl Harbor volunteered for the Marine Corps. At Guadalcanal he was seriously wounded trying to help a trapped scout patrol, and was awarded a Silver Star and the Distinguished Service Cross. After the war he became a staunch Zionist, smuggling guns into Israel after 1948. Two films draw on part of Ross's story – *Body and Soul* (1948) and *Monkey on My Back* (1957).

Thirties fiction and film is full of stories about dreams of individual success, stories of escaping poverty and rebuilding the family fortunes through sport or crime. Ross's employment choice (boxing or Al Capone) became emblematic, as the sportsman and the gangster were presented as related figures, both advancing as best they could in a world that barred more conventional routes. Once again Dempsey epitomized the fighter who could just as easily have become a criminal. In 1937 Paul Gallico described him, rather floridly, as the product of a 'hard rough world in which there was never any softness or any decency . . . I can see him as a surly, dangerous inhabitant of that spiteful nether world, just on the borderline of the criminal.'[13] The 'borderline' professions of prize-fighter and criminal were seen as glamorous alternatives to the breadline, and, for some, they were interchangeable, not only with each other, but with a new kind of movie star.[14] When Benny Lynch returned to Glasgow after winning the world flyweight title in 1937, he was hailed as both the 'Jack Dempsey of the small men' and the Gorbals Jimmy Cagney (illus. 102).[15]

Robert Sklar argues that through his portrayals of boxers and gangsters, James Cagney established a new 'cultural type': the urban tough guy – small, wiry and street-smart, the product of the ethnic neighbourhoods of Chicago and New York.[16] Cagney, in other words, was the Jack Dempsey of the big screen, and Benny Lynch was not the only one to think of the two men as comparable idols (illus. 103). Cagney first played a gangster in *The Public Enemy* (1931) and a boxer in *Winner Take All* (1932). As gangster Tom Powers, he operates from an office whose walls display pictures of John L. Sullivan, and he shows affection to his mother and friends with repeated short-fisted jabs. The main difference between being a boxer and being a gangster seems simply to be where your weapon is concealed. When Powers goes to get fitted for a suit, the dresser feels his biceps. 'Oh sir,' he campily says, 'here's where you need the room – such a muscle!' Powers, however, wants the extra room in his waistband – such a gun, is what he's counting on.[17]

The press was quick to praise the 'effortless authenticity' of Cagney's performances as both gangster and boxer. One review of *Winner Take All* concluded enthusiastically that he 'carries with him a veritable smell of the shower room, of sweating body and sodden leather'.[18] Nevertheless, a large part of the film is about his character's misguided attempt to rid himself of the authenticating marks of boxing, when he falls in love with a heartless 'society dame' called Joan (Virginia Bruce). As soon as she tells him that he might be handsome (and hence kissable) without his broken nose and cauliflower ear, he rushes off to a plastic surgeon. Fixed up, he then rushes back to Joan, saying, 'I want to be just like you want me, honey'. Joan, however, is not interested; as she later tells a friend, 'he's lost all the things that made him colourful and different; he's just ordinary now, like any other man. And one thing I can't stand is bad grammar spoken through a perfect Grecian nose.'[19] Joan is not the only one to reject the beautified Jim. The boxing crowd don't like the defensive style he adopts to protect his face and a newspaper headline accuses him of becoming a '"Powder Puff" Boxer'. All is put right at the end when Jim fights for the championship, damages his face and returns to the arms of his original working-class girlfriend. The film's reference to plastic surgery and powder puff boxers brings to mind the era of smooth-faced silent screen lovers and in particular, Rudolph Valentino. In evoking, but rejecting, that model, *Winner Take All* announced the birth of a new kind of Hollywood leading man.[20]

Cagney's sex appeal may have been sadistic and anarchic, but after 1932, the films in which he appeared were often promotional vehicles for Franklin D. Roosevelt's New Deal administration. Warner Brothers supported Roosevelt's campaign and even laid on a special train to bring stars to his inauguration in 1933.[21] The first of Warner's overtly New Deal films was released later that year. Although rather an ideological muddle, *Heroes for Sale* is determinedly optimistic

102
Fans watch as Benny Lynch trains.

about the capacity of Americans to survive the Depression; as one character puts it, 'it takes more than one sock on the jaw to lick a hundred and twenty million people'. As if to illustrate this point literally, many subsequent Warner's films involved socks on the jaws. In *Winner Take All*, a typical boxing melodrama, Cagney plays a worn-out fighter called Jim Kane. While in New Mexico for a rest cure, he meets Peggy (Marian Nixon), a young widow who can't pay her bills because the insurance company won't honour her husband's life insurance policy. Still in poor health, Kane offers to fight to pay her debt. Aaron Baker argues that this sequence of events embodies the 'hybrid ideology' of both the film and populism more generally: the community is to be redeemed by the efforts of a rugged individualist who labours not just for his own good, but for that of others.[22] The movie's emphasis on individualism is further bolstered by the terms under which the fight takes place. Initially, Jim is told that the loser's fee is $600, exactly the amount of Peggy's debt. But when the fight promoter learns this, he worries that Jim won't fight seriously. 'What guarantee do I have,' he asks, 'that you won't fold in the first round, just to get the loser's fee?' Instead, he proposes that the fight be 'winner take all' – $2,000 or nothing. The initial terms of the agreement might be read as representing those of the New Deal itself, including a measure of social insurance – a safety net of $600 for the loser. This deal, however, introduces an element of risk for the promoter/state, the risk that the fighter/worker will rely on the safety net and abandon the competitive incentives of boxing/work. A 'winner take all' system shifts the risk from the promoter to the fighter and represents *laissez-faire* capitalism at its starkest. This part of *Winner Take All* is set on the Mexican border, where such frontier economics were thought to flourish naturally.

The Mexican border was also the setting for King Vidor's 1931 box office hit, *The Champ*, a film with a rather different ideological slant (illus. 106). If Cagney's boxer is a model worker, Wallace Beery's is a drunken layabout. Beery stars as Andy, an ex-heavyweight champion who lives a dissolute life in Tijuana with his young son Dink (Jackie Cooper). One day, Dink's mother Linda (Irene Rich) reappears with her wealthy, hard-working second husband Tony (Hale Hamilton) and they offer to take the boy away to 'a better life'. The film is very sentimental about Andy's relationship with his son, and the separate all-male world that they create together. Nevertheless, the final outcome – in which Andy briefly pulls himself together and wins a fight, but dies shortly afterwards – was the one test audiences preferred. Dink, they knew, would be better off with a solid bourgeois life in the American heartland.

In both these early-thirties movies, boxing is portrayed as a business in which you can succeed with sufficient hard work. In films made just a few years later, however, hard work is hardly the issue as the business itself is shown to be corrupt to its core. The tragic consequences of that corruption were the subject of numerous *noir* films during the late 1940s – screenwriter Carl Foreman, for example, described *Champion* as drawing 'a parallel between the prize fight business and western society or capitalism in 1948'.[23] At the height of the Depression, a comic perspective was often more welcome. *The Milky Way* by Lynn Root and Harry Clork, a Federal Theater production that was filmed in 1936, is a comic fantasy about a Chaplinesque milkman who becomes middleweight champion.[24] The story is not one of talent rising to the top, but of financial dealings and deception. The milkman, Burleigh Sullivan (Harold Lloyd), is persuaded to become a boxer because he has embarrassed the current middleweight champion, whom the press, erroneously, believe he has knocked out. A scheme is hatched to build up the milkman's value over the course of six set-ups, and then to stage a sell-out match with the champ. The milkman enters the contract because his employers, the profit-driven Sunflower Dairy, want to send his sick horse to the knackers' yard. The film's comic resolution comes with the introduction of charity into the world of business. Burleigh, with six 'wins' under his belt, thinks himself a big shot and walks around with a lion on a leash (à la Battling Siki). His girlfriend tells him he has become a 'tiger' when he used to be a horse-loving 'humanitarian'.

Burleigh gets to redeem himself in the fight with the champ because the proceeds will go to Mrs Winthrope Lemoyne's Milk Fund Charity, an obvious allusion to Millicent Willson Hearst's Free Milk Fund for Babies. Everyone wins in this scenario. Paramount Pictures also did well, promoting the film in conjunction with the Borden Milk Company. Cardboard cutouts featuring Harold Lloyd were placed over milk bottles.[25]

While boxing was a popular sport in local gyms throughout America, boxing films of this period firmly locate the business of boxing in the heart of the city (usually Manhattan) – the downtown urban centre provides the settings both of the boxer's work (the changing room and the boxing ring) and that of his leisure (the hotel room and the nightclub). The gangster-managers are very much at home in this environment, but their fighters are brought in from elsewhere, from the countryside or the working-class neighbourhoods that surround the metropolitan centre. These two spaces – the country and the neighbourhood – are presented as roughly equivalent. Boys from the country are strong, wholesome, and easily, if only briefly, tempted. In Michael Curtiz's *Kid Galahad* (1937), Ward Guisenberry (Wayne Morris) moves to New York, home of 'fast-living spenders and punch-drunk gunmen', in order to earn enough money to buy his own farm. After enduring a temporary 'diet of cigar smoke and gymnasium fumes', he becomes champion, only to retire and marry the farm-girl sister of his manager. Meanwhile, the rival gangsters (Edward G. Robinson and Humphrey Bogart) dispose of each other in a shoot-out.[26] In *Palooka* (1934), the protagonist is happily selling eggs on his farm when his strength is discovered by Knobby Walsh (Jimmy Durante), presumably en route from one metropolis to another. The scrawny Knobby tries to persuade Joe Palooka to come with him, saying, 'It ain't healthy living in the country. Why look at me – raised on gasoline fumes and carbon monoxide, the picture of vigorous vitality!' After a series of unsuccessful urban adventures, Joe too ends up back on the farm with his rural sweetheart.[27]

Other thirties films give cynical city boxers the chance to escape Babylon: in *Winner Take All*, Jim and Peggy meet in the countryside and form the kind of authentic relationship that neither found possible back in New York; in *The Life of Jimmy Dolan* (1933), a prize-fighter (Douglas Fairbanks, Jr) accidentally kills a man at a party and flees to a health farm for invalid children. Gradually, he begins to lose his cynicism under the influence of the children and another pretty girl called Peggy (Loretta Young).[28] Andrew Bergman argues that these films have little to do with reality but set one myth, 'the shyster city', against another, 'the country as an idyll'; the real state of the economy, he points out, is ignored ('why, in 1933, go to a farm?').[29] But although these films are not interested in the realities of rural life, neither are they mere fantasies about cows and barns. The countryside itself is less important than the alternative, utopian communities that exist within it – Dr Betts's Rosario Ranch for asthmatic children and rundown boxers in *Winner Take All*, or the reform school farms of *The Life of Jimmy Dolan* and *Boys' Town*. These small, integrated communitarian ventures, like the co-operative farm in King Vidor's 1934 film, *Our Daily Bread* or the migrant workers' camp in John Steinbeck's 1939 novel, *The Grapes of Wrath*, are presented as collective alternatives to the individualistic and pugnacious city.[30] In another series of films, the urban hub is set in opposition to the romanticized working-class neighbourhood, where cultural and ethnic, rather than physical, health is the primary issue.[31] Both the farm and the neighbourhood are clearly defined spaces and operate with clearly defined values centred around family bonds and local solidarity; in contrast, the city (and this term is used to apply solely to the urban centre) is an amorphous entity, represented either by limitless vistas or by tightly enclosed spaces. Its values are those of impersonal capitalism.

The spatial mapping of the city versus the neighbourhood is particularly clear in *Golden Boy* (1939), Rouben Mamoulian's film adaptation of Clifford Odets's 1937 play (illus. 107).[32] *Golden Boy* was the most successful of Odets's plays for the Group Theatre, itself an 'oasis' within a city that was dominated by commercial theatre.[33] The film opens with shots of downtown Manhattan's skyscrapers before zeroing in on a sign advertising 'Tom Moody, Boxing Enterprises'. Moody needs $5,000 in order to pay for a divorce and remarriage to Lorna Moon (Barbara Stanwyck); 'I see a penthouse in your eyes', he tells her. No sooner has Moody discovered that his latest contender has been injured in the gym than Joe Bonaparte (William Holden) appears, offering to take his place. Joe phones home to tell his father he will be late, and we see Papa Bonaparte (Lee J. Cobb) answering the phone. Papa's place of work and home could not be more different. The Italian American Grocery is piled high both with goods and with communal values: it is a meeting-place as well as a selling-place, a bazaar as traditionally understood. More important, as the camera penetrates to the living-quarters behind the shop and then lingers admiringly, is the seamless fit of public and private life. The apartment is a shrine to traditional, bourgeois domestic comfort, stuffed full of chintz, doilies, velvet drapes, a painting of the Virgin and child, and a gilt-framed photograph of Joe playing the violin as a curly-haired child. Particular attention is given to this last image in contrast to representations of Joe as a close-cropped fighter (denuded of his Italian hair as well as culture) on numerous mass-produced posters in Moody's office. Joe is tempted away from his heritage by a desire for 'people to know who I am', and also by Lorna, an ambitious 'girl from Newark'. She takes him up on to the roof of a skyscraper to show him the open spaces of Manhattan. As he looks down, she tells him that 'it's a big city and little people don't stand a chance', but that he could make 'all that your carpet to walk on'. The film tells us that by abandoning the neighbourhood – a place of cultured ethnicity – for the metropolitan promise of celebrity, Joe has abandoned his identity; 'people' now know his name, but he no longer knows 'who he is'. Nevertheless, this process is easily reversed – in the film, if not the play. After a hearty dinner Lorna is converted and now tells him, 'you shouldn't be in the ring; you should be at home, with your violin'. There are a few complications involving gangsters to iron out first, but Joe takes her advice. The film ends with the couple held in the embrace of

Papa, as the camera shifts slightly to bring the painting of the Holy Family into view behind them.[34] Papa's faded oriental rug is now all the carpet Joe and Lorna need to walk on.

The ethnic neighbourhoods of Chicago provide the setting for much of Nelson Algren's fiction, and there too the 'way out' offered by boxing is questioned. In the Hemingway mould, Algren was also fond of the analogy between writers and fighters. In 'Nonconformity' (1951), Algren quoted Georges Carpentier on the fighter's need for 'viciousness' in order to argue that a writer needed similar qualities: 'the strong-armer isn't out merely to turn a fast buck any more than the poet is solely out to see his name on the cover of a book, whatever satisfaction that event might afford him. What both need most deeply is to get even'.[35] 'Getting even' was an impulse that Algren particularly associated with Chicago, 'the very toughest kind of town – it used to be a writer's town and it's always been a fighter's town'.[36] Hemingway provided a blurb for Algren's first novel, *Somebody in Boots* (1935), saying you shouldn't read it 'if you cannot take a punch'. Algren's subsequent works offer many punches; most directly, his last, posthumously published novel, *The Devil's Stocking*, was about the incarceration of middleweight contender Rubin 'Hurricane' Carter.

*Never Come Morning* (1942), is set in the thirties and draws on many of Warner Brothers' stock naturalistic plots and characters – the fallen woman, the juvenile delinquent and the boxer.[37] It tells the story of Bruno Bicek and his dream of becoming a boxing champion, and of how, turning 21, he instead ends up in jail on a murder charge. 'If they had stayed in the Old World,' Mama Bicek thinks, 'her son would have been a good son. There a boy had to behave himself or be put in the army.'[38] The local barber, and prime villain, Bonifacy, is reminiscent of the grandmother in *Yekl* in his incomprehension of 'young Poles with a purely amateur enthusiasm for a wop outfielder or a Jew welterweight . . . Life in the old world had been too hard to permit young men to play games'. (What he can appreciate is the value of boxing, and gambling, as a way of making money.) The neighbourhood boys also follow *Yekl* in compulsively adding American nicknames to their Polish surnames – Bruno (a.k.a. 'Lefty'; 'Biceps'; 'Powerhouse'; 'Iron-Man'; 'Killer') more compulsively than anyone. When arrested on a murder charge, he proudly tells the police that he is 'a citizen', 'a Polish-American citizen' and distinguishes himself from greenhorns who don't speak English properly. Nevertheless, all the enmities in the novel are expressed in terms of their Old World nationalities and loyalties – we don't know names, just the Jew, the Mex, the Polack, the Litvak and the Greek. Only the idea of the Great White Hope overrides these affiliations. In the fight that closes the book, Bruno is aware that the crowd are applauding him simply for 'being white'.[39] Algren originally called his book *White Hope*, perhaps with a nod to the unpublished novel that his friend Richard Wright was working on at the same time, *Black Hope*.[40]

Unlike the films discussed above, *Never Come Morning* does not romanticize, or indeed ever leave, the confines of the neighbourhood. Algren does not allow any moral or cultural alternative to Chicago's 'Little Polonia', an area bounded triangularly, and tightly, by three streets – Chicago, Ashland and Milwaukee Avenues. Within the triangle are further confined spaces – the brothel, the jail, the beer flat, the gang clubhouse, the poolroom, the barber shop (and the bird cage within it), the police station, the amusement park, and the boxing ring – each of which simply reinforces the enclosure of the others. The novel is framed by two fight scenes. In the opening sequence, Casey Benkowski dutifully takes a dive and returns to the barber's shop. The final chapter rests on whether Bruno will do the same. He doesn't, but his gesture of existentialist heroism proves futile. The police are waiting to take him to prison, just one more 'ropeless ring'. Algren uses these different places to create an insistently interlocking network of symbols. 'The Triangle's my territory,' boasts Bruno, and there is very little sense of the existence of a world, indeed of a city, beyond the boundaries of its three streets. Identities are so local that characters introduce each other by their street names ('Catfoot N. from Fry St', 'Bruno B. from Potomac and Paulina', 'Steffi R. from by the poolroom').[41] The wider world, the wider city even, only really exists for Bruno and the fellow members of his gang, the Warriors, through the magazines and movies that they consume. One of Algren's sources may have been a long-running series of films about a gang variously known as the Dead End Kids, the East End Kids and the Bowery Boys, films which emphasized the sociology behind the gangster myth and thus tried to undermine its glamour.[42] These films were about saving street kids from a life of crime, and in the muscular Christian tradition, a combination of religion and sport often play a large part in the cure. In *Angels with Dirty Faces* (1938), gangster Jimmy Cagney, just out of prison, is enlisted on to the basketball court by Father Connelly (Pat O'Brien); in *The Bells of St Mary's* (1945), Father O'Malley (Bing Crosby) and Sister Benedict (Ingrid Bergman) both don gloves in order to install discipline among their unruly charges. Spencer Tracy won an Oscar as Father Flanagan in *Boys' Town* (1938), which was based on the true story of a rural reform school which used boxing to produce 'sturdy young bodies and stout young hearts' (illus. 104). The 'boxer-and-the-priest' movie is one of the many genres parodically referred to by Nabokov in *Lolita* (1952). The plot of one, told to Humbert by Charlotte Haze, is typical: 'The boxer had fallen extremely low when he met the good old priest (who had been a boxer himself in his robust youth and could still slug a sinner).'[43]

Unfortunately Bruno Bicek does not have a priest or a reformed gangster to help him. He is obviously a keen movie-goer, however, and compares himself and his friends to Cagney, John Barrymore and others. The only time in the story that Bruno sees a movie, however, it is a boxing picture in a kinetoscope arcade, 'a scarred and faded film of the Dempsey–Willard fight'.

> With his fighter's heart and his fighter's mind, Bruno sensed the mind and heart of the other. He watched Willard on his knees, swinging his head like a blinded ox, and no spark of pity came to the watcher . . .

His fingers spread, resisting the urge to get in there for the kill himself. He watched the referee standing Dempsey off, and that bothered both Dempsey and Bicek. He turned the film as slowly as possible . . . Dempsey was circling, circling, trying to get the beaten man on the other side of the referee's arm. A warmth rose in Bruno: Jack was in on the bum – one – two – left to the heart – right to the jaw – to the heart – to the jaw – and his hand stopped cold on the film. There was nothing before him but a cracked square of yellow cardboard and he was sweating on his hands. 'We killed the bum fer life,' he assured himself, 'I'm a killer too.'

Algren employs several layers of irony in this passage. In the novel's closing boxing match, Bruno does become like his hero, Dempsey, when he metaphorically 'kills' his opponent, but the night after seeing the movie, he had already literally killed someone, and it is for this that he is arrested as the final bell of his own fight sounds. Identifying with Dempsey is a complicated business. Bruno is not primarily interested in the boxer's David-versus-Goliath-like success; rather it is his anger, his ruthlessness and his urge to 'prove himself' at whatever cost that appeal. 'No spark of pity came to the watcher', Algren comments. Identification means experiencing another man's battles (indeed, another man's sadism) as your own and in order to do this Bruno turns the fairground kinetoscope 'as slowly as possible', adapting it to suit his own needs. Dempsey's slow circling becomes the medium through which he experiences the self that he would like to be (later, in jail, he is 'swamped by an image of himself: as though he had been abruptly transplanted before a technicolor movie being reeled a little too fast').[44]

By the late thirties, the language of movie gangsters had become well-worn cliché. Damon Runyon's 1937 palooka of a gangster Tobias Tweeney complains

104
'Sturdy Young Bodies and Stout Young Hearts', postcard of Father Flanagan's Boys' Home, Nebraska.

that his wife wants to know why he cannot be a 'big gunman' like Edward G. Robinson or James Cagney.[45] But while Runyon viewed such behaviour as rather comical, others were less sanguine. James T. Farrell's trilogy *Studs Lonigan* (1932–5) recounts the short, delusional life of a Chicago-Irish boy who is constantly involved in a 'dream of himself'. This culminates in his death at the age of 29, and a fevered death fantasy, in which hard-as-nails Studs imagines himself walking 'along a strange city with a gun', as 'Al Capone Lonigan' and then 'entering a ring with two million people looking on', as 'Jack Dempsey Lonigan'.[46]

For Marxist critics of popular culture, identification such as this was pernicious, not only because it distracted the masses from the realities of their own lives, but because, by doing so, it made authentic choices and action impossible. In numerous naturalist novels of this period, those who succumb to the allure of popular culture end badly. The tragedy of John Steinbeck's *Of Mice and Men* (1937), for example, begins in mass-produced fantasies of movie and boxing glory. The son of a ranch boss in the Salinas valley, Curley is a Cagney-esque 'lightweight' who has 'done quite a bit in the ring'; we hear that he 'got in the finals for the Golden Gloves' and that 'he got newspaper clippings about it'. He walks about the ranch with his fists clenched and slips into 'a slight crouch' at the slightest provocation. His glance is 'at once calculating and pugnacious' and he fights dirty with a 'glove fulla Vaseline'. His unnamed wife of two weeks, meanwhile, is convinced she 'coulda been in the movies'; stuck on the ranch she contents herself by 'giving the eye' to every man around. The dangerous consequence of these fantasies is revealed when the couple encounters Lennie Small, a simple-minded gentle giant who comes to work on the ranch with his friend George Milton. The novella's tragedy lies less in Lennie's inability to control his immense strength than in his lack of understanding of mass media conventions. Lennie 'don't know no rules'.[47] He destroys, by failing to acknowledge them, both Curley's pretensions to be a Hollywood boxer and his wife's pretensions to be a Hollywood *femme fatale*. Readers in the thirties may have associated the mentally slow but 'strong as a bull' Lennie with Primo Carnera, who beat Jack Sharkey for the heavyweight title in 1933. Gangsters Owney Madden and Dutch Schultz stole much of Carnera's money and it has been speculated that most of his fights were fixed.[48] Unlike Carnera, however, Lennie relies on a man whose interest in his welfare is genuine. The ranch boss cannot understand this: 'what stake you got in this guy?' he asks George. The antithesis of a fight manager trying to make a buck, George, it seems, has 'no stake' in Lennie. The novella ends bleakly with his acknowledgment that Lennie cannot live in 'society'. In a gesture of love, George shoots his friend.[49]

THE SET-UP

'I just got through triple-crossing a double-crosser', Knobby Walsh (Jimmy Durante) cheerfully admits in *Palooka* (1934). Apparently, he was not alone. In 1931, J. F. Steiner complained that professional boxing had 'failed to free itself entirely of the undesirable associations that have so long clung to it'. While it had been hoped that legalisation would end boxing's links to crime, the connection flourished. 'More than any other sport', Steiner notes, boxing 'has been exploited for purposes of excessive financial gain by both its promoters and participants'.[50] This was partly because it is relatively easy to fix a boxing match – certainly much easier than fixing a baseball game which requires the co-operation of a whole team – and boxing, especially outside of New York, was virtually unregulated until the 1950s.[51] For a large part of the twentieth century, the plot twists of boxing fiction and film relied heavily on the many ways there were to fix a fight.[52]

Before legalization, boxing had largely been controlled by local politicians; afterwards, Prohibition bootleggers and gangsters took over. Notable figures in the twenties and thirties include Dutch Schultz and Owney Madden in New York, Boo Hoo Hoff in Philadelphia, and Al Capone in Chicago. 'By the Depression,' Riess notes, 'the sport's connection with organized crime was an open secret.'[53] In the middleweight division, Frankie Carbo ('Mr Big') held a virtual monopoly from the mid-thirties until the late fifties, exploiting his close ties with managers, matchmakers and promoters to fix fights at every level. One of his most useful contacts was Billy Brown, matchmaker at Madison Square Garden. Any fighter who refused to play along suffered greatly; a prime example was Jake La Motta, the top middleweight contender from 1943 to 1947. After years of being refused a shot at the title, La Motta accepted an offer to fight light heavyweight, Billy Fox, managed by one of Carbo's men, Blinky Palermo.[54] For $100,000 and the promise of a title shot, La Motta took part. But his naiveté proved his undoing. He refused to attack and protected himself so well that when a technical knockout was awarded to Fox in the fourth round, the crowd was convinced it was a set-up. An investigation cleared La Motta; he was fined $1,000 and suspended for seven months for 'concealing an injury', which was his excuse for a poor performance. He did not receive his title fight until 1949 (after paying $20,000 to champion Marcel Cerdan).

One of the first stories to explore the relationship between boxing and organized crime was Ernest Hemingway's 'The Killers' (1927).[55] Two men show up in a small-town café and hold the staff hostage as they wait for the man they want to kill, Ole Andreson, a former heavyweight boxer. When Nick Adams, who has been in the café, tells Andreson about the men, the boxer says that nothing can be done to save him and turns his face to the wall. Little more than a page of this eleven-page story is devoted to Nick's encounter with Andreson, but it changes everything. The gangsters dub Nick 'bright boy', but the story reveals how little he knows about power and powerlessness. In an attempt to escape his revelation – that the heavyweight, the epitome of masculinity, is not prepared to fight back – Nick decides to move on. 'I can't stand to think about him waiting in the room and knowing he's going to get it.' As in the case of 'The Battler' and 'The Light of the World', the story ends with Nick preparing to 'get out of this town'.[56]

If the dominant boxing setting of the 1920s was Madison Square Garden, during the thirties, forties and fifties, crime writers such as Hammett and Chandler, and so-called proletarian writers such as Algren and Farrell, focused on low-level professional boxing as a setting within which to examine delusion and corruption. If the dominant boxing motif of the twenties was the knockout, that of the following decades was the set-up. Damon Runyon even created a whole new vocabulary to describe fighters who accepted bribes: 'tank-fighter', 'ostrich' and the ultimate shady character who 'folds up' easily, a 'parasol'. 'Of course all the customers know very well that Chester is only fighting some parasol, for in Philadelphia, Pa., the customers are smartened up to the prize-fight game and they know they are not going to see a world war for three dollars tops'.[57]

While Hemingway's fighter in 'Fifty Grand' gambled on a $25,000 profit, James T. Farrell's Kid Tucker is willing to settle for $25. 'Twenty-five Bucks' (1930) revisits the territory of Jack London's 'A Piece of Steak' by matching a 'never-was of a palooka' with a young contender, but Farrell's naturalism, rejecting the consolations of sentimental animalism, is much harsher than London's. Kid Tucker's life comes to an end one evening after fifteen years of living 'in grease'. Psychologically damaged by his experiences in the trenches of the First World War and with a face 'punched to a hash', Tucker is usually paid simply to get beaten. 'He earned his living by taking smashes on the jaw.' In a metaphor that London would have approved of, Farrell says of Tucker's manager that he prepared his fighters 'as cattle were fed for the Chicago stockyards'. On one particular occasion, however, in order to make the bout look more authentic, he is instructed to put up the pretence of a fight, 'or no dough'. But 'the war and the prize ring had taken all the fight out of him', and Tucker cannot comply. At the end of the bout, as he lies unconscious on the floor, the manager, determined to prove the fight was 'on the level', makes a speech saying that he will not pay Tucker. Instead the purse will go to 'the boy who puts up the best fight here this evening' and the crowd can choose. But it does not matter. Tucker dies of a cerebral haemorrhage without regaining consciousness. For the Marxist Farrell, as for London, the manager and the members of the crowd (the manufacturer and the consumers) are ready partners in an economic system in which the individual boxer is mere labour, and as such expendable.[58]

This is certainly the way things work in Personville, Montana – better known as Poisonville – the setting of Dashiell Hammett's *Red Harvest* (1929), often described as the first 'hard-boiled' detective novel. An operative from San Francisco's Continental Detective Agency is sent to Poisonville to investigate a murder and clean up the town. Among the many poisons of the 'lousy burg' that he encounters is its crooked prize-fighting.

> We talked about the fights. Nothing more was said about me versus
> Poisonville . . . [The gambler] even gave me what seemed to be a straight
> tip on the fights – telling me any bet on the main event would be good
> if its maker remembered that Kid Cooper would probably knock Ike

Bush out in the sixth round. He seemed to know what he was talking about, and it didn't seem to be news to the others.[59]

The Continental Op tries to persuade Bush not to go ahead with the fix, and after much prevarication, Bush knocks out Cooper, an obvious 'palooka'. There is a 'short silvery streak' from the balcony, followed by a thud. 'Ike Bush took his arm out of the referee's hand and pitched down on top of Kid Cooper. A black knife-handle stuck out of the nape of Bush's neck.'[60]

This is a particularly dramatic ending, but the scenario that Hammett presents – in which the boxer defies the gangsters by refusing to throw the fight, and then immediately pays for it with his health or his life – soon became a staple in popular fiction and film. The plot often turned on the moment in which the boxer realizes that he has been duped by the mob, his crooked manager or the nightclub singer who has been stringing him along. In more socially conscious films, such *Golden Boy* and *Body and Soul* (1947), the death of a black man provides the prompt. In *Golden Boy*, Joe Bonaparte's conscience revives when he kills the Chocolate Drop Kid (James 'Cannonball' Green) in the ring. He leaves boxing behind, telling the gangsters, 'you used me like a gun'. In *Body and Soul*, Charley Davis (John Garfield) wakes up to the reality of his life when he finds out that his black sparring partner, Ben Chapman (Canada Lee) has died – neither man was told that Chapman had a blood clot. As Gerald Early notes in a different context, there is 'a very simple and very old idea here, namely, that the black male is metaphorically the white man's unconscious personified'.[61]

Charley's story is told in flashback, following an opening sequence in which he has agreed to throw a fight for $60,000. Although his mother has told him to 'fight for something, not for money', Charley is seduced by the prospect of 'lots of clothes, lots of money, lots of everything'. But after Ben's death, Charley fights to win. When the gangsters complain, he is scornful. 'What can you do?' he asks, 'Kill me? Everybody dies.'[62] Although *Body and Soul* was based on *Golden Boy* (as well as the biography of Barney Ross), scriptwriter Abraham Polonsky did not want to recreate Odets's original tragic ending or the film version's saccharine family reunion. Director Robert Rossen had wanted to close with Davis being shot by the mob, and falling into a barrel of garbage. Polonsky talked him out of this 'heroic' conclusion, arguing that it would be 'totally against the meaning of the picture, which is nothing more than a fable of the streets'.[63] *Body and Soul* ends with Garfield walking away with his girlfriend into the sunset, seemingly unharmed by his insubordination.

Stories such as these celebrate individual rebellion against collective tyranny, but where that tyranny lies is not always made clear. In the late forties, most audiences concentrated on the corruption of the criminally connected prize-fight world itself; just before *Body and Soul*'s release, the New York district Attorney's office launched an investigation of the La Motta-Fox fight. Today, however, the film is more often considered as a parable of defiance against the House Un-American Activities Committee, which only months later subpoenaed many of those involved in its making. Rossen, who had been an active member of the Communist Party, eventually offered other names to clear his own. Polonsky, also a communist, refused to name names and was blacklisted, as was Garfield.

The redemptive power of resistance is depoliticized and mythologized in Robert Wise's *The Set-Up* (1949). A third-rate boxer and his wife go to the ironically named Paradise City for one last fight. (Paradise City Athletic Club is next to a dance hall called Dreamland, and across the street from the Hotel Cozy.) Stoker Thompson (Robert Ryan) is fighting a much younger, stronger man, and everyone but him is aware that the fight is fixed. Everyone, including himself, will gain if he loses. In the classic *noir* gesture of integrity and futile defiance, when Stoker finds out about the set-up, he fights so hard that he wins. But his victory is limited to the confines of the square circle. After he leaves the gym, the gangsters work him over in the grim alley-way.[64] However Christ-like he is (and we are not allowed to forget it), Paradise City is really just another name for Poisonville after all.

The symbolism of the set-up was not confined to stories directly about the fight game. When, in James M. Cain's 1936 novel, *Double Indemnity*, insurance salesman Walter Huff conspires with Phyllis Nirdlinger to insure and then kill her husband, he talks of their plan as a 'set-up'. Huff maintains that insurance is itself a form of gambling. Billy Wilder's 1944 film adaptation, with the conspirators renamed Walter Neff and Phyllis Dietrichson, further highlights the sport- or game-like nature of the plan.[65] Dietrichson had been a college football player and is now a keen devotee of baseball on the radio; his daughter Lola, meanwhile, plays checkers with her stepmother and talks of going roller-skating. When she quarrels with her father, he describes Lola as 'a good fighter for her weight' (and this is something she will prove to be after the murder has been committed). Walter himself talks of the murder plan as something that should be followed 'move by move', and later, believes that his immediate boss, Keyes, is 'playing on our team' (the big boss, Norton, meanwhile, 'fumbled with the ball'). Most relevantly, the living room of Walter's apartment is decorated with four framed prints of nineteenth-century bareknuckle fighters. In the crucial scene in which Phyllis arrives to secure and plan the set-up, the camera makes sure that these prints are clearly visible. They are not images of fights, but of solitary men in fighting pose, much as Walter had seen himself up to this point. At the start Walter believes that by killing her husband, he is fighting for Phyllis and the money. By the end of the film, aware that he has won neither, he realizes that she is his real opponent, and in an embrace that is both sexual and a boxers' clinch, they shoot each other. Of his life before Phyllis, Walter says there were 'no visible scars'. The point of the film is not that he dies at the end, but that he dies with the 'visible scars' of a man who has chosen the wrong fight.[66]

The screenplay of *Double Indemnity* was written by Wilder and Raymond Chandler, and it may have been Chandler's idea to compare the insurance investigator to a boxer. Certainly Chandler had made frequent use of boxing metaphors in his 1939 novel *The Big Sleep*. Dressed in a 'powder-blue suit', Philip Marlowe describes himself as the start of the novel as 'neat, clean, shaved and sober'; in other words, 'everything the well-dressed private detective ought to be'. At this stage, there is still a possibility of 'me versus Poisonville'. But things start to fall apart only a page later when Marlowe meets his client's daughter, Carmen Sternwood, and she fails to recognize his carefully constructed and signalled identity. Instead she notices that he is 'awfully tall' and when he jokes that his name is Doghouse Reilly, she asks if he is a prize-fighter. 'Not exactly, I'm a sleuth,' he replies. Being a sleuth, Marlowe suggests, is not *exactly* the same as being a prize-fighter, but there is a similarity between the two professions. The prize-fighter analogy works against the novel's earlier suggestion that the detective is a kind of knight.[67] While Sherlock Holmes could equate the chivalric and meticulous codes of boxing to detective work, Marlowe does not really do much detection. 'I'm not Sherlock Holmes', he tells Sternwood.[68] 'Little methods of thought' are not what being a modern sleuth, or a modern prize-fighter, is all about. All Marlowe can do is take part in a series of dirty fights, double-crosses and set-ups.

If medieval codes of chivalry, and the English Queensberry rules, are obsolete in 'this rotten crime-ridden country', Marlowe still holds onto one rule, that opponents should be equally matched. He makes frequent references to the relative sizes and weights of the men and women he encounters, but most of the contests that he witnesses or participates in are mismatches. We assume Marlowe is a heavyweight; at any rate, he is, as Carmen points out, 'awfully tall'. (Chandler later described Marlowe as 'slightly over six feet and weigh[ing] about thirteen stone eight'.[69]) Most of his opponents are either smaller than him or homosexual, which seems to amount to the same thing. The only time Marlowe doesn't fight at all is when he encounters a real boxer, Eddie Mars's bodyguard, 'an obvious pug, a good-looking pale-faced boy with a bad nose and one ear like a club steak'. Compared to the boxer, Marlowe feels himself feminine: 'I turned around for him like a bored beauty modeling an evening gown'. Shortly afterwards, however, he is able to re-establish his masculinity when he takes on Carol Lundgren, 'a very handsome boy indeed', and the lover of the dead 'queen', Geiger. When Lundgren punches Marlowe on the chin, he backsteps and manages to avoid being knocked down. 'It was meant to be a hard one, but a pansy has no iron in his bones, whatever he looks like.' Marlowe tells Lundgren that he won't fight with him – 'You're giving away too much weight' – but Lundgren 'wants to fight'. Each man has a different strategy: Marlowe takes Lungren's neck 'in chancery'; Lundgren uses his hands 'where it hurt'; but there is a moment in which 'it was a balance of weights'. 'We seemed to hang there in the misty moonlight, two grotesque creatures'. On the threshold of what he describes as the 'poisonous room' in which homosexual sex and murder have taken place, Marlowe feels himself momentarily a 'grotesque' creature too. Then he finishes his opponent off, and starts to call him 'son'.[70]

In the novel's final pages Marlowe is finally matched with two opponents who equal him in size. The first is Eddie Mars's wife, Silver-Wig, who is 'tall rather than short, but no bean-pole', and whose hair, under her wig, is short and clipped, 'like a boy's'; the second is the confusingly purring but dog-like Canino (Marlowe's *nom de guerre* is, of course, Doghouse).[71] The fight begins with a warning scream from Silver-Wig, 'a beautiful thin tearing scream that rocked me like a left hook'. When Canino fires his gun, Marlowe contemplates allowing him to continue, 'just like a gentleman of the old school'. But he is no knight, no Sherlock Holmes, and so he shoots 'four times, the Colt straining against my ribs'.[72] (Walter Huff, in the novel *Double Indemnity*, experiences being shot as 'something hit[ting] me in the chest like Jack Dempsey had hauled off and given me all he had'.[73]) At the end Marlowe admits, over a couple of double scotches, that he is 'part of the nastiness now'.

## MEN 'TAKING IT' AND WOMEN WATCHING

In most Hollywood comedies of the thirties, it did not really matter if the boxer won or lost as long as he got paid. In *Cain and Mabel* (1936), for example, Larry Cain (Clark Gable) is about to clinch the match when he hears Mabel (Marion Davis) calling out to him. He turns to look and is knocked out. 'Gee, Mabel, I lost every penny I had in the world', he complains. 'Never mind,' she replies, 'I bet on the other guy and I've enough for both of us.' In *Nothing Sacred* (1937), Wally (Fredric March) and Hazel (Carole Lombard) decide to box so that Hazel will seem tired enough to convince a doctor she has radium poisoning and therefore deserve her free trip to New York (illus. 108). By the late 1940s, however, when economic conditions were much better, such cheerful pragmatism no longer seemed possible.[74]

In her 1949 study of gender differences, *Male and Female*, the anthropologist Margaret Mead commented on the importance for American boys of a willingness to fight. 'Both sexes are told not to fight, and then boys are watched very anxiously, girls almost as anxiously, to see if they show signs of being quitters, of not being able to take it.'[75] Boxing stories, in some way or another, are always about the anxieties of boys and the ways in which they test and define their masculinity. But at different times, different aspects of masculinity are foregrounded. In the thirties, Clifford Odets's Joe Bonaparte clenched his fists and explained that he became a fighter because 'I'd rather give it than take it'.[76] His aggression was clearly motivated and comprehensible. By the late forties, however, the test of manliness was not aggression – how much pain the boxer's body could inflict – but endurance – how much it could withstand. Being able to 'take it' was now all that one could expect of men.[77] In 1932, Kirstein had described Cagney's appeal as lying in his portrayal of 'the delights of violence'; in 1947, John Houseman concluded an article on 'today's hero', saying that, 'in all history I doubt there has been a hero whose life was so unenviable and whose aspirations had so low a ceiling'.[78] The 'semi-conscious sadism' of the thirties gangster film had, in other words, given way to the masochism of the forties *film noir*.[79]

Sports films tend to be optimistic about individual or team efforts to succeed, even against extreme odds, and *film noir* generally stayed clear of sporting stories. Boxing was an exception, since, as Andrew Dickos points out, 'the fight game encompasses many key noir features – its urban roots, the corruption of power and money and of the criminal element so often controlling it, and the violence and near-narcotic dynamism intrinsic in its exercise'.[80] The three most notable boxing *noirs* were *Body and Soul*, *Champion* and *The Set-Up*, although many movies, from *The Killers* (1946) to *The Big Combo* (1955), effectively used boxing settings to create an atmosphere of barely contained violence.[81]

Although these films often presented themselves as 'socially conscious', aiming to expose the brutality of boxing, they often seemed to relish the suffering that individual boxers endured.[82] In a 1949 essay attacking both the 'compulsion to grind away at a message' and the exaggerated degradation of most fight films, Manny Farber argued that their real impetus often seemed to be 'a pure imaginative delight in the mangling of the human body'.[83] This is apparent if we consider the endings of *Champion*, *Body and Soul* and *The Set-Up*. Each concludes, in seemingly traditional style, with the protagonist winning his big fight, but in each case, this physical sporting victory is shown as hollow rather than glorious. As I suggested earlier, the ostensible 'message' of these films is that some kind of spiritual or moral transcendence of the body is not only possible but absolutely necessary. It might be argued that in their rejection of the cult of the body these films, like *Raging Bull* some 30 years later, are the antithesis of the typical sports movie. However, the camera's lingering attention to the endurance as well as the 'mangling' of the human body, like the attention given by Renaissance artists to the crucified Christ, inevitably undermines the intentions of the artists: an asserted rejection or transcendence of the physical is always going to be less memorable than an all-too-present physicality. *Body and Soul*'s final image is of Charley and his girl walking respectably down the street together; after a final fight, he has left boxing and crime behind. The images that we remember, however, are those from the fight itself – Charley's spirited refusal to stop fighting and his bloodied, battered face, which cinematographer James Wong Howe shot with a handheld camera. Even more memorable is the final scene of *Champion*, in which Midge Kelly (Kirk Douglas) dies alone in his dressing room after a severe beating in the ring.[84] The scene parallels an earlier one in which a well-oiled Douglas, a 'quartzlike, malevolent show-off' according to Farber, preened as he trained. While generally disapproving of the film's sentimentality, Farber found the death scene 'unbearably moving'.

While scenes such as this put late-forties boxing films firmly into the category of the male weepie, it is worth remembering that the most important spectators *within* the films are always women. 'Boxing movies may describe the world of men and male values,' noted Ronald Bergan, 'but it is the women in the background that give them meaning.'[85] From the male point of view, the meaning of women is relatively straightforward and, in these films, largely negative: life would be simpler without them. Nevertheless, as the title of a 1939 Kenneth Patchen poem puts it, 'Boxers Hit Harder When Women Are Around'.[86] In the early twentieth century, representations of women spectators at men's boxing matches signalled a fascination with unabashed male display and active female choice in matters of sex. By mid-century, women were still seen as choosing, but the men seemed more anxious about being judged. Much of this anxiety is manifest in misogynist portrayals of women as sexual predators, *femme fatales* – lustful, cruel, bloodthirsty and, most of all, only really interested in hard cash. 'They're all alike', complained Midge in Ring Lardner's story 'Champion', 'Money, money, money'; a view supported by Bruno, in *Never Come Morning*: 'Dames don't care if a guy's puss is pushed in, so long as they ain't no dent in his wallet'. According to Jim Tulley's bruiser, 'the women who marry fighters, God save my ragged soul, are often crueler than the managers'.[87]

Women did not fare much better in the movies. In *Golden Boy*, Lorna (Barbara Stanwyck) tells the naïve Joe (William Holden) that she only likes men 'who reach for a slice of fame': 'do it', she urges, 'bang your way to the middleweight crown. Buy that car, give some girl the things she wants.' Lorna, as we have seen, is reformed by her exposure to Italian family life, but most *femmes fatales*, and most boxers, are not so lucky. Perhaps the most relentless exploration of what happens to a boxer when he hooks up with a bad girl is Robert Siodmak's *The Killers* (1947). The film begins with a fairly faithful adaptation of Hemingway's short story of the same title: the Swede (Burt Lancaster) is seen lying on his bed, passively awaiting his killers despite having muscles that actively strain his vest. While Nick Adams never learns why the Swede has given up, the film introduces an insurance investigator to delve into his past and solve the puzzle of his downfall.[88] The solution lies with torch-song singer Kitty (Ava Gardner); in Frank Krutnik's words, 'a lustrous incarnation of 1940s Hollywood eroticism'.[89] It is Kitty, we gradually learn, who has unmanned the Swede, who has transformed him from a prizefighter, the epitome of active masculinity, into a prone and passive figure lying on a bed.

Many *noir* films and novels rely on a clear distinction between bad girls and good girls, the ones who reject blood-soaked money and tell their men to stay at home. Good women shield their eyes at ringside, and really good women listen, wincing, to the radio at the hearth. Occasionally, *in extremis*, they appear at ringside to steer their men back to the true path. In *Spirit of Youth* (1938), Joe (Joe Louis) deserts his hometown sweetheart, Mary (Edna Mae Harris) for a cabaret singer called Flora (Mae Turner); finally awarded a shot at the title, Joe fights listlessly until Mary appears at ringside to urge him on. *Body and Soul* presents the competing influence of three women on Charley Davis: the film was advertised as 'The story of a guy that women go for!' (illus. 109). The bad girl, Alice (Hazel Brooks), who snuggles up in her fur coat and yells for him to kill his opponent, has no chance against the combined strength of Charley's Jewish mama (Anne Revere) and his neighbourhood girlfriend, Peg (Lilli Palmer). Peg leaves Charley when she sees him being corrupted, but returns when he defies the gangsters and shows that he's really a *mensch* after all.

Men may do the fighting, but stories like this suggest that without the guiding moral influence of a woman, they have no idea what is worth fighting for.

The male desire for glory is frequently declared to be rather pathetic. When, in *The Set-Up*, Stoker Thomson tells his wife that he's just a punch away from success, Julie counters mercilessly, 'Don't you see, Bill, you'll always be one punch away'. She refuses to use the ticket that he has bought her and in a dramatic scene rips it up and throws it over a bridge (we are encouraged to think that she is contemplating suicide, but that is hardly believable – unlike her husband, she is not prone to self-destruction). Throughout his fight, Stoker looks towards Julie's seat – in section C, row four – but it remains empty. From the other seats, stereotypically bad women shout out 'kill him', 'let him have it'. While Stoker is boxing, and afterwards, while he is being beaten up by the gangsters whose set-up he has refused to honour, Julie has been warming soup on the hot plate at the Hotel Cozy. Finally she sees him staggering out of the alley and rushes to his side. The religious symbolism of the film continues when she holds him in a classic *pietà* shot – he has become the fallen Christ.[90] But what is she? Stoker, hardly able to speak, gasps out that he had won that night. Looking at his broken hand, Julie smiles beatifically and says 'we've both won.' He has won his integrity, but lost his career, physical prowess and, it might be argued, his masculinity; certainly she has won control of their future.[91]

A rather more complex take on women as boxing spectators can be found in John Steinbeck's 1937 story, 'The Chrysanthemums', which, like *Of Mice and Men*, is set in the Salinas Valley. Steinbeck once described Salinas as a town dominated by a 'blackness – the feeling of violence just below the surface'. Although there were many forms of entertainment in town, he recalled, 'easily the most popular' was evangelist 'Billy Sunday in boxing gloves fighting the devil in the squared ring'.[92] 'The Chrysanthemums' is the first in a collection of stories which explore the dark enclosure of the town and its valley. The first sentence announces entrapment – 'The high grey-flannel fog of winter closed off the Salinas Valley from the sky and from all the rest of the world. On every side it sat like a lid on the mountains and made of the valley a closed pot' – and the story proceeds, in good naturalist fashion, to explore the forces contained within that closed pot. Most tightly constrained is Elisa Allen, the wife of a rancher, who tends her chrysanthemums, although their stems 'seemed too small and easy for her energy'. A chicken-wire fence divides her flower garden from the rest of the farm, and her conversations with her husband tend to take place with this fence between them. Critics have tended to read Elisa's flower garden as a symbol of repressed sexuality. Some argue that her husband is keeping her fenced in; more convincingly, Stanley Renner suggests that she represses her own physicality: she will not even garden without gloves.[93] The story then introduces a tinker, a 'big' man with 'calloused hands', whom she invites into the garden and to whom she gives a chrysanthemum in a different kind of pot ('the gloves were forgotten now'). When her husband comes home, he tells her that she looks 'different', 'strong and happy'. They decide to go to town for dinner; on the way, she sees the plant abandoned on the road – despite his talk, the travelling man was only interested in the pot. The story is rather insistent on the sexual meaning of gardens and flower pots. More relevant here is the way that Steinbeck links these to boxing. ('Sex is a kind of war', he later claimed.[94]) At the start of the story, Elisa's husband had joked about going to the fights. 'Oh no', she said breathlessly. 'No, I wouldn't like fights.' Later, after seeing the tinker's cart and her rejected flower, she asks her husband, 'Henry, at those prize fights, do the men hurt each other very much? . . . I've read how they break noses, and blood runs down their chests. I've read how the fighting gloves get heavy and soggy with blood.' Several words used here link back to moments earlier in the story – the reference to 'gloves' recalls Elisa's own pair, and 'heavy' resonates with Henry's comment, just a few lines earlier, that 'we get so heavy out on the ranch'. The prize-fights, of course, take place in a fenced-off square that echoes Elisa's garden, the flower beds within it and the Salinas Valley itself. So what is Steinbeck suggesting? Elisa, it seems, has the sexual energy and potential violence of a boxer, but, until that day, she has not allowed a real opponent into the ring with her. Having finally done so, and having even gone bareknuckled, she herself has now been badly bloodied. Bemused, Henry offers to take his wife to watch the fights, but all her own fight has gone. 'She relaxed limply in the seat . . . She turned up her coat collar so he could not see that she was crying weakly – like an old woman.'[95]

### 'JOE LOUIS IS THE MAN'

Chapter Two of *The Autobiography of Malcolm X* begins with 'the greatest celebration of race pride our generation had ever known': 'On June twenty-seventh of that year, nineteen thirty-seven, Joe Louis knocked out James J. Braddock to become the heavyweight champion of the world.' More than two decades had passed since a black American had held the title.

In the wake of this victory the thirteen-year-old Malcolm Little followed his brother to the gym. But while Philbert was 'a natural boxer', Malcolm was not. Pretending he was older he signed up for a bout with another novice, a white boy called Bill Peterson; 'I'll never forget him.'

> I knew I was scared, but I didn't know, as Bill Peterson told me later on, that he was scared of me, too. He was so scared I was going to hurt him that he knocked me down fifty times if he did once.
>
> He did such a job on my reputation in the Negro neighbourhood that I practically went into hiding. A Negro can't just be whipped by somebody white and return with his head up to the neighbourhood, especially in those days . . . When I did show my face again, the Negroes I knew rode me so badly I knew I had to do something.
>
> . . . So I went back to the gym, and I trained – hard. I beat bags and skipped rope and grunted and sweated all over the place. And finally I signed up to fight Bill Peterson again.

The rematch was no better:

The moment the bell rang, I saw a fist, then the canvas coming up, and ten seconds later the referee was saying 'Ten!' over me. It was probably the shortest 'fight' in history . . . That white boy was the beginning and the end of my fight career.[96]

It is interesting to consider why Malcolm X included this story in his *Autobiography*. Most straightforwardly, it seems that he was illustrating the impact of Louis in the late thirties – 'Every Negro boy old enough to walk wanted to be the next Brown Bomber' – and demonstrating his own tenacity. More importantly, however, the story allows him to compare the roles of black men, and black leaders, in the 1960s and in the 1930s, where 'sports and, to a lesser extent, show business, were the only fields open to Negroes, and when the ring was the only place a Negro could whip a white man and not be lynched.' Malcolm X's autobiography is all about the unexpected places in which he has been able to 'whip a white man', and the suggestion is that if he had been good at boxing he would not have become an exceptional leader. 'A lot of times in these later years since I became a Muslim, I've thought back to that fight and reflected that it was Allah's work to stop me: I might have wound up punchy.'[97] Nevertheless, the qualities that made him train 'hard' and go back for a second shot at Peterson are also, it is suggested, the qualities which made him the man he became.[98]

Born in 1914 in Lafayette, Alabama, Joe Louis Barrow moved with his family to Detroit's Black Bottom when he was twelve.[99] According to legend, his first boxing lessons were paid for with money his mother had given him for violin classes, and, when he began to fight, he dropped his surname to deceive her.[100] Louis trained at the Brewster gym, where he met local businessmen John Roxborough and Julian Black (both men dealt in real estate and Roxborough also ran Detroit's numbers racket, while Black ran a casino). While keen to manage Louis, neither man had any experience in boxing, so they enlisted the help of veteran trainer Jack Blackburn.

After winning the light heavyweight championship at the (unsegregated) Detroit Golden Gloves competition in 1933 and 1934, Louis turned professional. By the time he was twenty he had a record of twelve wins and no losses, and was starting to get noticed. Eventually Roxborough, Black and Blackburn decided that he would have a better chance at securing high-profile fights with white fighters if he also had a white manager, and in particular, one with the right connections. Mike Jacobs was employed by the Hearst organization and was therefore the most powerful promoter in the States; the 'pugilist-infested stretch' of 49th Street between Broadway and 8th Avenue was dubbed 'Jacobs' Beach'.[101] Jacobs joined the three-man management team in 1935, and subsequently had a major influence on the direction of Louis's career. Jacobs collected half the profits from Louis's fights and reduced Roxborough and Black to figureheads.[102] Because of this, Jacobs has been demonized. Louis's biographer, Chris Mead, for example, described Louis as 'getting into bed with a rattlesnake', while Jean-Michel Basquiat's 1982 painting *St Joe Louis Surrounded By Snakes* depicts the boxer in the pose of the Renaissance *sacra conversazione*, with Blackburn on his right, laying a supportive arm on his leg, and a hooked-nosed Jacobs, as a money-grubbing Judas on the left.[103] Louis recalled Jacobs more generously:

> If it wasn't for Mike Jacobs I would never have got to be champion. He fixed it for me to get a crack at the title, and he never once asked me to do anything wrong or phony in the ring . . . He made a lot of money through me, but he figured to lose, too.[104]

The key to success in 1930s America, Roxburgh and Jacobs realized, was for their fighter to behave in a manner as unlike Jack Johnson as possible. Roxborough laid down seven rules for Louis to follow. White America had been offended by Johnson's marriages to white women, so Louis agreed only to be photographed with black women. White America had been offended by Johnson's flamboyance, so Louis was to appear low key and unexpressive. He was never to gloat over a fallen opponent. He was never to get a speeding ticket. In short, he was to be, at all times, 'a credit to his race', blameless and bland.[105] As Langston Hughes put it,

> 'They say' . . . 'They say' . . . 'They say' . . .
> But the gossips had no
> 'They say'
> to latch onto
>     for Joe.[106]

Years later Louis admitted, 'I was just as vain as Muhammad Ali; I just had to be more discreet about it.'[107]

Louis's professional career was notable not simply for its brilliance – he retained his title for nearly twelve years – but because of what else was going on during those particular twelve years, 1937–49. Louis fought a lot of white men during that time, and each fight represented something slightly different. For Richard Bak, he is 'unquestionably the greatest metaphor the American prize ring has ever produced'.[108]

Louis's first metaphorical contest took place at Madison Square Garden in 1935, just a few months after the Harlem riots. His opponent was Primo Carnera, the Italian former heavyweight champion who had famously been photographed by Edward Steichen giving the Fascist salute. Carnera was a huge man and the press portrayed him as symbolic of the quarter of a million Italian troops poised to invade Ethiopia. The *Washington Post* printed a cartoon of the fighters with enormous shadows (representing Haile Selassie and Mussolini) behind them, and the New York *Sun* featured Louis kicking a boot called Carnera, while a similarly small figure named Ethiopia stood next to a giant map of Italy. The *Sun*'s caption asked, 'can the king of Abyssinia, descendant of King Solomon and the Queen of Sheba, do on a big scale in Africa what Joe Louis did on a small scale in Yankee Stadium?'[109]

Louis was not well known before the fight, but overnight he became famous. While Jack Johnson's celebrity was tied up with the development of film, and Muhammad Ali would later been seen as the saviour of television boxing, Louis's status as a national hero was associated with the spread of radio during the thirties.[110] Autobiographies of the period (by blacks and whites) almost invariably contain an account of listening to one of his fights. 'We'd be all crowded around the radio waiting to hear the announcer describe Joe knocking some motherfucker out,' recalled Miles Davis. 'And when he did, the whole goddamn black community of East St Louis would go crazy'.[111] Maya Angelou describes a crowd gathering in an Arkansas store to listen to radio coverage of the Louis–Carnera contest. Every piece of commentary brings forth a reaction from the listeners, as they imagine what is happening in the ring. When it seems Louis might be going down, Angelou reports:

> My race groaned. It was our people falling. It was another lynching, yet another Black man hanging on a tree. One more woman ambushed and raped. A Black boy whipped and maimed . . . This might be the end of the world.

The wider meanings of the fight are clear to everyone there. When the commentator reports, 'They're in a clench, Louis is trying to fight his way out', Angelou notes, 'some bitter comedian on the porch said, "That white man don't mind hugging that niggah now, I betcha."' And she herself 'wondered if the announcer gave any thought to the fact that he was addressing as "ladies and gentlemen" all the Negroes around the world who sat sweating and praying, glued to their "master's voice". Louis's eventual victory proved glorious: 'people drank Coca-Colas like ambrosia and ate candy bars like Christmas'. But Angelou, writing in 1969, was also conscious of the limitations of this moment. As the crowd dispersed, she notes that 'those who lived too far had made arrangements to stay in town'. 'It wouldn't do for a Black man and his family to be caught on a lonely country road on a night when Joe Louis had proved that we were the strongest people in the world.'[112]

In the months that followed his defeat of Carnera, Louis-mania flourished in diverse quarters. In June, the journal of the respectable NAACP, *The Crisis*, gave its seal of approval by putting him on the cover (illus. 105).[113] In September, Richard Wright (who had listened to Louis's defeat of Baer on the radio in a

105
Louis on the cover of *The Crisis*, June 1935.

BROWN BOMBER JOE LOUIS

**UNIONISM OUR ONLY HOPE**
By Frank R. Crosswaith

**RELIGION AND THE RACE PROBLEM**
By John M. Cooper

**SHARECROPPERS DROP COLOR LINE**
By Ward H. Rodgers

South Side tavern) wrote in the communist *New Masses* of Chicago's black population filling the streets as 'a fluid mass of joy':

> Four centuries of oppression, of frustrated hopes, of black bitterness, felt even in the bones of the bewildered young rose to the surface. Yes unconsciously they had imputed to the brawny image of Joe Louis all the balked dreams of revenge, all the secretly visualized images of retaliation AND HE HAD WON! . . . From the symbol of Joe's strength they took strength.[114]

Although he came from Detroit, Harlemites quickly claimed Louis as one of their own. Badly hit by the Depression, Harlem was still the symbolic centre of black American life, and as Ralph Ellison later recalled, 'a place of glamour'.

> Those were the days of the swinging big bands, days when the streets of Harlem were filled with celebration every time Joe Louis knocked somebody out in the ring, days when we danced the Lindy at the Savoy Ballroom, and nights when new stars were initiated on the stage of the Apollo Theater.[115]

When Louis beat Max Baer, the São Tomense poet Francisco José Tenreiro wrote that 'Harlem opened up in a wide smile', while little girls skipped and sang of Louis's 'socking' and Baer's 'rocking' as the 'dream of a viper'.[116]

While waiting for his title chance against Jim Braddock, Louis took on a number of ex-world champions, the most prominent of whom was Max Schmeling. Schmeling had come touted by Goebbels and Hitler as an exemplar of Aryan racial superiority (although Hitler was supposedly pleased to point out that Schmeling's manager, Joe Jacobs, was an American Jew, and hence 'Germany is not anti-Jewish'[117]). Boxing was important to Hitler, and in *Mein Kampf*, he had emphasized its role in training the youth of Germany:

> It is regarded as natural and honourable that a young man should learn to fence and proceed to fight duels right and left, but if he boxes, it is supposed to be vulgar! Why? There is no sport that so much as this one promotes the spirit of attack, demands lightning decisions, and trains the body in steel dexterity . . . If our entire intellectual upper crust had not been brought up so exclusively on upper-crust etiquette; if instead they had learned boxing thoroughly, a German revolution of pimps, deserters, and such-like rabble would never have been possible.[118]

In the years leading up to the war, Max Schmeling's every fight became a test case not only for Hitler's racial theories (German Jews had not been allowed to box professionally for some time) but also for the potential might of the German army.[119] In 1933 Schmeling had been defeated by Max Baer (whose Jewishness was questionable, but who often fought with a Star of David on his shorts), and the *American Hebrew* described the defeat as 'a huge joke at the expense of "Herr Hitler"' whose 'Nazi theory of Nordic superiority' had been made 'ridiculous'.[120] On 19 June 1936, however, Schmeling fought and beat Louis in twelve rounds. He had picked up Louis's only weakness as a fighter – a tendency to hold his left hand too low. Any fighter who circled to his left could defeat him, a jealous Jack Johnson had predicted, and he proved right. The American had been the 10–1 favourite. Johnson, however, had bet heavily on Schmeling and, after the contest, walked down 125th Street, waving his wad around.[121] (Johnson was also involved in the search for a white hope to defeat Louis: 'it's a commercial affair with me', he explained.[122])

The Nazi journal *Das Schwarze Korps* declared that 'Schmeling's victory was not only sport. It was a question of prestige for our race', and Goebbels used the fight footage in one of his most successful propaganda films, *Max Schmelings Sieg – Ein Deutscher* ('Schmeling's Victory, A Germany victory'). More than three million Germans saw the film in its first month.[123] (The Berlin Olympics began just six weeks later.) Meanwhile, *Der Weltkampf* wrote that France, England and 'white North America' should also celebrate the victory which had 'checked the arrogance of the Negroes and clearly demonstrated to them the superiority of white intelligence'.[124] At least one American paper, the *New Orleans Picayune*, agreed. A columnist cheerfully wrote of Louis's defeat, 'I guess this proves who really is the master race.'[125]

For blacks, Louis's defeat was made worse by the fact that it had taken place on Juneteenth, Emancipation Day.[126] Hundreds wept in the streets of Harlem, and Francisco José Tenreiro declared that 'The gong of the bell / Hangs in the air, screaming / The negro's defeat.'[127] Marcus Garvey, meanwhile, blamed Louis, accusing him of laziness, selfishness, and lack of racial pride. 'Schmeling knew that he had the responsibility of satisfying a watching and waiting Germanic world', but Louis, 'as is customary to us', 'thought only of himself': 'We hope Mrs Louis will not think hard of us, but we think Joe got married too early before securing his world championship.'[128] 'Don't be a Joe Louis' was a popular expression that summer and John Dos Passos wrote to his friend Ernest Hemingway, asking him what had happened to his 'little chocolate friend Joey Louis? Matrimony? Dope? Disease? Or is Hitler right?'[129]

On 22 June 1937 Louis's redemption began. Twenty-two years after Jess Willard had defeated Jack Johnson, Joe Louis broke the colour line in the heavyweight championship for good by defeating Jim Braddock, the 'Cinderella Man'.[130] The fight had been difficult to secure and Louis's manager, Mike Jacobs, finally agreed to pay Braddock, and his manager Joe Gould, 10 per cent of Louis's earnings for a decade. The Baltimore celebration was witnessed by British journalist Alistair Cooke. Cooke and a friend were attending a Fats Waller show in 'darktown', when 'far off from somewhere came a high roar like a tidal wave'. 'It was like Christmas Eve in darkest Africa . . . for one night, in all the lurid darktowns of America, the black man was king. The memory of that night has terrified and exhilarated me ever since.'[131] The *Daily Worker* was less

Conradian: 'The Negro people,' it declared, 'are going to smack Jim Crow right on the button like Louis hit Braddock.'[132]

But the real championship fight, and the fight that turned Louis into a potent symbol for white as well as black America, was the 1938 Schmeling rematch (illus. 110).[133] In the lead up to the contest, Franklin D. Roosevelt reputedly invited the boxer to the White House, felt his muscles, and said, 'Joe, we're depending on those muscles for America.'[134] Louis did not disappoint. After only 124 seconds he knocked out the 'sagging Teuton', the 'Nazi Nailer'; 'people who had paid as much as $100 for their chairs didn't use them' and many radio listeners who had not quite settled down for the fight said they missed it altogether.[135] 'It was a shocking thing, that knockout,' reported Bob Considine, 'short, sharp, merciless, complete'.[136] 'Hitler's pet,' wrote Richard Wright, 'looked like a soft piece of molasses candy left out in the sun.'[137] Nevertheless, Louis and Schmeling embraced. 'They both smiled,' noted Considine, 'and could afford to – for Louis had made around $200,000 a minute and Schmeling $100,000.' (Later, to salve opinion back in Germany, Schmeling claimed he had been fouled.)

In Harlem, 500,000 blacks took to the streets, saluting each other with Nazi salutes and shouting 'Heil Louis!' 'One joyous Negro passed it on to another and finally Seventh Avenue looked like a weird burlesque of Wilhelmstrasse in Berlin – staggering, yelling, singing, jumping, dancing, hugging, men and women jutting out their hands to one another in mock Nazi salute.'[138] In Georgia, things were slightly different. Jimmy Carter recalled hearing the fight on the family radio which had been propped up on the window sill so that their black neighbours could listen to it without entering the house. At the end of the fight, 'there was no sound from anyone in the yard, except a polite "Thank you, Mister Earl"', offered to Carter's 'deeply disappointed' father.

> Then, our several dozen visitors filed across the dirt road, across the railroad track, and quietly entered a house about a hundred yards away out in the field. At that point, pandemonium broke loose inside that house, as our black neighbours shouted and yelled in celebration of the Louis victory. But all the curious, accepted proprieties of a racially-segregated society had been carefully observed.[139]

Like the victory of the black American runner Jesse Owens at the 1936 Berlin Olympics, Louis's triumph had a powerful political impact.[140] For whites, American democracy had straightforwardly defeated German fascism. For blacks, however, Louis was primarily a 'race hero', fighting in (as well as for) Jim Crow America. Marcus Garvey now argued that Louis's punches were 'typical of our race in true action': Joe had 'had time for reflection and for the appreciation of the responsibility our race has placed on his shoulders'.[141] Richard Wright noted the political potential of the 'High Tide in Harlem' that Louis's victory inspired and tried to balance the claims of democracy vs. fascism with those of black

American racial justice.

> Carry the dream on for yourself; lift it out of the trifling guise of a prizefight celebration and supply the social and economic details and you have the secret dynamics of proletarian aspiration. The eyes of these people were bold that night. Their fear of property, of the armed police fell away. There was in their chant a hunger deeper than that for bread as they marched along.

For the communist Wright, this was a moment of potentially revolutionary significance. With Louis as a rallying point, the black proletariat might break out of the confines of their own square circle and recognize 'that the earth was theirs . . . that they did not have to live by proscription in one corner of it'.[142]

When Jack Johnson entered the ring in Reno in 1910 the band played 'All Coons Look Alike to Me'; in 1938, 'The Star-Spangled Banner' introduced Louis. After 1938, white newspaper cartoonists finally abandoned Sambo stereotypes to portray Louis in a flattering light.[143] Louis's nicknames proliferated as fast as his product endorsements. As Eugene McCartney noted in a 1938 scholarly article, 'Alliteration on the Sports Page':

> *Brown Bomber has finally emerged as his most popular name, but only after knocking out a score of others: Alabam' Assassin, Black Beauty, Brown Behemoth, Brown Bludgeon, Brown Embalmer, Dark Destroyer, Dark Dynamiter, Detroit Demon, Detroit Devastator, Detroit's Dun Demon, Jarring Joe, Jolting Joe, Licorice Lasher, Michigan Mauler, Ring Robot, Sable Sphinx, Sepia Slasher, Sepia Sniper, Tan Thunderbolt, Tan Thunderer, Tan Tornado, Wildcat Warrior.*[144]

Louis's reputation as an all-American hero was consolidated in 1942 when he risked his title against Max Baer and donated his winnings (approximately $70,000) to the Naval Relief Fund to help the families of those who had died at Pearl Harbor.[145] Paul Gallico declared that Louis ('Citizen Barrow') represented nothing less than 'simple good American integrity', perhaps forgetting that in 1935 he had dubbed him a 'calmly savage Ethiopian.' Many blacks were less happy about Louis's support of the discriminatory and oppressive Navy policies. After Walter White, Secretary of the NAACP, expressed the hope that Louis's patriotic actions would stir the American Navy toward desegregation, the Office of War Information and the War Department made statements insisting that it was necessary to the war effort to 'de-emphasize our many long standing internal dissensions'.[146] But the war simply highlighted those dissensions. In the May 1941 issue of *The Crisis*, labour leader A. Philip Randolph had called for a mass march on Washington to protest against employment inequalities in the National Defense industries, arguing that the present situation was 'a blow below the belt'. Six days before the scheduled march, Roosevelt issued an order barring racial discrimination in the defense industries, and Randolph cancelled the march. The effectiveness of the threat of nonviolent direct action had been demonstrated.[147]

After the fight, Louis enlisted and became a spokesman and recruiting agent for the army. In May 1942, he made a speech saying, 'We gon do our part, and we will win, because we're on God's side.' This immediately became a popular propaganda slogan, featuring on a recruitment poster with Louis and his gun.[148] Claudia Jones of the Young Communist League used the same image for the cover of a 1942 pamphlet, *Lift Every Voice for Victory!* (illus. 133). 'All victories won on the "home front" against discrimination today,' she argued, 'are inseparable from the struggle to defeat Hitler.'[149] Louis also appeared in a couple of propaganda films, including *This is The Army* (1943) – featuring an Irving Berlin song that urged the fashionable to 'take a look at Brown Bomber Joe' to find out what 'the well-dressed man in Harlem will wear' – and the groundbreaking *The Negro Soldier* (1944).[150] The film begins in a church where the black congregation listens to a young preacher, who departs from his prepared text to consider the contribution of blacks in the military. The preacher (played by Carlton Moss, who also wrote the script) begins by evoking Joe Louis's 1938 defeat of Schmeling. A newsreel clip of the fight is then shown with the preacher's words as a voiceover:

> In one minute and 49 seconds an American fist won a victory. But it wasn't a final victory. No, that victory's going to take a little longer and a whole lot more American fists. Now those two men that were matched in the ring that night are matched again, this time in a far greater arena and for much greater stakes.

The scene then shifts to Louis and Schmeling in training – Louis in uniform running through the countryside with his comrades, and Schmeling jumping out of a plane, learning to be a parachutist. In Germany, men are 'turned into machines', the preacher says; in America, he implies, even black men are at one with nature. The sermon continues:

> This time it's a fight not between man and man but between nation and nation, a fight for the real championship of the world, to determine which way of life shall survive – their way or our way. And this time we must see to it that there is no return engagement for the stakes this time are the greatest men have ever fought for.[151]

The film goes on to tell the story of black involvement in the American army since the Revolution. Although the Civil War and Abraham Lincoln are briefly mentioned, slavery is not.[152] In 1945, Louis was awarded a medal by the Legion of Merit. 'White America found it easier to give Joe Louis a medal than to integrate the army,' notes Chris Mead, 'easier to write an editorial praising Joe Louis than to hire a black reporter.'[153] Louis was not unaware of the political

106
Poster advertising *The Champ* (1931).

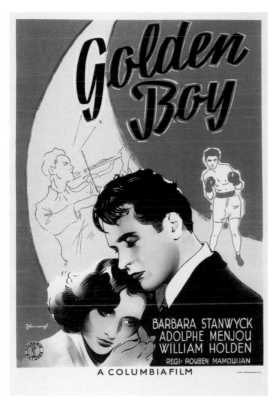

107
Poster advertising *Golden Boy* (1939).

108
Poster advertising *Nothing Sacred* (1937).

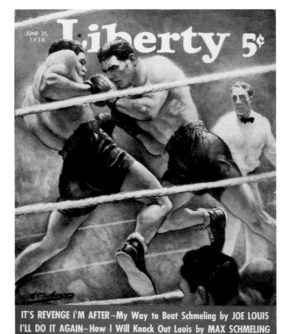

109
Poster advertising *Body and Soul* (1947).

110
Louis vs. Schmeling on the cover of *Liberty* magazine, 25 June 1938.

111
Benny Andrews, *The Champion*, 1968.

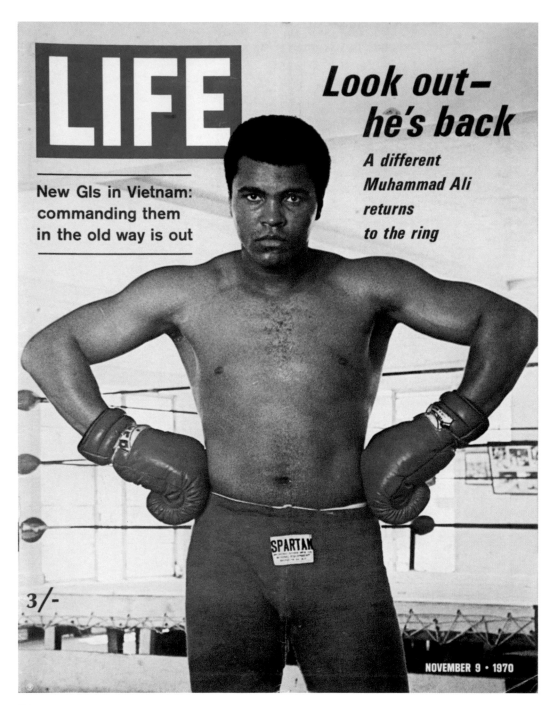

**LIFE**

New GIs in Vietnam:
commanding them
in the old way is out

Look out –
he's back

A different
Muhammad Ali
returns
to the ring

3/-

NOVEMBER 9 · 1970

112
'Look out – he's back', cover of *Life*, 9 November 1970.

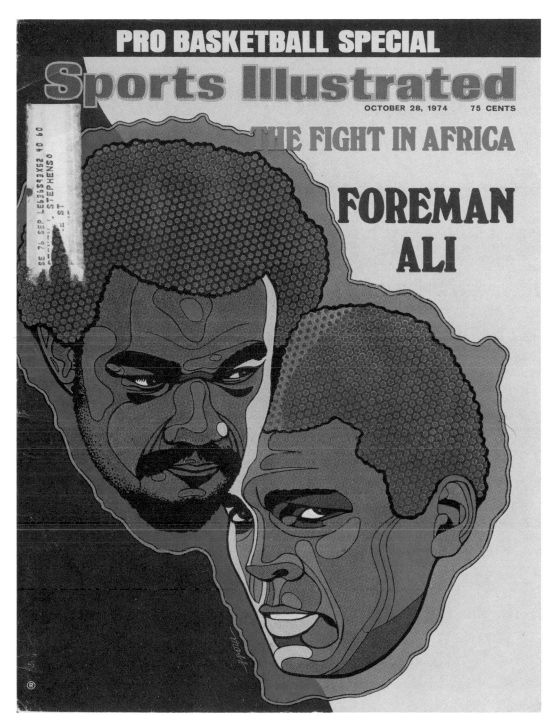

113
Cover of *Sports Illustrated*, 28 October 1974: 'The Fight in Africa'.

114
Andy Warhol, *Muhammad Ali: Hand on Chin*, 1977.

115
Cover of Ntozake Shange, *Float Like a Butterfly*, with illustrations by Edel Rodriguez (New York, 2002).

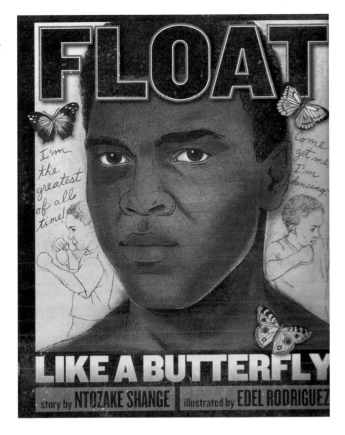

116
Poster advertising *When We Were Kings* (1996).

117
Poster advertising *a.k.a. Cassius Clay* (1970).

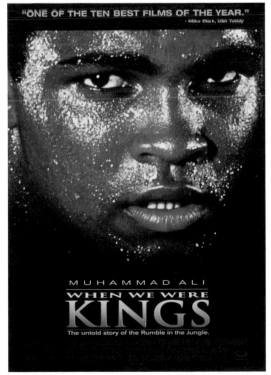

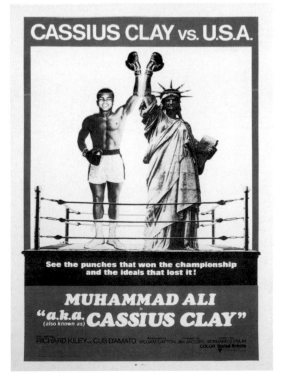

118
Elliott Pinkney (with
the assistance of
Sam Barrow and
Lloyd Goodney),
detail of *Visions and
Motions*, 1993.

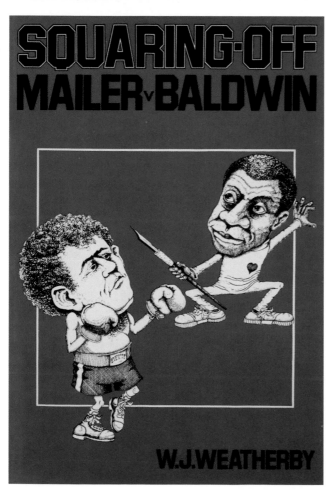

119
Harold King, cover
of W. J. Weatherby,
*Squaring Off: Mailer
v. Baldwin* (1977).

120
Sylvester Stallone in
*Rocky* (1976).

121
Cover of *Superman
vs. Muhammad Ali*,
DC Comics (1978).

122
Eduardo Arroyo, *Direct Panama*, 1984.

123
Keith Haring,
*Boxer*, 1988.

124
David Hammons, *Champ*, 1989.

125
Godfried Donkor, *Financial Times Boxers*, No. 2, 2001, collage on paper.

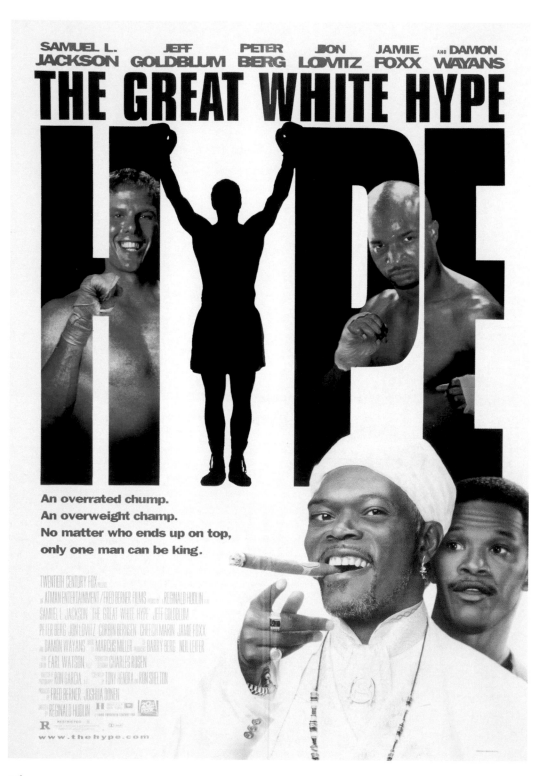

126
*The Great White Hype* poster, 1996.

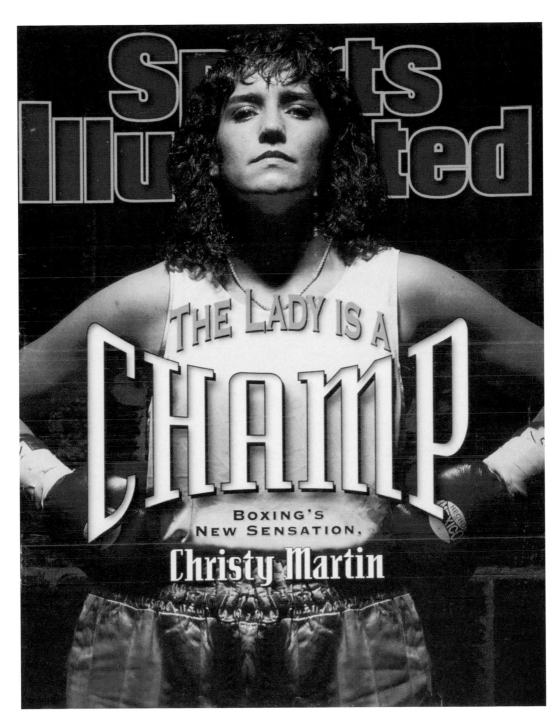

127
Christy Martin on the cover of *Sports Illustrated*, 1996.

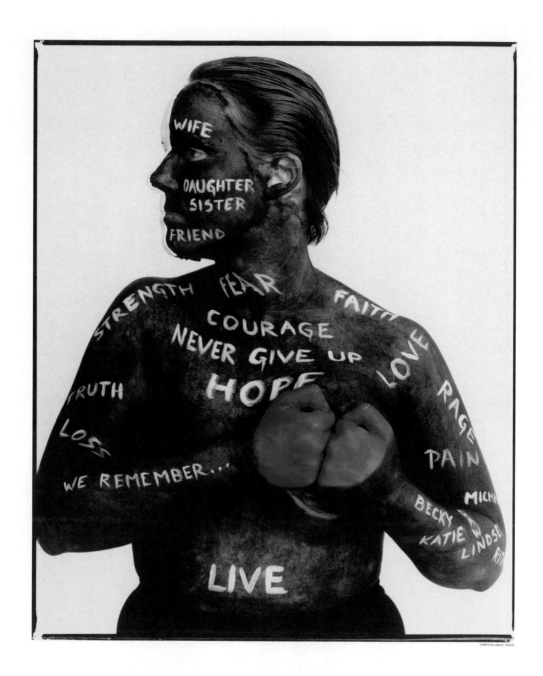

**WOMEN ANNIE LEIBOVITZ**
THE CORCORAN GALLERY OF ART OCTOBER 1999–FEBRUARY 2000

128
Annie Leibovitz, poster advertising *Women* exhibition, Washington, DC, 1999–2000.

129
*Battle of the Blues,*
vol. 4, album cover,
1959.

130
Emma Amos,
*Muhammad Ali,*
1998.

131
Peter Howson,
*Boxer 1,* 2002, pastel
on paper.

132
Paul-Felix Montez,
*The Gloves*, 2006,
model for a 70-foot
sculpture of steel
and bronze gloves
above granite,
shown at the *21st
Century Las Vegas
Monuments* exhibi-
tion, Las Vegas.

hypocrisies at play. Of his fights with Schmeling, he said, 'White Americans –
even while some of them still were lynching black people in the South – were
depending on me to K.O. Germany.'[154]

In 1946, Louis returned to boxing but he was not as strong or as fast as he
had been. He knocked out Billy Conn again – coining the slogan, 'He can run,
but he can't hide' – and won three other fights, including two with Jersey Joe
Walcott, before abdicating his title in 1949. However, because he needed money
to pay taxes – the IRS demanded a reported $1.2 million in back taxes, interest
and penalties – he returned to the ring. In 1950 he lost a one-sided decision to
Ezzard Charles and retired for good the following year when Rocky Marciano
knocked him out in front of a national television audience. Broke, Louis turned
to wrestling and refereeing and, following several stays in hospitals for cocaine
addiction and paranoia, he became an 'official greeter' at Caesars Palace in Las
Vegas. He died in 1981 at the age of 66 and was buried in Arlington National
Cemetery; Max Schmeling, who had become a good friend, was one of the pall-
bearers. Between 1937 and 1949 Louis defended his title 25 times, setting records
for any division in the number of defences and longevity as a continuous world
champion. Both records still stand.

For all that white America eventually embraced him, it was as a 'race hero'
that Louis flourished.[155] For some, he was simply the best-known black man in
America. In November 1938 Frank Byrd described trying to write an article on
a Harlem prostitute called Big Bess for the *Amsterdam News*, but being told by
the night deskman that his job was simply 'to tell me when Joe Louis gets some,
and if the Brown Bomber likes it . . . Sidney said an *Amsterdam* reader could not
care less whether Lenox Avenue Bess really had a heart; they'd read about her
if Joe Louis said so'.[156] For others, the Louis phenomenon merited proper academic analysis. In their seminal sociological study *Black Metropolis* (1945), Clair
Drake and Horace R. Cayton noted that from 1933 to 1938 Louis had more front-
page mentions (80) in the Chicago *Defender* than anyone else; Haile Selassie
came a poor second with 24 mentions.[157] In *Negro Youth at the Crossways* (1940),
E. Franklin Frazier reported Louis's popularity with high school students: 'Joe
Louis', Frazier wrote, 'enables . . . many Negro youths and adults in all classes
to inflict vicariously the aggressions which they would like to carry out against
whites for the discriminations and insults which they have suffered.'[158]

Louis soon became a quasi-religious figure, and in 1941 even *Time* magazine dubbed him 'a black Moses, leading the children of Ham out of bondage'.[159]
There are many examples of Louis being evoked in these terms, but none more
poignant than a story told by Martin Luther King in *Why We Can't Wait*:

> More than 25 years ago, on one of the southern states adopted a new
> method of capital punishment. Poison gas supplanted the gallows. In
> its earliest stages a microphone was placed inside the sealed death
> chamber so that scientific observers might hear the words of the dying
> prisoner to judge how the victim reacted in this novel situation. The

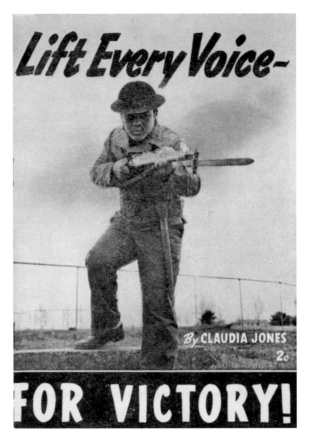

133
Cover of *Lift Every Voice for Victory!* by Claudia Jones (1942).

134
*Two Champions*. Postcard based on a photograph of Joe Louis and Martin Luther King taken at a benefit for the March on Washington, 1963.

first victim was a young Negro. As the pellet dropped into the container, and the gas curled upward, through the microphone came these words. 'Save me Joe Louis. Save me Joe Louis. Save me Joe Louis'.[160]

Writing in 1963, King described this cry as 'bizarre and naïve', and claimed that it had now been replaced by 'a mighty shout of challenge': the 'loneliness and profound despair of Negroes in that period', a despair manifest in the belief that 'not God, not government, not charitably minded white men, but a Negro who was the world's most expert fighter, in this last extremity, was the last hope' had finally been 'replaced by confidence' in the possibility of real political change (illus. 134).[161] During the sixties, another 'expert boxer' would come to represent political change, but at the height of the Depression, the dying prisoner was not the only American to believe that Louis was a Christ-like figure, the 'New Black Hope', the 'one Negro white men respect'.[162] After Louis beat Baer (in the first million-dollar gate since Dempsey), Richard Wright wrote that the feeling on the streets of Chicago 'was like a revival': 'After one fight really, there was a religious feeling in the air. Well, it wasn't exactly a religious feeling, but it was *something*, and you could feel it. It was a feeling of unity, of oneness.'[163]

The religious aura surrounding Louis meant that he was highly flexible as a political symbol.[164] Ironically, Louis's success in a sport that epitomized personal struggle and achievement was often used to harness support for political struggles that rejected individualist aspiration in favour of collective action. In 1942, Louis appeared in propaganda for the us Army; in 1946 he agreed to act as the honorary national chairman of the communist-linked United Negro Veterans of America, and was honoured (along with Duke Ellington and Frank Sinatra) by *New Masses*, the journal in which Richard Wright had dubbed him political 'dynamite'.[165] Along with movie stars such as Humphrey Bogart and Rita Hayworth, and performers such as Frank Sinatra and Benny Goodman, Louis could be found 'supporting Spanish Loyalists, raising money for anti-fascist refugees, playing benefits for Popular Front politicians, and promoting themselves in the *Daily Worker*'.[166] In July 1947 *The Worker* reported the presence of Louis and Sinatra, along with Edward G. Robinson and Harpo Marx, at a benefit for an inter-racial hospital.[167]

Novels of, and about, the 1930s and '40s abound with references to Louis and his capacity for political inspiration. V. S. Naipaul's *The Mimic Men* (1967) is set partly on the British-governed Caribbean island of Isabella. Ralph Singh, writing his memoirs in London, recalls a visit to the home of a black schoolfriend, Bertie Browne, in the early forties. 'On one wall, ochre-colored with white facings, there were framed pictures of Joe Louis, Jesse Owens, Haile Selassie, and Jesus.' Only a few years later, Browne becomes a 'black folk-leader', active in the island's struggle for independence.[168] A radio broadcast of Louis's 1941 fight against 'new White Hope', Billy Conn, is the stimulus for a prison rebellion in Lloyd L. Brown's 1951 novel, *Iron City*. For protagonist, Lonnie James, whose initials reverse those of the champion, each of Louis's victories has been 'a good sign'. On the night of the Conn fight, however, Louis seems to be struggling and the prison resounds with the sound of 'KILL THAT NIGGER!' The guards turn the radio off, but the prisoners protest:

> TURN ON THE RADIO! TURN ON THE RADIO! It was savage now, not pleading, and it seemed as though the granite walls would shatter from the pounding beat of the chant . . . Everything was in that outcry – the beatings, the Hole, the graft, the senseless rules, crooked cops, crooked judges – everything.

The guards give in and switch the radio back on. The fight is over, 'but the inmates would still hear the solemn announcement. THE *WINNAH* AND STILL HEAVYWEIGHT CHAMPION OF THE WORLD – JO-O-OE *LOUIS*! The prisoners fight back against the guards, just as Louis had fought against Conn, but there is an important difference in the two battles. Louis's victory had been an individual achievement, but that of the prisoners was a collective act. In the following chapter those same prisoners gather together to support Lonnie James's appeal against the death penalty. Louis's individual victory sparks collective action, and Brown links the fight to the German invasion of the Soviet Union (which took place just a few days later).[169]

But not everyone agreed that race heroes such as Louis could be effective as political models. Langston Hughes's poem 'To be Somebody' (1950) describes a little boy 'dreaming of the boxing gloves / Joe Louis wore' but for him there is no 'knockout' merely 'Bam! Bop! Mop!' 'There's always room,' the poem concludes, '*They say*, / At the top.'[170] A similar irony informs Chester Himes's first novel *If He Hollers Let Him Go* (1945), written in the wake of Louis's support of the segregated American Navy. Robert Jones, who works in a California shipyard, has been raised up – 'We made you a leader of your people, such as Joe Louis, the prize fighter, Marian Anderson, the singer, and others. We had confidence in you.' – only to be brought down, by a false accusation of rape. Jones says he doesn't want to fight, but he dreams constantly of killing. The novel ends when he joins the army.[171]

While Joe Louis, or his reputation, crop up in a wide variety of novels, the form of expression most often associated with him was undoubtedly the blues (illus. 135).[172] Within weeks of his 1935 defeat of Carnera, songs about the fighter were being released all over the country. The first was Texan Joe Pullum's 'Joe Louis is the Man', which praised him

135
'Joe Louis is the Man': Advertisement for Decca records, 1935.

Here are four great records dedicated to Joe Louis, the Brown Bomber, still our bet for the championship. Be sure to get these records.

**6071**—Joe Louis Is The Man and Peters' Blue—Voc.-Piano Acc. Joe Pullum ..............................59c
**7114**—Joe Louis Blues and Let's Have A New Deal—Vocal-Guit. Acc. Carl Martin ..............................59c
**7115**—Joe Louis Chant and Baby O' Mine—Voc. Orch. Acc. George Dewey Washington ..................59c
**3046**—Joe Louis Strutt and He's In The Ring Doing The Same Old Thing—Vocal with Orch. Acc. Sung by Memphis Minnie ..............................59c

less as a fighter than as a devoted son, while nine days later Memphis Minnie McCoy recorded the 'Joe Louis Strut' and 'He's In the Ring (Doin' the Same Old Thing)', a wonderful evocation of Joe's promise amid Depression hardship.

> I wouldn't even pay my house rent
> I wouldn't buy me nothing to eat
> Joe Louis said 'Come take a chance with me
> I'll bet I put you on your feet.'

Soon every victory was being celebrated, and even Louis's 1936 defeat by Schmeling was debated, most notably in a calypso by The Lion and Atilla: 'I wouldn't say it was dope or conspiracy, / but the whole thing look extremely funny to me.'[173] By the end of the thirties Louis was established as the greatest blues hero since John Henry, and literary figures such as Langston Hughes and Richard Wright joined in. In 1940 the NAACP Hollywood Theatre Alliance Negro Revue included a skit about Louis, which had as its climax Hughes's song 'America's Young Black Joe', a parody of Stephen Foster's 'Old Black Joe' (1861). Old Black Joe was a slave dreaming of leaving the cotton fields for heaven:

> I'm coming, I'm coming
> For my head is bending low
> I hear their gentle voices calling
> Old Black Joe.

Young Black Joe is also 'comin',

> But my head AIN'T bending low!
> I'm walking proud! I'm speaking loud!
> I'm America's Young Black Joe![174]

In 1941 Richard Wright's attempt, 'King Joe' (with music by Count Basie), was recorded by Basie's Orchestra, with Paul Robeson 'singing the blues for the first time in his life' (Jimmy Rushing stood by his side to beat time).[175] 'Wonder what Joe Louis thinks when he's fighting a white man,' Wright asked, 'Bet he thinks what I'm thinking, cause he wears a deadpan.'[176]

## JOE LOUIS VS. JACK JOHNSON

Joe Louis's enormous popularity did not mean that Jack Johnson was entirely forgotten.[177] If white fight fans liked to compare Joe Louis and Jack Dempsey, blacks pitted Louis against Johnson. The comparative experience of the two black heavyweight champions was also evoked as a barometer of the changing position of black Americans more generally. Richard Wright's first novel, *Lawd Today*, presents a Joycean day in the life of a Chicago South Side post office worker called Jake Jackson.[178] The day is 12 February 1937, Abraham Lincoln's birthday, and the novel draws parallels between the Civil War, boxing, and Jackson's daily struggles. At one point, Jake overhears part of a radio broadcast: 'In the latter part of 1862 Meade and Lee sparred and feinted cautiously for an opening to deal a telling blow.' It is also some months before Louis won the title, but the men at the post office think Louis will never be allowed to become champion.[179] After discussing Louis's 1936 defeat by Schmeling, they reminisce about Johnson's acts of defiance and the riots that took place in the wake of his victory over Jeffries. The Civil War is not over; the battling continues. Wright's choice of name for his protagonist seems deliberately ironic. Jackson is no hero, but a gullible and pathetic drunk whose only blows are directed at his wife. The novel ends with a knockout of sorts: she smashes a glass over his head and he falls into a drunken sleep.

A comparative reading of the careers of Jack Johnson and Joe Louis is also important to Ralph Ellison's *Invisible Man* (1952). The novel enacts a debate between the two great black heavyweight champions of the first half of the twentieth century, and considers each in turn as a model for the black writer in America. Ralph Ellison was born in the year before Johnson lost his title, in 1914, the same year as Joe Louis Barrow. If by the 1940s the colour line in heavyweight boxing had gone for good, it remained firm in what might be called heavyweight writing. When, in 1963, Ellison wanted to complain that Irving Howe's essay, 'Black Boys and Native Sons', was a 'Northern white liberal version of the white Southern myth of absolute separation of the races', he did so in the language of the boxing commentator: '[Howe] implies that Negroes can only aspire to contest other Negroes (this at a time when Baldwin has been taking on just about everyone, including Hemingway, Faulkner, and the United States Attorney General!), and must wait for the appearance of a Black Hope before they have the courage to move.'[180] Ellison repeatedly rejected the idea of a black-only tradition, asserting strongly the influence of writers such as Eliot, Joyce, Hemingway and Twain upon his work. 'While one can do nothing about choosing one's relatives,' he maintained, 'one can as an artist, choose one's "ancestors".' Richard Wright was, in this sense, a 'relative'; Hemingway an 'ancestor'.[181] This is an interesting and much-discussed distinction, but within both words, 'relative' and 'ancestor', I would suggest, another nestles – 'opponent'. Ellison goes even further in his determination to throw off the influence of Wright, when he maintains in the same essay: 'I did not need Wright to tell me how to be a Negro or to be angry or to express anger – Joe Louis was doing that very well.'[182]

Ellison's metaphor of the writer as fighter recalls his 'ancestor'/ opponent Hemingway's famous 1949 letter to Charles Scribner in which he claimed to be 'a man without any ambition, except to be champion of the world'.[183] As Hemingway took on all-comers, living or dead, Ellison wanted to be seen as taking on all-comers, black or white. Ellison wanted to be considered 'a real contender' and part of that involved demonstrating the ambition necessary to be thought so. But while Hemingway's only ambition was 'to be champion of the world', Ellison extends the fighterly metaphor, and makes it more precise and, in a way, more problematic. Wright may have given him faith 'in his ability to compete', but Joe Louis had taught him how 'to be a Negro . . . to be angry . . . to express anger'.[184]

*Invisible Man* is a book full of 'bouts with circumstance', in and out of the boxing ring, bouts which are repeatedly presented as commentaries on questions of verbal expression and communication.[185] How much is writing, or boxing, Ellison asks, about 'expressing anger' or indeed any other form of self-expression or self-assertion? How much are both simply about performing? The best-known fight in the novel comes in its opening chapter, in the battle royal scene, which was first published as a short story.[186] The battle royal (which only featured blacks) was a popular form of boxing event in the early twentieth-century south, and was often the opening event on a boxing card. Most often, battle royals involved adolescent boys, who, often blindfolded and sometimes with one arm tied behind their backs, would compete to be the last one standing. 'Manufactured disunity among blacks was the barely concealed plot,' Andrew Kaye argues, 'redolent of the old days on the plantation.'[187] In Ellison's novel, the protagonist has been invited to speak before 'a gathering of the town's leading white citizens' – the crowd will 'judge truly [his] ability' and it will be a 'triumph for [the whole black] community'. In fact what happens is that several black boys his age are forced to watch a dance performed by a naked white woman with 'a small American flag tattooed upon her belly', and then are blindfolded and made to fight each other before scrambling for the coins that are their 'reward'.[188] Initially ten boys are involved, but soon the number is reduced to two: Invisible Man and Tatlock.[189] When Invisible Man suggests, 'Fake it like I knocked you out, you can have the prize,' Tatlock replies, 'I'll break your behind'. 'For *them*?' the narrator asks. 'For *me*, sonofabitch!'[190] Unlike his opponent, Invisible Man is convinced that a fight between black men in front of a white audience cannot be a genuine competition, and certainly not 'sport'. Budd Schulberg's description of boxing as 'show business with blood' is reinforced here, and throughout the novel, by references to the circus (the white woman, the unattainable prize, is described as a circus kewpie doll).[191] But Invisible Man's awareness that his expected role is as an entertainer does not extend to the speech he is about to give. Indeed, during the fight, he can only think of his speech, and despite the humiliation he is suffering, of impressing the white audience. The fight is thus a commentary on that imminent verbal performance.[192]

In numerous interviews Ellison spoke of the battle royal episode as a type of initiation rite involving acceptance of white supremacy, a version of the initiation fights that he would have read about in Richard Wright's autobiography, *Black Boy* (1945).[193] Like *Invisible Man*, *Black Boy* is structured around a series of flights and fights. The most striking fight comes in Chapter Twelve in which Wright describes working in an optical factory in Memphis, a city he had hoped would be more enlightened than his native Jackson, Mississippi. Two incidents disabuse him of this belief. First, he witnesses the transformation, for a mere 25c, of one of his most intelligent co-workers, the 'hardheaded, sensible'

Shorty, into 'a clown of the most debased and degraded type'. This is merely the prelude to his own degradation. Worn down by insistence, Wright is goaded to fight Harrison, who works for a rival company, for $5 apiece. When Wright objects, arguing that 'those white men will be looking at us, laughing at us', Harrison is dismissive: 'What have we got to lose?' Wright's acknowledgment of having nothing to lose is what makes him both willing to take part in a performance designed to 'fool them white men', and so physically angry that he cannot help going beyond the performance and hurting Harrison.

> The shame and anger we felt for having allowed ourselves to be duped crept into our blows and blood ran into our eyes, half blinding us. The hate we felt for the men whom we had tried to cheat went into the blows we threw at each other.

Afterwards, Harrison and Wright avoid each other. 'I felt that I had done something unclean, something for which I could never properly atone.' The symbolism of this fight is the antithesis of the glorious defeat of Covey, or Carnera, or Schmeling. Wright and Harrison fight in the spotlight ('a bright electric bulb glowed above our heads') but it is not that of Madison Square Garden. If the 'white folks formed a kind of superworld', black folks operate in the underworld. The performance takes place 'in the basement of a Main Street building' before an all-male, all-white audience.[194]

Perhaps the most obvious point to note about Ralph Ellison's version of the rite is the gap between the narrator's retrospective understanding of its significance and the understanding of his adolescent self. Invisible Man (as a young man) does not realize what is going on, and so the novel repeats the rite of initiation, again and again, through a series of real and metaphorical fights. The repetition is so insistent that the chapters of the novel begin to seem less like episodes in a picaresque adventure than rounds in a boxing match. I want to concentrate on two particular episodes and consider how attention to the boxing allusions can aid in their interpretation.[195]

In Chapter Three, Invisible Man takes the college benefactor Norton, upset and in need of whisky after his encounter with Trueblood, to a bar called The Golden Day. Many have noted the allusion to the title of Lewis Mumford's 1924 pioneering study of the American Renaissance, and argued that Ellison is taking issue with Mumford's lack of attention to slavery.[196] But there is another allusion at the beginning of the chapter. When the narrator approaches the bar, he overhears a man describing the 1910 Johnson–Jeffries fight in a virtuoso blend of anatomical detail, invective and graveyard humour. The description ends with the phrase, 'Naturally, there was no other therapy possible.'[197] The allusion to the 'Golden Day' of American literature is thus complicated by an allusion to the day (4 July no less) when the Man with the Golden Smile challenged assumptions of white supremacy. The fight the men recall is one which was not simply, as in the case of the battle royal, a performance, but a genuine victory – an effective form of 'therapy'.[198] Here, however, black power manifests itself as stylistic barroom bravado in what seems to be an imitation of the pub scene in Joyce's 'Cyclops', where Alf Bergan and Joe Hynes discuss the recent Keogh-Bennett bout.[199]

At this stage, the narrator is unable to grasp the possibility of any kind of bravado, as becomes clear in the remainder of the chapter. This scene is followed almost immediately by a real fight when the veterans turn on their attendant, and give *him* some 'therapy'. The narrator says of the men in the bar that they 'hooted and yelled as at a football game', or, we might add, a boxing match. He describes feeling 'such an excitement that I wanted to join them' and his chance to get involved comes soon after, when he goes looking for Norton, hiding under the stairs. His response, when confronted close-up with a white man, is, however, far from that of Jack Johnson:

> some of the milling men pushed me up against him and suddenly a mass of whiteness was looming up two inches from my eyes; it was only his face but I felt a shudder of nameless horror. I had never been so close to a white person before. In a panic I struggled to get away.[200]

The competing rhetoric of fighting and the circus (both structured performances) and running (a refusal of structure or a recognition of its absence) are here, and throughout the novel, set up as alternatives.[201] They come together again in one of the final scenes in the book. Shortly before the riots which end the novel, the narrator comes across a huge woman with a beer barrel, sitting on a milk wagon and singing:

> If it hadn't been for the referee,
> Joe Louis woulda killed
> Jim Jeffrie
> Free beer!!

In the song she confuses Joe Louis (a credit to the race) with bad Jack Johnson.[202] By substituting the names, Ellison seems to be suggesting that despite the 'deadpan', Louis is carrying on Johnson's work, work that the heavyweight woman also participates in as, with her 'enormous hand[s]', she 'sends quart after quart of milk crashing into the street'. But although this action, and the riots that follow, are intended to be a form of 'therapy', the reference to the circus (she is 'like a tipsy fat lady in a circus parade'), reminds us again that therapy is also a performance.[203]

*Invisible Man* proper concludes with the narrator 'plung[ing] down' a manhole as once again, he runs away, this time from two white men with baseball bats. 'I was just fixing to slug the bastard,' one says. Underground, he finds himself 'beyond the point of exhaustion, too tired to close my eyes.' The fight, though, is not over. He has not been knocked out. He is in 'a state neither of dreaming nor of waking, but somewhere in between'. And it is in this state, and under the influence of marijuana and Louis Armstrong's 'What Did I Do to Be So Black and Blue', that he tells the story of the yokel and the prize-fighter:

> Once I saw a prize fighter boxing a yokel. The fighting was swift and amazingly scientific . . . He hit the yokel a hundred times while the yokel held up his arms in stunned surprise. But suddenly the yokel, rolling about in the gale of boxing gloves, struck one blow and knocked science, speed, and footwork as cold as a well-digger's posterior. The smart money hit the canvas . . . The yokel had stepped inside of his opponent's sense of time.[204]

Invisible Man is here 'outside of time' but what I suggest he (and Ellison) learn through his 'hibernation' is how to step 'inside': how to fight differently, how to become the yokel inside of modernism.

A possible way of reading the epilogue then is that Invisible Man decides to get up and go back to the fight, before he is counted out. In the final pages, the narrator acknowledges, with an ironic nod to Hemingway, that 'it's "winner take nothing" that is the great truth of our country or any country', and recognizes that although 'there's still a conflict within me', now 'I am invisible, not blind'. What he calls the 'victory of conscious perception' has been won.[205] If we read the novel as a *künstlerroman*, we can see that the progress 'from ranter to writer' is also one from bodily inarticulacy and blindness – represented by the blind-folded boys in the battle royal – to a disembodied articulacy.[206] Yet this very disembodiment is still imagined in terms of bodies. Invisible Man's version of Stephan Dedalus's dedication to 'silence, exile and cunning' is yet again to talk about boxers.

With these questions in mind, I want to return to Ellison's comparison of writing and fighting and how it might enable a consideration of style and form. Asserting frequently that 'technique' was what was needed 'to free ourselves', Ellison asked where that 'technique' could be learned.[207] His customary answer was that it lay in 'vernacular idiom in the arts'; indeed there, 'lessons are to be learned in everything from power to elegance'. When challenged in an interview with the claim that 'the black masses are uninterested in elegance', he responded (in terms that recall Weldon Johnson on Jack Johnson 50 years earlier):

> Elegance turns up in every aspect of Afro-American culture, from sermons to struts . . . Aesthetically speaking, when form is blended successfully with function, elegance results. Black Americans expect elegance even from their prizefighters and basketball players and much of the appeal of Jack Johnson and Joe Louis sprang from the fact that each was as elegant as the finest of ballet dancers.[208]

Connecting the world of sport and that of art for Ellison is not simply the bringing together of 'power' and 'elegance', although this combination is important.

314

Sport and art could also be seen as related forms of 'symbolic action', to use Kenneth Burke's term.[209] Ellison was a close friend of Burke and was very interested in his anthropological understanding of literary works as forms of ritual.[210] Burke's critical method, which drew on psychoanalysis, Marxism and linguistics, as well as anthropology, repeatedly stressed the importance of understanding the effect the work of art has on the reader.[211] What the work is *in itself* is less important than what it allows its author to express and its audience to experience.[212] 'All action', Burke proclaimed, 'is poetic'; the only difference being that 'some people write their poems on paper, and others carve theirs out of jugular veins.'[213] Or, as Ellison reworked these ideas, some 'act' 'poetically' by boxing, others by writing novels. It was high praise indeed, therefore, for Ellison to recall Wright as 'a Negro American writer as randy, as courageous, and irrepressible as Jack Johnson'. 'We literary people', he went on, should always keep a sharp eye on what's happening in the unintellectualized areas of our experience.'[214] Bringing together novels and boxing, or Keats and the carving of jugular veins, does more, however, than simply initiate a form of cultural studies based on performativity. Boxing is 'show business *with blood*'; in acknowledging the show business in Burke's theory, and in the fiction of Wright and Ellison, we should not forget the aggression, the desire for therapeutic blood-letting, which both enact.

In recent years, the tendency has been to regard Ellison as a quintessential fifties liberal – and thus a figure of deadpan complicity.[215] But a fuller understanding of what boxing meant to him would suggest that there was more of the Johnsonian golden grin in Ralph Ellison than the Louis deadpan.[216] Ellison himself said as much in a 1956 letter to Albert Murray:

> with writing I learned from Joe and Sugar Ray (though that old dancing master, wit, and bull-balled stud, Jack Johnson is really my mentor, because he knew that if you operated with skill and style you could rise above all that being-a-credit-to-your-race-crap because he was a credit to the human race and because he could make that much body and bone move with such precision to his command all other men had a chance to beat the laws of probability and anything else that stuck up its head and if he liked a woman he took her and told those who didn't like it to lump it and that is the way true studs have always acted).[217]

# 9

# King of the Hill, and Further Raging Bulls

Many of the first experiments with television (as with cinema) focused on sporting events. The 1936 Olympic Games was watched by 15,000 viewers stationed at 27 'TV locales' throughout Berlin; the following year, the BBC covered the Oxford and Cambridge boat race; and in May 1939, the American NBC broadcast footage of a college baseball game. Two weeks later, Lou Nova's defeat of Max Baer at the Yankee Stadium became the first televised heavyweight boxing match. Sport provided the new medium of television with a ready-made cast of stars, and provided numerous events to fill out the initially sparse schedules of the networks.[1]

Boxing proved as amenable to early television as it had to early cinema. Until post-war developments brought larger screens, close-ups, slow motion, colour and instant replays, team sports like baseball were not easy to follow on television – the field was too big, the players too dispersed, the ball too small and too fast-moving. Boxing, however, with its well-lit enclosed setting and cast of only two, was ideal for the TV screen, and during the late forties and early fifties, the sport became 'television's darling', with prime-time fights broadcast almost every evening.[2] In 1950, only 9 per cent of American homes had TV, and most men watched the fights in neighbourhood bars (illus. 136). By 1955, however, 55.7 per cent of homes had sets, and commentators marvelled at the very idea of sport being available 'from a sofa!'[3] Television, one journalist remarked, 'has all the impact of one of Marciano's punches', but he was sorry when it 'tossed Joe Louis right into our living room on his back'.[4]

If memoirs of the thirties tended to depict the family gathered around the radio listening to reports of Joe Louis, those of the fifties repeated the scene but substituted television and Rocky Marciano or Sugar Ray Robinson.[5] 'The most vibrant memories I bear from my childhood,' writes Gerald Early, 'are of my uncles crowded around a very small black-and-white television, drinking beer and watching the Gillette Friday-night fights'.[6] Henry Louis Gates, meanwhile, describes how his home town of Piedmont, Virginia, 'was transformed from a radio culture to one with the fullest range of television, literally overnight'. 'What interracial sex was to the seventies, interracial sports were to the fifties.

136
'Joe's Tavern',
*The Ring*, April 1959.

137
Advertisement for
Pabst Blue Ribbon
and Wednesday
Night Fights, *The
Ring*, July 1956.

138
Advertisement for
'TV Fights', *The Ring*,
February 1955.

Except for sports, we rarely saw a colored person on TV.'[7]

Boxing's success as a television sport was partly due to the fact that the structure of a bout – three-minute rounds separated by one-minute intermissions – seemed custom-made for advertising. The two main sponsors during the fifties were Pabst Blue Ribbon beer, associated with CBS's Wednesday night fights, and Gillette razors, the promoter of NBC's Friday night Cavalcade of Sport (illus. 137).[8] These products suggest that the market mainly consisted of men, but boxing was often promoted as family entertainment. The cover of the February 1955 issue of *TV Fights* magazine, for example, imagines a white-collared fan being joined by his wife and son to watch the boxing; inside an article explains 'How women score TV fights' (illus. 138). The idea of boxing entering the domestic sphere inspired mid-twentieth-century cartoonists as much as it had their nineteenth-century equivalents. A recurrent claim was that the 'live' fights that took place in suburban sitting rooms were better viewing than those on screen (illus. 139).

Boxing commentators were quick to note the impact that the new medium was having on the sport, and most of their conclusions were negative. Sports-

writing itself was offered as an alternative
to 'this ridiculous gadget called television':
writers such as John Lardner and A. J.
Liebling (both in *The New Yorker*) suggested that both boxing and what might
be called boxing *belles lettres* were endangered species in need of careful preservation. Between 1947 and 1951, Lardner
published a series of essays entitled 'That
was Pugilism', vividly evoking the era of
his father, Ring Lardner, as a time of wild
adventures and idiosyncratic figures.
'Things are not the same in the wake of the
Second World War,' he complained, 'The
fighters are more businesslike; their train-

"I've seen you and Mama do Better".

139
Cartoon in *The Ring*,
April 1956.

ing camps are respectable and dull . . .; the managers and "characters" on the
fringe of the show are organized and syndicated.'[9]

Liebling saw his essays as a direct response to 'the anticipated lean aesthetic
period induced by television'. His unlikely model for the rearguard defence of
boxing was Pierce Egan, whom he declared 'the greatest writer about the ring
who ever lived'. *The Sweet Science*, a collection of Liebling's *New Yorker* pieces,
was, he declared, an 'Extension of the GREAT HISTORIAN's Magnum Opus'; the
title itself is a phrase of Egan's. The Regency commentator is evoked and praised
as the Herodotus, the Holinshed, the Edward Gibbon (among others) of the
English prize ring, while *Boxiana* is dubbed its *Mille et Une Nuits*.[10] Liebling's
concern, like Egan's, was as much with the subculture of boxing as with the
sport; in mid-century America, he felt that both were under threat. But, unlike
newspaper columnists such as Dan Parker and Jimmy Cannon, he was not
interested in exposing mobsters or the machinations of corporate interests.[11]
Instead, *The Sweet Science* offered itself as an elegy to the last of boxing's pictur-
esque oddballs and to 'the verbal dandyism of Egan'.[12] As Fred Warner points
out, few readers who encountered Liebling's work in *The New Yorker* cared much
about boxing. They accepted 'exposure to a brutal and alien sport because they
loved good prose'.[13] Liebling's writing is often witty and always digressive, and
he worked hard to charm and flatter his readers with frequent allusions to
literature and art. Floyd Patterson, after his defeat of Archie Moore, is described
as being in the position 'of a Delacroix who has run out of canvas'.[14] *The New
Yorker*, as Robert Warshaw pointed out in 1947, 'has always dealt with experience
. . . by prescribing the attitude to be adopted toward it'.[15]

Much as he deplored television's devotion to 'the sale of beer and razor
blades', Liebling's objections extended beyond commercialization. In an essay
called 'Boxing with the Naked Eye', he argued that the experience of watching
boxing was much diminished by television, and that you could only have a 'feeling of participation' by being there in the stadium. 'For one thing', he quipped,

'you can't tell the fighters what to do'.[16] This was partly an expression of snobbery, a feeling that the aficionado was being ousted by the 'big and silly television audience', and one that sat easily among *The New Yorker*'s advertisements for imported whisky and Spode dinnerware 'for the hard-to-please'. 'The masses are asses,' an old fighter called Al Thoma told Liebling, 'There are no connoisseurs. The way most of these guys fight, you'd think they were two fellows having a fight in a barroom.'[17]

More importantly, Liebling argued that by creating a monopoly on boxing, television had fundamentally distorted the nature of the sport. First of all, the live audience was severely diminished (ticket sales at Madison Square Garden were down by as much as 80 per cent). Furthermore, he maintained, 'the clients of the television companies, by putting on a free boxing show almost every night of the week, have knocked out of business the hundreds of small-city and neighbourhood boxing clubs where youngsters had a chance to learn their trade and journeymen to mature their skills'. One of Liebling's most famous (and most Egan-like) coinages was to dub the famous New York gym, Stillman's, the 'University of Eighth Avenue'.[18] This proved the unlikely prompt for a scene in Stanley Donen and Gene Kelly's 1955 musical satire, *It's Always Fair Weather*. Fight manager Ted Riley (played by Kelly) arranges to meet television executive, Jackie Leighton (Cyd Charisse), at the gym. Arriving early, she is instructed in the history of the place – 'Why these old walls are as steeped in tradition as the ivy-covered walls of Harvard!' – before joining the residents in a song-and-dance tribute to their 'alma mater', 'Stillman's, Dear Old Stillman's' (illus. 140).[19] But these high educational standards were under threat. Television's constant demand for fresh boxers resulted in the closure of many of the small clubs in which the sport's traditional apprenticeship had taken place. Meanwhile, 'the peddlers' public' was asked to believe that 'a boy with perhaps ten or fifteen fights' was a 'topnotch performer.' On occasion, this could prove fatal. In 1954, for example, Ed Sanders died after being knocked out in the eleventh round of a televised bout, his ninth professional fight. 'In more normal pre-television times,' noted Liebling, 'a fellow out of the amateurs would spend three years in four-, six-, and eight-round bouts in small clubs before attempting ten.'[20] More TV deaths followed. In 1963, Davey Moore died after being knocked out by Sugar Ramos, inspiring

140
Rocky Graziano and Lou Stillman outside Stillman's Gym, from *Somebody Up There Likes Me: My Life So Far* (New York, 1955).

protest songs by Bob Dylan and Phil Ochs. The previous year, Benny Paret had died a week after having been knocked unconscious by Emile Griffith during the world welterweight title fight. Many tuned in to ABC to see the final, fatal punches via a new replay system.

The story of boxing (and indeed of most sports) from the early nineteenth century onward has been one of gradual transformation into mass-market entertainment. Each new technological development (film, radio and television) has brought a larger audience to individual contests. These changes in method of consumption have, at every stage, been accompanied by changes in methods of

**LET'S FACE IT . . . HE DOESN'T LOOK GOOD ON TV.**

141
Cartoon in *The Ring*, 1951.

production – in the supply and control of boxers and fights. Television signalled the biggest shift (illus. 141). After 1950, if an up-and-coming boxer wanted a chance at a title, it was no longer enough to hook up with the manager who happened to have connections at Madison Square Garden (as Dempsey and Louis had done). 'Commercial-driven televised bouts promised riches beyond the rewards possible from ticket sales in even the biggest arenas', recalls Truman Gibson.[21] A member of the newly established International Boxing Club (IBC), Gibson, along with Jim Norris and Arthur Wirtz, became one of the most powerful boxing promoters of the fifties. As Gibson later told the Senate Subcommittee on Antitrust and Monopoly, 'during the period 1950 to 1959, practically all of the championships in the major weight categories were staged by one or the other of our organizations or in conjunction with our television presentations'.[22] The boxing world was still closely tied in with that of organized crime, although Gibson maintains it was often 'more a matter of appearance than substance'.[23] Nevertheless, forties operators such as Frankie Carbo and Blinky Palermo were still around, and fights were still routinely fixed.[24] More importantly, the IBC (popularly known as 'the Octopus') needed 'a plentiful supply of fighters': 'a hundred fights a year required us to come up with four hundred fighters', Gibson reckoned; two for each 'main event' and two waiting in the wings in case of a quick knockout. 'Television ruled us . . . We didn't care whether managers or promoters cozied up to Carbo or warred with him.'[25]

If the 'fight racket' remained 'the swill barrel of sports', as sportswriter Jimmy Cannon had declared in 1948, this suited Hollywood very well.[26] After 1950, however, *noir* fatalism gradually gave way to a reformist zeal more familiar in the social-problem cinema of the Depression. Consider, for example, Elia Kazan's *On the Waterfront* (1954), in which Marlon Brando played Terry Molloy, a washed-up prize-fighter who famously thinks he 'coulda been a contender', the 'next Billy Conn'. Terry finally gets his big fight in the real world, when, after much soul-searching, he decides to expose the underworld infiltration of the longshoremen's union and to confront a mob leader directly. 'Everybody's got a racket', he says; the 'hawks' always prey on the 'pigeons' down below.[27] Fifties boxing films (like many other Cold War dramas) tend to suggest that the worst possible thing to be is an 'organization man' – never mind whether the organization is the mob, the union, the Communist Party or the army.[28] By contrast, the free man is 'inner directed', to borrow another term from fifties sociology, and his integrity often derives from saying no.[29] In James Jones's *From Here to Eternity* (1951; filmed in 1953), Private Prewitt, having once blinded a man in the ring, refuses to join the regimental boxing team. 'I don't see why a man should fight unless he wanted to,' he tells the disbelieving captain. 'A man has to decide for himself what he has to do.'[30]

*The Harder They Fall* (1956), based on Budd Schulberg's 1947 novel, focused on the culpability of Eddie Willis (Humphrey Bogart in his final role), a has-been sportswriter who, in order to get 'a bank account', becomes the press agent for Toro Moreno (illus. 142). Loosely based on the thirties heavyweight, Primo Carnera, the gigantic Moreno can hardly put two punches together. Although it seems that size is still everything, the days in which all that a set-up needed was a crooked manager and a willing fighter are long gone; Willis is just one of many

142
Advertisement for
*The Harder They Fall*,
1956.

employees hired by Nick Benko (Rod Steiger) to steer Moreno towards a lucrative title fight. There are lots of management meetings and the talk is always of 'business'. When his wife, Beth, objects to the nature of this business, Eddie responds, 'You sell a fighter, you sell soap. What's the difference?' The question is repeated several times, but the answer is always the same. We are never in doubt that by becoming Nick's publicity agent, Eddie has made a deal with the devil. In order to build Moreno's reputation before the big fight in New York, Eddie uses every trick he can think of, including touring the country in a garishly painted bus (a gimmick that Cassius Clay later copied). These traditional methods are fine, but as Nick points out, the introduction of 'coast-to-coast telecasts' has made publicity much easier.[31] (At one point, Beth watches a fixed Californian fight at Benko's comfortable home in New York – the whole family gather around the set, and Nick's little girl watches from his knee.[32]) Everyone describes Eddie as 'a good man', and at first he thinks he can be so simply by adjusting the system a little bit – by making sure Moreno's 'tank fighters' are paid directly; by helping them 'look good' to save their pride. Even after a man dies in the ring, he persuades Toro to keep going so that they can both get the final pay-off. But, after a careful consideration of the cooked books reveals Toro's share of the million-dollar gate to be a measly $49.07, Eddie quits. In the final scene, he threatens to expose Nick in a series of muckraking articles. 'People still know how to read,' he says. 'The people, the people,' mocks Nick, 'The little people, they sit and get fat and fall asleep in front of the television set with a belly full of beer.' But Eddie, like Schulberg, and Liebling, believes that the integrity of the individual's written word can triumph over the opiate power of the television freak show. The film ends as he sits down at his battered old typewriter, and the camera closes in on the sentence he types: 'Professional boxing should be banned even if it takes an Act of Congress to do it.'[33]

As the decade drew to a close, boxing's appeal for television began to diminish. In 1952, fight-nights attracted 31 per cent of the prime-time audience; by 1959, their share had shrunk to 11 per cent. There were several reasons for this. Most important was the fact that viewers now had considerably more choice in their viewing, including in 1956, Rod Serling's play *Requiem for a Heavyweight*, welcomed as an 'indictment' of a 'so-called sport'.[34] Boxing itself was losing its appeal. After Rocky Marciano retired in 1956, his successors (Moore, Patterson, Johansson and Liston) did not attract the same support from the sponsors, networks or viewers. Prolonged congressional hearings highlighted boxing's links to organized crime, and reports of fighters dying from injuries sustained in the ring (nineteen in 1953) further sullied its image.[35] In 1959, Carbo was sent to jail and the Supreme Court declared the IBC to be an illegal monopoly; the following year, NBC announced that it was dropping its Friday night fights. It was not until Cassius Clay emerged on the scene that television boxing revived.

## AMERICAN DILEMMAS

The difference between a history of boxing and a history of the cultural representation of boxing becomes apparent if we consider the part played in each by Sugar Ray Robinson (illus. 143). While Sugar Ray is revered by many as the all-time best 'pound-for-pound' fighter, he never became a cultural symbol in the way that Johnson, Dempsey, Louis or Ali did. This is both partly because less attention is paid to welter- and middleweights (he fought as both), the fact that during the late forties and fifties there was no obvious story to be told about his victories.[36] Sugar Ray Robinson is a kind of interregnum figure in the history of culturally and politically significant boxers, between Louis (whom he idolized) and Ali (who idolized him). Welterweight champion from 1945 to 1951, he reinvented himself as a middleweight and won the title five times between 1951 and 1960. In 1957, as Maya Angelou notes, he 'lost his middleweight title, won it back, then lost it again, all in a matter of months'. Angelou uses Robinson's status as an on-again, off-again

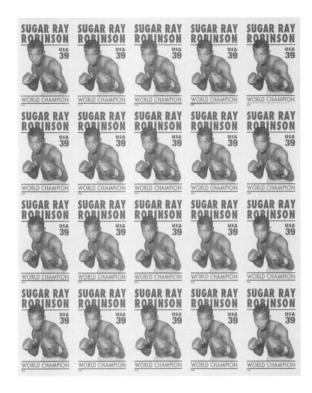

143
Sugar Ray Robinson
on US commemora-
tive stamps, 2006.

champion as a metaphor for 'the maze of contradictions' that was the civil rights movement in the late fifties.[37] Out of the ring, the contradictions continued. Sugar Ray set up numerous businesses on Harlem's Seventh Avenue, and he and his stylish wife, Edna Mae, were dubbed 'the Prince and Princess of Harlem'. In 1953, however, the couple moved to the white suburb of Riverdale and their dream home was featured on the cover of *Ebony* magazine. Well-known for his processed hair, pink Cadillacs, and appearances on the Ed Sullivan Show, Sugar Ray Robinson was also often outspoken about racial discrimination.[38]

The fifties may have witnessed the first moves towards desegregation, but boxing fans (and therefore TV networks) still wanted to see interracial contests. Robinson's most publicized fights were a series of six (between 1942 and 1951) against Jake La Motta. Because of Martin Scorsese's film, *Raging Bull*, La Motta is now better remembered than his rival, but Robinson, 'the matador', won all but one fight. At the weigh-in for the last round of the 'bitter feud', Arna Bontemps noted (in a biography intended for children) that the men 'exchanged nostalgic remarks': '"Jake, I made you," Ray kidded. "I done all right for you," the Bull chuckled.'[39] Ten rounds later, however, La Motta conceded that 'the black bastard' had given him 'about as bad a beating as I've ever had'.[40] These remarks were not quoted by Bontemps.

Another awkward but powerful puncher who appealed to white fans was Rocky Marciano, 'the archetypal working-class stiff from blue-collar Brockton'.[41] After defeating the aging Louis on national television in 1951, Marciano became the 'white hope' of the Southern press, while sportswriters in the North merely noted that 'it would be a change-of-pace to have a white boy on top after all these years'.[42] Because of his slugging style, Marciano was frequently described as 'the new Dempsey' and considered 'good for boxing' – a phrase which Russell Sullivan translates as 'black champion versus Great White Hope made dollars and cents'.[43] Although the majority of title-holders since the thirties (including Louis and Sugar Ray) had been black, their challengers were usually white; 'promoters rarely offered the same money for bouts against equally tough black challengers'.[44] As a plausible white hope, Marciano had a relatively straightforward passage to a title shot. From 1952, when he took the championship from Jersey Joe Walcott, to 1956, when he retired undefeated with a record of 49 wins, he was largely matched against black opponents.[45] The vacant title was filled when the 21-year-old Floyd Patterson beat Archie Moore to become the youngest ever heavyweight champion. The era of white vs. black heavyweight fights seemed to be over, except for a brief interlude in 1959 and 1960, when Patterson fought the Swedish boxer, Ingemar Johansson (he lost the first and won the second).[46] The attention given to those fights suggests the symbolism of black vs. white boxing was still very much alive.

The novelist Harvey Swandos wrote an essay about the first Patterson–Johansson fight for a new literary journal called *Noble Savage* (where it appeared alongside 'And Hickman Arrives', an extract from Ralph Ellison's unfinished second novel).[47] For Swandos, the fight had 'no racially symbolic overtones'. 'The position of the American Negro,' he maintained, 'has changed so greatly that it is no longer necessary for a Negro heavyweight champion to be a hero to his people; when he is beaten it is no longer inevitable that the defeat will be regarded by Negroes as a racial setback (or by whites as a white conquest).' In this 'new era', boxers should no longer consider themselves 'Walking Symbols'.[48] John Lardner's 'That Was Pugilism' series in *The New Yorker* also located racial prejudice firmly in the past. For Lardner, the success of Louis, and then Patterson, had put racism, and thus the concept of the 'white hope', to rest.[49] Noting the crowd's support (both in cheers and bets) for Patterson in 1959, Liebling concurred: 'I felt a warm glow of gratification – we were a solid *patrie*, where American citizenship meant more than race or color'.[50] Unsurprisingly, black commentators responded rather differently to the story of Patterson and Johansson, a story that many felt did still carry 'racially symbolic overtones'. In 1970 Addison Gayle Jr recalled the fight as emblematic of the daily struggles of men like himself. Gayle tells the story of a humiliating incident in which he was refused a job because of his race, but 'like the ex-heavyweight champion, I was on my feet searching for another job less than fifteen minutes after absorbing a crushing blow to my psyche.[51] A more radical interpretation of Patterson's symbolism was offered by Eldridge Cleaver. Whites, he argued, 'despised' Johansson for knocking out Patterson because it contradicted their image of the 'black man as the Supermasculine Menial'.[52]

After 1960, interracial fighting increasingly took place in the realms of white fantasy. Although *Esquire* magazine liked to imagine Dempsey defeating the current crop of black boxers, fight fans were mostly faced with a choice between two black boxers.[53] This could be problematic for blacks as well as whites. Ollie Harrington's popular comic strip character Bootsie complains to his wife as they watch television: 'why don't the NAACP make 'em stop usin' cullud boys to fight one 'nother. Don't they realize that causes a whole lot of confusion 'mongst us fight fans?' (illus. 144)[54] When Patterson fought Johansson, black fans had no trouble picking sides, but when he took on Sonny Liston, they faced what James Baldwin called a 'terrible American dilemma'. Whether or not Baldwin was consciously evoking Gunnar Myrdal's classic 1944 study of 'the Negro Problem and Modern Democracy', *An American Dilemma*, the problem he identified was one of political stance. 'I feel terribly ambivalent, as many Negroes do these days,'

"... AN' WHY DONT THE NAACP MAKE 'EM STOP USIN' CULLUD BOYS TO FIGHT ONE 'NOTHER. DONT THEY REALIZE THAT CAUSES A WHOLE LOT OF CONFUSION 'MONGST US FIGHT FANS ? "

Baldwin wrote, 'since we are all trying to decide, in one way or another, which attitude, in our terrible American dilemma, is the most effective: the disciplined sweetness of Floyd, or the outspoken intransigence of Liston'.[55] That choice was particularly acute in the midst of the Civil Rights struggles of 1962, and not every black intellectual opted for Baldwin's ambivalence. LeRoi Jones saw it as a 'simple conflict'.

> "They" painted Liston Black. They painted Patterson White . . . Which way would the black man go? . . . A lot of Negroes said Patterson. (That old hope come back on you, that somehow this is my country, and ought'n I be allowed to live in it, I mean, to make it. From the bottom to the top? Only the poorest black men have never fallen, at least temporarily, for the success story.) A lot of Negroes said Liston.[56]

If Patterson was a model of integrationist politics – Jones described him as a 'black Horatio Alger, the glad hand of integration' and Norman Mailer dubbed him 'a liberal's liberal' – Sonny Liston, with his prison record and mob connections, was boxing's 'ultimate bad ass' – 'the big black negro in every white man's hallway', said Jones; 'Faust', said Mailer.[57] In a telling echo of Roosevelt's meeting with Louis before the second Schmeling fight, Kennedy invited Patterson to the White House and reputedly told him, 'you've *got* to beat this guy'.[58]

Unable to fulfil his President's wishes, Patterson was knocked out by Liston (who outweighed him by more than 25 pounds) in the first round. 'Before the referee could count to ten,' William Nack wrote, 'Liston had become a mural-sized American myth, a larger-than-life John Henry with two hammers, an 84-inch reach, 23 knockouts (in 34 bouts) and 19 arrests'.[59] The 1963 rematch did little to change anyone's perceptions. Some objected to Liston because of his connections with the mob. Other were more concerned that he was an unsuitable role model for black America at a time when the news was filled with images of non-violent freedom marchers being swept away by fire hoses and attacked by police dogs. Martin Luther King saluted Patterson for joining the 'bruising combat' endured by the protesters in Birmingham, Alabama.[60] After winning a fight in 1961, Archie Moore too had announced his support for the Freedom Riders: he planned to donate a significant amount of his purse to their cause and use the rest to buy a life membership of the NAACP.[61] But when a white reporter asked Liston why he had not gone to Birmingham, the boxer replied, 'I ain't got no dog-proof ass.'[62] By 1970 Liston was dead, in mysterious circumstances, from an overdose. Joe Louis was a pall-bearer at his funeral.

### 'A NEW HERO COMES ALONG'

In March 1962, A. J. Liebling went to see Cassius Clay, then preparing to fight Sonny Banks. Although uncertain about the young man's power, Liebling admitted that his 'skittering style' was 'good to watch', and that the 'poet' had a certain 'talent': 'Just when the sweet science appears to lie like a painted ship upon a painted ocean, a new Hero, as Pierce Egan would term him, comes along like a Moran tug to pull it out of the doldrums.'[63] Around the same time, Clay introduced himself to Malcolm X at a Nation of Islam rally. 'He acted as if I was supposed to know who he was', Malcolm recalled, 'So I acted as though I did. Up to that moment, though, I had never even heard of him'.[64]

The rise of Cassius Clay, and his transformation into the now legendary figure of Muhammad Ali, is well-known and amply documented. The legend begins in 1954 when the twelve-year-old Cassius fought the boy who had stolen his brand-new bicycle. Along came Joe Martin, a policeman whose sideline was teaching boxing at a local gym. Persuaded to join, Clay was not obviously talented, but Martin recalled that 'the little smart aleck' was 'easily the hardest working kid I ever taught'.[65] Six years later, he won a gold medal at the Rome Olympics. When Clay was asked by a Russian reporter to comment on segregation, he answered that America, the 'best country in the world', would sort it out.[66]

Clay soon became known as a boxer of rare speed and agility, with a knack for skilful combinations of punches. His fondness for extravagant bragging and prophesy also singled him out as an entertaining performer. In 1962 Liebling dubbed him 'Poet and Pedagogue', and described his habit of reciting while doing sit-ups – 'he is probably the only poet in America who can recite this way. I would like to see T. S. Eliot try.'[67] Liebling joked about Clay's 'career as a poet' from the start, even while acknowledging the commercial value of 'self-advertising' through rhyme. Perhaps, he joshed, it was wrong to consider the present age as 'one of mediocre culture': 'Could Paul Valery have filled the Vel' d'Hiv . . . or Keats Her Majesty's Theatre?'[68] The joke continued in 1963, when Clay released an album *I Am the Greatest!*, with jacket notes by modernist poet Marianne Moore (who compares him to Sir Philip Sidney and describes him as a 'master' of alliteration, concision and hyperbole).[69] Moore had already written a sonnet with Clay, alternating one line each. He speedily produced rhymes while she hesitated with hers until finally he took over and finished within a couple of minutes. Describing him as a 'defender of poesie', she entitled the poem 'Much Ado About Cassius'.[70]

Whether he was prophesying his opponent's doom in rhyme, posing with The Beatles or creating 'pop culture in the ring', American TV audiences found Clay 'totally loveable'.[71] 'A popular good-looking youngster with a clean background', the sportswriters enthused; he was not only 'precisely what the stricken fight industry needed', but 'the perfect American ambassador to the world'.[72] In 1972, Budd Schulberg looked back at this time as one of innocence. 'Imagine,' he told his readers, 'a time before the Bay of Pigs, before Dallas, before Watts, before the attempted Americanization of Indochina, before assassination became an annual horror' and so on.[73] Imagine, in other words, a time before the fall, before Cassius Clay became Muhammad Ali.

In the months leading up to his title fight with Liston, rumours circulated about Clay's involvement with the Nation of Islam. He had first attended a Nation meeting when he was seventeen, while participating in a Chicago Golden Gloves tournament in 1959. With his brother Rudolph, he attended meetings secretly for the next three years, believing that if his membership of the organization was known he 'wouldn't be allowed to fight for the title.'[74] Until he became champion, the Nation's inner circle was equally keen to remain at a distance. Although Malcolm X quickly and astutely recognized Ali's potential value for the organization, he and his followers were chastised for 'fool[ing] around with fighters'.[75]

Founded in the 1930s, the Nation of Islam adopted many of the themes and practices of early twentieth-century Christian racial uplift – laying great emphasis on thrift, propriety, industry and temperance, but recasting them in terms that had only a tangential connection to mainstream Islam.[76] It recruited most successfully in prisons and among the poorest communities of black America. Despite its anti-white rhetoric, the Nation was less interested in confrontation than in persuading American blacks to reject the 'slave' ways of 'the so-called Negro' (including the 'filthy temptation' of sport) and to situate themselves instead within a separate, and international, framework.[77] 'Self-determination' meant abandoning the goals of integration and establishing independent educational, economic and political, as well as religious, structures. 'I know how to dodge boobytraps and dogs,' Clay told reporters after the Liston fight, 'I dodge them by staying in my own neighbourhood.'[78]

Relations between the charismatic Malcolm and the Nation's leader, Elijah Muhammad, had been gradually deteriorating when, in December 1963, against explicit orders, Malcolm made a scathing remark about the assassination of President Kennedy, characterizing his murder as just another case of the 'chickens coming home to roost'. He was immediately suspended from his public speaking position, a punishment that was originally set to expire in 90 days, but later became 'indefinite'.[79] Malcolm's decision to visit Clay's Miami training camp in January 1964 was a conscious act of defiance.

As Clay waited to fight Liston, he was given a lot of advice. Sugar Ray Robinson instructed him to think like a matador (as he had done with the Raging Bull); Malcolm, meanwhile, suggested that he prepare for 'modern Crusades – a Christian and a Muslim facing each other with television to beam it off Telstar for the whole world to see what happens!' 'Do you think Allah has brought about all this', Malcolm asked, 'intending for you to leave the ring as anything but the champion?'[80] Although Liston was the 7-1 favourite, and, as Early points out, 'an unusually inappropriate symbol for either Christianity or the West', Clay was convinced that he was destined to become champion.[81] And on 24 February 1964, he did.

After the fourth round Clay complained of stinging in his eyes, and it was suggested that Liston had put something on his gloves. Then, at the start of the seventh round, Liston stayed on his stool, claiming that his shoulder was injured and that he could not get up. Many suspected a fix, but despite numerous investigations, nothing was proven – 'a result,' observes Sammons, 'that can be attributed more to a lack of commitment than to the circumstances'.[82] Ali won the 1965 rematch easily again – knocking Liston down in the first round with what he called an 'anchor punch', a quotation from Jack Johnson via the elderly vaudevillian, Stepin Fetchit, now a Muslim and part of his retinue. For most fans, however, it was not merely a fix but a 'flaunted fix'.[83] Even the poets complained when Liston 'sat down / wobbly as a dowager'. Jay Meek quoted the bartenders who reputedly announced:

Next time he's gonna fight some fruit
from a garbage scow on the Atlantic.
Out there he can really take a dive.[84]

With Clay champion and 'the most famous Black Muslim in the country', the Nation's leaders put their reservations about boxing on hold. The organization had found 'a new star, another powerful drawing card', and, Michael Gomez argues, this directly contributed to Malcolm's 'expendability'.[85] After the fight, the leadership approached Clay directly, and took the unusual step of bestowing on him 'his divine name rather than a simple X'.[86] This was a great honour, but it also served to distinguish him from Malcolm and reflected the Nation's desire to shift to a 'less threatening stance'.[87] Ali gave a press conference and famously declared himself 'free to be what I want'.[88] In response, Edward Lassman, president of the World Boxing Association, chastised him for 'setting a very poor example to the youth of the world', while Joe Louis set aside his deadpan to predict that the new champion would 'earn the public's hatred'. 'The way I see it, the Black Muslims want to do just what we have been fighting against for a hundred years.'[89] Martin Luther King, however, congratulated Ali on his victory.[90]

On 6 March, at Elijah Muhammad's insistence, Ali broke with Malcolm, and two days later, Malcolm formally broke with the Nation.[91] Ali's choice of Elijah Muhammad over Malcolm was the subject of much debate. Floyd Patterson, for example, argued that he was 'trapped', while LeRoi Jones attributed the decision to Ali's lack of political sophistication: 'He is still a "homeboy", embracing the folksy vector straight out of the hard spiritualism of poor negro aspiration.'[92]

From the start, the NOI recognized Ali's potential, and not just in America.[93] In the spring of 1964, the new champion was sent on a month-long tour to Ghana, Nigeria and Egypt, attracting extensive press coverage and considerably larger crowds than either Elijah Muhammad or Malcolm X had ever done.[94] While in Ghana, Ali coincided with Malcolm X, but he refused to acknowledge his former friend.[95] Malcolm nevertheless continued to associate himself with the boxer, mentioning him frequently (and always as Clay) in speeches and lectures. The most important was an April 1964 address in Detroit, now famous as 'The Ballot or the Bullet', which attacked many of the goals and strategies of the Civil Rights Movement. While Martin Luther King had advocated 'meeting physical force with soul force' through peaceful demonstration based on prayer and song, Malcolm declared himself a 'black Nationalist Freedom fighter' and announced that it was 'time to stop singing and start *swinging*.'[96] 'Cassius Clay can sing. But singing didn't help him to become the heavyweight champion of the world. *Swinging* helped him become the heavyweight champion.' Later, Malcolm described his quarrel with Elijah Muhammad as resulting from being 'kept from doing something' about white racist attacks; the equivalent, he said, of being put in the ring with Liston or Clay. 'No, don't tie my hands, unless you're going to tie up their hands too.'[97]

Ali's hands (or at least his box office drawing power) had themselves been tied up by his change of name and religion. After the 1965 Liston rematch, he fought Floyd Patterson who promoted the fight as a 'moral crusade' (the Cross vs. the Crescent, part 2) and insisted on talking about 'Clay'. Ali responded by dubbing him 'rabbit' and 'white America' and beating him severely. What some saw as a 'spectacle of cruelty' lost him further support, although Eldridge Cleaver declared the result 'symbolic proof of the victory of the autonomous over the subordinate Negro' and declared Ali the first 'free black champion', the 'black Fidel Castro of boxing'.[98] A useful corrective to the hyperbole of both the sportswriters' disgust and Cleaver's allegory is Patterson's own account of events. At a press conference before the fight, Ali reputedly interrupted a bout of 'screaming and bragging' to whisper, 'You want to make some money, don't you Floyd? You want to make lots of money, don't you?'[99]

Seriously in debt, the following year Ali launched a series of 'humpty-dumpty fights against humpty-dumpty fighters', most of which took place outside of America.[100] As Malcolm had predicted, the Telstar satellite allowed 'the whole world to see' Ali's fights, and they paid well. Most lucrative was a match with Henry Cooper (the first world heavyweight title to be held in Britain since 1908). 'Hundreds of millions were going to see it on their screens in places like Tokyo, Bangkok, Dortmund, Mexico City and Beunos Aires,' marvelled Cooper; 'it was a fantastic thought.'[101]

## A MUSLIM ST SEBASTIAN

In 1966 the Pentagon launched Project 100,000 to induct men like Ali who had previously been rejected. Although Defence Secretary Robert McNamara claimed this was to assist the 'educationally disadvantaged', the Defense Department later conceded that the programme was introduced simply because the army needed to enlist more men. When his application for conscientious objector status on religious grounds was refused, Ali declared that, regardless, he would follow the example of Elijah Muhammad who had served a three-year jail sentence for refusing the draft during the Second World War.[102] 'I'm a member of the Black Muslims, and we don't go to no wars unless they're declared by Allah himself. I don't have no personal quarrel with those Viet Congs.'[103] In April 1967, Ali's title was withdrawn and in June, a Texas jury convicted him of violating the Selective Service Laws and awarded the maximum sentence, five years in prison and a $10,000 fine. The conviction was finally overturned in 1971.

These events resonated with both the anti-war and the burgeoning Black Power movements, and Ali became a hero for both. In July 1967, just a few days after the city erupted in riots, the National Conference on Black Power met in Newark. Among many conference resolutions was one to boycott all sponsors of television boxing until Ali's title was restored. 'Why', wonders historian Jerry Gafio Watts, 'was such an inconsequential issue brought up at a conference formulating national black priorities?'[104] But while a boxing title may in itself be politically inconsequential, and while most black radicals viewed the Nation of Islam with some scepticism after Malcolm X left, Ali himself was widely admired as a symbol of militancy. The Black Power Movement was less concerned with the processes of mainstream politics than in exerting a direct influence in schools and universities, the media and the sports industry. If, as Debbie Louis has argued, the Movement's success was largely a consequence of its ideological vagueness, Ali's case, which easily served as a rallying point for activists with very different agendas, was a gift.[105]

The stripping of Ali's title became one of the pivotal events in what sociologist/activist Harry Edwards termed 'the revolt of the black athlete'. A generation earlier, athletes such as Jackie Robinson, Jesse Owens and Joe Louis had simply fought for sports to be integrated; now, Edwards argued, black athletes and their spokesmen should consider the terms of their inclusion. He questioned the lack of black involvement in team captaincy, management and coaching, reflecting on what happened to athletes after they retired. 'Participation without power' was not enough; black athletes should be 'leaders and spokesmen . . . rather than puppets and dupes'.[106] The revolt reached its apotheosis in the Olympic Project for Human Rights, which sought to boycott the 1968 Mexico City games. Once again, one of the first demands was that Ali's title be restored. Around this time, comparisons between the 'castration' of Ali and Jack Johnson began to be made. For Edwards, however, there was a clear difference between the two men. While Johnson was a 'classic, tragic loser', he said, Ali was nothing less than 'a god'.[107]

Because of his stand on Vietnam, Ali also became the 'White Liberal Hope' of the anti-war movement, a position that was enhanced by his 1968 college lecture tour and appearance alongside Dr Spock and H. Rap Brown at the 1967 Peace Action Council.[108] For ex-champions such as Louis, Tunney and 'slacker' Dempsey, the involvement of the heavyweight champion in an anti-war movement was insupportable.[109] But for anti-war activists, Ali's participation both encouraged the conviction that refusing to fight could be more manly than going, and challenged the 'lily-white' image of the New Left.[110]

Ali's 'martyrdom' (rather than, say, 'rebellion') became a common theme in New Left discourse; his situation enabling a timely revival of the old story in which 'the black male is metaphorically the white man's unconscious personified.'[111] Budd Schulberg wrote of Ali's having 'received into his beautiful black body' all the 'poisoned arrows' of the decade: 'Wounded by all those arrows of our social misfortune, he refused to die.'[112] 'When Cassius Clay became a Muslim,' echoed George Lois, 'he also became a martyr'. Membership of a 'counterrevolutionary organisation that basically endorsed . . . a bourgeois fantasy of regeneration through respectability' had turned Ali into a hero of the left; now conversion to Islam made him the perfect model for Christian symbolism.[113] Lois (who designed covers for *Esquire* magazine and who had famously cast Sonny Liston as Santa Claus) decided that Ali should be photographed as Botticini's *St Sebastian* for the April 1968 cover. 'At the studio, I showed him a postcard of the painting to illustrate the stance,' Lois recalled, 'He studied it with enormous concentration. Suddenly he blurted out, "Hey George, this cat's a Christian!" . . . Before we could affix any arrows to Ali, he got on the phone with . . . Elijah Muhammad.'[114] After Ali had explained the painting 'in excruciating detail' and Lois had endured a 'lengthy theological discussion' with the Black Muslim leader, the project was given the go-ahead. The cover was later reproduced and sold as a protest poster. In 2005 the American Society of Magazine Editors ranked the image third in the top ten magazine covers of the last 40 years.[115]

A rather less glossy version of Ali's martyrdom, but one no less informed by Christian iconography was Benny Andrews's mixed-media collage *The Champion*

(1968) (illus. 111). The boxer is depicted sitting on a corner stool, with a towel 'made of a piece of rumpled and pigment-stiffened cloth' draped over his head.[116] His glazed look and mashed-up face (made-up of appropriately rough layers of plastic, glue and resin) recalls the classical 'pugilist at rest', but Andrews's champion stares back at the viewer.[117] Drawing on Ali's political struggle and the fate of Joe Louis, at that time receiving treatment in a Colorado psychiatric hospital, the painting, Andrews said, was about 'the strength of the black man, the ability to persevere in the face of overwhelming odds'.[118]

The Nation of Islam, unsurprisingly, had no desire to portray Ali as either a victim or a martyr. His photograph regularly appeared in *Muhammad Speaks* but always as 'physically strong, pious, and devoted to Elijah Muhammad'.[119]

As disenchantment with the war and opposition to the draft became more prevalent, support for Ali also grew. In 1967, the majority of black soldiers felt that Ali 'had given up being a man' when he refused to be inducted; by 1970, 69 per cent approved of his decision.[120] Among white liberals, Ali benefited from the fact that the 'intensely brooding, beautiful black rebel' had become the latest thing in 'radical chic'.[121] Panthers appeared on the Johnny Carson Show, cultural nationalists sold their novels to Random House, and in November 1969, *Esquire*'s cover once again campaigned on Ali's behalf – an assortment of luminaries (from Dick Cavett to Elizabeth Taylor) pointed a finger at the camera, demanding Ali's 'right to defend his title'.[122] The following month Ali appeared (for seven nights) as a militant black leader in the Broadway musical *Buck White*.[123] The highlight was his rendition of Oscar Brown Jr.'s song, 'It's All Over Now, Mighty Whitey'.

In 1970, Ali was granted a boxing licence in Atlanta to fight Jerry Quarry (illus. 112). While the Governor of Georgia called for a boycott of the fight and some tried to enlist Quarry as a white hope, the audience at the closed-circuit television screening at Madison Square Garden cheered Ali's victory.[124] America was divided and once again the boxing ring provided a space for allegory. In March 1971, three months before the Supreme Court overturned his draft-evasion conviction, Ali took on champion Joe Frazier in the first of what would become a 'heroic trilogy' of fights between the pair. Once again political opposition – this time, 'law-abiding pragmatism vs. quixotic ideology' or 'radical chic' vs. 'Agnewian *angst*' – was expressed in terms of race and style.[125] Ali was Black Power's white dancer ('Nureyev') and Frazier, the white man's primitive ('Caliban').[126] This, anyway, was the kind of thing that white commentators such as Schulberg and Mailer wrote. But Gwendolyn Brooks, doyenne of the Black Arts Movement, and author of 'Black Steel', a poem specially commissioned for the official fight programme, refused to play the game. 'Black Steel' celebrates the 'roaring-thing' of both fighters, 'the Uttermost of Warriors in the world', and demands only that 'black love survive the Calculated Blaze'.[127] Boxing aficionados felt that by fighting Frazier, Ali was finally facing a real test (the Liston fights were suspect; the others not really challenging enough), and after fifteen hard-contested rounds, they concluded that he was no longer a 'magical untried

Prince'.[128] Ali's defeat, it seemed, made the story even better. By losing, by getting hit, yet remaining on his feet until the end of the contest – in other words, by resembling La Motta more than Sugar Ray – Ali had shown that he had 'heart' as well as talent.[129] 'He was a man,' Mailer declared. 'He could bear moral and physical torture and he could stand.'[130]

In 1973, Frazier lost his title to George Foreman and a few months later he was defeated by Ali (by decision) in a $25 million Madison Square Garden rematch. The following year, Ali signed to meet Foreman for a title fight in Kinshasa, Zaire (illus. 113). The event was the brainchild of Don King, who promoted it as a celebration of black political and economic independence: 'A fight between two Blacks in a Black Nation, organized by Blacks and seen by the whole world; that is a victory for Mobutism.'[131]

Again the politics were complicated – King was exploiting black America's interest in all things African, but it was not clear that the newly independent government of Mobutu, installed with the help of the CIA and already an oppressive 'cult of the king', deserved such a boost. King promised Ali and Foreman $5 million each; Mobutu guaranteed the sum out of Zaire's treasury.[132] In any case, what King dubbed 'the Rumble in the Jungle' was 'an event impossibly rich for the imagination'.[133] Ali, the self-proclaimed champion of Pan-Africanism, would fight a man who, on winning a gold medal at the 1968 Mexico City Olympics, had defied the clenched-fisted Black Power protests by waving an American flag and calling for 'United States Power'.[134] Foreman was the most powerful heavyweight Ali had encountered since Liston, and it was thought that Foreman would win easily. Ali's unexpected victory (mythologized in Norman Mailer's *The Fight* and Leon Gast's *When We Were Kings*) is famous as his 'most cerebral' or trickster-like – by lying back on the ropes and protecting his head until Foreman tired himself out, he claimed to have invented a new technique, the 'Rope-a-Dope'.[135] In fact, it was a classic defensive strategy and, for José Torres, what was most admirable was Ali's subsequent skill in 'patenting' it as his own.[136] In the eighth round, Ali knocked Foreman out. The photograph of the knockout has, as Charles Lemert notes, become 'one of the iconic images in all of sports': 'Ali towers above the fallen Foreman, fist cocked, holding back the final punch that in being withheld asserted Ali's reserve of prowess and, one must add, aesthetic taste.'[137]

Ali's third and final meeting with Frazier took place in 1975 in the Philippines. Dubbed the 'Thrilla in Manila', it is sometimes cited as the greatest fight in boxing history. Although both men were 'dinosaurs', the fight went fourteen rounds until finally Frazier was unable to continue.[138] Ali later described the fight as the 'hardest' of his life, the 'deadliest and most vicious', and the tenth round as the 'closest thing to dying I know'.[139] For Joyce Carol Oates, 'Ali-Frazier I . . . and Ali-Frazier III . . . are boxing's analogues to *King Lear* – ordeals of unfathomable human courage and resilience raised to the level of classic tragedy'.[140] Aired live to paying subscribers via satellite by HBO, the Manila fight was also the 'breakthrough event' that launched the cable industry.[141]

Ali continued to fight for another six years. In 1978, he lost and then regained his title for the third time in two fights with Leon Spinks.[142] Retiring in 1979, he returned in 1980 to be carried through eleven rounds by Larry Holmes (it was, said Sylvester Stallone, 'like watching an autopsy on a man who's still alive').[143] When, the following year, Ali fought Trevor Berbick, a tremor (later diagnosed as Parkinson's Syndrome) was already noticeable.

## FROM *GREATEST* TO G.O.A.T.

In 1975, in the wake of the Rumble, Ali published his autobiography, *The Greatest: My Own Story*. Although the jacket credits Ali 'with Richard Durham', the book's authorship is more complicated. The managing editor of the Nation of Islam's newspaper, *Muhammad Speaks*, but a Marxist rather than a Muslim, Durham taped Ali's conversations with a variety of people, and sent the tapes to Random House. Toni Morrison, a senior editor there, used the tapes to construct a book. Finally Herbert Muhammad approved the text, which is full of praise for his role as Ali's 'other self'.[144] A 'self-consciously political construct' – one in which, for example, Malcolm X is written out except for a mention of the threat posed by his 'people' – *The Greatest* is still often treated as the definitive account of Ali's life.[145]

The book begins in 1973, with Ali returning to Louisville after his defeat by Ken Norton, and ends with his victories against Foreman in Kinshasa and Frazier in Manila – a structure which Gerald Early reads as representing more than simply an upward trajectory. For Early, the book is a version of 'Odysseus returning home from the black male exile'.[146] When Ali overhears someone saying 'Norton beat that nigger!', the book's theme is introduced: the racism of 'White America' is what motivates Ali. 'Only this morning,' he notes, 'Norton was a "nigger" like me. But tonight he's The Great White Hope'. The story of Jack Johnson (the 'ghost in the house') is evoked throughout.[147]

*The Greatest* treats boxing as at best a suspect activity (a recurrent 'nightmarish image' is of 'two slaves in the ring' before their masters) and focuses on Ali's experience as a 'freedom fighter' in the 'real fighting ring, the one where freedom for black people in America takes place'.[148] At the heart of the story is Ali's religious conversion and refusal of the draft; what the narrative needs to do is explain how Ali came to make these decisions. Two incidents in particular are singled out as shaping the development of his political consciousness. The first is the story of his reaction to the 1955 lynching of the fourteen-year-old Emmett Till. A close-up of Till's battered face had appeared in *Jet* magazine and Ali describes the effect of seeing 'his head . . . swollen and bashed in, his eyes bulging out of their sockets, and his mouth twisted and broken'.

> I felt a deep kinship to him when I learned he was born the same year and day I was. I couldn't get Emmett Till out of my mind, until one evening I thought of a way to get back at white people for his death.[149]

In the story that follows, Ali and his friend, Ronnie, walked to the railway station where they saw a poster of Uncle Sam. After hurling stones at the poster, they place some shoe rests on the track and later watch as a train is derailed. Two days later, Ali returns to the scene and looks again at the image. He concludes the story, 'I always knew that sooner or later he would confront me, and I would confront him.'[150]

The next key story concerns Ali's brief 'holiday as a White Hope' following the 1960 Olympics. Ali describes himself as immediately wary of the role that was being thrust upon him: 'Of course I understood they would prefer that the White Hope be white. But, Hopes having come upon hard times in boxing, I could see they would settle for a Black White Hope . . . until a real White White Hope came around.'[151] Disillusion comes quickly. Back in Louisville, while wearing his medal, he is refused entry to a Louisville restaurant. In disgusted response, and 'feeling tight and warm as though the bell had rung for the round,' Ali says he threw his medal in the Ohio river.[152] By 1967, Ali is firmly established as both the '"Jack Johnson" of [his] time', and a Pan-African statesman.[153]

Like Alex Haley's *Roots*, the bestselling book of 1976, *The Greatest* presents the story of a powerful black man who survives hardship to come good in America but never forgets his African origins. Both Ali and Haley use slavery as a metaphor for the experience of American blacks long after Emancipation, both confess that, prior to visiting the continent, their knowledge of Africa was derived from 'Tarzan movies', and both experience their return as a 'peak experience'.[154] In his review of *Roots*, considering the passage in which the baby Kunta Kinte is told his name, James Baldwin reinforced the connection. 'Even way up here in the 20th century,' he wrote, 'Muhammad Ali will not be the only one to respond to the moment that the father lifted his baby up with his face to the heavens, and said softly, "Behold – the only thing greater than yourself".'[155]

For all *The Greatest*'s talk of Ali's estrangement from white America, white America was appreciating and buying into Ali like never before. Ronald Bergan describes the 1977 film adaptation (featuring Ali as his 22-year-old self, James Earl Jones as Malcolm X, and George Benson singing 'The Greatest Love of All') as 'rather like an extended commercial advertising a renowned and well-loved product'.[156] Ali's commercial potential was also apparent to the master of pop iconography, Andy Warhol. In August 1977, Warhol visited Ali's training camp in order to photograph him for a series of ten silk-screen portraits of athletes (illus. 114). Victor Bockris recorded the event and quoted Ali's delight that 'white people gonna pay $25,000 for my picture!'[157] Warhol found Ali boring but very handsome.[158] For Mike Marqusee, Warhol's portrait marks 'the moment of symbolic appropriation, the transition of Ali from a divisive to a consensual figure'.[159] By the time Ali lit the torch to open the Atlanta Olympics in 1996 (accompanied by loudspeakers broadcasting Martin Luther King's 'I have a dream' speech), the transformation was complete. During the games he was given a replacement gold medal to replace the one he'd purportedly thrown into the Ohio River.[160] *When We Were Kings*, a film of the 1974 'Rumble', was released later that year, followed by Michael Mann's bio-pic, *Ali*, starring Will Smith, in 2001. In 1999, BBC viewers awarded Ali 'Sports Personality of the Century', and in 2001 *Sports Illustrated* noted that Ali commanded $100,000 (more than any other retired athlete) for a single public appearance.[161]

Marquesee argues that the 'Ali offered up for veneration in the 1990s' is a 'mere caricature of the original', a postmodern pastiche stripped of all political meaning.[162] But Ali's protean political usefulness never really ended. The subject of illegal FBI surveillance for a decade, in 1975 Ali accepted an invitation to the White House as part of Gerald Ford's attempt to 'heal the wounds of racial division, Vietnam and Watergate'.[163] In 1976, he campaigned for Jimmy Carter, who sent him to Africa to gather support for a boycott of the Moscow Olympics. On a visit to the USSR in 1978, Ali described America as the 'best country in the world' (the exact phrase he'd used in 1960): it was almost as if the past eighteen years hadn't happened.[164] In 1980, he supported Ronald Reagan's presidential campaign and in 1990, flew to Iraq to try to secure the release of the American hostages held by Saddam Hussein.

The shift in Ali's political positioning was connected to changes in his religious affiliation. After Elijah Muhammad's death in 1975, the Nation of Islam split. Ali chose to remain with Wallace D. Muhammad, who reinvented the organization along more orthodox Islamic lines, renaming it the American Muslim Mission, rather than following Louis Farrakhan who revived the old-style Nation. After the World Trade Center attack in 2001, Ali appeared on national television as the 'exemplary African-American Muslim' and declared that 'Islam is peace. It's against killing, murder and the terrorists and the people who are doing that in the name of Islam are wrong. And if I had a chance I'd do something about it.'[165] In December 2001 he made a short film designed to persuade America's Muslims to support the war effort and the following year visited Kabul.[166] He was awarded the Presidential Medal by George W. Bush in 2005.

Ali has also become a kind of New Age spiritual guru; his Parkinson's Syndrome merely adding poignancy to his story. God, he claimed, was keeping him 'humble' and showing him that 'I'm just a man, like everybody else.'[167] Recent years have seen the publication of books on Ali's 'life lessons' by his daughters Hana and Laila, as well as Ali himself.[168] He is also frequently evoked in inspirational books aimed at young people, and features in the memoirs of those who claim to have been inspired by his example (illus. 115).[169]

Memoirs form the basis of Leon Gast's 1996 film *When We Were Kings*. The soundtrack features Wyclef Jean's 'Rumble in the Jungle', a song which follows the nationalist argument of *The Greatest*, to suggest that the fight represents an attempt 'to reconnect 400 years' and that the film is a way to 'give love . . . / To the man who made the fam' remember when we were kings'. Wyclef ends by connecting the past to the present moment in which 'we need a ghetto Messiah'. The film itself, however, is purely nostalgic. While Foreman and Ali appear in the 1974 footage, we don't learn what they remember of the fight (or, indeed, what any Zairians thought of the occasion).[170] Instead, Gast intercuts scenes from the fight and its buildup with the recollections and primitivist interpretations of Norman Mailer and George Plimpton.[171] As Julio Rodriguez points out, this means that the 'we' of the title mostly refers to the old sportswriters and, by extension, Gast whose cinematography, he suggests, is as 'lustful' as Mailer's talk.[172] The film was advertised by a poster featuring a close-up of Ali's sweat-drenched face; his lips are slightly open and his eyes narrowed in concentration (illus. 116). The image suggests that Ali has transcended his previous movie personae, both that of boxer and that of political symbol, and become a work of primitivist art (illus. 117).

Ali also remains a promising resource for academic discussion. For cultural critics such as Grant Farred, he is more than a 'cultural icon', he is a 'vernacular intellectual'; someone whose 'physical actions . . . are indistinguishable from his cerebral contemplations' and who, by changing his name, 'narrativizes himself as postcolonial figure'.[173] Farred has high standards for Ali and suggests, for example, that by fighting in Jakarta without 'speaking out against the Indonesian genocide,' the boxer 'compromised himself ideologically'.[174] Ali's self-confessed prettiness has also been the subject of much speculation. On the simplest reading, when Ali announced, 'I am the prettiest thing that ever lived', he was simply making the classic boxer's boast of avoiding his opponent's gloves – 'I don't have a mark on my face'.[175] Ishmael Reed, however, worried that 'when he refers to himself as "pretty" he might mean his Caucasian features' – a thesis that was supported by Ali's habit of denigrating his opponents with racial insults.[176] More recently, Ali's prettiness has been read as a sign of late twentieth-century 're gendering' or 'cross-gendered wholeness'.[177]

As the new century began, Ali and his managers consolidated the 'brand' in a series of new ventures (illus. 145). In 2004, Taschen Books published a limited edition 'tribute' to Ali entitled *G.O.A.T.* – the acronym of 'Greatest of All Time'. The volume exemplified excess in every respect – twenty inches squared, it numbered 800 pages, weighed 75 pounds, and retailed at $3,000. The first 1,000 copies (the 'Champ's Edition' at $7,500) contained four silver gelatin prints by Howard Bingham and a self-assembly plastic sculpture by the master of kitsch consumerism, Jeff Koons. The following year, the Muhammad Ali Center, an interactive 'museum,

145
'Ali, Now and Then';
cover of *Esquire*,
October 2003.

peace, and conflict resolution center', assumed a central role in the regeneration of the still segregated city of Louisville and in April 2006, Ali sold 80 per cent of the marketing rights to his name and image to the entertainment rights firm CKX for $50 million.[178] A statement purportedly from Ali announced that the move will 'help guarantee that, for generations to come, people of all nations will understand my beliefs and purpose'.[179] In June, his corporation took advantage of the latest moral panic (childhood obesity) to launch G.O.A.T. snacks, shaped like punch bags and boxing gloves, and meant to be eaten in seven 'rounds' throughout the day.[180]

Ali has always been very astute about his ability to appeal to diverse constituents – to pretty girls 'because I say things that attract them'; to 'redneck white folks' who want to see 'the nigger' get 'a whoppin'; to 'black militants that don't like the whites'; to 'long-haired hippies, because I don't go to war'; to Muslims 'because of the name Muhammad Ali' and, finally, to 'the Israelis, who don't get along with the Muslims'. 'So you add it all up,' he once said, 'I got a helluva crowd.'[181]

In the remainder of this chapter, I look in greater detail at the appeal and challenge of Ali's celebrity for some of that crowd – first the Black Arts Movement; then Bob Dylan and Norman Mailer. Finally, I consider three 'white hope' tales: *Rocky*, *Raging Bull* and the comic book, *Superman vs Muhammad Ali*.

## 'SAY IT LOUD – I'M BLACK AND I'M PROUD'

Drawing variously on aesthetic, entrepreneurial, religious and therapeutic discourses, the aims and ambitions of late sixties and early seventies black cultural nationalism were constantly being debated and reformulated. At times it seemed that what unified its various agendas was simply blackness and, as Amiri Baraka later said, 'that meant many things to many people'.[182] Nevertheless, three dominant themes emerged: self-determination, pride and masculinity.[183] 'Black is beautiful and it's so beautiful to be black', read the student placards; 'say it loud, I'm black and I'm proud', sang one-time boxer James Brown; 'I am the greatest,' declared Muhammad Ali; 'We're the Greatest,' echoed the Alabama Black Panthers' bumper stickers.[184] These assertions were backed up by what Vincent Harding remembers as an extraordinary burst of cultural activity.

> Conventions and conferences on Black history, music, art, politics and religion were meeting almost weekly. New journals, new institutions, new African and Islamic names seemed to rise up continuously in a period of tremendous Black energy and creative force. It was a time of renaissance far more powerful than the celebrated period of Harlem's rise in the 1920s.[185]

Essential for many of these activities was the recovery of 'cultural roots', which were largely conceived in terms of the example provided by individual achievement.[186] When Sonia Sanchez asked, 'who's gonna give our young / blk people new heroes,' there was no shortage of offers.[187] 'Rip those dead white people off / your walls,' instructed another poet, Jayne Cortez, and in their place, she urged, erect 'A Black Hall of Fame / so our children will know / will know and be proud'.[188] While the most popular subject was undoubtedly Malcolm himself, 'the epic hero of our struggle', heroes were found far and wide – in traditional folklore (Railroad Bill, Shine), black history (Nat Turner, Frederick Douglass), contemporary popular culture (Charlie Parker, John Coltrane and James Brown) and sports (Muhammad Ali and Jack Johnson).[189] Ali may have chosen Elijah Muhammad over Malcolm X, but it is Malcolm beside whom he is commemorated in literary, musical and visual Halls of Fame.

The representation of heroes was the driving force behind much activity in the visual arts. In 1967 the Organization of Black American Culture (OBAC), intent on producing an art work that would be in, as well as of, the community, created the 'Wall of Respect' on an abandoned building in inner-city Chicago. Influenced by the heroic murals of Aaron Douglas, as well as the Mexican and WPA traditions, the Wall was intended 'to inspire the South Side black community with faces of black success, creative genius, and resistance' – faces that included Malcolm X, Marcus Garvey, John Coltrane, Nina Simone and, standing victorious in the centre of a bay window, Muhammad Ali.[190] After the mural was featured in *Ebony* magazine, further walls of respect, as well as 'truth', 'consciousness' and 'dignity', were produced all over the country, creating numerous 'Black Museum[s] in the inner city'.[191] Today 'motivational' murals featuring Ali and others remain a frequent sight on the walls of schools and youth centres all over the United States. In 1993, for example, Elliott Pinkney (with the assistance of Sam Barrow and Lloyd Goodney) created *Visions and Motions* for the Community Youth Sports and Arts Foundation in Los Angeles (illus. 118). Designed 'to encourage young people', it 'depicts men and women who had visions to become great and then set about setting those dreams in motion'.[192] One of those men is Muhammad Ali.

Jack Johnson also became a popular subject for commemoration.[193] After 1966, parallels began to be drawn between Ali's refusal of the draft and subsequent ban from boxing, and Johnson's 1910 conviction under the Mann Act. Jack Johnson seemed 'tailor made' for a 'generation looking for forceful, independent leaders'.[194] But although Ali asserted that his exile from boxing was 'history all over again', different political and social issues were at play.[195] Johnson was considered dangerous because he challenged the caste system in and out of the ring. White women and white hopes were largely irrelevant to Ali's career, except as a way of making money; he espoused racial separatism. It seemed, however, that if Ali was not going to be a Joe Louis, then he had to be a Jack Johnson, as if these were the only possibilities. Johnson was represented in many different ways by both black and white artists. *The Young Jack Johnson* (1967), one of several 'hero portraits' by Reginald Gammon, draws on an often-reproduced photograph of Johnson standing with folded arms and staring directly at the camera.

Gammon's painting emphasizes the boxer's musculature and challenging look, and surrounds him with bands of red, black and green, the Black Nationalist colours.[196] Raymond Saunders's series of mixed media portraits of Johnson took a very different approach. Saunders disrupts the figurative representation of Johnson by overlaying it with Abstract Expressionist paintwork and a collage of tickets and other documents. Saunders was very critical of the Black Art Movement and, in a privately printed pamphlet, *Black is a Color* (1969), argued against an aesthetic based on 'perpetual anger'. 'For the artist,' he said, 'this is aesthetic atrophy'.[197] Nevertheless, it is hard not to see political intent in Saunders's choice of Johnson as a subject and in his mode of representation. In one painting, Johnson's head is cropped and his arms obscured by red paint. The painting is dominated by his white-trousered legs with his crotch as its focal point.[198]

In 1967 Howard Sackler wrote a play, *The Great White Hope*, closely based on Johnson's newly reissued autobiography. James Earl Jones, who played Jefferson (the Johnson character), claimed that his performance was partly based on observations of Ali, and when he stepped down from the role, it was suggested that Ali himself could take over.[199] Although he needed work and said he loved the 'Jack Johnson image', Ali refused the part.[200] He may have emulated the role of 'the nigger white folks didn't like', but,he added, 'a black hero chasing white women was a role I didn't want to glorify'.[201] Keen to appeal to the increasingly lucrative young black audience, Twentieth Century Fox decided to film the play and gave it a comparatively large budget.[202] The release of *The Great White Hope* coincided with Ali's return to the ring, and, as publicity for both, he was happy to spar with Jones for photographers. 'If you just change the time, date and details, it's about me!' he said.[203] The film, however, was unpopular with both blacks and whites. Blacks disliked the 'glorification of a black man's love of a white woman' and the fact that more time was spent considering Johnson's final defeat than his victory over Jeffries (dealt with rapidly in close-ups of Jones laughing and punching). White audiences, meanwhile, resented the film's 'all-purpose accusation and rhetoric' and 'guilt-mongering advertising campaign': the posters read, 'He could beat any white man in the world. He just couldn't beat all of them!' (illus. 146).[204]

146
Poster advertising
*The Great White Hope* (1970).

He could beat any white man in the world.
He just couldn't beat all of them.

From the play and performances that won The Pulitzer Prize, The New York Critics Award and The Tony Award

20th Century-Fox Presents A Lawrence Turman-Martin Ritt Production.

**The Great White Hope**

Starring James Earl Jones, Jane Alexander.

Produced by Lawrence Turman. Directed by Martin Ritt.
Screenplay by Howard Sackler based on his play.
Produced on the New York Stage by Herman Levin. PANAVISION® Color by DE LUXE®

The following year, a feature-length documentary *Jack Johnson*, directed by Jim Jacobs and produced by William Cayton, was shown at the Whitney Museum.[205] Today the film, which presents Johnson as a prototype Black Power activist, is largely remembered for its Miles Davis soundtrack. Davis's score makes no attempt to be historical; rather, he marries his jazz horn with the rock influences of electric bass and guitar.[206] Davis felt the score fitted the movie 'perfectly' – his aim, he said later, was to make music that Jack Johnson could have danced to, music that had a 'black rhythm', that was 'black enough'.[207] Davis had been a keen amateur boxer since his youth, and had idolized Sugar Ray Robinson.[208] The black subcultures of boxing and jazz had traditionally overlapped, and while musicians tapped in to the masculine mythology of the prize-fighter, boxers wanted to be thought of as stylish and artful.[209] Percussion and dancing skills, both of which required a sense of rhythm and timing, were particularly transferable to the ring.[210] Sugar Ray had begun as a tap dancer, imitating Bill 'Bojangles' Robinson; later he played drums with his friend Max Roach.[211] While both activities depended on constant practice until they became 'instinctive', as well as 'science and precision', what makes a great boxer, Davis maintained, is the same thing that makes a great musician – a distinctive style. While working on *Jack Johnson*, Davis was sparring regularly and he claimed to have written the piece with 'that shuffling movement boxers use' in mind.[212] But Johnson's influence was more than stylistic. In his sleevenotes for the 1971 album *A Tribute to Jack Johnson*, Davis said that 'Johnson portrayed Freedom' – 'His flamboyance was more than obvious. And no doubt mighty Whitey felt "No Black man should have all this." But he did and he'd flaunt it.'[213] Davis wanted his album to be seen as a comparable gesture of stylish masculine flamboyance, a reproof to 'white envy'.[214]

The comparison of Ali to Johnson was often situated in the context of discussions about the relationship between the Black Arts Movement and the Harlem Renaissance. For Ishmael Reed, for example, the 'glamorous, sophisticated, intelligent, international, and militant' Ali not only represented the 'New Black of the 1960s', but was an obvious successor to the 'New Negro of the 1920s'.[215] The status of Ali in the Black Arts Movement was, however, just as complicated as that of Jack Johnson in the Harlem Renaissance 40 years earlier. In the twenties, debates focused on whether Johnson was a suitable role model for the aspirant middle classes. Was the heavyweight championship the best 'measurement' of black progress? asked James Weldon Johnson. Would an interest in sport distract blacks from the importance of education? wondered W.E.B. Du Bois. In Chapter Five, I argued that one way to reconcile the celebration of a sports hero with a belief in the importance of artistic achievement was to consider boxing as itself an art form or analogous to art. In the late sixties, debates about Ali's suitability as a role model had a slightly different emphasis. The rhetoric of Black Power tended to associate proper blackness with proper masculinity.[216] There was much talk of 'emasculation' and 'eunuchs', while numerous works debated the 'price of being a black man in America', and the nature of 'black masculinity', which was defined in essentialist terms.[217] 'The question for the black critic today,' declared LeRoi Jones and Larry Neal in 1968, is 'how far has the work gone in transforming an American Negro into an African-American or black man?'[218]

One way of considering this question (and its possible answers) is to read it as emerging from the debates that followed the American publication of Franz Fanon's work. Fanon's books provided a framework within which many intellectuals and activists located the condition and consciousness of black American men (again women are largely ignored). It became commonplace to speak of Black America as an internal colony and its literature as 'a literature of combat'.[219] In *Black Skin, White Masks* (first published in English in 1968) Fanon considered 'the singularly eroticised' body of the black athlete as an example of the association of 'the Negro' with 'the biological'. In a word-association test conducted on 'some 500 members of the white race – French, German, English, Italian', he inserted the word 'Negro': '*Negro* brought forth biology, penis, strong, athletic, potent, boxer, Joe Louis, Jesse Owens, Senegalese troops, savage, animal, devil, sin.'[220] But Fanon wanted to do more than simply expose white stereotyping; he wanted black men to think about themselves differently. In order to be truly free, he argued, they must actively resist being 'locked into' their bodies.[221] These themes were elaborated in Eldridge Cleaver's 1968 essay 'Allegory of the Black Eunuchs', an extended complaint that 'the white man wants to be the *brain* and he wants us to be the muscle, the *body*'.[222]

As reigning heavyweight champion, Ali was, of course, the ultimate performer of a 'slave sport', the ultimate representative of the 'singularly eroticised' Body, the biological essence. 'The Heavyweight Champion of the World is, most of all, a grand hunk of flesh,' wrote Ishmael Reed, 'capable of devastating physical destruction when instructed by a brain, or a group of brains. He may be brilliant, but even his brilliance is used to praise his flesh.'[223] Writers such as Cleaver did not, however, want to forego the male body. If racism had 'negated masculinity' by separating brain and body, Black Power must bring them together again. It was just a question of emphasis. While whites such as Norman Mailer celebrated Ali's athleticism and laughed at his poetry and philosophy, Cleaver and LeRoi Jones took Ali's excellence as a boxer largely for granted and concentrated on his out-of-ring activities: first, as 'loud-mouthed Clay because, after all, it takes at least a bird-brain to run a loud-mouth, and the white man despises even that much brain in a black man', and then, even better, as Ali, the man-of-principle who sacrificed his considerable physical assets for his beliefs.[224] Of course, the loud-mouth-become-political icon would scarcely have been worth celebrating if he did not also remain beyond doubt the incarnation of masculinity. Side-stepping Ali's profession was made much easier by the fact that between 1967 and 1970 – the height of the Black Power Movement – he was not boxing at all.

In his 1962 address to the American Society for African Culture, LeRoi Jones argued that America had not yet produced a 'legitimate Negro art', with the result that Jack Johnson remained a 'larger cultural hero than any Negro writer'. Boxing (or more precisely, the symbolism of Johnson's career) and music assumed a 'legitimacy of emotional concern' that literature had been unable to achieve.[225] This legitimacy, or authenticity, was the one thing that white culture could not steal. White blues singers may sing the same words as their black counterparts but, Jones maintained, the songs were not the same. 'It is a different quality of energy they summon. The body is directly figured in it.' Similarly, he went on, 'a white man could box like Muhammad Ali, only *after* seeing Muhammad Ali box. He could not initiate that style. It is no description, it *is* the culture.'[226] The white appropriation of black style was a much-discussed subject.[227] Ishmael Reed wrote extensively about the way in which American art depended on 'a secret understanding that the oppressor shall always prevail and make off with the prizes, no matter how inferior his art to that of his victims'.[228] For the black artist to survive, Reed argued, he must emulate such 'conjure men' as Railroad Bill, Nat Turner, Malcolm X and Jack Johnson, all of whom resisted attempts to steal their magic.[229]

LeRoi Jones also alluded to Johnson and Ali in his attempts to create a literature that, he said, would reflect the 'singular values' (often conceived in emotional or bodily terms) of black life. His 1964 poem, 'Black Dada Nihilismus', for example, is an attempt to create an aesthetic based on medieval alchemy, Egyptian astrology and the exorcising 'black scream', as well as a tribute to a series of exemplary rebels and entertainers who include Johnson.[230] Three years later, Jones prefaced a short story about space invaders searching for jazz records in Newark with the following poem:

*Can you die in airraid jiggle*
*torn arms flung through candystores*
*Touch the edge of an answer. The waves of nausea*
*as change sweeps the frame of breath and meat.*

'Stick a knife through his throat,'
he slid
in the blood
got up running toward
the blind newsdealer. He screamed
about 'Cassius Clay', and slain there in the
street, the whipped figure of jesus, head opened
eyes flailing against his nose. They beat him to
pulpy answers. We wrote Muhammad Ali across his
face and chest, like a newspaper of bleeding meat.[231]

The narrator of the poem seems uncertain about his position is relation to the violent attack. The mob is both a 'they', who beat the man to a paper-like pulp, and a 'we' whose number includes a 'newsdealer' and who transform the pulp into a 'newspaper of bleeding meat'. We don't know anything about the victim of the mob other than the fact that he screams the name Cassius Clay and, to the ambivalent narrator, becomes a Christ-like martyr. But that, it seems, is all we need to know. The 'news' that needs to be conveyed is that Clay is now Ali. That shift (mirrored the following year when Jones changed his name to Amiri Baraka) is of course the shift from the rhetoric of Civil Rights to that of Black Power; from 'We Shall Overcome' to 'Up Against the Wall, Motherfucker!'[232] In aesthetic terms, this move meant rejecting a poetry of reflection and analysis for one of immediacy and direct expression: 'reflect never did shit for any of us. Express would. Express. Now Now Now Now Now Now.'[233] But there was, however, only so far that an aesthetic based on the 'Black scream' could go, and by the late sixties, in works such as 'It's Nation Time' or *Black Fire*, an enormously influential anthology that he edited with Larry Neal, Baraka returned to his earlier emphasis on cultural nationalism.[234]

Neal's introduction to *Black Fire* argued that the Black Arts Movement must learn from the mistakes of the Harlem Renaissance which, he said, had failed to 'address itself to the mythology and the life-styles of the black community' and had not spoken 'directly to black people'.[235] By 1970, Neal had begun to evoke Ralph Ellison as an alternative model; Ellison's work displayed a complex appreciation of 'the aesthetic all around . . . preachers, blues singers, hustlers, gamblers, jazzmen, boxers, dancers, and itinerant storytellers'. It was not enough, Neal maintained, simply to name heroes; black literature must recognize the diverse sources of its strengths and singularity – in boxing, music, politics and religion. There was no need to invent a new black aesthetic; one simply had to locate it.[236]

Ostensibly an essay on the 1971 Ali–Frazier fight, 'Uncle Rufus Raps on the Square Circle' is Neal's masterclass on the black aesthetic.[237] Its epigraph is the prize-fighter versus yokel passage from *Invisible Man*, and its barroom setting alludes to the Golden Day scene in Ellison's novel. Uncle Rufus suggests Uncle Remus, and there are also mentions of minstrel shows, Jelly Roll Morton, and Melvin B. Tolson's epic poem, *Harlem Gallery*. The story-cum-essay's most important models, however, are the barber shop and barroom debates of Ollie Harrington's Bootsie comic strip and Langston Hughes's Simple stories – both of which were syndicated in black newspapers.[238] Set in a Harlem bar, Hughes's stories generally featured a conversation between the middle-class narrator, Boyd, and Jesse B. Semple or Simple, a working-class 'race man', on topics ranging from politics and history to music and sport.[239] Introduced as a boxer-turned-minstrel-performer, and a friend of 'the real John Henry', Uncle Rufus is the embodiment of black culture and history, the conscience of his race. Although Larry, the narrator, just wants to talk about Ali–Frazier, Uncle Rufus takes him through the history of black boxing – from Molineaux to Johnson to Battling Siki to Joe Louis – all of whose fights he seems to have witnessed. 'I once saw two slaves beat each other to death,' he says. At this point (two pages into the story), the naturalistic conversation is interrupted by an italicized paragraph (in the style of *Invisible Man*) in which a first person narrator describes the fight – '*I am inside of a bull of a man named Silas*'.[240] Rufus then carries on as if this scene has been spoken aloud, 'You got the right idea son.' Larry has begun to learn something about his history; in Ellison's terms, has 'stepped inside of his opponent's sense of time.' Rufus then moves on to consider boxing and music as comparable expressions of 'rhythmic style', and compares Ali to riffing 'body bebop' and Frazier to slow 'stomp-down blues'; in other words, a reformulation of the prize-fighter and the yokel.[241] In suggesting the varieties of black styles, Neal provides a corrective to the seemingly inevitable translation of every stylistic contest between blacks (from Liston vs. Patterson to Ali vs. Frazier) into one between black and *faux* white. For someone like Mailer (or indeed Jones or Cleaver), there only ever seems to be one legitimate black style, one legitimate black winner. Rufus's final lesson for Larry, and one that requires a full understanding of black history and culture, is that it is possible to celebrate very different styles.

Celebrating his boxing style, Neal does not extend his analysis to Ali's other contributions to black popular culture (illus. 147). Others, however, were eager to claim him as a 'modern mass communication comedian' in the tradition of Langston Hughes, and to argue, further, that being a 'good black poet in the '60s', meant capturing his 'rhythms . . . on the page'.[242] The late 1960s and '70s saw a proliferation of studies defining the 'specific rhetorical devices and linguistic patterns inherent in Black verbal style', and the ways in which they informed the

147
Muhammad
Ali, *Float Like a
Butterfly, Sting Like
a Bee*, c. 1979.

new black poetry.[243] Particular attention was paid to 'Black verbal rituals', such as the dozens, toast, signification, and call-and-response. Most relevant to a consideration of Ali is the rhyming, boasting narrative tale known as the toast (what Kimberley Benston and Henry Louis Gates later punned as 'trope-a-dope').[244] The 'overriding theme' of the toast, argued Geneva Smitherman, was 'the omnipotence of Black folks as symbolized in the lone figure of the black hero. Full of braggadocio, [the Toast-Teller] is always talkin bout how bad he bees, and his boasting consumes a good portion of the Toast's content.'[245]

Since Homer's Epeios declared himself the greatest, fighting and boasting have always gone together, and in 1934 Zora Neale Hurston identified both as fundamental 'Characteristics of Negro Expression'.[246] 'Threats', Hurston maintained, are integral to fighting, and 'a great threatener must certainly be considered an aid to the fighting machine'.[247] Ali's every fight was aided by threats (he preferred to call them predictions), and hyperbolic boasts. His first 'campaign poem' (and in 1975 still his favourite) begins, 'It started twenty years past. / The greatest of them all was born at last.' The imagery of 'Feats of Clay' is predictable ('I'm strong as an ox and twice as tough'), but Ali was soon to invent narratives, metaphors and boasts which do not look out of place alongside the work of Black Arts poets.[248] Compare, for example, Ali on stage in 1964,

> I am so modest I can admit my own fault.
> My only fault is I don't realise how great I really am.

with Nikki Giovanni's 'Ego Tripping', published in 1970:

> I am so hip even my errors are correct.
> . . .
> I cannot be comprehended except by my permission.[249]

Or, consider these two dream visions:

> Last night I had a dream. When I got to Africa, I had one hell of a rumble. I had to beat Tarzan's behind first for claiming to be King of the Jungle. I done something new for this fight. I done wrestled with an alligator. That's right. I have wrestled with an alligator. I done tussled with a whale. I done handcuffed lightning, thrown thunder in jail. That's bad! Only last week I murdered a rock, injured a stone, hospitalised a brick! I'm so mean I make medicine sick!

> I am a cowboy in the boat of Ra. Ezzard Charles of the Chisholm Trail. Took up the bass but they blew off my thumb. Alchemist in ringmanship but a sucker for the right cross.[250]

The first is Ali-as-Davy-Crockett, speaking to the press before fighting Foreman in 1974; the second, a verse of Ishamel Reed's often-anthologized poem 'I am a Cowboy in the Boat of Ra', a modernist interweaving of Egyptian, Christian and West African mythology narrated by a shape-shifting narrator (cowboy-cum-jazz-musician-cum-boxer).[251]

What Reed admired about Ali's verse was the way in which, like Reed himself, he supplemented the standard folk repertoire with characters drawn from television and comic books.[252] Ali was particularly keen on space imagery. Before fighting Liston, he recited a poem predicting that his powerful punch would lift his opponent 'clear out of the ring' and into space. After describing the audience's restlessness and the referee's anxiety about whether or not to start the count, Ali continues the story:

> But our radar stations have picked him up
> He's somewheres over the Atlantic.
> Who would have thought
> When they came to the fight
> That they'd witness the launching
> Of a human satellite.
> Yes, the crowd did not dream
> When they put down their money
> That they would see
> A total eclipse of the Sonny.[253]

After the second Liston fight, Ali declared himself 'the astronaut of boxing' (compared to Joe Louis and Dempsey, who were 'just jet pilots') and he often spoke of his ambition to become champion of the universe, defeating 'slick shiny-headed green men' from Venus or Mars. There was, Ali admitted in 1965, 'one problem': 'they might not let me on that ship . . . I'm going to contact Martin Luther King and see if he can integrate those ships because they will send two men on the planet and I want to be the first coloured one.'[254] These remarks provided the starting point for Raymond Washington's 1969 poem, 'Moon bound'. The only way 'black folks going to the moon', Washington jokes bitterly, is if it proves unfit for human habitation but good for growing cotton. Then, 'Stokely on the moon / Muhammad Ali on the moon / Rap on the moon . . . white folks / going to send blackfolks to the moon / whether they like it or not'.[255]

The ability to translate a 'tendency to boast and brag' into a successful career as a 'celebrity' poet, rapping in 'Black style' with 'Black exaggerations', is the subject of John Oliver Killens's 1971 satire, *The Cotillion*. But even Killens's narrator, Ben Ali Lumumba, wearies of those who aspire to a 'world of total Blackness' and the way in which 'the competition went on and on, never ending, to determine the World Individual Champeenship of Blackness'.[256] Black Arts' 'champeenship' competitions took place in cafés, theatres, little magazines and small presses all over America. Meanwhile, Muhammad Ali was introducing 'black oral rhyming culture into the mainstream' world of network television.[257]

Ali's involvement with television began almost as soon as he started boxing. One of the attractions of the Columbia police gym in Louisville was the fact that the club fights were televised in a Saturday night show called *Tomorrow's Champions*. ('I watch you all the time on TV,' the girl who first kissed him is reputed to have said.[258]) When he turned professional, commentators declared that he was 'made for' television and that television 'seemed to be invented' for him.[259] Ali himself later wrote about the importance of television in the development of his style inside and outside of the ring. Inside, he had 'hated the sight on TV of big, clumsy, heavyweights plodding' and so determined to be 'as fast as lightweight'; outside, he had seen the theatrical entrances of the wrestler Gorgeous George, and realised that 'if I talked even more, there was no telling how much money people would pay to see me'.[260]

In 1908, Jack London drew on a long tradition that Jessie Fauset dubbed 'the black American as a living comic supplement' and cast Jack Johnson in the role of 'clown', claiming that 'his face beamed with all the happy, care-free innocence of a little child'.[261] Nearly 50 years later, a *Newsweek* poll revealed that the most popular stereotype that whites held about blacks was that they 'laugh a lot'. Some worried that Ali, who 'laughed and smiled more in public in a week than Joe Louis did in his entire life', simply confirmed that view.[262] But however much he smiled, Ali was acutely aware of the possibilities of television, using it as a tool to be exploited for his own ends (financial and otherwise).[263] Never mind the ring – every chat show, press conference and weigh-in became a space for oratory as well as theatre. 'I liked being who I was,' he once said, 'because they would put me on television and when I say, "I'm the greatest, I'm pretty," that means that little black children and people who felt like nothing say, "We got a champion"'.[264]

## TWO NICE JEWISH BOYS IN THE AGE OF ALI

During the 1960s neither Norman Mailer nor Bob Dylan much liked discussing their middle-class Jewish upbringing. Instead both adopted a variety of popular American outlaw personae, including those of fighter and fight fan.[265]

Dylan's first public association with boxing came in 1964 when he wrote 'Who Killed Davey Moore?', a reworking of 'Who Killed Cock Robin?', about the death of a young black boxer and the refusal of his manager, the referee, and the anonymous mass of gamblers, boxing writers and spectators to admit any responsibility. All are players in 'the old American game', and all, Dylan suggests, are to blame.[266] In 1976, Dylan took up the cause of another black boxer-victim, Rubin 'Hurricane' Carter. Once a middleweight contender, Carter had been convicted for three murders in 1967 and 1976 and, despite several appeals, had been in prison ever since. In 1974 Carter published his autobiography, *The Sixteenth Round*, and his case quickly became a *cause célèbre*.[267] Nelson Algren moved to Paterson, New Jersey, to research the case (his fictional version, *The*

*Devil's Stocking*, was published posthumously), while George Lois, designer of *Esquire* magazine covers, established a trust fund for legal expenses. Lois persuaded celebrities from Burt Reynolds to Muhammad Ali to add their support. 'I know you all came here to see me, because Bob Dylan just ain't that big,' Ali told a largely white audience at the Madison Square Garden benefit concert, but 'you've got the connections and the complexion to get the protection'.[268] Dylan's 'Hurricane' tells the story of Carter in cinematic detail, before concluding, 'To see him obviously framed / Couldn't help but make me feel ashamed to live in a land / Where justice is a game.'[269] The first retrial ended with Carter's reconviction; he was finally freed after a further trial in 1985, and in 1993 became the first boxer to receive an honourary championship belt.

In 1964 and in 1976 Dylan was able to write 'finger-pointin'' songs like 'Davey Moore' and 'Hurricane' with equanimity: in fact 'Hurricane' became the centrepiece of the Rolling Thunder Revue, a tour which self-consciously tried to conjure up the good 'old days' of 'civil rights rallies down in Mississippi'.[270] In the intervening years, however, Dylan was often anxious about being labelled as spokesman for any particular cause. This anxiety first manifested itself in a 1964 album which offered to reveal *Another Side of Bob Dylan*. In a song entitled 'I Shall Be Free No. 10', Dylan announces that he is 'just average, common', no 'different from anyone'. Soon, however, he is imagining himself as a contender for the heavyweight crown. Protesting about Davey Moore in the Guthrie-Ochs tradition is abandoned in favour of a performance *as* Cassius Clay, with Dylan determined 'to match the Louisville Lip rhyme for rhyme, boast for boast.'[271]

> I was shadow-boxing earlier in the day
> I figured I was ready for Cassius Clay
> I said "Fee, fie, fo, fum, Cassius Clay, here I come
> 26, 27, 28, 29, I'm gonna make your face look just like mine
> Five, four, three, two, one, Cassius Clay you'd better run
> 99, 100, 101, 102, your ma won't even recognize you
> 14, 15, 16, 17, 18, 19, gonna knock him clean right out of his spleen.[272]

Dylan's self-mockery manifests itself in both the ridiculousness of his giant-killing rhetoric and the casual improvisation of rhyming 'clean' with 'spleen' (and later 'poet' with 'blow it').

In 1969, Simon and Garfunkel released a single called 'The Boxer' which was 'widely interpreted' as being about Dylan's career up to 1969.[273] Unsuccessful in the folk community ('I come looking for a job, but I get no offers'), Dylan-the-boxer ends up succumbing to what Simon calls the 'come-ons from the whores on Seventh Avenue', that is, the bosses of Columbia Records. Eventually, everything falls to pieces when the protagonist finds that he has 'squandered [his] resistance on a pocket full of mumbles'; in other words, his singing voice has become unintelligible and his lyrics less concerned with 'resistance' than with surreal juxtapositions and obscure allusions. The final line of 'The

Boxer', on this reading, acknowledges that the protagonist, although beaten down, remains 'a fighter by his trade'. In 1970 Dylan recorded the song on *Self Portrait*, an album of covers in which he again questions the idea of a fixed and knowable identity. The album was a self-conscious attempt to send out what he would later call 'deviating signals'.[274] 'The Boxer' is only one of many personae at play here, and Dylan further undermines any claim to identifying the singer with the song by recording it on two simultaneous but discordant tracks.

The boxer-motif recurred in 2004 when Dylan published the first volume of his memoirs, entitled *Chronicles*. The book begins with his arrival in New York in 1961. John Hammond, of Columbia Records, had introduced Dylan to publisher Lou Levy, and the story opens with Levy taking the singer to dinner at Jack Dempsey's Restaurant, a restaurant whose slogan was 'Love Matches are made in heaven, Fight Matches are made at Jack Dempsey's' (illus. 148). (It is also the place where Michael Corleone goes to meet his father's rival in Mario Puzo's *The Godfather*, a meeting that will transform him into a gangster.[275]) When Levy introduced Dylan to Dempsey, the great champion mistook the young man for a fighter. '"You look too light for a heavyweight kid, you'll have to put on a few pounds. You're going to have to dress a little finer, look a little sharper – not that you'll need much in the way of clothes when you're in the ring – don't be afraid of hitting somebody too hard."'[276] Dempsey is quickly put right about Dylan's profession, and the story moves on. Why does Dylan begin his story here? Certainly it's true that signing contracts with Levy and Hammond was the beginning of his success, but something additional seems to be implied. Dylan – always seeking to appropriate new identities in order to be 'true to [him]self' – seems to relish Dempsey's mistake and to take on his advice.[277] Much of the book is about becoming famous and working out how to live in the public spotlight, naked in the ring. It is also important that Dylan meets Dempsey, Depression hero of the white working class, and not some other boxer. To be mistaken for a boxer by Dempsey (the Woody Guthrie of his sport) is tantamount to being acknowledged by Guthrie himself, 'the starting place for my identity and destiny'.[278]

After quickly achieving celebrity, Dylan devotes most of his chronicles to an account of his resistance to it, to feeling 'like a piece of meat that someone had thrown to the dogs'.[279] Halfway through the book, he tells another boxing story – that of Jerry Quarry's fight against Jimmy Ellis in 1967.

Jimmy Ellis was a 'take the money and go home' kind of guy – boxing was a job to

148
Advertisement for Dempsey's Restaurant, Broadway, New York, 1955.

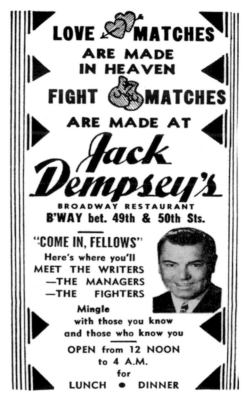

350

him, no more no less. He had a family to feed and didn't care about becoming a legend . . . Jerry Quarry, a white boxer, was being touted as the new Great White Hope – an odious designation. Jerry . . . wanted no part of it. The white vigilante groups who came to cheer him didn't move Quarry . . . he wouldn't accept their bigoted allegiance and resisted the dementia swirling around him.[280]

'I identified with both Ellis and Quarry,' Dylan concludes, 'and drew an analogy between our situations and responses to it.' Like Ellis, 'I too had a family to feed'. The analogy with Quarry is rather odder. 'I wasn't going to acknowledge being an emblem, symbol or spokesman', he says, as if representing folk music or the New Left was equivalent to being a symbol for white supremacism.

Like Dylan, Norman Mailer did everything he could to break free from his childhood self, 'the one personality he found absolutely insupportable' – in his case, that of the 'nice Jewish boy' from Brooklyn rather than Minnesota. Being a nice Jewish boy meant being gentle, clean, and above all, 'modest' – 'he had been born to a modest family, had been a modest boy, a modest young man, and he hated that, he loved the pride and the arrogance and the confidence and the egocentricity he had acquired over the years'.[281] While Dylan alluded to journeymen boxers such as Ellis and Quarry to express his distaste for celebrity, Mailer sought only 'the greatest', a title that he applied seriously to Ali and less seriously to himself. 'Champ' was just one of many 'half-heroic and three-quarters comic' advertisements for himself that 'Norman' or 'Mailer' cultivated.[282] In *The Armies of the Night* (1968), for example, he noted the instability of his speaking voice at the Pentagon demonstration against the Vietnam war; how, without any plan, his accent shifted from Irish to Texan, from 'Marlon Brando's voice in *The Wild One*' to some 'Woo-eeeee's and grunts' which showed 'hints of Cassius Clay.' Eventually he tried 'to imitate a most high and executive voice', but that too came out as 'shades of Cassius Clay'.[283] Mailer's versions of American masculinity are elaborately constructed masquerades, many of which, he acknowledges, are the result of a 'wretched collaboration with the multimillion-celled nausea machine, that Christ-killer of the ages – television'.[284] Even as he asserts a hyper-masculinity, Mailer's deadpan humour underlines its anxieties; even as he cultivates celebrity, he attacks the means by which it is produced.

Mailer's writing is obsessed with America, both in reality and as an idea. 'The grandson of immigrants', he said that he could never really *be* an American; he could, nonetheless, 'have a love affair with America', and occasionally even feel '*like* an American'.[285] In order to do this, Mailer (not unlike Abraham Cahan 60 years earlier) had to find both an appropriate subject matter and an appropriate language or style. From the mid-fifties onward, boxing played a part in both.[286] This is not to say that, like Cahan and others, he was interested in the ways in which a subculture (and its slang) could represent a nation. For Mailer, 'America' and 'boxing' were much less concrete than that. Instead the boxing match provided a 'metaphor' of the 'schizoid' nature of 'modern life', a useable structure within which to explore many of the violently felt debates of Cold War America: debates about sex, gender, sexuality and race, about vitalism and the death wish, about literary style, and, all too often, about literary rivalry.[287] I will say a little about these different debates, but really they are all the same. Mailer presents every concept in absolute and rather abstract terms: an essential masculinity is pitted against an essential femininity, an idealized heterosexuality confronts a mythical homosexuality; imaginary 'blacks' encounter imaginary 'whites'. The continuing clash of one against each other is what constitutes 'existential politics', and 'form' is 'the record of a war . . . as seen in a moment of rest'.[288] In fiction then, Mailer's characters became the embodiments of opposing positions which need to be argued through; in non-fiction, he favoured the Q&A in which he could have 'a rousing club fight' with an interviewer, or sometimes enter the 'arena' with an imagined alter ego.[289] And sometimes genres – in particular, fiction and history – argue with each other.[290] 'The element which is exciting, disturbing, nightmarish perhaps, is that incompatibles have come to bed'.[291]

If all relationships have the same dialectic structure, then it makes equal sense to use the language of sex to describe boxing – the first fifteen seconds of a fight are equivalent 'to the first kiss in a love affair' – and the language of boxing to describe sex.[292] For the narrator of 'The Time of Her Time' (1959), boxing provides a grammar for 'the language of bodies', while the 'dialectic' of sex stages conflicts between Jewishness and non-Jewishness, high culture and low culture, and even the competing therapeutic claims of Sigmund Freud and Wilhelm Reich.[293] If conflict is the model for the relationship between men and women, men additionally face an internal battle between heterosexuality and homosexuality (women don't seem to have this problem). The brutal outcome of the 1962 fight between Emile Griffith and Benny (Kid) Paret is said to dramatize the 'biological force' with which men disavow their inherent homosexuality.[294] Paret had taunted Griffith with homophobic remarks at the weigh-in and during the fight, and Griffith responded by beating him to death.[295] For Mailer, this is an example of the ring not doing its usual job of containing and controlling (or sublimating) sexual desire.[296] Since Ali and Frazier can 'kiss' as long and hard as they like inside the ring, they have no need to do so elsewhere. Nor do they need to kill each other.

The boxing ring also enacts and thus contains another conflict that Mailer sees as fundamental to American culture, one between blacks and whites. Again his definitions recycle familiar essentialist stereotypes: whites are civilized, sophisticated, cerebral, literate and literary, while blacks are primitive, illiterate, 'physically superior', attuned to the 'pleasures of the body', and fluent in its language.[297] James Baldwin (and many others) complained about Mailer's tendency to see 'us as goddam romantic black symbols'.[298] While this is undoubtedly true, it is not surprising – Mailer sees everyone and everything symbolically.

Mailer first started to think about literary style in relation to boxing in the mid-fifties, when he sought out a new and more 'muscular' style for his third novel, *The Deer Park*. It is the story of an Irish-American orphan called Sergius

O'Shaughnessy who before the story begins had 'boxed [his] way into the middleweight semi-finals of an Air Force enlisted man's tournament' and therefore into flying school.[299] O'Shaughnessy goes first to Hollywood where the producers are initially dismissive ('I didn't even know the athlete could read') and then, when he gets depressed (becoming 'a boxer without a punch'), to Mexico. There he plans to learn to be the 'first great and recognized American matador', but finally he gives up his novel on bullfighting as 'inevitably imitative' of Hemingway.[300] O'Shaughnessy's crisis of confidence reflected that of his creator; on receiving the proofs, Mailer decided *The Deer Park* needed substantial revision. He would abandon the novel's 'poetic style', rip up its 'silk', smash its 'porcelain', create a first-person voice 'bigger' than himself, and think much more closely about pace.[301] That bigger voice and controlled pace would restore the book's punch.[302]

Mailer's next book was, he later said, 'the first one to be 'written in what became my style'.[303] *Advertisements for Myself* (1959) spanned Mailer's career to date and included stories, essays, interviews and drafts of *The Deer Park*; there are two contents lists and one offers the book as a 'biography of style'. Mailer opens the book by declaring his arrival as a major American writer, an identity which, it seemed, required both a new style and a new persona. 'I started as a generous but very spoiled boy, and I seem to have turned into a slightly punch-drunk and ugly club fighter who can fight clean and fight dirty, but liked to fight.'[304] If fighting (clean and dirty) was part of that style (the making of an American), so too, it seemed, was an obsession with celebrity culture and one's own place in it. Even while working on his fourth novel, *An American Dream*, Mailer was shifting toward an 'enormously personalized journalism' which would explore the 'dream life of the nation' as embodied in the iconic figures of John F. Kennedy, Marilyn Monroe and Muhammad Ali.[305] Kennedy was first. Mailer believed that 'Superman Comes to the Supermarket', which presented Kennedy as a Brando-like 'personality', was the 'act of propaganda' that won him the election. JFK was not a boxer, but, exploiting the fact that the convention was held in a sports arena, Mailer described him and his brother Bobby as fighters, 'hungry' to take on totalitarianism at home and abroad. More generally, the essay established the method that Mailer would use in his subsequent pieces on Griffith and Paret, Liston and Patterson, Ali and Frazier – a method that is said to have kick-started the decade's revival of the long, digressive essay.[306]

The sixties and seventies are often thought of as a 'kind of golden age in magazine writing'.[307] Despite Liebling's fears, television had not destroyed idiosyncratic sports reporting; instead it whetted the public's appetite for stories about 'the public figures whom they had just seen flash on the screen'. Reporters who, in another era, had worked on a piece for a day or two, now spent up to two months honing them for up-market men's magazines such as *Esquire* or *Playboy*. And by writing journalism that 'read like a novel', Tom Wolfe argued, the New Journalism 'would wipe out the novel' and become 'literature's main event'.[308]

Mailer's first 'existential' boxing essay was 'Ten Thousand Words a Minute', ostensibily about the Liston vs. Patterson fight, but also covering Griffith vs. Paret, Mailer's own 'club fight' with William Buckley, and his ongoing 'quarrel' with James Baldwin. All of these feed into a Lawrentian meditation on the anti-Establishment 'religion of blood'. Mailer clearly wanted the essay to be regarded as much more than a sports report, and he devotes quite a lot of space to dismissing the traditional sportswriter as someone who endlessly rehashes tired statistics for stories that come out 'like oats in a conveyor belt'. The fight reporter is also compared to a tailor taking measurements, a welfare officer offering 'facts', or, the ultimate insult, 'an old prizefight manager, which is to say, . . . an old cigar butt.' If traditional hurried journalism is mere 'chores', then the new, 'enormously personalized' and carefully crafted, journalism (Mailer announced that he'd spent seven weeks on the article) is a creative art more worthy of a boxer than a fight manager.[309]

For all that Patterson and Liston might represent on Mailer's political and 'psychic seismograph' – Art vs. Magic; Love vs. Sex; God vs. the Devil – the two men are described in very similar and conventionally stereotypical terms. Patterson, when bad, is the 'dreamy Negro kid who never knew the answer in class'; when good, 'a jungle cat', jumping from his tree to 'swipe at a gorilla swinging by on a vine'. Liston too is both an animal and a child – his eyes remind Mailer of both a 'halfway reptile and sleepy leopard' and 'beautiful colored children, three or four years old'. The essay ends in a comic scene in which the drunken Mailer (having defeated Buckley and 'buried' his quarrel with Baldwin) offers to arrange a Patterson-Liston rematch. '"Listen," said I, leaning my head closer, speaking from the corner of my mouth, as if I were whispering in a clinch.'

> Out of Liston's eyes stared back the profound intelligence of a profound animal. Now we understood each other, now we could work as a team. 'Say,' said Liston, 'that last drink really set you up. Why don't you go and get me a drink, you bum.'
>
> 'I'm not your flunky,' I said.
>
> It was the first jab I'd slipped, it was the first punch I'd sent home. He loved me for it. The hint of a chuckle of corny old darky laughter, cottonfield giggles peeped out a moment from his throat. 'Oh sheet, man!' said the wit in his eyes. And for the crowd who was watching, he turned and announced at large, 'I like this guy'.

A knowing exchange of insults allows Mailer to stop being an analytic, metaphor-driven liberal and become the kind of person (a hipster, a White Negro, a real American, a real man) whom Liston, the epitome of all these things, understands and likes. The moment soon passes, but Mailer can leave the conference feeling 'not too unclean'.

It would be 1971 before Mailer wrote another essay on boxing. 'Ego' (later collected as 'King of the Hill'), an account of the first Ali–Frazier fight, is a much more tightly focused on its subject than its predecessor. Much more than either Liston or Patterson, Ali was the epitome of the existential hero, a man whose life was a work of art and who embodied 'the very spirit of the twentieth century.' Mailer is concerned with exploring the self-contained dialectical struggle at the heart of 'America's Greatest Ego': the fact that 'the mightiest victim of injustice in America' was also 'the mightiest narcissist in the land' proved that 'the twentieth century was nothing if not a tangle of opposition'.[310]

The essay is also, again, partly about writing, and in particular about style. Boxing is imagined as a kind of writing, a 'dialogue between bodies'. The white style is simple, clumsy and masculine; 'close to rock' and with 'guts'. The black style is 'complex', 'tricky' and feminine. Since all the 'dialogues between bodies' that Mailer describes take place between two black boxers, his dialectic requires him to suggest that, on each occasion, one black boxer has a 'white style'. Joe Frazier, as 'the greatest brawler of them all', thus becomes 'the white man's fighter' while Ali, 'the greatest artist of pugilism' with 'the exquisite reflexes of Nureyev', is feminized. Mailer tries to emulate the 'conversational exchange' between these two bodily styles in the body of his essay. For the heavy relentless boxing style of Frazier, he uses long steady sentences (sentences that tire you to read aloud), punctuated with bursts of onomatopoeia:

> Frazier went on with the doggedness, the concentration, the pumped-up fury of a man who has so little in his life that he can endure torments to get everything, he pushed the total of his energy and force into an absolute exercise of will so it did nor matter if he fought a sparring partner or the heavy bag, he lunged at each equally as if the exhaustions of his own heart and the clangor of his lungs were his only enemies, and the head of the fighter or the leather of the bag as it rolled against his own head was nothing but some abstract thunk of material, not a thing, not a man, but thunk! thunk! something of an obstacle, thunk! thunk! thunk! to beat into thunk! oblivion.

The speed and variety of Ali's punches, on the other hand, are translated into a prose of short rhythmic units, of constantly changing similes and metaphors:

> he played with punches, was tender with them, laid them on as delicately as you would put a postage stamp on an envelope, then cracked them in a riding crop across your face, stuck a cruel jab like a baseball bat held head on into your mouth, next waltzed you into a clinch with a tender arm around your neck, winged out of reach on flying legs, dug a hook with a full swing of a baseball bat hard into your ribs, hard pokes of a jab into the face, a mocking flurry of pillows and gloves, a mean forearm cutting you off from coming up to him, a cruel wrestling of your neck in a clinch, then elusive again, gloves snake-licking your face like a whip.

For Mailer, the triumph of the fight's end is that Ali has somehow managed to combine both white masculine endurance (he could stand) and black feminine grace (he could dance).[311]

*The Fight*, Mailer's final meditation on the 'vortex' of heavyweight boxing, borrows more than its title from Hazlitt.[312] Like Mailer, Hazlitt found the opposition of boxing a useful metaphor for discussing a wide variety of subjects, but especially style. The boxing match detailed in 'The Fight' is presented as a clash between an English style of solid empiricism and a rapid, skilful French style (although both fighters are English). In the various battles I have described here Mailer reworks these stylistic oppositions – he just gives them different names. Hazlitt's solid English style becomes 'white' style (even when employed by black fighters), while the artful French style becomes the hipster style of both 'real' blacks and 'white Negroes'.

Hazlitt once wrote of prose style that 'every word should be a blow: every thought should instantly grapple with its fellow'. In *The Fight* stylistic variation is expressed almost wholly through an ever-shifting repertoire of metaphors and similes, presented here as the equivalent of punches.[313] This is a risky strategy, for much of the time, when describing the training process or early rounds, Mailer mimics the fighters' boredom and lack of imagination by restricting his imagery to the most banal and predictable formulations: Foreman is a 'sleepy lion', an 'ox', a 'child'; working on the heavy bag, he's like a 'sledgehammer hitting a tree' or 'steamhammer driving a channel of steel into clay'. Ali is no more interesting: on the speedbag, he's like a 'potter working his wheel'; after running, he's an 'overheated animal'.[314] Like the boxers, Mailer is reserving his best work for the main event.

The fight itself is presented in three chapters, comparable, Mailer says, to the three acts of a play, another metaphor that he borrows from Hazlitt. During the first two rounds (Chapter Thirteen), the metaphors remain fairly dull. The boxers are again likened to animals (bulls, pumas and tigers) and their punches compared to gun shots. Occasionally, something more interesting occurs – Foreman's head, for example, is described as a rivet under a riveting gun – but Mailer acknowledges that two rounds have felt like eight because he has been 'trying to watch' (that is, write) with the 'fighters' sense of time'.[315] During Chapter Fourteen (rounds three to five), Foreman's effort increases and Mailer ups his figurative game to match – Foreman boxes 'like a bricklayer running up a ladder', his legs are 'like wheels with a piece chipped out of the rim'.[316] Ali holds back but occasionally he (and therefore Mailer) unleashes something unexpected – a punch from the ropes is 'like a housewife sticking a toothpick in a cake to see if it is ready'. The chapter's title 'The Man in the Rigging' refers to Ali's rope-a-dope, but also to Melville's *Moby-Dick* (a novel he'd mentioned earlier in the essay). If Foreman is the whale, and Ali is Ahab, then, Michael Cowen suggests, Mailer becomes Ishmael, the observer who has 'climbed the mast into a squall of magical forces'.[317] In the final three rounds of the fight (the final act, the final chapter), Foreman continues to fight in the same fashion and so Mailer continues to describe him in the routine language of artillery fire and bulls. Ali, however, surprises with a range of unexpected shots, the consequences of which Mailer expresses in elaborate metaphors. As Foreman struggles to cope with Ali's punches his legs begin to 'prance like a horse high-stepping along a road full of rocks'; when Ali finally hits the decisive blow, he falls to the floor, 'like a six-foot sixty-year-old butler who has just heard tragic news'.[318]

Hazlitt's 'The Fight' began with the narrator-protagonist keen to escape the sentimental complications of daily life. Mailer is similarly keen for diversion, but, in his case, the disappointing love affair is not with a woman but with himself. His thoughts have been 'mediocre' and repetitive, 'like everyone else's'. At 51, he is feeling old. Moreover, his 'love affair with the Black soul, a sentimental orgy at its worst' had not held up under several 'seasons of Black Power'. All of these feelings are expressed in the language of indigestion and constipation.[319] Hazlitt travelled companionably to the heart of the country, discussing Cobbett and Rousseau en route; Mailer flies Pan Am to Conrad's 'Heart of Darkness' in Vachel Lindsay's 'Congo', and on the return journey, plays dice with the air stewardess.[320] Both men experience a 'restoration of being' through journeys to watch boxing. But while Hazlitt ends by acknowledging the ephemeral achievement of both the boxing match and his essay, Mailer wants more, nothing less in fact than the restoration of the title 'champ among writers'.[321] The book plays with various versions of magical thinking, but all are designed to the same end – 'the powers of regeneration in an artist'. Ali works magic on Mailer by showing him that regeneration is possible; set against his example is that of Hemingway, whose suicide fourteen years earlier haunts the book.[322]

Mailer wrote many pieces on Hemingway, who remained for him the representative American, the model for hard-won manliness as well as (not coincidentally) authorial stardom.[323] On Mailer's reading, Hemingway's notion of writers competing for an elusive championship belt seems not so much an act of macho posturing as one of psychic compensation. Mailer adopted and developed this metaphor at some length, with additional pathos. For while 'Punching Papa' faced the likes of Fitzgerald, Dos Passos, Steinbeck, Farrell and Faulkner, the second half of the twentieth century had not, Mailer thought, provided opposition of similar quality. In the age of Malamud, Pynchon, Bellow, Cheever, Updike and Vidal, he felt it was no great claim for him to say, 'I'm going to be the champ until one of you knocks me off'.[324] If Hemingway was comparable with Ali, Mailer declared himself merely the 'Ezzard Charles of the heavyweight division'.[325]

Leaving Hemingway behind (if not actually beating him), Mailer rejects the modernist credo of technique (which he dismisses as mere 'craft', 'a grab bag of procedures, tricks, lore, formal gymnastics, symbolic superstructures, methodology in short' – the kind of thing he elsewhere identified with light and middleweight fighters) in favour of an 'existentially' informed prose (the writer, like the heavyweight, aware that he is 'the big toe of God').[326] While the great writers of the twenties worried about lean prose style, the 'great writer' of the sixties was more concerned with keeping his 'consciousness in shape' and not letting it get 'flabby'.[327]

For all Mailer's talk of style, he is ultimately less interested in boxing as a way of explaining the processes of writing than in the fight as a metaphor for the public life of the writer. Byron had dismissed 'quarrels of authors' as an inferior form of sparring, mere evidence of 'an irritable set'.[328] Mailer, however, believed that regular spats with other male writers was an essential part of 'keeping in shape'. Asked by an interviewer whether he let anyone see his work in progress, Mailer replied, 'I do it the way I box: I pick my sparring partners carefully. Usually I'll box with people who are so good that I'm in no danger of getting hurt because they consider it obscene to damage me. Or I'll box with friends where we understand each other and are trying to bring out the best in each other as boxers. The same thing with an early stage of a manuscript.'[329] Once a book was published, however, the gloves came off and the real competitive business of being a writer began: at parties, during marches and (a sign of the times) on television.[330]

Sparring on television, it seemed, made a proper celebrity fighter, even if the show in question was *Saturday Night* with David Frost rather than the Gillette Sport Cavalcade – for 'maybe', Mailer wrote, 'he had never been as aware before of all America out there . . . a million homes tuning [in].'[331] And if Frost is imagined as Henry Cooper – 'David had come at him like a British heavyweight mauler, no great skill, but plenty of shove' – then it seems to follow that Mailer is the Ali of on-the-couch guests.[332] (And like Ali, Mailer is pleased to note how 'telegenic' he is – 'he appeared even better on TV, he thought, than in the mirror'.[333]) The chat show provided the ideal forum for literary quarrels which Mailer easily and repeatedly refigured as boxing matches. After an appearance with Nelson Algren, he concludes that 'two middleweight artists had fought a draw'.[334] His much-publicized quarrel with Gore Vidal on *The Dick Cavett Show* in 1971 was a less satisfactory affair. Sharing the couch with the two men was Janet Flanner (whom Mailer accused of being 'Mr Vidal's manager' instead of the 'referee'); at the end of the Show, Cavett asked the audience to 'let us know who you think won'.[335]

The most interesting of Mailer's 'quarrels with authors' was that with James Baldwin (illus. 119). The two men became friends in 1956, and, Morris Dickstein argues, the 'precedent' of Baldwin's long, digressive essays, which interwove autobiographical, philosophical and political meditations, made 'Mailer's own breakthrough thinkable'. For Dickstein, *Advertisements* would not have been possible without the example of Baldwin's 1955 *Notes of a Native Son*, while *The Armies of the Night* was 'quite deliberately' Mailer's version of *The Fire Next Time*.[336] Not that Mailer acknowledged these debts. Instead he dismissed Baldwin as 'too charming a writer to be major' and his writing as 'noble toilet water'.[337] In 1961 Baldwin responded to this undisguised homophobia (and to 'The White Negro') by publishing an essay, 'The Black Boy Looks at the White Boy', which parodies both Mailer's 'boxer mannerisms' and his conflation of boxing (and, by inference, black men) with sex.[338] What, in other words, we are invited to ask, does Mailer mean when he says he wants to 'slug' his friend?[339] Baldwin designates the essay a 'love letter' and describes Mailer as both 'charming' and, in the way he jabs his 'short, prodding forefinger', faintly ridiculous. Their 'circling around each other' expresses a fear that 'the other would pull rank', but also the fact that they 'liked' but could not understand one another.[340]

The following year, both men were commissioned by men's magazines to cover the Patterson-Liston fight and both ended up writing essays that are partly about their own quarrel. Mailer openly notes that the empty ringside seat between Baldwin and himself reflected the 'chill' that had come between them – 'Not a feud, but bad feeling'. But all is resolved when Patterson is knocked down – 'in the bout's sudden wake', he is pleased to acknowledge, they 'buried' their quarrel. Mailer is, however, unable to let things be. When Baldwin asks after his sister, he replies, 'why didn't he consider marrying her, quick as that, which put me one up on old Jim again, and we shook our writer's hands'.[341] Baldwin is less direct, merely mentioning that his 'weird and violent' depression was due to having had 'a pretty definitive fight with someone with whom I had hoped to be friends'. His personal depression is, he suggests, linked to a depression about the subject matter which he found himself writing about. Boxing had very different connotations for Baldwin than it did for Mailer (and this was something that his friend did not seem able to appreciate). In 'My Dungeon Shook', Baldwin wrote of the need of 'every Negro boy' to find 'a "thing", a gimmick, to lift him out, to start him on his way'. Before he became a writer Baldwin chose the church, but he explained that that was partly because he saw few other options in the Harlem of his youth. 'I could not become a prizefighter,' he wrote; 'many of us tried but very few succeeded. I could not sing. I could not dance. I had been well conditioned by the world in which I grew up, so I did not yet dare take the idea of becoming a writer seriously'.[342] Elsewhere he cited the fact that his 'first hero was Joe Louis' as evidence of the way in which the 'Negro children of [his] generation' had been limited and 'controlled by white America's image' of them.[343]

'There aren't many ways to describe a fighter in training,' Baldwin begins his account of Patterson vs. Liston, 'it's the same thing over and over'. But what's worse for him than banality is the recognition that boxing is simply another version of white boys looking at black boys and seeing 'only the Negro they wished to see'.[344]

> It doesn't appear to have occurred yet to many members of the press that one of the reasons their relations with Floyd [Patterson] are so frequently strained is that he has no reason, on any level, to trust them, and no reason to believe that they would be capable of hearing what he had to say, even if he could say it.

If Baldwin admires Patterson as 'the least likely fighter in the history of the sport', then, as Early notes, Baldwin was the 'least likely' person to write about it.[345] This identification may have been in Baldwin's mind ten years later when, recalling his success with *The Fire Next Time*, he noted, 'I was, in some way, in those years, without entirely realizing it, the Great Black Hope of the Great White Father.'[346]

## GREAT WHITE HOPES AND HYPES

In the midst of the 'Ali-mania' of the late seventies, it was perhaps not surprising that stories about white boxers flourished. Consolatory tales of Anglo-Saxon triumph had first become popular in 1909, after Jack Johnson assumed the mantle of heavyweight symbolism. Apart from an interlude of Dempsey-mania in the twenties, it became increasingly difficult to imagine white boxing in terms of triumph. For the rest of the century, the only thing that white boxers symbolized was stubborn endurance, a belief that survival is more admirable than victory.

In Chapter Four, I outlined a model of the naturalist story as one of a rapid rise to a biological peak, followed by a long decline into age and exhaustion. Most of life, on this model, is the story of decline. What Philip Fisher terms the 'chronicle of subtraction' was, I suggested, particularly appropriate for stories about the short careers of boxers.[347] For example, Leonard Gardner's ironically titled 1969 novel *Fat City* (filmed by John Huston in 1972) presents the decline of 29-year-old Billy Tully alongside the rise (in a minor way) of eighteen-year-old Ernie Munger. By the story's end, it is clear that Ernie's life is assuming the same shape as Billy's. In *On the Waterfront*, Terry Malloy famously complains to his brother that he was unable to reach his 'peak' 'that night at the Garden', the one night when he 'coulda been a contender'. But even Terry never doubts that he was always going to go 'downhill' after that. For a boxer, victory is always temporary. 'Only . . . defeat is permanent'.[348]

If *Raging Bull* (1980) were ever remade to follow the lines of a conventional naturalist plot, Jake La Motta's peak would be identified as the night he defeated Marcel Cerdan to become middleweight champion. This is certainly how La Motta himself describes it in his autobiography: 'There can't be a high any higher than being a world's champion,' he notes, before adding 'and – though I didn't recognize it then – I was on my way to my lowest low.'[349] Scorsese's film pays very little attention to the highest high (and indeed has La Motta complain about his small hands and how he'll never be able to fight Joe Louis, 'the best there is').[350] The championship fight is over in minutes and the next scene jumps ahead a year to present an overweight La Motta at home, eating a hero sandwich as he tries to get the TV to work. No longer a compelling bodily spectacle on the screen but mere spectating body – the film suggests that it is inevitable to be one or the other – his distended stomach blocks the picture. All that is left of the hero is the sandwich. The closest the film comes to providing a 'peak' is the fight in which La Motta loses his title to Sugar Ray Robinson. That peak is achieved through the fetish of La Motta's blood, a kind of holy water. We see him sponged down with blood-infused water and receive a punch that splatters the ringside spectators in slow-motion sweat and blood. This is both a familiar indictment of the atavistic crowd (including, of course, the cinema audience) and a debased holy blessing. The fight was stopped in the thirteenth round, with La Motta still on his feet and declaiming, 'I never went down. You never got me down.' 'If this scene cannot be interpreted as an instance of erectile pride,' quips Allen Guttmann, 'then Dr. Freud labored in vain.'[351] Robinson (Johnny Barnes) incidentally has no lines in the scene or indeed the whole film. He is simply there so that Jake can stand up to him.

The naturalist chronicle of subtraction becomes, in La Motta's case, a chronicle of addition, as he (or rather DeNiro in the apotheosis of method acting) puts on 55 pounds.[352] This is hardly surprising since, as Steven Kellman notes, more of the movie is set in kitchens and restaurants than in the ring.[353] From the start, we see both versions of La Motta: in his prime – the Bronx Bull entering the ring in a leopard-skin robe and complaining about an overcooked steak and threatening to eat his neighbour's dog; and in his decline – a 'fat pig' performing in a nightclub, a 'fucking gorilla' bothering teenage girls. When he smashes his head against the prison wall, and yells 'I'm *not* an animal', we don't believe him. While *Fat City*, *Rocky* and even Jack London's 'A Piece of Steak' qualify their meaty mysticism with accounts of the economic or psychological factors that lead men to plot their lives in bodily terms, *Raging Bull* serves it raw.[354] 'Jake is an elemental man,' said Scorsese.[355]

If the story told by *Raging Bull* proper is unrelenting, the film's narrative frame suggests a way out. The final title (on a black screen) is a biblical quotation from John, 9: 24–26, which ends, 'All I know is this: once I was blind and now I can see.' Connecting Jake as a 'sinner' to Jesus Christ, this instructs us to reinterpret what we have just seen as a story of 'redemption through physical pain, like the Stations of the Cross, one torment after another'.[356] But if the bloody fight with Robinson becomes a version of the crucifixion, it is hard to locate a risen or redeemed La Motta – unless we think redemption can be signified simply by an awkward hug with his brother and a rote recitation of 'I coulda been a contender' in the debased setting of the nightclub, a church whose creed is simply 'that's entertainment'.[357] Indeed that scene ironically recalls the film's opening sequence during which (in between segments of the opening credits) La Motta is seen shadowboxing languidly to the strains of the intermezzo from *Cavalleria rusticana*.[358] The camera stays outside the ring and observes the distant and solitary boxer through three thick ropes. This is a transcendent world, a dream world without messy relationships, a world in which the boxer in his monk-like robe can be truly an artist; no longer an entertaining, bloody bull but, finally, a dancer like Sugar Ray or Ali. But lyricism and Christianity can only exist outside of the film's narrative. Within the story, we remain fully immersed in the secular, Darwinian world of La Motta's pointless pain. There is no progression from body to soul.

Clearly attracted to the naturalism of mid-century boxing films, Scorsese did not simply want to copy it. Rather, *Raging Bull* both emulates and strives to disrupt the style of the many films that it quotes and borrows from: *The Set-Up* (a bloody gum-shield dropping to the canvas); *The Harder They Fall* (sweat knocked off a boxer's face); *The Quiet Man* (the pop of flashbulbs accompanying the memory of a fatal bout); *The Day of the Fight* (a through-the-boxer's-legs camera angle).[359] Scorsese was determined that each fight scene should have a 'different aura', and to that end endlessly varied the camera angle, movement and speed (sometimes, cinematographer Michael Chapman noted, he shifted from 24 frames per second to 48 frames per second to 96 frames per second and back to 24 within a single shot.)[360] Against these rapid temporal shifts, the choreographic rhythm of the fights is created by a soundtrack of photographers' exploding flash bulbs and powerfully amplified punches which not only acts like 'scoring music' to what we see, but makes it even more surreal and abstract.[361] *Raging Bull*'s stylized and operatic naturalism signals its auteur's mastery and transcendence of the B-movies he quotes.[362] 'To call it a boxing picture is ridiculous,' Scorsese said.[363]

The most emphatic stylization comes through the film's photography, designed to make it look 'like a tabloid' from the forties or fifties.[364] This was the heyday of stroboscopic photography – a method of freezing action at 1/3,000th to 1/30,000th of a second through the explosive illumination of stroboscopic speed lighting. Weegee made the technique famous, but it was also used to startling effect by Charles Hoff in his sports pictures for the New York *Daily News*. Hoff's pictures document the exact and decisive moment in which a blow is landed, and as such were often used as evidence in controversial cases. They also record the precise, if momentary, distortions to the face of the punch's recipient, creating a realism of a particular grotesque and abstract kind – one that says this particular 1/30,000th of a second is the moment that counts. Such concentration on the instant runs counter to the naturalist narrative which characteristically describes gradual decline by means of an accumulation of increasingly sordid detail. It is also a 'reality' that is heightened and stylized by stark flash lighting effects. Announced as signifying an adherence to a particular kind of gritty truth, this kind of black and white photography (as used by Hoff in the *Daily News* and Chapman in *Raging Bull*) inevitably aestheticizes and mythologizes – reducing the murky palette of life to images of clear-cut tabloid contrast.

Sylvester Stallone first got the idea for *Rocky* in 1975. He was unemployed and feeling sorry for himself when he saw a journeyman fighter called Chuck Wepner take on Muhammad Ali. 'I identified with Wepner,' Stallone later said, 'the guy is going to get hammered.' Wepner had been working in a series of menial jobs until Don King (in the guise of 'equal opportunity employer') transformed him into a lucrative white hope.[365] Against all expectations, Wepner managed to knock down Ali in the ninth round and stay standing to the end.[366] Stallone went home and hammered out the first draft of *Rocky* in three days. Originally, Rocky was retired, but Stallone was easily encouraged to make him still an active fighter. 'I thought, "Let me try to make this a redemptive thing." And I tried to work this Christ symbol, this religious overtone'.[367]

If *Raging Bull* presented the foundation of redemption in bloody defeat, *Rocky* suggests that it begins in reinvention-through-hard-work, a Protestant American myth epitomized by Horatio Alger's *Ragged Dick* (1868). Early in the book, Alger makes plain how indebted he is to fairy tales of transformation such as Dick Whittington or Cinderella. When Dick is given a new set of clothes by his benefactor, he looks in the mirror and exclaims, '"that isn't me, is it? . . . It reminds me of Cinderella, when she was changed into a fairy princess."'[368] Reinvention starts by changing one's appearance by changing one's clothes. Cinderella needed a new dress before she could leave the kitchen and go to the ball. Dressed in his new suit, Dick can move in very different circles than he had in his rags. For the boxer, however, physical transformation must take place at a more fundamental level – that of the body itself. Filmed in blockbuster 'bright colours, strong reds and blues' (complained Scorsese), *Rocky* is a pure example of such a fairy tale.[369]

Walking the streets of South Philadelphia in a vaguely comical hat, Rocky Balboa (Sylvester Stallone) is 'just another bum from the neighbourhood', but unlike all the others, he is given the fairy-tale chance of fighting the World Heavyweight Champion, Apollo Creed (played by Carl Weathers in a thinly disguised caricature of Muhammad Ali).[370] Most of the film focuses on the training process, on Rocky's willing effort to transform his body and his life. This is not confined to the gym, and we see him pounding meat in the local abattoir, and running through the neighbourhood, the local Italian community literally behind him (illus. 120).[371] Presumably Apollo Creed has the backing of the black community, but we never see any local popular support for him – he is presented simply as the product of corporate (i.e. false and ugly) America.

Apollo Creed's great crime, the film suggests, is assuming that *he* represents America – he enters the title fight dressed as Uncle Sam and on his float adopts the garb and pose of George Washington crossing the Delaware. But he is an illegitimate Uncle Sam, not only because he is black, but because, without any suggestion of a political or religious affiliation, he is made to represent both greedy capitalism and the savvy and articulate (for which we are encouraged to read glib) values of the counterculture.[372] Rocky – an inarticulate boy from 'the neighbourhood' – is really what 'the land of opportunity' wants to be all about. He is both white ethnic – the 'Italian Stallion' – and American: indeed, while Creed's race excludes him from 'true' Americanness, Rocky is uniquely qualified by his ethnicity (Italian, 'not *that* white').[373] His very name aligns him to the great Italian-American champions of the fifties – Graziano and, the 'last great white heavyweight', Marciano (whose picture hangs on his wall).[374] 'You know you kinda remind me of the Rock?' Rocky's trainer, Mickey (Burgess Meredith) says at one point. 'You move like him and you have heart like he did.'

Fantasies of the Rock's return had begun in the late sixties, when Murray Woroner, a Miami boxing promoter and radio producer, fed details of Ali's and Marciano's records into a computer and asked it to predict a winner. The computer decided that Marciano (equipped with 'a boxing style edited down to its bare essentials') would knock out the stylish Ali in the thirteenth round. Woroner then persuaded the two men to enact the 'superfight' on film.[375]

By 1976, however, Ali had regained his title and so all that could be asked of Rocky is that he regain his pride (and that of the country) by 'going the distance'.[376] A self-conscious bicentennial fantasy, *Rocky* is set in the city of the Founding Fathers, Philadelphia, but for all the shots of the museum steps, the film's nostalgia is for a national spirit based on local values. As in the boxing films of the 1930s and forties, those values are embodied in the fighter's neighbourhood girlfriend. Unconcerned that he has not won, Rocky's only impulse at the end of the fight is to call out 'Adrian'.

If *Raging Bull* and *Rocky* were fantasies of white indestructibility (and grievance) in the face of superior black talent, Neal Adams and Dennis O'Neil's *Superman vs. Muhammad Ali* (DC Comics, 1978) offered a different kind of consolation.[377] Ostensibly a tale of 'the fight to save earth from star-warriors', it is really a black-and-white 'buddy' story in the tradition of James Fenimore Cooper's classic American frontier novel, *The Last of the Mohicans* (1826).[378] Just as Natty Bumppo must go to the woods and learn the soon-to-be-lost Indian ways (from Chingachgook) before he can take on the alien French, so Superman must absorb Ali's 'native skills' before he can defeat the alien 'Scrubb'. The story begins with Clark Kent, Lois Lane and Jimmy Olsen walking through an 'inner-city ghetto' in 'downtown Metropolis' – they are, we are told, 'as out of place as they look'. They no longer seem to be employed by the *Daily Planet* but a TV network and they are looking to record an interview with Ali. Eventually they find him shooting hoops and 'moving among the neighbourhood youth with casual ease'.[379] The unlikeliness of Ali being there is ignored; this is, we are supposed to believe, his 'natural' setting. Suddenly the playground is invaded by an alien messenger. The Scrubb nation threatens to take over the earth if its laboratory-created abysmal brute, Hun'Ya, can defeat the greatest champion of the earth. Ali and Superman both offer their services, and they agree to hold a fight to decide who should take on Hun'Ya. It is this fight that is featured on the cover – and in many ways, the alien invasion is simply an excuse to stage it (illus. 121). Before they can compete, Ali agrees to train Superman (who has his superhuman powers deactivated for the occasion). A page is devoted to a demonstration of Ali's best punches and Superman finally concedes that 'I never realized that there is so much to ringmanship. It's more than adding fist to face.' The big fight attracts a huge crowd – 'intelligent beings from a thousand worlds' undertake 'the most massive migration in the history of the universe' to be there – while millions more, 'in the far corners of the universe', watch courtesy of the 'interstellar television network', with Olsen providing the commentary. It soon becomes apparent that, like Rocky in the sequels, Superman 'has copied Ali's fighting style to a "T"!' – they are like 'mirror images of each other', Olsen says. 'How strange it must be for Ali be fighting . . . to well . . . himself!!'[380] Natty Bumppo has learnt his lesson well.

Ali, however, is still the greatest fighter and in the later rounds, Superman gets badly beaten.[381] Like Rocky (and Jake La Motta), he won't 'fall down'; since the alien referee refuses to intervene, Ali finally refuses to continue. The story then moves on to Ali's fight against Hun'Ya, whose Foreman-like strength forces Ali to reprieve the 'rope-a-dope' (the fight also recalls the mythic battle of Amycus and Polydeuces). Ali seems to be weakening when the alien Emperor Rat'Lar comes to his corner and offers him a deal – 'if your governments agree to deed the peoples of earth to us as our slaves, we will spare them!'. The word 'slave' is enough to ignite Ali and he finally knocks Hun'Ya out of the ring (in a pastiche of Bellows's *Dempsey and Firpo*). The 'universe goes wild', but Rat'Lar won't accept the victory. All seems to be lost.

At this point Superman comes back into the story. The defeat and injuries he sustained in the Ali fight were, it turns out, part of a cunning plan. Disguised as Ali's black trainer, Bundini Brown, Superman is free to roam the universe. 'The man of steel' dispatches the alien armada, and the comic's final double-page frame shows him shaking hands with Ali, who acknowledges that 'We are the Greatest!'[382]

Superman's liberal credentials can be traced to his creation in 1938. The invention of two Jewish artists, Jerry Siegel and Joe Shuster, Superman, it has been suggested, is perhaps Jewish too.[383] He's certainly a foreigner, an alien from Krypton, an immigrant who has to be taught 'truth, justice and the American way' by the rural Yankee Kent family. Passing successfully (if anxiously) as the chisel-featured WASP, Clark Kent, he fought rapacious capitalists and Nazis throughout the thirties and forties.[384] It is, perhaps, not surprising therefore to find him making the familiar liberal move of putting on blackface in order to save the earth. *Superman vs. Muhammad Ali* is nothing if not liberal. The fight attracts the crème of multicultural American celebrities (172 are depicted on the cover, accompanied by a who's who), and television viewers who are not just multicultural but multi-planetary. The TV commentator tells them that 'on earth, we don't show our intentions by fighting with our neighbours, but by showing what good friends we can be!'[385] He also explains that Superman is wearing his cape because otherwise 'many of our alien spectators wouldn't be able to tell the fighters apart! Except for subtle changes in hue, all humans look exactly alike to them.'[386] Intended as a dig at racist stereotyping, this remark nevertheless encourages us to think about the ways in which the story, like *The Last of the Mohicans*, distinguishes between its heroes. Ali's greatness lies in his perfection of a human skill (fighting) very much associated with the past. Superman needs to learn this skill and use it, much as Natty Bumppo had to learn the tactics of survival in the wild. But when things come to the crunch, when he needs to defeat Magua, Natty Bumppo rises above the level of the Indians he had thus-far been emulating. Reaching for his rifle, he tells Chingachgook, 'I leave the tomahawk and knife to such as have a natural gift to use them.'[387] In the limited confines of the ring, Superman may have had to learn from Ali, but fists are finally not enough for the battles of space and time. Those require both superhuman powers and a superior human intelligence ('Got to think!! Got to think!!' reads one frame). As his ability to manipulate sophisticated technology reveals, Superman, not Ali, is 'the man of tomorrow'. Here at least, there is no 'Black Superman'.[388]

# Conclusion

No one would call the last decades of the twentieth century a golden age of boxing. There have been some great fighters – Sugar Ray Leonard, Roberto Durán, Thomas Hearns, Marvin Hagler, Julio Cesar Chávez, Oscar De La Hoya and Roy Jones Jr stand out – but the general feeling is that the sport is in decline.[1] This is particularly true of the heavyweight division.[2] Who today can name the heavyweight champion of the world? And if so, which one? Twenty years ago things seemed different.

At first the story of Mike Tyson promised to be one of Hollywood simplicity – a fourteen-year old black boy with a Brooklyn 'Dickensian childhood' is taken in hand, and to the country, by a kindly old white man (Cus D'Amato, already famous for making champions of Floyd Patterson and José Torres); the old man experiences a new lease of life before sadly dying, and, eighteen months after turning professional, the bad boy becomes the youngest-ever heavyweight champion of the world (illus. 149).[3] Boxing fans assured each other that the post-Ali slump was over. 'A terrible beauty is born', declared Joyce Carol Oates.[4]

Tyson's early record was impressive: winning eleven first-round knockouts in fifteen fights in 1985; straight wins and the WBC title in 1986; and ten months later, unifying the various strands of the heavyweight championship.[5] Tyson hit his peak the following year when he knocked out the previously undefeated Michael Spinks in the first round of his title defence. Soon afterwards, however, 'it all started to go wrong'; the story switched genres.[6] In 1990, Tyson lost his title to the little-regarded Buster Douglas; two years later, he was convicted of the rape of a beauty queen and served three years in prison.[7] Even before the trial, Robert Lipsyte predicted that Tyson would become a 'symbolic character in various morality plays, a villain-victim of the Gender War, the Race War, the Class War, and the Backlash Against Celebrity Excess'.[8] Some spoke of Tyson's 'tragedy' and described his new manager Don King as the 'Iago' who had fuelled the paranoia of an insecure Othello.[9] Others compared Tyson to Richard Wright's Bigger Thomas, doomed from the start.[10]

But Tyson's story was not over. On emerging from jail, his knockout style and 'dependably shocking' behaviour made him once again a huge box-office draw.[11] After all, as Ellis Cashmore notes, 'the Tyson of the imagination [did]

not have to win rounds' or even fight decent opponents.[12] By the mid-nineties, boxing accounted for more than half of all pay-per-view programming, with Tyson again participating in the most successful single event – his November 1996 fight against the 'Christian Warrior', Evander Holyfield. Approximately 1.65 million households paid $49.95 each to watch and the fight grossed more than $80 million.[13] In their rematch the following year, Tyson bit off a piece of Holyfield's ear, to the delighted horror of the media.[14] Nevada revoked his licence for a year and fined him $3 million (actually only 10 per cent of his fee).[15] No longer heroic or tragic, Tyson was now seen as a character in a horror movie: an 'ogre', a 'prehistoric creature rising from a fearful crevice in our collective subconscious', or maybe just Hannibal Lecter.[16] As he acted out scenes from his favourite movies – ear-biting threats from *Raging Bull,* pigeon-fancying from *On the Waterfront* – he seemed to believe in the persona he had so carefully created.[17] After a series of losses and injuries, he announced his retirement from boxing in 2005. In October 2006 he began a world tour of exhibition fights.

In 1987, Joyce Carol Oates had predicted that Tyson would be 'the first heavyweight boxer in America to transcend issues of race'.[18] This did not prove to be true. Many of the gains of the Civil Rights movement were eroded during the eighties and, as Jesse Jackson observed, racism of various sorts became 'fashionable again'.[19] When Don King staged a 'coronation' for Tyson, *Time* magazine described the champion as a jewel-encrusted King Kong.[20] Much as it had in the 1910s, the dramatization of racial conflict meant money; only now it was a black promoter who dredged up white hopes. In 1982, King achieved great

149
Mike Tyson (2000).

success with a much-hyped but ultimately one-sided fight between Larry Holmes and Gerry Cooney, whom he marketed relentlessly as a white hope. A similar occasion was staged to celebrate Tyson's release from prison in 1995. His 89-second, ten-punch demolition of Peter McNeeley generated $63 million gross, and inspired the Hollywood satire, *The Great White Hype* (illus. 126).[21] The eighties also saw a substantial increase in the geographical and cultural gap between the black middle and working class. In inner-city ghettos, conditions sharply deteriorated and sociologists began to speak of a black urban 'underclass', immured in crime and drugs.[22] Tyson's emergence coincided then with what Cornel West described as a new nihilism in black America, a nihilism which led to a revival of sixties-style Black Nationalism.[23] From the start King used its rhetoric and imagery to promote his star. As Tyson became 'public enemy' and the hero of hip hop culture, the black middle class distanced itself from his image. Some complained that 'we all have to live him down every day; we can't exult in, say, Colin Powell without having to address Mike Tyson', while others argued that 'progress' could be measured in the fact that the boxer's behaviour was 'a disgrace – but only to himself.'[24]

None of this was likely to change the minds of the doctors who, since the early 1980s, had embarked on a sustained, international campaign to abolish both amateur and professional boxing. Prompted by a new spate of ring deaths and growing evidence of short- and long-term neurological damage, the medical profession spoke out, condemning the sport as 'a throwback to uncivilized man' and urging their colleagues not to participate in its management.[25] But it was not only uncivilized man who kept on boxing. Despite new evidence of boxing's dangers, increasing numbers of women took up the sport.[26] The breakthrough for professional women's boxing came in 1995 when Christy Martin fought Deirdre Gogarty on the undercard of the Tyson-Bruno match in Las Vegas. The main event was a desultory affair and sportswriters focused, with relief, on the competitive and exciting women's contest. Martin appeared to much acclaim on the cover of *Sports Illustrated*; inside, photographed with a vacuum cleaner, she said that she was 'not out to make a statement about women in boxing . . . This is about Christy Martin' (illus. 127)[27] Since 1996, a small number of professional women boxers have made a name for themselves. Some, like Lucia Rijker, came to boxing from the martial arts; others, like Laila Ali, Jacqui Frazier and Freeda Foreman, capitalized on their famous names and often fought each other. The language used to describe these celebrity fixtures was either humorously patronizing – Laila Ali was 'a manicurist on a mission' who 'stings like a butterfly' – or, more usually, spitting with moral outrage.[28] The *New York Post* described the $2-million fight between Ali and Jacqui Frazier as a 'perversion', while the London *Daily Mail* complained that the debut of 'fat girl' Freeda Foreman meant that boxing finally had reached the (long-anticipated) 'depths of depravity'.[29] When, in 1998, Jane Couch won her legal challenge against the British Board of Boxing Control's refusal to issue licences to women, the British Medical Association spoke of a 'demented extension of equal opportunities'.[30] Male sportswriters tended to agree. 'Would it have made any difference,' Harry Mullan asked, 'if more of the spectators were women? Perhaps. It is the edge of sexual voyeurism which heightens my discomfort'.[31]

Sexual voyeurism is probably the main reason why women's boxing has flourished as vigorously in Hollywood as anywhere else. Since Barbra Streisand played coach to Ryan O'Neal's contender in *The Main Event* (1979), there have been scores of films about women boxers, coaches, and managers.[32] They range in style from soft-porn to comedy – Romy and Michele prepare for their high school reunion, the equivalent of the big fight, by attending boxercise class.[33] Most, however, tout a feel-good feminist message and simply substitute a boy for a girl in a conventional plot. In *Blonde Fist* (1991) and *Knockout* (2003), girls fulfil their father's thwarted ambitions by winning a belt; in *Girlfight* (2000), *The Opponent* (2000) and *Honeybee* (2002), they dispense with their abusive boyfriends both in and out of the ring.[34] Singers such as Christina Aguilera and Pink regularly dress up as boxers to suggest that they're feisty and feminist and in control, an image that advertisers also use to sell a variety of products from deodorant with 'a different kind of strength' to vitamins with 'extra PUNCH'.

Several women amateur boxers have published memoirs which explore 'what happens when you transpose generic female motivations and confusions into the boxing ring'.[35] Kate Sekules, for example, reports that she had no problem fighting men, but had to work hard to overcome her reluctance to hit other women, while Leah Hager Cohen describes how boxing helped her to come to terms with anorexic and suicidal impulses and, finally, allowed her to fuse 'erotic and aggressive impulses' (à la Melanie Klein).[36] In 1999, Annie Leibovitz chose an image of a naked woman in boxing stance (with red gloves and a feminist text painted on her blacked-up body) to advertise an exhibition of photographs of American women at the millennium (illus. 128).

But just as women put the notion of the gym as a male sanctuary to rest, so men reasserted it in the familiar terms of Rooseveltian strenuousness.[37] Partly due to the popularity of Chuck Palahniuk's 1996 novel and David Fincher's 1999 film adaptation, *Fight Club*, white-collar boxing has flourished in recent years.[38] While the story presents the spread of bare-knuckle fight clubs as the first step to anarchism, the real life (and usually gloved) versions tended to advertise their socially stabilizing function.[39] 'We thought that if people had boxing matches,' one teenager was quoted as saying, 'they could get it out instead of killing people in schools, or whatever.'[40] Fincher's film was also evoked as a model when, in August 2000, an American promoter introduced 'executive sparring' into a British context. At an event organized in the heart of the City, London's financial district, a group of hedge-fund managers and IT specialists fought it out before an audience of 2,000.[41] Soon men too were writing memoirs of the psychologically therapeutic benefits of their experiences as 'modern-day Corinthians'.[42]

If then, in recent times, boxing has not entered a new golden age, neither has it shown any signs of disappearing. The same could be said of the boxing story. Alessandro Baricco's *City* (1996) is about a thirteen-year-old boy who invents a boxing story whose plot and characterization are borrowed from a hundred 'black-and-white movies'.[43] Asked why he wrote about boxing, Baricco replied that the sport had 'everything' a writer might want: 'it's all very well telling yourself that Jack London has already done it. Sooner or later you fall for it.'[44] Writers, film-makers and artists have continued to fall for it, and not always in the name of postmodern pastiche. Boxers crop up in sculptures and paintings, installations and performances, in books for toddlers and teenagers, and in films and novels of every genre, from romance to the detective story to fantasy.[45] Boxing metaphor is endemic, in fiction, poetry, art and journalism, and in commentary on almost every other sport.

In describing this material I have had to be highly selective. My aim is less to offer a comprehensive survey than to propose further lines of enquiry. Contemporary cultural uses of boxing, like those explored in previous chapters, fall into three broad, overlapping, categories: dialectical, iconographic, and naturalist. Artists and writers who use boxing *dialectically* are most interested in the sport as a metaphor for opposition: the performed fight between two people dramatizes an interaction between points of view or ideas. Those who use boxing *iconographically* are more interested in considering the symbolism of boxing's personnel and paraphernalia – that is, interpreting the meaning, and exploiting the aura, of the ring, gloves and mouthguards as well as individual boxers and fights. Finally, boxing lends itself to the *naturalist* desire to imagine formlessness, decline, damage and mortality. The naturalist boxer is not an icon but a piece of matter – his authenticity evident in his sweat, bruises and blood. In what follows, I will briefly discuss a range of examples of each of these methods.

## THE DIALECTICS OF BOXING

Many times boxing is evoked simply as an assertively masculine way of expressing competition or even collaboration. In 1988, for example, Andy Warhol and Jean-Michel Basquiat's joint exhibition was famously promoted by posters presenting the two artists as fighters engaged in interracial and intergenerational fisticuffs (illus. 150).[46] And when the subject of literary rivalry comes up, few resist the temptation to talk about championship bouts with Hemingway or Mailer. In Charles Bukowski's 'Class', the writer-narrator enters the ring with 'Ernie'. After boxing 'like Sugar Ray' and hitting 'like Dempsey', he knocks Papa out. 'Nobody wins them all,' he tells the older man, 'Don't blow your brains out.'[47] Max Apple's 1976 short story 'Inside Norman Mailer' imagines a bout between the young aspiring author and his mentor for the literary heavyweight title.[48] (Apple later said that the story contained 'one of the best lines I've ever written': 'I was describing all that prize-fighting stuff and then I said, "You've all seen it – imagine it yourself!" That was a wonderful shortcut because I didn't want to write five pages describing prize-fighting.'[49]) From Hemingway to Mailer to Apple and Bukowski, a fairly straightforward genealogy of masculine ego (an imitation of the 'series of punches on the nose' said to connect John

150
Michael Halsband's
photograph of Andy
Warhol and Jean-
Michel Basquiat as
boxers, 10 July 1985.

L. Sullivan to Lennox Lewis) is being mapped out as well as mocked.[50] But what happens when a woman wants to join in? Joyce Carol Oates is not known for ego; indeed her cultivation of 'invisibility', the stereotypical female position, is much commented upon.[51] Her 1987 essay *On Boxing* was praised for its refreshing avoidance of 'hot competitive drive' and she herself has dismissed Hemingway's 'equation of masculinity with greatness in literature'.[52] Nevertheless, Oates too has used boxing to think about her career as a writer and she too has felt the need to raise her fists to Mailer. She was not, however, simply concerned with status.[53] More precisely Oates wanted to challenge the widely held assumption of female incomprehension of boxing, and by extension of men *per se*.[54] In published extracts from her journal, she notes that while Mailer would be unable to consider the sport 'through a woman's eyes', she can easily imagine what it must mean 'through a man's eyes'. 'Am I being too self-assured?' she hesitates, momentarily, before concluding, 'I'd like to eat Mailer's heart – is that it!'[55] Only by absorbing the male/Mailer perspective into the female perspective could Oates finally write, she claims, as a genderless 'aficionado'.[56]

Even more competitive than writers, jazz musicians have often compared themselves to fighters. Battles of the bands were a notable feature of the turn-of-the-century New Orleans jazz scene and carried on into the swing and bebop eras, when the music press pitted bop against traditional jazz 'with the zest of boxing promoters'.[57] Jam sessions or cutting contests between individual musicians were also frequently imagined as fights: from the twenties, when a 'southpaw' called Seminole 'dethroned' Count Basie, to the alternating solos of tenor saxophonists Dexter Gordon and Wardell Gray in the late forties.[58] Gordon and Gray's most successful albums were called *The Chase* and *The Hunt*, but remembering them later, producer Ross Russell adopted the less rural image of a 'contest between evenly matched boxers of contrasting skills, a Dempsey against a Joe Louis, a Marciano against a Muhammad Ali'.[59] Observing his twelve-year-old brother Lester's eagerness to join in such contests, Lee Young said, 'he really wanted to see who was the better man; it would be just like a prize fighter or a wrestler'.[60] 'You defended your honour with your instrument,' recalled Duke Ellington.[61]

In *Invisible Man*, Ralph Ellison compares Louis Armstrong's ability to 'bend' the military trumpet into a 'beam of lyrical sound' to a prize-fighter who disrupts an existing rhythm by slipping 'into the breaks'.[62] Boxing, in other words, has its equivalent to the 'true jazz moment' of improvisation, which Ellison elsewhere defines as springing 'from a contest in which each artist challenges the rest'.[63] In Chapter Nine, I considered Miles Davis's improvisation-as-boxing in *Jack Johnson*, but twenty years earlier Babs Gonzalez used Charlie Parker's 'Ornithology' (itself an outgrowth of 'How High the Moon') as the starting point for 'Sugar Ray', a track which celebrated the boxer as the epitome of 'cool'.[64] In 2003, Matthew Shipp recorded an album in which his own free jazz piano 'boxed' with the experimental rap of Antipop Consortium.[65]

Prize-fighting imagery is not restricted to jazz. Volume three of the 1959 *Battle of the Blues* series presented two musicians in dinner jackets and boxing gloves; volume four retained the boxing motif, expressed on the cover by an image of two smiling women in bathing suits and gloves (illus. 151). Meanwhile, Jamaican reggae (born at the height of Ali's fame) has often imagined 'soundboy killings' between rival DJs as boxing matches.[66] In 2004, Beenie Man declared himself 'King of the Dancehall', a title his 2006 album *Undisputed* seeks to uphold (illus. 151).[67] The Jamaican DJ-ing battle and blues boasts in turn provide models for the seemingly endless confrontations of rap.[68] Numerous songs have

151
Posters advertising Beenie Man, *Undisputed*, New York, 2006.

been devoted to proclamations about the MC's prowess, his rival's uselessness and/or homosexuality, and their 'rhyme for rhyme, word for word, verse for verse' battles.[69] Big Daddy Kane disses his opponent as a 'featherweight' whose rhymes won't earn points; Coolio announces that 'the championship belt is what I taste and claim'; Sticky Fingers proclaims himself a 'heavyweight (and still undisputed)'; and Q-Tip complains that his hands are blistered from tightly holding the mic that knocked out his opponent.[70] Too often, laments George Nelson, hip hop turns itself into a new version of the battle royal – 'young African-American men bashing each other for a predominantly white audience'.[71]

Rivalry is not the only way in which the dialectics of boxing functions. Often it expresses a more complicated relationship between 'polar opposites'.[72] The scope of the encounter (as well as the medium in which it is expressed) varies considerably. The oppositions might be cultural or conceptual, political or stylistic, purely abstract or deeply personal. Senam Okudzeto's *Long Distance Lover* (1999–2000), for example, places delicately painted boxers on British Telecom phone bills revealing calls from London to Ghana and the United States. 'The idea', Okudzeto said, 'is that you see a person in argument with herself. The two figures represent conflicting opinions, ideologies and identities within the same psyche.'[73] Elsewhere boxing is used to dramatize a sexual encounter or fantasy. John Updike's Rabbit Angstrom masturbates to thoughts of a 'hefty coarse Negress' with 'big cocoa-colored breasts' which 'swing into his face like boxing gloves with sensitive tips'.[74]

Boxing provides just one of many overwrought images for Updike. For other writers, however, it reflects an enduring preoccupation with duality and conflict. Joyce Carol Oates's fiction is populated by twins and doubles – the ego and the alter-ego; the good girl and the bad girl; the public self and the private self.[75] Enid Maria Stevick, the protagonist of *You Must Remember This* (1987) is a typical Oates 'double personality' – both a 'nice Catholic girl' who plays the piano, and a bad girl who has an affair with her half-uncle, Felix, an ex-boxer.[76] Throughout the novel, their relationship is figured as a competitive boxing match. The story begins with the fifteen-year old swallowing a bottle of aspirin after Felix tries to break off the relationship with a slap to her face – 'she hadn't seen it coming and her head knocked against the side of the window and for an instant she was stunned, astonished'.[77] Her suicide attempt, however, provides the counterpunch that their relationship/fight needs. Felix now recognizes that they have a 'blood bond as if between two men who'd fought each other to a draw'.[78] He finds this much more satisfying than his initial rape of Enid, her body then merely offering 'some small unwitting resistance'.[79] The 'blood bond' between Enid and Felix is broken when she forms an alternative bond by getting pregnant and then by having an abortion.

Felix gave up boxing when the 'joy of the body' was overtaken by a realization (again in the form of an unanticipated punch) that 'he was going to die'. Enid's bodily education (a progression of suffering from rape to attempted suicide to abortion) is also compared to a series of unexpected, and near-deathly, blows.[80] At the same time as Oates asserts the incommensurability of gender, she argues that pain and the fear of death provide a level playing-field on which men and women can compete. The masculine world (epitomized by boxing) and the feminine world (epitomized by reproductive and sexual trauma) seem comparable in the amount of suffering each entails. Ultimately, however, Oates believes that women cope much better than men with that suffering.[81] *You Must Remember This* ends with Enid winning a scholarship to music college and Felix being beaten to death in the toilets of a diner.

The frequently interchangeable categories of boxing and sex also appeal to artists less interested with pitting an essential masculinity against an essential femininity than with exploring oppositions within these categories.[82] Occasionally, the relationship is reciprocal – in Rita Mae Brown's *Southern Discomfort*, one woman tells another that love means 'you're in my corner and I'm in yours', while Keith Haring's shiny red and blue steel *Boxers* (1988) thrust their arms symmetrically through one another's bodies (illus. 123) – but usually a balance of power is at stake.[83] Judith Halberstam, for example, argues that the figure of the woman boxer, the 'raging bull dyke', epitomizes the 'masculine woman', the kind who prefers to 'give than to take'.[84] Tony Kushner, meanwhile, uses an allusion to the Brown Bomber in his play *Angels in America* (1990–93) to explore political tension within the gay community of eighties New York. At first Reaganite Joe and liberal Louis find their ideological disputes sexy – Joe tells Louis that 'Freedom is where we bleed into one another. Right and Left' – but eventually their arguments turn serious and physical.[85]

In writing by men, a series of familiar fantasies recur: aristocrats eulogize working class toughs; white men dream about black men; soft men desire hard men; and Jean Genet writes poems to his 'thief-boxer', a 'muscled rose'.[86] Usually thought of as an elegy for the *'belle epoque'* before AIDS, Alan Hollinghurst's *The Swimming-Pool Library* (1988) exposes the power relations involved in such fantasies. The narrator, Will Beckwith, and the man he works for, Lord Charles Nantwich, belong to 'that tiny proportion of the population that . . . owns almost everything' and who therefore treat the world like a 'great big public school'. Public school provides a model for the homosocial, and mostly homosexual, London that Will inhabits. Swimming (in the West End Corinthian Club) is the book's central metaphor for the escape and freedom offered by that world; boxing (in an East End Boys' Club) provides a contrasting image of the violence it can contain.[87]

Nantwich's love of boxing began during his Edwardian schooldays at Winchester College. He then became a colonial administrator in the Sudan (where he developed a passion for young black men) and on his return to London, set up a club in Limehouse to teach 'rough boys' how to box.[88] The link between his boxing and colonial interests is encapsulated in the portrait of a beautiful black man he keeps on the wall of his London house. The man Will identifies as 'an eighteenth-century colonial servant' turns out to be the boxer and trainer Bill Richmond, who had boxed with Byron. Will is happy to note how times have changed since Nantwich went to prison for soliciting, and indeed since Byron's day, but Hollinghurst also wants to draw attention to the ways in which times haven't changed. Will visits the boxing club and admires a boy with 'pink and gold colouring like my own' (and also 'like the inmate of a penitentiary as imagined by Genet') fighting a black boy. He is 'moved' by the occasion, finding an 'innocence' in it. He admires the 'careless fondness' with which the golden boy embraces his opponent at the end. This 'little manly world', he suggests, is 'in some ideal Greek way' maintained with 'an ethos of sport rather than violence'. In the wider world, Will knows that fights degrade and damage (a view that is confirmed when he is beaten up by 'sexy' skinheads on the street), but he likes to think that the homosocial worlds he inhabits are different. Hollinghurst, however, encourages his readers to notice the gap between Will's interpretation of events and his descriptions. For an occasion intended to symbolize Greek sportsmanship, the boys club fight is a rather gruesome affair. The white boy hits the black boy with a 'vicious jab' and the spectators are said to have heard 'a strange, squinching little sound, as of the yielding of soft, adolescent bone and gristle'. Will notices that the white boy's glove, raised in victory, is smeared with 'the bright trace of blood'. Nevertheless, he goes on to talk of innocence and tenderness.[89]

In other 'little manly worlds' (many of which are described as hot and enclosed, like a boxing ring), the encounters between men are also often violent and described in terms that recall the Limehouse fight. Arthur, a young black boy from the East End, takes refuge in Will's West End flat and turns the heating up. Torn between 'disgust' and a desire to 'save' Arthur, Will initiates sex. This takes the form of 'a few seconds brutal fumbling' accompanied by Arthur's 'shouts of pain'. Once more, Will is 'moved'. Later he has sex with working-class, ex-boxer Phil at a hotel called the Queensberry (Wilde's adversary was also the man who established the modern rules of boxing). There, in a 'small bed' which reminds him of school, he again takes sexual 'command' and again his passion is 'almost cruel'. Will bites Phil's lips 'brutally' until they bleed and, at one point, their 'skulls cracked together quite painfully'. Phil, despite his 'hard' body, is 'powerless'. Mapping the history of gay oppression in Britain, *The Swimming-Pool Library* also exposes forms of oppression within the public-school version of gay culture.[90]

While Hollinghurst contrasts the violence of boxing with the meditative activity of swimming, Douglas Oliver compares it to meditation itself. 'The Jains and the Boxer' is a poetic dialogue between the 'unending harmlessness' of Jainism and the boxer's desire to punch 'harm into harm in sadistic rhymes'. This is partly autobiographical (Oliver trying to reconcile the memory of his 'schizophrenic' boyhood spent reading and boxing) but mostly a matter of poetics and philosophy. What Oliver wants to do is find a way of expressing the relationship between continuity (poetically, the 'brief interval' in which 'the vowel continues unharmed') and violent change (in poetic terms, the 'purity' of the vowel is 'destroyed by a diphthong glide or a consonant.')[91] Julio Cortázar had other concerns. For him, the novel and the short story are the contenders. Either might triumph, but 'the novel would win by points and the short story by a knockout'.[92] Yet another debate about aesthetics informs R. B. Kitaj's 1992 painting *Whistler vs. Ruskin (Novella in Terre Verte, Yellow and Red)*, a reworking of Bellows's *Dempsey and Firpo*.[93] Reviewing Whistler's *Nocturne in Black and Gold: The Falling Rocket* in 1877, John Ruskin famously wrote that he'd 'never expected to hear a coxcomb ask two hundred guineas for flinging a pot of paint in the public's face'.[94] Whistler brought a libel suit against Ruskin and won, although the judge only awarded him a farthing in damages. By presenting the quarrel in terms of both a famous boxing painting and a famous boxing match Kitaj is inviting viewers to think about his painting as a 'novella', a story about characters that Victorian viewers like Ruskin might have enjoyed. By drawing attention to the painting's colours, however, Kitaj seems to be siding with Whistler and the purely aesthetic gaze. The painting includes a self-portrait as the referee.

Dada's boxing pranks also continue to influence artists interested in shock and repudiation. One of Guy Debord's heroes was Arthur Cravan, whose aesthetic of pugilistic provocation informs Debord's conception of 'détournement', or the 'mutual interference of two worlds of feeling'.[95] Debord's 1952 film, *Hurlements en faveur de Sade (Hurls for Sade)*, juxtaposes scenes of riots, battles and a boxing match, while *Guy Debord: Son Art et Son Temps* (1994) includes footage from the 1916 Cravan vs. Johnson newsreel.[96] In 1972, meanwhile, as part of the Documenta 5 exhibition, Joseph Beuys established an Information Office for the 'Organisation for Direct Democracy Through Referendum'. For 100 days he discussed the nature of democracy with visitors. During the course of these debates, his pupil Abraham David Christian invited him to take part in a 'Boxing match for Direct Democracy' and this became the exhibition's closing event. Beuys fought on behalf of direct democracy while Christian represented delegated democracy. Another of Beuys's pupils, Anatol Herzfeld, acted as referee and afterwards reported that Beuys had won on points. His 'direct hits' had established the case for direct democracy.[97] For Debord and Beuys (as for Tzara and Cravan), the punch provides a metaphor for unmediated address; it represents that which cannot be faked, and as such, is the obverse of the 'society of the spectacle'. When Beuys wanted to attack television culture in 1966, he staged a performance in which he punched himself in the face in front of a felt-covered television set.[98] Since then, and for similar reasons, performance artists and art galleries have periodically staged boxing matches.[99]

For the American novelist Philip Roth, the very idea of direct and authentic address has always been suspect. Nevertheless, on occasion, he too has relied on descriptions of punches to make his point. In Chapter Six, I considered Roth's trips with his father to see fights at Newark's Laurel Garden and his adolescent obsession with Jewish boxers.[100] Later he reflected that boxing was a 'strange deviation from the norm' of Jewish culture and 'interesting largely for that reason'.[101] Boxing imagery crops up throughout Roth's fiction as a way of describing the contradictions of his childhood and beyond. On the one hand are bouts between Jewish and Gentile identities (dramatized through his father's interest in watching Jews fight men of other ethnicities); on the other, is the contest between different versions of a Jewish-American childhood (the Jewish 'norm' vs. the 'strange deviation' of boxing).

The first kind of competition (Jews vs. Gentiles) is enacted in Roth's first novel, *Portnoy's Complaint* (1969). There the Jew is the narrator, Alex Portnoy, and his opponents, a variety of Gentile girlfriends. First Alex draws a parallel between the 'rough' and unsatisfying 'hand-job' he has received from Bubbles Girardi and the exploits of her brother 'Geronimo' Girardi in the Hoboken boxing world. Soon boxing provides a way of expressing the fact that sex is less about the girls than their 'backgrounds – as though through fucking I will discover America'. So, weighing 170 pounds, 'at least half of which is undigested halvah and hot pastrami', and wearing 'black pubic hair', Alex 'The Shnoz' Portnoy takes on Sarah Abbott Maulsby, 114 pounds of 'Republican refinement', wearing 'fair fuzz'.[102]

Fighting the goyim is 'clear', a 'good, righteous, guilt-free punch up'.[103] Contests between the 'mirrored fragments' of Jewishness are more complicated.[104] This second kind of bout is staged in *The Ghost Writer* (1979). There the narrator Nathan Zuckerman finds himself arguing with his father at a New York intersection about whether he is the 'kind of person' who would write a story making fun of Jews like his family. 'I *am*', he says; 'You're not', his father says, shaking him 'just a little'.

> But I hopped up onto the bus, and then behind me the pneumatic door, with its hard rubber edge, swung shut with what I took to be an overly appropriate thump, a symbol of the kind you leave out of fiction. It was a sound that brought back to me the prize fights at Laurel Garden, where once a year my brother and I used to wager our pennies with one another, each of us alternating backing the white fighter or the colored fighter . . . What I heard was the heartrending thud that follows the roundhouse knockout punch, the sound of the stupefied heavyweight hitting the canvas floor. And what I saw was . . . my bewildered father, alone on the darkening street-corner by the park that used to be our paradise, thinking himself and all of Jewry gratuitously disgraced and jeopardized by my inexplicable betrayal.[105]

What Nathan *hears* (the heartrending thud that reminds him of Laurel Garden) and what he *sees* (his neatly dressed father and the 'park that used to be our paradise') are of course at odds. One childhood memory is set against another, as are the two interpretations of Nathan's short story. His father thinks the story is about 'one thing and one thing only . . . kikes and their love of money'; Nathan retorts, 'I was administering a bear hug'. Love vs. Hate. Neither man concedes to the other at that New York intersection. 'Nor was that the end,' begins the next paragraph.

*The Ghost Writer* was the first in what would become a trilogy of novels featuring Nathan Zuckerman; novels which continued to debate what kind of writer, what kind of Jew, what kind of man he should be. After an interval writing other works, Roth returned to his alter ego in 1997 for a second trilogy of novels. Nathan now became the chronicler of the central 'historical moments in postwar American life': late-sixties radicalism, the McCarthy witch hunts of the fifties, and their equivalents in the late-nineties 'culture wars'.[106] Each novel also tells the story of an athlete. 'Swede' Levov is 'our household Apollo', a Jew who is 'as close as a goy as we were going to get'; Ira Ringold is a six-foot six-inch Jew who looks like a prize fighter; Coleman Silk is black but passes successfully as both a Jewish classics professor and a Jewish boxer.[107] I don't have space here to discuss the trilogy's sustained (and rather Nietzschean) classicism except to note that an 'aura of heroic purity' surrounds each of these men and that each is also marked with an all-too-human stain.[108]

In *American Pastoral*, high school sports represent the golden goyische image which post-war Jews like Zuckerman fear and desire. In *I Married a Communist*, Roth narrows his focus to boxing and uses it as a metaphor for the various 'fights' – with received wisdom, 'tyranny and injustice', their employers and wives, the House Un-American Activities Committee, and, finally, old age – that Murray and Ira (Iron Man) Ringold undertake.[109] Zuckerman too is drawn into the fight. Because of his association with the Ringolds, he fails to get a Fulbright scholarship. 'I wuz robbed,' he later jokes to Murray – a boxing allusion that both men would surely recognize. In 1932, when Max Schmeling lost his title to Jack Sharkey by a dubious decision, his Jewish manager Joe Jacobs famously protested 'We wuz robbed'.[110]

The Ringolds are an inspiration to Nathan not only because of their size and athletic 'strenuousness', but also because they represent to him the possibility of 'forceful, intelligent manliness', the possibility of being an 'angry Jew' and having 'convictions'. They teach him that it is possible to talk about politics, boxing and books in the same way. 'Not opening up a book to worship it or to be elevated by it or to lose yourself to the world around you. No, *boxing* with the book.' 'The Ringolds were the one-two punch promising to initiate me into the big show, into my beginning to understand what it takes to be a man on the larger scale.'[111]

*I Married a Communist* has something of the Socratic dialogue about it – with Nathan as the young acolyte sitting at the feet of a series of books and 'men to whom I apprenticed myself'.[112] At college, he is introduced to another teacher, Leo Glucksman, who offers an alternative perspective to that of the Ringolds. If they believe in the (heterosexual) power of the word to change the world, he is a (homosexual) advocate of art for art's sake – 'You want a lost cause to fight for? Then fight for the *word*.'[113] Nathan fluctuates. Ultimately, he rejects the 'zealotry' or 'purity' of any one position – associated with Leo and also with Ira's hardline communist mentor, Jack O'Day – for an uncertainty that he shares with the flawed Ira.[114] Late in the novel, he recalls Murray acting out *Macbeth*, another story about manliness and betrayal, for his high school class. The most memorable lines come from an exchange between Malcolm and Macduff: 'Dispute it like a man,' orders Malcolm; 'I shall do so,' replies Macduff, 'But I must also feel it as a man.'[115] The 'dichotomies' of the heart, its 'thousand and one dualities', are, Nathan concludes, what makes us human and alive.[116] To find a situation in which there is 'no antagonism', we have to look to the stars; in other words, we have to die.

Coleman Silk, in *The Human Stain*, also inspires Zuckerman. If the Ringolds are 'extra fathers', Silk is an extra big brother. Although they only meet as old men, it transpires that they grew up less than five miles apart and nearly coincided in after-school boxing classes.[117] The connection is reinforced by the game Roth seems to be playing with their names – the story of a black man – coal man – presented in parallel to that of a Jewish – Zucker or, with more boxing connotations, Sugar – man. (In *I Married a Communist*, Nathan had sought guidance from irate Ira, a.k.a. 'Iron Man', and Glucksman, or Lucky Man).[118] If the Sugar Ray Robinson association seems stretched, it might be worth noting that the boxer was commonly known as Smitty. 'Call me Smitty,' began Roth's 1973 *The Great American Novel*. It would hardly be surprising to find the much-pseudonymed Roth emulating the typical prize-fighter's penchant for inventing names. Coleman's ring name is 'Silky Silk', smooth and slippery in the ring and in life.[119]

'My impulse,' Roth once said, 'is to problematize material . . . I like when it's opposed by something else, by another point of view.'[120] In *The Human Stain*, the material to be problematized is that of fixed identity (in particular racial and ethnic identity) and the impulse to present it in opposition is considered through the metaphor of the counterpunch. Coleman may believe that '*self-discovery – that* was the punch to the labonz' (after all, says Nathan, that's the 'drama that underlines America's story') – but his whole life has been based on playing a part.[121] As a young man Coleman had been a keen boxer, and in particular, a counterpuncher, a style that Zuckerman believes he also adopts outside of the ring.

> All the other kids were always blabbing about themselves. But that wasn't where the power was or the pleasure either. The power and pleasure were to be found in the opposite, in being counterconfessional in the same way you were a counterpuncher . . .

The culture (the 'other kids') requires the declaration or exposure of an overtly marked identity. It jabs Coleman with its demand for confession. He replies by 'slipping the punch' and offering, in return, a counterlife – an identity that is neither black nor white, but Jewish. One 'impersonates best the self that best gets one through'.[122]

Zuckerman too is concerned with impersonation. He freely admits that his version of Coleman Silk's life is a fiction and one that he is constructing with his own preoccupations in mind. Is the story so much about boxing simply because Zuckerman has put a framed photograph of Coleman as a 'boy boxer' on his writing desk?[123] But there are different styles of boxing. The main lesson that big 90-year-old Murray Ringold taught Zuckerman was how to achieve a 'state of ardorlessness'; in him, 'human dissatisfaction has met its match', Zuckerman notes with awe. He concludes that 'the man who first taught me how you box with a book is back now to demonstrate how you box with old age'. The lesson that the 70-year-old Silk teaches the now impotent, continent and deeply depressed Zuckerman is quite different. He is all ardour, all 'allure' and dancing 'magnetism', a counterpuncher. A 'goat-footed Pan', Silky Silk dances Nathan back to life.[124]

Coleman's favourite book is the *Iliad* and throughout Zuckerman's tale he adopts many Homeric roles: after the death of his wife, he is 'adrenal Achilles' ('they meant to kill me and they got her instead'); with Faunia, his 'Helen of Troy', he is Paris.[125] Most importantly, however, he plays Patroclus to Zuckerman's Achilles. Wearing on his shoulders the armour of both Zuckerman's Jewishness and 'sexual rapacity', Coleman had taken Zuckerman's place on the battlefields of the American culture wars.[126] In his honour, funeral games must be performed. Standing at Coleman's graveside, he confesses, 'I was completely seized by his story . . . and then and there, I began this book.'[127] Zuckerman does not stage an athletic contest (an imitation of military combat) but, with the photograph of the boy boxer on his desk, writes a counterpunching novel (the form which he believes best imitates the 'antagonism that *is* the world').[128] Like the funeral games, art can sometimes seem to defy death. Zuckerman goes to hear the pianist Yefim Bronfman. Another boxer-type, 'conspicuously massive through the upper torso', Bronfman plays 'with such bravado as to knock morbidity clear out of the ring'.[129]

## THE ICONOGRAPHY OF BOXING

Today much of the visual representation of boxing capitalizes on, or interrogates, the symbolic resonance of specific individuals, objects and events. Certain fights have a particularly powerful resonance or aura – a 'uniqueness' that can only be understood by saying 'I was there', or 'I knew someone who was there', or, at the very least, 'I remember where I was when it happened'.[130] Every boxing fan can name the special fights – from Louis vs. Schmeling to the Rumble in the Jungle, memorialized by one man in Don DeLillo's *White Noise* (1984) as 'the southernmost point I've ever brushed my teeth at'.[131] In *White Noise*, boxing matches and rock concerts mark historical milestones in individual lives; in DeLillo's more portentous *Underworld* (1997), sports events become 'measures of the awesome' and represent the possibility of a communal history. *Underworld* begins with an iconic baseball game – the Giants' defeat of the Dodgers in 1951. DeLillo imagines Russ Hodges, the radio 'voice of the Giants', anticipating the game ahead and feeling lucky because 'something big's in the works'.

But he finds himself thinking of the time his father took him to see Dempsey fight Willard in Toledo and what a thing that was, what a measure of the awesome, the Fourth of July and a hundred and ten degrees and a crowd of shirtsleeved men in straw hats, many wearing handkerchiefs spread beneath their hats and down to their shoulders, making them look like play-Arabs, and the greatness of the beating big Jess took in that white hot ring, the way the sweat and blood came misting off his face every time Dempsey hit him. When you see a thing like that, a thing that becomes a newsreel, you begin to feel you are a carrier of some solemn scrap of history.[132]

Hodges, and DeLillo, following Walter Benjamin, want to mark a sharp distinction between the experience of the thing itself and that of its mechanical reproduction (here, the newsreel). But it may also be possible to think of the kind of aura that did not only survive mechanical reproduction but flourished because of it, through the star-making technologies of film, television, video and DVD. Perhaps we could speak of an after-aura in the same way that we speak of an after-image. DeLillo himself only knows the Dempsey-Willard fight through a 1919 film. The after-aura of the Rumble in the Jungle (and two other Ali fights) was the subject of Paul Pfeiffer's video installation *The Long Count* (2000–2001) in which the boxers themselves have been removed from the footage. As the ropes bulge and bounce back, we sense their ghostly presence.[133]

Hip hop's interest in boxing is usually an attempt to tap into the much-mediated after-aura of heavyweight heroes. Occasionally, rappers talk of 'knocking niggers out like Jack Dempsey' or Rocky Balboa, but most compare themselves to either Ali or Tyson.[134] Allusions to Ali tend to refer to his reputation as a stylist, both as a boxer and as a prototypical punning, rhyming and boasting rap artist.[135] Ali's status as Greatest or G.O.A.T. is also one that many rappers want to emulate, and many rhyme 'Manila' with descriptions of themselves as a 'killer' or claim that they too could 'float like a butterfly / sting like a bee' (rhymed with MC).[136] In the ever-more-hyperbolic world of rap lyrics, the butterfly's floating has been superseded by helium and the bee's sting replaced by the pique of the scorpion or Tabasco.[137] More seriously, Chuck D of Public Enemy (a group that has been described as 'rap's conscience') instructed black 'entertainers and athletes' to follow Ali's example and use their celebrity to inspire, uplift and talk about 'the untalked about'.[138]

If Ali suggested skill, grace and political commitment, Tyson represented both the possibility of instant stardom and the endurance of a 'fierce, reckless fury'. That is why Tyson, rather than any single musician, says Nelson George, 'embodied hip hop' in the eighties.[139] Tyson's name is mentioned in 'scores of rap records' over the last 30 years. LL Cool J declared himself 'bad' – 'like Tyson icin' I'm a soldier at war', while Will Smith in his self-mocking Fresh Prince persona boasted 'I Think I Can Beat Mike Tyson'.[140] The 'perfect fighter for the MTV generation', Tyson also became a popular figure in music videos and computer games.[141] Just after his release from jail in 1995, he appeared as himself in *Black and White*, James Toback's film about hip hop culture's attraction for wealthy white teenagers. Tyson appears as a guru for the black rappers (Wu-Tang Clan) and a sexual magnet for the white tourists (played by Brooke Shields, Robert Downey Jr and Claudia Schiffer).[142]

Nelson sees a parallel between the progression of Tyson's career and that of hip hop itself. After 1990, he maintains, both lost their way: a process that culminated in Tupac Shakur's murder on leaving a Tyson fight in 1996, and in Tyson's biting a piece of Holyfield's ear, 'a testament to the impatience and unfocused rage that often mar contemporary black youth culture'.[143] In 1998, LL Cool J (responding to an attack on his reputation by Canibus, featuring Tyson), released 'The Ripper is Back', a homophobic attack on 'that convicted rapist' which demanded to know what the 'Ear Biter taught you', and in 2002, Motion Man boasted of his ability to attack 'human flesh like I'm Tyson or Jeffrey Dahmer'.[144] Since then Roy Jones Jr (title holder in every division from middle to heavyweight) has released two rap albums, which, his website says, try to promote a 'positive lifestyle'. In the first, he introduces himself, 'I'm Roy Jones . . ./ the legend . . . you found one.'[145]

The iconography of boxers has also been important for Spike Lee, whose film-making career has its roots in the eighties revival of Black Nationalist rhetoric and imagery, particularly the idea of the 'Wall of Respect'. *School Daze* (1988) opens with a montage of still photographs of familiar figures – from Douglass to Jesse Jackson to Louis and Ali – accompanied by the spiritual, 'I'm Building Me a Home'.[146] Walls of respect also play an important part in *Do the Right Thing* (1989), the story of a summer day on a single block in Bedford-Stuyvesant, Brooklyn.[147] The film asks what the 'right thing' to do might be, but gives no simple answer. The old 'American dilemma' (assimilation vs. separatism; peaceful struggle vs. violent self-defence) is expressed in quotations from Malcolm X and Martin Luther King that end the film, and in the two large knuckle rings inscribed with the legends 'love' and 'hate' worn by a character called Radio Raheem (Bill Nunn).[148] At one point we see him rapping while shadow-boxing, thrusting first love and then hate at the camera.[149] As the action moves inexorably toward the riots with which the film ends, Lee provides what has been described as an almost Brechtian commentary through the music that emanates from the streets (jazz, blues, soul, rock, funk, and most insistently, Public Enemy's 'Fight the Power'), and through images on the street walls.[150] These images include graffiti, signs and advertisements for numerous products and events; the camera describes them carefully, using them to reflect on the narrative action.[151] One image that is frequently passed, and significantly lingered upon, by the camera is a mural of Mike Tyson performing a right hook (next to a piece of graffiti instructing voters to 'dump' New York Mayor Koch).[152] A huge billboard of Tyson, 'Brooklyn's own', looms above Sal's Famous Pizzeria in counterpoint to the Italian-American Hall of Fame (featuring Sinatra, DiMaggio and DeNiro) that decorates the interior. Buggin' Out (Giancarlo Esposito) wages a campaign for black heroes to be represented in the pizzeria since blacks are the main customers, but Sal won't listen. As Buggin' tries to persuade the local kids to boycott the pizzeria, Sal (Danny Aiello) does a DeNiro-as-La Motta impression and the camera shifts to the image of Tyson.[153]

*Raging Bull* is an important point of reference for *Do the Right Thing* in several ways.[154] The two squabbling brothers, Vito (Richard Edson) and Pino (John Turturro), recall Jake and Joey La Motta, and the opening credits allude to the famous shadow-boxing credit sequence in Scorsese's film. But while Robert DeNiro dances operatically to the strains of *Cavalleria rustina*, Tina (Rosie Perez) performs a hip hop boxing dance to 'Fight the Power', a track that Tyson himself used for his entrances.[155] This allusiveness is one of the ways in which, as Andrew Ross suggests, the film signalled a deliberate 'challenge to the reign of Italian-American figures as the favored, semi-integrated ethnic presence in Hollywood film'.[156] Lee said much the same in a 1991 interview in which he spoke about the necessity of black people 'owning stuff ', because then 'you can do the hell what you want to do'.[157] In 2006 he was said to be at work on a film (written with Budd Schulberg) about the Louis-Schmeling fights.[158]

In some ways, Lee seems to think that all black American men (whatever their profession) are boxers. In *Jungle Fever* (1991), the issue is interracial sex. A playful curbside argument between married architect Flipper Purify (Wesley Snipes) and girlfriend Angie Tucci (Annabella Sciorra) about 'whose people' produced the best fighter (Ali or Marciano, etc.) turns into an affectionate sparring match. Two policemen arrive and point a gun to Flipper's head. For the protagonist of *She Hate Me* (2004), sex is like boxing not because it involves black vs. white, but because you get paid for it. John Henry Armstrong is named for two black heroes – the mythical John Henry whose portrait (with hammer) hangs on his wall, and thirties welterweight champion Henry Armstrong. After he loses his job as an executive in a corrupt biotech company, Armstrong establishes a career as a sperm donor for lesbian couples. We see him in training for the task (running up stairs, eating vitamins, etc.) and when prospective customers come to his apartment they sit under a twelve-foot portrait of Joe Louis.[159] Later he and his friend wonder how much Ali's sperm would cost.

The memorialization of heroic individuals also remains the starting point for much recent work in the visual arts, much of which explores the nature of commemoration itself.[160] Carrie Mae Weems's 1991 series of golden rimmed decorative souvenir plates, *Commemorating*, includes one in which Ali is thanked, alongside Malcolm X and murdered Civil Rights activist Medgar Evers, 'for providing the vision', while Emma Amos's series of portraits of *The Hero* reworks the 'African custom of printing commemorative fabrics to honor leaders and important people'.[161] Amos's *Muhammad Ali* (1998), a painting on the back of a boxer's robe bordered in woven African fabric, celebrates his status as a Pan-African, as well as personal, hero (illus. 130).[162]

Elsewhere, the celebration of heroes has proved less straightforward. Consider, for example, the controversy surrounding Robert Graham's *Monument to Joe Louis*, a 24-foot-long horizontal forearm with clenched fist suspended within

a pyramid of steel beams, which was unveiled in 1986 (illus. 152). Some thought the sculpture evoked the Black Power fist of the sixties, while others complained that it reduced Louis to a mere function or fetish, one that, in addition, had phallic associations.[163] Much recent work by black artists uses the figure or idea of the boxer to examine such reductions. Depersonalization is the critical intention rather than simply the consequence of Godfried Donkor's *Financial Times Boxers* (2001) and Danny Tisdale's 1991 series *Twentieth Century Black Men* (subjects included Rodney King and Buster Douglas). Both adapt the Warholian serial portrait, taking as their starting point a pre-existing image and multiplying it repeatedly. The individual figure is thus transformed into a mechanically and, it could be argued, traumatically reproduced commodity – something that Donkor reinforces by using the *Financial Times* as his grid (illus. 125).[164]

The ambiguities of sports iconography and commemoration were also important to Jean-Michel Basquiat. No individual is represented in *Famous Negro Athlete* (1981); the work consists solely of the title, with a drawing of a baseball below and a crown above. Basquiat's critics have had trouble deciding whether he is being serious or ironic.[165] His use of the word 'Negro', however, surely suggests a sardonic tone, as does the fact that there is no 'famous' athlete. While *Famous Negro Athlete # 47* (1981) features a crowned man, he too is unnamed. But does the crown that Basquiat attaches to these words simply reflect a desire to confer a long-denied 'regal status on the black man'?[166] Or is the championship crown simply another brand, like Blue Ribbon, sponsors of boxing, whose beer bottle top also recurs in Basquiat's iconography? Is Basquiat commenting on the 'Black male body's history as property, pulverized meat, and popular entertainment', an identity presented as particularly American in *Per Capita* (1981), in which another boxer, this time haloed, holds up a burning torch in the manner of the Statue of Liberty?[167] Here too, the boxer is unnamed, except by the brand of his shorts, Everlast. In 1982, however, Basquiat produced a series of paintings commemorating specific boxers (depicted by a roughly sketched mask or skull-like face) with crowns – *Jersey Joe Walcott*, *Jack Johnson*, and *Untitled (Sugar Ray Robinson)*. The only uncrowned figures are Joe Louis (he has a halo in *St Joe Louis Surrounded by Snakes*, a very different work from the others) and Ali, since in the painting he is still *Cassius Clay* and not yet champion.[168]

The various objects and practices which transform fighting into boxing (ring, gloves, punch bags, brand names) have also become popular with Pop-meets-Conceptual artists concerned with the 'processes and productions of *signification*'.[169] Aiming to reduce boxing to its structural essence and to demystify that essence, such works nevertheless often re-mystify or fetishize their chosen objects.[170] For Roderick Buchanan, five bean bags, each of which corresponds to the pre-match weight of a soon-to-be-knocked-out boxer, suggests *Deadweight* (2000), while Glenn Ligon and Byron Kim's *Rumble, Young Man, Rumble* (1993), consisting of two suspended canvas punchbags carefully stencilled with extracts from Ali's autobiography to emphasize the words 'white' and 'battle', evokes the 'legibility of race'.[171]

Boxers themselves tend to fetishize gloves, hanging replicas from keyrings and car mirrors, and wearing miniatures as earrings, cufflinks and necklaces – a custom that has its origin in the Golden Gloves competition, named for the miniature golden glove awarded to every champion. One of the most poignant moments in *Rocky v* (1990) is when, in a flashback, we see his trainer Mickey give him 'the favorite thing that I have on this earth', a golden glove necklace, once Rocky Marciano's cufflink. 'I'm givin' it to you and it, it's gotta be like a, like an angel on your shoulder see?' Now retired, Rocky passes on the talisman to Rocky Jr. For Paul-Felix Montez, gloves are the key to boxing, the 'impact point' of offence and defence, and as such were the obvious choice to represent the sport in a series of

'21st century Las Vegas Monuments'.[172] (Gambling is represented by dice and singing by microphones.) *The Gloves* is planned as a 70-foot-tall sculpture, in which a stainless steel glove and a bronze glove 'touch' vertically (as before the first and fifteenth rounds of a fight) above a black granite pool (illus. 132).

While Montez's heavyweight gloves reach to the sky, David Hammons's *Champ* (1989) hangs down (illus. 124). One of many works by Hammons to use salvaged rubbish, *Champ* consists of a tyre's deflated inner tube with a red glove at either end. The irony implied by the title of Benny Andrews's 1968 collage of rumpled cloth, *The Champion* (discussed in the previous chapter) is taken a step further. Here the 'champ' is nothing more than a piece of limp rubber and gloves, 'an emblem of deflated hopes and the certainty of going nowhere fast'.[173] Gary Simmons and Satch Hoyt also associate boxers with their gloves primarily to suggest their status as commodities. Simmons's white gloves *Everforward* (1993) argues for the continuing power of white capitalism behind the punch, while Hoyt's series of figures made of miniature leather gloves and set in fighting stances – named Joe Louis, Sugar Ray Robinson, Floyd Patterson and Jack Johnson – has the collective title, *DonKingDom*.[174]

The ring has also lent itself to numerous works on the meaning of boxing and boxers. For Keith Piper, the ring is a place in which debates about different versions of, and attitudes toward, black masculinity are staged. *Four Corners: A Context of Opposites* (1995) consists of a square 'ring' each side of which contains a video projection of a black heavyweight boxer and the attitude he adopted toward, or provoked from, a white audience: Jack Johnson is Consternation; Joe Louis, Conciliation; Ali, Contravention; Tyson, Confirmation.[175] For Thomas Kilpper, recovering forgotten names was more urgent than interpreting their meanings. Kilpper created *The Ring* (2000) in a soon-to-be-demolished office building (once a major boxing venue; see illus. 74) in Southwark, London. He carved a 400-square-metre woodcut of a boxing ring with a surrounding audience in the parquet of the building's tenth floor, then hung 80 portraits (twenty of which featured boxers), printed on a variety of found materials, on washing lines above.[176] While *The Ring* sought to memorialize both the site and its inhabitants, Jane Mulfinger and Graham Budgett's *A Grey Area* (1995) expresses the transience of boxing fame by presenting the names of various champions embossed into a mixture of plasticine and astro-turf.[177] Alix Lambert used more enduring materials in her 2005 sculpture, *Wild Card* – an empty cement and steel ring containing only a corner stool and discarded pair of cast bronze gloves – but she seemed to be saying much the same thing, that we don't remember individual fighters for long.[178] Finally, Gary Simmons's 1994 *Step into the Arena (The Essentialist Trap)* – a full-size boxing ring in which dance-step patterns are placed on the floor and tap shoes hang over the ropes – is less interested in commemorating individuals than in making a point about the continuing restriction of black men to the parallel industries of sport and entertainment.[179]

I began this section with the fight in which Jack Dempsey won the heavyweight title, and end it with the fight in which he tried, and failed, to regain it.

While DeLillo was concerned with Dempsey as the focal point of a communal memory, James Coleman's *Box (ahhareturnabout)* (1977) tries to recreate the experience of fighting Dempsey. Coleman wants to know what it must have felt like to *have been* Tunney. He is, in other words, interested in both the iconography and what might be called the phenomenology of boxing.[180] His critics have argued about which is more important to the piece.[181] *Box* consists of a continuous seven-minute loop of film, consisting of fragments from the 1927 footage of Tunney's title defence against Dempsey. This is spliced with black leaders (perhaps to suggest 'momentary blackouts'), and accompanied by a soundtrack of words and phrases 'syncopated to evoke the beat of a heart and/or the jabs of a punching glove'. The film was projected in a dark 'tunnel-like space' to create the feeling of 'inhabiting the skull of the boxer'.[182] The subtitle of the piece is said to refer to Tunney's state of anxiety, a never-resolved since endlessly repeated moment of crisis, because Jean Fisher argues, 'at that moment he was both "champ" and "not-champ".'[183] The work explores the relationship between Tunney as a familiar visual icon (expressed in the visual fragments of the fight) and a version of some unknown 'inner' or 'real' Tunney (expressed in the auditory fragments that accompany the images). This 'inner Tunney' is of course as much a dramatic creation as the outer since Coleman himself wrote the script in which Tunney meditates on Irish nationalism and colonial history.

## THE NATURALISM OF BOXING

In 1991, the former Smiths frontman Morrissey performed his first full-length solo concert in Dublin's National Stadium. That it was a boxing venue was appropriate for during the next few years Morrissey became increasingly interested in boxers as emblems of a threatened white working-class Englishness. For all its hyper-masculine glamour, that Englishness is never about winning. It's about embarrassment and humiliation, about 'losing in front of your home crowd' and wishing 'the ground / would open up and take you down'.[184] Morrissey's wistful talk of going down draws on naturalism's perennial narrative concern with small-town losers rather than world champions, and old, worn-out fighters rather than the young and up-and-coming. If naturalists consider the young, it's to imply that they too will soon be old and worn-out, or to have them be hit with the unlucky punch that fate had in store for them.[185] Boxing, they conclude, is a 'cruel sport characterized by shattered bodies, broken dreams and hopeless futures.'[186]

Since the 1890s, the life of a boxer has been taken to exemplify the span or trajectory of a human life. Both might be expressed in terms of 'the distance'. For Rocky, going the distance just means holding on until the end of a single fight, but the distance can also be measured in terms of a whole life or career. Carlo Rotella uses the term to compare the 'resilience' of his Sicilian grandmother to that of similarly 'old-school' boxers. If, as he suggests, life sets 'regeneration' against 'exhaustion', exhaustion always ultimately wins.[187] The difference between the downward trajectory of biology and that of boxing is simply speed.

Rotella's grandmother was still going strong into her 80s; his boxers were finished in their 30s. After one fight too many, the narrator of Thom Jones's story 'The Pugilist at Rest' thinks that he's 'grown old overnight'.[188]

If the arena represents the peak of performance, if not always triumph, the gym is the place of promise and decline, both a factory production line and a kind of 'second home', a refuge for kids in need of a kind but firm parent, and a place 'where men are allowed to be kind to one another' without a 'shadow of impropriety' or 'question of motive'.[189] 'Part of what I'm falling in love with,' Kate Sekules writes of Gleason's Gym, 'is the thing my presence here will help subvert; that is, boxing as it used to seem – an arcane testosterone ghetto, photogenic and romantic, adoringly treated in black-and-white'.[190] In Clint Eastwood's film *Million Dollar Baby* (2004), the arrival of Maggie Fitzgerald (Hilary Swank) initially threatens to upset the homeliness of the gym, but not for long. Frankie (Eastwood) and Eddie (Morgan Freeman) find that gaining a daughter is not that different from gaining a son.[191] In stories like this, problems begin when you have to leave the safe womb-like world of gym and enter the less-controlled worlds of either the arena (which proves the death of Maggie) or life itself. Thom Jones's story 'Sonny Liston was a Friend of Mine' ends when Kid Dynamite realizes that boxing is 'over' and that the 'real world, which had seemed so very far away all these years, was upon him'. He knows, however, that the 'thing' that has made him good in the gym is the 'very thing' that will make life outside 'impossible'.'[192]

Of course life outside the gym means different things to the protagonists of the stories considered above and to middle-class memoirists and artists. For the latter, the journey from the healthclub to 'authentic' Gleason's repeats the story of descent described by nineteenth-century investigators into the slums, and they linger lovingly on its squalor and, particularly, its sounds and smells.[193] Boxers breathe and grunt through suspended speakers as a soundscape accompaniment to Satch Hoyt's 2003 installation piece *Inside Out*, consisting of 350 used mouthpieces and 44 handwraps encased in a plexiglass and steel metal box.[194] Arlene Shulman complements her black and white photographs of the Times Square Gym with a detailed written description of its 'beaten and broken chairs' and 'soiled canvas held together by peeling tape'. 'The ceiling sagged, its floor creaked, the moldy shower stank,' and most noticeable of all, the place 'stank of damp leather, lockers stuffed with forgotten, sweaty clothes, and perspiration that stuffed your nose and clung to your clothes'.[195]

For many, such scents provide an olfactory reminder of the land of their fathers, the 'irretrievable past' of the (usually white) industrial working class. Robert Anasi, for example, finds in Bernie's gym, 'a fragment of an old San Francisco, the blue-collar city of the longshoreman's general strike'.[196] The gym is a part of a past in which men worked with their hands, and in which a 'mashed-in mug, all rough and ugly' meant 'heart'.[197] Craig Raine's poem 'A Hungry Fighter' imagines his father in 1932, with only a 'featherweight of whiteness' to sell, both training (where 'juice erupts in tiny sacs / like smallpox through the vaseline') and losing his title challenge. 'The gym is rubble now', he notes, a 'bathos of bricks', and all he can do, he says, is gaze at his father's relics (vest, licence, cup) 'longer than someone in love'.[198] In fact, he does something more. Raine included the poem in *Rich*, a 1984 collection which presents a dialogue between the idea and experience of being 'rich' (the title of part 1) and that of being 'poor' (part 3). His father's world, he sentimentally concludes, was the rich one.

A fascination with the stories and settings of decline is usually accompanied by a fascination with the signs of that decline or damage in the material of the boxer's body itself. Prettiness may represent sustained success – Ali, Leonard and de La Hoya were not hit repeatedly on the nose, eye or ear – but the accumulation of visible scar tissue nevertheless has its own aura, serving as a badge of courage and endurance as well as defeat. 'I never got busted-up bad or nothing,' Scrap confides in F. X. Toole's story 'Frozen Water'; 'Nose be broke enough so I don't hardly have a nose, and one eye droop because of cuts and the dead nerve in the lid, but nothing serious'.[199] Lit cinematically from above and viewed from below so that his forearms seem enormous slabs of meat, the bare-knuckle fighter in Peter Howson's drawing *Boxer 1* (2002) transcends his scraggy neck and desperate eyes and becomes a monstrous monument (illus. 131).[200] And when a group of retired fighters appear at a charity event, Carlo Rotella imagines the crowd being 'transported' to 'a mythical era' by the 'time and damage tallied' in their faces.[201]

Sometimes a fascination with bodily damage seems more akin to a grotesque pornography than to expressionist mythology, the bloody and detachable bits of the body offering an enduring 'secret pleasure' to both white-collar memoirists and naturalist novelists.[202] Noticing some 'purple and red bruises' on her knuckles, Lynn Snowden Picket reaches for a Polaroid camera before stroking 'each bruise with reverence'.[203] Or consider Breece D'J Pancake's 'scrapper', who wishes he could knock out his opponent's eye 'and step on it, to feel its pressure building under his foot . . . pop', but instead finds he has bitten off part of his own tongue.[204] Or this description of a fight between two small-time Arizona boxers, from Luis Alberto Urrea's *In Search of Snow*:

> [Castro's fist] came down like an ax blow, straight into the top of Turk's head. *Crack*, The skin of Turk's scalp blew open like an egg yolk. Snot flew from his nose. He fell to his knees. The room was silent. Mike saw a flake of tooth on Turk's lip. Blood cascaded off Turk's head, filling his ears and eye sockets . . . Ramses Castro leaned over him and said, 'You lose, asshole.'[205]

When Mike Tyson bit Holyfield's ear, it was widely agreed that he had failed to recognize that what he was being paid to do was simply *perform* violently. But while descriptions of eyeballs, snot and flakes of teeth are not meant to intrude into the fantasy worlds of Las Vegas or television, in stories such as these, detailed accounts of 'the body turned inside out' announce that what is offered is real.[206]

The hard, muscled body of the gym and the 'theatrical dressing' of 'gaudy shorts' and 'pompous entrances' are, such works imply, merely temporary constructions; the 'twitching body on the stretcher' is what boxing is 'all about'.[207] This is certainly the view of the medical associations that call for the sport to be banned.

To accept that the 'essence' or 'basic fact' of boxing is 'the fact of meat and body hitting meat and bone' is to reject, or at least downplay, the intricate conceptual and iconographic constructions that surround it.[208] 'It takes constant effort,' writes Rotella, 'to keep the slippery, naked, near-formless fact of hitting swaddled in layers of sense and form.'[209] While art (by definition) can never wholly discard 'swaddling', artists often claim to have devised methods that allow them to get 'near' formlessness. When Cindy Sherman described Larry Fink's black and white boxing photographs as provoking a reflex 'to duck a punch or avoid a spray of sweat', she was offering him the highest praise – there was, she suggested, no aestheticizing 'layer' between reality and image.[210] This is not a new claim. Artists and writers keen to detach themselves from academic or artificial styles have, from the earliest times, associated the 'low' activity of boxing and, in particular, the abject body of the injured boxer with an aesthetic or ethos of waiting-to-be-recovered authenticity. Of course, authenticity is always a fantasy, but it's a necessary and fruitful fantasy. This kind of naturalism always occurs as a reaction (a counterpunch, we might say) to an existing, often overworked, paradigm. In classical times, the counterpunch was choosing to depict bruises in bronze rather than muscles in smooth marble; in the early nineteenth century, it meant slipping some flash slang into a lyric poem; in the early twentieth century, it meant preferring the sports arena to the theatre. To evoke boxing is always to dissociate oneself from the sentimental, the refined and the feminine. The ideology of boxing is always masculine, even when adopted by women. Today this means opting for black and white (rather than colour) photography, for plain (rather than figurative) language, and for a 'carnal' ethnography in place of an abstract sociology.[211]

Like boxing itself, art and literature about boxing thrive on the back and forth of dialectic: naturalism vs. iconography; the raw vs. the cooked. And while this binary opposition is itself an 'artificial creation of culture', it is one which culture cannot resolve.[212] At its most cooked, boxing remains raw; at its most bloody, it can still tell a story. Although, as Sonny Liston pointed out, it's always the same story – the good guy versus the bad guy – new versions of good and bad are forever forthcoming. Throughout its long and eventful history as a sport, boxing has remained unfailingly eloquent. At the beginning of the twenty-first century, our appetite for its stories remains undiminished.

# References

## Introduction

1 Albert Camus, 'The Minotaur, or The Stop in Oran' (1954), in *Lyrical and Critical Essays*, ed. Philip Thody, trans. Ellen Conroy Kennedy (New York, 1970), p. 123.
2 Quoted in John Eligon, 'Even in Defeat, Jones Remains Center of Attention', *New York Times*, 3 October 2005, Section D, p. 5.
3 Plato, *Protagoras*, trans. W.K.C. Guthrie (Harmondsworth, 1956), p. 73. See also Plato, *Gorgias*, trans. Walter Hamilton (Harmondsworth, 1960), pp. 34–5; Debra Hawhee, *Bodily Arts: Rhetoric and Athletics in Ancient Greece* (Austin, TX, 2004).
4 Gary Wills, 'Muhammad Ali' (1975), in *I'm a Little Special: A Muhammad Ali Reader*, ed. Gerald Early (London, 1999), p. 166.
5 *When We Were Kings*, dir. Taylor Hackford and Leon Gast (1997).
6 A. J. Liebling, *The Sweet Science* (1956) (Harmondsworth, 1982), p. 5. On the endemic nostalgia of boxing commentators, see A. J. Liebling, 'The University of Eight Avenue', *A Neutral Corner* (New York, 1990), p. 31.
7 Philostratus, *Gymnasticus*, in Waldo E. Sweet, *Sport and Recreation in Ancient Greece: A Sourcebook with Translations* (Oxford, 1987), p. 223.

## 1 The Classical Golden Age

1 Philostratus, *Gymnasticus*, in Stephen G. Miller, *Arete: Greek Sports from Ancient Sources* (Berkeley, CA, 1991), p. 31. On Greek nostalgia in this period, see Michael Poliakoff, *Combat Sports in the Ancient World: Competition, Violence, and Culture* (New Haven, CT, 1987), p. 4; Jason König, *Athletics and Literature in the Roman Empire* (Cambridge, 2005), ch. 7. On comparable late-Victorian nostalgia, see Donald G. Kyle, 'E. Norman Gardiner and the Decline of Greek Sport', in *Essays on Sport History and Sport Mythology*, ed. Donald G. Kyle and Gary D. Stark (College Station, TX, 1990), pp. 7–44.

2 On the ritual significance of the Thera paintings, and in particular the boys' shaved heads, see Ellen N. Davis, 'Youth and Age in the Thera Frescoes', *American Journal of Archaeology*, 90, no. 4 (October 1986), 399–406. See also Nanno Marinatos, *Art and Religion in Thera: Reconstructing a Bronze Age* (Athens, 1984). On the implications of the skeletal disorder of one of the figures, see Susan Ferrence and Gordon Bendersky, 'Deformity in the "Boxing Boys"', *Perspectives in Biology and Medicine*, 48, no. 1 (Winter 2005), pp. 105–23.
3 R. A. Hartley, *History and Bibliography of Boxing Books* (Alton, Hants, 1988), p. 6.
4 Poliakoff, *Combat Sports in the Ancient World*, p. 153. On boxing in Samoan funeral games, see James Frazer, 'The Killing of the Divine King', in *Aftermath: A Supplement to The Golden Bough* (London, 1990), p. 314.
5 Clifford Geertz, 'Deep Play: Notes on the Balinese Cockfight', in *The Interpretation of Cultures* (London, 1993), pp. 412–53.
6 Réne Girard, *Violence and the Sacred*, trans. Patrick Gregory (Baltimore, 1977), p. 8.
7 Andrew Stewart, *Art, Desire and the Body in Ancient Greece* (Cambridge, 1997), p. 32; Virgil Nemoianu, 'René Girard and the Dialectics of Imperfection', in *To Honor René Girard*, ed. Alphonse Juilland (Saratoga, CA, 1986), p. 8. See also *Violent Origins: Ritual Killing and Cultural Formation*, ed. Robert G. Hamerton-Kelly (Stanford, CA, 1987).
8 Michael Silk, *Homer: The Iliad* (Cambridge, 1987), p. 104.
9 James M. Redfield, *Nature and Culture in the Iliad* (Durham, NC, 1994), p. 210.
10 Jasper Griffin, *Homer on Life and Death* (Oxford, 1980), p. 193.
11 Homer, *Iliad*, trans. Martin Hammond (Harmondsworth, 1987), p. 382.
12 Homer, *Odyssey*, trans. Richmond Lattimore (New York, 1991), pp. 124–6.
13 Homer, *Odyssey*, pp. 270–73.
14 On the suitors' attitudes to games see Leslie Kurke, *Coins, Bodies, Games and Gold: The Politics of Meaning in Archaic Greece* (Princeton, 1999), p. 255.
15 Poliakoff, *Combat Sports in the Ancient World*, p. 70.

16 Tom Winnifrith, 'Funeral Games in Homer and Virgil', in *Leisure in Art and Literature*, ed. Tom Winnifrith and Cyril Barrett (London, 1992), p. 16.

17 Winnifrith, 'Funeral Games in Homer and Virgil', p. 24. Baron Pierre de Courbertin's assertion that 'the important thing . . . is not to win but to take part' is not in the spirit of Greek competitiveness. See Waldo E. Sweet, *Sport and Recreation in Ancient Greece* (Oxford, 1987), p. 118; Poliakoff, *Combat Sports in the Ancient World*, p. 115. An Edwardian view of Greek 'fair play' can be found in K. T. Frost, 'Greek Boxing', *The Journal of Hellenic Studies*, 26 (1906), pp. 213–25.

18 See Thomas F. Scanlon, 'Boxing Gloves and the Games of Gallienus', *The American Journal of Philology*, 107, no. 1 (Spring 1986), pp. 110–14.

19 'Virgil's Æneis', in *The Poems of John Dryden*, ed. James Kinsley (Oxford, 1958), vol. III, p. 1185.

20 Apollonius, *Jason and the Golden Fleece (The Argonautica)*, trans. Richard Hunter (Oxford, 1993), p. 38; Virgil, *The Georgics*, trans. L. P. Wilkinson (Harmondsworth, 1982), p. 107. See Richard Hunter, 'Bulls and Boxers in Apollonius and Vergil', *The Classical Quarterly*, new series, 39, no. 2 (1989), pp. 557–61. Mesopotamian cylinder seals often featured friezes of animal contests. In the Akkadian period, pairs of contesting figures sometimes included human-headed bulls or bull-men.

21 Ernest Hemingway, *The Sun Also Rises* (London, 1976), p. 116; Norman Mailer, *The Fight* (London, 1976), p. 156.

22 Richard Heinze, *Virgil's Epic Technique* (1982), trans. Hazel and David Harvey and Fred Robertson (Bristol, 1993), pp. 121–41.

23 Virgil, *The Aeneid*, trans. David West (Harmondsworth, 1990), pp. 115–19.

24 Achilles stops the wrestling match at the funeral games. Homer, *Iliad*, p. 383.

25 Joseph Farrell, '*Aeneid 5*: Poetry and Parenthood', in *Reading Vergil's Aeneid*, ed. Christine Perkell (Norman, OK, 1999), p. 102; R.G.M. Nisbet, 'Aeneas Imperator: Roman Generalship in an Epic Context', in *Oxford Readings in Vergil's Aeneid*, ed. S. J. Harrison (Oxford, 1990), p. 382. See also König, *Athletics and Literature in the Roman Empire*, pp. 238–9.

26 Homer, *Iliad*, p. 382. See Poliakoff, *Combat Sports in the Ancient World*, p. 113. Tacitus and Quintilian mention boxing in arguments about skill specialization. See H. A. Harris, *Sport in Greece and Rome* (London, 1972), p. 65.

27 Homer, *Iliad*, pp. 331, 334.

28 Michael C. J. Putnam, *The Poetry of the Aeneid* (Cambridge, MA, 1965), p. 215, fn. 22.

29 The Athenian develops the analogy fully. If they ran out of sparring partners, they would use dummies, and if they had none of those, they would 'box against their own shadows – shadow-boxing with a vengeance!' Plato, *The Laws*, trans. Trevor J. Saunders (Harmondsworth, 1975), pp. 323–4; *The Republic*, trans. Desmond Lee (Harmondsworth, 1974), p. 188.

30 Plutarch, *Moralia*, in Miller, *Arete*, p. 35; Marcus Auerelius, *Meditations*, trans. A.S.L. Farquharson (London, 1946), p. 38.

31 Aristotle, *The Nichomachean Ethics*, trans. David Ross, revised. J. L. Ackrill and J. O. Urmson (Oxford, 1980), pp. 70–71.

32 1 Corinthians, 9: 26–7.

33 Onomastos of Smyrna is credited (by Sextus Julius Africanus) with drawing up the basic rules, while Pythagoras of Samos is reputed to have introduced scientific boxing to the 48th Olympiad in 588 BC. See Poliakoff, *Combat Sports in the Ancient World*, p. 80; Sweet, *Sport and Recreation in Ancient Greece*, p. 71.

34 Pausanias, *Guide to Greece*, trans. Peter Levi (Harmondsworth, 1971), vol. II, p. 259. See also König, *Athletics and Literature in the Roman Empire*, ch. 4; Zahra Newby, *Greek Athletics in the Roman World* (Oxford, 2005), ch. 7.

35 Suetonius, 'Augustus', in *The Twelve Caesars*, trans. Robert Graves (London, 1962), p. 63.

36 Tacitus also reports an anxiety that Greek practices such as boxing will distract young men from their duties as warriors. *Annals* (Harmondsworth, 1956), p. 323.

37 Suetonius, *The Twelve Caesars*, p. 63.

38 Cicero, *Laws*, trans. Niall Rudd (Oxford, 1998), p. 137.

39 Horace, *Epistles*, in *Satires, Epistles and Ars Poetica*, trans. H. Rushton Fairclough (London, 1929), pp. 412–13; Terence, *Eunuch*, in Harris, *Sport in Greece and Rome*, pp. 51–2.

40 St Augustine, *Confessions*, trans. R. S. Pine-Coffin (Harmondsworth, 1961), pp. 121–2. For a very different view of spectatorship, see Philostratus's account of an exceedingly violent wrestling match. *Imagines*, trans. Arthur Fairbanks (London, 1960), p. 151.

41 This is Horace's definition of the scope of lyric, as opposed to epic, poetry in *The Art of Poetry*, in *Satires, Epistles and Ars Poetica*, pp. 456–7.

42 Bacchylides, Ode I, in *Epinician Odes and Dithyrambs of Bacchylides*, trans. David R. Slavitt (Philadelphia, 1998), p. 11.

43 Deborah Steiner, *The Crown of Song: Metaphor in Pindar* (London, 1986), p. 111.

44 Bacchylides, Ode III, *Epinician Odes and Dithyrambs*, p. 21.

45 Pindar, 'Olympian X', trans. C. M. Bowra, *The Odes* (Harmondsworth, 1969), pp. 106–7. Pausanias's version of the founding of the Olympics has the games beginning in a heavenly contest between the gods. *Guide to Greece*, p. 216.

46 See, for example, Pindar, 'Olympian X', in *Odes*, p. 110; and, on athlete-heroes, Poliakoff, *Combat Sports in the Ancient World*, pp. 128–9.

47 Richmond Lattimore, 'A Note on Pindar and His Poetry', *The Odes of Pindar* (Chicago, 1964), p. viii. Epinicians for events such as the chariot race (which the wealthy inevitably won) were more 'sumptuous' than those for events like running or boxing, which athletes won. Robert Fogles, *Bacchylides: Complete Poems*, trans. Fogles (New Haven, CT, 1961), p. xxii.

48 Pindar, 'Olympian VII', in *Odes*, pp. 164–9; and 'Olympian V', in *Odes*, pp. 94–5.

49 In *The Art of Poetry*, Horace declares that should he fail to maintain poetic forms such as the epinician, he would not deserve to be called a poet. *Satires, Epistles and Ars Poetica*,

pp. 456–9. See, for example, *Odes*, Book 4, Ode 3 in *The Complete Odes and Epodes*, trans. David West (Oxford, 1997), pp. 115–16.

50 Dio Chrysostom, 28th Discourse, in *Dio Chrysostom*, trans. J. W. Cohoon (London, 1939), vol. 5, pp. 360–63. On gladiatorial exhibitions, see the 31st Discourse, p. 121, and Cohoon's comments, p. 358.

51 See König, *Athletics and Literature in the Roman Empire*, ch. 3.

52 Winckelmann, 'On the Imitation of the Painting and Sculpture of the Greeks' (1755), in *Winckelmann: Writings on Art*, ed. David Irwin (London, 1972), p. 64.

53 Winckelmann, 'Imitation', p. 62; James Davidson, 'Tall and Tanned and Young and Lovely', *London Review of Books*, 18 June 1998, p. 26.

54 The Greek physician, Galen, complained that training inflicted as many wounds as conflict. See Poliakoff, *Combat Sports in the Ancient World*, p. 93.

55 Dio Chrysostom, 28th Discourse, p. 365.

56 Heinze, *Virgil's Epic Technique*, p. 132.

57 Idyll 22, 'The Dioscuri', in Theocritus, *Idylls*, trans. Anthony Verity (Oxford, 2002), pp. 61–6.

58 In Apollonius's version of this story (which most scholars argue preceded Theocritus), Amcyus is killed by Polydeuces.

59 In *Vera Historia*, Lucian too sets a modern athlete (Areios) against a Homeric hero (Epeios). See König, *Athletics and Literature in the Roman Empire*, pp. 77, 237.

60 Mark Golden, *Sport and Society in Ancient Greece* (Cambridge, 1998), p. 59, fig. 3.

61 The sculpture is also known as the Terme Boxer. *The Baths of Diocletian* (Rome, 2002), pp. 103–5.

62 Thom Jones, 'The Pugilist at Rest', in *The Pugilist at Rest* (London, 1994), pp. 18–19. Jones's narrator speculates that the statue depicts Theogenes.

63 Harris, *Sport in Greece and Rome*, p. 23. König notes that 'mangled ears occur so frequently that they seem to have been taken as a standard means of identifying an athlete as a wrestler or boxer.' *Athletics and Literature in the Roman Empire*, p. 115.

64 Lucilius, in *The Greek Anthology*, trans. W. R. Paton (London, 1918), vol. v, p. 111.

65 *Greek Anthology*, vol. v, p. 111; see also vol. v, p. 109.

66 *Ibid.*, p. 109.

67 Philostratus, *Gymnasticus*, in Miller, *Arete*, p. 18.

68 *Greek Anthology*, vol. iv, p. 343.

69 Plato, *The Republic*, p. 229.

70 Ovid, 'Letter XVI: Paris to Helen', in *Heroides*, trans. Harold Isbell (Harmondsworth, 1990), p. 153.

71 Propertius, 'The advantage of Spartan athletics', in *The Poems*, trans. Guy Lee (Oxford, 1994), pp. 90–91. Propertius also frequently imagined sex as a kind of combat sport ('let bruises show that I've been with my mistress'). See Golden, *Sport and Society in Ancient Greece*, pp. 128–9; Poliakoff, *Sport and Recreation in Ancient Greece*; ch. 20.

72 Anacreon, fragment 369; Sophocles, *Trachiniae*, 441, in Scanlon, *Eros and Greek Athletics*, p. 261. Eros is, however, more commonly imagined as a wrestler than as a boxer. For athletic Cupids, see Philostratus, *Imagines*, p. 25.

73 Lucilius, *Greek Anthology*, p. 111.

74 Scanlon, *Eros and Greek Athletics*, p. 227.

## 2 The English Golden Age

1 John Marshall Carter, *Medieval Games: Sports and Recreations in Feudal Society* (Westport, CT, 1992), pp. 102, 140.

2 See Alison Sim, *Pleasures and Pastimes in Tudor England* (Stroud, 1999).

3 Elliott J. Gorn, *The Manly Art: Bare-knuckle Prize-fighting in America* (Ithaca, NY, 1986), pp. 23–4.

4 Peter Burke, *Popular Culture in Early Modern Europe* (London, 1978), p. 249.

5 *The Dairy of Samuel Pepys*, ed. John Warrington (London, 1953), vol. II, p. 87.

6 This is the claim made by T. B. Shepherd, who includes the report in his anthology, *The Noble Art* (London, 1950), p. 88.

7 Hester Lynch Piozzi, *Anecdotes of the late Samuel Johnson, LL.D. during the last twenty years of his life*, ed. S. C. Roberts (Cambridge, 1925), p. 7. Until recently Figg's card was attributed to Hogarth; today it is thought to be a late-eighteenth-century forgery. Boxing booths continued to feature in British fairgrounds until the 1980s; one features prominently in Alfred Hitchcock's 1927 film *The Ring*. See Vanessa Toulmin, *A Fair Fight: An Illustrated Review of Boxing on British Fairgrounds* (Oldham, 1999), and Tony Gee, *Up to Scratch* (Harpenden, 1998).

8 Pierce Egan, *Boxiana, or Sketches of Ancient and Modern Pugilism: A Selection*, ed. John Ford (London, 1976), pp. 21–2.

9 *The London Journal*, 31 August 1723, cited in Christopher Johnson, '"British Championism": Early Pugilism and the Works of Fielding', *Review of English Studies*, new series, 47 (August 1996), p. 343, n. 33.

10 Quoted in James Peller Malcolm, *Anecdotes of the Manners and Customs of London during the Eighteenth Century* (London, 1808), p. 334. On 'mixed doubles', see pp. 42–3, 339. See also Dianne Dugaw, *Warrior Women and Popular Balladry, 1650–1850* (Cambridge, 1989), pp. 122–6.

11 Zacharias Conrad von Uffenbach, *London in 1710*, trans. W. H. Quarrell and Margaret Mare (London, 1934), pp. 90–91; Martin Nogüe, *Voyages et Aventures* (1728); William Hickey, *Memoirs (1749–1809)*, ed. Alfred Spenser (London, 1913–15), vol. I, pp. 82–3.

12 Pierre Jean Grosley, *A tour to London, or, New observations on England and its inhabitants*, trans. Thomas Nugent. (Dublin, 1772), vol. I, p. 64.

13 For an account of the context in which this print was made, see Ben Rogers, *Beef and Liberty* (London, 2003), pp. 123–8.

14 *The Gentleman's Magazine*, August 1754, quoted in Liza Picard, *Dr Johnson's London* (London, 2000), p. 208. See also George Rudé, *Hanoverian London* (Trupp, 2003), pp. 74–5.

15 Dennis Brailsford, *Bareknuckles: A Social History of Prize-fighting* (Cambridge, 1988), p. 28. Casanova reported coming upon a man dying 'from a blow he had received in boxing' in the streets of London. On inquiring about medical

assistance, he was told that this was not possible since two men had bet 20 guineas on his death or recovery. Wilmarth Sheldon Lewis, *Three Tours Through London in 1748, 1776, 1797* (New Haven, 1941), pp. 62–3.

16  H. D. Miles, *Pugilistica: A history of British Boxing* (Edinburgh, 1906), vol. I, pp. vii, 9, 10. Captain John Godfrey's *Treatise on the Useful Science of Defence*, which includes a chapter on boxing, was published in 1747. Prior to this, fist fighting was only one of several forms of 'prize-fighting'. Other forms involved cudgels, quarterstaffs and backswords.

17  Brailsford, *Bareknuckles*, p. 2. Norbert Elias argues that it was not until these rules were introduced that boxing 'assumed the characteristics of a "sport"'. 'The Genesis of Sport as a Sociological Problem', in *Quest for Excitement: Sport and Leisure in the Civilising Process*, ed. Norbert Elias and Eric Dunning (Oxford, 1986), p. 21.

18  *The Daily Advertiser*, February 1747, in Miles, *Pugilistica*, vol. I, p. 26.

19  Egan, *Boxiana: A Selection*, p. 54.

20  William Maginn, 'An Idyl on the Battle', in *Miscellaneous Writings*, ed. Skelton Mackenzie (New York, 1855–7), vol. I, p. 277. The battle in question is the 1823 fight between Bill Neate and Tom Spring.

21  James Faber's portraits of Broughton and Figg are reproduced and discussed in Sarah Hyde, 'The Noble Art: Boxing and Visual Culture in Early Eighteenth-Century Britain', in *Boxer: An Anthology of Writings on Boxing and Visual Culture*, ed. David Chandler, John Gill, Tania Guha and Gilane Tawadros (London, 1996), pp. 93–7.

22  The games stopped in 1643 as a result of the Civil War and were revived soon after the Restoration. They finally ended in 1853, after complaints of increasingly rowdy crowds.

23  Michael Drayton, 'To My Noble Friend Mr. Robert Dover on his brave annual Assemblies upon Cotswold', and John Stratford, 'To my kind Cosen, and Noble Friend Mr Robert Dover, on his Sports Upon Cotswold', in *Robert Dover and the Cotswold Games: Annalia Dubrensia*, ed. Christopher Whitfield (Evesham, 1962), pp. 102, 179–180.

24  John Suckling, 'A Session of the Poets', in *Fragmenta Aurea* (London, 1646), p. 7.

25  See Seymour Howard, 'Some Eighteenth-Century "Restored" Boxers', *Journal of the Warburg and Courtauld Institutes*, 56 (1993), pp. 238–55.

26  Moses Browne, 'A Survey of the Amphitheatre', in *The New Oxford Book of Eighteenth Century Verse*, ed. Roger Lonsdale (Oxford, 1984), p. 292.

27  John Byrom, 'Extempore Verses Upon a Trial of Skill Between the Two Great Masters of the Noble Science of Defence, Messrs. Figg and Sutton', in *Miscellaneous Poems* (Manchester, 1773), vol. II, p. 47. Greek gore as well as grace characterizes Paul Whitehead's 'The Gymnasiad, or The Boxing–Match' (1744), a mock-heroic account of Broughton's victory over George Stephenson in three books. An extract from Book III is included in *The New Oxford Book of Eighteenth Century Verse*, pp. 373–4. Jonathan Swift's 'The Battle of the Books' (1704) satirized the

ongoing debate between 'Ancients' and 'Moderns'.

28  Christopher Anstey, *The Patriot* (Cambridge, 1767), pp. 5, 7, 19. See Martin S. Day, 'Anstey and Anapestic Satire', *English Literary History*, XV/2, p. 145.

29  Christopher Anstey, *Memoirs of the Noted Buckhorse, Wherein That Celebrated Hero is Carried Into High Life* (London, 1756), vol. I, p. 4. Simon Dickie considers the *Memoirs* as an example of the 'ramble' novel in *In the Mid-Eighteenth Century*, PhD dissertation, Stanford, 2001 (http://novel.stanford.edu/ archive2.htm).

30  Anstey, *Memoirs of the Noted Buckhorse*, vol. II, p. 265.

31  Fielding learnt to box at Eton, which he attended from 1719 to 1724. In various essays and poems from the 1730s he mentions attending Figg's amphitheatre. Martin C. Battestin, *A Henry Fielding Companion* (Westport, CT, 2000), pp. 63–4.

32  Henry Fielding, *Tom Jones* (Oxford, 1996), p. 615.

33  Ibid., p. 181.

34  Henry Fielding, *Shamela*, in *Joseph Andrews and Shamela* (London, 1973), pp. 18–19. Fielding mentions two contemporary women fighters in a burlesque of Juvenal's Sixth Satire: 'Have you not heard of fighting Females / Whom you rather think to be Males? / Of Madam *Sutton*, Mrs. *Stokes* / Who give confounded Cuts and Strokes?' *Miscellanies*, ed. Henry Knight Miller (Oxford, 1972), vol. I, p. 111.

35  Fielding, *Tom Jones*, p. 156.

36  Henry Fielding, *Joseph Andrews* (New York, 1987), pp. 109–10.

37  Fielding, *Tom Jones*, p. 68.

38  Ibid., p. 447. In case the reader does not know the phrase Fielding explains it in a footnote, as he later does with 'muffled' (p. 615).

39  Broughton's 'most favourite blow was the projectile, and when directly planted in the pit of the stomach, generally proved decisive'. [William Oxberry], *Pancratia, or a History of Pugilism* (London, 1812), p. 44. The spot just above the liver became known as 'Broughton's Mark'. Bob Mee, *Bare Fists: The History of Bare-Knuckle Prize-Fighting* (Woodstock, NY, 2001), p. 14.

40  Fielding, *Tom Jones*, pp. 614–15.

41  Bonnell Thornton and George Colman (as 'Mr Town'), *The Connoisseur* 22 August, 1754, reprinted in *Boxing in Art and Literature*, ed. William D. Cox (New York, 1935), p. 59.

42  Oxberry, *Pancratia*, p. 37.

43  Anstey, *Memoirs of the Noted Buckhorse*, vol. I, p. 66.

44  Fielding, *Tom Jones*, p. 434.

45  Fielding, 'An Essay on the Knowledge of the Characters of Men' (1743), reprinted as an appendix to *Joseph Andrews*, p. 327.

46  Fielding, *Joseph Andrews*, p. 108.

47  See Johnson, '"British Championism"', for an account of the full range of boxing references in Fielding.

48  John Richetti says this is the effect, and intent, of the novel's many forms of repetition. *The English Novel in History, 1700–1780* (London, 1999), p. 124.

49  Samuel Richardson, as Johnson points out, ends *Clarissa* with a duel in which Morden kills Lovelace: '"British Championism"', p. 348.

50  *Tom Jones*, pp. 230–31. See also p. 220. Anstey gently mocks

this attitude in *Memoirs of the Noted Buckhorse*. At one point his hero knocks out a dragoon, and after the fallen man has had a chance to set 'his Hair and other matters to rights', Buckhorse clasps and shakes his hand, saying, 'I never love a Man till I have box'd him' (p. 131).

51 Daniel Mendoza, *The Memoirs of the Life of Daniel Mendoza*, ed. Paul Magriel (London, 1951), p. x.

52 Jenny Uglow, *Hogarth* (London, 1997), p. 423.

53 Henri Misson, *M. Misson's memoirs and observations in his travels*, trans. John Ozell (London, 1719), vol. I, p. 304.

54 Grosley credited boxing for the fact that London was the 'only great City in Europe where neither murders nor assassinations happen', and supported the conventional view of English magnanimity. He also noted the adoption of the sport in Brittany, whose inhabitants 'still practise it with certain modifications'. The modified sport, which combined hand and foot fighting, became known as *boxe-française*. *A tour to London*, vol. 1, pp. 62–3, 67, 94.

55 *Boswell's London Journal, 1762–1763*, ed. Frederick A. Pottle (New Haven, 1950), p. 278.

56 Pierce Egan, *Boxiana; or Sketches of Ancient and Modern Pugilism* (London, 1818), vol. I, p. 19; Piozzi, *Anecdotes of the late Samuel Johnson*, pp. 150, 7.

57 Christopher Johnson notes that while the words 'box' or 'boxing' do not appear in translations of the epics by Dryden (1697, 1700) or Pope (1715–20, 1725–6), Cowper's 1791 version of the *Iliad* refers to 'the boxer's art': '"British Championism"', p. 332, n. 5.

58 Brailsford, *Bareknuckles*, ch. 2.

59 Whitehead, 'The Gymnasiad', l.29. See, for example, the *London Evening Post* of 23 October 1764, quoted in Picard, *Dr Johnson's London*, p. 126.

60 *Boxing in Art and Literature*, ed. Cox, p. 57. See Lance Bertelsen, *The Nonsense Club: Literature and Popular Culture, 1749–1764* (Oxford, 1986), ch. 2.

61 Oliver Goldsmith, *The Vicar of Wakefield* (Harmondsworth, 1982), pp. 98, 188.

62 See Tony Gee, 'From Stage-Fighting Fame to the Gallows at Tyburn: James Field – Pugilist and Criminal', in *The British Board of Boxing Control Boxing Yearbook 2006*, ed. Barry J. Hugman (Harpenden, 2005), pp. 55–8.

63 Godfrey, *Treatise upon the Useful Science*, p. 56.

64 Nat Fleischer and Sam Andre, *A Pictorial History of Boxing* (London, 1959), p. 18.

65 *The World*, 10 January 1788, quoted in Ruti Ungar, 'On Shylocks, Toms and Bucks: Images of Minority Boxers in Late Eighteenth and Early Nineteenth Century Britain', in *Fighting Back? Jewish and Black Boxers in Britain*, ed. Michael Berkowitz and Ruti Ungar (London, 2007), p. 25.

66 See Adam Chill, 'The Performance and Marketing of Minority Identity in Late Georgian Boxing', in *Fighting Back?*, pp. 33–49.

67 See Mendoza, *Memoirs*, ch. 3, 'A Verbal Contest with Humphreys'. David Liss's thriller, *A Conspiracy of Paper* (London, 2000) draws on the *Memoirs* for the life of pugilist Benjamin Weave, although the novel is set in 1719 and deals with the South Sea Bubble. Mendoza's great-granddaughter was the mother of actor Peter Sellers.

68 On 'earning a living from sport' at this time, see Adrian Harvey, *The Beginnings of a Commercial Sporting Culture in Britain, 1793–1850* (London, 2004), pp. 198–202.

69 In 1834 Francis Place rather optimistically noted that Mendoza's school had 'put an end to the ill-usage of the Jews': 'the art of boxing as a science . . . soon spread among young Jews and they became generally expert at it.' Todd M. Endelman, *The Jews of Georgian England, 1714–1830* (Ann Arbor, MI, 1999), p. 219. In 1787 the *Times* observed that the school was near the Bank of England and that this was consistent with Mendoza's 'character as a Jew'. Ungar, 'On Shylocks', p. 25.

70 G. M. Trevelyan, *English Social History* (1944) (London, 1973), p. 503. See John Ford, *Prizefighting: The Age of Regency Boximania* (Newton Abbot, 1971).

71 Robert Southey, *Letters from England*, ed. Jack Simmons (London, 1951), p. 451.

72 Joseph Moser, *The Adventures of Timothy Twig, Esq.* (London, 1794), vol. I, pp. 45, 47.

73 Mendoza, Preface to *The Memoirs*, p. xi. For examples of such attacks see Grosley, *A Tour to London*, vol. I, p. 96.

74 Richard Steele, *The Tatler*, 7 July 1709; in *The Tatler*, ed. D. F. Bond (Oxford, 1987), vol. I, pp. 271–2.

75 Mendoza, Preface to *The Memoirs*, p. xi.

76 On English fair play, see Paul Langford, *Englishness Identified: Manners and Character 1650–1850* (Oxford, 2000), pp. 148–57. For the importance of fair play to the seventeenth-century Venetian ritual *pugni*, see Robert C. Davis, *The War of the Fists* (Oxford, 1994), p. 94.

77 *M. Misson's memoirs*, vol. I, pp. 305–6

78 Egan, *Boxiana: A Selection*, pp. 44–5.

79 Ibid., p. 74.

80 Diary entry for 27 October 1792, quoted in Robert Wyndham Ketton-Cremer, *The Early Life and Diaries of William Windham* (London, 1930), pp. 257–8.

81 Quoted in The Earl of Roseberry, 'Introduction', *The Windham Papers* (London, 1913), vol. I, pp. 6–7.

82 Don Herzog, *Poisoning the Minds of the Lower Orders* (Princeton, 1998), p. 333. See also Harvey, *The Beginnings of a Commercial Sporting Culture*, pp. 64–71.

83 *The Windham Papers*, vol. II, p. 351–2.

84 Linda Colley, *Britons: Forging the Nation, 1707–1837* (London, 2003), p. 303.

85 Egan, *Boxiana; or Sketches of Ancient and Modern Pugilism*, vol. I, pp. 481–2.

86 Colley, *Britons*, p. 303.

87 In 1733 a Venetian boxer Alberto di Carni fought Bob Whiteaker. A song celebrating di Carni's defeat proclaimed, 'Your foreigners may be allow'd to be bringers, / Of Eunuchs and Fiddlers and Singers, / But must not pretend to Bring Boxers or Flingers'. *Whiteacre's Glory* (Dublin, 1733). See also Godfrey, *Treatise upon the Useful Science*, pp. 58–60. Venetian boxing had a long history. Throughout the sixteenth and seventeenth centuries, groups of artisans regularly fought *guerre dei pugni* on the city's bridges. See Davis, *The War of the Fists*.

88  Egan, *Boxiana: A Selection*, p. 110.

89  *Black Ajax* by George MacDonald Fraser (London, 1997) is a thoroughly researched fictional account of the fights, presented through the eyes of (and in the styles of) real and imaginary witnesses. See also Peter Radford, 'Lifting the Spirits of the Nation: British Boxers and the Emergence of the National Sporting Hero at the Time of the Napoleonic Wars', *Identities: Global Studies in Culture and Power*, 12, no. 2 (April–June 2005), pp. 249–70.

90  Thomas Jefferson, letter to J. Bannister, 15 October 1785, in *Living Ideas in America*, ed. Henry Steele Commager (New York, 1951), p. 557.

91  D. K. Wiggins, 'Good Times on the Old Plantation', *Journal of Sport History*, 4, no. 3 (1977), pp. 260–84.

92  Egan, *Boxiana: A Selection*, p. 101.

93  Ibid., pp. 100–101. Egan probably wrote the letter.

94  Quoted in Peter Fryer, *Staying Power: The History of Black People in Britain* (London, 1984), p. 447. Appendix 1 consists of short biographies of boxers from 1791 to 1902. For a detailed account of Cribb's training, see Peter Radford, *The Celebrated Captain Barclay* (London, 2001), pp. 167–74.

95  Quoted in Christopher Hibbert, *Wellington: A Personal History* (London, 1997), p. 184.

96  Thomas Moore, 'Epistle from Tom Cribb to Big Ben concerning some Foul Play in a Late Transaction' (1818), in *Poetical Works* (London, 1891), pp. 588–9.

97  Peter Bailey, *Leisure and Class in Victorian England* (London, 1987), p. 36.

98  Claims made for duelling in France were not dissimilar from those made for boxing in England: *Masculinity and Male Codes of Honor in Modern France* (Berkeley, CA, 1998), p. 145. On the British tendency to associate France (and its culture) with effeminacy, see Tim Fulford, *Romanticism and Masculinity* (London, 1999).

99  William Cobbett, 'In Defence of Boxing', *The Political Register* (August 1805), in *Cobbett's England*, ed. John Derry (London, 1968), pp. 172–80.

100  The eponymous narrator of Arthur Conan Doyle's *Rodney Stone* (1896) justified prizefighting's widespread public support in the 1800s in terms of the fact that there was no conscription into the British army and navy; the army and navy depended on 'those who chose to fight because they had fighting blood in them'. *Rodney Stone* (London, 1912), p. 12.

101  Boxing infiltrated lowland Scots society and some academies were set up – notably under George Cooper. Scott's familiarity with boxing culture emerges in surprising places. For example, an 1803 letter to George Ellis begins by announcing, 'My conscience has been thumping me as hard as if it had studied under Mendoza.' *The Letters of Sir Walter Scott, 1787–1807*, ed. H.J.C. Grierson (London, 1932), vol. I, p. 196.

102  Walter Scott, 'The Two Drovers', in *Two Stories* (Edinburgh, 2002), pp. 43, 51. See Christopher Johnson, 'Anti-Pugilism: Violence and Justice in Scott's "The Two Drovers"', *Scottish Literary Journal*, 22, no. 1 (May 1995), pp. 46–60.

103  Scott, 'The Two Drovers', pp. 67–8.

104  Egan, *Boxiana: A Selection*, p. 58.

105  Richard Holmes, in *Romantics and Revolutionaries*, exh. cat., National Portait Gallery, London (London, 2002), pp. 128–9. In Dickens's *Oliver Twist* (1837–8), such dandyism is mocked in the figure of the villain, Bill Sikes, who sports a 'black velveteen coat' and 'a dirty belcher handkerchief round his neck, with the long frayed ends of which, he smeared the foam from the beer as he spoke'; like Belcher, Sikes is famously accompanied by a bull-terrier. *Oliver Twist* (Harmondsworth, 2002), p. 98. In *The Old Curiosity Shop* (1841), Dick Swiveller's fantasy of life as a convict involves a leg iron 'restrained from chafing . . . [his] ankle by a twisted belcher handkerchief.' *The Old Curiosity Shop* (Harmondsworth, 2000), p. 259. The eponymous hero of William Thackeray's *Barry Lyndon* (1844) complains that he can no longer tell the difference between 'my lord and his groom' since 'every man has the same coachman-like look in his belcher and caped coat.' *Barry Lyndon* (Oxford, 1984), p. 248.

106  In 'Advice to a Youth', Cobbett argued that 'natural beauty of person . . . always has, it always will and must have, some weight even with men, and great weight with women. But this does not want to be set off by expensive clothes.' *Cobbett's England*, p. 157. He might also be alluding to Belcher's reputation as the 'Napoleon of the Ring', a name bestowed partly because he was 'so successful in battle' and partly because he was said to look like the Frenchman. Egan, *Boxiana; or Sketches of Ancient and Modern Pugilism*, vol. I, p. 144. See also *The Celebrated Captain Barclay*, pp. 74–5.

107  Quoted in the OED.

108  Robert Fergusson, 'Auld Reikie', in *The Poems of Robert Fergusson*, ed. Matthew P. McDiarmid (Edinburgh, 1954–6), vol. II, p. 112. See Edwin Morgan, 'A Scottish Trawl', in *Gendering the Nation*, ed. Christopher Whyte (Edinburgh, 1995), pp. 208–9.

109  Anstey, *The Patriot*, pp. 19–20.

110  See, for example, Colley, *Britons*, ch. 6, and *A History of Private Life*, ed. Michelle Perrot (Cambridge, MA, 1990). In 1804, Richard Bisset satirized Mary Wollstonecraft, author of *The Rights of Women* (1792), as longing for the day 'when the sex would acquire high renown in boxing matches'. *Modern Literature: A Novel* (London, 1804), vol. III, p. 200; quoted in Dugaw, *Warrior Women*, p. 141.

111  [B. W. Proctor], 'On Fighting', *Fraser's Magazine*, May 1820, p. 519. A friend of Keats, Proctor trained with Tom Cribb and published verse and biographies under the pseudonym Barry Cornwall.

112  *Tom Moore's Diary: A Selection*, ed. J. B. Priestley (Cambridge, 1925), p. 18. Entry for 4 December 1818.

113  Miles, *Pugilistica*, vol. I, p. 97.

114  [Eaton Stannard Barrett], *Six Weeks at Long's* (London, 1817), vol. III, pp. 200–201. John Jackson, under the pseudonym Milo Gymnast, plays an important role in the story.

115  William Cobbett, quoted in Steven Parissien, *George IV: The Grand Entertainment* (London, 2001), p. 309. See also Fulford, *Romanticism and Masculinity*, ch. 5. The Prince separated from Caroline a year after their marriage in 1795. Although they lived apart and both had numerous indiscreet

affairs, she felt entitled to take her place as his Queen in 1821.

116 Byron, 'Hints from Horace' (1811), in *Complete Poetical Works*, ed. Frederick Page (Oxford, 1970), p. 138.

117 Thomas Moore, *The Letters and Journals of Lord Byron* (London, 1875), pp. 116–17.

118 Byron, in *Selected Letters and Journals*, ed. Peter Gunn (Harmondsworth, 1972), p. 142

119 Byron, Notes to *Don Juan*, in *Complete Poetical Works*, p. 918.

120 Moore, *The Letters and Journals of Lord Byron*, p. 24.

121 Thomas Moore noted that, after his death, Byron's friends found it hard to recall which of his feet was lame (they settled on the right): 'Mr Jackson, his preceptor in pugilism, was, in like manner, obliged to call to mind whether his noble pupil was a right or left hand hitter before he could arrive at the same decision.' *Life and Letters of Lord Byron*, p. 1062.

122 See Bohun Lynch, 'Lord Byron's Fire-Screen', *The Field*, December 1922, pp. 7–9; Aubrey Noakes, '70 Years of Prize Ring History', *Boxing News*, 20 August 1947, pp. 8–9; Elizabeth Stewart-Smith, *Byron's Screen* (Mansfield, 1995).

123 Cecil Y. Lang, 'Narcissus Jilted: Byron, *Don Juan* and the Biographical Imperative', in *Historical and Literary Criticism*, ed. Jerome McGann (Madison, 1985), pp. 154–5.

124 *Don Juan*, *Complete Works*, pp. 758, 765.

125 Letter to Elizabeth Pigot, 13 July 1807, in Moore, *The Life and Letters of Lord Byron*, p. 90; *Don Juan*, in *Complete Works*, p. 796.

126 Egan, *Boxiana: A Selection*, p. 168. For a list of 'sporting houses kept by pugilists', see pp. 185–6.

127 Quoted in Jon Hurley, *Tom Spring* (Stroud, 2002), p. 104.

128 Byron, *Selected Letters and Journals*, p. 131.

129 Hurley, *Tom Spring*, p. 117. *Life in London* became a theatrical hit, adapted in various forms throughout Britain and the United States. Exhibition bouts were included as part of the evening's entertainment.

130 Jonathan Bate, *John Clare: A Biography* (London, 2003), p. 264.

131 Byron, *Letters and Journals*, vol. I, pp. 135–6. Letter to Elizabeth Pigot, 26 October 1807.

132 Egan, *Boxiana: A Selection*, pp. 168, 172.

133 Egan, *Life in London. Or the Day and Night Scenes of Jerry Hawthorn, Esq. and his elegant friend Corinthian Tom, accompanied by Bob Logic, The Oxonian, in their Rambles and Sprees through the Metropolis* (London, 1821), pp. 19–20.

134 Washington Irving, 'Buckthorne, or the Young Man of Great Expectations', in *Tales of a Traveller, by Geoffrey Crayon, Gent.*, ed. Judith Giblin Haig (Boston, 1987), p. 121. The 'murderer on the gibbett' is probably John Thurtell, a boxing promoter who was executed for murder in January 1824. Pierce Egan's *Account of the Trial* and his *Recollections of John Thurtell* were published later that year. Buckthorne is surely a play on the eighteenth-century prize-fighter, Buckhorse.

135 Byron, *Selected Letters and Journals*, p. 128. He is quoting Virgil, *Eclogues* iii.59.

136 Ibid., p. 145. Entry for 10 April 1814.

137 Moore, *Life and Letters of Lord Byron*, p. 213.

138 Robert Gittings, *John Keats* (Harmondsworth, 1971), p. 390. Jack Randall defeated Ned Turner after 34 rounds.

# 3 Pugilism and Style

1 Cassius Clay, 'Do You Have to Ask?, in *I am the Greatest!* (Rev-Ola, 1964).

2 Christopher Ricks, *Keats and Embarrassment* (Oxford, 1974), p. 75.

3 Byron, *Selected Letters and Journals*, ed. Peter Gunn (Harmondsworth, 1972), pp. 332, 131. Entries for 15 October 1821 and 24 November 1813.

4 Byron, *Selected Letters and Journals*, p. 217. Letter to Thomas Moore, 1 June 1818.

5 'Hints from Horace', in *Complete Poetical Works*, ed. Frederick Page (Oxford, 1970), p. 138. Of Jeffrey's attack on *Hours of Idleness* in 1807, he said, 'it 'knocked me down', but 'I got up again.' Quoted in Elizabeth Longford, *Byron* (London, 1976), pp. 16–17.

6 [William Maginn], 'A Letter to Pierce Egan, Esq. By Christopher North', *Blackwood's Magazine* (March 1821), pp. 672–3. For a full account of his career, see J. C. Reid, *Bucks and Bruisers: Pierce Egan and Regency England* (London, 1971).

7 Pierce Egan, *Boxiana: A Selection*, ed. John Ford (London, 1976), pp. 199–200.

8 Gregory Dart, '"Flash Style": Pierce Egan and Literary London, 1820–28', *History Workshop Journal*, 51 (2001), p. 198. Mark Parker argues that the magazine was 'the preeminent literary form of the 1820s and 1830s in Britain'. *Literary Magazines and British Romanticism* (Cambridge, 2000), p. 1.

9 This is not quite the same as saying it was a 'classless language': Dart, '"Flash Style"', p. 191.

10 *Blackwood's Magazine*, July 1822, pp. 105–6.

11 Thomas De Quincey, 'Sketch of Professor Wilson [Part II]', *Edinburgh Literary Gazette*, 11 July 1829, in *Works*, ed. Robert Morrison (London, 2000), vol. VII, p. 16. See also Robert Morrison, '*Blackwood's* Berserker: John Wilson and the Language of Extremity', *Romanticism on the Net*, 20 (November 2000).

12 Hugh MacDiarmid, *Scottish Eccentrics* (London, 1936), pp. 99, 105.

13 Quoted in Christine Alexander, 'Readers and Writers: *Blackwood's* and the Brontës', *The Gaskell Society Journal*, 8 (1994), p. 57.

14 *Blackwood's Magazine*, May 1820, p. 187. In October 1820, *Boxiana* published a sonnet 'On the Battle Between Mendoza and Tom Owen, at Banstead Downs', also supposedly by W. W., with a lengthy note on the difference between the Fancy and fancy. For other examples of parodies using pugilism for bathetic effects, see Gary Dyer, *British Satire and the Politics of Style, 1789–1832* (Cambridge, 1997), p. 56.

15 The term was coined by Jon Bee in *Fancyana* (1824).

16 Egan, *Boxiana: A Selection*, p. 13.

17 *Letters of John Keats: A Selection* ed. Robert Gittings (Oxford, 1970), p. 311. Letter to George and Georgiana Keats, 17–14

September 1819. Hazlitt noted the 'oddity of the contrast' between the serious and 'flashy' passages in *Don Juan*. 'Lord Byron', *Lectures on the English Poets and The Spirit of the Age* (London, 1910), p. 241.

18 Byron, *Don Juan*, in *Complete Poetical Works*, pp. 790–1. By Canto xv, stanza xi, the narrator tells us that 'since in England', his mind has 'assumed a manlier vigour' (p. 833).

19 Byron, *Don Juan*, in *Complete Poetical* Works, p. 918.

20 P. W. Graham, *Lord Byron's Bulldog: The Letters of John Cam Hobhouse to Lord Byron* (Columbus, OH, 1984), p. 32; Thomas Moore, *The Letters and Journals of Lord Byron* (London, 1875), p. 446.

21 Gary Dyer, 'Thieves, Boxers, Sodomites: Being Flash to Byron's *Don Juan*', *PMLA* (2001), pp. 562–78 (p. 564).

22 Moore, *Poetical Works* (London, 1829), p. 159.

23 Benita Eissler, *Byron* (London, 1999), p. 103.

24 Washington Irving, 'Buckthorne, or the Young Man of Great Expectations', in *Tales of a Traveller, by Geoffrey Crayon, Gent.* (1824), ed. Judith Giblin Haig (Boston, 1987), p. 121.

25 Robert Southey, *Letters from England*, ed. Jack Simmons (London, 1951), p. 451.

26 [Henry Luttrell], *Advice to Julia: A letter in rhyme* (London, 1820), p. 32.

27 *Tom Moore's Diary: A Selection*, ed. J. B. Priestley (Cambridge, 1925), pp. 17–18. Entry for 29 November and 4 December 1818.

28 John Hamilton Reynolds, *The Fancy: A Selection from the Poetical Remains of the Late Peter Corcoran, of Gray's Inn, Student of Law, with a Brief Memoir of His Life* (1820), reprinted with a prefatory memoir and notes by John Masefield and illustrations by Jack B. Yeats (London, 1905), pp. 64, 74.

29 Reynolds, *The Fancy*, p. xxi.

30 Thomas De Quincey, 'The Pretensions of Phronology', in *Works*, ed. David Groves (London, 2000), vol. v, p. 323.

31 Thomas De Quincey, 'To a Reader; Invitation to a *Set-To* on Greek Literature', in *Works* (London, 2000), vol. vi, p. 226.

32 Andrew Crichton, *Edinburgh Evening Post*, 28 June 1828, in De Quincey, *Works*, vol. vi, p. 194.

33 William Hazlitt, 'Introduction to Elizabethan Literature', in *The Fight and Other Writings*, ed. Tom Paulin and David Chandler (Harmondsworth, 2000), p. 64; 'William Godwin', in *The Fight and Other Writings*, p. 280; 'Mr. Wordsworth', *The Fight and Other Writings*, p. 306.

34 Hazlitt, 'On Shakespeare and Milton' (1818), in *The Fight and Other Writings*, pp. 92, 97, 101. In a later essay, 'Poetry' (1829), he describes Perdita's speech on flowers in *The Winter's Tale* as 'knock[ing] down' English readers: *The Fight and Other Writings*, p. 208.

35 Hazlitt, 'Gusto' (1817), in *The Fight and Other Writings*, pp. 78, 80.

36 Hazlitt, 'On the Prose-Style of Poets' (1826), in *The Fight and Other Writings*, p. 406.

37 Linda Colley, 'I am the Watchman', *London Review of Books*, 20 November 2003, p. 16.

38 William Hazlitt, 'Character of Cobbett' (1821), in *The Fight and Other Writings*, p. 129.

39 Hazlitt, 'Character of Cobbett', p. 133. The allusion here is

to *Don Quixote*. A more general essay, on 'Parliamentary Eloquence', repeats the claim that, a 'repetition of blows . . . is of no use, unless they are struck in the same place': *The Fight and Other Writings*, p. 323.

40 The phrase is used in a newspaper clipping describing the fight which is glued on to Byron's screen.

41 Peter Radford, *The Celebrated Captain Barclay: Sport, Money and Fame in Regency Britain* (London, 2001), p. 23.

42 Hazlitt, 'Character of Cobbett', p. 138.

43 Hazlitt, 'Jack Tars', in *The Fight and Other Writings*, p. 157.

44 Hazlitt, 'Jack Tars', p. 158.

45 Much of Hazlitt's language is Lockean: 'The idea of *solidity* we receive by our touch; and it arises from the resistance which we find in body to the entrance of any other body into the place it possesses . . .'; '"hard" and "soft" are names that we give to things only in relation to the constitutions of our own bodies'. John Locke, *An Essay Concerning Human Understanding*, ed. A. D. Woozley (Glasgow, 1984), pp. 103, 105. See also Tom Paulin, *The Day-Star of Liberty: William Hazlitt's Radical Style* (London, 1998), p. 31.

46 Hazlitt, 'Madame Pasta and Mademoiselle Mars', in *The Fight and Other Writings*, p. 483, 485.

47 Hazlitt, 'A Farewell to Essay-Writing', in *The Fight and Other Writings*, p. 540.

48 'Letter to Pierce Egan, Esq.', quoted by Duncan Wu in his 'Introductory Note' to *Table Talk*, ed. Wu (London, 1998), p. xii.

49 John Hamilton Reynolds, *London Magazine*, 7 (May 1823), quoted in Wu, 'Introductory Note', *Table Talk*, p. xv.

50 Hazlitt, 'The Fight', in *The Fight and Other Writings*, p. 140, quoting *Hamlet*, II. ii 600–1.

51 John Milton, *Paradise Lost*, Book II, ll. 714–16.

52 David Bromwich, *Hazlitt: The Mind of a Critic* (New Haven, 1983), pp. 436–7, n. 10. The deleted passage, which Bromwich quotes, comes in the third paragraph, after 'I passed Hyde Park Corner', and before, 'Suddenly I heard the clattering of the Brentford stage'. For a full discussion about the ways in which Hazlitt negotiates between sentiment and its 'apparent opposite', see David Higgins, 'Englishness, Effeminacy, and the New Monthly Magazine: Hazlitt's *The Fight* in Context', *Romanticism*, 10 (2004), pp. 170–90. See also Gregory Dart, 'Romantic Cockneyism: Hazlitt and the Periodical Press', *Romanticism*, 6 (2000), pp. 143–62.

53 William Hazlitt, *Liber Amoris* (London, 1957), p. 89.

54 Hazlitt, 'On Going a Journey', in *Table Talk*, p. 166.

55 Arguing against the introduction of class distinctions into literary criticism in an 1821 essay, Hazlitt quoted Jem Belcher's response when asked how he felt when facing a larger opponent: 'An' please ye, sir, when I am stript to my shirt, I am afraid of no man.' 'Pope, Lord Byron, and Mr. Bowles', *London Magazine* (June 1821), p. 594.

56 Hazlitt, 'The Indian Jugglers' (1821), in *The Fight and Other Writings*, p. 125. On the competing claims of androgynous and masculine prose for Coleridge, see Tim Fulford, *Romanticism and Masculinity* (London, 1999), ch. 4.

57 Hazlitt, 'The Indian Jugglers', pp. 115–16.

58 Hazlitt, 'On the Qualifications Necessary to Success',

*London Magazine* 1 (June 1820), p. 653 fn.

59 Hazlitt, 'Prose-Style and the Elgin Marbles', in *The Fight and Other Writings*, p. 240.

60 Sir Joshua Reynolds, *Discourses on Art*, ed. Robert R. Wark (San Marino, CA, 1959), p. 171.

61 Hazlitt, 'On the Pleasure of Painting', in *The Fight and Other Writings*, pp. 22–3; 'On the Elgin Marbles', Part II, in *The Fight and Other Writings*, pp. 225, 231; 'On Hogarth's Marriage-à-la-Mode', Part II, in *The Fight and Other Writings*, p. 167; 'Prose-Style and the Elgin Marbles', in *The Fight and Other Writings*, p. 240.

62 William Hogarth, *The Analysis of Beauty*, ed. Ronald Paulson (New Haven, CT, 1997), p. 67.

63 Reynolds complained that the Boxers 'are engaged in the most animated action with the greatest serenity of countenance. This is not recommended for imitation'. *Discourses on Art*, p. 181.

64 Francis Haskell and Nicholas Penny, *Taste and the Antique: The Lure of Classical Sculpture, 1500–1900* (New Haven, 1981), p. 339.

65 John Flaxman, *Lectures on Sculpture* (London, 1829), pp. 119–20.

66 Pierce Egan, *Boxiana; or Sketches of Ancient and Modern Pugilism* (London, 1818), vol. I, p. 20. See also Sarah Hyde, 'The Noble Art: Boxing and Visual Culture in Early Eighteenth-Century Britain', in *Boxer: An Anthology of Writings on Boxing and Visual Culture*, ed. David Chandler, John Gill, Tania Guha and Gilane Tawadros (London, 1996), pp. 93–7, and Ronald Paulson, *Hogarth* (Cambridge, 1991), vol. I, pp. 23–4.

67 Jenny Uglow offers allegorical readings of Figg's presence: in *Southwark Fair*, he 'could suggest that old political prize-fighters too should be wary of challengers'; in *The Rake's Progress*, he represents 'the old squirarchical pleasures' that the Rake is rejecting. *Hogarth*, pp. 243, 248.

68 William Hazlitt, 'On Genius and Common Sense' (1821), in *The Fight and Other Writings*, p. 535. Tom Oliver defeated Ned Painter in May 1814. On Kean's interest in the 'aesthetic of boxing', see Jeffrey Kahan, *The Cult of Kean* (London, 2006), pp. 13–19.

69 Haydon's interest extended beyond the life class. His diary records trips to the Fives Court and the eager perusal of a fight report. *The Diary of Benjamin Robert Haydon*, ed. Willard Bissell Pope (Cambridge, MA, 1960), vol. II, pp. 220, 452.

70 *The Diary of Joseph Farington*, ed. Kathryn Cave (New Haven, 1982), vol. IX, pp. 3300-1.

71 Hogarth, *The Analysis of Beauty*, p. 68. Some years later Thomas Carlyle, arguing for the importance of the 'Intuitive' over the 'Logical', asked 'does the boxer hit better for knowing that he has a flexor longus and a flexor brevis?' 'Characteristics', *Edinburgh Review*, 59 (December 1831).

72 *The Diary of Joseph Farington*, vol. IX, p. 3306; Sir Charles Bell, *The Anatomy and Philosophy of Expression with the Fine Arts* (London, 1890), pp. 10–11.

73 *The Diary of Joseph Farington*, vol. IX, pp. 3320–21. In 1744

74 On representations of Dutch Sam, see Ruti Ungar, 'On Shylocks, Toms and Bucks: Images of Minority Boxers in Late Eighteenth and Early Nineteenth Century Britain', in *Fighting Back? Jewish and Black Boxers in Britain*, ed. Michael Berkowitz and Ruti Ungar (London, 2007), pp. 19–31.

75 Milton, *Paradise Lost*, Book I, l.330. According to Michael Levey, the painting was 'generally accounted a failure'. *Sir Thomas Lawrence, 1769–1830*, exh. cat., National Portrait Gallery, London (London, 1979), p. 34.

76 *Boxiana: A Selection*, p. 48.

77 For fuller accounts of these paintings, and *Homer Reciting His Poems to the Greeks*, in which Jackson appears in the foreground as the young victor in the foot race, see Douglas Goldring, *Regency Portrait Painter: The Life of Sir Thomas Lawrence, P.R.A.* (London, 1951), pp. 74–5, 110–11, 196, and Radford, *The Celebrated Captain Barclay*, pp. 43–6, 64.

78 On the more general use of boxing prints for political and satirical purposes, see Seymour Howard, 'Boxing Broadsides', in *Popular Art: Essays on Urban Imagery*, ed. Elizabeth Adan (Berkeley, CA, 1992), pp. 18–19.

79 See Lorenz E. A. Eitner, *Géricault: His Life and Work* (London, 1983), p. 91.

80 See Maureen Ryan, 'Liberal Ironies, Colonial Narratives and the Rhetoric of Art: Reconsidering Géricault's *Radeau de la Méduse* and the *Traite des Nègres*', in *Théodore Géricault: The Alien Body / Tradition in Chaos*, exh. cat., Morris and Helin Belkin Gallery, University of British Columbia (Vancouver, 1997), pp. 18–51.

81 John Masefield, 'Introduction', to Reynolds, *The Fancy*, p. 19.

82 Quoted in Carol Bock, '"Our Plays": the Brontë juvenilia', in *The Cambridge Companion to the Brontës*, ed. Heather Glen (Cambridge, 2002), p. 48. In Charlotte Brontë's *Corner Dishes* (1834), the young Duke of Zamorna employs a pugilist as his private secretary and sparring companion. Christine Alexander and Margaret Smith, *The Oxford Companion to the Brontës* (Oxford, 2003), pp. 414–15.

83 Patrick Branwell Brontë, *Works*, ed. Victor Neufeldt (New York, 1997), vol. I, p. 177.

84 See Mary Butterfield, *Brother in the Shadow: Stories and Sketches by Patrick Branwell Brontë* (Bradford, 1988), pp. 121–5, and Christopher Heywood, '"Alas! Poor Caunt": Branwell's Emancipationist Cartoon', *Brontë Society Transactions*, 21, no. 5 (1995), pp. 177–85.

85 Juliet Barker, *The Brontës* (London, 1999), p. 229.

86 John Clare, *Autobiographical Writings*, ed. Eric Robinson (Oxford, 1983), p. 144.

87 Iain McCalman and Maureen Perkins, 'Popular Culture', in *The Oxford Companion to the Romantic Age*, ed. Iain McCalman (Oxford, 1999), p. 220.

88 Jonathan Bate, *John Clare: A Biography* (London, 2003), p. 438.

Jack Broughton modelled for the arms of Michael Rysbrack's sculpture *Hercules*, housed in the Stourhead Pantheon. See Richard Warner, *Excursion from Bath* (London, 1801), p. 111; M. I. Webb, 'Sculpture by Rysbrack at Stourhead', *The Burlington Magazine*, 92 (November 1950), p. 311.

89 John Clare, *Letters*, ed. Mark Storey (Oxford, 1985), p. 648 n.

90 Northampton MS. Jotting, quoted in *Clare: The Critical Heritage*, ed. Mark Storey (London, 1973), p. 3. See also Edward Strickland, 'Boxer Byron: A Clare Obsession', *The Byron Journal*, 17 (1989), pp. 57–76.

91 Clare, *Letters*, p. 647.

92 H. D. Miles, *Pugilistica* (Edinburgh, 1906), vol. I, pp. 442 3. The fight took place on 18 April; the Battle of Waterloo on 18 June. The image is reproduced in Christine Alexander and Jane Sellars, *The Art of the Brontës* (Cambridge, 1995), p. 95.

# 4 'Fighting, Rightly Understood'

1 'Punch's Theatre', *Punch*, 25 September 1841, p. 131.

2 Matthew Arnold, *'Culture and Anarchy' and Other Writings*, ed. Stefan Collini (Cambridge, 1993), pp. 109, 114–15. Arnold takes his description of the Barbarians from Tennyson's 'The Princess' (1847).

3 Quoted in Carol Lansbury, 'Sporting Humor in Victorian Literature', *Mosaic*, 9, 4 (Summer 1976), p. 70.

4 John Ford, *Prizefighting* (Newton Abbot, 1971), p. 188.

5 William Hazlitt, 'Rev. Mr. Irving' (1825), in *Lectures on the English Poets and The Spirit of the Age* (London, 1910), p. 205.

6 Vincent Dowling, *Bell's Life*, 2 October 1825, in Ford, *Prizefighting*, pp. 189–90.

7 William Cobbett, 'In Defense of Boxing' (1805), in *Cobbett's England*, ed. John Derry (London, 1968), p. 178.

8 Charles Dickens, *The Pickwick Papers* (Oxford, 1986), p. 295.

9 George Borrow, *Lavengro* (Oxford, 1982), pp. 157–9.

10 Thomas Hardy links modern prizefighting to the ghosts of 'gladiatorial combat', both of which prefigure the 'mortal commercial combat' in which Henchard and Farfrae are engaged. *The Mayor of Casterbridge* (Harmondsworth, 1978), pp. 141, 142, 186.

11 Jon Hurley, *Tom Spring* (Stroud, 2002), p. 75.

12 Borrow, *Lavengro*, p. 167. *Lavengro* and its sequel, *The Romany Rye* (1857), are full of fights and stories of old-school pugilists.

13 Elliot J. Gorn, *The Manly Art: Bare-Knuckle Prize Fighting in America* (Ithaca, NY, 1986), p. 40.

14 Viscount Knebworth, *Boxing* (London, 1931), pp. 36–7.

15 Quoted in Alan Lloyd, *The Great Prize Fight* (London, 1977), p. 9.

16 Ibid., pp. 13, 7. See also Arthur Conan Doyle, 'Bendy's Sermon', in *Songs of the Road* (1911).

17 Quoted in Hershel Parker, *Herman Melville: A Biography* (Baltimore, 1996), vol. I, pp. 501–2.

18 Herman Melville, *Moby-Dick, or, The Whale* (Harmondsworth 1972), p. 266.

19 Gorn, *The Manly Art*, pp. 148–9.

20 This claim was made in *All the Year Round* (19 May 1860). The author, John Hollingshead, felt it necessary to begin his piece by announcing that it was with the 'encouragement' of 'my friend the Conductor of this Journal' (that is, Dickens) that he both attended the fight and wrote about it. The essay begins, 'There was a period, not more than some six months ago, when most of us thought we could not publicly state that we had seen a prize fight.' H. D. Miles, *Tom Sayers, Sometime Champion of England, His Life and Pugilistic Career* (London, 1866), Appendix, pp. xx-xxxii.

21 Heenan had worked in the foundries of the Pacific Mail Steamship Company in Benicia. Forty years later the teenage Jack London briefly worked, and drank, there. See *John Barleycorn* (1913), ch. 12. In England, the name provided opportunities for numerous jokes. *Punch* pretended it was a girl's name; Surtees adopted it for the name of a wayward stag. 'The Wrong Ring for Ladies', *Punch*, 3 March 1860, p. 87; R. S. Surtees, *Mr Facey Romford's Hounds* (London, 1865).

22 Lloyd, *The Great Prize Fight*, pp. 72–3.

23 Ibid., pp. 113–15.

24 Farnborough was easily served by both the South Eastern and South Western lines. Railways, and special excursion trains, made it possible for a much wider social spectrum, as well as greater numbers, of spectators to attend sporting events. James Walvin, *Leisure and Society, 1830–1950* (London, 1978), pp. 24–7. For an account of the journey to Farnborough, see Miles, *Tom Sayers*, pp. 164–6.

25 See Hugh Walpole's *The Fortress* (London, 1932), Part IV, for a fictional account of the fight.

26 Lloyd, *The Great Prize Fight*, p. 145.

27 Quoted in *Punch*, 26 May 1860, p. 210.

28 Charles Dickens, 'The Uncommercial Traveller: Shy Neighbourhoods', in *The Uncommercial Traveller and other Papers, 1859–70*, ed. Michael Slater and John Drew (London, 2000), p. 119.

29 Lloyd, *The Great Prize Fight*, p. 133.

30 *The Times*, 16 June 1904, p. 9.

31 James Joyce, *Ulysses* (Harmondsworth, 1992), p. 311. See J. Lawrence Mitchell, 'Joyce and Boxing', *James Joyce Quarterly*, 31, 2 (1994), pp. 21–9.

32 Benjamin Disraeli, *Sybil* (Harmondsworth, 1980), pp. 395, 397.

33 Ibid., p. 58.

34 George Eliot, *Letters*, ed. Gordon S. Haight (New Haven, 1954), vol. III, pp. 289–90. The following year Lewes's son, Thornton, sent his father an excited letter telling him of his fight with a 'Mr. R'. He concludes the letter, 'That is all, as Sayers said to Heenan, when he split the latter's eye open'. Eliot, *Letters*, ed. Gordon S. Haight (New Haven, 1978), vol. VIII, pp. 294–5. Black eyes are also the mark of prize-fighters in Anthony Trollope's *The Small House at Allington* (Harmondsworth, 1991), p. 382.

35 William Allingham, *A Diary, 1824–1889* (Harmondsworth, 1985), pp. 85–6.

36 William Makepeace Thackeray, 'On Some Late Great Victories', in *Roundabout Papers*, ed. John Edwin Wells (New York, 1925), pp. 41–7. Thackeray also published (anonymously) 'The Fight of Sayerius and Heenanus: A Lay of Ancient London', a parody of 'Horatius', one of Macaulay's *Lays of Ancient Rome* (1842). *Punch* (28 April 1860), p. 177.

37 William Makepeace Thackeray, 'De Juvente', in *Roundabout*

*Essays*, pp. 83–4.

38  William Makepeace Thackeray, 'John Leech's Pictures of Life and Character', *Quarterly Review*, 191 (December 1854).

39  William Makepeace Thackeray, *Vanity Fair* (Oxford, 1983), p. 70.

40  Ibid., pp. 112, 128, 113. On more recent Oxford University boxing, see *Blue Blood*, dir. Stevan Riley (2006).

41  Ibid., pp. 424–5, 427–8, 430.

42  *Vanity Fair*'s villain, Lord Steyne is modelled on the Earl of Yarmouth, a patron of Gentleman John Jackson. Lord Yarmouth spoke on 'the national unity of the pugilistic art' at the inaugural dinner of the Pugilistic Club in 1814. Peter Radford, *The Celebrated Captain Barclay* (London, 2001), p. 222. Yarmouth is also the model for Lord Monmouth in Disraeli's *Coningsby* (1844).

43  Thackeray, *Vanity Fair*, p. 685.

44  Robert Browning, 'A Likeness', in *Robert Browning: A Critical Edition of the Major Works*, ed. Adam Roberts (Oxford, 1997), pp. 341–2. The eponymous hero of Washington Irving's 'Buckthorne' recalls his Oxford college room as 'decorated with whips of all kinds, spurs, fowling pieces, fishing rods, foils and boxing gloves.' *Tales of a Traveller, by Geoffrey Crayon, Gent.*, ed. Judith Giblin Haig (Boston, 1987), pp. 95–127. Schoolboy studies were decorated in a similar style. See Thomas Hughes, *Tom Brown's Schooldays* (Oxford, 1999), p. 94.

45  George Eliot, *Middlemarch* (Harmondsworth, 1994), pp. 557–8.

46  George Eliot, *Adam Bede* (Harmondsworth, 1980), p. 8.

47  Ibid., p. 19. By the end of the novel, Eliot suggests that Adam's moral sensibility has developed 'like a muscle' to match his physical prowess (p. 489). On Eliot's debt to Thomas Hughes, see Maureen M. Martin, '"Boys who will be Men": Desire in *Tom Brown's Schooldays*', *Victorian Literature and Culture*, 30, 2 (2002), pp. 483–502.

48  Eliot, *Adam Bede*, pp. 62–3, 163, 165.

49  Ibid., p. 302.

50  Darwin distinguishes Natural Selection, the 'struggle for existence', from Sexual Selection, the 'struggle between the males for possession of the females', in which 'special weapons confined to the male sex' ensure victory. *The Origin Of Species* (Oxford, 1996), p. 73. I am not claiming a direct influence. *Adam Bede* was published in February; Eliot read *The Origin of Species* shortly after it appeared in November.

51  Eliot, *Adam Bede*, p. 310.

52  In R. D. Blackmore's *Lorna Doone* (1869), schoolboy John Ridd speculates on the roots of the expression: 'whether that word hath origin in a Greek term meaning a conflict, as the best-read boys asserverated, or whether it is nothing more than a figure of similitude, from the beating arms of a mill . . . it is not for a man devoid of scholarship to determine'. *Lorna Doone* (London, 1967), pp. 28–9.

53  In 'On Some Late Great Victories', Thackeray personified Morality as a woman, only to interrupt her, 'Have the great kindness to stand a LEETLE aside, and just let us see one or two more rounds between the men' (p. 43).

54  See, for example, Samuel Warren, 'The Thunder Struck and the Boxer' (1832), in *Tales of Terror from Blackwood's Magazine*, ed. Robert Morrison and Chris Baldick (Oxford, 1995), pp. 243–80.

55  Thomas Ingoldsby, 'The Ghost', in *The Ingoldsby Legends, or Mirth and Marvels* (London, 1840), pp. 96–7.

56  George Eliot, *The Mill on the Floss* (Harmondsworth, 1985), pp. 90, 107, 237, 258, 447–8, 506, 537.

57  George Bernard Shaw, 'Preface' to *Cashel Byron's Profession* (London, 1925), p. xvii.

58  Thackeray, *Vanity Fair*, pp. 49, 50. This reworks a similar scene set in an 1843 short story, 'Mr. And Mrs. Frank Berry'. See *The Fitz-Boodle Papers* and *Men's Wives* (London, 1857), p. 59. The school is called 'Slaughter House'; Thackeray attended Charterhouse, where he broke his nose in a fight.

59  Thackeray, *Vanity Fair*, p. 54. Although Dobbin is named for the fruit his father sells, Thackeray may also be alluding to the prize-fighter James Figg.

60  An example of this interchange was Thomas Moore's description of Waterloo as 'that great day of *milling*, when blood lay in lakes, / When Kings held the bottle, and Europe the stakes.' 'Epistle from Tom Cribb to Big Ben' (1818), in *Poetical Works* (London, 1891), pp. 588–9.

61  Asa Briggs, *Victorian People* (Harmondsworth, 1965), p. 152.

62  So said *Blackwood's Magazine* (February 1861), p. 131.

63  The phrase 'muscular Christianity' was first used in T. C. Sandars's review of Charles Kingsley's *Two Years Ago* (1857). Donald E. Hall, 'Introduction', *Muscular Christianity: Embodying the Victorian Age* (Cambridge, 1994), ed. Hall, p. 7. See also J. A. Mangan, 'Bullies, beatings, battles and bruises: "great days and jolly days" in one mid-Victorian public school', in *Disreputable Pleasures*, ed. Mike Huggins and J. A. Mangan (Abingdon, 2004), pp. 23–5.

64  Bruce Haley, *The Healthy Body and Victorian Culture* (Cambridge, MA, 1978), p. 4.

65  Hughes, *Tom Brown's Schooldays*, pp. 281–2.

66  E. S. Turner, *Boys Will be Boys* (London, 1948), pp. 247.

67  Ibid., p. 254.

68  Hughes, *Tom Brown's Schooldays*, pp. 282, 301. On Hughes's debt here to Thomas Carlyle, see David Rosen, 'The volcano and the cathedral: muscular Christianity and the origins of primal manliness', in *Muscular Christianity*, ed. Hall, p. 25.

69  On Hughes's concern with the concept of England, see Dennis W. Allen, 'Young England: muscular Christianity and the politics of the body in *Tom Brown's Schooldays*', in *Muscular Christianity*, ed. Hall, pp. 114–32.

70  1 Corinthians, 9: 26–7. Hughes makes this observation as Tom is about to have his first taste of a 'town and gown row'. *Tom Brown at Oxford* (London, 1861), vol. I, pp. 198–200. Hughes attended Oriel College, which he described as 'the accepted home of the noble science of self-defence'. Edward C. Mack and W.H.G. Armytage, *Thomas Hughes* (London, 1952), p. 28. At Cambridge, Thomas Welsh, better known as Massa Sutton, taught Charles Kingsley to box. Peter Fryer, *Staying Power: The History of Black People in Britain* (London, 1984), p. 451.

71 See Richard Jenkyns, *The Victorians and Ancient Greece* (Oxford, 1980), pp. 280–97, and Alex Potts, *Flesh and the Ideal* (New Haven, 1994), pp. 239–53.

72 Walter Pater, 'The Age of Athletic Prizemen', in *Greek Studies* (London, 1910), pp. 276, 279. Pater compares ancient athletes with modern cricketers.

73 Walter Pater, 'Winckelmann' (1867), in *The Renaissance* (Oxford, 1989), p. 137; 'The Age of Athletic Prizemen', in *Greeks Studies*, p. 280.

74 Pater, 'The Age of Athletic Prizemen', p. 295 (my emphasis).

75 Norman Vance finds a 'possible meeting point' between Muscular Christian ideals and Pater's aestheticism in the 'moralised Hellenism' of the Revd. E. C. Lefroy. *The Sinews of the Spirit* (Cambridge, 1985), p. 185. James Eli Adams argues that Carlyle is their common root. 'Pater's muscular aestheticism', in *Muscular Christianity*, ed. Hall, pp. 215–38.

76 Briggs, *Victorian People*, p. 160.

77 In his personal life, the Marquess was also pugnacious. Best known as the father of Oscar Wilde's lover, Lord Alfred Douglas (Bosie), and Wilde's great antagonist, the police intervened to stop him fighting on the street with his son Percy. The Tenth Marquess of Queensberry, *The Sporting Queensberrys* (London, 1942), p. 141.

78 Donald Thomas, *The Victorian Underworld* (New York, 1998), p. 195.

79 Marquess of Queensberry, *The Sporting Queensberrys*, p. 116.

80 The Native Americans opposed the election of foreigners to office, and demanded the repeal of naturalization laws. See Herbert Asbury, *The Gangs of New York* (London, 2002), ch. 5; Edward Van Every, *Sins of New York as 'exposed' by the Police Gazette* (New York, 1930); Gorn, *The Manly Art*, ch. 3. On the wider context, see Richard B. Stott, *Workers in the Metropolis: Class, Ethnicity, and Youth in Antebellum New York City* (Ithaca, NY, 1990).

81 Gorn, *The Manly Art*, p. 164. The Rev. Gilbert Haven compared Ulysses S. Grant to Morrissey, describing him as 'but a boxer on a bigger scale', who 'fights with others' fists'. *National Sermons* (Boston, 1869), p. 617.

82 Thomas Wentworth Higginson, 'Saints and Their Bodies', in *Major Problems in American Sport History*, ed. Steven A. Riess (Boston, 1997), pp. 83–85.

83 Oliver Wendall Holmes, 'The Autocrat of the Breakfast Table', *Atlantic Monthly*, 1 (May 1858), p. 881.

84 Walt Whitman, 'A Song of Joys', in *Leaves of Grass* (Oxford, 1990), p. 143. See also Whitman, 'Pugilism and Pugilists' (1858), in *I Sit and Look Out: Editorials from the Brooklyn Daily Times*, ed. Emory Holloway and Vernolian Schwarz (New York, 1932), pp. 105–6.

85 Henry James, *The American* (Harmondsworth, 1991), pp. 33–4, 52–3, 56. Eric Haralson connects Newman's 'corporeal and capitalist energies'. 'Henry James's *The American*: A (New)man is Being Beaten', *American Literature* 64 (1992), p. 478. Jeffory A. Clymer links the novel to changes in late nineteenth-century boxing, most of which, however, occurred after the novel's publication. 'The Market in Male Bodies: Henry James's *The American* and Late-Nineteenth-Century Boxing', *The Henry James Review*, 25 (2004),

pp. 127–45.

86 Henry James, *The Bostonians* (Harmondsworth, 1976), p. 290.

87 Duffield Osborne, 'A Defence of Pugilism', *North American Review*, April 1888, pp. 434–5. Frederick Jackson Turner's 'The Significance of the Frontier in American History' (1893) is the classic expression of this anxiety.

88 Theodore Roosevelt, 'The Strenuous Life' (1900), in *Works* (New York, 1926), vol. XIII, p. 319. On Roosevelt as a Harvard student boxer, see Jacob A. Riis, *Theodore Roosevelt, The Citizen* (New York, 1903), pp. 29–31.

89 Theodore Roosevelt, *An Autobiography* (New York, 1985), p. 42.

90 Vance, *Sinews of the Spirit*, p. 52.

91 The difference is made clear by Colin, the protagonist of Frances Hodgson Burnett's 1911 novel, *The Secret Garden*. Happy to acquire muscles that 'stand out like lumps', Colin is appalled by the thought that he might resemble a prize-fighter. *The Secret Garden* (Oxford, 2002), pp. 250, 270.

92 Mack and Armytage, *Thomas Hughes*, p. 98.

93 Ibid., pp. 79–80. See J. Llewelyn Davies, *The Working Men's College 1854–1904* (London, 1904).

94 Walter Besant, *East London* (London, 1901), p. 172.

95 Walter Besant, *All Sorts and Conditions of Men* (Oxford, 1997), p. 182. Harry's father, it turns out, had in 'his Corinthian days . . . often repaired to Seven Dials to see noble sportsmen *chez* Ben Caunt'. *All Sorts and Conditions of Men*, p. 225.

96 Besant, *East London*, pp. 329–31.

97 See J. S. Reed, 'Ritualism Rampant in East London – Anglo-Catholicism and the Urban Poor', *Victorian Studies*, 31, 3 (1988), pp. 375–403; John Springhall, 'Building character in the British boy: the attempt to extend Christian manliness to working-class adolescents, 1880–1914', in *Manliness and Morality*, ed. J. A. Mangan and James Walvin (Manchester, 1987), pp. 52–74; and on a similar phenomenon in 1930s Chicago, Gerard R. Gems, 'Selling Sport and Religion in American Society: Bishop Sheil and the Catholic Youth Organization', in *The New American Sport History*, ed. S. W. Pope (Urbana, IL, 1997), pp. 300–11.

98 Robert Baden-Powell suggested that boxing might help combat 'the deterioration of our race' noted after the Boer War. *Scouting for Boys* (Oxford, 2005), pp.184, 192. He recommends A. J. Newton's 1904 manual, *Boxing*. A rabbi's son learns to box at Manchester's Jewish Lads' Brigade in 1916 in Louis Golding, *Magnolia Street* (Nottingham, 2006), pp. 329–30.

99 Vladimir Nabokov, *The Annotated Lolita* (Harmondsworth, 1980), p. 45.

100 John Pearson, *The Profession of Violence: The Rise and Fall of the Kray Twins* (London, 1984), pp. 41, 43. See also Michael Berkowitz, 'Jewish Blood-Sport: Between Bad Behavior and Respectability', in *Fighting Back? Jewish and Black Boxers in Britain*, ed. Michael Berkowitz and Ruti Ungar (London, 2007), pp. 67–82.

101 William Booth, *In Darkest England and the Way Out* (London, 1890).

102 Arthur Morrison, *A Child of the Jago* (London, 1996), p. 80.

103 Ibid., p. 173.

104 George Orwell, *Shooting an Elephant and Other Essays* (Harmondsworth, 2003), p. 91.

105 John Carey, *The Violent Effigy* (London, 1973), p. 28.

106 Charles Dickens, *Letters*, vol. VI, ed. Graham Storey, Kathleen Tillotson and Nina Burgis (Oxford, 1988), p. 777.

107 Dickens, *The Pickwick Papers*, p. 528. See also James E. Marlow, 'Popular Culture, Pugilism and Pickwick', *Journal of Popular Culture*, 15, no. 4 (1982), pp. 16–30.

108 Charles Dickens, *The Old Curiosity Shop* (Harmondsworth, 2000), pp. 111, 25, 106, 29.

109 Joseph Addison, *The Spectator* (London, 1907), vol. I, p. 123.

110 Dickens, *The Old Curiosity Shop*, p. 225. On Victorian pubs run by ex-boxers, see Walvin, *Leisure and Society*, pp. 35–6.

111 Dickens, *Nicholas Nickleby*, p. 373.

112 Charles Dickens, *Dombey and Son* (Harmondsworth, 2002), pp. 313, 577, 622, 442.

113 Charles Dickens, *Bleak House* (Harmondsworth, 1996), p. 304.

114 An earlier example than those given in the OED can be found in Washington Irving's 'Buckthorne' (1824). The narrator says, 'I felt as if I could have fought even unto the death; and I was likely to do so; for he, was, according to the boxing phraze, "putting my head into Chancery" . . .'; *Tales of a Traveller*, p. 111.

115 'Legal Pugilism', *Punch*, 7 August 1841, p. 41.

116 Charles Dickens, *The Mystery of Edwin Drood* (London, 1996), p. 46.

117 Dickens, *Nicholas Nickleby*, p. 1. See Lois E. Chaney, 'The Fives' Court', *Dickensian*, 81 (1985), pp. 86–7.

118 Charles Dickens, *Great Expectations* (Harmondsworth, 1996), p. 298.

119 Dickens, *The Pickwick Papers*, p. 537.

120 After calling Mr Pickwick 'a humbug' in the book's opening chapter, Mr Blotton says 'he had used the word in its Pickwickian sense'. Dickens, *The Pickwick Papers*, p. 6.

121 Charles Dickens, *David Copperfield* (Harmondsworth, 1996), pp.170, 246, 650, 652. Mr Jarndyce, in *Bleak House*, is also occasionally 'floored': when Esther rejects his plum pudding in Chapter Three and when she describes Mrs Jelleby as 'a little unmindful of her home' in Chapter Six.

122 Charles Dickens, *Hard Times* (Harmondsworth, 1985), p. 50.

123 Dickens, *Nicholas Nickleby*, pp. 279–80. 'Backing the little one' is a principle of chivalry for Roboshobery Dove in Arthur Morrison's *Cunning Murrell* (London, 1900), p. 206.

124 Charles Dickens, *Oliver Twist* (Harmondsworth, 2002), pp. 47–8. Martin Chuzzlewit decides to go to America after attempting to strike Pecksniff. *Martin Chuzzlewit* (Oxford, 1982), pp. 182–3.

125 Dickens, *Nicholas Nickleby*, p. 99. Nicholas also knocks down the comic tragedian Mr. Lenville in ch. 29 and the villainous Sir Mulberry Hawk in ch. 32.

126 Carey, *The Violent Effigy*, p. 29

127 Dickens, *David Copperfield*, p. 157.

128 Ibid., pp. 253–7. Thackeray's Barry Lyndon has tussles with local lads for similar reasons: *Barry Lyndon* (Oxford, 1984), pp. 17, 22.

129 Dickens, *David Copperfield*, pp. 261, 266, 282.

130 Ibid., pp. 356, 476, 530, 531, 354, 567, 571–2, 689, 697–8.

131 Ibid., pp. 395, 678, 735. See Juliet John, *Dickens's Villains* (Oxford, 2001), pp. 175–82. Charlotte Brontë was equally severe on latter-day Byronism. Jane Eyre's overbearing rival, Miss Ingram, disapproves of modern young men as 'absorbed in care about their pretty faces and their white hands'. *Jane Eyre* (Toronto, 1999), pp. 257–8.

132 Dickens, *Great Expectations*, pp. 60, 62–3. See also Robin Gilmour, *The Idea of the Gentleman in the Victorian Novel* (London, 1981), p. 122.

133 Ibid., pp. 90–92. Mary Edminson dates the main action of the novel as roughly 1807 to 1823; that is the era of Regency boximania. 'The date of the action of *Great Expectations*', *Nineteenth Century Fiction*, 13 (1958), p. 31.

134 Dickens, *Great Expectations*, p. 93.

135 Ibid., pp. 47, 140–42, 225.

136 Dickens, *David Copperfield*, p. 283.

137 Dickens, *Great Expectations*, pp. 181, 185.

138 Wilkie Collins's muscular Christians are more sinister. Geoffrey Delamayn fights with 'stuffed and padded gloves' but they are only 'apparently harmless weapons'. *Man and Wife* (Oxford, 1998), p. 174.

139 Dickens, *The Mystery of Edwin Drood*, pp. 45–6.

140 Charles Dickens, *Speeches*, ed. K. J. Fielding (London, 1988), p. 123.

141 Dickens, *The Mystery of Edwin Drood*, pp. 175–6.

142 Arthur Conan Doyle, *Rodney Stone* (London, 1912), p. 12.

143 Francis Galton, 'On the Anthropometric Laboratory at the Late International Health Exhibition', *Journal of the Anthropological Institute*, 14 (1884), p. 211.

144 Fitzsimmons is claimed by several nations. He was born in Cornwall in 1863, moved to New Zealand as a child, learned to box in Australia and was an American citizen when he won the heavyweight title.

145 Angus Wilson, *The Naughty Nineties* (London, 1976), pp. 6–7.

146 David Christie Murray, *The Making of a Novelist* (London, 1894), pp. 196–7, 198–99, 212.

147 The French Revolution and its aftermath was a popular subject for 1890s historical fiction. See Sandra Kemp, Charlotte Mitchell and David Trotter, *Edwardian Fiction* (Oxford, 1997), pp. 185–6. *Rodney Stone* had its origins in a play which Conan Doyle wrote as a vehicle for Sir Henry Irving in 1894. *The House of Temperley: A Melodrama of the Ring* ended with a lengthy boxing match. Although, or perhaps because, reviewers praised its 'life-like' quality, the play did not attract large audiences. Daniel Stashower, *Teller of Tales* (New York, 1999), pp. 268–9. Other historical novels of this period featuring boxing include Arthur Morrison's *Cunning Murrell* (1900) and, a favourite of the young Norman Mailer, Jeffrey Farnol's *The Amateur Gentleman* (1913). Many of Georgette Heyer's 1930s novels include Regency boxing.

148 Doyle, *Rodney Stone*, p. 251.

149 Stashower, *Teller of Tales*, p. 192.

150 Ibid., p. 35.

151 Arthur Conan Doyle, *The Exploits of Brigadier Gerard* (1903);

see, in particular, his encounter with the Bristol Bustler in 'How the King Held the Brigadier'. See also Conan Doyle's 'The Lord of Falconbridge', in which Tom Spring is tricked into fighting the Lord, 'Jackson's favourite pupil'. *The Last Galley* (1911).

152 A prize-fighter also features as a bodyguard to a diamond magnate in 'A Costume Piece' by Conan Doyle's brother-in-law, E. W. Hornung. The presence of this 'paid bully' provides an added challenge to Hornung's gentleman thief, Raffles. *The Amateur Cracksman* (Harmondsworth, 2003), pp. 23–38.

153 Arthur Conan Doyle, *The Sign of Four* (Harmondsworth, 1982), p. 41.

154 Hughes, *Tom Brown's Schooldays*, p. 355.

155 Arthur Conan Doyle, *The Memoirs of Sherlock Holmes* (Harmondsworth, 1950), p. 76.

# 5 'Like Any Other Profession'

1 Michael T. Isenberg, *John L. Sullivan and His Times* (London, 1988), p. 13.

2 Tom Wolfe, Foreword, *The Police Gazette*, ed. Gene Smith and Jayne Barry (New York, 1972), p. 10. See also Howard P. Chudacoff, *The Age of the Bachelor: Creating an American Subculture* (Princeton, 1999), pp. 193–210.

3 Smith, 'Introduction', *The Police Gazette*, pp. 15–16.

4 See Frank Butler, *A History of Boxing in Britain* (London, 1972), ch. 5.

5 José Martí, 'Letter from New York', in *José Martí: Selected Writings*, ed. and trans. Esther Allen (Harmondsworth, 2002), pp. 107–15.

6 Robert Frost, 'New Hampshire', in *Complete Poems* (London, 1951), pp. 193–4. The poem was published in 1925 during the heyday of William Jennings Bryan's fundamentalist crusade against teaching the theory of evolution in public schools.

7 Theodore Dreiser, *A Book about Myself* (London, 1929), pp. 150–51.

8 In 1903, depressed by the reception of *Sister Carrie*, Dreiser went to a sanatorium run by William Muldoon, Sullivan's trainer-manager, and later portrayed him in a 1919 story, 'Muldoon, the Strong Man'. *Fulfilment and Other Tales of Women and Men*, ed. T. D. Nostwich (Santa Rosa, CA, 1992), pp. 341–84. See Kathy Frederickson, 'Working Out to Work Through: Dreiser in Muldoon's Body Shop of Shame', in *Theodore Dreiser and American Culture*, ed. Yoshinobu Hakutani (Newark, NJ, 2000), pp. 115–37.

9 Theodore Dreiser, *Sister Carrie* (Harmondsworth, 1981), pp. 165, 43. In creating McTeague Frank Norris may also have thought of Sullivan. Norris drew on a newspaper report of a murder case, which said of the accused, Collins: 'Fancy a first cousin of John L. Sullivan's in Collins' dress and situation and you have the man.' *San Francisco Examiner*, 14 October 1893, in *McTeague* (New York, 1977), p. 260.

10 Vachel Lindsay, 'John L. Sullivan, The Strong Boy of Boston', in *Collected Poems* (New York, 1925), pp. 93–5. The poem is dedicated to Louis Untermeyer and Robert Frost. In 1921 Frost wrote to another poet, Sara Teasdale, proposing to include Lindsay's poem in a collection of poetry about Sullivan. The collection never materialized. Philip Cronenwett, 'Frost to Teasdale: A New Letter', *Friends of the Dartmouth Library Newsletter*, no. 31 (July 2001), p. 3.

11 Edward Bellamy imagined that people of the future would associate Bostonians with pugilistic skills. *Looking Backward, 2000–1887* (New York, 2000), p. 26.

12 Lindsay used the phrase 'Higher Vaudeville imagination' when introducing his poems in *Poetry, A Magazine of Verse* in 1913. The editor, Harriet Monroe, reprinted his comments in her introduction to his collection *The Congo and Other Poems* (New York, 1914).

13 Patrick Myler, *Gentleman Jim Corbett* (London, 1998), pp. xiv, 46.

14 Ibid., pp. 216–21. Alan Woods argues that the marketing of Corbett marks 'a major step in the American commercialization of both sport and theatre.' 'James J. Corbett: Theatrical Star', *Journal of Sport History* (Summer 1976), p. 175.

15 Mark Twain, *Selected Letters*, ed. Charles Neider (New York, 1982), p. 224. Corbett ends his autobiography with his version of this anecdote. He refers to Twain as 'dear old Mark, another good friend of mine'. *The Roar of the Crowd* (New York, 1925), p. 328. Twain had described Sullivan as the kind of 'man of prowess' who would have done well in the Middle Ages. *A Connecticut Yankee in King Arthur's Court*, in *Historical Romances* (New York, 1994), p. 304.

16 For a full account of the Texan fight promoter Dan Stuart's attempts to stage the fight, see Leo N. Mitetich, *Dan Stuart's Fistic Carnival* (College Station, TX, 1994).

17 Myler, *Gentleman Jim Corbett*, p. 141; Theodore Roosevelt, *Autobiography* (New York, 1985), p. 43.

18 Quoted in Steven A. Riess, 'In the Ring and Out: Professional Boxing in New York, 1896–1920', in *Sport in America: New Historical Perspectives*, ed. Donald Spivey (Westport, CT, 1985), p. 97.

19 From 1911 to 1918, a state commission ran these clubs, bringing in around $49,000 in revenue a year. The 1920 Walker Bill was modelled on the examples of the British National Sports Club and Army, Navy and Civilian Board of Control. In a 1906 short story, 'The Coming-out of Maggie', O. Henry describes 'the legal duress that constantly threatened' the Give and Take Athletic Association of New York's East Side. *The Four Million* (London, 1947), p. 53.

20 Upton Sinclair, *The Jungle* (New York, 1960), pp. 96, 250. Sinclair may have drawn on Alexander R. Piper's *Report of an Investigation of the Discipline and Administration of the Police Department of the City of Chicago* which described how Joseph Kipley, Police Superintendent during the late 1890s, supported an ultimately unsuccessful scheme to hold illegal prizefights to aid a 'Police Relief Fund'. Piper, *Report* (Chicago, 1904), pp. 5–11. See Perry R. Duis, *The Saloon: Public Drinking in Chicago and Boston, 1880–1920* (Urbana, IL, 1983), p. 240.

21 Jack London, *John Barleycorn* (Oxford, 1989), p. 3. See also pp. 12, 27, 33.

22 G. Stanley Hall, *Life and Confessions of a Psychologist* (New

York, 1923), pp. 578–9. Although Hall officially disapproved of prize-fights in his non-confessional writings, he vociferously championed the moral and physical benefits of amateur boxing. See *Adolescence* (New York, 1904), p. 218; *Youth* (New York, 1904), pp. 3, 78, 102–3.

23 Eakins's interest in professional, rather than amateur, boxing only began in the late 1890s, but once introduced to the sport, Lloyd Goodrich notes, he attended the arena 'several times a week . . . watching [the fights] with such intensity that he would go through all the motions'. At 'polite parties he would draw friends aside to discuss the latest bouts'. Lloyd Goodrich, *Thomas Eakins* (Cambridge, MA, 1982), vol. II, p. 144.

24 *Salutat* alludes to *Hail Caesar! We Who Are About To Die Salute You* (1859) by Eakins's Paris teacher, Jean-Léon Gérôme. In 1866 Eakins wrote from Paris to his father about the American reputation for boxing. Quoted in Goodrich, *Thomas Eakins*, vol. I, p. 21. Eakins described Gérôme's painting as depicting 'cold cruel barbarians' who kill each other 'for love of fighting' while 'the fat hideous Caesar' is raised far above them in his elaborate throne. Goodrich, *Thomas Eakins*, vol. I, pp. 45–6.

25 Goodrich, *Thomas Eakins*, vol. II, p. 277.

26 Quoted in Martin A. Berger, *Man Made: Thomas Eakins and the Construction of Gilded Age Manhood* (Berkeley, CA, 2000), p. 113.

27 Michael Hatt, 'Muscles, morals, mind: the male body in Thomas Eakins' *Salutat*', in *The Body Imaged*, ed. Kathleen Adler and Marcia Pointon (Cambridge, 1993), p. 68.

28 Bennard B. Perlman, *Painters of the Ashcan School: The Immortal Eight* (New York, 1988), p. 56.

29 Quoted in Perlman, *Painters of the Ashcan School*, p. 89.

30 David E. Shi, *Facing Facts: Realism in American Thought and Culture, 1850–1920* (Oxford, 1995), p. 258.

31 Edward Lucie-Smith, *American Realism* (New York, 1994), p. 69.

32 Bellows, quoted in Marianne Doezema, *George Bellows and Urban America* (New Haven, 1992), p. 213, n. 58.

33 Doezema, *George Bellows and Urban America*, p. 100.

34 Charles Belmont Davis, 'The Renaissance of Coney', in *Tales of Gaslight New York*, ed. Frank Oppel (Edison, NJ, 1985), p. 29.

35 Doezema, *George Bellows and Urban America*, p. 100.

36 Quoted in Doezema, *George Bellows and Urban America*, p. 215, n. 84.

37 See, for example, Robert Haywood, 'George Bellows's *Stag at Sharkey's*: Boxing, Violence, and Male Identity', *Smithsonian Studies in American Art*, 2 (Spring 1988), pp. 3–15.

38 James Huneker, 'Seen in the World of Art', *New York Sun* (5 March 1911). The 'mere manliness of Mr. Bellows's style is enough to distinguish him' from the general 'American school of painting' in which 'there is so much that is effeminate,' wrote Henry McBride: *New York Sun* (20 November 1921). Bellows is 'a real man, with "pep" enough for half a dozen' declared the *Boston Evening Transcript* (13 January 1919). All are quoted in Shi, *Facing Facts*, p. 267.

39 George Santayana first used the phrase in his 1911 lecture 'The Genteel Tradition in American Philosophy'.

40 Frank Norris, 'The True Reward of the Novelist', in *The Responsibilities of the Novelist and Other Literary Essays* (London, 1903), pp. 15–22.

41 Michael Holroyd, *Bernard Shaw* (Harmondsworth, 1990), vol. I, p. 114. George Bernard Shaw, 'Note on Modern Prizefighting' (1901), appended to *Cashel Byron's Profession* (London, 1925), p. 341.

42 A film of the novel, *Román Boxera*, was made in Czechoslovakia in 1921. Michael Holroyd, *Bernard Shaw* (Harmondsworth, 1993), vol. III, p. 374.

43 Shaw, 'Preface', *Cashel Byron's Profession*, pp. xii–xiii.

44 P. G. Wodehouse, 'The Pugilist in Fiction', *The Independent Shavian*, 30, nos 1–2 (1992), pp. 2–14. A schoolboy boxer at Dulwich, Wodehouse often wrote about boxers. See, for example, 'The Debut of Battling Billson', in *He Rather Enjoyed It* (1924) and *Bachelors Anonymous* (1973).

45 Norman Clark, '"Come to Lunch!" – G. Bernard Shaw: Exclusive Interview' in *Shaw: Interviews and Recollections*, ed. A. M. Gibbs (Iowa City, IA, 1990), pp. 94–5.

46 Clark, '"Come to Lunch!"', p. 195.

47 George Bernard Shaw, 'Joe Beckett v Georges Carpentier', in *Punches on the Page*, ed. David Rayvern Allen (Edinburgh, 1998), pp. 41–7; Arnold Bennett, 'The Prize Fight', in *Boxing in Art and Literature*, ed. William D. Cox (New York, 1935), pp. 139–45.

48 Holroyd, *Bernard Shaw*, vol. III, pp. 208–9. See also Jay Tunney, 'The Playwright and the Prizefighter: Bernard Shaw and Gene Tunney', *SHAW: The Annual of Bernard Shaw Studies*, 23 (2003), pp. 149–54; and '*Cashel Byron's Profession*: A Catalyst to Friendship – Life Imitates Art', *SHAW: The Annual of Bernard Shaw Studies*, 25 (2005), pp. 52–8.

49 Shaw, 'Preface' to *Cashel Byron's Profession*, p. xv.

50 Shaw, *Cashel Byron's Profession*, pp. 4, 7, 24, 141–2, 276.

51 Arthur Conan Doyle, 'The Croxley Master', *The Green Flag* (London, 1905), pp. 104–70.

52 Shaw, *Cashel Byron's Profession*, p. 167; Shaw, 'Joe Beckett v Georges Carpentier', p. 47.

53 Holroyd, *Bernard Shaw*, vol. I, p. 114.

54 Shaw, 'Modern Prizefighting', pp. 345–6.

55 George Bernard Shaw, Preface, *Plays Pleasant and Unpleasant* (London, 1898), vol. I, pp. xxv–xxvi.

56 Thorstein Veblen, *The Theory of the Leisure Class* (New York, 1953), pp. 172, 178–9, 182.

57 Theodor W. Adorno, 'Veblen's Attack on Culture', *Prisms* (1967), trans. Samuel and Shierry Weber (Cambridge, MA, 1981), p. 81. For an example of an extended development of this idea, see, Jean-Marie Brohm, *Sport – A Prison of Measured Time*, trans. Ian Fraser (London, 1978).

58 Horace Fletcher, *The A.B.–Z of Our Own Nutrition* (1903). See Donald J. Mrozek, *Sport and the American Mentality, 1880–1910* (Knoxville, TN, 1983), pp. 91–7, 196–9.

59 Jack London, *The Call of the Wild, White Fang and Other Stories* (Oxford, 1990), p. 22.

60 The raw is always preferable to the cooked. In *Tarzan of the Apes*, Edgar Rice Burroughs contrasts the fastidious Lord Greystoke who 'sent back his chops to the club's *chef*

because they were underdone, and when he had finished his repast he dipped his finger-ends into a silver bowl of scented water and dried them upon a piece of snowy damask' with his nephew Tarzan, who 'gobbled down a great quantity of the raw flesh' before wiping 'his greasy fingers upon his naked thighs'. Burroughs, *Tarzan of the Apes* (London, 1917), p. 77.

61 Charles Dickens, *Oliver Twist* (Harmondsworth, 2002), p. 53.

62 Jon Hurley, *Tom Spring* (Stroud, 2002), p. 18; Moses Browne, 'A Survey of the Amphitheatre', in *The New Oxford Book of Eighteenth Century Verse*, ed. Roger Lonsdale (Oxford, 1984), p. 292. See Ben Rogers, *Beef and Liberty: Roast Beef, John Bull and the English Nation* (London, 2003).

63 Quoted in *The Great Prize Fight* (London, 1977), pp. 80–81.

64 Norman Mailer, *The Fight* (London, 1975), pp. 27–8.

65 Quoted in *Tom Spring*, p. 26. See also Peter Radford, *The Celebrated Captain Barclay* (London, 2001), pp. 169–70.

66 Benjamin Disraeli, *Sybil* (Harmondsworth, 1980), p. 119.

67 Daniel Mendoza, 'Observations on the Art of Pugilism', Appendix to *The Memoirs of the Life of Daniel Mendoza*, ed. Peter Magriel (London, 1951), p. 113.

68 Arthur Morrison, 'Three Rounds', in *Tales of Mean Streets* (London, 1927), pp. 85–96. Stan Shipley has written on the difficulty of conceiving boxers as a labour force in this period. 'Tom Causer of Bermondsey – A Boxer Hero of the 1890s', *History Workshop*, 15 (1983), pp. 28–59.

69 In an early comic story, 'Shorty Stack, Pugilist' (1897), Frank Norris too depicts the effects of stodge (here, potato salad) on a boxer's stomach. *The Apprenticeship Writings*, ed. Joseph R. McElrath, Jr and Douglas K. Burgess (Philadelphia, 1996), vol. I, pp. 187–95.

70 Jack London, 'A Piece of Steak', in *The Portable Jack London*, ed. Earle Labor (Harmondsworth, 1994), pp. 232–48.

71 See, for example, his remarks on the 1905 'Britt Nelson Fight' in *Jack London Reports*, ed. King Hendricks and Irving Shepard (New York, 1971), p. 258.

72 Jack London, 'The Somnambulists', in *Revolution and Other Essays* (London, 1910), pp. 46–7, 50. The Federal Meat-Inspection Act, designed to prevent adulterated livestock from being sold as food, and to ensure that meat was slaughtered and processed under sanitary conditions, was passed in 1906. For London, Darwin's ideas could be pretty much be reduced to 'the law of meat', the title of Chapter Five of *White Fang* (1906). See also Jack London, *Smoke Bellew* (1911), chs. 1 and 2.

73 London wrote an almost identical sentence in *John Barleycorn*, only substituting drinking for boxing (p. 66). 'Certainly prize-fighting is not half as brutalizing or demoralizing as many forms of big business,' concurred *Theodore Roosevelt: An Autobiography*, p. 43.

74 George Orwell, 'Introduction to *Love of Life and Other Stories* by Jack London', in *The Collected Essays, Journalism and Letters*, ed. Sonia Orwell and Ian Angus (Harmondsworth, 1970), vol. IV, p. 45.

75 Orwell, 'Introduction to *Love of Life*', p. 47. Orwell concludes that 'if [London] had been a politically reliable person he would probably have left behind nothing of interest' (p. 48).

76 London described Battling Nelson as both 'the abysmal brute' and 'the lean and hungry proletarian' in his report of the 1905 Nelson–Britt prize-fight: *Jack London Reports*, pp. 254–5. Nelson became known by the first rather than the second title, and dedicated his 1909 autobiography to London, thanking him for 'paying me the biggest compliment ever accorded me by any writer.' David Mike Hamilton, *'The Tools of My Trade': The Annotated Books in Jack London's Library* (Seattle, 1986), pp. 212–13. London revived the phrase as the title for a 1911 novella, in which Pat Glendon, a bear-eating, Browning-reading 'creature of the wild' retires when the corrupt nature of capitalist boxing becomes clear to him.

77 *Champion* (1949) starred Kirk Douglas as Midge. The film was based on Ring Lardner's 1915 short story of the same title.

78 Non-capitalist fights can occur in nature. See Buck vs. Spitz in *The Call of the Wild* (1903), ch. 3. Mark Seltzer describes the protagonists of London's animal stories as 'men in furs': *Bodies and Machines* (New York, 1992), p. 166.

79 Jack London, 'The Mexican', in *The Portable Jack London*, pp. 291–313.

80 Philip Fisher, *Hard Facts: Setting and Form in the American Novel* (Oxford, 1986), pp. 171–2.

81 Dreiser, *Sister Carrie*, p. 338.

82 Pierce Egan, *Boxiana: A Selection*, ed. John Ford (London, 1976), p. 15.

83 Roland Barthes, 'The World of Wrestling', in *Mythologies*, trans. Annette Lavers (New York, 2000), pp. 15–25.

84 Jack London, *A Daughter of the Snows* (London, 1964), p. 46. London's formulation is close to that of one his favourite writers, Herbert Spencer, who maintained that 'the amount of vital energy which the body at any moment possesses is limited; and that being limited, it is impossible to get from it more than a fixed quantity of results.' *Education: Intellectual, Moral and Physical* (London, 1861), p. 268. Although stories such as 'A Piece of Steak' or 'Three Rounds' suggest that decline in muscle stock was an individual phenomenon, reversible with the ingestion of a good meal, many argued that it affected whole populations. See H. Llewellyn Smith, 'Influx of Population (East London)', in Charles Booth et al., *Life and Labour of the People in London*, 1st series (London, 1902), vol. III, p. 110. For a full account of various applications of thermodynamic language in this period, see Anson Rabinbach, *The Human Motor: Energy, Fatigue and the Origins of Modernity* (Berkeley, CA, 1990).

85 Jack London, 'Jeffries Never Wasted Energy', in *Jack London Reports*, pp. 287–90.

86 Jack London, 'What Life Means to Me', in *No Mentor but Myself*, ed. Dale L. Walker and Jeanne Campbell Reesman (Stanford, CA, 1999), pp. 90–91. Compare George Orwell's remark that 'a novelist does not, any more than a boxer or a ballet dancer, last for ever. He has an initial impulse which is good for three or four books, perhaps even for a dozen, but which must exhaust itself sooner or later.' 'As I Please', in *Collected Essays, Journalism and Letters*, vol. IV, p. 293.

87 See Christopher Wilson, *The Labor of Words: Literary*

*Professionalism in the Progressive Era* (Athens, GA, 1985), pp. 92–112.

88 London, *John Barleycorn*, pp. 134–5; Jack London, *Martin Eden* (Harmondsworth, 1967), pp. 104–5.

89 Shaw, 'Modern Prizefighting', p. 335.

90 Ibid., p. 336.

91 Myler, *Gentleman Jim Corbett*, p. 129.

92 Gorn, *The Manly Art*, p. 205.

93 Ibid., p. 205.

94 Karl Marx, *The Poverty of Philosophy* (1847), in *Collected Works of Karl Marx and Frederick Engels* (London, 1975), vol. VI, p. 127. See also E. P. Thompson, 'Time, Work-Discipline and Industrial Capitalism', *Past and Present*, 38 (1967), pp. 56–97.

95 Gorn, *The Manly Art*, p. 205.

96 The first automatic timing device was used in California for the 1891 Corbett vs. Jackson fight. It was not adopted in New York until 1925 when the new Madison Square Gardens opened. Myler, *Gentleman Jim Corbett*, p. 42.

97 Arthur Morrison, *Cunning Murrell* (London, 1900), pp. 210–12. The chapter is entitled 'The Call of Time'.

98 John Masefield, 'The Everlasting Mercy' (1911), in *Poems* (London, 1946), pp. 37–79. The pub call of time – 'HURRY UP PLEASE IT'S TIME' – was to play a significant part in 'A Game of Chess', Section II of T. S. Eliot's *The Waste Land* (1922).

99 'Between Rounds' is also the title of an O. Henry story in which the ongoing fight between a husband and wife is briefly interrupted by the news of a missing child. *The Four Million* (1906).

100 Carl Smith contrasts the 'peaceful' nature of these paintings with George Bellows's lithographs, *Between Rounds* (1916), where 'the two exhausted fighters slump on their stools and over the ropes as they gasp for life', and *A Knockout* (1921), where 'the upright fighter does not stand back . . . but, tasting blood, bulls his way past the referee to finish the slaughter'. 'The Boxing Paintings of Thomas Eakins', *Prospects*, 4 (1979), p. 408. See Emma S. Bellows, *George Bellows: His Lithographs* (New York, 1927).

101 Michael Fried, *Realism, Writing, Disfiguration* (Chicago, 1989), p. 71. Eakins here depicts his friend, sportswriter Clarence Cranmer (the man raising his hat in *Salutat*) as the timekeeper.

102 Martin A. Berger describes *Salutat* is 'an apparent reworking' of Eakins's 1875 *Gross Clinic*, another setting in which professional activity becomes a spectacle. Berger, *Man Made*, p. 112.

103 See Susan Danly and Cheryl Leibold, *Eakins and the Photograph* (Philadelphia, 1994).

104 Eakins studied in Paris from 1866 to 1869. In 1867, Courbet and Manet were rejected from the Exposition Universale and famously showed their work in a building outside. Eakins wrote home about the Exposition, but did not mention Manet. Goodrich, *Thomas Eakins*, vol. I, p. 30.

105 Emile Zola, 'The Experimental Novel', in *Documents of Modern Literary Realism*, ed. and trans. George J. Becker (Princeton, 1963), p. 171.

106 Frank Norris, 'Zola as a Romantic Writer', in *Literary Criticism*, ed. Donald Pizer (Austin, TX, 1964), p. 72.

107 London, *Martin Eden*, p. 118. The mechanical model of the body had changed considerably in 75 years. In 1818 Pierce Egan had compared the boxer's muscles to 'springs and levers, which execute the different motions of the body'. *Boxiana* (London, 1818), vol. I, pp. 37–8.

108 Terry Ramsaye, *A Million and One Nights: History of the Motion Picture Through 1925* (New York, 1986), p. 88. Laurent Mannoni notes that 'from 14 April 1894 to 1 April 1895 the takings of the New York Kinetoscope Parlor were $16,171.56.' Laurent Mannoni, *The Great Art of Light and Shadow* (1995), trans. Richard Crangle (Exeter, 2000), p. 400.

109 In an earlier novel, London described a sense of being both actor and spectator as being characteristic of dreams. Jack London, *Before Adam* (London, 1929), p. 109. See David Trotter, *Cinema and Modernism* (Oxford, 2007), p. 19.

110 Films of animal fights were also popular and presumably to London's taste. The first boxing kangaroo was exhibited by Professor Landermann at the London Aquarium in 1892. Paul Gallico's *Matilda* (1970; filmed in 1978) is the story of a kangaroo which knocks out the middleweight champion.

111 Mannoni, *The Great Art of Light and Shadow*, p. 427. See also Luke McKernan, 'Sport and the First Films', in *Cinema: the Beginnings and the Future*, ed. Christopher Williams (London, 1996), p. 109; Charles Musser, *The Emergence of Cinema: The American Screen to 1907* (New York, 1990), pp. 82–3.

112 Myler, *Gentleman Jim Corbett*, p. 96.

113 McKernan, 'Sport and the First Films', p. 110. The Lumières had projected film before this, but not commercially. The *New York World* advertised the event: 'You'll sit comfortably and see fighters hammering each other, circuses, suicides, hangings, electrocutions, shipwrecks, scenes on the exchanges, street scenes, horse-races, football games, almost anything, in fact, in which there is action, just as if you were on the spot during the actual events. And you won't see marionettes. You'll see people and things as they are.' Quoted in Musser, *The Emergence of Cinema*, p. 96.

114 Although celebrated as new, this was the same punch as Jack Broughton's 'projectile', discussed by Fielding's Tom Jones.

115 Quoted in Musser, *The Emergence of Cinema*, pp. 196–7.

116 Ramsaye, *A Million and One Nights*, p. 288. Staged re-enactments, based on newspaper reports, were also popular. See Musser, *The Emergence of Cinema*, pp. 196, 201; Dan Streible, 'Fake Fight Films', in *Le cinéma au tourant du siècle*, ed. Claire Dupré La Tour, André Gaudreault, and Roberta Pearson (Québec, 1999), pp. 63–79.

117 Quoted in Leon Edel, *Henry James: The Treacherous Years, 1895–1901* (Philadelphia, 1969), p. 175.

118 James Joyce, *Ulysses* (Harmondsworth, 1992), p. 323.

119 Miletich, *Dan Stuart's Fistic Carnival*, pp. 95, 229–30; William A. Brady, *The Fighting Man* (Indianapolis, 1916), pp. 148–50. Corbett had earned $5,000 for his first film, the six-round staged contest against Courtney in 1894, but also received royalties of $150 per week (later reduced to $50) for each set of films on exhibition in the kinetoscopes. Musser, *The Emergence of Cinema*, p. 84.

120 Shaw, 'Modern Prizefighting', p. 340. Jack London's 'abysmal brute' earns 'from twenty to thirty thousand dollars a fight, as well as equally large sums from the moving picture men'. Jack London, *The Abysmal Brute* (Lincoln, NE, 2000), pp. 62–3.

121 Dan Streible, 'A History of the Boxing Film', *Film History*, 3 (1989), pp. 235–47; McKernan, 'Sport and the First Films', p. 107. Equally bold are the claims made by Noel Burch, *Life to those Shadows*, trans. Ben Brewster (London, 1990), p. 143.

122 Kevin Brownlow, *The Parade's Gone By* (Berkeley, CA, 1968), p. 2.

123 Ramsaye, *A Million and One Nights*, p. 116.

124 I am quoting from a poster advertising a 20 June 1898 showing of the Corbett-Fitzsimmons film at the Argyle Theatre of Varieties, Birkenhead, which is on display at the Bill Douglas Centre for the History of Cinema and Popular Culture, University of Exeter.

125 Vachel Lindsay, *The Art of the Moving Picture* (New York, 2000), pp. 136–7.

126 Quoted in Streible, 'A History of the Boxing Film', p. 238.

127 Frederick A. Talbot, *Moving Pictures: How They are Made and Worked* (London, 1912), p. 122.

128 On 29 January 1912, for example, the Argyle Theatre of Varieties, Birkenhead, advertised Phil Rees's Stable Lads in their Novel Racing Act, 'Not a Crook', introducing New Songs, Dances, and Comic Boxing. The Bill Douglas Collection, University of Exeter. After 1900, boxing films in America were largely shown at burlesque houses. Richard Abel, *The Red Rooster Scare: Making American Cinema, 1900–1910* (Berkeley, CA, 1999), pp. 3–12.

129 Musser, *The Emergence of Cinema*, p. 116

130 Dennis Gifford, *The British Film Catalogue* (London, 2000), vol. I, p. 13; John Barnes, *The Beginnings of Cinema in England, 1894–1901* (London, 1992), vol. IV, p. 239.

131 *The Knockout* was completed on 29 May and released on 11 June 1914; *Mabel's Married Life* (dir. Chaplin and Mabel Normand) was released on 20 June.

132 *Bioscope* (3 June 1915) described Chaplin as fighting 'with the agility of a boxing kangaroo and with almost as much disregard for the rules of warfare'. Glen Mitchell, *The Chaplin Encyclopedia* (London, 1997), p. 97.

133 Chaplin may have picked up this gag from *The Knockout* where Fatty Arbuckle instructs the camera to move away while he is changing. See also William Paul, 'Charles Chaplin and the Annals of Anality', in *Comedy/Cinema/Theory*, ed. Andrew Horton (Berkeley, CA, 1991), pp. 109-30.

134 Mark Winokur, *American Laughter: Immigrants, Ethnicity, and 1930s Hollywood Film Comedy* (London, 1996), p. 104.

135 Chaplin attended fights in Hollywood and, with Fatty Arbuckle, acted as a second at the LA Athletic Club. He was often photographed with boxers. Charles Chaplin, *My Autobiography* (Harmondsworth, 1996), pp. 185–8, 273; David A. Yallop, *The Day the Laughter Stopped: The True Story of Fatty Arbuckle* (London, 1976), p. 79.

136 Thomas Burke, 'The Chink and the Child', *Limehouse Nights* (London, 1916).

137 *The Abysmal Brute* was the title of a 1911 Jack London novella; it was filmed in 1923. See also Karl Brown, *Adventures with D. W. Griffith* (London, 1973), p. 241.

138 Dudley Andrew, '*Broken Blossoms*: The Vulnerable Text and the Marketing of Masochism', *Film in the Aura of Art* (Princeton, 1984), p. 21.

139 Brigitte Peucker, *Incorporating Images: Film and the Rival Arts* (Princeton, 1995), p. 61.

140 Estimates varied; one source suggested that in Chicago 60 per cent of spectators were women. Musser, *The Emergence of Cinema*, p. 200.

141 Miriam Hansen, *Babel and Babylon: Spectatorship in American Silent Film* (Cambridge, MA, 1991), p. 1.

142 Dan Streible, 'Female Spectators and the Corbett–Fitzsimmons Fight Film', in *Out of Bounds: Sports, Media and the Politics of Identity*, ed. Aaron Baker and Todd Boyd (Bloomington, IA, 1997), pp. 34–5, 41. Women also attended his stage performances. William Brady, *Showman* (New York, 1937), p. 107. Sherwood Anderson recalled shadow-boxing in front of a girl he was trying to impress in hope that 'she will take me for . . . a young Corbett'. *A Story Teller's Story* (New York, 1924), p. 202.

143 Nellie Bly, 'A Visit with John L. Sullivan', in *Punches on the Page*, ed. Allen, pp. 11–16. London includes a lengthy scene in which a woman journalist interviews a prize-fighter in *The Abysmal Brute*, p. 79.

144 Streible, 'Female Spectators and the Corbett–Fitzsimmons Fight Film', p. 31. On Annie Laurie, see Barbara Belford, *Brilliant Byline: A Biographical Anthology of Notable Newspaper Women in America* (New York, 1986), p. 140.

145 Quoted in Miletich, *Dan Stuart's Fistic Carnival*, p. 196.

146 Corbett, *The Roar of the Crowd*, p. 264.

147 Ashton Stevens, 'Tragedy is Mirrored in the Face of Britt's Father', *San Francisco Examiner*, 10 September 1905, quoted in Michael Oriard, 'Introduction' to Jack London, *The Game* (Lincoln, NE, 2001), p. XV.

148 Streible, 'A History of the Boxing Film', p. 241.

149 Quoted in Riess, 'In the Ring and Out', p. 113. See also Jeffrey T. Sammons, *Beyond the Ring: The Role of Boxing in American Society* (Urbana, IL, 1990), pp. 53–9.

150 Charles Darwin, *The Origin of Species* (Oxford, 1996), p. 73.

151 Shaw, *Cashel Byron's Profession*, pp. 28, 41–2. For a comparison with a similar scene in *Lady Chatterley's Lover*, see Elsie B. Adams, 'A "Lawrentian" Novel by Bernard Shaw', *The D. H. Lawrence Review*, 2 (1969), pp. 245–53.

152 Shaw, Preface to *Cashel Byron's Profession*, p. xi. Corbett first played the role in 1901; he also appeared in a Broadway production in 1906. See Benny Green, *Shaw's Champions* (London, 1978), ch. 3.

153 Shaw, *Cashel Byron's Profession*, pp. 49, 266, 277.

154 London, *Martin Eden*, p. 303. See also London, *A Daughter of the Snows*, p. 10.

155 The best account of the novella is Michael Oriard's introduction to the 2001 edition, pp. vii–xviii; see also Christian Messenger, 'Jack London and Boxing in *The Game*', *Jack London Newsletter*, 9 (1976), pp. 67–72.

156 London, *The Game*, pp. 9, 13.

157 Ibid., p. 41.

158 In 1883, actress Ann Livingston reportedly 'dressed as a boy' to attend a fight between her boyfriend, John L. Sullivan, and Charlie Mitchell. Nat Fleischer and Sam Andre, *A Pictorial History of Boxing* (London, 1959), p. 61. In 1909, London's wife, Charmian, attracted controversy when, undisguised, she accompanied him to the Johnson–Burns contest in Sydney. Clarice Stasz, *American Dreamers: Charmain and Jack London* (New York, 1988), p. 192. See also 'The Birth Mark: A Sketch written for Robert and Julia Fitzsimmons', in which a girl dresses up in a man's tuxedo and sneaks into the West Bay Athletic Club for a bet. There she meets Fitzsimmons who, although he knows she's a girl, strings her along for a while. Jack London, *The Human Drift* (New York, 1917).

159 London, *The Game*, p. 53.

160 Ibid., pp. 61–5. Michael Hatt compares London's description of Joe with Thomas Eakins's depiction of boxer Billy Smith in *Salutat*, which he claims 'requires an imaginary female viewer'. 'Muscles, morals, mind: the male body in Thomas Eakins' *Salutat*', p. 68.

161 London, *The Game*, pp. 80, 84, 98–9.

162 A similar moment of incomprehension can be found in *The Sea-Wolf* when Maud Brewster tries to intervene in some dangerous 'man-play'. Jack London, *Novels and Stories* (New York, 1982), p. 641.

163 See Jean Pfaeflzer, *The Utopian Novel in America, 1886–1896: The Politics of Form* (Pittsburgh, 1984), p. 145–6.

164 William H. Bishop, *The Garden of Eden, USA: A Very Possible Story* (Chicago, 1895), pp. 148, 198.

165 *The Police Gazette*, ed. Smith, p. 120.

166 Quoted in Vanessa Toulmin, *A Fair Fight* (Oldham, 1999), p. 33. Belle Gordon regularly used a punch bag as part of her vaudeville act, and is named as the author of *Physical Culture for Women* (New York, 1913). Other women's boxing movies include *Gordon Sisters Boxing* (Edison, 1901), based on Bessie and Minnie Gordon's stage act; *The Physical Culture Girl* (Edison, 1903), in which a young woman wakes up, stretches, and hits a punch bag; and *Boxing Ladies* (Mitchell and Kenyon, early 1900s) in which two women fairground boxers rescue a man from a gang of thieves. See also Lauren Rabinovitz, *For the Love of Pleasure: Women, Movies, and Culture in Turn-of-the-Century Chicago* (New Brunswick, NJ, 1998), p. 33.

167 J. K. Huysmans, *Against Nature*, trans. Robert Baldick (Harmondsworth, 1959), p. 110; George Gissing, *The Odd Women* (London, 1980), p. 102. See Stephen Kern, *The Culture of Love: Victorians to Moderns* (Cambridge, MA, 1992), p. 71.

168 Frank Norris, 'A Girl of Twenty Who has the Frame of a Sandow', in *The Apprenticeship Writings*, pp. 238–40. Many of Norris's heroines recall Capitaine. For example, Moran, the daughter of a Norwegian sea captain, is 'massive': 'even beneath the coarse sleeve of her oilskin coat one could infer that the biceps and deltoids were large and powerful'. Norris describes her as more powerful than the hero, Ross Wilbur, but when they fight, he wins. *Moran of the Lady Letty* (New York, 1898), pp. 70–72.

169 London, *A Daughter of the Snows*, p. 17. As the novel goes on, Frona becomes less interested in physical activity and comes to represent an alternative moral position. Compare the unnamed heroine of 'Amateur Night', whose 'vigorous daintiness . . . gave an impression of virility with none of the womanly left out.' Jack London, *Moon-Face and Other Stories* (New York, 1906), p. 60. See Clarice Stasz, 'Androgyny in the Novels of Jack London', in *Jack London: Essays in Criticism*, ed. Ray Wilson Ownbey (Santa Barbara, CA, 1978), pp. 54–65.

170 London, *A Daughter of the Snows*, pp. 52, 53, 55.

## 6 Fresh Hopes

1 Frank Norris, 'The True Reward of the Novelist', in *The Responsibilities of the Novelist and Other Literary Essays* (London, 1903), p. 19.

2 On the role of sport in the development of a national ethos in this period, see S. W. Pope, *Patriotic Games: Sporting Traditions in the American Imagination, 1876–1926* (Oxford, 1997).

3 Irving Howe, *World of Our Fathers* (New York, 1976), p. 128.

4 Abraham Cahan, *Yekl: A Tale of the New York Ghetto*, in *The Imported Bridegroom and Other Stories* (New York, 1996), p. 168.

5 Sabine Haenni, 'Visual and Theatrical Culture, Tenement Fiction, and the Immigrant Subject in Abraham Cahan's *Yekl*', *American Literature*, 71, 3 (1999), p. 513.

6 Cahan, *Yekl*, p. 185.

7 Ibid., p. 173.

8 Jules Chametzky, *From the Ghetto: The Fiction of Abraham Cahan* (Amherst, MA, 1977), p. 53.

9 Initially rejected by magazines such as *Harper's* as being of no interest to 'the American reader', *Yekl* was eventually published in 1896. A translation also appeared in a Yiddish magazine. Saul Scott, *Homing Pidgins: Immigrant Tongues, Immanent Bodies in Abraham Cahan's Yekl* (Stanford, CA, 1995), p. 17. On *Yekl*'s reception, see Jules Chametzky, *Our Decentralized Literature* (Amherst, MA, 1986), pp. 61–2.

10 Chametzky, *From the Ghetto*, p. 55. Werner Sollors also finds that Jake's 'bastardized language' is rendered 'quite derogatorily'. *Beyond Ethnicity: Consent and Descent in American Culture* (Oxford, 1986), p. 164. For a more subtle reading, see Gavin Jones, *Strange Talk: The Politics of Dialect Literature in Gilded Age America* (Berkeley, CA, 1999), ch. 5.

11 Cahan, *Yekl*, p. 194.

12 Howe, *World of Our Fathers*, p. 473.

13 Cahan, *Yekl*, pp. 170–71.

14 See Sander Gilman, *The Jew's Body* (New York, 1991), pp. 53–4. On the revival of interest in Mendoza at this time, see Michael Berkowitz, *The Jewish Self-Image: American and British Perspectives, 1881–1930* (London, 2000), p. 75. Muscular Judaism was promoted by the Maccabi movement. By 1914, there was over 100 Maccabi clubs in Europe. For an example from Weimar Germany, see Hermann von Wedderkop, 'Jüdischer Box-Klub Machabi', *Querschnitt*, 6 (1926), p. 887.

15 Israel Zangwill, *The Children of the Ghetto* (London, 1998), pp. 8–9.

16 Paul Breines, *Tough Jews* (New York, 1990), pp. 19–49.

17 Quoted in Howe, *World of Our Fathers*, p. 128.

18 Patrick Myler, *The Fighting Irish* (Dingle, 1987), p. 49.

19 In this period, a 'move from racial to cultural identity appears to replace essentialist criteria of identity (who we are) with performative criteria (what we do).' Walter Benn Michaels, *Our America* (Durham, NC, 1995), pp. 14–15.

20 O. Henry, 'The Coming-out of Maggie', *The Four Million* (London, 1947), pp. 51–8. In 1905 the *National Police Gazette* noted that although 'Celtic names' still dominated boxing, many of them belonged to Italians ('the stiletto of one generation being succeeded by the hard knuckles of the next'). *Major Problems in American Sport History*, ed. Steven A. Riess (Boston, 1997), pp. 280–81.

21 Steven A. Riess, *Sport in Industrial America, 1850–1920* (Wheeling, IL, 1995), p. 104.

22 James. T. Farrell, *Young Lonigan*, in *Studs Lonigan* (New York, 1977), pp. 82, 143. On the experience of Jewish immigrants in Irish Harlem at this time, see Henry Roth, *A Star Shines Over Mt. Morris Park* (London 1995), p. 30. The 1927 film, *East Side, West Side* is the story of an Irish-American boxer made-good (played by George O'Brien) and his Jewish girlfriend. See Frederick V. Romano, *The Boxing Filmography: American Features, 1920–2003* (Jefferson, NC, 2004), pp. 53–4.

23 Randy Roberts, *Papa Jack: Jack Johnson and the Era of White Hopes* (New York, 1983), p. 13. See also Patrick Myler, *Gentleman Jim Corbett* (London, 1998), ch. 5, and David Berzmozgis, 'Choynski', *Natasha and Other Stories* (London, 2004), pp. 113–26.

24 James Corbett, *The Roar of the Crowd* (New York, 1925), p. 65.

25 'The *National Police Gazette* Supports the Rise of Italian Boxing, 1905', *Problems in Sport History*, ed. Riess, p. 281.

26 See John Harding with Jack Berg, *The Whitechapel Windmill* (London, 1987). An opera based on the book, written by Berg's cousin Howard Frederics and Jacob Sager Weinstein, was performed in London in 2005.

27 Quoted in Allen Bodner, *When Boxing was a Jewish Sport* (Westport, CT, 1997), p. 19. In Joseph Roth's 1929 story 'Strawberries', eight brothers disperse from their Eastern European birthplace; 'one became a boxer in America'. Joseph Roth, *The Collected Stories*, trans. Michael Hoffmann (New York, 2002), p. 143. The wicked son in the parable of the four sons in the Haggadah was sometimes presented as a boxer. Douglas Century, *Barney Ross* (New York, 2006), p. 27.

28 John Dos Passos, *Nineteen Nineteen*, in *USA* (London, 1950), pp. 667–8.

29 Philip Roth, *Patrimony* (London, 1999), p. 203. The book he gave his father was Ken Blady, *The Jewish Boxers' Hall of Fame* (New York, 1988).

30 Philip Roth, *The Facts* (New York, 1997), p. 28.

31 Farrell, *Young Lonigan*, 145.

32 Peter Levine, *Ellis Island to Ebbets Field: Sport and the American Jewish Experience* (Oxford, 1992), p. 152.

33 Nat Fleischer, *Leonard the Magnificent* (Norwalk, CT, 1947), p. 87.

34 Simon Lovish, *Monkey Business: The Lives and Legends of the Marx Brothers* (London, 1999), pp. 121, 301.

35 Groucho Marx and Richard J. Anobile, *The Marx Bros. Scrapbook* (New York, 1974), p. 40; Lovish, *Monkey Business*, p. 134.

36 Budd Schulberg, 'The Great Benny Leonard', *Ring Magazine* (May 1980), pp. 32–7.

37 Levine, *From Ellis Island to Ebbets Field*, pp. 145 6.

38 Charles E. Van Loan, 'No Business', in *Taking the Count: Prize Ring Stories* (New York, 1915), pp. 147–73. Hemingway was a fan of Van Loan's fight stories. In 1924, while working on *In Our Time*, he gave a copy to a friend, and in 1925 he sent his bullfight story, 'The Undefeated' to George Lorimer of the *Saturday Evening Post*, with a letter explaining that he was trying 'to show it the way it actually is, as Charles E. Van Loan used to write fight stories'. *Hemingway: Selected Letters, 1917–1961*, ed. Carlos Baker (London, 1985), p. 148; Michael Reynolds, *Hemingway: The Paris Years* (New York, 1989), p. 249.

39 Cohn was based on Harold Loeb, whose mother was related to the Guggenheims. Loeb and Hemingway had a famous, drunken almost-fight in Pamplona in 1925. Harold Loeb, *The Way It Was* (New York, 1959), pp. 294–7; Reynolds, *Hemingway: The Paris Years*, pp. 304–5. Hemingway's satire may also have been directed at Princeton-educated Scott Fitzgerald. See James Plath, 'The Sun Also Rises* as 'A Greater Gatsby", in *French Connections: Hemingway and Fitzgerald Abroad*, ed. J. Gerald Kennedy and Jackson R. Bryer (London, 1999), pp. 257–75; Carlos Baker, *Ernest Hemingway: A Life Story* (London, 1969), p. 107.

40 Ernest Hemingway, *The Sun Also Rises* (London, 1976), pp. 7–8. Compare with Loeb, *The Way It Was*, p. 218.

41 On Santayana and the Ivy League 'spirit', see Ronald Berman, *Fitzgerald, Hemingway, and the Twenties* (Tuscaloosa, AL, 2001), ch. 6.

42 Hemingway, *The Sun Also Rises*, pp. 11, 39, 40, 135, 148, 158–61, 167–9, 172.

43 Michaels, *Our America*, p. 27.

44 Hemingway, *The Sun Also Rises*, pp. 8, 32.

45 Herman Melville, *Typee* (London, 1993), p. 234. This view was widely assumed, despite contrary evidence from works such as Captain Cook's accounts of his voyages to the South Sea. See John Hoberman, *Darwin's Athletes* (Boston, 1997), p. 105.

46 James Weldon Johnson, *Black Manhattan* (New York, 1991), pp. 59–60.

47 James Weldon Johnson, *The Autobiography of an Ex-Colored Man* (Penguin, 1990), pp. 76–8. See also, Johnson, *Black Manhattan*, pp. 74–8.

48 Frederick Douglass, *Narrative of the Life of Frederick Douglass, An American Slave* (Oxford, 1999), pp. 70, 74. See also Henry Bibb, *Narrative of the Life and Adventures of Henry Bibb, An American Slave, Written by Himself* (1849), in *Puttin' on Ole Massa*, ed. Gilbert Osofsky (New York, 1969), p. 68; and the Rev. W. P. Jacobs, quoted in *Weevils in the Wheat: Interviews with Virginia Ex-Slaves*, ed. Charles L. Perdue, Jr, Thomas E. Barden and Robert K. Phillips (Charlottesville, VA, 1976), p. 155.

49 Douglass, *Narrative*, pp. 68, 57. On the book's debt to the American jeremiad, see David Blight, Introduction, *Narrative of the Life of Frederick Douglass* (Boston, 1993), p. 8. See also Robert O'Meally, 'Frederick Douglass's 1845 *Narrative*: The Text Was Meant to be Preached', in *Afro-American Literature*, ed. Dexter Fisher and Robert Stepto (New York, 1979).

50 David L. Dudley, *My Father's Shadow* (Philadelphia, 1991), pp. 27–8.

51 Jenny Franchot, 'The Punishment of Esther: Frederick Douglass and the Construction of the Feminine', in *Frederick Douglass: New Literary and Historical Essays*, ed. Eric J. Sundquist (Cambridge, 1990), p. 141.

52 Richard Yarborough, 'Race, Violence and Manhood: The Masculine Ideal in Frederick Douglass's "The Heroic Slave"', in *Frederick Douglass*, ed. Sundquist, p. 174. See also Donald B. Gibson, 'Reconciling Public and Private in Frederick Douglass's *Narrative*', *American Literature*, 57 (Dec 1985), p. 563.

53 Douglass, *Narrative*, p. 67. 'He has borne himself with gentleness and meekness, yet with true manliness of character,' concluded William Lloyd Garrison: Preface to Douglass, *Narrative*, p. 5.

54 Frederick Douglass, *My Bondage and My Freedom* (New York, 1969), pp. 242–6.

55 David Leverenz, *Manhood and the American Renaissance* (Ithaca, NY, 1989), p. 112.

56 See Bernard R. Boxill, 'The Fight with Covey', in *Existence in Black: An Anthology of Black Existential Philosophy*, ed. Lewis R. Gordon (New York, 1997), pp. 273–90.

57 Legree delegates Tom's whipping to 'two gigantic negroes'. He wants to make Tom an overseer for which he believes 'hardness' is the prerequisite. In refusing to beat others, Tom remains physically soft but morally firm. Harriet Beecher Stowe, *Uncle Tom's Cabin*, in *Three Novels* (New York, 1982), p. 415. In *My Bondage*, Douglass wrote, 'while slaves prefer their lives, with flogging, to instant death, they will always find christians enough, like unto Covey, to accommodate that preference.' In taking on Covey, Douglass 'had reached the point, at which I was *not afraid to die*' (p. 247). On 'Douglass's preference for death', see Paul Gilroy, *The Black Atlantic* (London, 1993), pp. 61–4.

58 See Susan F. Clark, 'Up Against the Ropes: Peter Jackson as "Uncle Tom" in America', *The Drama Review*, 44, no. 1 (2000), pp. 157–82; Linda Williams, 'Versions of Uncle Tom: Race and Gender in American Melodrama', in *New Scholarship from BFI Research*, ed. Colin McCabe and Duncan Petrie (London, 1996).

59 Douglass, *My Bondage and My Freedom*, pp. 246–7.

60 Frederick Douglass, 'Fighting the Rebels with One Hand', in *The Frederick Douglass Papers*, ed. John W. Blassingham and John R. McKivigan (New Haven, 1991), Series 1, vol. III, pp. 473–88.

61 Frederick Douglass, 'Men of Color, To Arms', in *Life and Times* (Cleveland, OH, 2005), pp. 397–8. Douglass is alluding to Byron's *Childe Harold's Pilgrimage*: 'Hereditary bondsmen! know ye not / Who would be free themselves must strike the blow?'. He also attached this stanza to the end of his accounts of the Covey fight in *My Bondage* and *Life and Times*.

62 Frederick Douglass, 'What the Black Man Wants', in *The Frederick Douglass Papers*, Series 1, vol. IV, p. 69.

63 The fight is 'the primal scene in male African American autobiography'. Dudley, *My Father's Shadow*, pp. 26–7.

64 Kelly Miller, 'Frederick Douglass', *Voice of the Negro*, 1 (1904), pp. 463–4; John Henry Adams, 'Rough Sketches: The New Negro Man', *Voice of the Negro*, 1 (1904), p. 450.

65 Paul Lawrence Dunbar, 'Frederick Douglass', in Helen Pitts Douglass, *In Memoriam Frederick Douglass* (Freeport, NY, 1971), p. 168.

66 Booker T. Washington, *Frederick Douglass* (New York, 1969) pp. 40–41.

67 James Weldon Johnson, *Along This Way* (New York, 1935), p. 208. In an 1892 interview with R. Thomas Fortune, Douglass described Jackson as 'one of our best missionaries abroad. ' Quoted in *The Frederick Douglass Papers*, Series 1, vol. V, pp. 500–501.

68 W.E.B. Du Bois, *The Souls of Black Folk* (New York, 1995), p. 54. See D. K. Wiggens, 'From Plantation to Playing Field', *Research Quarterly for Exercise and Sport*, 57, no. 2 (1986), pp. 101–16.

69 Dale A. Somers, *The Rise of Sports in New Orleans, 1850–1900* (Baton Rouge, LA, 1972), pp. 181–3.

70 David K. Wiggens, 'Peter Jackson and the Elusive Heavyweight Championship: A Black Athlete's Struggle Against the Late Nineteenth Century Color-Line', in *A Question of Manhood: A Reader in US Black Men's History and Masculinity*, ed. Ernestine Jenkins and Darlene Clark Hine (Bloomington, IA, 2001), vol. II, p. 293.

71 Corbett, *The Roar of the Crowd*, p. 118. See also Leo N. Miletich, *Dan Stuart's Fistic Carnival* (College Station, TX, 1994), p. 214.

72 Patrick Myler, *Gentleman Jim Corbett* (London, 1998), pp. 37–45.

73 Clark, 'Up Against the Ropes', p. 173. Sullivan also appeared in a production of the play, as Simon Legree. Nat Fleischer, *John L. Sullivan* (London, 1952), p. 165.

74 Winston Churchill's drawing of the fight is reproduced in *The Fireside Book of Boxing*, ed. W. C. Heinz (New York, 1961) p. 205.

75 Guy Deghy, *Noble and Manly: The History of the National Sporting Club* (London, 1956), pp. 104–5. The story of the Jackson-Slavin fight is recounted by an English bartender in the opening chapter of Budd Schulberg's novel, *The Harder They Fall* (1947).

76 On Jackson's gentlemanliness, see Kasia Boddy, 'Peter Jackson and Jack Johnson Visit Britain', in *Fighting Back? Jewish and Black Boxers in Britain*, ed. Michael Berkowitz and Ruti Ungar (London, 2007), pp. 51–66.

77 Johnson, *Black Manhattan*, p. 73. See, for example, Frank Harris, *My Life and Loves* (New York, 1991), p. 650.

78 Richard Wright, 'The Ethics of Living Jim Crow', *Uncle Tom's Children* (New York, 1993), p. 14. Wright included this passage in his 1945 memoir *Black Boy* (London, 1970),

p. 202. The only change is the addition of the Fifteenth Amendment.

79  Al-Tony Gilmore, *Bad Nigger! The National Impact of Jack Johnson* (Washington, NY, 1975), pp. 27–8.

80  Jack Johnson, *In the Ring and Out* (New York, 1977), p. 48. Out of print for many years, Johnson's autobiography was reissued at the height of Black Power under the title, *Jack Johnson is a Dandy* (1969).

81  Jack London, 'Burns-Johnson', in *Jack London Reports*, ed. King Hendricks and Irving Shepard (New York, 1970), pp. 258–9, 260, 261, 263. In his autobiography, Johnson felt obliged to note that 'to me it was not a racial triumph.' Johnson, *In the Ring and Out*, p. 53.

82  Roberts, *Papa Jack*, p. 53. On 'the black American as a living comic supplement,' see Jessie Fauset, 'The Gift of Laughter' in *The New Negro: An Interpretation*, ed. Alain Locke (New York, 1997), pp. 161–7.

83  See William H. Wiggens, Jr. 'Boxing's Sambo Twins: Racial Stereotypes in Jack Johnson and Joe Louis Newspaper Cartoons, 1908–1938', *Journal of Sport History*, 15, no. 3 (Winter 1988), pp. 242–54.

84  Roberts, *Papa Jack*, pp. 24–6.

85  In 1901, Jim Jeffries had seen Johnson defeat his brother in five easy rounds. Roberts, *Papa Jack*, p. 21.

86  Rudyard Kipling, 'The White Man's Burden', *McClure's Magazine*, 12 (February 1899).

87  Quoted in Johnson, *Black Manhattan*, p. 66.

88  Lovish, *Monkey Business*, pp. 70–71.

89  Quoted in Finis Farr, *Black Champion: The Life and Times of Jack Johnson* (New York, 1965), p. 105.

90  Arthur Conan Doyle, *Rodney Stone* (London, 1912), p. 164; 'Both in Fine Condition', *New York Times*, 3 July 1910, p. 2; Jack London, *Jack London Reports*, pp. 266, 273. See John Hoberman, *Darwin's Athletes*, pp. 11–12

91  'Johnson's Mother Happy', *New York Times*, 5 July 1910, p. 3.

92  Louis Armstrong, *Satchmo: A Life in New Orleans* (New York, 1986), p. 31; Henry Crowder, 'Hitting Back', in *Negro: An Anthology*, ed. Nancy Cunard (New York, 2002), p. 119.

93  Allen Guttmann, *Sports Spectators* (New York, 1986), p. 119.

94  Quoted in Lerone Bennett, Jr, 'Jack Johnson and the Great White Hope', *Ebony* (October 1976), p. 80. The Johnson years coincided with the founding of the NAACP (1909), the National Urban League (1911) and the Universal Negro Improvement Association (1918).

95  Tad, 'Keeping Pace with Jack Johnson', Preface to Johnson, *In the Ring and Out*, p. 19.

96  John Lardner, 'That Was Pugilism: The White Hopes – I', *The New Yorker*, 25 June 1949, p. 59. See also Graeme Kent, *The Great White Hopes: The Quest to Defeat Jack Johnson* (Sutton, 2005).

97  William A. Phelon, 'Fitzsimmons and the White Hopes', *Baseball Magazine*, 4 (February 1914), p. 51.

98  Georges Carpentier, *Carpentier by Himself*, trans. Edward Fitzgerald (London, 1958), p. 89.

99  Jack London, *The Abysmal Brute* (Lincoln, NE, 2000), pp. 5, 16.

100  Edgar Rice Burroughs, *The Mucker* (New York, 1974), pp. 183–4.

101  W.R.H. Trowbridge, *The White Hope* (London, 1913), pp. 61, 293, 303.

102  Gilmore, *Bad Nigger!*, pp. 75–90.

103  James Weldon Johnson, 'The Passing of Jack Johnson', in *The Selected Writings*, ed. Sandra Kathryn Wilson (Oxford, 1995), vol. I, p. 126. See W. Stephen Bush, 'Arguments of Fight Films', *The Moving Picture World*, 15 May 1915, pp. 1049–50; Edward de Grazia and Roger K. Newman, *Banned Films: Movies, Censors and the First Amendment* (New York, 1982), pp. 185–6; Dan Streible, 'Race and the Reception of Jack Johnson Fight Films', in *The Birth of Whiteness*, ed. Daniel Bernardi (New Brunswick, NJ, 1996), pp. 170–200; Lee Grieveson, *Policing Cinema: Movies and Censorship in Early Twentieth-Century America* (Berkeley, CA, 2004), ch. 4; Richard Maltby, 'The Social Evil, The Moral Order and the Melodramatic Imagination, 1890–1915', in *Melodrama*, ed. Jacky Bratton, Jim Cooke and Christine Gledhill (London, 1996), p. 226.

104  Theodore Roosevelt, 'Recent Prize-Fight', *Outlook*, 16 July 1910, p. 551.

105  W.E.B. Du Bois, 'The Prize Fighter', in *Writings* (New York, 1986), p. 1162.

106  W.E.B. Du Bois, 'The Problem of Amusement', in *W.E.B Du Bois on Sociology and the Black Community*, ed. Dan S. Green and Edwin D. Driver (Chicago, 1978), pp. 226–37.

107  W.E.B. Du Bois, *The Crisis*, April 1926, p. 270; 'As to Pugilism', *Pittsburgh Courier*, 7 April 1923, p. 6.

108  Ida B. Wells, *Crusade for Justice* (Chicago, 1970), p. 359. Johnson later ran the Harlem Club de Luxe, which became the Cotton Club. See Johnson, *In the Ring and Out*, pp. 58–60; Ted Vincent, *Keep Cool: The Black Activists Who Built the Jazz Age* (London, 1995), p. 70; Kevin J. Mumford, *Interzones: Black/White Sex Districts in Chicago and New York in the Early Twentieth Century* (New York, 1997), pp. 3–18.

109  Booker T. Washington, *Up from Slavery* (New York, 1996), p. 57. On black dandies, see Eric Lott, *Love and Theft: Blackface Minstrelsy and the American Working Class* (Oxford, 1993), pp. 133–4.

110  *The Booker T. Washington Papers*, ed. Louis R. Harlan and Raymond W. Smock (Urbana, IL, 1981), vol. X, pp. 75–6.

111  Nick Carraway laughs at the sight of 'a limousine, driven by a white chauffeur, in which sat three modish negroes'. F. Scott Fitzgerald, *The Great Gatsby* (Harmondsworth, 1990), p. 75.

112  Johnson married Etta Duryea in late 1910 or early 1911. She committed suicide in September 1911, and in 1912 he married Lucille Cameron. They divorced in 1924 and the following year he married Irene Pineau. On interracial marriage in this period, see W.E.B. Du Bois , 'Intermarriage', *Crisis*, 5 (February 1913), pp. 180–81; Mary Frances Berry and John W. Blassingame, *Long Memory: The Black Experience in America* (Oxford, 1982), pp. 130–41.

113  Roberts, *Papa Jack*, p. 145; Geoffrey C. Ward, *Unforgiveable Blackness: The Rise and Fall of Jack Johnson* (New York, 2004), ch. 10. On white slavery in the movies, see Grieveson, *Policing Cinema*, ch. 5.

114  Booker T. Washington, 'A Statement on Jack Johnson for the

United Press Association', 23 October 1912, in *The Booker T. Washington Papers*, vol. XII, ed. Louis R. Harlan and Raymond W. Smock (Urbana, IL, 1982), pp. 43–4. For Johnson's response, see Gilmore, *Bad Nigger*, p. 102.

115 Johnson, *In the Ring and Out*, p. 70.

116 'Actions Against Jack Johnson: Assault on a Music-Hall Artist', *The Times*, 2 March 1916, p. 4. See also Boddy, 'Peter Jackson and Jack Johnson Visit Britain'.

117 Immediately after the fight Johnson said nothing, but within a year, he sold his 'confessions' to Nat Fleischer, editor of *The Ring*, for $250. Footage of the fight, recovered by Jim Jacobs and included in his film *Jack Johnson* (1970), suggests that Johnson really was knocked out.

118 Claude McKay, *Home to Harlem* (Boston, 1987), pp. 66–7, 71–2, 273. He later recalled being told that he 'did not look like the boxer-type [portraits] . . . that were reproduced with the reviews of *Home to Harlem*.' Claude McKay, from *A Long Way Home*, in *The Portable Harlem Renaissance*, ed. David Levering Lewis (Harmondsworth, 1994), p. 165.

119 George Hutchinson, *The Harlem Renaissance in Black and White* (Cambridge, MA, 1995), p. 364. For the full story, see Jon-Christian Suggs, '"Blackjack": Walter White and modernism in an unknown boxing novel', *Michigan Quarterly Review*, 38, no. 4 (Fall 1999), pp. 514–40.

120 Jim Tully had been a professional featherweight boxer (1907–1915) and in 1937 published a prize-fight novel, *The Bruiser*. He is best known, however, as author of *Beggars of Life: A Hobo Autobiography* (1924), which was filmed in 1928.

121 Quoted in Martin Duberman, *Paul Robeson: A Biography* (New York, 1988), pp. 103–4. Langston Hughes attended one of the 37 performances. Langston Hughes, *The Big Sea: An Autobiography* (New York, 1993), p. 251. See Gerald Bordman, *American Theatre: A Chronicle of Comedy and Drama, 1914–1930* (Oxford, 1995), pp. 297–8; and Theophilus Lewis's review, in *The Messenger Reader*, ed. Sondra Kathryn Wilson (New York, 2000), p. 247.

122 See Barbara Foley, *Spectres of 1919: Class and Nation in the Making of the New Negro* (Urbana, IL, 2003).

123 Henry Louis Gates, 'Canon-Formation, Literary History and the Afro-American Tradition: From the Seen to the Told', in *Afro-American Literary Study in the 1990s*, ed. Houston A. Baker and Patricia Redmond (Chicago, 1989), p. 33.

124 James Weldon Johnson, 'Inside Measurement', in *The Selected Writings*, ed. Wilson, vol. I, pp. 260–61.

125 James Weldon Johnson, *The Book of American Negro Poetry* (New York, 1931), p. 9.

126 W.E.B. Du Bois , 'The Talented Tenth', in *The Negro Problem* (New York, 1903), pp. 33–75.

127 Johnson, 'The Passing of Jack Johnson', p. 125.

128 Johnson, *Along This Way*, p. 208.

129 James Weldon Johnson, 'The Negro in American Art', in *Selected Writings*, vol. I., p. 262. Robert Coady was the editor of *The Soil* (1916–17) which argued that America's distinctive culture was found outside its museums. He interspersed photographs of figures such as Johnson and the comedian Bert Williams among reproductions of primitive and European art. See Wanda Corn, *The Great American*

*Thing: Modern Art and National Identity, 1915–1935* (Berkeley, CA, 1999), pp. 81–89.

130 In a 1924 article in the *Messenger*, A. Philip Randolph imagined Du Bois and Marcus Garvey as boxers and gave a round by round account of their contest. A. Philip Randolph, 'Heavyweight Championship Bout for Afro-American-West-Indian Belt, Between Battling Du Bois and Kid Garvey . . . Referee – Everybody and Nobody', in *Voices of a Black Nation: Political Journalism in the Harlem Renaissance*, ed. Theodore G. Vincent (San Francisco, 1973), p. 122.

131 George S. Schuyler, 'The Negro-Art Hokum', in *The Portable Harlem Renaissance*, ed. Lewis, p. 97.

132 Claude McKay, *A Long Way from Home* (New York, 1937), p. 61.

133 Denzil Batchelor, *Jack Johnson and His Times* (London, 1956), p. 178.

134 The song was recorded and reproduced by folklorist J. Mason Brewer in *Worser Days and Better Times: The Folklore of the North Carolina Negro* (Chicago, 1965), p. 178.

135 J. 'Berni' Barborn, 'The Black Gladiator', quoted in Streible, 'Race and the Reception of Jack Johnson Fight Films', p. 195 n. 17.

136 Roberts, *Papa Jack*, p. 134. The song adapts an urban toast featuring a character called Shine. See Larry Neal. 'And Shine Swam On', in *Black Fire*, ed. LeRoi Jones and Larry Neal (New York, 1968), p. 638. For two versions, see *The Norton Anthology of African American Literature*, ed. Henry Louis Gates, Jr. and Nellie Y. McKay (New York, 1997), pp. 51–2. Legend had it that Johnson was refused a ticket for the *Titanic*, but in April 1912 he was in Chicago arranging a fight with Jim Flynn. After Johnson defeated Flynn, the *Chicago Defender* described him as 'the pugilistic *Titanic* of the Caucasian race'. Roberts, *Papa Jack*, p. 134.

137 William J. Maxwell, *New Negro, Old Left: African-American Writing and Communism Between the Wars* (New York, 1999), p. 64. McKay later dismissed what he called 'the highly propagandized Negro renaissance period'. Claude McKay, *A Long Way from Home*, p. 154.

138 Claude McKay, 'If We Must Die', in *Harlem Shadows: The Poems* (New York, 1922), p. 53.

139 See Henry Louis Gates, Jr. 'The Trope of the New Negro and the Reconstruction of the Image of the Black', in *The New American Studies*, ed. Philip Fisher (Berkeley, CA, 1991), p. 325.

140 Rollin Lynde Hartt, 'The New Negro. When He's Hit, He Hits Back', *Independent*, 15 January 1921, pp. 59–60, 76. The term 'New Negro' had been in circulation since the 1890s but was used increasingly in the period following the postwar race riots. See Foley, *Spectres of 1919*.

141 W. A. Domingo, Editorial, *The Messenger*, September 1919, and J. A. Rogers, 'Who Is the New Negro, And Why?', March 1927, reprinted in *The Messenger Reader*, ed. Wilson, pp. 308–12, 335–7.

142 Zora Neale Hurston, *Mules and Men* (1935), in *I Love Myself When I Am Laughing: A Zora Neale Hurston Reader*, ed. Alice Walker (New York, 1979), p. 83; Hurston, 'High John de

Conquer' (1943), in *Mother Wit from the Laughing Barrel: Readings in the Interpretation of African-American Folklore*, ed. Alan Dundes (Jackson, MI, 1981), pp. 541–8. See also Harry Ostler, 'Negro Humor: John and Old Master', in *Mother Wit*, ed. Dundes, pp. 549–60.

143 See H. C. Brearley, 'Ba-ad Nigger', in *Mother Wit*, ed. Dundes, pp. 578–85; John W. Roberts, *From Trickster to Badman: The Black Folk Hero in Slavery and Freedom* (Philadelphia, 1989), ch. 5; William H. Wiggens, 'Jack Johnson as Bad Nigger: The Folklore of His Life', *Black Scholar* (January 1971), pp. 4–19.

144 Crowder, 'Hitting Back', pp. 117–19.

145 Alain Locke, 'Sterling Brown: The New Negro Folk-Poet', in *Negro*, ed. Cunard, pp. 88–92.

146 Sterling Brown, 'Strange Legacies', in *The Collected Poems*, ed. Michael S. Harper (New York, 1980), pp. 86–7. Johnson meanwhile compared himself to Job. Johnson, *In and Out the Ring*, p. 167.

147 Johnson, *In and Out of the Ring*, pp. 168–9.

148 Roberts, *Papa Jack*, p. 212.

149 Claude McKay, *The Negroes in America*, trans. Robert J. Winter, ed. Alan L. McLeod (Port Washington, NY, 1979), p. 3. The original text was lost; this version was translated from Russian back into English.

150 For a reading of McKay as 'a precursor – and Marxian pre-critic – of black cultural studies', see Maxwell, *New Negro, Old Left*, pp. 86–87.

151 McKay, *The Negroes in America*, pp. 53–5. See also Wayne F. Cooper, *Claude McKay* (Baton Rouge, LA, 1996), pp. 185–9.

152 Langston Hughes, 'Prize Fighter', *Fine Clothes to the Jew* (New York, 1927), p. 33.

153 Jean Toomer, 'Box Seat', in *Cane* (New York, 1988), p. 67.

154 See Darwin T. Turner, 'Contrasts and Limitations in *Cane*', reprinted in Toomer, *Cane*, p. 210; and Thomas Fahy, 'Exotic Fantasies, Shameful Realities: Race in the Modern American Freak Show', in *A Modern Mosaic: Art and Modernism in the United States*, ed. Townsend Ludington (Chapel Hill, NC, 2000), pp. 75–82.

155 On the popularity of the 'fistic quarrel' in minstrel shows, see Lott, *Love and Theft*, pp. 126–8.

156 Arthur Conan Doyle, 'The Adventure of the Three Gables', in *The Penguin Complete Sherlock Holmes* (Harmondsworth, 1981), pp. 1023–4. See also 'Nig' Coston, a Tyson-like biter, in P. G. Wodehouse, *Psmith Journalist* (Harmondsworth, 1970), p. 105.

157 William Carlos Williams, *The Autobiography* (New York, 1967), p. 141.

158 Joyce Carol Oates, 'George Bellows: The Boxing Paintings', in *(Woman) Writer: Occasions and Opportunities* (New York, 1988), p. 295. See also Marianne Doezema, *George Bellows and Urban America* (New Haven, 1992), p. 101.

159 McKay, *Home to Harlem* p. 106. Whites who attended 'nigger clubs' justified their visits as nostalgia for a childhood spent among 'little darkies'. Paul Lawrence Dunbar, *The Sport of the Gods* (New York, 1981), p. 103.

160 See Emma S. Bellows, *George Bellows: His Lithographs* (New York, 1927). Compare *The White Hope* with *The Saviour of his Race*, an etching which Bellows published in *Masses* the month after Willard beat Johnson. The white fighter is depicted with arms outstretched against the corner post in an obvious crucifixion allusion. Doezema, *George Bellows and Urban America*, p. 218.

161 Ernest Hemingway, 'A Matter of Colour', in *Ernest Hemingway's Apprenticeship. Oak Park, 1916–1917*, ed. Matthew J. Bruccoli (Washington, DC, 1971), pp. 98–100. See also David Marut, 'Out of the Wastebasket: Hemingway's High School Stories', in *Ernest Hemingway: The Oak Park Legacy*, ed. James Nagel (Tuscaloosa, AL, 1996), pp. 81–95; Gregory Green, '"A Matter of Color": Hemingway's Criticism of Race Prejudice', *Hemingway Review*, 1 (Fall 1981), pp. 27–32. Hemingway began boxing lessons in 1916. See Carlos Baker, *Ernest Hemingway: A Life Story* (London, 1969), pp. 43–4; Peter Griffin, *Along with Youth: Hemingway, the Early Years* (Oxford, 1985), pp. 23–4.

162 Hemingway, *The Sun Also Rises*, p. 60. His model seems likely to have been the 1922 Siki-Carpentier fight. James L. Martine, 'Hemingway's "Fifty Grand": The Other Fight(s)', in *The Short Stories of Ernest Hemingway: Critical Essays*, ed. Jackson J. Benson (Durham, NC, 1975), p. 200; Peter Benson, *Battling Siki* (Fayetteville, AR, 2006), pp. 251–2.

163 Hemingway, *The Sun Also Rises*, p. 14.

164 Reynolds, *Hemingway: The Paris Years*, p. 297. The fight took place on 9 June; Hemingway changed it to 20 June.

165 Ernest Hemingway, 'The Light of the World', in *Winner Take Nothing* (London, 1977), pp. 67–73.

166 Ketchel's real name was Stanislaus Kiecal.

167 Ketchel's knockdown of Johnson was widely believed, even at the time, to have been staged for the film cameras. The painter John Sloan wrote appreciatively in his diary of seeing 'the cinematograph pictures of the recent fight between Ketchel and the negro Jack Johnson. The big black spider gobbled up the small white fly – aggressive fly – wonderful to have this event repeated.' Quoted in *John Sloan's New York Scene*, ed. Bruce St John (New York, 1965).

168 Walter Benn Michaels, 'The Souls of White Folk', in *Literature and the Body*, ed. Elaine Scarry (Baltimore, 1988), p. 193.

169 Philip Young, *Ernest Hemingway* (Philadelphia, 1966), p. 50. On the story's relationship to Holman Hunt's painting of Jesus with a lantern, see Michael Reynolds, 'Holman Hunt and "The Light of the World"', *Studies in Short Fiction*, 20 (Winter 1983), pp. 317–19.

170 Roberts, *Papa Jack*, pp. 81–4. In a 1922 letter, Hemingway described Ketchel as 'too small for that damned smoke'. *Selected Letters, 1917–1961*, ed. Carlos Baker (London, 1985), p. 64. See also William J. Collins, 'Taking on the Champion: Alice as Liar in "The Light of the World"', *Studies in American Fiction*, 14, no. 2 (Autumn 1986), pp. 225–32; James J. Martine, 'A Little Light on Hemingway's "The Light of the World"', in *The Short Stories of Ernest Hemingway*, ed. Jackson, pp. 196–8.

171 See Howard L. Hannum, 'Nick Adams and the Search for Light', in *New Critical Approaches to the Short Stories of Ernest Hemingway*, ed. Jackson L. Benson (Durham, NC, 1990), pp. 321–30.

172 Hemingway described the story as being about a 'busted down pug and a coon'. *Selected Letters*, ed. Baker, p. 157. Baker argues that Ad was an amalgam of Ad Wolgast and Bat Nelson, and that Bugs was based on the trainer who had looked after Wolgast, a one-time opponent of Steve Ketchel. The story was originally called 'A Great Little Fighting Machine'. Baker, *Ernest Hemingway: A Life Story*, pp. 178–9.

173 The opening story of *In Our Time*, 'Indian Camp', introduces the recurrent motif of a safe-seeming camp which turns out to be a violent and dangerous place.

174 Ernest Hemingway, 'The Battler', in *In Our Time* (New York, 1986), pp. 53–62. He sent the manuscript to his publisher with a letter claiming it had 'a good 3/1 chance' at success. 'And I never bet on Jeffries at Reno nor Carpentier not other sentimental causes.' Hemingway was only 11 in 1910, but he did bet, and lose, on Carpentier in 1921. *Selected Letters*, pp. 155, 52.

175 Thomas Strychacz, 'Dramatizations of Manhood in Hemingway's *In Our Time* and *The Sun Also Rises*', *American Literature*, 61, no. 2 (May 1989), p. 252.

176 See, for example, George Monteiro, '"This is My Pal Bugs": Ernest Hemingway's "The Battler"', in *New Critical Approaches*, ed. Jackson, pp. 224–8. Consider also Hemingway's reported comments to Gertrude Stein: 'when you were a boy and moved in the company of men, you had to be prepared to kill a man, know how to do it and really know that you would do it in order not to be interfered with.' *A Moveable Feast* (London, 1982), pp. 21–2.

177 The novel makes much of the 'mingled virtues' of Johnny's mixed blood, or 'sanguinary cocktail'. Alin Laubreaux, *Mulatto Johnny*, trans. Coley Taylor (London, 1931), p. 204. See also John Frederick Matheus, 'Some Aspects of the Negro interpreted in Contemporary American and European Literature', in *Negro*, ed. Cunard, pp. 86–7.

178 Joseph Moncure March, *The Set-Up* (Garden City, NJ, 1931), pp. 123, 200.

179 Mae West, *The Constant Sinner* (London, 1995), p. 6. The original American edition had the title *Babe Gordon*; the working title was *Black and White*. Marybeth Hamilton, *The Queen of Camp: Mae West, sex and popular culture* (London, 1996), p. 138.

180 Bearcat McMahon was a White Hope of the teens. Stories about the feats of Mae's father, 'Battling Jack West, Champion of Brooklyn New York', and various boyfriends, can be found in West's autobiography, *Goodness Had Nothing to Do with It* (London, 1996) pp. 2–3, 17, 23–5, 136. Boxers reputed to have had affairs with West include Jim Corbett, Johnny Indrisano, William 'Gorilla' Jones, Kid Berg and Joe Louis. See Maurice Leonard, *Mae West: Empress of Sex* (New York, 1991), pp. 292–4 and passim.

181 *The Constant Sinner*, pp. 47, 17, 90, 103, 109–10, 212. When the novel was adapted for Broadway in 1931, Money Johnson was played by a white actor in blackface. Hamilton, *The Queen of Camp*, p. 148. See also West, *Goodness Had Nothing To Do With It*, p. 148.

182 Wallace Thurman, *Infants of the Spring* (New York, 1999), pp. 22, 40, 43, 74. On the fashion among white women to

have black lovers and 'Negro' annoyance at Jack Johnson's white wives, see Heba Jannath, 'America's Changing Color Line', in *Negro*, ed. Cunard, pp. 64–5. Although the OED dates the use of 'johnson' as a slang equivalent of 'penis' to 1863, Clarence Major argues that its use in African-American slang 'probably stems from the image of Jack Johnson pounding his opponent'. *Juba to Jive: A Dictionary of African-American Slang* (Harmondsworth, 1994), p. 261.

183 Thurman, *Infants of the Spring*, pp. 79, 87, 156, 169.

184 William Faulkner, *Absalom, Absalom!* (Harmondsworth, 1971), pp. 13, 19–25, 36, 38, 115.

185 Stanislaus Joyce, *My Brother's Keeper* (London, 1958), p. 62.

186 The advertisement ran in *The Freeman's Journal* on 19 and 28 April 1904 (p. 4 each day) and described an upcoming 'civil and military' boxing tournament to be held at Earlsfort Terrace Rink, including a ten-round fight between M. L. Keogh of Dublin and Garry of the Sixth Dragoons. On the 30th, we learn that Keogh has won. Joyce changed the names slightly to avenge himself on Percy Bennett, the consul-general in Zurich whom he sued in 1918. Bennett had supported Henry Carr, another member of the consulate, in a row concerning Joyce's theatre company, the English Players. Carr is avenged in 'Circe'. Richard Ellmann, *James Joyce* (Oxford, 1982), pp. 436–42, 472. See also Robert Martin Adams, *Surface and Symbol: The Consistency of Ulysses* (New York, 1967), p. 70.

187 See Tracy Mishkin, *The Harlem and Irish Renaissances: Language, Identity and Representation* (Gainsville, FL, 1998).

188 James Joyce, *Ulysses* (Harmondsworth, 1992), pp. 219–20. Ted Keogh, who managed a prizefighter, may have been a model for Blazes Boylan. Ellmann, *James Joyce*, p. 389.

189 Joyce, *Ulysses*, pp. 412–4.

190 Ibid., p. 432. Valente argues that Bloom here is merely providing 'a colonial impersonation of manhood'. Joseph Valente, '"Neither fish not flesh"; or how "Cyclops" stages the double-bind of Irish manhood', in *Semicolonial Joyce*, ed. Derek Attridge and Marjorie Howes (Cambridge, 2000), p. 120. See also Richard Brown, 'Cyclopean Anglophobia and Transnational Community: Re-Reading the Boxing Matches in Joyce's *Ulysses*', in *Twenty-First Joyce*, ed. Ellen Carol Jones and Morris Beja (Gainsville, FL, 2004), pp. 82–96; Tracey Teets Schwarze, '"Do You Call That a Man?": The Culture of Anxious Masculinity in Joyce's *Ulysses*', in *Masculinities in Joyce*, ed. Christine Van Boheemen-Saaf and Colleen Lamos (Amsterdam, 2001), pp. 113–35.

191 See Valente, '"Neither fish not flesh"'; Vincent Cheng, 'Catching the Conscience of a Race', in *Joyce, Race and Empire* (Cambridge, 1995), pp. 15–56.

192 Joyce, *Ulysses*, pp. 496, 745–6, 764.

193 Stuart Gilbert argues that this chapter, 'Eumaeus', was meant to represent both physical and linguistic exhaustion, and that Bloom was perhaps deliberately trying to send Stephen to sleep. Quoted in Ellman, *James Joyce*, p. 372, n.

194 Joyce, *Ulysses*, pp. 444–5, 805. Later still, Bloom rejects 'retribution' against his wife's lover, Blazes Boylan – 'Duel by combat? No', pp. 863, 866. On Mendoza's 1791 visit to Ireland, see Myler, *The Fighting Irish*, pp. 19–22.

195 While Bloom is walking home, Molly lies in bed reminiscing

about the attentions paid to her by various men. She remembers a fish supper that a King's Counsel gave her 'on account of winning over the boxing match'. His silk hat recalls those worn by the spectators in the nineteenth-century print seen by Stephen. Joyce, *Ulysses*, pp. 925–6.

196 Joyce misquotes the title (deliberately?) as *Physical Strength and How to Obtain It*. See Hugh Kenner, 'Bloom's Chest', *James Joyce Quarterly*, 16.4 (1979), pp. 505–8; Cheryl Herr, *Joyce's Anatomy of Culture* (Urbana, IL, 1986), pp. 193–5; Brandon Kershner, 'The World's Strongest Man: Joyce or Sandow', *James Joyce Quarterly*, 30.4/31.1 (1993–94), pp. 667–96.

197 Bloom first thinks of Sandow on his way back from buying his breakfast kidney, when, after reading a Zionist pamphlet, he becomes depressed at the thought of the 'dead sea in a dead land' and his own ageing body. 'Must begin again those Sandow exercises. On the hands down.' (Sandow wrote of the benefits of his system for 'the inner organs' as well as visible muscles.) He remembers them again in 'Calypso' and in 'Circe' when he develops a stitch. In 'Ithaca', the narrator notes that the exercises would also have given him 'a most pleasant repristination of juvenile agility.' Bloom is 11st 4lb and wears a size 17 collar. His 'before and after' measurements are also given. Joyce, *Ulysses*, pp. 73, 567, 797, 779, 835, 850. Chapter Seven of *Strength and How to Obtain It* is entitled 'Physical Culture for the Middle-Aged'.

198 Eugen Sandow, *Strength and How to Obtain It* (London, 1900), pp. 89–95; Eugen Sandow, *Sandow on Physical Training: A Study in the Perfect Type of the Human Form* (London, 1894), pp. 19, 113.

199 Joyce, *Ulysses*, pp. 564, 572, 578.

200 Shortly after *Ulysses* was published, Joyce told Arthur Power that, 'in realism you are down to the facts on which the world is based: that sudden reality which smashes romanticism into a pulp.' *Conversations with James Joyce*, ed. Clive Hart (New York, 1974), p. 98.

201 Joyce, *My Brother's Keeper*, p. 62.

202 Joyce, *Stephen Hero*, pp. 34, 82.

203 George Bernard Shaw, 'Preface' (1901) to *Cashel Byron's Profession* (London, 1925), p. xiv. Boxing could easily have been included in the litany of 'British Beatitudes': 'beer, beef, business, bibles, bulldogs, battleships, buggery and bishops'. Joyce, *Ulysses*, p. 556.

204 The Keogh-Bennett fight, and Joyce's battle with the Zurich consulate is again evoked as Carr drunkenly announces that Bennett's his 'pal' – 'I love old Bennett'. Joyce, *Ulysses*, pp. 579, 686, 687, 69. See Ellmann, *James Joyce*, p. 442.

205 Joyce, *Ulysses*, pp. 689, 696, 697. The scene also reworks one in *Stephen Hero* in which a drunken 'bandy-legged little' clerk argues with a medical student about 'the art of self-defence'. There is again great relish in the quoted lingo of 'props', 'mits' and 'smashing'. Joyce, *Stephen Hero*, pp. 211–12. That scene may in turn rework an incident from Joyce's early life. See Ellmann, *James Joyce*, p. 156.

206 James Joyce, *Finnegans Wake* (Harmondsworth, 1992), p. 18.

207 If the Irish were often described as blacks, then perhaps occasionally blacks were Irish. See Noel Ingatiev, *How the Irish Became White* (New York, 1995).

208 Joyce, *My Brother's Keeper*, p. 62; Ellmann, *James Joyce*, p. 371.

209 Joyce, *Finnegans Wake*, pp. 16–18, 338–55, 609–10.

210 Gilbert Seldes, *The Seven Lively Arts* (New York, 1924), p. 216; Bud Fisher, *A. Mutt, 1907–1908* (Westport, CT, 1977), p. 51. The pair did not make it into the English or Irish press until 1918 when they appeared as soldiers – Mutt as an American, Jeff as British. Joyce may also have encountered Mutt and Jeff in one of over 500 animated silent cartoons produced between 1917 and 1928. See Donald Crafton, *Before Mickey: The Animated Film, 1908–1928* (Cambridge, MA, 1984), pp. 196–200.

211 Dan Schiff, 'Joyce and Cartoons', in *Joyce in Context*, ed. Vincent J. Cheng and Timothy Martin (Cambridge, 1992), pp. 210, 212. See also Ellmann, *James Joyce*, p. 61.

212 William York Tindall compares the knockout to Private Carr's biffing of Stephen in 'Circe'. Tindall, *A Reader's Guide to Finnegans Wake* (New York, 1969), p. 181. See also Schiff, 'Joyce and Cartoons', p. 209.

213 Joyce, *Finnegans Wake*, pp. 301, 302, 304.

214 Joyce described this part of the book as 'the most difficult of all': 'the technique here is a reproduction of a schoolboy's (and schoolgirl's) old classbook complete with marginalia by the twins, who change sides at half time, footnotes by the girl (who doesn't), a Euclid diagram, funny drawings etc.' James Joyce, *Letters*, ed. Stuart Gilbert (London, 1957), p. 406.

215 Jimmy Wilde, known as the Mighty Atom, held British, European and World flyweight titles between 1916 and 1923. Heavyweight Jack Sharkey (born Joseph Chusauskas of Lithuanian parents) adopted the Irish name of his hero Tom Sharkey, and fought against Dempsey, Schmeling and Louis in the 1930s. He was briefly champion in 1932. In 1918, Katherine Mansfield told Middleton Murry that, despite her new iron supplements, 'Jimmy Wilde is more my size than Jack Johnson.' *The Collected Letters of Katherine Mansfield*, ed. V. O. Sullivan and M. Scott (Oxford, 1987), vol. II, p. 222.

216 Joyce, *Finnegans Wake*, p. 269.

## 7 Sport of the Future

1 In Cameron Crowe's 1989 film *Say Anything*, Lloyd Dobler (John Cusack) memorably declares *kickboxing* the 'sport of the future'.

2 Bruce J. Evensen, 'Jazz Age Journalism's Battle Over Professionalism, Circulation, and the Sports Page', *Journal of Sports History*, 20, no. 3 (Winter 1993), p. 231; Paul Gallico, *A Farewell to Sport* (1937) (London, 1988), p. 15.

3 'Jack Dempsey, New Heavyweight Champion, Announces He Will Draw the Color Line', *New York Times*, 6 July 1919, p. 20. W.E.B. Du Bois wrote that 'Dempsey develops a weak heart because of Texas Rickard's strenuous efforts to protect him from the Willis wallop'. *The Crisis*, April 1926, p. 270.

4 Thomas Healey, *A Hurting Business* (London, 1996), p. 17.

5 Quoted in Tom Clark, *The World of Damon Runyon* (New York, 1978), p. 123.

6 Peter Heller, *In This Corner!* (London, 1973), p. 55; Joyce Carol Oates, *On Boxing* (London, 1988), p. 88.

7 Gallico, *Farewell to Sport*, p. 16.

8 A species of cichlid, Cichlasoma biocellatum, was nicknamed 'Jack Dempsey' and 'renowned for the fairness of his fighting'. This was not, however, the boxer's reputation. Konrad Lorenz, *On Aggression*, trans. Marjorie Latzke (London, 1967), p. 94.

9 Damon Runyon, *New York American*, 5 July 1919, p. 1.

10 Jack Dempsey, with Jack Cuddy, *Championship Fighting* (London, 1950), pp. 8–9. Dempsey and Willard were reunited in the 1933 film, *The Prizefighter and the Lady*. Dempsey says, 'A little bit of a problem we had in Toledo that day' and Willard replies, 'I don't remember much about that day, Jack'.

11 Melvin B. Tolson, 'Omega', *Harlem Gallery, Book 1: The Curator* (New York, 1969), p. 149.

12 Damon Runyon, *New York American*, 5 July 1919, p. 1.

13 Clark, *The World of Damon Runyon*, pp. 11–14, 124.

14 'The Psychology of Boxing' is the subject of a chapter in Georges Carpentier, *My Methods, or Boxing as a Fine Art*, trans. F. Hurdman-Lucus (London, n.d.).

15 Gallico, *Farewell to Sport*, p. 17. During the Second World War, Dempsey wrote a book about 'down and dirty' techniques. One illustration caption reads '"Remember . . . he's the enemy. Break off his arm and hit him over the head with it."' Jack Dempsey, *How to Fight Tough* (Boulder, CO, 2002), p. 125.

16 Roderick Nash, *The Nervous Generation: American Thought, 1917–1930* (Chicago, 1970), p. 127.

17 The original Madison Square Garden, a converted railroad station, opened at Madison Square in 1874; in 1891, a new sports arena dedicated chiefly to boxing, opened on the site. In 1968 the Garden moved to its current location on top of Penn Station at 33rd Street and Seventh Avenue.

18 Max Schmeling, *An Autobiography*, trans. George B. von der Lippe (Chicago, 1998), p. 53.

19 Ernest Hemingway, 'Fifty Grand', *Men Without Women* (New York, 1986), p. 86.

20 See Elliott J. Gorn, George Plimpton and Marianne Doezema's short essays on the painting in *Frames of Reference: Looking at American Art, 1900–1950*, ed. Beth Venn and Adam D. Weinberg (New York, 1999), pp. 146–57.

21 The Lynds, *Middletown* (New York, 1929), p. 226. See Jesse Frederick Steiner, 'Spectatorism versus Participation', in *Americans at Play: Recent Trends in Recreation and Leisure Time Activities* (New York, 1933), pp. 100–102.

22 Stuart Chase, *Men and Machines* (London, 1929), pp. 259–60.

23 Peter Standish, *Understanding Julio Cortázar* (Columbia, SC, 2001), pp. 47–8; Julio Cortázar, 'Circe', *Breve Antologia de Cuentos* (Buenos Aires, 1991), p. 12; Garrison quoted in Ray Barfield, *Listening to Radio, 1920–1950* (Westport, CT, 1996), p. 80. Firpo's story forms the basis for Julio Cortázar, 'Torito', *Final del juego* (1956). See also Cortázar, 'The Noble Art', in *Around the Day in Eighty Worlds* (New York, 1986).

24 Richard Bak, *Joe Louis: The Great Black Hope* (New York, 1998), p. 25.

25 Stanley Woodward, *Sports Page* (New York, 1949), p. 38. In the first two decades of the twentieth century, there had been a 50 per cent rise in sports coverage in 63 of America's largest papers. Between 1920 and 1925, newspaper circulation increased by 5 million. Evensen, 'Jazz Age's Journalism', pp. 234, 236.

26 Gallico, *Farewell to Sport*, pp. 103–5. Within months of buying the *New York Journal* in 1895, William Randolph Hearst quadrupled its sports coverage and introduced the first dedicated sports section. His circulation wars with Joseph Pulitzer were partly fought over their respective coverage of Corbett's title defence against Charlie Mitchell, the fight that Abraham Cahan's Yekl reads about. Evensen, 'Jazz Age Journalism', p. 238. The New York *Daily News*, Hearst's 'first conspicuously successful tabloid', was launched in 1919. Frederick Allen Lewis, *Only Yesterday* (New York, 1964), p. 3. 'A journal for the home' called *Cosy Moments* is transformed into 'red-hot stuff' by the introduction of crime and boxing in P. G. Wodehouse's 1915 novel, *Psmith Journalist* (Harmondsworth, 1970), pp. 9, 32.

27 See Leo Lowenthal, 'The Triumph of Mass Idols', *Literature, Popular Culture, and Society* (Palo Alto, CA, 1968), pp. 109–41.

28 Heywood Broun, 'Sport for Art's Sake', in *The Best American Sports Writing of the Century*, ed. David Halberstam (Boston, 1999), p. 133.

29 Lowenthal, 'The Triumph of Mass Idols', p. 133.

30 Ibid., pp. 131–4.

31 Damon Runyon, 'The Big Umbrella', in *On Broadway* (Harmondsworth, 1990), p. 441.

32 William K. Everson, *American Silent Film* (New York, 1998), p. 269.

33 Kevin Brownlow, *The Parade's Gone By* (Berkeley, CA, 1968), pp. 448–56.

34 Paul Gallico, *The Golden People* (New York, 1965), pp. 13–28.

35 Robert K. Murray, *Red Scare: A Study in National Hysteria, 1919–1920* (Minneapolis, 1955), p. 241.

36 F. Scott Fitzgerald, 'Echoes of the Jazz Age', in *The Crack-Up* (Harmondsworth, 1965), p. 10; Lewis, *Only Yesterday*, p. 155.

37 John Dos Passos, 'Newsreel XL', *Nineteen Nineteen* (1932), in *USA* (London, 1950), pp. 665–6.

38 Carpentier's Hollywood films include *The Wonder Man* (1920), *A Gypsy Cavalier* (1922) and *The Show of Shows* (1929).

39 Quoted in Claude Meunier, *Ring Noir* (Paris, 1992), pp. 74–5. A full translation appears in Carpentier's autobiography, *Carpentier by Himself*, trans. Edward Fitzgerald (London, 1958), pp. 135–8.

40 Broun, 'Sport for Art's Sake', pp. 131, 134. Eugene O'Neill supposedly once told Harry Kemp, a Byronic Provincetown poet who often talked about boxers, that he would have 'liked to have been a prizefighter, too – but I got a blow once that loosened all my teeth.' Edmund Wilson, *The Twenties* (New York, 1976), p. 338.

41 Ring Lardner, 'The Battle of the Century', in *Some Champions*, ed. Matthew J. Bruccoli and Richard Layman (New York, 1992), pp. 134–49. When Lardner died in 1933, Scott

Fitzgerland described him as a 'disillusioned idealist': 'It was never that he was completely sold on athletic virtuosity as the be-all and end-all of problems; the trouble was that he could find nothing finer.' F. Scott Fitzgerald, 'Ring', in *The Crack-Up*, pp. 37–8.

42 Gene Tunney, 'My Fights with Jack Dempsey', in *The Aspirin Age, 1919 1941*, ed. Isabel Leighton (London, 1950), p. 159.

43 Tunney studied Dempsey's fights in detail. 'My Fights with Jack Dempsey', pp. 155–7.

44 F. Scott Fitzgerald, *The Great Gatsby* (Harmondsworth, 1990), p. 125. See Elliot J. Gorn, 'The Manassa Mauler and the Fighting Marine: An Interpretation of the Dempsey–Tunney Fights', *Journal of American Studies*, 19, no. 1 (1985), pp. 27–45.

45 Jeffrey T. Sammons, *Beyond the Ring* (Urbana, IL, 1990), p. 72.

46 Quoted in Sammons, *Beyond the Ring*, p. 71; 'The Manassa Mauler and the Fighting Marine', p. 29.

47 In 'The Bear' (1942), William Faulkner described the never-ending conversation about the fight between the bear, Old Ben, and the dog, Lion, as anticipating the way 'people later would talk about Sullivan and Kilrain and, later still, about Dempsey and Tunney.' Faulkner's story is set in the early 1880s. If the Kilrain-Sullivan fight of 1889 signalled the beginning of the development of modern commercial boxing, the Tunney-Dempsey contests of 1926 and 1927 represented its apotheosis. This is just one manifestation in the story of capitalism's encroachment on the 'doomed wilderness'. Faulkner, *Go Down, Moses* (Harmondsworth, 1960), pp. 175, 147.

48 See Randy Roberts, *Jack Dempsey, The Manassa Mauler* (Baton Rouge, LA, 1979), pp. 258–63.

49 Sherwood Anderson, 'Prize Fighters and Authors', in *No Swank* (Philadelphia, 1934), p. 20.

50 Lewis, *Only Yesterday*, p. 174; Clark, *The World of Damon Runyon*, p. 189. 'G. B. Shaw's Letters to Gene Tunney', are in *Collier's Magazine*, 23 June 1951. See also Jay Tunney, 'The Playwright and the Prizefighter: Bernard Shaw and Gene Tunney', *SHAW: The Annual of Bernard Shaw Studies*, 23 (2003), pp. 149–54; Benny Green, *Shaw's Champions* (London, 1978).

51 Michael Holroyd, *Bernard Shaw* (Harmondsworth, 1993), vol. III, p. 208. See Gene Tunney, 'What People Want To Know About Me', *The American Legion Monthly Magazine*, March 1927, and 'The Ring and the Book: A Champion Surveys the Literary Champions who have written of the Glories of the Fight', *The Golden Book Magazine*, April 1934. See also David Margolick, 'The Reader in the Ring', *New York Review of Books*, 31 May 2007, pp. 46–8.

52 Harrison S. Martland, 'Punch Drunk', *Journal of the American Medical Association*, 91, 13 October 1928, pp. 1103–7. The OED cites the first use of 'punch drunk' in 1918.

53 Anderson, 'Prize Fighters and Authors', pp. 17–20.

54 James T. Farrell, 'A Remembrance of Ernest Hemingway', in *Literary Essays, 1954–1974*, ed. Jack Alan Robbins (Port Washington, NY, 1976), pp. 88–9. Robert Frost asked Tunney how Hemingway bloodied his nose. Nelson Algren, *Notes from a Sea Diary: Hemingway All the Way* (New York, 1966), p. 128.

55 Ernest Hemingway, 'Banal Story' *Men without Women*, pp. 126–8. Hemingway is referring to Laird S. Goldsborough, 'Big Men – Or Cultured', *Forum*, 73 (February 1925), 209–14. The story was first written for the *Little Review*'s 'Banal Issue'. Hemingway wrote to the editor Jane Heap, 'Now don't go and switch numbers on me and put it in A Great White Hopes number.' Reynolds, *Hemingway: The Paris Years*, pp. 265–6. See also Wayne Kvam, 'Hemingway's "Banal Story"', in *New Critical Approaches to the Short Stories of Ernest Hemingway*, ed. Jackson J. Benson (Durham, NC, 1990), pp. 215–23.

56 Mina Loy, 'Perlun', *The Last Lunar Baedeker*, ed. Roger L. Conover (Manchester, 1997), pp. 75, 96; Roger Kahn, *A Flame of Pure Fire: Jack Dempsey and the Roaring '20s* (New York, 1999), p. 249.

57 Gösta Adrian-Nilsson's 1926 collage *Bloody Boxing Debut* (1926), figure 7.18, in Christopher Wilk, 'The Healthy Body Culture', in *Modernism: Designing a New World, 1914–1939*, ed. Wilk, exh. cat., Victoria and Albert Museum, London (London, 2006), pp. 263, 285n.

58 Djuna Barnes, 'My Sisters and I at a New York Prizefight' (1914), in *New York*, ed. Alyce Barry (Los Angeles, 1989), pp. 168–73.

59 Djuna Barnes, 'Jess Willard Says Girls Will Be Boxing for a Living Soon', in *I Could Never Be Lonely Without a Husband* (London, 1987), p. 137.

60 Djuna Barnes, 'Dempsey Welcomes Female Fans', in *I Could Never Be Lonely*, p. 285.

61 Katharine Fullerton Gerould, *Ringside Seats* (New York, 1937), pp. 208–26.

62 Quoted in Brian Gallagher, *Anything Goes* (New York, 1987), p. 98.

63 Mae West, *The Constant Sinner* (London, 1995), p. 59.

64 Colette, *Chéri*, trans. Roger Senhouse (London, 2001), p. 14, 18.

65 Ibid., p. 25. When Léa meets Chéri again after the war, he appears 'scraggy' to her; no longer like a pugilist, but 'like a fighting cock'. Colette, *The Last of Chéri* (1926), trans. Roger Senhouse (London, 2001), pp. 51–2.

66 Anne Chisholm, *Nancy Cunard* (Harmondsworth, 1979), p. 219.

67 Rosamund Lehmann, *The Weather in the Streets* (London, 1981), pp. 146–7. In the second volume of Ford Madox Ford's war tetralogy, *Parade's End* (1924–28), Captain Christopher Tietjens refuses a soldier home-leave on the grounds that he will be killed by his wife's lover, a prize-fighter. Ironically, a bomb gets him instead. *Parade's End* (Harmondsworth, 1982), pp. 309–10.

68 Jane Bowles, 'Going to Massachusetts', in *My Sister's Hand in Mine: The Collected Works* (New York, 1978), p. 460.

69 Zelda Fitzgerald, *Save Me the Waltz*, in *The Collected Writings*, ed. Matthew J. Bruccoli (London, 1993), pp. 98, 100. A lack of ability to fight is linked to lack of virility elsewhere in the novel. See also Matthew J. Bruccoli, *Some Sort of Epic Grandeur: The Life of F. Scott Fitzgerald* (Columbia, SC, 1981), p. 199.

70 William Carlos Williams, *The Autobiography* (New York, 1967), pp. 224, 226.

71 Schmeling, *An Autobiography*, pp. 49–50; Erik Jensen, 'Crowd Control: Boxing Spectatorship and Social Order in Weimar Germany', in *Histories of Leisure*, ed. Rudy Koshar (Oxford, 2002), pp. 93–4.

72 See Frederick V. Romano, *The Boxing Filmography, 1920–2003* (Jefferson, NC., 2004), pp. 152–4; Frank Ardolino, 'Shadow Boxing: Max Baer on Canvas and On Screen', *Aethlon*, 9, no. 1 (Fall 1991), pp. 67–71. The film was banned in Germany because 'the relationship of the Jewish man – who . . . is a quite Negroid type . . . – with the non-Jewish women in the film is . . . a violation of the National Socialist sentiment as interpreted by the new film law of February 16'. David Hull, *Film in the Third Reich* (Berkeley, CA, 1969), p. 47.

73 Jensen, 'Crowd Control', p. 93.

74 Tom Dardis, *Keaton: The Man Who Wouldn't Lie Down* (New York, 1979), pp. 133, 190.

75 Quoted in Marion Meade, *Buster Keaton: Cut to the Chase* (New York, 1995), p. 160.

76 Dardis, *Keaton*, p. 133.

77 Walter Kerr, *The Silent Clowns* (New York, 1980), p. 243.

78 H. L. Mencken, 'Appendix to Moronia, part 3: Valentino', in *Prejudices: Sixth Series* (London, 1927), p. 311.

79 Quoted in Gaylen Studlar, *This Mad Masquerade. Stardom and Masculinity in the Jazz Age* (New York, 1996), p. 185. If Valentino was not sufficiently a boxer, Garbo was too much of one. Kenneth Tynan complained that she walked 'like a middleweight boxer approaching an opponent'. 'Garbo', *Sight and Sound*, 23, no. 4 (April–June 1954), p. 189. See also Miriam Hansen, *Babel and Babylon: Spectatorship in American Silent Film* (Cambridge, MA, 1991).

80 Emily W. Leider, *Dark Lover: The Life and Death of Rudolph Valentino* (London, 2003), p. 374.

81 John Dos Passos, 'Adagio Dancer', *The Big Money*, in *USA*, pp. 861, 863–4.

82 Dorothy Parker, 'The Sheik' (1922), in *The Uncollected Dorothy Parker*, ed. Stuart Y. Silverstein (London, 2001), p. 115.

83 Quoted in Chase, *Men and Machines*, p. 258.

84 Quoted in *Envisioning America: Prints, Drawings and Photographs by George Grosz and his Contemporaries, 1915–1933*, exh. cat., Busch-Reisinger Museum, Harvard University (Cambridge, MA, 1990), p. 10.

85 George Grosz, *An Autobiography*, trans. Nora Hodges (Berkeley, CA, 1997), p. 228.

86 Wanda Corn, *The Great American Thing: Modern Art and National Identity, 1915–1935* (Berkeley, CA, 1999), p. 57.

87 Guillaume Apollinaire, 'Montparnasse', *Le Guetteur mélancolique suivi de Poèmes Retrouvés* (Paris, 1970), pp. 180–81.

88 William Carlos Williams, *Spring and All*, in *Imaginations* (New York, 1970), pp. 97, 103.

89 See Mary Nolan, *Visions of Modernity: American Business and the Modernization of Germany* (Oxford, 1994).

90 Although by the 1920s, boxing was thought of as an American sport, it was initially popularized by young Germans who had learned to box in British prisoner-of-war camps during the war. Jensen, 'Crowd Control', p. 81.

91 Hannes Meyer, 'Die Neue Welt' (1926), in *The Weimar Republic Sourcebook*, ed. Anton Kaes, Martin Jay and Edward Dimendberg (Berkeley, CA, 1994), p. 447. See also 'The Healthy Body Culture', pp. 249–96.

92 Herbert Jhering, 'Boxing', in *The Weimar Republic Sourcebook*, p. 686.

93 John M. Hoberman, *Sport and Political Ideology* (London, 1984), p. 19.

94 Quoted in David Bathrick, 'Max Schmeling on the Canvas: Boxing as an Icon of Weimar Culture', *New German Critique*, 51 (Autumn 1990), p. 119. See *Der Querschnitt: Facsimile Querschnitt durch den Querschnitt 1921–1936*, ed. Wilmont Haacke (Frankfurt, 1977), p. 146.

95 Quoted in Jensen, 'Crowd Control', pp. 89–90.

96 Willi Wolfradt's discussion of impersonality in Baumeister's 1929 series, *Sport und Maschine*, is quoted in John Willett, *The New Sobriety, 1917–1933: Art and Politics in the Weimar Period* (London, 1978), pp. 105–6.

97 Belling's sculpture is reproduced in Bärbel Schrader and Jürgen Schebera, *The 'Golden' Twenties: Art and Literature in the Weimar Republic* (New Haven, CT, 1980), pp. 144, 174.

98 Schmeling, *An Autobiography*, pp. 28–30; Grosz, *An Autobiography*, p. 195. The painting is reproduced in Willett, *The New Sobriety*, p. 103.

99 Schmeling won the title because Sharkey was disqualified. The following year he defended it against Stribling, and in 1932 lost, by a dubious decision, to Sharkey. 'We wuz robbed,' Joe Jacobs famously yelled. *An Autobiography*, pp. 4, 65–6, 75–6, 81–3, 91, 102–5.

100 Schmeling, *An Autobiography*, pp. 32–3; Peter Kühnst, *Sport: A Cultural History in the Mirror of Art*, trans. Allen Guttmann (Dresden, 1996), p. 331. Hemingway later said of Dietrich, 'The Kraut's the best that ever came into the ring'. Lillian Ross, *Reporting* (London, 1966), p. 204.

101 Bertolt Brecht, *Diaries 1920–1922*, trans. and ed. John Willett (London, 1979), p. 74; Bertolt Brecht, *Poems, 1913–1956*, ed. John Willettt and Ralph Manheim (New York, 1987), pp. 57–8.

102 Grosz, *An Autobiography*, p. 188.

103 Bertolt Brecht, 1954 note on *In the Jungle of Cities*, trans. Gerhard Nellhaus, ed. John Willett and Ralph Manheim (London, 1970), pp. 71–2.

104 Quoted in Battrick, 'Max Schmeling on the Canvas', p. 122. Brecht wanted to write a novel or play about Dempsey vs. Carpentier. *Das Renomee: Ein Boxerroman*, *Werke* (Frankfurt/Main, 1989), vol. XVII, pp. 421–39.

105 Brecht, *Poems 1913 to 1956*, ed. Willett and Manheim, pp. 1534.

106 Bertolt Brecht, *Man Equals Man* in *Collected Plays: Two*, ed. John Willett and Ralph Manheim (London, 1994), pp. 75, 90; Franco Ruffini, 'A Little More Healthy Sport! Bertolt Brecht and Objective Boxing', *Mime Journal* (1996), p. 5.

107 Brecht, Note on *In the Jungle of Cities*, p. 65. See also p. 53.

108 Bertolt Brecht, *The Rise and Fall of the City of Mahagonny* (1927), trans. W. H. Auden and Chester Kallman, in *Collected Plays: Two*, p. 211.

109 The protagonist of 'Hook to the Chin' is roughly based on Samson-Körner. Bertolt Brecht, *Collected Short Stories*, ed. John Willett and Ralph Manheim (London, 1992), pp. 68–71. For an unfinished fragment of 'Life Story of the Boxer Samson-Körner', see Brecht, *Collected Stories*, pp. 207–24.

110 Schmeling, *An Autobiography*, pp. 19, 22.

111 Quoted in *Brecht on Theatre: The Development of an Aesthetic*, ed. John Willett (London, 1974), p. 551. Samson-Körner's 1925 essay 'Jugend und Sport' is discussed in Theodore F. Rippey, 'Athletics, Aesthetics, and Politics in the Weimar Press', *German Studies Review*, 28, no. 1 (2005), pp. 91–2.

112 Maximillian Sladek, 'Our Show' (1924), in *The Weimar Republic Sourcebook*, p. 556. See also Peter Jelavich, *Berlin Cabaret* (Cambridge, MA, 1993), pp. 165–75.

113 Quoted in *Envisioning America*, p. 14.

114 'Girls' Prizefights Entertain Dempsey', *New York Times*, 2 May 1922, p. 27.

115 Quoted in Kahn, *A Flame of Pure Fire*, p. 295. In 1924, a quintet of 'athletic fräuleins from the land of the pretzel and schnapps' embarked on a tour of American vaudeville houses. *The Boxing Blade* (12 April 1924). In England, there was outrage when a boxer called Annie Newton challenged Dempsey. The niece of A. J. Newton, author of a 1904 boxing manual, Annie later featured in a documentary on *Women London Boxers* (Gaumont, 1931).

116 'Berlin Wickedness Shocks Dempsey', *New York Times*, 4 May 1922, p. 27.

117 Antonio Gramsci, 'Americanism and Fordism', in *Selections from the Prison Diaries*, ed. and trans. Quintin Hoare and Geoffrey Nowell Smith (London, 1971), p. 318.

118 Wyndham Lewis, *Tarr* (Harmondsworth, 1982), p. 85.

119 George Du Maurier, *Trilby* (Oxford, 1995), pp. 3–4, 89, 91–2, 144, 229–30. Although set in the 1850s, the novel includes much 1890s detail.

120 Claude Meunier, *Ring Noir* (Paris, 1992), pp. 111–13. See also Daniel Karlin, *Proust's English* (Oxford, 2005), p. 14.

121 Marcel Proust, *A l'ombre des jeunes filles en fleurs*, in *A la recherche du temps perdu*, Pléiade edition (Paris, 1987), vol. II, p. 200, trans. C. K. Scott Moncrieff and Terence Kilmartin, revised by D. J. Enright (London, 2002), vol. II, p. 490; *Sodome et Gomorrhe*, Pléiade, vol. III, p. 23, English translation, vol. IV, p. 25; *La Prisonnière*, Pléiade, vol. III, p. 710, English translation, vol. V, p. 229. In *Le Temps retrouvé*, the Baron imagines the war as a gigantic boxing match: Pléiade, vol. IV, p. 373, English translation, vol. VI, p. 129. I am grateful to Danny Karlin for drawing my attention to these passages.

122 Arthur Cravan, 'To Be or Not To Be . . . American', in *Oeuvres*, ed. Jean-Pierre Begot (Paris, 1992), pp. 121–4. Terry Hale's translation is in *Four Dada Suicides*, ed. Roger Conover, Terry Hale and Paul Lenti (London, 1995), p. 34. See also André Dunoyer de Segonzac on the arrival of American boxing, in Meunier, *Ring Noir*, pp. 35–6. Dunoyer de Segonzac later illustrated Tristan Bernard's *Tableau de la boxe* (1922) and Jean Giraudoux's *Le Sport* (1924).

123 Carpentier, *My Methods, or Boxing as a Fine Art*, p. 22; *Carpentier by Himself*, p. 60.

124 Carpentier, *My Methods*, p. 23.

125 Orio Vergani, *Poor Nigger*, trans. W. W. Hobson (London, 1930), p. 193.

126 Colette, *Contes des Mille et Un Matins* (Paris, 1970), some are quoted in Meunier, *Ring Noir*, pp. 46–49. Cocteau, quoted in Alexis Philonenko, *Histoires de la Boxe* (Paris, 1991), p. 400 (my translation). On Hemingway's coaching of Masson and Miró, see Carolyn Lanchner, *André Masson* (New York, 1976), p. 86. Man Ray attended a 1929 fight with Hemingway; his photographs are reproduced in Jean-Michel Bouhours, 'Les Mystères du Château du dé', in *Man Ray: directeur du mauvais movies*, ed. Jean-Michel Bouhours and Patrick de Haas (Paris, 1997), p. 97. On Hemingway's encounter with Jean Prévost, see Noel Riley Fitch, *Sylvia Beach and the Lost Generation: A History of Literary Paris in the Twenties and Thirties* (Harmondsworth, 1983), pp. 189–90. On Bonnard's 1931 self-portrait *The Boxer*, see Graham Nickerson, in *Pierre Bonnard, Stealing the Image: Works on Paper*, exh. cat., New York Studio (New York, 1997). See also Yvette Sánchez, 'Un round de littérature française et la boxe', *Versant*, 40 (2001), pp. 159–71.

127 Vladimir Nabokov, *The Annotated Lolita* (Harmondsworth, 1995), p. 26.

128 Quoted in Tyler Stovall, *Paris Noir: African Americans in the City of Light* (Boston, 1996), p. 68. See also Petrine Archer-Straw, *Negrophilia* (London, 2000).

129 Ivan Coll, 'The Negroes are Conquering Europe', in *The Weimar Republic Sourcebook*, p. 559; Paul Colin, quoted in Karen C. C. Dalton and Henry Louis Gates, Jr., 'Josephine Baker and Paul Colin: African American Dance Seen Through Parisian Eyes', *Critical Inquiry*, 24 (Summer 1998), p. 921; 'Ring du Coliseum' is included in *Josephine Baker*, footage from the Cinématheque de la Danse archives (Paris, 1998); many thanks to Sarah Wood for showing me this.

130 Quoted in Katia Samaltanos, *Apollinaire: Catalyst for Primitivism, Picabia and Duchamp* (Ann Arbor, MI, 1984), p. 53.

131 Stovall, *Paris Noir*, pp. 67–8. See Michel Fabre, 'The Ring and the Stage: African Americans in Parisian Public and Imaginary Space before World War I', in *Space in America: Theory History Culture*, ed. Klaus Benesch and Kerstin Schmidt (Amsterdam, 2005), pp. 521–8. For a fictional life of Sam McVea, see Guillaume Apollinaire, 'Distiques pour plaire à Dupuy', in *Poésies libres* (Paris, 1978), p. 51.

132 Bennetta Jules-Rosette, *Black Paris: The African Writers' Landscape* (Urbana, IL, 1998), p. 11.

133 Quoted in Jules-Rosette, *Black Paris*, p. 29. See also Eduardo Arroyo, *Panama Al Brown* (Paris, 1998), pp. 106–8.

134 Stovall, *Paris Noir*, pp. 3–4, 75. See also Craig Lloyd, *Eugene Bullard: Black Expatriate in Jazz-Age Paris* (Athens, GA, 2000).

135 Gwendolyn Bennett, 'Wedding Day', in *The Sleeper Wakes: Harlem Renaissance Stories by Women*, ed. Marcy Knopf (New Brunswick, NJ, 1993), p. 54. See also Alice Morning's 'Something Alive in Paris', *The New Age* (11 March 1920), pp. 302–3. Morning describes 'modern life' at the 'Nothing-Happens Bar'. The cast of characters includes 'a negro boxer', 'a short woman, sports variety' and 'an American sausage-king', and the story, a scene in which 'the negro boxer mistakes

his place in the sun and pays court to the sportswomen, for which Uncle Sam taps him on the head from behind and knocks him out.' Morning describes this as a 'scene of gilded savagery'.

136 Claude McKay, *The Negroes in America* (Port Washington, NY, 1979), p. 50. Individuals too did not always fare so well. In 1913, Jack Johnson was refused rooms at the city's best hotels. Roberts, *Papa Jack*, p. 186.

137 John Lardner, *White Hopes and other Tigers* (New York, 1951), pp. 118–36.

138 The first African–American to contest a title after Johnson was Tiger Flowers who won the world middleweight title in 1926. See Andrew M. Kaye, *The Pussycat of Prizefighting: Tiger Flowers and The Politics of Black Celebrity* (Athens, GA, 2004).

139 Hemingway wired this description of Siki to the *Toronto Star* two days before the fight. Michael Reynolds, *Hemingway: The Paris Years* (New York, 1989), p. 73.

140 Lincoln Steffens, 'The Carpentier-Siki Fight', in *The World of Lincoln Steffens*, ed. Ella Winter and Herbert Shapiro (New York, 1962), p. 249.

141 Bob Scanlon, 'The Record of a Negro Boxer', in *Negro*, ed. Nancy Cunard (New York, 2002), p. 210.

142 Orio Vergani's Siki-like hero, George Boykin, fights a French opponent and finds 'the primeval savagery of his race' has been 'unloosed'. Vergani, *Poor Nigger*, p. 160. Despite this language, the novel portrays Boykin as a victim of prejudice. In 2004, it was adapted by Extramondo-Theatri 90 for the Milan stage as *Knock Out* (dir. Michela Blasi). P. C. Wren, author of *Beau Geste*, also wrote a novel about Siki, *Soldiers of Misfortune*. M'Bongu is 'so much lower in the scale of creation' than his white opponent that he is impossible to beat. (New York, 1929), p. 20.

143 'Battling Siki as a Dark Cloud on the Horizon', *Literary Digest*, October 1922, pp. 62–5; 'Battling Siki Shot Dead in the Street', *New York Times*, 16 December 1925, p. 3; Gerald Early, 'Battling Siki', *The Culture of Bruising* (Hopewell, NJ, 1994), p. 68. See also Gerald Early, 'Three Notes Toward a Cultural Definition of The Harlem Renaissance', *Callaloo*, 14, no. 1 (1991), p. 142.

144 Steffens, 'The Carpentier-Siki Fight', p. 250.

145 Blaise Diagne, *Le Populaire*, 1 December 1922. A slightly different translation is quoted in Benson, *Battling Siki*, p. 258. When Diagne became Under Secretary of State for the Colonies in 1931, an American magazine reminded its readers that he was the deputy who had risen 'magnificently in the Chamber in 1922 in defense of his compatriot Battling Siki, kinky-haired light heavyweight'. 'Butcher's Son's Cabinet', *Time*, 9 February 1931.

146 David Trotter, *The Making of the Reader* (London, 1984), p. 73.

147 Carlos Baker, *Ernest Hemingway: A Life Story* (London, 1969), pp. 132, 162. See also *Selected Letters, 1917–1961*, ed. Carlos Baker (London, 1985), p. 139. When Hemingway wrote his memoir of that period, *A Moveable Feast*, in the late 1950s, his reputation as a boxer-writer was firmly established. It therefore seems deliberately provocative to preface the book with the announcement that it will contain 'no mention of

the Stade Anastasie where the boxers served as waiters at the tables set out under the trees and the ring was in the garden. Nor of training with Larry Gains, nor the great twenty-round fights at the Cirque d'Hiver.' Ernest Hemingway, *A Moveable Feast* (London, 1984).

148 Morley Callahan, *That Summer in Paris* (New York, 1963), p. 122. See David L. Inglis, 'Morley Callaghan and the Hemingway Boxing Legend', *Notes on Contemporary Literature*, 4, no. 4 (1974), pp. 4–7; Scott Donaldson, *Hemingway vs. Fitzgerald* (London, 1999), pp. 138–44.

149 Hemingway, *Selected Letters*, p. 673.

150 On Hemingway's encounter with Wallace Stevens, see Kenneth Lynn, *Hemingway* (London, 1987), p. 437. Hemingway's contest with William Carlos Williams took place on the tennis court. Williams, *The Autobiography* (New York, 1967), p. 218.

151 Hemingway, *Selected Letters*, p. 116.

152 Ibid., pp. 205, 210.

153 Sherwood Anderson, *Selected Letters*, ed. Charles Modlin (Knoxville, TN, 1984), p. 80.

154 Judy Jo Small and Michael Reynolds, 'Hemingway v. Anderson: The Final Rounds', *The Hemingway Review*, 14, no. 2 (Spring 1995), p. 4. In an earlier draft the fighter had been called Nerone; Hemingway changed the name to Anderson and then, finally, to Andreson. Anderson responded with a story about two 'substantial-looking' men whose fight settles nothing. Sherwood Anderson, 'The Fight', in *Death in the Woods and Other Stories* (New York, 1961), pp. 95–108.

155 Hemingway, *Selected Letters*, p. 649.

156 Wyndham Lewis, *Blasting and Bombardiering* (London, 1967), p. 277. On teaching Pound to box, see Hemingway, *Selected Letters*, pp. 62, 65. See also Fitch, *Sylvia Beach and the Lost Generation*, p. 123.

157 Wyndham Lewis, 'The "Dumb Ox" in Love and War', in *Twentieth-Century Interpretations of 'A Farewell to Arms'*, ed. Jay Gellens (Englewood Cliffs, NJ, 1970), pp. 72–90.

158 Hemingway, *A Moveable Feast*, pp. 75–6.

159 On this passage, see David Trotter, *Paranoid Modernism* (Oxford, 2001), p. 287.

160 Ezra Pound, 'Patria Mia', in *Selected Prose 1909–1965*, ed. William Cookson (New York, 1973), pp. 109–10. A few pages earlier Pound relates a story about 'Bill Donohue, a pugilist' who is forced to lift pianos to amuse the 'civilised peoples of the world' (p. 105). Again American virility has been made to perform with the tools of effete European culture, to little appreciation.

161 Wyndham Lewis, 'A Soldier of Humour', in *The Wild Body* (London, 1927), pp. 27–8. See Trotter, *The Making of the Reader*, pp. 76–7.

162 See Trotter, *Paranoid Modernism*, pp. 305–11.

163 For an argument that being an American is a profession in itself, see Cravan, *Oeuvres*, pp. 121–4.

164 Ezra Pound, 'A Retrospect', in *Literary Essays of Ezra Pound*, ed. T. S. Eliot (London, 1954), p. 10.

165 Ezra Pound, *Selected Letters, 1907–1941*, ed. D. D. Paige (London, 1950), p. 13.

166 Ezra Pound, 'On Technique', in *Selected Prose*, pp. 32–3.

167 Ezra Pound, *The Pisan Cantos*, ed. Richard Sieburth (New York, 2003), p. 47. Siki is mentioned in Canto 74 (l.704) in the context of a passage about undergraduates and the First World War. The students with their bayonets are 'inferior gorillas'; Siki, it seems, is the real thing. *The Pisan Cantos*, p. 23. On Dempsey and Tunney, see Ezra Pound, *ABC of Reading* (London, 1951), pp. 86–7.

168 Pound, *Selected Letters*, p. 348.

169 Conrad Aiken, 'King Bolo and Others', in *T. S. Eliot: A Symposium*, ed. M. J. T. Tambimuttu and Richard March (London, 1948), pp. 20–23. See also Conrad Aiken, *Ushant* (London, 1963), pp. 133–7. Attending Harvard in 1910, Quentin Compson is 'boxed . . . all over the place' by a fellow student who has learnt to fight by 'going to Mike's every day, over in town'. William Faulkner, *The Sound and the Fury* (Harmondsworth, 1964), pp. 149–50.

170 O'Donnell advertised in the MIT newspaper *The Tech*: 'Boxing and Physical Culture taught by STEVE O'DONNELL Boxing Instructor at Harvard University First class gymnasium all the latest Spaulding machines, hot and cold shower baths. Guaranteed no black eyes or marks. 8 E. Concord St., cor Wash.' Available at http://www-tech.mit.edu/ archives/ VOL_026/TECH_V026_S0129_P004.pdf.

171 T. S. Eliot, 'Portrait of a Lady', in *The Complete Poems and Plays* (London, 1969), p. 20.

172 The facsimile of *The Waste Land* includes a satirical reference to Fresca as 'Minerva in a crowd of boxing peers'. Valerie Eliot glosses this by naming the peers as the 8th Marquis of Queensberry and the 5th Earl of Lonsdale. *The Waste Land: A Facsimile and Transcript of the Original*, ed. Valerie Eliot (London, 1971), pp. 29, 127. Eliot retained an interest in boxing throughout his life. In 1963, he attacked television, but admitted that he nevertheless liked to watch boxing. David E. Chinitz, *T. S. Eliot and the Cultural Divide* (Chicago, 2003), p. 228. In 1963 Groucho Marx began a correspondence with Eliot and joked that he shared a first name with Tom Gibbons, 'a prizefighter who once lived in St. Paul'. *The Groucho Letters* (London, 1969), pp. 127–9.

173 Nevill Coghill, 'Sweeney Agonistes (An anecdote or two)', in *T. S. Eliot: A Symposium*, p. 86.

174 Dos Passos, *USA*, pp. 402, 404.

175 Fitzgerald, *The Great Gatsby*, p. 12. See Christian Messenger, 'Tom Buchanan and the Demise of the Ivy League Athletic Hero', *Journal of Popular Culture*, 8, no. 2 (Fall 1974), pp. 402–10. By 1931, Fitzgerald was complaining that 'except for a short period in school, we were not turning out to be an athletic people like the British, after all.' 'Echoes of the Jazz Age', in *The Crack-Up*, pp. 15–16.

176 Ernest Hemingway, *The Sun Also Rises* (London 1976), pp. 10, 9, 13, 33–4, 116, 140, 144, 178, 181, 14.

177 In *Save Me the Waltz*, David tells his wife, Alabama, who is trying to establish a career as a ballet dancer, 'I hope you realize that the biggest difference in the world is between the amateur and the professional in the arts.' Zelda Fitzgerald, *The Collected Writings*, p. 138. See also F. Scott Fitzgerald, 'Early Success', in *The Crack-Up*, pp. 58, 61.

178 F. Scott Fitzgerald, *Tender is the Night* (Harmondsworth,

1986), p. 196. This is perhaps a dig at Hemingway, for Fitzgerald adds that 'Dick was ashamed at baiting the man, realizing that the absurdity of the story rested in the immaturity of the attitude combined with the sophisticated method of its narration.'

179 Fitzgerald, *Tender Is the Night*, pp. 102, 198, 245, 261. For an account of Hemingway's mid-Atlantic boxing, see Baker, *Ernest Hemingway: A Life Story*, pp. 112–13.

180 Discussions of 'diving' in the period include James T. Farrell's story, 'Twenty-Five Bucks', in which a manager warns his fighter, 'that ring ain't no swimming pool'. *The Short Stories* (New York, 1962), p. 185. Damon Runyon coined numerous phrases to describe the phenomenon, including 'a header into the wash bowl' and 'watermen'. Quoted in Daniel L. Schwarz, *Broadway Boogie Woogie: Damon Runyon and the Making of New York City Culture* (London, 2003), p. 22. See also Runyon's column, 'The Lost Art of Diving', quoted in Clark, *The World of Damon Runyon*, p. 237.

181 Quoted in Joshua Taylor, *Futurism* (New York, 1961), pp. 124–7.

182 See Filippo Marinetti, 'Some Episodes from the film *Futurist Life*', in *Selected Writings*, trans. R. W. Flint and Arthur A. Coppotelli (London, 1972), pp. 135–6; Mario Verdone and Günter Berghaus, '*Vita Futurista* and Early Futurist Cinema', in *International Futurism in Art and Literature*, ed. Günter Berghaus (Berlin, 2000), pp. 398–421.

183 The Hylaea group (later renamed Cubo-Futurists), 'Slap in the Face of Public Taste', in *Russian Futurism through its Manifestoes, 1912–1928*, ed. Anna Lawton (Ithaca, NY, 1988), pp. 51–2; D. H. Lawrence, *The Letters*, ed. Aldous Huxley (London, 1932), p. 196; Denis Mack Smith, *Mussolini: A Biography* (New York, 1982), p. 114.

184 T. E. Hulme, 'Modern Art, I: The Grafton Group' (1914), in *The Collected Writings*, ed. Karen Csengeri (Oxford, 1994), pp. 263–7; 'Mr. Epstein and the Critics', in *Collected Writings*, p. 260. See also Patrick Bridgwater, *Nietzsche in Anglosaxony* (Leicester, 1972), pp. 135–8.

185 Wyndham Lewis, *The Letters*, ed. W. K. Rose (London, 1963), pp. 54–6. See also Michael Levenson, *A Genealogy of Modernism* (Cambridge, 1984), pp. 121–3; Trotter, *Paranoid Modernism*, pp. 231–3.

186 Friedrich Nietzsche, *The Will to Power* (1888), trans. Walter Kaufman and R. J. Hollingdale (New York, 1968), pp. 428–9.

187 *Russian Futurism through its Manifestoes*, p. 149.

188 Antonello Negri, *Aligi Sassu*, trans. Susan Scott (Lugano, 1998), pp. 12–13.

189 Quoted in Marianne Doezema, *George Bellows and Urban America* (New Haven, 1992) p. 215.

190 Robert Musil, *The Man without Qualities*, trans. Sophie Wilkins (London, 1995), vol. I, pp. 7–8, 21–2, 24–5.

191 Musil's first novel, *The Confusions of Young Törless* (1906), is a school story in which the pupils are required to 'be constantly ready to engage in quarrels and fist-fights'. Unlike Tom Brown and the rest, Törless does not fight for the weaker boy's honour but lets him become a scapegoat. The old rules do not apply. Robert Musil, *The Confusions of Young Törless*, trans. Shaun Whiteside (Harmondsworth, 2001),

pp. 11, 42, 119, 143.

192 Wyndham Lewis, 'The New Egos', *Blast*, no. 1 (Santa Barbara, CA, 1981), p. 141. Although the magazine 'blasts' sport, it 'blesses' six prize-fighters (Young Ahearn, Colin Bell, Dick Burge, Petty Officer Curran, Bandsman Rice and Bombadier Wells). *Blast*, pp. 17, 28. See Richard Cork, *Vorticism and Abstract Art in the First Machine Age* (London, 1976), p. 250; William C. Wees, *Vorticism and the English Avant-Garde* (Manchester, 1972), pp. 22–7, 171.

193 Wyndham Lewis, 'Inferior Religions', in *The Wild Body*, pp. 235–6. A couple of comic types battle it out in Lewis's 1929 painting *Boxing at Juan-les-Pins*. See Paul Edwards, *Wyndham Lewis: Painter and Writer* (New Haven, 2000), pl. 216.

194 Although Bergson was one of the thinkers whom Lewis 'blasts' in his magazine, his rejection of the 'isolated figure' in favour of insect-like intersection derives from Bergson's philosophy of 'creative evolution' which was very much in vogue before the war. In the same, first, issue of *Blast*, Lewis presented his unperformable 'Vorticist drama', 'The Enemy of the Stars', in which two antagonists Hanp and Arghol (workers in a wheelwright's yard, and uneasy doubles) argue and then fight. See Wees, *Vorticism and the English Avant-Garde*, pp. 182–5; David Graver, 'Vorticist Performance and Aesthetic Turbulence in *Enemy of the Stars*', *PMLA*, 107, no. 3 (1992), pp. 482–96.

195 For a comparison of 'Combat No. 2' (in which three couples battle) with 'The New Egos' and Lewis's story 'Bestre', which describes 'phases of combat or courtship in the Insect-world', see David Ayers, *Wyndham Lewis and Western Man* (London, 1992), pp. 27–9.

196 Wyndham Lewis, *Time and Western Man* (London, 1927), p. 332.

197 Ibid., pp. 36–7.

198 Wyndham Lewis, *The Art of Being Ruled* (New York, 1926), pp. 115–16. In the first of his 1935 series of lectures, *Introduction to Metaphysics*, Heidegger cited two symptoms of the 'spiritual decline of the earth': 'when a boxer counts as a great man of a people; when the tallies of millions at mass meetings are a triumph'. In a later lecture, Heidegger hailed the 'inner truth and greatness' of the National Socialist movement as a possible solution. *Introduction to Metaphysics*, trans. Gregory Fried and Richard Polt (New Haven, 2000), pp. 40, 213. By 1935, Lewis too was a sympathetic supporter of Hitler. See Edwards, *Wyndham Lewis: Painter and Writer*, ch. 11.

199 Fitch, *Sylvia Beach and the Lost Generation*, pp. 191–2. See also Constant Lambert's ballet score *Prize Fight* (1924–7).

200 This was also true for Le Corbusier, who illustrated the proposition that 'lesson of the machine lies in the pure relation of cause and effect' with pictures of ships' guns, airplane propellers and a boxing match between a black and white fighter. Le Corbusier, *The Decorative Art of Today* (1925), trans. James I. Dunnett (London, 1987), pp. xxiv, 170. Consider also the comparison of Raymond Hood's Radiator Building (clad in black brick with gilded details and a golden crown) and 'Jack Johnson's golden smile'. Robert A. M.

Stern, Gregory Gilmartin and Thomas Mellins, *New York 1930* (New York, 1994), p. 576.

201 George Antheil, *Bad Boy of Music* (Hollywood, 1990), p. 139. See also Carol J. Oja, 'George Antheil's *Ballet Mécanique* and Transatlantic Modernism', in *A Modern Mosaic*, ed. Townsend Ludington (Chapel Hill, NC, 2000), pp. 175–202.

202 *391*, no. 19 (October 1924). See Roger Conover's note in Loy, *The Lost Lunar Baedeker*, p. 196. Duchamp bet, and lost, on Carpentier when he fought Dempsey. *Affectionately, Marcel: The Selected Correspondence of Marcel Duchamp*, ed. Francis M. Nuamann and Hector Obalk Ludion, trans. Jill Taylor (Ghent, 2000), pp. 99–100.

203 See *The Green Box* in *The Writings of Marcel Duchamp*. See also Craig E. Adcock, *Marcel Duchamp's Notes from the Large Glass* (Epping, 1983). The photomontage was first published as a leaflet in *TNT*, March 1919. The magazine is reprinted in *New York Dada*, ed. Rudolf E. Kuenzli (New York, 1986). 'Combat de Boxe' appears on p. 150. 'The Boxing Match' (1913) and the 1919 photomontage can also be found in Arturo Schwarz, *The Complete Works of Marcel Duchamp* (London, 1997), vol. II, pp. 583, 641.

204 Quoted in Jerrold Seigel, *The Private Worlds of Marcel Duchamp* (Berkeley, CA, 1995), p. 106.

205 Dawn Ades, Neil Cox and David Hopkins, *Duchamp* (London, 1999), p. 99.

206 Calvin Tompkins, *Duchamp: A Biography* (New York, 1996), p. 10.

207 Jean Suquet, 'Possible', in *The Definitely Unfinished Marcel Duchamp*, ed. Thierry De Duve (Cambridge, MA, 1992), p. 101.

208 Quoted in Calvin Tompkins, *The Bride and the Bachelors: The Heretical Courtship in Modern Art* (New York, 1965), p. 24, and in James Johnson Sweeney, 'Marcel Duchamp', in *Wisdom: Conversations with the Elder Wise Men of Our Day*, ed. James Nelson, (New York, 1958), p. 99.

209 André Breton, 'Lighthouse of the Bride' (1935), *View* (March 1945), pp. 6–9, 13.

210 Tyrus Miller compares the mechanical operation of desire in the *Large Glass* and Djuna Barnes's *Nightwood*. *Late Modernism* (Berkeley, CA, 1999), pp. 164–8.

211 Djuna Barnes, *Nightwood* (London, 2001), pp. 69, 71, 84, 133, 146. See also Tim Armstrong, *Modernism, Technology and the Body* (Cambridge, 1998), pp. 123–9.

212 Tristan Tzara, *Seven Dada Manifestos and Lampisteries*, trans. Barbara Wright (London, 1992), pp. 12–13.

213 Tzara, *Seven Dada Manifestos*, p. 28; Tzara, 'Memoirs of Dadaism', in Edmund Wilson, *Axel's Castle*, London, 1984), p. 243.

214 Tzara, *Seven Dada Manifestos*, p. 5; Tzara, 'Zurich Chronicles (1915–1919)', in *The Dada Painters and Poets*, ed. Robert Motherwell (Cambridge, MA, 1989), p. 236.

215 See Jill Lloyd, *German Expressionism: Primitivism and Modernity* (New Haven, 1991), ch. 6.

216 John D. Erickson, 'The Cultural Politics of Dada', in *Dada: The Coordinates of Cultural Politics*, ed. Stephen C. Foster (New York, 1996), p. 25.

217 Malcolm Cowley, *Exile's Return* (Harmondsworth, 1994),

pp. 169–70. The previous year Cowley published a poem, 'Valuta', in which he declared the 'four angels' of modern America to be Theodore Roosevelt, Charlie Chaplin, Jack Johnson and an anonymous fiddle player. Quoted in Michael North, *Reading 1922* (Oxford, 1999), p. 166.

218 David Gascoyne, *A Short Survey of Surrealism* (London, 2000), p. 44. Jacques Rigaut, quoted in Patrick Waldberg, *Surrealism* (London, 1965), p. 63.

219 Anna Balakian, *Surrealism: The Road to the Absolute* (Chicago, 1986), pp. 135, 137. Breton's *Poem-Objet*, 1941 is reproduced and discussed in Diane Waldman, *Collage, Assemblage, and the Found Object* (London, 1992), pp. 157–8.

220 Arthur Cravan, 'Oscar Wilde Lives!', in *Oeuvres*, pp. 49–63; translation in *Four Dada Suicides*, pp. 49–61. See also Maria Lluïsa Borràs, *Arthur Cravan: Une stratégie du scandale* (Paris, 1996); *Arthur Cravan: Poète et Boxeur*, exh. cat., Galerie 1900/2000, Paris (Paris, 1992).

221 Cravan, 'Poet and Boxer', in *Oeuvres*, pp. 87–92; translation in *Four Dada Suicides*, pp. 40–44.

222 Cravan, 'Exhibition of the Independents', in *Oeuvres*, pp. 67–79; translation in *The Dada Painters and Poets*, ed. Motherwell, pp. 3–13. See also Gabrielle Buffet-Picabia, 'Arthur Cravan and American Dada', in *The Dada Poets and Painters*, pp. 13–17; Steven Watson, *Strange Bedfellows: The First American Avant-Garde* (New York, 1991), p. 376.

223 Roger Shattuck, *The Banquet Years: The Arts in France, 1885–1918* (New York, 1955), p. 272.

224 Quoted in Virginia M. Kouidis, *Mina Loy: American Modernist Poet* (Baton Rouge, LA, 1980), p. 10.

225 Nina Hamnett, *Laughing Torso: Reminiscences of Nina Hamnett* (London, 1932), pp. 51–2. Van Dongen painted a full-size portrait of Johnson, naked and holding a jewel-studded cane and a top hat, against a backdrop of palms and exotic flowers. See Fabre, 'The Ring and the Stage', p. 527.

226 Cravan, 'André Gide', in *Oeuvres*, pp. 33–7; translation in *Four Dada Suicides*, p. 40; 'Notes', in *vvv*, issues 1 and 2/3 (June 1942 and March 1943), in *Oeuvres*, pp. 105–17, translated by Terry Hale in *Four Dada Suicides*, p. 79; Geoffrey C. Ward, *Unforgivable Blackness: The Rise and Fall of Jack Johnson* (New York, 2004), p. 388. On Johnson in Paris, see *Ring Noir*, chapter one. Cravan said of Johnson, 'After Poe, Whitman, Emerson, he is the most glorious American.' 'Arthur Cravan vs. Jack Johnson', *The Soil*, 1, no. 4 (April 1917), quoted in Francis M. Naumann, *New York Dada, 1915–23* (New York, 1994), pp. 165–6.

227 Quoted in George Plimpton, *Shadow Box* (London, 1989), pp. 57–9.

228 Leon Trotsky, *My Life: An Attempt at an Autobiography* (New York, 1930), p. 268.

229 See Roger Conover, 'Mina Loy's Colossus: Arthur Cravan Undressed', in *New York Dada*, ed. Kuentzli, pp. 102–19. Fictional accounts of the story include Antonia Logue, *Shadow Box* (London, 1999); Mike Richardson and Rick Geary, *Cravan: Mystery Man of the Twentieth Century* (Milwaukie, OR, 2005).

230 James Riordan, *Sport in Soviet Society* (Cambridge, 1980), pp. 9, 19, 79.

231 Riordan, *Sport in Soviet Society*, p. 98. See also *Sport and Political Ideology*, ch. 7. American popular culture remained popular in Soviet Russia. See, for example, Lev Kelshov, 'Americanism' (1922), in *The Film Factory: Russian and Soviet Cinema in Documents, 1896–1939*, ed. Richard Taylor and Ian Christie (London, 1988), pp. 72–3.

232 Vladimir Mayakovsky, 'Comrades, discuss Red Sport!' (1928), unpublished translation by Tanya Frisby. Some 40 years later, the Soviet poet Yevgeny Yevtushenko echoed Mayakovsky's words. The sports star should display more than mere 'athletic narcissism'; he should be an 'educator'. 'A Poet Against the Destroyers', *Sports Illustrated*, 12 December 1966, p. 106.

233 Quoted in Riordan, *Sport in Soviet Society*, p. 104. On Lunacharsky, see Huntly Carter, *The New Spirit in the Russian Theatre, 1917–1928* (London, 1929), pp. 37–46.

234 Vil Bykov, 'Jack London in the Soviet Union', *Book Club of California Quarterly Newsletter*, 24, no. 2 (1959), pp. 52–8.

235 Mike O'Mahony, *Sport in the USSR: Physical Culture-Visual Culture* (London, 2006), p. 84.

236 Irina Makoveeva, 'Soviet Sports as a Cultural Phenomenon: Body and/or Intellect', *Studies in Slavic Culture*, 3 (2002), p. 11.

237 Martin Amis, *Visiting Mrs Nabokov and Other Excursions* (Harmondsworth, 1994), p. 118.

238 Vladimir Nabokov, 'Breitensträter-Paolino', in *Sobranie sochinenii russkogo perioda v piati tomakh*, ed. A. Dolinin et al. (St Petersburg, 1999), vol. I, pp. 749–54. I am quoting from an unpublished translation by Thomas Karshan. 'The Fight' was written a few months earlier. The narrator of the story is 'enthralled' by 'the play of shadow and light' on the bodies of two fighting men. Vladimir Nabokov, *The Stories* (New York, 1997), pp. 141–54. *Glory* (1932), Nabokov's Cambridge novel, includes a virtuoso fight over a girl between the protagonist and a boxing Blue called Darwin. *Glory*, trans. Dmitri Nabokov (Harmondsworth, 1974), pp. 115–19. Nabokov's poem 'The Boxer's Girl' (1924) is written from the point of view of the girl happy to see her violent lover knocked out. *Sobranie sochinenii russkogo perioda v piati tomakh*, vol. I, pp. 622–3. See also Brian Boyd, *Vladimir Nabokov: The Russian Years* (Princeton, 1990), pp. 242–3, 257.

239 Frederick Winslow Taylor, *The Principles of Scientific Management* (London, 1993), p. 13.

240 Taylor, *The Principles*, pp. 39, 63, 68, 85.

241 Marie Seton, *Sergei M. Eisenstein* (London, 1952), p. 47. See also Janne Risum, 'The Sporting Acrobat: Meyerhold's Biomechanics', *Mime Journal* (1996), pp. 67–111.

242 Sergei Eisenstein, *Film Form* (New York, 1949), pp. 7–8. See also Seton, *Sergei M. Eisenstein*, pp. 42–3, and Robert Leach, 'Eisenstein's Theatre Work', in *Eisenstein Rediscovered*, ed. Ian Christie and Richard Taylor (London, 1993), pp. 110–20.

243 Dziga Vertov, 'The Cine-Eyes. A Revolution' (1923), in *The Film Factory*, ed. Taylor and Christie, p. 92.

244 S. M. Eisenstein, 'Our "October". Beyond the Played and the Non-Played', in *Selected Works*, ed. Richard Taylor (London, 1988), vol. I, p. 103.

245 S. M. Eisenstein, 'The Montage of Attractions', in *Selected Works*, vol. I, p. 33.

246 Discussions of theatrical productions which draw on boxing conventions include Gerhard P. Knapp, 'From *Lilla helvetet* to the Boxing Ring: Strindberg and Dürrenmatt', in *Structures of Influence: A Comparative Approach to August Strindberg*, ed. Marilyn Johns Blackwell (Chapel Hill, NC, 1981), pp. 226–44; Howard Quackenbush, 'Pugilism as Mirror and Metafiction in Life and in Contemporary Spanish American Drama', *Latin American Theatre Review* (Fall 1992), pp. 23–41; Franco Ruffini, *Teatro e Boxe* (Bologna, 1994).

247 Etienne Decroux, 'Words on Mime', trans. Mark Piper, *Mime Journal* (1985), p. 14. See also Thomas Leabhart, 'The Theatre/Sport Connection', *Mime Journal* (1996), pp. 32–65.

248 Antonin Artaud, *The Theater and Its Double* (1938), trans. Victor Corti (London, 1993), pp. 88–9.

249 Bertolt Brecht, 'More Good Sports', in *The Weimar Republic Sourcebook*, p. 537. See also 'Is the Drama Dying?', in *The Weimar Republic Sourcebook*, pp. 538–9; Jensen, 'Crowd Control', p. 82.

250 Brecht, *In the Jungle of Cities*, p. 2. Nellhaus translates 'ringkampf' as wrestling. Compare Brecht's programme notes for the 1928 Heidelberg production, section 3, pp. 69–71.

251 Bertolt Brecht, 'Difficulties of the Epic Theatre', in *The Weimar Republic Sourcebook*, p. 540. See Hans Ulrich Gumbrecht, *In Praise of Athletic Beauty* (Cambridge, MA, 2006), pp. 211–12.

252 *Brecht on Theatre*, pp. 44, 231, 33.

253 Schmeling, *Autobiography*, p. 38.

254 Jean Arp, 'Flyweight Glory', in *Collected French Writings*, trans. Joachim Neugroschel and ed. Marcel Jean (London, 2001), p. 259.

## 8 Save Me, Jack Dempsey; Save Me, Joe Louis

1 Irwin Shaw, 'I Stand By Dempsey', *Sailor off the Bremen* (New York, 1939), pp. 21–31. The following year, Gene Tunney imagined Dempsey knocking Louis out. 'Dempsey Knocks Out Louis in Mythical Ring Battle', *Look*, 13 February 1940.

2 A. J. Liebling, *The Sweet Science* (Harmondsworth, 1982), p. 2.

3 Quoted in David Margolick, *Beyond Glory: Max Schmeling vs. Joe Louis, and a World on the Brink* (London, 2005), p. 86. See also Roger Kahn, *A Flame of Pure Fire: Jack Dempsey and the Roaring '20s* (New York, 1999), pp. 430–31.

4 Jo Sinclair, *Wasteland* (New York, 1946), p. 263.

5 Horace Gregory, 'Dempsey, Dempsey', in *Proletarian Literature in the United States: An Anthology*, ed. Granville Hicks, Michael Gold, et al. (London, 1935), pp. 161–2.

6 Budd Schulberg, *On the Waterfront* (London, 1988), p. 231.

7 Jesse Frederick Steiner, *Americans at Play: Recent Trends in Recreation and Leisure Time Activities* (New York, 1933), p. 96. In 1923 the Chicago *Tribune* decided to supplement the Amateur Athletic Union tournaments with something locally based; in 1927, the New York *Daily News* copied the idea and Paul Gallico, then sports editor, dubbed the competition 'Golden Gloves'.

8 Otis L. Graham, Jr., 'Years of Crisis: America in Depression and War', in *The Unfinished Century*, ed. William Leuchtenburg (Boston, 1973), p. 381.

9 Frederick Lewis Allen, *Since Yesterday: The 1930s in America* (New York, 1986), p. 147.

10 Barney Ross and Martin Abramson, *No Man Stands Alone* (London, 1959), pp. 65, 70.

11 Steven Riess, *City Games: The Evolution of American Urban Society and the Rise of Sports* (Urbana, IL, 1989), p. 112.

12 Ross, *No Man Stands Alone*, pp., 22, 65, 75. For a more reliable version, see Douglas Century, *Barney Ross* (New York, 2006).

13 Paul Gallico, *Farewell to Sport* (London, 1988), pp. 21, 27. Jim Tully dedicated a novel to Dempsey, 'my fellow road-kid'. Tully, *The Bruiser* (London, 1937).

14 Leger Grindon, 'Body and Soul: The Structure of Meaning in the Boxing Film Genre', *Cinema Journal*, 35, no. 4 (Summer 1996), pp. 54–69. Grindon argues that after 1934, when the Production Code constrained the gangster film, boxing films 'served to both mute and deliver key elements made popular by the urban crime film'.

15 John Burrowes, *Benny: The Life and Times of a Fighting Legend* (Edinburgh, 1982), pp. 199, 151. See also Kasia Boddy, 'Scottish Fighting Men: Big and Wee', in *Scotland in Theory*, ed. Eleanor Bell and Gavin Miller (Amsterdam, 2004), pp. 183–96.

16 Robert Sklar, *City Boys: Cagney, Bogart, Garfield* (Princeton, 1992), p. 12.

17 In *The Roaring Twenties* (1939), Cagney plays Eddie Bartlett, a World War I veteran who becomes a gangster after failing to get a job in 1919 (a year characterized in the film by reference to the Dempsey–Willard fight). 'I can't go around shadow-boxing any more,' he says.

18 Frederick V. Romano, *The Boxing Filmography: American Features, 1920–2003* (Jefferson, NC, 2004), pp. 207–9. Cagney, a dancer, was not surprised to find his footwork praised. *Cagney by Cagney* (New York, 1976), p. 53.

19 In *Night After Night* (1932) George Raft plays an ex-boxer who takes etiquette lessons to impress an heiress. His cover is blown when his brash ex-girlfriend, Mae West in her film debut, shows up.

20 Cagney also appeared as a boxer in *The Irish in Us* (1935) and *City for Conquest* (1940). See Romano, *The Boxing Filmography*, pp. 32–4, 95–7. After 1934, the studios began to recast gangsters and boxers as crime-fighting government employees. In 1936's *Great Guy*, Cagney plays an ex-boxer who works for the Bureau of Weights and Measures. *Great Guy* was advertised with the slogan – 'Ex-Boxer Johnny Cave has a New Opponent: CORRUPTION!'

21 Cass Warner Sperling and Cork Millner, with Jack Warner Jr., *Hollywood Be Thy Name: The Warner Brothers Story* (Lexington, KY, 1998), p. 161. The release of *42nd Street* was announced as 'The Inauguration of a New Deal in Enter-

tainment'. Richard Barrios, *A Song in the Dark: The Birth of the Musical Film* (Oxford, 1995), p. 377.

22  Aaron Baker, 'A Left/Right Combination: Populism and Depression-Era Boxing Films', in *Out of Bounds: Sports, Media, and The Politics of Identity*, ed. Aaron Baker and Todd Boyd (Bloomington, IN, 1997), p. 165.

23  Quoted in Brian Neve, *Film and Politics in America* (London, 1992), p. 115.

24  In 1946, *The Milky Way* was remade as *The Kid from Brooklyn*, a musical starring Danny Kane. The most recent version is *The Calcium Kid* (2003), in which a South London milkman (Orlando Bloom) defeats a slick American.

25  Romano, *The Boxing Filmography*, pp. 133–5.

26  *Kid Galahad* was remade as an Elvis Presley musical in 1962.

27  'Palooka' became slang for an incompetent boxer in the twenties. *Palooka* (1936) spawned a series that ran from 1947 to 1951 and which was 'a veritable film school of budding left-wing directors and writers'. Paul Buhle and Dave Wagner, *Blacklisted* (London, 2003), pp. 113–14.

28  *The Life of Jimmy Dolan* was remade by Warners in 1939 as *They Made Me a Criminal*, starring John Garfield, Gloria Dickson and the Dead End Kids.

29  Andrew Bergman, *We're in the Money: Depression America and Its Films* (New York, 1992), p. 73.

30  On 'communitarian ventures' at this time, see Warren I. Sussman, 'The Thirties', in *The Development of an American Culture*, ed. Stanley Coben and Lorman Ratner (Englewood Cliffs, NJ, 1970), p. 183.

31  Rural and ethnic values are combined in Mama Donati's farm in *Kid Galahad* (1937). When her son Nick (Edward G. Robinson) visits, he drops his wise-guy persona and starts speaking Italian.

32  In 1964 Charles Strouse and Lee Adams turned the play into a successful Broadway musical about a black boxer. Sammy Davis, Jr. starred. See Stanley Green, *Broadway Musicals Show by Show* (New York, 1996), p. 210.

33  Harold Clurman, *The Fervent Years: The Story of the Group Theatre and the Thirties* (New York, 1957), p. 197. See also Gabriel Miller, *Clifford Odets* (New York, 1989), pp. 62–79.

34  The play ended with a rather different homecoming. On learning that Joe and Lorna have been killed in a car crash, Papa Bonaparte closes the play saying, 'Come, we bring-a him home . . . where he belong'. Clifford Odets, *Golden Boy and Other Plays* (Harmondsworth, 1963), p. 111.

35  Nelson Algren, *Nonconformity* (New York, 1996), pp. 33–4. Hemingway is the source for Carpentier's line 'viciousness in the ring is essential'. Nelson Algren, *Notes from a Sea Diary: Hemingway All the Way* (New York, 1966), p. 29.

36  Nelson Algren, *Chicago: City on the Make* (New York, 1951), p. 69. On getting even, see, for example, Nelson Algren, 'The Face on the Barroom Floor', *The Neon Wilderness* (New York, 1986), p. 129.

37  Warner Bros. was famously 'the studio of the working class'. David A. Cook, *A History of Narrative Film* (New York, 1996), p. 290. See Thomas Schatz, *The Genius of the System: Hollywood Filmmaking in the Studio Era* (New York, 1988), chs. 9 and 12.

38  Nelson Algren, *Never Come Morning* (New York, 1987), p. 16. The story originated in a short story, 'A Bottle of Milk for Mother', in *The Neon Wilderness*, pp. 73–90.

39  *Never Come Morning*, pp. 3, 111, 122, 261. See also Ian Peddie, 'Poles Apart? Ethnicity, Race, Class and Nelson Algren', *Modern Fiction Studies*, 47, no. 1 (Summer 2001), pp. 118–44.

40  Hazel Rowley, *Richard Wright: The Life and Times* (New York, 2001), pp. 187–9, 354, 202; Bettina Drew, *Nelson Algren: A Walk on the Wild Side* (London, 1990), p. 125.

41  Algren, *Never Come Morning*, pp. 59, 60, 87, 118.

42  The gang first appeared in Sidney Kingsley's 1937 hit play, *Dead End*, and then in the film version, written by Lillian Hellman and directed by William Wyler. Approximately 85 films featuring either the Dead End Kids or Bowery Boys followed. See *We're in the Money*, Chapter Eleven.

43  Vladimir Nabokov, *The Annotated Lolita* (Harmondsworth, 1980), p. 45. Other films featuring boxing priests include: *The Leather Saint* (1955), in which a priest fights to get medical supplies for the parish hospital, and *The Big Punch* (1948) in which a boxer retires to enter the church. *On the Waterfront* (1954) presents the parallel crises of conscience of ex-pug, Terry Malloy (Marlon Brando), and priest ('and something of an amateur boxer in his college days'), Father Barry (Karl Malden). Budd Schulberg, *On the Waterfront*, p. 43.

44  Algren, *Never Come Morning*, pp. 57–8, 89, 90–91. See also Kasia Boddy, 'Detachment, Compassion and Irritability: The Naturalism of *Never Come Morning*,' in *Nelson Algren: A Collection of Critical Essays*, ed. Robert Ward (Madison, NJ, 2007), pp. 72–94

45  Damon Runyon, 'Tobias the Terrible', in *On Broadway* (Harmondsworth, 1990), p. 88.

46  James T. Farrell, Epilogue, *Studs Lonigan* (Urbana, IL, 1993), p. 865. The death fantasy sequence was not published in 1935; much was lost and this edition is the first to include fragments. Al Capone was a great fan of Dempsey's and the boxer had to dissuade him from trying to fix the Tunney rematch. Kahn, *A Flame of Pure Fire*, p. 412.

47  John Steinbeck, *Of Mice and Men* (Harmondsworth, 1949), pp. 25–6, 31, 47, 54, 74.

48  See Jeffrey T. Sammons, *Beyond the Ring* (Urbana, IL, 1990), pp. 86–91.

49  Steinbeck, *Of Mice and Men*, pp. 22–3, 26, 54, 55, 76. Steinbeck recalled that he had once been 'fairly good at boxing, mainly because I hated it and wanted to get it over with and to get out. This is not boxing but fighting.' 'Then My Arm Glassed Up' (1965), in *Of Men and Their Making: The Selected Non-Fiction of John Steinbeck*, ed. Susan Shillinglaw and Jackson J. Benson (London, 2002), p. 127.

50  Steiner, *Americans at Play*, p. 96.

51  It was not, of course, impossible to fix team sports. In 1919, the Chicago White Sox conspired with a betting syndicate to throw the World Series.

52  On some of these ways, see Riess, *City Games*, p. 179.

53  Riess, *City Games*, p. 177

54  Ike Williams, Testimony to the US Congress Senate Judiciary

Committee, *Professional Boxing: Hearings Before Subcommittee on Antitrust and Monopoly*, 1960, in *Major Problems in American Sport History*, ed. Steven A. Riess (Boston, 1997), pp. 401–8.

55 The other boxing-and-crime story in *Men without Women*, 'Fifty Grand', is much lighter in tone. See Robert P. Weeks, 'Wise-Guy Narrator and Trickster Out-Tricked in Hemingway's "Fifty Grand"', in *New Critical Approaches to the Short Stories of Ernest Hemingway*, ed. Jackson L. Benson (Durham, NC, 1990), pp. 275–81.

56 Ernest Hemingway, 'The Killers', in *Men Without Women* (New York, 1955), pp. 45–55. On the three stories in which Nick Adams encounters the 'perplexing behaviour of boxers', see Gerry Brenner, 'From "Sepi Jingan" to "The Mother of a Queen": Hemingway's Three Epistemologic Formulas for Short Fiction', in *New Critical Approaches*, pp. 156–71.

57 Damon Runyon, 'Leopard's Spots', in *More Guys and Dolls* (Garden City, NY, 1951), p. 68. Heavyweight parasols are 'big umbrellas'. 'The Big Umbrella' is one of several stories about Spider McCoy, a manager on the look-out for 'some sausage' who might be 'the next heavy-weight champion of the world'; see particularly 'Bred for Battle'. Both are in *On Broadway*.

58 James T. Farrell, 'Twenty-Five Bucks', in *The Short Stories* (New York, 1962), pp. 183–96.

59 Dashiell Hammett, *Red Harvest* (London, 1974), p. 63.

60 Ibid., p. 72.

61 Gerald Early, 'I Only Like It Better When the Pain Comes: More Notes toward a Cultural History of Prizefighting', *Tuxedo Junction* (Hopewell, NJ, 1989), p. 138. Early is discussing Mailer's *The Fight*. On race in *Body and Soul*, see Michael Rogin, *Blackface, White Noise: Jewish Immigrants in the Hollywood Melting Pot* (Berkeley, CA, 1996), ch. 7.

62 Odets also makes the distinction between fighting for money and fighting for things you 'believe in'. *Golden Boy*, p. 108.

63 Quoted in Neve, *Film and Politics in America*, p. 133.

64 Only at this point, argue Borde and Chaumeton, does the film become *noir*. Raymond Borde and Étienne Chaumeton, *Panorama du film noir américain, 1941–1953* (Paris, 1955), p. 3.

65 In 1949 T. V. Smith argued that 'the game' was a 'fitting symbol' of all aspects of American life during this period; 'deal' evoked poker as well as business. T. V. Smith, 'The New Deal as Cultural Phenomenon', in *Ideological Differences and World Order*, ed. F.S.C. Northrop (New Haven, 1949), p. 209. On precoccupation of New Deal stories with insurance, see Michael Szalay, *New Deal Modernism* (Durham, NC, 2000).

66 Neff's wound is usually read as a mark of castration. See, for example, Claire Johnston, '*Double Indemnity*', in *Women in Film Noir*, ed. E. Ann Kaplan (London, 1998), p. 92. Neff loses the 'game' because he fails to anticipate all the correct 'moves' – if Dietrichson had taken out accident insurance, he would have made a claim after breaking his leg.

67 Raymond Chandler, *The Big Sleep*, in *The Chandler Collection* (London, 1983), vol. I, pp. 9–11. As the novel goes on, Marlowe and others compare his job to a variety of occupations: the detective is also a pornographer (trying to 'take a photo-

graph with an empty camera'), a Proustian 'connoisseur in degenerates', a 'stooge . . . in search of a comedian', a 'killer', and a 'soldier'. *The Big Sleep*, pp. 41, 51, 60, 128, 180.

68 Chandler, *The Big Sleep*, pp. 133, 178.

69 Raymond Chandler, letter to D. J. Ibberson, 19 April 1951, in *Selected Letters of Raymond Chandler*, ed. Frank MacShane (London, 1981), p. 270. Humphrey Bogart, who played Marlowe in John Huston's 1946 film adaptation, was only 5' 8", and the film jokes about him being too short to be a private eye. In the film, a picture of a boxer in a crouch can be seen on his office wall.

70 Chandler, *The Big Sleep*, pp. 10–11, 53, 66, 85–90.

71 Canino had killed Harry Jones, 'a very small man' in love with a woman 'too big' for him. To get to Canino, Marlowe must first endure a knockdown blow from Art Huck, who fights above his weight by fighting dirty. Chandler, *The Big Sleep*, pp. 137, 139, 142, 156–60.

72 Ibid., pp. 161, 163, 169–70.

73 James M. Cain, *Double Indemnity* (London, 2002), p. 112.

74 See David Reid and Jayne L. Walker, 'Cornell Woolrich and the Abandoned City', in *Shades of Noir*, ed. Joan Copjec (London, 1993), pp. 64–5; Joan Mellen, *Big Bad Wolves: Masculinity in the American Film* (New York, 1977), p. 164; Frank Krutnik, *In a Lonely Street* (London, 1991), ch. 5.

75 Margaret Mead, *Male and Female* (London, 1950), p. 278.

76 Odets, *Golden Boy*, p. 96.

77 Joyce Carol Oates says that this is what boxing is always 'about'. *On Boxing* (London, 1988), p. 25.

78 Lincoln Kirstein, 'James Cagney and the American Hero', *Hound And Horn* (April/June 1932), pp. 466–7; John Houseman, quoted in Krutnik, *In a Lonely Street*, p. 89.

79 Kirstein, 'James Cagney and the American Hero', p. 467.

80 Andrew Dickos, *Street with No Name: A History of the Classic American Film Noir* (Lexington, KY, 2002), p. 197.

81 These films are very different from historical boxing dramas such as *Gentleman Jim* (1942) and *The Great John L.* (1945) that were popular during the war. Errol Flynn played Corbett in *Gentleman Jim*; he also fought frequently with Bette Davis on the set of *The Private Lives of Elizabeth and Essex* (1939). She hit him 'in the most beautiful technical way' and harder than he'd ever been hit 'even in the boxing ring'. Errol Flynn, *My Wicked, Wicked Ways* (London, 1960), pp. 221–8.

82 James Naremore, *More Than Night: Film Noir in Its Contexts* (Berkeley, CA, 1998), p. 103.

83 Manny Farber, 'Fight Films', in *Negative Space* (New York, 1971), p. 65.

84 This scene was shown in studies on the effects of screen violence on viewers. Richard B. Felson, 'Mass Media Effects on Violent Behavior', in *Screening Violence*, ed. Stephen Prince (Piscataway, NJ, 2000), pp. 237–66.

85 Roland Bergan, *Sport in the Movies* (New York, 1982), p. 16.

86 Kenneth Patchen, *The Collected Poems* (New York, 1968), p. 71.

87 Ring Lardner, 'Champion', in *The Best Short Stories of Ring Lardner* (New York, 1957), p. 119; Tully, *The Bruiser*, pp. 107–8; Algren, *Never Come Morning*, p. 24. Sometimes women are

not bad but just young and stupid. See also Irwin Shaw, 'Return to Kansas City', in *Sailor off the Bremen*, pp. 47–58; a film adaptation is in *Women and Men 2: In Love There Are No Rules* (1991).

88 Robert Siodmak claimed that *The Killers* was 'the only film of a Hemingway story that Hemingway actually likes!': 'Hoodlums: The Myth', *Films and Filming*, 5, no. 9 (1959), p. 10

89 Krutnik, *In a Lonely Street*, p. 116. For a full discussion of the film, see pp. 114–24.

90 See James M. Welsh, 'Knockout in Paradise: An Appraisal of *The Set-up*', *American Classic Screen*, 2, no. 6 (1978), pp. 14–16.

91 Another boxer's girlfriend confesses to doping his tea to get him 'out of the game'; he tells her he's been a 'blind fool' and thanks her. Robert E. Howard, 'Iron Men' (1930), in *Boxing Stories*, ed. Chris Gruber (Lincoln, NE, 2005), pp. 239–41.

92 John Steinbeck, 'Always Something to Do in Salinas' (1955), in *Of Men and Their Making*, pp. 6–7.

93 Stanley Renner, 'The Real Woman Inside the Fence in "The Chrysanthemums"', *Modern Fiction Studies*, 31, no. 2 (Summer 1985), pp. 305–17.

94 *John Steinbeck: A Life in Letters*, ed. Elaine Steinbeck and Robert Wallsten (London, 1975), p. 509.

95 John Steinbeck, 'The Chrysanthemums', in *The Long Valley* (London, 1958), pp. 7–19

96 Malcolm X, with Alex Haley, *The Autobiography of Malcolm X* (London, 1965), pp. 97–8.

97 Haley, *Autobiography of Malcolm X*, p. 98.

98 Nelson Mandela also described boxing as preparation for political leadership. *Long Walk to Freedom* (London, 1995), pp. 192–3.

99 A major destination during the Great Migration, Detroit saw its black population grow from 5,000 in 1910 to about 120,000 in 1930. Richard Bak, *Joe Louis: The Great Black Hope* (New York, 1998), p. 13.

100 Bak, *Joe Louis*, p. 26. The seeming dichotomy between boxing and violin-playing proved popular. It was picked up in *Kid Galahad*, in which fight manager Donati (Edward G. Robinson) declares that 'a fighter's a machine, not a violin player', and developed at length by Odets in *Golden Boy*.

101 Damon Runyon coined the phrase after seeing a group of fight managers taking the sun on colourful chairs outside Jacobs's ticket store. Barney Nagler, *James Norris and the Decline of Boxing* (New York, 1964), p. 47.

102 Margolick, *Beyond Glory*, p. 73.

103 Chris Mead, *Champion: Joe Louis Black Hero in White America* (New York, 1985), p. 40; Milly Heyd, *Mutual Reflections: Jews and Blacks in American Art* (New Brunswick, NJ, 1999), pp. 192–3 and fig. 100.

104 Quoted in *Joe Louis: The Great Black Hope*, p. 87.

105 Bak, *Joe Louis*, pp. 74–5. Although never photographed with them, Louis had affairs with several white women including Sonja Henie and Lana Turner. In 1939 *Look* magazine published an article about his womanizing. Louis's lawyer later admitted that the article was largely true, but it conflicted with Louis's carefully cultivated image. 'So we

sued. And *Look* settled.' Truman K. Gibson, *Knocking Down Barriers* (Chicago, 2005), pp. 75–6.

106 Langston Hughes, 'Joe Louis', in *Montage of a Dream Deferred* (1951), in *Selected Poems* (London, 1999), p. 265.

107 Quoted in Al-Tony Gilmore, 'The Myth, Legend and Folklore of Joe Louis: The Impression of Sport on Society', *South Atlantic Quarterly*, 82 (1983), p. 259. Andrew M. Kaye quotes this line in his comparison of the personae cultivated by Louis and Tiger Flowers. See *The Pussycat of Prizefighting: Tiger Flowers and the Politics of Black Celebrity* (Athens, GA, 2004), pp. 134–9.

108 Bak, *Joe Louis*, p. 293.

109 Quoted in Wilson Jeremiah Moses, *Black Messiahs and Uncle Toms: Social and Literary Manipulations of a Religious Myth* (Philadelphia, 1993), p. 157.

110 See William Barlow, *Voice Over: The Making of Black Radio* (Philadelphia, 1999), ch. 3; Allen Guttmann, *Sports Spectators* (New York, 1986), pp. 132–4.

111 Miles Davis, with Quincy Troupe, *The Autobiography* (London, 1990), pp. 8–9.

112 Maya Angelou, *I Know Why the Caged Bird Sings* (London, 1984), pp. 129–32.

113 A couple of months later, *The Crisis* felt it necessary to add a note of caution, advising 'our race' not to 'hitch its wagon to a boxer'. Quoted in John Hoberman, *Darwin's Athletes* (Boston, 1997), p. 27.

114 Richard Wright, 'Joe Louis Uncovers Dynamite', *New Masses*, 17 (8 October 1935), pp. 18–19. Wright's essay followed Saul Green's piece on the lynching of Richard Lee, entitled 'Lessons'. See also Michel Fabre, *The Unfinished Quest of Richard Wright*, trans. Isabel Barzun (Urbana, IL, 1993), p. 125.

115 Ralph Ellison, 'Bearden', in *The Collected Essays of Ralph Ellison*, ed. John F. Callahan (New York, 1995), pp. 833–4. Forty years earlier Ellison had described Harlem as a place where 'surreal fantasies' were regularly acted out. For example, 'a man beating his wife in the park uses boxing "science" and observes Marquess of Queensberry rules (no rabbit punching, no blows beneath the belt).' *Shadow and Act* (New York, 1972), p. 297.

116 Quoted in James de Jongh, *Vicious Modernism: Black Harlem and the Literary Imagination* (Cambridge, 1990), p. 120.

117 Quoted in Peter Levine, *Ellis Island to Ebbets Field* (Oxford, 1992), p. 180.

118 Adolf Hitler, *Mein Kampf*, trans. Ralph Manheim (Boston, 1971), pp. 407–12. Goebbels was particularly fond of using boxing metaphors to illustrate military progress or setbacks. After the Battle of Stalingrad, for example, he reassured Germany, 'We wipe the blood from our eyes in order to see clearly, and, when it is time to enter the ring for the next round, our legs stand firm once again.' On Goebbels's boxing metaphors, see Victor Klemperer, 'Boxing', in *The Language of the Third Reich*, trans. Martin Brady (New York, 2002), pp. 231–5. The absurdity of boxing, with all its rules and claims to fair play, in the midst of the death camps is made very clear in Primo Levi, *The Truce* (1963), trans. Stuart Woolf (London, 1987), pp. 374–5, and Paul Steinberg, *Speak*

*You Also*, trans. Linda Coverdale with Bill Ford (Harmondsworth, 2001), pp. 17–27. A camp survivor feed. his son boxing 'tales from an invented past' to make him tough in Jurek Becker, *The Boxer* (New York, 2002), p. 202. See Sander Gilman, *Jewish Self-Hatred: Anti-Semitism and the Hidden Language* (Baltimore, 1985), pp. 341–44.

119 Margolick, *Beyond Glory*, p. 30

120 Quoted in Levine, *Ellis Island to Ebbets Field*, p. 182.

121 Geoffrey C. Ward, *Unforgivable Blackness: The Rise and Fall of Jack Johnson* (New York, 2004), p. 441.

122 Margolick, *Beyond Glory*, p. 124.

123 Ibid., p. 185.

124 Quoted in Clarence Lusone, *Hitler's Black Victims* (London, 2002), pp. 220–21.

125 The Chicago *Defender* surveyed the racial prejudice of the Southern papers and concluded that 'it took the defeat of Joe Louis to uncover this condition'. Lewis A. Erenberg, *The Greatest Fight of Our Generation: Louis vs. Schmeling* (Oxford, 2006), p. 101. On the *Saturday Evening Post*'s coverage of Schmeling, see Kathryne V. Lindberg, 'Mass Circulation versus The Masses: Covering the Modern Magazine Scene', *boundary 2*, 20, no. 2 (Summer 1993), pp. 51–83.

126 Juneteenth celebrations commemorated 19 June 1865, when the Union soldiers, led by Major General Gordon Granger, landed at Galveston, Texas, with news that the war had ended and that the enslaved were free. This was two and a half years after President Lincoln's Emancipation Proclamation, which had become official on 1 January 1863.

127 Quoted in *Vicious Modernism*, p. 121.

128 Quoted in Moses, *Black Messiahs and Uncle Toms*, p. 159.

129 Margolick, *Beyond Glory*, p. 193; John Dos Passos, *The Fourteenth Chronicle: Letters and Diaries*, ed. Townsend Ludington (London, 1974), p. 485.

130 Damon Runyon dubbed Braddock Cinderella Man in 1935 after he had surprisingly outboxed Max Baer to win the title. Peter Heller, *In This Corner* (London, 1989), p. 173. See also Jeremy Schaap, *Cinderella Man* (Boston, 2005), the main source for the movie of the same title.

131 Alistair Cooke, 'Joe Louis', *Letters from America, 1946–1951* (Harmondsworth, 1951), pp. 56–61 (p. 57).

132 Quoted in Margolick, *Beyond Glory*, p. 231.

133 In 1937 Goebbels had wanted Braddock to come to Germany to fight Schmeling. Braddock's manager, Joe Gould, had three conditions. Goebbels agreed to the first two (concerning the fee and referee), but the deal fell through when Gould asked 'that you get Hitler to stop kicking the Jews around'. Quoted in *James Norris and the Decline of Boxing*, p. 14. See also Budd Schulberg, *Loser and Still Champion: Muhammad Ali* (London, 1972), pp. 31–2.

134 Quoted in Moses, *Black Messiahs and Uncle Toms*, p. 159. Margolick thinks the story apocryphal. *Beyond Glory*, p. 98 fn.

135 Ray Barfield, *Listening to the Radio, 1920–1950* (Westport, CN, 1996), pp. 80, 196. 64 per cent of all American radio owners are estimated to have listened in (97 per cent in New York). Only two of Roosevelt's fireside chats drew more listeners. Bak, *Joe Louis*, p. 163. See also Wideman,

*Sent for You Yesterday*, p. 202.

136 Bob Considine, 'Louis Knocks Out Schmeling', in *The Best American Sports Writing of the Century*, ed. David Haleberstam (Boston, 1999), pp. 138–9.

137 Richard Wright, 'How He Did It – And Oh! – Where Were Hitler's Pagan Gods?', *Daily Worker*, 24 June 1938, pp. 1, 8.

138 Quoted in Moses, *Black Messiahs and Uncle Toms*, p. 159.

139 Jimmy Carter, *Why Not the Best?* (New York, 1976), pp. 36–7

140 Donald McRae, *White and Black: The Untold Story of Joe Louis and Jesse Owens* (New York, 2002).

141 Quoted in Moses, *Black Messiahs and Uncle Toms*, p. 159.

142 Richard Wright, 'High Tide in Harlem', in *Speech and Power*, ed. Gerald Early (Boston, 1992), vol. I, p. 157. Ralph Ellison had tickets to the fight, but missed it. Lawrence Jackson, *Ralph Ellison: Emergence of a Genius* (New York, 2002), p. 203.

143 William H. Wiggens, Jr. 'Boxing's Sambo Twins: Racial Stereotypes in Jack Johnson and Joe Louis Newspaper Cartoons, 1908–1938', *Journal of Sport History*, 15, no. 3 (Winter 1988), pp. 251–4.

144 Eugene S. McCartney, 'Alliteration on the Sports Page', *American Speech*, 13, no. 1 (February 1938), p. 31. On Louis's endorsements, see St Clair Drake and Horace R. Cayton, *Black Metropolis* (New York, 1962), vol. II, p. 462.

145 One of the heroes of Pearl Harbor was another black boxer, Dorie Miller, heavyweight champion of the USS *West Virginia*. The first black sailor to be awarded the Navy Cross, for rescuing numerous other sailors and remaining on board to operate an anti-aircraft machine gun, he was killed while on active service in 1943.

146 Quoted in Lauren Sklaroff, 'Constructing G.I. Joe Louis: Cultural Solutions to the "Negro Problem" during World War II', *Journal of American History*, 89, no. 3 (December 2002), p. 972, 959.

147 A. Philip Randolph, 'The March-on-Washington Movement', in *Sources of the African-American Past: Primary Sources in American History*, ed. Roy E. Finkenbine (London, 1997), p. 151. During the war, many southern blacks and whites migrated to ports and industrial cities in search of work. This led to frequent racial disturbances and in 1943 full-scale riots broke out in Detroit and many other cities. Membership of the NAACP soared during the war, growing from 50,000 in 1940 to 450,000 in 1947.

148 Louis's remark also inspired a popular poem by Carl Byoir, 'Joe Louis Named the War', *Collier's*, 16 May 1942.

149 Claudia Jones, *Lift Every Voice for Victory!* (New York, 1942), p. 9.

150 Irving Berlin, 'That's What the Well-Dressed Man in Harlem Will Wear', in *Perfect in their Art*, ed. Robert Hedin and Michael Waters (Carbondale, IL, 2003), p. 30.

151 Thanks to Mark Whalan for lending me a video copy. Intended to promote a segregated army, the film led to some integration in postwar Hollywood. Thomas Cripps and David Culbert, '*The Negro Soldier* (1944): Film Propaganda in Black and White', in *Hollywood as Historian*, ed. Peter C. Rollins (Lexington, KY, 1983), pp. 109–33. Louis also appeared in the loosely autobiographical 'race film' *Spirit of Youth* (1937). Coley Wallace played him in *The Joe Louis Story*

(1953). See Romano, *The Boxing Filmography*, pp. 101–2, 187–9.

152 Lillian Hellman wrote the original script for *The Negro Soldier*. In her version, John, a young black soldier meets another young black man called Chris on the 80th anniversary of the Emancipation Proclamation. 'In the course of the evening, which included Joe Louis's fight over the radio, the recounting of a lynching, and a concert of Paul Robeson at the Lincoln Memorial, John succeed. in convincing Chris that the America of Lincoln is worth fighting for even though the lynchers are present both inside and outside the United States.' Saverio Giovacchini, *Hollywood Modernism: Film and Politics in the Age of the New Deal* (Philadelphia, 2001), p. 259.

153 Mead, *Joe Louis, Champion*, p. 236.

154 Joe Louis, with Edna Rust and Art Rust, *My Life* (Boston, 1997), p. 137.

155 Drake and Cayton, *Black Metropolis*, vol. II, p. 391. See also Lawrence W. Levine, *Black Culture and Black Consciousness* (New York, 1977), pp. 420–40.

156 Frank Byrd, 'Private Life of Big Bess', in *A Renaissance in Harlem: Lost Essays of the WPA*, ed. Lionel C. Bascom (New York, 2001), pp. 163–4.

157 Drake and Cayton, *Black Metropolis*, vol. II, p. 403.

158 E. Franklin Frazier, *Negro Youth at the Crossways* (New York, 1967), p. 179.

159 Quoted in Moses, *Black Messiahs and Uncle Toms*, p. 156.

160 Martin Luther King, *Why We Can't Wait* (New York, 1963), pp. 110–11. The story is retold in Madison Smartt Bell, *Save Me, Joe Louis* (Harmondsworth, 1993), pp. 305–6, and Ernest J. Gaines, *A Lesson Before Dying* (New York, 1994), p. 91. See also Ernest J. Gaines, *The Autobiography of Miss Jane Pittman* (New York, 1971), p. 203.

161 On the need for both Louis and King to adopt 'the mutually antagonistic roles of racial crusader and "Uncle Tom"', see Moses, *Black Messiahs and Uncle Toms*, ch. 10.

162 Moses, *Black Messiahs and Uncle Toms*, p. 157; Frazier, *Negro Youth at the Crossroads*, p. 179.

163 Wright, 'Joe Louis Uncovers Dynamite', p. 18.

164 Melvin B. Tolson reversed the usual metaphor and claimed that 'the First Lady has a punch like Joe Louis.' 'The Four Freedoms of Mrs Roosevelt', in *Caviar and Cabbage: Selected Columns by Melvin B. Tolson from the Washington Tribune, 1937–1944*, ed. Robert Farnsworth (Columbia, MO, 1982), p. 157.

165 'Recognition: "New Masses" Honors Outstanding Artists', *New Masses*, 58, no. 7 (12 February 1946), pp. 16–17; Earl Ofari Hutchinson, *Blacks and Red.: Race and Class in Conflict, 1919–1990* (East Lansing, MI, 1995), pp. 197–8.

166 Michael Denning, *The Cultural Front* (London, 1997), p. 155.

167 Simon Louvish, *Monkey Business: The Lives and Legends of the Marx Brothers* (London, 2000), p. 419.

168 V. S. Naipaul, *The Mimic Men* (London, 2002), pp. 160, 262. An inhabitant of Anguilla describes Louis as the 'one man' in his generation to have made a difference: V. S. Naipaul, 'The Shipwrecked Six Thousand', in *The Writer and the World* (London, 2002), p. 88.

169 Lloyd L. Brown, *Iron City* (New York, 1951), pp. 239–43. See also Alan M. Wald, *Writing from the Left* (London, 1994), ch. 18; Barfield, *Listening to the Radio, 1920–1950*, p. 41.

170 Langston Hughes, 'To Be Somebody', *Phylon*, 11, no. 4 (1950), p. 311.

171 Chester Himes, *If He Hollers Let Him Go* (London, 1986), pp. 37, 153, 202.

172 See, for example, Louise Meriwether, *Daddy was a Number Runner* (London, 1986), pp. 91–3, 170, 175–6; John Edgar Wideman, *Sent for You Yesterday* (London, 1986), pp. 200, 202; Jewelle Gomez, 'Joe Louis was a Heck of a Fighter', in *To Be Continued: Take Two*, ed. Michele Karlsberg and Karen X. Tolchinsky (Ann Arbor, MI, 1999), pp. 53–71.

173 All on *Joe Louis: An American Hero*, compiled by Rena Kosersky, with an essay by William H. Wiggens, Jr (Sony, 2001). 'Joe Louis Strut' is on *Memphis Minnie: Queen of the Blues* (Columbia/Legacy, 1997). See Paul Oliver, *Blues Fell This Morning* (Cambridge, 1994), pp. 274–6; Oliver, *Screening the Blues: Aspects of the Blues Tradition* (London, 1968), pp. 148–9.

174 The complete lyrics are quoted in a letter to Carl Van Vechten, *Remember Me to Harlem. The Letters of Langston Hughes and Carl Van Vechten, 1925–1964*, ed. Emily Bernard (New York, 2001), p. 175. See also Denning, *The Cultural Front*, p. 312.

175 Fabre, *The Unfinished Quest of Richard Wright*, p. 237.

176 On *Joe Louis: An American Hero*.

177 Robert Hayden's poems frequently considered the role of boxers as inspirational 'dark dream figures' for American blacks. 'Summertime and the Living . . .' (1955) presents a child's recollection of a Depression summertime in which hope exists in the vision of 'big splendiferous / Jack Johnson in his diamond limousine'. Johnson 'set the ghetto burgeoning/ with fantasies/of Ethiopia spreading her gorgeous wings.' *Poems* (New York, 1975), pp. 6–7. See Michael F. Cooke, *Afro American Literature in the Twentieth Century* (New Haven, 1984), pp. 137–9; Edward M. Pavlić, *Crossroads Modernism* (Minneapolis, 2002), pp. 163–70.

178 Written in the thirties, *Lawd Today* was not published until 1963, after Wright's death. He also attempted 'a psychological study of bronze-sepia, firm-fleshed Jack Johnson', which he intended to form part of his uncompleted second novel, *Tarbaby's Dawn*. Rowley, *Richard Wright: The Life and Times*, pp. 103, 113, 304, 538. See also William Burrison, '*Lawd Today*: Wright's Tricky Apprenticeship', in *Richard Wright: Critical Perspectives Past and Present*, ed. Henry Louis Gates, Jr and K. A. Appiah (New York, 1993), pp. 98–109.

179 Richard Wright, *Lawd Today* (London, 1969), pp. 106, 171.

180 Ralph Ellison, 'The World and the Jug', in *Shadow and Act*, p. 115. Ellison was responding to Howe's essay, 'Black Boys and Native Sons', in *A World More Attractive* (New York, 1963), pp. 98–122. On their debate, see Emily Buddick in *Jews and Blacks in Literary Conversation* (Cambridge, 1998).

181 Ellison, 'The World and The Jug', p. 140. See Robert G. O'Meally, 'The Rules of Magic: Hemingway as Ellison's "Ancestor"', in *Ralph Ellison's Invisible Man: A Casebook*, ed. John F. Callahan (Oxford, 2004), pp. 149–87.

182 Ellison, 'The World and The Jug', p. 141. See Joseph T.

Skerrett, Jr., 'The Wright Interpretation: Ralph Ellison and the Anxiety of Influence', in *The Critical Response to Ralph Ellison*, ed. Robert J. Butler (Westport, CT, 2000), pp. 149–59.

183 Ernest Hemingway, *Selected Letters: 1917–1961*, ed. Carlos Baker (London, 1981), p. 673.

184 Ralph Ellison, 'A Very Stern Discipline', in *Going to the Territory* (New York, 1987), p. 283. On Ellison's 'ambitions toward literary upward mobility', see T. V. Reed, *Fifteen Jugglers, Five Believers* (Berkeley, CA, 1992), p. 71. On Ellison's 'belief in his ability to compete', see Stanley Crouch, 'Introduction' to *The All-American Skin Game* (Vintage Books, 1997), pp. x–xi. On Crouch's own pugilistic persona, see Robert S. Boynton, 'The Professor of Connection', *The New Yorker*, 6 November 1995, p. 95.

185 Ralph Ellison, Introduction, *Invisible Man* (New York, 1995), p. xxi.

186 Ralph Ellison, 'The Invisible Man', *Horizon*, 16 (October 1947), pp. 104–18.

187 Kaye, *The Pussycat of Prizefighting*, p. 62.

188 Ellison, *Invisible Man*, pp. 17–24.

189 The ten boys, and later, the ten drops of black paint added to 'optic white', are surely an allusion to W.E.B. Du Bois' notion of the Talented Tenth, to which the narrator feels he naturally belongs. Gerald Early, 'The Black Intellectual and the Sport of Prizefighting', in *The Culture of Bruising* (Hopewell, NJ, 1994), p. 25.

190 Ellison, *Invisible Man*, p. 24.

191 Budd Schulberg, *The Harder They Fall* (New York, 1947), p. 85.

192 The speech itself seems to allude to James Weldon Johnson's *The Autobiography of an Ex-Colored Man*. (Harmondsworth, 1990), p. 31. The narrator's friend Shiny delivers a graduation speech to a largely white audience in 'tones of appealing defiance'. The narrator compares him to 'a gladiator tossed into the arena'.

193 See Ellison, *Shadow and Act*, pp. 174–5; *Going to the Territory*, pp. 49, 177.

194 Richard Wright, *Black Boy* (London, 1970), pp. 200–13. For an account of a battle royal as 'comedy', see James Brown, with Bruce Tucker, *James Brown: The Godfather of Soul* (Fontana, 1988), p. 27. See also Gordon Parks, *The Learning Tree* (New York, 1963), pp. 119–25.

195 Others that should be considered include the narrator's speech for the Brotherhood in an auditorium where a prizefighter had lost his sight, and the narrator's intervention in a fight between Ras and Clifton. On the latter, see Jonathan Baumbach, *The Landscape of Nightmare* (New York, 1965), p. 71. The blind prize-fighter may have been based on Sam Langford (1886–1956). In 1944 he was destitute and living in Harlem when Al Laney tracked him down and wrote two pieces for the New York *Herald Tribune* in order to establish a trust fund. See *The Fireside Book of Boxing*, ed. W. C. Heinz (New York, 1961), pp. 226–8. Other allusions are more incidental: see *Invisible Man*, pp. 471, 520, 523. Some may be drawn from Len Zinberg's *Walk Hard – Talk Loud* (1940) which Ellison reviewed. Zinberg describes a blind black prize-fighter and a battle royal, during which the narrator

thinks, 'what am I cutting up this poor slob for? To make those damn whites yell?' Len Zinberg, *Walk Hard – Talk Loud* (New York, 1950), pp. 123, 161. See Ralph Ellison, 'Negro Prize Fighter', *New Masses*, 17 December 1940, pp. 26–7.

196 The golden age of American literature is located in the period 1830 to 1860 in Lewis Mumford, *The Golden Day* (1924). Ellison commented, 'It wasn't that I didn't admire Mumford. I have owned a copy of *The Golden Day* since 1937 . . . I was simply upset by his implying that the war which freed my grandparents from slavery was of no real consequence to the broader issues of American society and its culture.' Quoted in Alan Nadel, *Invisible Criticism: Ralph Ellison and the American Canon* (Iowa City, IA, 1988), p. 158.

197 Ellison, *Invisible Man*, p. 65.

198 He later remembers the Golden Day as a place which 'had once been painted white; now its paint was flaking away with the years, the scratch of a finger being enough to send it down.' *Invisible Man*, p. 201.

199 James Joyce, *Ulysses* (Harmondsworth, 1992), pp. 412–14. Ellison frequently acknowledged Joyce as a model for the intertwining of high and low cultural references. See *Shadow and Act*, pp. 15, 58, 168, 174. See also Craig Hansen Werner, *Paradoxical Resolutions: American Fiction Since James Joyce* (Urbana, IL, 1982), pp. 133–43; Robert N. List, *Dedalus in Harlem: The Joyce-Ellison Connection* (Washington, DC, 1982). On Ellison's debt to Homer's *Odyssey*, see William W. Cook 'Ellison's Modern Odysseus', *Humanities* (May–June 1992), 13, no. 3, pp. 26–8.

200 Ellison, *Invisible Man*, pp. 71, 72, 74. Compare this with Bledsoe's ability to 'touch a white man with impunity'. Bledsoe describes the narrator as 'a nervy little fighter' and says that 'the race need. good, smart, disillusioned fighters'. He misquotes James Weldon Johnson's poem 'Prodigal Son', 'Young man, young man, / Yo' arms too short/ To box with God', substituting 'me' for 'God'. James Weldon Johnson, *God's Trombone* (New York, 1927), p. 21. Ellison also quotes these lines in 'Flying Home', in *Flying Home and Other Stories*, ed. John F. Callahan (Harmondsworth, 1998), p. 166.

201 After the battle royal and speech, Invisible Man is given his 'prize' – a briefcase with a piece of paper inside, his scholarship to the college. That night he dreams that the paper read 'To whom it May Concern, Keep This Nigger-Boy Running.' *Invisible Man*, p. 33.

202 The correct version of the song (with Johnson instead of Louis) appeared in Ellison's short story, 'Afternoon', in *Flying Home and Other Stories*, pp. 33–44.

203 Ellison, *Invisible Man*, p. 544. For an alternative reading of this passage, see Michael Oriard, *Sporting with the Gods: The Rhetoric of Play and Game in American Culture* (Cambridge, 1991), pp. 318–20.

204 Ellison, *Invisible Man*, pp. 565, 568. Early describes this scene as 'the story of the tortoise and the hare . . . Brer Fox and Brer Rabbit'. In Early's analysis, the prize fighter is black and the yokel white. 'The Black Intellectual', p. 5. See also Floyd R. Horowitz, 'Ralph Ellison's Modern Version of Brer Bear and Brer Rabbit in *Invisible Man*', in *The Critical Response to Ralph Ellison*, ed. Butler, pp. 45–9. In 'Hidden

Name and Complex Fate', Ellison figures the world as Tar Baby, 'that enigmatic figure from Negro folklore', and also a boxer, Sonny Liston. *Shadow and Act*, p. 147.

205 Ellison, *Invisible Man*, pp. 576, 577, 581. *Winner Take Nothing* was the title of a 1933 collection of Hemingway's short stories. There is a lot more that could be said about the ways in which *Invisible Man* relates to Hemingway's work, *The Sun Also Rises* in particular. In both novels, for example, the protagonist encounters a man selling boxing dolls on the street.

206 Ralph Ellison, 'Change the Joke and Slip the Yoke', in *Shadow and Act*, p. 57.

207 Ralph Ellison, 'Hidden Name and Complex Fate', in *Shadow and Act*, p. 147.

208 Robert B. Stepto and Michael S. Harper, 'Study and Experience: An Interview with Ralph Ellison', in *Conversations with Ralph Ellison*, ed. Maryemma Graham and Amritjit Singh (Jackson, MI, 1998), p. 329.

209 Kenneth Burke, *Language as Symbolic Action* (Berkeley, CA, 1966).

210 Burke dedicated his first book of poems, *Book of Moments* (1915), to 'my sparring partners, and long may we spar without parting.' See Kenneth Burke, 'Ralph Ellison's Truebloodsed *Bildungsroman*', in *Ralph Ellison's Invisible Man: A Casebook*, ed. Callahan, pp. 65–79. See also Robert G. O'Meally, 'On Burke and the Vernacular: Ralph Ellison's Boomerang of History', in *History and Memory in African-American Culture*, ed. Genevieve Fabre and Robert G. O'Meally (Oxford, 1994), pp. 244–60; James M. Albrecht, 'Saying Yes and Saying No: Individualist Ethics in Ellison, Burke, and Emerson', *PMLA*, 114.1 (1999), pp. 46–63; Timothy Parish, 'Ralph Ellison, Kenneth Burke, and the Form of Democracy', *Arizona Quarterly*, 51, no. 3 (Autumn 1995), pp. 117–48; Donald E. Pease, 'Ralph Ellison and Kenneth Burke: The Nonsymbolizable (Trans)Action', *boundary 2*, 30, no. 2 (Summer 2003), pp. 65–96.

211 Literature is 'designed for the express purpose of arousing emotion'. Kenneth Burke, *Counter-Statement* (Berkeley, CA, 1968) p. 123.

212 On Burke's inability to discriminate high from low, see R. P. Blackmur, *Language as Gesture* (New York, 1952), p. 393; René Wellek, *A History of Modern Criticism* (London, 1986), vol. VI, p. 255; Angus Fletcher, 'Volume and Body in Burke's Criticism', in *Representing Kenneth Burke*, ed. Hayden White and Margaret Brose (Baltimore, 1982), p. 172.

213 Kenneth Burke, *Permanence and Change* (Berkeley, CA, 1984), pp. 102, 275. Since Burke felt that 'all life' can be linked to 'the writing of poetry', it was not a big step to suggest 'a "dyslogistic" adjective is the equivalent of a blow – and enough of them can lead to one'. *Permanence and Change*, pp. 101, 320. Burke described literary criticism (in terms that recall Pound and Brecht) as 'a game [that] is best to watch, I guess, when one confines himself to the single unit and reports on its movements like a radio commentator broadcasting the blow-by-blow description of a prizefight'. Kenneth Burke, 'Symbolic Action in a Poem by Keats', in *A Grammar of Motives* (Berkeley, CA, 1969), p. 451.

214 Ralph Ellison, 'Remembering Richard Wright', in *Going to the Territory*, pp. 215–16.

215 See, for example, Harold Cruse, *The Crisis of the Negro Intellectual* (New York, 1967), pp. 505–11; Lloyd L. Brown, 'The Deep Pit', in *The Critical Response to Ralph Ellison*, ed. Butler, pp. 31–3; Larry Neal, 'Ellison's Zoot Suit', in *Ralph Ellison's Invisible Man: A Casebook*, ed. Callahan, pp. 81–108; John S. Wright, 'To the Battle Royal: Ralph Ellison and the Quest for Black Leadership in Postwar America', in *Recasting America*, ed. Larry May (Chicago, 1987), pp. 246–66.

216 In the posthumously published fragment of Ellison's last novel, the Rev. Hickman preaches the need to 'Roll with the punches like ole Jack Johnson.' Ralph Ellison, *Juneteenth*, ed. John F. Callahan (Harmondsworth, 2000), p. 129.

217 Ralph Ellison, *Trading Twelves: The Selected Letters of Ralph Ellison and Albert Murray*, ed. Murray and John F. Callahan (New York, 2000), p. 132. On this letter and Ellison as 'a Jack Johnson intellectual', see Tim Parrish, 'The Fight to be a Negro Leader', in *The Cambridge Companion to Ralph Ellison*, ed. Ross Posnock (Cambridge, 2005), p. 147.

## 9 King of the Hill, and Further Raging Bulls

1 Jeff Neal-Lunsford, 'Sport in the Land of Television: The Use of Sport in Network Prime-Time Schedules 1946–50', *Journal of Sport History*, 19, no. 1 (Spring 1992), pp. 56–76.

2 Randy Roberts, 'The Wide World of Muhammad Ali: The Politics and Economics of Televised Boxing', in *Muhammad Ali, The People's Champ*, ed. Elliott J. Gorn (Urbana, IL, 1995), p. 28.

3 Quoted in Benjamin Rader, *In Its Own Image: How Television Transformed Sports* (New York, 1984), p. 18.

4 Quoted in Thomas Doherty, *Cold War, Cool Medium* (New York, 2003), p. 6.

5 See, for example, Mary Pat Kelly, *Martin Scorsese: A Journey* (London, 1992), p. 122; Joyce Carol Oates, *On Boxing* (London, 1988), p. 82; Herb Boyd, with Ray Robinson II, *Pound for Pound: A Biography of Sugar Ray Robinson* (New York, 2005), pp. 3–4; Paul Zimmer, *After the Fire* (Minneapolis, 2002), p. 100. Robinson and Louis both also appeared on Ed Murrow's CBS *Person to Person* series. J. Fred MacDonald, *Blacks and White TV: Afro-Americans in Television since 1948* (Chicago, 1983), p. 37.

6 Gerald Early, 'The Passing of Jazz's Old Guard', in *Tuxedo Junction* (Hopewell, NJ, 1989), p. 307.

7 Henry Louis Gates, Jr., *Colored People* (New York, 1995), p. 20. See also *Cold War, Cool Medium*, p. 73, n. 5.

8 The association was very profitable – Gillette saw its share of the razor market rise from 16 per cent in the 1930s to more than 60 per cent in the late 1950s.

9 John Lardner, 'That Was Pugilism: Toledo, 1919', *The New Yorker*, 6 December 1949, p. 71.

10 A. J. Liebling, *The Sweet Science* (Harmondsworth, 1982), pp. 100, 156, 201, 181. In further essays, determined not to use the same name twice, he referred to Egan as the Thucydides, Colly Knickerbocker, and Sainte-Beuve of the London Prize Ring. *A Neutral Corner*, ed. Fred Warner and James Barbour (New York, 1990), pp. 3, 46, 129, 136, 158, 162, 192.

11 David Remnick, *King of the World: Muhammad Ali and the Rise of an American Hero* (London, 1999), p. 46.

12 David Remnick, 'Reporting It All', *The New Yorker*, 29 March 2004, p. 52. See also Gerald Early, '"I Only Like It Better When The Pain Comes": More Notes Toward a Cultural Definition of Prizefighting', *Tuxedo Junction*, pp. 144–6.

13 Fred Warner, 'Afterword', *A Neutral Corner*, p. 239.

14 Liebling, *A Neutral Corner*, p. 87.

15 Robert Warshaw, *The Immediate Experience* (Cambridge, MA, 2001), p. 75.

16 Liebling, *The Sweet Science*, pp. 15–29. Joyce Carol Oates, not a fan of Liebling, nevertheless agreed with him about television. *On Boxing*, pp. 50, 53, 82. Wole Soyinka also complained about the 'cosy insulation' of 'teleglow'. 'Muhammad Ali at Ringside, 1985', in *Mandela's Earth* (New York, 1990), p. 47. Norman Mailer was more confident of his ability to communicate with boxers 'through the tube'. *Pieces and Pontifications* (London, 1985), p. 76. See also Carlo Rotella, *Cut Time* (Boston, 2003), pp. 6–10.

17 A. J. Liebling, 'The Reporter at Large: The Neutral Corner Art Group', *The New Yorker*, 18 December 1954, p. 75.

18 Liebling, *A Neutral Corner*, pp. 16–44. Descriptions of Stillman's can be found in Budd Schulberg, *The Harder They Fall* (New York, 1947), pp. 89–92; Bert Randolph Sugar, 'Boxing Gyms: A Brief History', in *Shadow Boxers*, ed. John Gattuso (Milford, NJ, 2005), pp. 21–4; Ronald K. Fried, *Corner Men* (New York, 1991), pp. 31–53; Rocky Graziano, with Roland Barber, *Somebody Up There Likes Me* (New York, 1956), pp. 159–60. On Graziano's book, see Gerald Early, 'The Romance of Toughness', *The Culture of Bruising* (Hopewell, NJ, 1994), pp. 101–69.

19 Another film in which a boxing manager is put right by a feisty feminist is *Pat and Mike* (1952).

20 Liebling, *The Sweet Science*, p. 223, n.

21 Truman K. Gibson, Jr., *Knocking Down Barriers: My Fight for Black America* (Chicago, 2005), p. 249.

22 Quoted in Nick Tosches, *Night Train: The Sonny Liston Story* (Harmondsworth, 2001), p. 75.

23 Gibson, *Knocking Down Barriers*, p. 260.

24 Tosches, *Night Train*, pp. 81, 128–9. See also Jeffrey T. Sammons, *Beyond the Ring* (Urbana, IL, 1980), ch. 6; Barney Nagler, *James Norris and the Decline of Boxing* (New York, 1964).

25 Gibson, *Knocking Down Barriers*, pp. 251, 273.

26 Jimmy Cannon, 'This Prize-Fight Racket', in *The Esquire Treasury*, ed. Arnold Gingrich (London, 1954), pp. 410–17.

27 Schulberg subsequently reworked the screenplay as a novel in order to 'put Terry Malloy in proper focus'. *On the Waterfront* (London, 1992), p. x.

28 Organization men were 'the ones of our middle class who have left home, spiritually as well as physically, to take the vows of organization life'. William H. Whyte, *The Organization Man* (Philadelphia, 2002), p. 3. Paul Buhle and Dave Wager describe the film as a 'narrative alibi' for the filmmakers' testimonies before the HUAC. *Blacklisted* (London, 2003), p. 166. See also 'Schulberg Tells of Red Dictation: Move To Control His Writing Caused Him to Leave Party, Novelist Says in Inquiry', *The New York Times*, 24 May 1951, p. 16.

29 David Riesman, *The Lonely Crowd* (New York, 1950), pp. 17–53, 133–88.

30 James Jones, *From Here to Eternity* (New York, 1953), pp. 48, 701.

31 In the pre-TV setting of the novel, publicity relies on placing the right photographs in the papers. Schulberg, *The Harder They Fall*, pp. 177, 88, 257. Heinz contrasts an empathetic sportswriter with a 'sadistic' chat-show hostess. W. C. Heinz, *The Professional* (Boston, 2001), pp. 202, 235. See also Dennis Barone, '"This Great Spectator Nation": Budd Schulberg's *The Harder They Fall* and the Parallel Growth of the Entertainment Industries', *Aethlon*, 16, no. 2 (Spring 1999), pp. 67–75.

32 In 1950s boxing films good women still tried to avoid watching fights, although this was made more difficult by the fact of television. In Stanley Kubrick's *Killer's Kiss* (1955), a WASP private dancer struggles as her Latino boss tries to kiss her, while, even worse, making her watch an interracial boxing match on TV. The film cuts between the seduction scene and the fight. On Kubrick's roots as a boxing photographer, see Rainer Crone, *Stanley Kubrick: Dreams and Shadows, Photographs 1945–1950* (London, 2005). Kubrick's first film, *The Day of the Fight* (1950), developed out of a photo story.

33 The novel has a classic naturalistic downward trajectory and avoids the redemptive finale. Schulberg, *The Harder They Fall*, pp. 281, 342. Schulberg did not want boxing to be banned, only reformed. Schulberg, *Loser and Still Champion: Muhammad Ali* (London, 1972), p. 13.

34 Jack Gould, 'Rod Serling's Drama Scores a Knockout', *New York Times¸* 12 October 1956.

35 Arthur R. Ashe, Jr., *A Hard Road to Glory* (New York, 1993), vol. III, p. 83. In 1952, the first sustained sociological analysis of 'boxing culture' concluded that it 'tends to work to the eventual detriment of the individual boxer'. S. Kirson Weinberg and Henry Arond, 'The Occupational Culture of the Boxer', *American Journal of Sociology*, 57, 5 (March 1952), p. 468.

36 See, however, Daniel A. Nathan, 'Sugar Ray Robinson, the Sweet Science, and the Politics of Meaning', *Journal of Sport History*, 26, no. 1 (Spring 1999), pp. 163–74.

37 Maya Angelou, *The Heart of a Woman* (London, 1986), p. 3.

38 Boyd, *Pound for Pound*, pp. 50, 58–9, 131–2; Sammons, *Beyond the Ring*, p. 191.

39 Arna Bontemps, *Famous Negro Athletes* (New York, 1964), p. 54.

40 Jake La Motta, with Joseph Carter and Peter Savage, *Raging Bull: My Story* (New York, 1997), p. 148; Boyd, *Pound for Pound*, p. 118.

41 William Nack, 'The Rock', in *The Best American Sportswriting 1994*, ed. Tom Boswell (Boston, 1994), p. 227.

42 Russell Sullivan, *Rocky Marciano: The Rock of His Times* (Urbana, IL, 2005), p. 75, 84.

43 Sulllivan, *Rocky Marciano*, p. 74. A version of Cole Porter's 'You're The Top', in *Anything Goes* (1956), includes the line 'You're a Met soprano, You're Marciano'.

44 Remnick, *King of the World*, p. 25.

45 Marciano holds the record for the longest undefeated run by a heavyweight and for being the only World Heavyweight Champion to go undefeated throughout his career. He defended his title only six times.

46 'Ingemar and Floyd' is a popular children's game in Lasse Hallström's film *My Life as a Dog* (1985), which is set in a small Swedish village in the months leading up to the fight.

47 *Noble Savage*, edited by Jack Ludwig, Keith Botsford and Saul Bellow, was launched in 1959. According to Bellow, it was not to be 'too literary' but should allow writers 'to write in the good old ranging way that was natural to novelists in the '20s'. James Atlas, *Bellow* (London, 2000), pp. 278–9. Five issues were published between March 1960 and October 1962.

48 Harvey Swandos, 'Exercise and Abstinence', *Noble Savage*, 1 (1960), pp. 159–75.

49 John Lardner, 'That Was Pugilism: The White Hopes – I', *The New Yorker*, 25 June 1949, p. 56. See also Mary F. Corey, *The World Through a Monocle: The New Yorker at Midcentury* (Cambridge, MA, 1999), pp. 87–91.

50 Liebling, *A Neutral Corner*, p. 127. In 1953, however, the Hollywood bio-pic *The Joe Louis Story* was unable to get distribution in the South. Ronald Bergan, *Sports in the Movies* (New York, 1982), p. 43.

51 Addison Gayle Jr, *The Black Situation*, in *New Black Voices*, ed. Abraham Chapman (New York, 1972), p. 531.

52 That is also why, he continued, less plausibly, 'the whites applauded Joe for crushing Schmeling'. Eldridge Cleaver, 'The Allegory of the Black Eunuchs', *Soul on Ice* (London, 1968), p. 112.

53 'The Greatest Fights of the Century', *Esquire* (December 1963), discussed in LeRoi Jones, 'The Dempsey-Liston Fight', *Home: Social Essays* (New York, 1966), pp. 155–60.

54 'Dark Laughter', featuring Bootsie, began in the Harlem *Amsterdam News* in 1935; the cartoon was later syndicated in a number of black newspapers.

55 James Baldwin, 'The Fight: Patterson vs. Liston', in Early, *Tuxedo Junction*, p. 333.

56 Jones, *Home*, p. 156.

57 Richard Bak, *Joe Louis: The Great Black Hope* (Cambridge, MA, 1998), p. 276; Jones, *Home*, p. 155; Norman Mailer, *The Presidential Papers* (London, 1964), pp. 240, 242.

58 Remnick, *King of the World*, p. 14. Kennedy and Patterson pose together on the cover of Patterson's autobiography, *Victory Over Myself* (1962). Gerald Early, 'The Unquiet Kingdom of Providence: The Patterson-Liston Fight', in *The Culture of Bruising*, p. 50.

59 William Nack, 'O Unlucky Man', in *The Fights: Photographs by Charles Hoff*, ed. Richard Ford (San Francisco, 1996), p. 66.

60 Martin Luther King, *Why We Can't Wait* (New York, 1963), p. 111.

61 Liebling, *A Neutral Corner*, pp. 160–1.

62 Nack, 'O Unlucky Man', p. 73.

63 Liebling, *A Neutral Corner*, p. 166.

64 Malcolm X, with Alex Haley, *The Autobiography of Malcolm X* (London, 1965), p. 382.

65 Thomas Hauser, *Muhammad Ali: His Life and Times* (London, 1997), p. 19.

66 Jack Olsen, *Cassius Clay: A Biography* (London, 1967), p. 71.

67 Liebling, *A Neutral Corner*, p. 164.

68 Ibid., pp. 215, 217. See also p. 234.

69 Marianne Moore, *The Complete Prose*, ed. Patricia C. Willis (Harmondsworth, 1986), pp. 659–60.

70 See George Plimpton, *Shadow Box* (London, 1989), p. 125.

71 Schulberg, *Loser and Still Champion*, p. 41; Robert Lipsyte, quoted in David W. Zong, 'The Greatest: Ali's Confounding Character', in *Sport and the Color Line*, ed. Patrick B. Miller and David K. Wiggins (London, 2004), p. 290.

72 Olsen, *Cassius Clay*, p. 44.

73 Schulberg, *Loser and Still Champion*, p. 39.

74 Ali gave several different accounts of his introduction to the Nation. Muhammad Ali, with Richard Durham, *The Greatest: My Own Story* (London, 1976), pp. 199–201; Henry Hampton and Steve Fayer, *Voices of Freedom: An Oral History of the Civil Rights Movement* (New York, 1991), pp. 324–5; Olson, *Cassius Clay*, pp. 150–54; Hauser, *Muhammad Ali*, pp. 89–100.

75 Hauser, *Muhammad Ali*, p. 97.

76 See Richard Brent-Turner, *Islam in the African-American Experience* (Bloomington, IN, 2003).

77 See, for example, the Messenger's Address, 28 March 1964, in *The Negro Since Emancipation*, ed. Harvey Wish (Englewood Cliffs, NJ, 1964), p. 178; Olsen, *Cassius Clay*, p. 146.

78 Mike Marquesee, *Redemption Song: Muhammad Ali and the Spirit of the Sixties* (London, 1999), pp. 56–7.

79 Manning Marable, *Race, Reform and Rebellion: The Second Reconstruction in Black America, 1945–1990* (London, 1991), pp. 87–91.

80 *The Autobiography of Malcolm X*, pp. 385.

81 Gerald L. Early, 'Muhammad Ali as Third World Hero', in *This is Where I Came In: Black America in the 1960s* (Lincoln, NE, 2003), p. 7.

82 Sammons, *Beyond the Ring*, p. 182. James Ellroy's byzantine thriller *The Six Cold Thousand* (2001) intertwines Liston and the mob with the CIA, FBI, KKK and the Mormon Church. 1940s boxing provides background material to *The Black Dahlia* (London, 1987).

83 Tosches, *Night Train*, pp. 221–4.

84 William Trowbridge, 'Liston'; Jay Meek, 'Sonny Liston', in *Perfect in Their Art: Poems on Boxing from Homer to Ali*, ed. Robert Hedin and Michael Waters (Carbondale, IL, 2003), pp. 202, 145.

85 Michael A. Gomez, *Black Crescent: The Experience and Legacy of African Muslims in the Americas* (Cambridge, 2005), p. 361.

86 Doctrine stated that the believer was not to know his 'original' name until the second coming of the Nation's founder, Wallace D. Fard Muhammad. Early, 'Muhammad Ali as Third World Hero', p. 10.

87 Sammons, *Beyond the Ring*, p. 195.

88 Hauser, *Muhammad Ali*, pp. 81–4; Marquesee, *Redemption Song*, p. 8.

89 Marquesee, *Redemption Song* p. 9; Bak, *Joe Louis*, p. 278.

90 Frederic Cople Jaher, 'White America Views Jack Johnson,

Joe Louis, and Muhammad Ali', in *Sport in America*, ed. Donald Spivey (Westport, CT, 1985), p. 171.

91 Gomez, *Black Crescent*, pp. 360–61.

92 Jones, *Home*, p. 159.

93 Jeffrey O. G. Ogbar, *Black Power: Radical Politics and African American Identity* (Baltimore, 2004), p. 131.

94 Early, 'Muhammad Ali as Third-World Hero', p. 15.

95 See Maya Angelou, *All God's Children Need Travelling Shoes* (London, 1991), pp. 143–4, 146; *The Autobiography of Malcolm X*, pp. 438–9; Alex Haley, in Hampton and Fayer, *Voices of Freedom*, pp. 329–30.

96 Martin Luther King, 'I Have a Dream', in *A Call to Conscience: The Landmark Speeches of Dr Martin Luther King, Jr.*, ed. Clayborne Crason and Kris Shepard (New York, 2001), p. 83; Malcolm X, 'The Ballot or The Bullet', in *The Norton Anthology of African American Literature*, ed. Henry Louis Gates, Jr and Nellie Y. McKay (New York, 1997), p. 93.

97 Malcolm X, 'Discussion with young civil rights fighters', 1 January 1965, in *Malcolm X talks to Young People*, ed. Steve Clark (New York, 1991), p. 96. See also 'On Afro-American History', 24 January 1965, in *Malcolm X on Afro-American History* (New York, 1967), p. 25.

98 Mark Kram, *Ghosts of Manila* (New York, 2001) p. 123; Hampton and Frayer, *Voices of Freedom*, pp. 326–7; Ali, *The Greatest*, p. 120; Cleaver, *Soul on Ice*, pp. 92–3. See also Robert Lipsyte, 'Clay Knocks Out Patterson in the 12th', *The New York Times*, 23 November 1965.

99 Floyd Patterson with Gay Talese, 'In Defense of Cassius Clay', in *I'm A Little Special: A Muhammad Ali Reader*, ed. Gerald Early (London, 1999), p. 66. In praise of Patterson's essays, see Gerald Early, 'The Black Intellectual and the Sport of Prizefighting', in *The Culture of Bruising*, p. 14.

100 Olson, *Cassius Clay*, p. 195.

101 Henry Cooper, *An Autobiography* (London, 1974), p. 115. Cooper's claim to fame was that he had knocked Ali down in 1963.

102 Ali was not exceptional in this; most blacks had 'great difficulty' in obtaining conscientious objector status. Mary Frances Berry and John W. Blassingame, *Long Memory: The Black Experience in America* (Oxford, 1982), p. 331.

103 Hauser, *Muhammad Ali*, pp. 142–201; Ali, *The Greatest*, pp. 124–5, 160. As early as 1965, SNCC members had declared that blacks should not 'fight in Vietnam for the white man's freedom, until all the Negro people are free in Mississippi'. Marable, *Race, Reform and Rebellion*, p. 85

104 Thomas A. Johnson, 'Boycott of Sports by Negroes Asked', *New York Times*, 24 July 1967, pp. 1, 16. Jerry Gafio Watts, *Amiri Baraka: The Politics and Art of a Black Intellectual* (New York, 2001), p. 305. The 1968 Black Power Conference also issued a statement condemning 'all pretenders to the heavyweight crown of Muhammad Ali as traitors, hypocrites, or both'. Harry Edwards, *The Revolt of the Black Athlete* (New York, 1969), p. 182.

105 Debbie Louis, *And We Are Not Saved: A History of the Movement as People* (New York, 1970), pp. 296–7.

106 William L. Van Deburg, *New Day in Babylon: The Black Power Movement and American Culture, 1965–1975* (Chicago, 1992),

p. 84; Edwards, *The Revolt*, pp. 179, 190. See also Othello Harris, 'Muhammad Ali and the Revolt of the Black Athlete', in *Muhammad Ali*, ed. Gorn, pp. 54–69.

107 Edwards, *The Revolt*, p. 74.

108 Ishmael Reed, 'The Greatest, My Own Story', in *Shrovetide in Old New Orleans* (New York, 1978), p. 122; Fred Halstead, *Out Now!* (New York, 1978), p. 308; Victor Bockris, *Muhammad Ali in Fighter's Heaven* (London, 2000), pp. 38–9; Wayne Glaster, *Black Students in the Ivory Tower* (Amherst, 2002), pp. 29–32.

109 Joe Louis attacked Ali as being 'a guy with . . . a dime's worth of courage'. Quoted in George Whiting, *The Ring*, February 1967, p. 6. Dempsey avoided the First World War and was a dubbed a 'slacker' in his fights with war heroes Carpentier and Tunney (who said Ali 'disgraced' the American flag). Like Louis, however, Dempsey participated in army propaganda in the Second World War. Jaher, 'White America Views Jack Johnson, Joe Louis, and Muhammad Ali', pp. 173–4.

110 Marqusee, *Redemption Song*, pp. 174–5. In general black activists had 'reservations about participating in anti-war organizations dominated by white liberals and leftists'. Marable, *Race, Reform and Rebellion*, p. 101.

111 Early, 'I Only Like It Better', p. 138.

112 Schulberg, *Loser and Still Champion*, p. 39

113 Early, 'Muhammad Ali as Third World Hero', p. 31. See also Elizabeth A. Castelli, 'The Ambivalent Legacy of Violence and Victimhood: Using Early Christian Martyrs to Think With', *Spiritus*, 6 (2006), pp. 1–24.

114 George Lois, *Covering the '60s: The Esquire Era* (New York, 1996), p. 61. On Lois's other boxer-covers, James Hughes, 'The Graphic Arts: George Lois', *Stop Smiling*, no. 20 (2005), pp. 22–3.

115 Mark Feeney, 'Judged by their Covers', *Boston Globe*, 18 October 2005, C3. See Leonard Shechter, 'The Passion of Muhammad Ali', *Esquire* (April 1968), pp. 128–60.

116 Holland Cotter, 'Benny Andrews at the Studio Museum in Harlem', *Art in America*, 77 (September 1989), p. 212.

117 Andrews may also have been thinking of Robert Riggs's lithograph, *Little Brown Brother* (1932).

118 Quoted in Sharon F. Patton, *African-American Art* (Oxford, 1998), p. 191. The fate of the ex-fighter was the subject of Clay Goss's one-act play, 'Of Being Hit', first produced at Howard University in 1970. *Homecookin': Five Plays* (Washington, DC, 1974), pp. 65–80. On the retiring boxers, see Nathan Hare, 'The Study of the Black Fighter', in *Speech and Power*, ed. Gerald Early (Hopewell, NJ, 1992), vol. I, pp. 158–66.

119 An exception was a political cartoon, reprinted in the magazine in 1968. There, 'Ali is seen hung on the cross, arms outstretched, hands covered by boxing gloves. Several pairs of white hands rip off Ali's clothes, which are imprinted with the caption, "World Champion". One pair of white hands throws dice.' Below the cartoon, the editorial states: 'Christian Cross, which is responsible for so much oppression of Black people, was depicted recently . . . as the instrument by which Muhammad Ali was "crucified" at hands of white

America.' Quoted in Edward E. Curtis IV, 'Islamizing the Black Body: Ritual and Power in Elijah Muhammad's Nation of Islam', *Religion and American Culture*, 12, no. 2 (Summer 2002), pp. 170–71. Ali also featured in a controversially anti-Semitic cartoon which was published in the SNCC newsletter in the summer of 1967, as an accompaniment to an article about the Six-Day War. Ali and Nasser are depicted with nooses around their necks; a hand marked with a Star of David and dollar signs is holding the rope; an arm, inscribed 'Third World Liberation Movements', is poised to cut it. Robert G. Weisbord and Richard Kazarian Jr., *Israel in the Black American Perspective* (Westport, CT, 1985), pp. 33–5. See also Melani McAlister, 'One Black Allah: The Middle East in the Cultural Politics of African American Liberation, 1955–1970', *American Quarterly*, 51, no. 3 (1999), pp. 622–56.

120 Wallace Terry, 'Bringing the War Home', *Black Scholar*, 2, no. 3 (1970), pp. 6–18; Terry, *Bloods: An Oral History of the Vietnam War* (New York, 1984), p. xvi.

121 Quoted in Thomas Cripps, 'The Noble Black Savage: A Problem in the Politics of Television Art', *Journal of Popular Culture*, 8, no. 4 (Spring 1975), p. 693. For a comparison of 'the courting of pet primitives such as . . . José Torres' by sixties New Yorkers to the courting of prizefighters by the Regency aristocracy, see Tom Wolfe, *Radical Chic and Mau-Mauing the Flak Catchers* (New York, 1971), pp. 39, 65.

122 'No matter what we say to Whitey, we always end up as his entertainment'. John Oliver Killens, *The Cotillion* (New York, 1971), p. 180. *Esquire*'s list of signatories included Ralph Ellison, Kenneth Burke and Katherine Anne Porter.

123 The musical was adapted by Oscar Brown Jr. from Joseph Dolan Tuotti's play, *Big Time Buck White*, which was first performed by Budd Schulberg's Watts Writers Workshop. See *The Grove Press Reader, 1951–2001*, ed. Stanley Gonferski (New York, 2001), pp. 258–65; Ali, *The Greatest*, pp. 239–42.

124 Jaher, 'White America Views Jack Johnson, Joe Louis, and Muhammad Ali', pp. 175–6. On the Quarry fight, José Torres, *Sting Like a Bee* (London, 1971), ch. 1. On the importance of closed-circuit television for boxing in this period, see Anna McCarthy, '"Like an earthquake!" theater television, boxing, and the black public sphere', *Quarterly Review of Film and Video*, 16, nos 3–4 (1999), 307–23.

125 Schulberg, *Loser and Still Champion*, pp. 108, 144.

126 Ibid., ch. 6.

127 Gwendolyn Brooks, *Black Steel: Joe Frazier and Muhammad Ali* (Detroit, 1971). In 1935 Brooks had written a very different 'Song for Joe Louis': 'Unspoken words are stronger / Ungiven smiles are sweet; / Staid ice is best cover / For strength's resourceful heat.' Quoted in George E. Kent, *A Life of Gwendolyn Brooks* (Lexington, KY, 1990), p. 36.

128 Norman Mailer, *Existential Errands* (New York, 1973), p. 41.

129 Oates, *On Boxing*, pp, 25, 79.

130 Mailer, *Existential Errands*, p. 42.

131 Norman Mailer, *The Fight* (London, 1975), p. 22; V. S. Naipaul, *The Writer and the World* (London, 2002), p. 207.

132 Charles Lemert, *Muhammad Ali: Trickster in the Culture of Irony* (London, 2003), pp. 145–6.

133 Christian K. Messenger, 'Norman Mailer: Boxing and the Art of His Narrative', *Modern Fiction*, 33, 1 (Spring 1987), p. 98.

134 Edwards, *The Revolt*, pp. 106–7.

135 Kram, *Ghosts of Manila*, p. 163; Lemert, *Muhammad Ali*, p. 147.

136 José Torres, 'Ex-Fighter's Notes on the Champion', in *I'm a Little Special*, ed. Early, p. 177. Kram argues that Ali learnt this, like much else, from Archie Moore. *Ghosts of Manila*, pp. 70–1.

137 Lemert, *Muhammad Ali*, p. 24.

138 Ali, *The Greatest*, pp. 258, 412.

139 Kram, *Ghosts of Manila*, p. 185.

140 Joyce Carol Oates, 'The Cruellest Sport', in *I'm a Little Special*, p. 264.

141 Mark Tobichaux, *Cable Cowboy: John Malone and the Rise of the Modern Cable Business* (New York, 2002), p. 46. Pay Cable began in 1972 as a regional service. In 1973, HBO transmitted the Foreman vs. Frazier fight from Kingston, Jamaica. By 1996, boxing accounted for 57 per cent of all pay-per-view programming. Howard J. Blumenthal and Oliver R. Goodenough, *The Business of Television* (New York, 1998), p. 83; Walter Ciciora, James Farmer, David Large and Michael Adams, *Modern Cable Television Technology* (San Francisco, 2004), p. 11.

142 See Richard Pryor's monologue on Ali vs. Spinks, *Live in Concert* (1979).

143 Quoted in Oates, 'The Cruellest Sport', p. 264.

144 Ali, *The Greatest*, p. ix; Remnick, *King of the World*, p. 90. On Durham's 'frustrating' experience writing the book, see Leon Forrest, 'Elijah', in *Relocations of the Spirit* (Wakefield, RI, 1994), p. 69. Forrest worked with Durham on the staff of *Muhammad Speaks* and took over as managing editor in 1972. See also Maureen Smith, '*Muhammad Speaks* and Muhammad Ali', in *With God on Their Side: Sport in the Service of Religion*, ed. Tara Magdalinski and Timothy J. L. Chandler (London, 2002), pp. 177–96.

145 Ali, *The Greatest*, pp. 117, 193. Gerald Early, 'Some Preposterous Propositions from the Heroic Life of Muhammad Ali: A Reading of *The Greatest: My Own Story*', in *Muhammad Ali*, ed. Gorn, p. 71–2.

146 Early, 'Some Preposterous Propositions', p. 83.

147 Ali, *The Greatest*, pp. 21, 320.

148 Ibid., p. 52, 244.

149 Ibid., p. 34. See also Ogbar, *Black Power*, pp. 38–9.

150 Ibid., p. 35.

151 Ibid., p. 63.

152 Ibid., pp. 69, 76. On the apocryphal nature of this story, see Remnick, *King of the World*, p. 89.

153 Ibid., p. 197. Ali also adopted some of his predecessor's lines and gimmicks. 'Just like him to pick up some crazy notion from that film', complained Angelo Dundee. Plimpton, *Shadow Box*, pp. 151–4. See Ali A. Mazrui, 'Boxer Muhammad Ali and Soldier Idi Amin as International Political Symbols', *Comparative Studies in Society and History*, 19, no. 2 (April 1977), pp. 189–215.

154 Ali, *The Greatest*, p. 62. Alex Haley, *Roots* (London, 1977), pp. 627, 628.

155 James Baldwin, 'How One Black Man Came to be an American: Review of *Roots*', *The New York Times Book Review*, 26 September 1976, pp. 1–2.

156 Bergan, *Sport in the Movies*, pp. 39–40.

157 Bockris, *Muhammad Ali in Fighter's Heaven*, p. 118.

158 Ibid., p. 126.

159 Marqusee, *Redemption Song*, p. 286.

160 Ibid., p. 2.

161 Lemert, *Muhammad Ali*, p. 22.

162 Marqusee, *Redemption Song*, p. 5.

163 Marable, *Race, Reform and Rebellion*, p. 131; Hauser, *Muhammad Ali*, p. 281. William Klein's film of the Liston fights, *Muhammad Ali, The Greatest*, was released in 1974.

164 Jaher, 'White America Views Jack Johnson, Joe Louis, and Muhammad Ali', p. 178.

165 Brent-Turner, *Islam in the African-American Experience*, p. xxix; Weisbord and Kazarian Jr., *Israel in the Black American Perspective*, p. 46; Michael Ellison, 'Muhammad Ali joins the fight with TV message to win over Muslims', *The Guardian*, 24 December 2001, p. 9.

166 Marqusee, *Redemption Song*, p. 5.

167 Quoted in Davis Miller, *The Zen of Muhammad Ali* (London, 2002), pp. 17, 37.

168 Hana Ali, *More Than A Hero* (New York, 2000); Hana Ali and Muhammad Ali, *The Soul of a Butterfly: Reflections on Life's Journey* (New York, 2004); Laila Ali, with David Ritz, *Reach: Finding Strength, Spirit and Personal Power* (New York, 2003).

169 Jim Stynes, Paul Currie and Jon Carnegie, *Heroes: a guide to realizing your dreams* (London, 2003), p. 10; Michele Ingber Drohan, *Learning About Strength of Character from the Life of Muhammad Ali* (New York, 1999); Ntozake Shange, *Float Like a Butterfly*, with illustrations by Edel Rodriguez (New York, 2002). 'Because of Ali, after nearly ten years of trying, I am finally able to eke out a living as a writer', admits Miller, *The Zen of Muhammad Ali*, p. 23. See also Ian Probert, *Rope Burns* (London, 1999).

170 Gerald Early, 'Ali's Rumble', *Sight and Sound*, 7, 5 (May 1997), pp. 10–12.

171 Sam B. Girgus finds no problem in the fact that a film which 'glorifies all things black' depends on Mailer and Plimpton as its sole 'informed participants and commentators'. Girgus, *America on Film* (Cambridge, 2002), p. 104. See also Lemert, *Muhammad Ali*, pp. 143–4 and Grant Farred, 'Feasting on Foreman: *When We Were Kings* as Hagiography', *Camera Obscura*, 39 (September 1996), pp. 52–77.

172 Julio Rodriguez, 'Documenting Myth: Racial Representation in Leon Gast's *When We Were Kings*', in *Sports Matters: Recreation, Race and Culture*, ed. John Bloom and Michael Nevin Willard (New York, 2002), pp. 209–22.

173 Grant Farred, *What's My Name?: Black Vernacular Intellectuals* (Minneapolis, 2003), pp. 8, 29, 47–9.

174 Farred, *What's My Name?*, p. 87.

175 Hauser, *Muhammad Ali*, p. 78.

176 '*The Greatest, My Own Story*', p. 124. Cassius was nearly called Rudolph Valentino Clay. His younger brother was given the name instead. Ali, *The Greatest*, pp. 78, 144; Kram, *Ghosts of Manila*, pp. 27–8, 55, 129, 169; Hauser, *Muhammad Ali*, p. 313; Ogbar, *Black Power*, p. 27.

177 Michael Oriard, 'Muhammad Ali: The Hero in the Age of Mass Media', in *Muhammad Ali*, ed. Gorn, p. 10; Jeffrey T. Sammons, 'Rebel with a Cause: Muhammad Ali as Sixties Protest Symbol', in *Muhammad Ali*, ed. Gorn, p. 161. 'The World's Greatest Athlete is in danger of being our most beautiful man, and the vocabulary of Camp is doomed to appear', opens Mailer, *The Fight*, p. 9. See also bell hooks, *We Real Cool Men: Black Men and Masculinity* (London, 2004), p. 22.

178 Lemert, *Muhammad Ali*, pp. 7–8; Douglas Rogers, 'The Greatest Show on Earth, Round Two', *The Guardian*, 15 April 2006, p. 3.

179 Greg Levine, 'The "Greatest" Deal: Muhammad Ali Sells Name, Image', *Forbes*, 12 April 2006.

180 Michael Marriott, 'With Food Line, Ali Makes Obesity an Opponent', *New York Times*, 28 June 2006.

181 Bockris, *Muhammad Ali in Fighter's Heaven*, pp. 40–41.

182 Amiri Baraka, *The Autobiography*, in *The LeRoi Jones/Amiri Baraka* Reader, ed. William J. Harris (New York, 1991), p. 389.

183 Ogbar, *Black Power*, p. 2; Early, 'Muhammad Ali as Third World Hero', p. 4.

184 James H. Cone, *Martin and Malcolm and America* (Maryknoll, NY, 1991), p. 229; Marqusee, *Redemption Song*, p. 193. James Brown, 'Say It Loud – I'm Black and I'm Proud (Part I)' was released in Spring 1968. See also James Brown, *The Godfather of Soul* (London, 1988), pp. 26–7, 37–8. By the mid-seventies, Baraka, now a Maoist, rejected what he termed 'so called nationalism': an Ali-inspired 'I AM THE GREATEST-ISM', he declared, was just another form of sectarianism. Quoted in Werner Sollors, *Amiri Baraka/LeRoi Jones: The Quest for a 'Populist Modernism'* (New York, 1978), p. 230.

185 Vincent Harding, 'A Long Time Coming: Reflections on the Black Freedom Movement 1955–1972', in *Transition and Conflict: Images of a Turbulent Decade, 1963–1973*, exh. cat., Studio Museum in Harlem (New York, 1985), p. 41.

186 'The restoration of our cultural roots and history,' Malcolm X declared, 'will restore dignity to the black people in this country.' *Malcolm X: Speeches at Harvard*, ed. Archie Epps (New York, 1968), p. 142. See Van Deburg, *New Day in Babylon*, pp. 272–80.

187 Sonia Sanchez, 'Blk/rhetoric', in *We a BaddDDD People* (Detroit, 1970), p. 15. 'The work of the poets', wrote Carolyn Gerald in 1969, is 'to give us back our heroes and to provide us with new ones'. Quoted in Abby Arthur Johnson and Ronald Maberry Johnson, *Propaganda and Aesthetics: The Literary Politics of Afro-American Magazines in the Twentieth Century* (Amherst, MA, 1979), p. 171. On the limited politics of hero worship, see William Keorapetse Kgositsile, 'Paths to the Future', in *The Black Aesthetic*, ed. Addison Gayle, Jr (New York, 1970), p. 255.

188 Jayne Cortez, 'How Long Has Trane Been Gone' (1969), in *The Norton Anthology of African American Literature*, pp. 1957–9.

189 Soul Brother # 44 (Ernest White) provided a Civil Rights

family tree, Dr and Mrs M. L. King are 'Pa' and 'Ma', Rosa Parks is 'Sister' and Ali 'Brother'. *Why We March* (New York, 1969), p. 87. See also Larry Neal, 'Some Reflections on the Black Aesthetic', in *The Black Aesthetic*, ed. Gayle, pp. 13–16; Malcolm X, *By Any Means Necessary* (New York, 1970), pp. 124–5. Numerous poems and songs imagined a future nation of 'chocolate cities' in which Ali occupied the White House, or at the very least was warmly celebrated in the names of streets. Parliament, 'Chocolate City', *Chocolate City* (Casablanca, 1975); Van Deburg, *New Day in Babylon*, p. 286. Today Louisville has a Muhammad Ali Boulevard and Plaza.

190 At the dedication ceremony, Gwendolyn Brooks and Don L. Lee read poems to the 'mighty black wall'. Don L. Lee, 'The Wall', in *Understanding the New Black Poetry*, ed. Stephen Henderson (New York, 1973), pp. 334–5; Gwendolyn Brooks, 'Two Dedications, Part 2, The Wall', in *The Norton Anthology of African American Literature*, p. 1594. See also Michael D. Harris, 'Urban Totems: The Communal Spirit of Black Murals', in James Pigolf and Robin H. Dunitz, *Walls of Heritage, Walls of Pride: African American Murals* (San Francisco, 2000), p. 24. On the influence of Mexican mural art, Mary Schmidt Campbell. *Transition and Conflict*, p. 49; see also pp. 56–7.

191 The *Wall of Respect* led to 'more than 1,500 murals in virtually every urban black community in the nation'; by 1975, there were 200 in Chicago alone. The *Wall of Dignity* was painted in Detroit in 1968, the *Wall of Truth* in Chicago in 1969 and the *Wall of Consciousness* in Philadelphia in 1972. Atlanta and St Louis also had Walls of Respect. See Jeff R. Donaldson and Geneva Smitherman Donaldson, 'Upside the Wall', in *The People's Art: Black Murals, 1967–1978* (Philadelphia, 1986).

192 Pinkney, quoted in Pigolf and Dunitz, *Walls of Heritage, Walls of Pride*, p. 188.

193 See, for example, Ishmael Reed, 'white hope', in *Conjure. Selected Poems, 1963–1970* (Amherst, MA, 1972), p. 68.

194 Randy Roberts, *Papa Jack: Jack Johnson and the Era of White Hopes* (London, 1986), p. 228. See also Al Buck, 'Clay–Johnson Parallels Warn Cassius Beware', *The Ring* (June 1966), p. 12.

195 Remnick, *King of the World*, p. 224; Hauser, *Muhammad Ali*, p. 206.

196 Samella Lewis, *African American Art and Artists* (Berkeley, CA, 2003), p. 163.

197 Quoted in Elsa Honig Fine, *The Afro-American Artist* (New York, 1982), pp. 262–3. *Le Noir est une Couleur* was the title of an exhibition of European avant-garde painting shown at the Galerie Maeght in Paris in 1946.

198 Lewis, *African American Art and Artists*, pp. 147–9; Milly Heyd, *Mutual Reflections: Jews and Blacks in American Art* (New Brunswick, NJ, 1999), p. 192. See also Richard J. Powell, *Black Art and Culture in the 20th Century* (London, 1997), pp. 125–6.

199 Jones also claimed to have drawn on William H. Grier and Price M. Cobbs's *Black Rage* (1968) as a 'socio-psychological aid'. James Earl Jones, 'Jack Johnson is Alive and Well . . . On Broadway', *Ebony* (June 1969), p. 60.

200 Remnick, *King of the World*, p. 224.

201 Ali, *The Greatest*, p. 317. In 1979 Ali appeared as a Reconstruction senator in the NBC adaptation of Howard Fast's novel, *Freedom Road*. Although stories of slavery and Reconstruction remained popular during the seventies, black athletes were no longer cast as Uncle Tom. Instead, Ken Norton played a sexy fighting buck in *Mandingo* (1975) and *Drum* (1976), and the football star O.J. Simpson played a boxer in *Goldie and the Boxer* (1979). MacDonald, *Blacks and White TV*, p. 232; Donald Bogle, *Toms, Coons, Mulattoes, Mammies and Bucks* (New York, 1986), p. 243.

202 See Nicholas Naylor, 'Muhammad Ali, Jack Johnson, and the "Problem" of Interracial Relationships: A Re-view of Martin Ritt's *The Great White Hope* (1970)'; *Scope: An Online Journal of Film Studies*: http://www.scope.nottingham.ac.uk.

203 Vincent Canby, '"Great White Hope" Brought to Screen', *New York Times*, 12 October 1970, p. 46. During the Quarry fight, Drew Bundini Brown famously yelled that there was a 'ghost in the house' – Johnson's ghost was watching. Ali, *The Greatest*, p. 320.

204 Bergan, *Sports in the Movies*, p. 36. See also Pauline Kael, 'The Current Cinema: Clobber-Movie', *The New Yorker*, 17 October 1970, pp. 155–7.

205 Cayton and Jacobs had long been keen collectors of historical fight films and their rights. Some of these were shown in a popular TV show, 'Greatest Fights of the Century', that followed Gillette's Friday Night Fights from 1948 to 1954. The two men eventually amassed a library of 16,000 boxing films, Big Fights Inc., which they used as the basis for numerous documentaries, including *Legendary Champions* (1968) and *a.k.a. Cassius Clay* (1970). Hauser, *Muhammad Ali*, pp. 195–6.

206 Davis's approach was very different from that of Wynton Marsalis, who, for the soundtrack to Ken Burns's PBS documentary *Unforgivable Blackness* (Blue Note, 2004), drew faithfully on the ragtime and blues of Johnson's era.

207 Miles Davis, with Quincy Troupe, *The Autobiography* (London, 1990), p. 305.

208 Davis, *The Autobiography*, p. 164.

209 Gerald Early, 'The Art of the Muscle: Miles Davis as American Knight and American Knave', in *Miles Davis and American Culture*, ed. Early (St Louis, 2001), pp. 3–23. See also Peter Relic, 'Knockout! The Potent Presence of boxing in the life and music of Miles Davis', *Stop Smiling*, no. 20 (2005), pp. 32–7. Billie Holiday boxed as a teenager but stopped after another girl hit her on the nose. 'I took my gloves off and beat the pants off her. The gym teacher got so sore, I never went near the school gym again.' Her brother Henry 'grew up to be a prize fighter and then a minister'. Billie Holiday, with William Dufty, *Lady Sings the Blues* (New York, 1976), pp. 10, 7.

210 'When I look at a drummer,' said Davis, 'it's just like when I look at a fighter'. Arthur Taylor, *Notes and Tones: Musician-to-Musician Interviews* (London, 1983), p. 12.

211 Boyd, *Pound for Pound*, p. 18; Taylor, *Notes and Tones*, p. 119.

212 Davis, *The Autobiography*, p. 305.

213 Miles Davis, *A Tribute to Jack Johnson* (Columbia Records, 1971).

214 The film did not do well commercially and so Davis's album was largely ignored. Today it is much admired and in 2003 Columbia released *The Complete Jack Johnson Sessions*, including tributes to Roberto Durán, Archie Moore, Johnny Bratton, Sugar Ray Robinson and Ali. Davis also recorded 'Ezz-thetic', George Russell's tribute to Charles Ezzard, on *Conception* (Prestige, 1951).

215 Ishmael Reed, 'The Fourth Ali' (1978), in *God Made Alaska for the Indians* (New York, 1982), p. 62. Reed's 1972 novel *Mumbo Jumbo* explored parallels between 'the black cultural and political spectrum' of the twenties and that of the sixties. See Reed, *Shrovetide in Old New Orleans*, pp. 130–31. When the book was published, Reed's friend Richard Brautigan presented him with the 'original front-page description of Jack Johnson's defeat of Jim Jeffries'. Reed said this amounted to 'overpraise', and suggested his style was closer to that of Larry Holmes. Ishmael Reed, *Writin' Is Fightin'* (New York, 1988), pp. 3–8.

216 See Philip Brian Harper, *Are We Not Men? Masculine Anxiety and the Problem of African-American Identity* (Oxford, 1996), p. 50.

217 James Baldwin, in *James Baldwin & Nikki Giovanni, A Dialogue* (London, 1975), p. 39; Larry Neal, 'And Shine Swam On', in *Black Fire: An Anthology of Afro-American Writing*, ed. LeRoi Jones and Larry Neal (New York, 1968), p. 646; Albert Murray, *The OmniAmericans* (New York, 1970), p. 30.

218 Jones and Neal, Introduction to *Black Fire*, p. xxiii. See also Geneva Smitherman 'The Power of the Rap: The Black Idiom and The New Black Poetry', *Twentieth Century Literature*, 19, no. 4 (October 1973), pp. 259–74; Michele Wallace, *Black Macho and the Myth of the Superwoman* (London, 1979), p. 47; Robyn Wiegman, *American Anatomies* (Durham, NC, 1995), pp. 108–10; Marable, *Race, Reform and Rebellion*, pp. 95, 164–6.

219 Franz Fanon, *The Wretched of the Earth*, trans. Constance Farrington (New York, 1963), p. 240. See Marable, *Race, Reform and Rebellion*, pp. 107–8; Alvin Pouissant, 'An Overview of Fanon's Significance to the American Civil Rights Movement', in *International Tribute to Frantz Fanon*, Record of the Special Meeting of the UN Special Committee Against Apartheid, 3 November 1978, pp. 59–66. Stokely Carmichael's and Charles V. Hamilton's preface to *Black Power: The Politics of Liberation in America* ends with a quote from Fanon. *Black Power* (New York, 1967), p. xii.

220 Franz Fanon, *Black Skin, White Masks*, trans. Charles Lam Markmann (London, 1986), pp. 158, 166.

221 Fanon, *Black Skin, White Masks*, p. 225.

222 Cleaver, 'Allegory', p. 111. See also Jones, *Home*, p. 229; John Hoberman, *Darwin's Athletes* (Boston, 1997), ch. 5.

223 Reed, 'The Fourth Ali', p. 39.

224 Sonny Liston remained 'the mindless Body' and for Cleaver, that was the source of his appeal to whites. Cleaver, 'Allegory', p. 112. After Liston was defeated by 'the lippy punk from Louisville', William Trowbridge wrote, 'We felt / Betrayed, diminished, tongue tied by that /Prattling dancer with the couplets and pretty face. / We wanted blood, teeth. Nothing fancy.' *Perfect in Their Art*, p. 202.

225 Jones, *Home*, pp. 109–10.

226 Jones, 'The Changing Same (R&B and New Black Music)', in *Black Fire*, ed. Jones and Neal, pp. 121–2. See also *Home*, p. 170.

227 Van Deburg, *New Day in Babylon*, pp. 285–6.

228 Ishmael Reed, *19 Necromancers From Now* (1970), in *New Black Voices*, ed. Chapman, pp. 519–20. See also 'Ishmael Reed – Self Interview', p. 129.

229 Ishmael Reed, 'Railroad Bill, A Conjure Man', in *Chattanoga* (New York, 1973), pp. 9–15.

230 LeRoi Jones, 'Black Dada Nihilismus', in *The Dead Lecturer* (New York 1964), pp. 61–4. Jones recorded the poem with the New York Art Quartet on their eponymous 1965 album. See Sollors, *Amiri Baraka/LeRoi Jones*, pp. 90–94; Kimberly W. Benston, *Performing Blackness* (London, 2000), pp. 217, 219; Aldon Lynn Nielsen, *Black Chant: Languages of African-American Postmodernism* (Cambridge, 1997), pp. 190–94.

231 LeRoi Jones, 'Answers in Progress', *Tales*, in *The Fiction of LeRoi Jones/Amiri Baraka* (Chicago, 2000), p. 219.

232 The protagonist of Jones's 1964 play *Dutchman* is a 'would-be poet' called Clay Williams; 'too pretentious to be a Jackson or a Johnson'. *The LeRoi Jones/Amiri Baraka Reader*, p. 84. Ali was named after a noted Kentucky emancipationist; he said Clay was not only a slave name but meant dirt. Hauser, *Muhammad Ali*, p. 84. The phrase 'up against the wall, motherfucker!' first appeared in Jones's 1967 poem, 'Black People', in *The Jones/Baraka Reader*, p. 224. 'One year later, it served as a motto for both the Black Panthers and dissent students at Columbia University.' Johnson and Johnson, *Propaganda and Aesthetics*, p. 172.

233 Jones, 'New-Sense', in *The Fiction of LeRoi Jones/Amiri Baraka*, pp. 195–9.

234 When, following the Newark rebellion, Baraka was tried for illegal possession of firearms, his poem 'Black People!' was produced as evidence of his 'diabolical' intentions. Sollors, *Amiri Baraka/LeRoi Jones*, pp. 199–203.

235 Larry Neal, 'The Black Arts Movement', in *Visions of a Liberated Future: Black Arts Movement Writings*, ed. Michael Schwartz (New York, 1989), p. 78.

236 Neal, 'And Shine Swam On', pp. 654–5; Neal, 'Ellison's Zoot Suit', in *Ralph Ellison's Invisible Man: A Caesebook*, ed. James Callahan (Oxford, 2004), p. 98. See also Houston A. Baker, 'Critical Change and Blues Continuity: An Essay on the Criticism of Larry Neal', *Callaloo*, 23 (Winter 1985), pp. 70–85.

237 Always fond of a boxing analogy, Stanley Crouch said of Neal's early death: 'He was just shaking off the conventions of black nationalist thought that had driven his intellect to the canvas, was in the process of taking a few rounds, and had a grand strategy for what he was going to do all the way through the fifteenth when he left the ring feet first.' Stanley Crouch, 'The Incomplete Turn of Larry Neal', in *Visions of a Liberated Future*, pp. 3–6.

238 'Bootsie' had its origins in the conversations that Harrington observed at the Elite Barber Shop on 7th Avenue: 'Each Saturday morning some of America's top second class citizens filled the Elite air with spirited public debate . . . When Joe Louis was in the chair, traffic was tied up on both

sides of Seventh Avenue.' Oliver Harrington, *Why I Left America* (Jackson, MI, 1993), p. 29. Hughes wrote an introduction for *Bootsie and Others* in 1958. Between 1943 and 1965 Hughes wrote a weekly sketch for the Chicago *Defender* which was widely syndicated. After 1960 it appeared in *Muhammad Speaks.*

239 See Donna A. S. Harper, *Not So Simple: The 'Simple' Stories by Langston Hughes* (St Louis, 1995).

240 Larry Neal, 'Uncle Rufus Raps on the Squared Circle', *Partisan Review* (Spring 1972), in *Speech and Power*, vol. I, ed. Early, pp. 186–92.

241 Compare Langston Hughes's Simple story, 'Bop', in *Black Voices*, ed. Abraham Chapman (New York, 1968), pp. 103–5. See also Early, 'Black Intellectual', p. 18.

242 Terry Baker, 'Humor Collected from a World of Pain', *Phylon*, 28, no. 2 (1967), p. 213; Ishmael Reed, 'The Fourth Ali', p. 44. Elsewhere Reed claimed that Ali's poetry was 'as competent as any of that produced by the New York School although literary critic Joe Frazier commented "Shhhiiit!"' 'The Greatest, My Own Story', in *Shrovetide in Old New Orleans* (New York, 1978), p. 123.

243 Smitherman, 'The Power of the Rap', p. 263. Seminal essays include John Dollard, 'The Dozens: Dialectic of Insult' (1939) and Roger D. Abrahams, 'Playing the Dozens' (1962), in *Mother Wit from the Laughing Barrel*, ed. Alan Dundes (Jackson, MI, 1981), pp. 277–94, 295–309. These form the basis of a 'theory of African-American literary criticism' in Henry Louis Gates, Jr., *The Signifying Monkey* (Oxford, 1988).

244 Gates, *The Signifying Monkey*, pp. 52, 76.

245 Smitherman, 'The Power of the Rap', p. 268. See H. Rap Brown, *Die Nigger Die*, in *Mother Wit*, p. 355; also published as 'Rap's Poem', in *Understanding the New Black Poetry*, ed. Henderson, pp. 187–8.

246 On the importance of 'bragging and scoffing matches' in the 'most diverse cultures', see Johann Huizinga, *Homo Ludens, A Study of the Play Element in Culture* (London, 1970), p. 86. See, for example, Achilles and Agamemnon in the *Iliad*, Book I.

247 'There is nothing so exhilarating as watching well-matched opponents go into action. The entire world likes action, for that matter. Hence prize-fighters become millionaires.' Zora Neale Hurston, 'Characteristics of Negro Expression' in *Negro: An Anthology*, ed. Nancy Cunard (New York, 2002), pp. 28–9.

248 Ali, *The Greatest*, p. 97.

249 Cassius Clay, 'I am the Double Greatest', on *I am the Greatest!*; Nikki Giovanni, 'Ego-Tripping', in *Re: Creation* (Detroit, 1970), pp. 37–8.

250 Ali, in *When We Were Kings*; Ishmael Reed, 'I am a Cowboy in the Boat of Ra', in *New and Collected Poems* (New York, 2006), pp. 21–3.

251 See Shamoon Zamir, 'The Artist as Prophet, Priest and Gunslinger: Ishmael Reed's "Cowboy in the Boat of Ra"', *Callaloo* (Fall 1994), pp. 1205-35.

252 Reed, 'The Fourth Ali', p. 44. Ishmael Reed, interviewed by John O'Brien, in Joe David Bellamy, *The New Fiction* (Urbana, IL, 1974), p. 131.

253 Clay on the eighth round of his up-coming fight with Liston. Part of the 'Will the Real Sonny Liston Fall Down' is on *I Am the Greatest!* A version, 'Clay Comes Out to Meet Liston', is in *Perfect in Their Art*, pp. 16–17.

254 Olson, *Cassius Clay*, pp. 198–9.

255 Raymond Washington, 'Moon bound', in *New Black Voices*, ed. Chapman, pp. 389–90. See also Faith Ringgold's 1969 painting, *Flag for the Moon: Die Nigger*; Paul Gilroy, *Against Race* (Cambridge, MA, 2000), ch. 9.

256 Killens, *The Cotillion*, pp. 1–3, 75, 176. Don L. Lee's poem, 'Gwendolyn Brooks', also satirizes 'nonsensical attempts of Blacks to "outBlack" one another'. Quoted in Smitherman, 'The Power of the Rap', p. 266.

257 Imani Perry, *Prophets of the Hood: Politics and Poetics in Hip Hop* (Durham, NC, 2004), p. 58.

258 Ali, *The Greatest*, pp. 46–7, 89; Olson, *Cassius Clay*, p. 61; Hauser, *Muhammad Ali*, p. 18.

259 Roberts, 'The Wide World', p. 39; Kram, *Ghosts of Manila*, p. 64.

260 Hauser, *Muhammad Ali*, p. 39; Ali, *The Greatest*, pp. 104, 127.

261 Jack London, 'Burns-Johnson', in *Jack London Reports*, ed. King Hendricks and Irving Shepard (New York, 1970), p. 263; Jessie Fauset, 'The Gift of Laughter' in *The New Negro*, ed. Alain Locke (New York, 1997), pp. 161–7.

262 Quoted in Ogbar, *Black Power*, p. 138; Early, *I'm A Little Bit Special*, p. xiv.

263 On TV as 'the chosen instrument of the black revolution', see Cripps, 'The Noble Black Savage', p. 690. Before meeting Malcolm X, Ali knew his face and voice from 'numerous TV debates'. Ali, *The Greatest*, p. 99.

264 Hampton and Fayer, *Voices of Freedom*, p. 325. Ralph Wiley remembers his delight when Ali refused a TV interviewer's demand to 'shut up', while Maxi Jazz of Faithless raps, 'My release from low self esteem / Came when I saw you rapping on my TV screen'. Wiley, *Serenity* (Lincoln, NE, 2000), p. 63; 'Muhammad Ali', on *Outrospective* (Arista, 2001). Occasionally television caused problems for Ali. See Kram, *Ghosts of Manila*, pp. 96–7; Marqusee, *Redemption Song*, pp. 248–9.

265 Mailer, however, complained of Dylan that 'there's something a little boring about a man who comes from a fine Jewish family in Minneapolis sounding like an Oklahoma Okie'. *Pieces and Pontifications*, p. 69.

266 Bob Dylan, 'Who Killed Davey Moore?', on *The Bootleg Series, 1961–1991* (Sony, 1991). Daniel Karlin notes Dylan's habit of opposing a named figure to an anonymous group. 'Bob Dylan's Names', in *Do You, Mr. Jones?*, ed. Neil Cocoran (London, 2003), p. 33. Phil Ochs also wrote a song about Davey Moore, the chorus of which declares, rather predictably, that 'the fighters must destroy as the poets must sing, / as the hungry crowd must gather for the blood upon the ring.' On *The Early Years* (Vanguard, 2000).

267 Rubin Carter, *The Sixteenth Round: From Number One Contender to #45472* (New York, 1974). See also Sam Chaiton and Terry Swinton, *Lazarus and The Hurricane* (New York, 1991).

268 Robert Shelton, *No Direction Home: The Life and Music of Bob Dylan* (London, 1986), pp. 460–61.

269 Bob Dylan and Jacques Lévy, 'Hurricane', on *Desire* (Columbia, 1975). Carter's story forms the basis of *The Hurricane* (1999), directed by Norman Jewison and starring Denzel Washington. Christopher Bruce of Ballet Rambert created a short ballet to accompany Dylan's song. Luke Jennings, 'The Boxer Takes All', *Evening Standard*, 3 May 2001, p. 52.

270 Dylan quoted in Clinton Heylin, *Bob Dylan: Behind the Shades Revisited* (London, 2003), p. 97; Larry Sloman, *On the Road with Bob Dylan: Rolling with the Thunder* (New York, 1978), p. 26. See also Shelton, *No Direction Home*, p. 461; Clinton Heylin, *Dylan: Behind Closed Doors: The Recording Sessions (1960–1994)* (Harmondsworth, 1996), p. 113.

271 Marqusee, *Redemption Song*, p. 152.

272 Bob Dylan, 'I Shall Be Free No. 10', on *Another Side of Bob Dylan* (Columbia, 1964).

273 Simon and Garfunkel, 'The Boxer', on *Bridge Over Troubled Water* (Columbia, 1970). Heylin suggests that Simon borrowed the 'singer/boxer motif' from Elvis's performance in *Kid Creole* and reports that Dylan was 'quite taken with the song'. Heylin, *Bob Dylan: Behind The Shades Revisited*, p. 310. Many thanks to Jim Clemens for drawing this to my attention. Simon had openly parodied Dylan in 'A Simple Desultory Phillipic', on *The Paul Simon Songbook* (1965), and then, with revised lyrics, on the 1966 Simon and Garfunkel album, *Parsley, Sage, Rosemary and Thyme*. The original version includes the line, 'Walter Brennan punched out Cassius Clay'. Both versions of the song make fun of Dylan's tendency to name-drop.

274 Bob Dylan, *Chronicles* (New York, 2004), vol. I, p. 120.

275 Mario Puzo, *The Godfather* (London, 1970), p. 150. Mordecai Richler also presents Dempsey's Bar as a site for fantasies of success in '*real* America'. Richler's protagonist Jake Hersh imagines breaking the jaw of Rocky Graziano (who calls him Hymie), thus wrecking his chances against Tony Zale. *St Urbain's Horseman* (London, 1972), pp. 91–2.

276 Dylan, *Chronicles*, p. 3. The chapter is entitled 'Markin' Up the Score'.

277 Ibid., p. 115

278 Ibid., p. 229.

279 Ibid., p. 119.

280 Ibid., p. 128.

281 Norman Mailer, *The Armies of the Night* (Harmondsworth, 1968), pp. 88, 145.

282 Mailer, *Pieces and Pontifications*, p. 153.

283 Mailer, *The Armies of the Night*, p. 61, 123, 48, 60. See Mary V. Dearborn, *Mailer* (Boston, 1999), p. 109.

284 Mailer, *Pieces and Pontifications*, p. 17. See Joe Moran, *Star Authors* (London, 2000), pp. 70–74.

285 Mailer, *The Armies of the Night*, p. 58.

286 Mailer's second father-in-law had been a professional boxer and 'was always putting on the gloves with me'. *Advertisements for Myself* (London 1985), p. 265. His first encounter with the sport, however, seems to have been through an English novel, Jeffrey Farnol's *The Amateur Gentleman* (1913). Dearborn, *Mailer*, p. 18.

287 The 'unendurable demand' of mid-century was 'to restore metaphor'. Norman Mailer, *Cannibals and Christians* (London 1969), p. 352. Mailer frequently described modernity as 'schizoid'. See, for example, *Advertisements for Myself*, p. 165.

288 Mailer, *Cannibals and Christians*, p. 413. D. H. Lawrence was a 'great writer because he contained a cauldron of boiling opposites'. Norman Mailer, *The Prisoner of Sex* (New York, 1971), p. 137. Richard Poirier sees war as Mailer's key metaphor, while J. Michael Lennon, who argues for Mailer's debt to American Transcendentalism, argues that he is 'interested in RELATION, an idea larger than war and which subsumes it under its rubric.' Poirier, *Mailer* (London 1972), pp. 9–24; J. Michael Lennon, 'Mailer's Cosmology', in *Critical Essays on Norman Mailer*, ed. Lennon (Boston, 1986), p. 150.

289 Mailer, *The Presidential Papers*, pp. 125–48; *Existential Errands*, pp. 195–9.

290 *The Armies of the Night* is subtitled 'History as a Novel, The Novel as History'; *Marilyn* (1973) is a 'novel biography'. Tom Wolfe argues that Mailer uses these phrases because of his 'dread' of being termed a 'journalist'. 'The new journalism', in *The New Journalism: An Anthology*, ed. Tom Wolfe and E. W. Johnson (London, 1975), p. 42.

291 Mailer, *Advertisements for Myself*, p. 275.

292 Mailer, *Existential Errands*, pp. 36. Training is like making love to one's wife with 'carnal indifference'; making 'comfortable love' with a sparring partner is dangerous. When Ali starts fighting like a southpaw, Mailer thinks Foreman must feel like he's 'making love to a brunette when she is wearing a blonde wig'. When Ali lies back on the ropes, he's like a 'working man getting back into bed after a long day to be treated to a little of God's joy by his hardworking wife'. Mailer, *The Fight*, pp. 11, 64, 167, 175.

293 Mailer, *Advertisements for Myself*, pp. 392–416. When Stephen Rojack kisses Cherry Melanie he feels as though he'd 'been sparring with a bigger man and got hit with a full right hand, not a bare fist but a hand in a boxing glove'. Cherry, however, simply compliments him on being 'such a sweet kisser.' *An American Dream* (London, 1965), pp. 113–14.

294 Mailer, *The Presidential Papers*, p. 243.

295 Emile Griffith, in *In This Corner . . .!*, ed. Peter Heller (London, 1989), pp. 383–7. The story forms the basis of Oliver Mayer's play, *Blade to the Heat* (New York, 1996). See David Richards, 'The Boxing Ring as a Parable on Manhood', *The New York Times*, 4 November 1994.

296 For a reading of the fight which concludes that boxing is 'virtually antihomosexual theater', see Gerald Early, 'James Baldwin's Neglected Essay: Prizefighting, the White Intellectual, and the Racial Symbols of American Culture', *Tuxedo Junction*, p. 189.

297 Mailer, *Advertisements*, pp. 269–89.

298 Quoted in W. J. Weatherby, *Squaring-Off: Mailer v. Baldwin* (London, 1977), p. 78.

299 Mailer, *Advertisements*, p. 187.

300 Mailer, *The Deer Park* (New York, 1957), pp. 43, 170, 276, 300.

301 Mailer later totted up the reviews much in the manner of a

boxer's scorecard – 'seven good and eleven bad'. *Advertisements*, p. 211.

302 Ibid., pp. 205–6.

303 Mailer, *Pieces and Pontifications*, p. 145.

304 Mailer, *Advertisements*, p. 21.

305 Ibid., pp. 390–91; *Pieces and Pontifications*, pp. 145–7, 189; *The Presidential Papers*, p. 38.

306 Bobby Kennedy was 'the kind of man never to put on the gloves with if you wanted to do some social boxing, because after two minutes it would be a war, and ego-bastards last long in a war'. JFK, meanwhile, 'carried himself . . . with a cool grace which seemed similar to the poise of a fine boxer, quick with his hands, neat in his timing, and two feet away from his corner when the bell ended the round'. Faced with 'a competition between totalitarianisms', Mailer argued, 'the first maxim of the prizefighter would doubtless apply: "Hungry fighters win fights."' America, it seemed, needed a boxer or two. *The Presidential Papers*, pp. 36, 45, 43–4.

307 David Halberstam, Introduction to *The Best American Sports Writing of the Century* (Boston, 1999), p. xxxi.

308 According to Wolfe, the first piece of journalism that worked 'like a short story' was Gay Talese's 'Joe Louis: the King as a Middle-aged Man' (1962). 'The New Journalism', pp. 23–4.

309 Mailer, *The Presidential Papers*, pp. 213–67; *Pieces and Pontifications*, p. 134.

310 Mailer, *Existential Errands*, pp. 15–42.

311 Messenger, 'Norman Mailer and the Art of His Narrative', pp. 97–8.

312 Mailer, *The Fight*, p. 110. Hazlitt's 'The Fight' was often discussed as an antecedent to the New Journalism. Wolfe disagreed. See 'The New Journalism', pp. 58–9.

313 Mailer guards his territory carefully and finds the very idea of Ali as a purveyor of poetic images disturbing. *The Fight*, pp. 17, 18, 29.

314 Ibid., pp. 13, 19, 43, 47, 54, 57, 83.

315 Ibid., pp. 156, 163, 164.

316 Ibid., pp. 168–70.

317 Michael Cowan, 'The Quest for Empowering Roots: Mailer and the American Literary Tradition', in *Critical Essays on Norman Mailer*, ed. Lennon, pp. 170–71.

318 Mailer, *The Fight*, pp. 179–80.

319 Ibid., pp. 24, 40, 42, 77, 84.

320 Ibid., pp. 93–4.

321 Ibid., pp. 34, 207.

322 Ibid., pp. 109, 142.

323 For Mailer, Hemingway's masculinity lay in a constant struggle with 'cowardice' and an ability to carry 'within him a weight of anxiety' which would have 'suffocated any man smaller than himself.' He wrote these lines in a 1963 book review, and in 1998 reprinted them as a 'prelude', and therefore presumably a self-defining statement, to his greatest-hits-volume, *The Time Of Our Time* (New York, 1998), pp. 3–4. See also *Cannibals and Christians*, p. 192.

324 Mailer, *Advertisements*, pp. 378–88. See also *Cannibals and Christians*, pp. 131–61.

325 Mailer, *Pieces and Pontifications*, p. 69–70. Later he compared himself to Leon Spinks in that, with the publication of his first novel, *The Naked and the Dead*, he became 'champ before he . . . [knew] whether he . . . [could] really fight or not'. Both Ali and Hemingway, Mailer suggests, 'come out of that same American urgency to be the only planet in existence. To be the sun.' In the end, however, Ali is more admirable than Hemingway because 'after Ali got old he still won a couple of great fights', while Hemingway 'didn't make the big knockout . . . in his later books'. *Pieces and Pontifications*, pp. 159–62.

326 Mailer, *Existential Errands*, p. 20.

327 Mailer evokes the example of Harry Greb, 'completely a fighter, the way one might wish to be completely a writer'. *Christians and Cannibals*, pp. 254–5; *Pieces and Pontifications*, p. 23.

328 Byron, *Selected Letters and Journals*, ed. Peter Gunn (Harmondsworth, 1972), p. 142.

329 Mailer, *Pieces and Pontifications*, p. 148.

330 Protesting at the Pentagon in 1967, for example, he tussles with Robert Lowell, a master of feinting with faint praise. *The Armies of the Night*, pp. 29–32.

331 See Mailer, 'Of a Small and Modest Malignancy', pp. 27, 29.

332 Mailer, *Pieces and Pontifications*, pp. 51–2.

333 Ibid., p. 39.

334 Mailer, *Cannibals and Christians*, pp. 210–13. Algren had just published a satirical account of one Norman Manlifellow, the author of *Look Ma, My Fly is Open. Who Lost an American?* (London, 1963), p. 19. Mailer does not mention this attack, but recalls his own swipe at Algren in *Advertisements*, p. 382. As they leave the studio, the talk shifts to middleweights and they shake hands.

335 Mailer, *Pieces and Pontifications*, pp. 65, 67, 73.

336 Morris Dickstein, *Gates of Eden: American Culture in the Sixties* (Cambridge, MA, 1997), p. 162.

337 Mailer, *Advertisements*, pp. 386–7. Later he modified this view, dismissing Baldwin's novels but praising his essays. *Christians and Cannibals*, p. 143.

338 Weatherby, *Squaring-Off*, p. 34.

339 Ibid., p. 112.

340 James Baldwin, *Nobody Knows My Name* (New York, 1961), pp. 216–41.

341 Mailer, *The Presidential Papers*, pp. 250, 256, 266; Weatherby, *Squaring-Off*, pp. 78–82.

342 James Baldwin, *The Fire Next Time* (Harmondsworth 1964), p. 29.

343 Baldwin, *Nobody Knows My Name*, pp. 79–81.

344 Ibid., p. 96.

345 Early, 'James Baldwin's Neglected Essay', p. 192. See also, Early, 'The Unquiet Kingdom of Providence', pp. 57–61.

346 James Baldwin, *No Name in the Street*, in *The Price of the Ticket: Collected Non-fiction, 1948–1985* (London, 1985), p. 498.

347 Philip Fisher, *Hard Facts: Setting and Form in the American Novel* (Oxford, 1986), pp. 171–2.

348 Oates, *On Boxing*, p. 61.

349 La Motta, *Raging Bull: My Story*, p. 189.

350 See David Bordwell and Kristin Thompson, *Film Art: An Introduction* (Boston, 2001), p. 393.

351 Allen Guttmann, *The Erotic in Sports* (New York, 1996), p. 111. Sam B. Girgus, however, sees it as a scene of 'symbolic castration' which makes La Motta equal to the 'feminized' Robinson. *America on Film*, p. 85.

352 According to Louis Menand, the real subject of the film is DeNiro's performance: boxing serves as a metaphor for acting. 'Methods and Madnesses', in *Perspectives on Raging Bull*, ed. Steven G. Kellman (Boston, 1994), pp. 60–68.

353 Steven G. Kellman, 'Introduction', *Perspectives on Raging Bull*, p. 9.

354 Scorsese complained that the book *Raging Bull* was 'very bad' because 'they tried to give a reason for everything Jake did in his life, for his guilt and for his violence.' Quoted in *Scorsese on Scorsese*, ed. Ian Christie and David Thompson (London, 2003), p. 76. His film, however, teases us with possible reasons: La Motta is pathologically jealous of his wife, perhaps struggles with an 'unacknowledged homosexual urge', has been a contender too long, and is angry when he has to throw a fight. He says that he has done 'a lot of bad things', but we don't know what they are.

355 Quoted in Fred Ferretti, 'The Delicate Art of Creating a Brutal Film Hero', *New York Times*, 23 November 1980, D1, p. 28.

356 Screenwriter Paul Schrader, quoted in *Schrader on Schrader*, ed. Kevin Jackson (London, 1990), p. 133. Schrader complained that Scorsese was 'imposing salvation on his subject by fiat'.

357 Scorsese described this as the 'redemption scene' and said that the film was 'about a man who loses everything and then regains it spiritually'. Elsewhere he described the film as a kind of expressionist autobiography; dramatizing La Motta's problems allowed him to 'express' his own. *Scorsese on Scorsese*, pp. 76–7; Les Keyser, *Martin Scorsese* (Boston, 1992), p. 120. Most critics elaborate on this reading. See, for example, Girgus, *America on Film*, pp. 75, 86; Lawrence S. Friedman, *The Cinema of Martin Scorsese* (New York, 1998), pp. 125–6.

358 In the opera, the intermezzo 'suggests a momentary religious sanctuary before a violent confrontation prompted by jealousy'. Barry Leeds, 'Scorsese vs. Mailer: Boxing as Redemption in *Raging Bull* and *An American Dream*', in *Perspectives on Raging Bull*, pp. 134–5.

359 Scorsese said that Buster Keaton, director of *Battling Butler*, was 'the only person who had the right attitude about boxing in movies'. *Scorsese on Scorsese*, pp. 78, 80. Pauline Kael described the film as 'a biography of the genre of prize-fight films'. *Taking It All In* (New York, 1984), pp. 106–12.

360 Dennis Schaefer and Larry Salvato, *Masters of Light: Conversations with Contemporary Cinematographers* (Berkeley, CA, 1984), pp. 122–4.

361 *Scorsese on Scorsese*, p. 83. In real life, a punch does not necessarily make much of a noise; in cinema, 'the sound of the impact is well-nigh obligatory'. Visually punches are so fast that they would 'get lost' on screen; sound 'rubber stamps' the image. Michel Chion, *Audio-Vision*, trans. Claudia Gorman (New York, 1994), pp. 60–2. *Fat City* is one of the very few boxing films which did not amplify the sound of its punches.

362 *Scorsese on Scorsese*, p. 78. Seen as a version of repetitive religious ritual, genre leads to a transcendence of itself. See Leo Braudy, 'The Sacraments of Genre: Coppola, De Palma, Scorsese', *Film Quarterly*, 39, no. 3 (Spring 1986), pp. 17–28.

363 Ferretti, 'The Delicate Art of Creating a Brutal Film Hero', p. 28.

364 Quoted in *Martin Scorsese: A Journey*, p. 125.

365 Marqusee, *Redemption Song*, p. 285.

366 Hauser, *Muhammad Ali*, pp. 296–302.

367 Mike Figgis, 'Sylvester Stallone', in 'Hollywood Film-Makers on Film-Making', *Projections*, 10 (1999), p. 113.

368 Horatio Alger, Jr., *Ragged Dick, Or, Street Life in New York with the Boot Blacks* (New York, 1990), p. 24.

369 *Scorsese on Scorsese*, p. 78. '*Raging Bull* seemed an anti-*Rocky*, a tale of the fall down the museum steps and not the run up.' Keyser, *Martin Scorsese*, p. 110.

370 The relationship between Rocky and Creed reflected that between Stallone and Weathers as well as between Wepner and Ali. This is Stallone's version of how they met: 'Carl Weathers walked in . . . and he had all this arrogance. . . He goes, "You wanna see my body?" He takes his shirt off and he's really built. He says, "I can box a little bit." So I get up with him and he's sort of banging me in the forehead. And then he . . . goes, "You know, I could do a lot better if I was with a real actor." He thought I was the office boy. John says, "Well, he is Rocky. That's the guy." Carl goes, "Huh! Well, I see I won't be having any problem with this movie." I said, "Hire him, immediately. This is exactly what I want." Figgis, 'Sylvester Stallone', p. 113.

371 To become a local hero, Rocky had first, however, to appear on national television. See also Claude Brown, *Manchild in the Promised Land* (New York, 1965), p. 368.

372 Some of Apollo Creed's dialogue is Ali's. Jan Phillip Reemtsma, *More Than A Champion: The Style of Muhammad Ali*, trans. John E. Woods (New York, 1999), p. 83.

373 Matthew Frye Jacobson, *Roots Too: White Ethnic Revival in Post-Civil Rights America* (Cambridge, MA, 2006), p. 101. Both Rocky's habit of training in a meat freezer and running up the steps of the Philadelphia Art Museum were copied from Joe Frazier, who had worked in a slaughterhouse. Kram, *Ghosts of Manila*, p. 58.

374 Early, 'The Romance of Toughness', p. 86.

375 Nack, 'The Rock', p. 227. Woroner staged his initial elimination contests (which included a Jim Jeffries victory over Ali) as radio plays, before approaching Ali and Marciano to make a film. *The Superfight* (1970) had a single showing in 1,500 closed-circuit theatres across the United States and Europe. Since it 'made people in Europe mad' to see Ali lose to Marciano, the BBC produced a different version in which Ali stopped Marciano 'on cuts'. Hauser, *Muhammad Ali*, pp. 196–7. The film was released on DVD in 2005. In 1971 Norman Mailer presented his own imaginary 'superfight', between Marciano and Frazier. 'Nothing could be more strangely sentimental and filled with longing,' says Early,

'The Romance of Toughness', p. 86. See also Romano, *The Boxing Filmography*, pp. 195–7.

376 In *Rocky II*, Creed loses his title, and by III and IV the two men are friends, 'a fantasy', as Tim O'Brien notes, 'that implies that interracial harmony only blossoms as soon as the white man wins'. *The Screening of America* (New York, 1990), p. 87.

377 Jacobson, *Roots Too*, p. 98.

378 The 'White Negro', Mailer wrote in 1957, is a kind of 'frontiersman'. *Advertisements*, p. 272. Sam B. Girgus compares Michael Mann's 1992 adaptation *The Last of the Mohicans* and 2001 bio-pic *Ali* as stories about 'individual and cultural rebirth'. *America on Film*, p. 111.

379 *Superman vs. Muhammad Ali*, DC Comics, no. C–56 (1978), pp. 2–4. The story was by Dennis O'Neil and Neal Adams, with the cover and pencil work by Adams and inks by Dick Giordano and Terry Austin.

380 Ibid., pp. 19, 28, 33–34. On how the sequels enact Rocky's transformation into Ali, see Reemtsma, *More Than a Champion*, pp. 86–114. On Creed's transformation into an 'old-style, self-sacrificing tom', see Donald Bogle, *Toms, Coons, Mulattoes, Mammies and Bucks*, p. 275. On *Rocky Balboa* (2007), see Kasia Boddy, 'Rocky's American Dreams', *opendemocracy.com*, 19 January 2007.

381 After meeting Ali in 1978, Ishmael Reed noted that he had shaken hands 'with the black man they let beat up Superman'. 'The Fourth Ali', p. 42.

382 *Superman vs. Muhammad Ali*, pp. 50, 55, 64, 72–3.

383 Goebbels reputedly thought he was. See Werner Sollors, *Beyond Ethnicity: Consent and Descent in American Culture* (Oxford, 1986), pp. 100–101; Scott Rabb, 'Is Superman Jewish?' in *Superman at Fifty*, ed. Denis Dooley and Gary Engle (New York, 1987); Simcha Weinstein, *Up, Up and Oy Vey!* (New York, 2006), ch. 1.

384 See, for example, Thomas Andrae, 'From Menace to Messiah: The History and Historicity of Superman', in *American Media and Mass Culture*, ed. Donald Lazere (Berkeley, CA, 1987), pp. 124–38.

385 *Superman vs. Muhammad Ali*, p. 42

386 Ibid., p. 33.

387 Natty's use of sophisticated technology relies on his ability to calculate distances and 'a reasoning aim'. James Fenimore Cooper, *The Last of the Mohicans* (Oxford, 1990), pp. 52, 208, 234.

388 *Superman vs. Muhammad Ali*, p. 65. Inspired by Ali's habit of describing himself as a black Superman (and occasionally posing in a cape), Johnny Wakelin, a white singer from Sussex, wrote 'Black Superman'. The song became a hit in 1975 and appeared along with his other Ali-inspired hit, 'In Zaire', on *Reggae, Soul and Rock 'n' Roll*. Two faster reggae versions, one by Derrick Morgan and the other by The Aggrovators, can be found on *Sucker Punch: Jamaican Boxing Tributes* (Trojan Records, 2004). 1977 saw the release of *Abar, the First Black Superman* (dir. Frank Packard), followed, in 1978, by *Superman – The Movie*, the 'ultimate immigrant saga'. *Beyond Ethnicity*, p. 12.

# Conclusion

1 Ralph Wiley describes 1978 to 1982 as 'a Golden Age'. *Serenity* (Lincoln, NE, 2000), p. 51. See also Hugh McIlvanney, *McIlvanney on Boxing* (London, 1990). On the symbolism of fights between black and Hispanic boxers, see Gerald Early, 'Hot Spinks Versus Cool Spades: Three Notes Toward a Cultural Definition of Prizefighting', in *Tuxedo Junction* (Hopewell, NJ, 1989), pp. 115–29; James Ellroy, *Destination: Morgue!* (London, 2005), pp. 3–28. See also L. Howard Quackenbush, 'Pugilism as Mirror and Metafiction in Life and in Contemporary Spanish American Drama', *Latin American Theatre Review* (Fall 1992), pp. 23–41; Gregory Rodriguez, 'Boxing and Masculinity: The History and (Her)story of Oscar de la Hoya', in *Latino/a Popular Culture*, ed. Michelle Habell-Pallán and Mary Romero (New York, 2002), pp. 252–68. For the story of a Mexican girl in LA who decides to 'snag' the local 'Big Brown Hope', with tragic consequences, see Yxta Maya Murray, *What It Takes to Get to Vegas* (New York, 1999), pp. 41, 141. Diego Luna's documentary *Chávez* was released in 2007.

2 Thomas Hauser, *Chaos, Corruption, Courage and Glory: A Year in Boxing* (Toronto, 2005), pp. 89–95. On recent FBI investigations into criminal practices in boxing, see pp. 221–8.

3 Robert Lipsyte, 'Tyson's Story Could Have More Chapters', in *Iron Mike: A Mike Tyson Reader*, ed. Daniel O'Connor (New York, 2002), p. 238. In some versions of the story, D'Amato seems like Frankenstein at work in the 'laboratory' of the Gramercy Gym. William Plummer, 'Cus D'Amato', in *Iron Mike*, p. 5. 'More than me or Patterson,' said Torres, 'Tyson is a clone of Cus's dream. Cus changed both of us, but he made Mike from scratch.' Tom Callahan, 'Boxing's Allure', *Time* (27 June 1988), p. 68. D'Amato's fighters were recognizable by their 'peek-a-boo defense and power hooks'. Katherine Dunn, 'School of Hard Knocks', in *Shadow Boxers*, ed. John Gattuso (Milford, NJ, 2005), p. 35.

4 Joyce Carol Oates, *(Woman) Writer: Occasions and Opportunities* (New York, 1988), p. 238.

5 The television era is marked by a proliferation of weight divisions, governing organizations, and hence championship fights. On the complex, and shifting, politics of these organizations and their associations with promoters such as Don King, Bob Arum and Frank Warren, see Harry Mullan, *Boxing: Inside the Game* (Cambridge, 1998), pp. 33–42; Jim Brady, *Boxing Confidential* (Lytham, 2002); Thomas Hauser, *The Black Lights: Inside the World of Professional Boxing* (New York, 1991). The respected website Cyber Boxing Zone ignores 'Alphabet titles' and lists only lineal champions, 'The Man Who Beat the Man'.

6 Mullan, *Boxing: Inside the Game*, p. 147. The Spinks fight was the highest-grossing one-day event in sports history to date – ringside seats cost $1,500, while cable and closed-circuit TV rights amounted to $58 million.

7 Tyson's trial was compared to that of O.J. Simpson and O.J.'s lawyer Johnnie Cochran was described as 'modern-day Joe Louis'. Michael Eric Dyson, *Between God and Gangsta Rap* (Oxford, 1996), p. 27. Others described Tyson's trial as itself

a kind of rape, or adopting Clarence Thomas's term, a 'high-tech lynching'. All three men were said to be victims of 'the myth of rapacious black sexuality'. Earl Ofari Hutchinson, *The Assassination of the Black Male Image* (New York, 1996), pp. 67, 70; Jack Lule, 'The rape of Mike Tyson: Race, the press and symbolic types', *Critical Studies in Mass Communication*, 12 (June 1995), pp. 176–95; Robert Wright, 'Tyson vs Simpson', in *Iron Mike*, pp. 187–90. Tyson's trial and incarceration form the basis of Walter Hill's 2002 film *Undisputed*.

8 Robert Lipsyte, 'From Spark to Flame to a Roaring Blaze', *New York Times*, 12 February 1992, section 2, p. 13.

9 Montieth Illingworth, *Mike Tyson* (London, 1992), p. 428; McIlvanney, *McIlvanney on Boxing*, p. 222. King gave Tyson Jawanza Kunjufu's 1990 *Countering the Conspiracy to Destroy Black Boys*, 'a very short and easy-to-read piece of racial paranoia'. Gerald Early, 'Mike's Brilliant Career', *Transition*, 71 (1996), p. 48.

10 June Jordan, *Technical Difficulties: African-American Notes on the State of the Union* (New York, 1992), pp. 221–6. On Tyson as 'a kind of three-penny Raskolnikov and Bigger Thomas', see David Remnick, 'Tyson's Corner', *The New Yorker*, 27 June 2005, p. 34. See also Ishmael Reed, 'Bigger and OJ', in *Birth of a Nation'hood: Gaze, Script, and Spectacle in the O.J. Simpson Case*, ed. Toni Morrison and Claudia Brodsky Lacour (New York, 1997).

11 Ralph Wiley, 'Open Mike for the Ratings', *ESPN.com: Page 2*, 29 May 2003.

12 Ellis Cashmore, *Tyson: Nurture of the Beast* (London, 2005), p. 45. John Duncan's *In the Red Corner: A Journey into Cuban Boxing* (London, 2000) is an account of the journalist's 1996 attempt to lure Cuban Olympic champion Felix Savón to fight Tyson. Before the Revolution, Cuba produced several great professional boxers, notably Kid Chocolate and Kid Gavilan. Nicolás Guillén's 1929 poems 'Sports' and 'Small Ode to a Black Cuban Boxer' warn Kid Chocolate of the racism of the 'hard and cruel' North. Nicolás Guillén, *Man-Making Words: Selected Poems*, trans. and ed. Robert Marquez and David Arthur McMurray (Havana, 1975), pp. 47–55. On Kid Gavilan, see Philip Levine, 'Shadow Boxing' in *Perfect in Their Art: Poems on Boxing from Homer to Ali*, ed. Robert Hedin and Michael Waters (Carbondale, IL, 2003), p. 127. Since professional sports were outlawed in 1962, Cuba has dominated international amateur boxing. Invited to turn professional, three-time Olympic heavyweight champion, Teófilo Stevenson famously responded, 'What is one million dollars compared to the love of eight million Cubans?' Savón said much the same thing. Paula J. Pettavino and Geralyn Pye, *Sport in Cuba* (Pittsburgh, 1994), p. 161.

13 Howard J. Blumenthal and Oliver R. Goodenough, *This Business of Television* (New York, 1998), pp. 89–90. 'Up to 1999, Tyson had appeared in six of the eight most-viewed ppv fights ever. His fights accounted for one-third of all ppv boxing revenues'. Cashmore, *Tyson*, p. 51.

14 As a corrective to this, see Joyce Carol Oates, 'Fury and Fine Lines', *New York Times*, 3 July 1997; Katherine Dunn,

'Defending Tyson', in *Iron Mike*, pp. 247–55; Tony Sewell, quoted in Cashmore, *Tyson*, pp. 79–80.

15 Cashmore, *Tyson*, p. 81

16 McIlvanney, *McIlvanney on Boxing*, pp. 238–41; Oates, quoted by George Plimpton, *Iron Mike*, p. xiv; David Remnick, 'Kid Dynamite Blows Up', *The New Yorker*, 14 July 1997, p. 58. Oates groups Tyson with Jeffrey Dahmer and Timothy James McVeigh under the heading 'Three American Gothics' in *Where I've Been, And Where I'm Going: Essays, Reviews, and Prose* (New York, 1999), pp. 232–42.

17 Rudy Gonzalez, 'No Happy Ending', in *Iron Mike*, p. 301; Wiley, *Serenity*, p. 185. Tyson's threat to eat Lennox Lewis's children may also be a film quotation. Cashmore, *Tyson*, p. 53.

18 Oates, *(Woman) Writer*, p. 239.

19 During the seventies, membership of the KKK tripled. Manning Marable, *Race, Reform and Rebellion* (London, 1991), pp. 174, 178.

20 Callahan, 'Boxing's Allure', p. 71.

21 King is also caricatured, as George Washington Duke in *Rocky V* (1990) and as Lucius Sweet in 'The Homer They Fall', *The Simpsons*, (1996). In 1997, he was the subject of a docudrama, *Don King: Only in America* and appeared as himself in *The Devil's Advocate* (1997), which, like *Snake Eyes* (1998) and *Celebrity* (1998), uses Atlantic City boxing as a setting.

22 See, for example, Douglas G. Glasgow, *The Black Underclass* (San Francisco, 1980); Ken Auletta, *The Underclass* (New York, 1982). On the validity of the concept, see Garry L Rolison, 'An Exploration of the term underclass as it relates to African-Americans', *Journal of Black Studies*, 21, 3 (March 1991), pp. 287–301; Loïc Wacquant, 'L' "underclass" urbaine dans l'imaginaire social et scientifique américain', in *L'Exclusion. L'état des servoirs* (Paris, 1996), pp. 248–62.

23 Cornel West, 'Nihilism in Black America', in *Black Popular Culture*, ed. Gina Dent (Seattle, 1992), pp. 37–47. Since the eighties, black nationalism has been 'primarily a cultural affair'. Michael Eric Dyson, *Reflecting Black: African-American Cultural Criticism* (Minneapolis, 1993), p. 131. See also Trey Ellis's influential essay, 'The New Black Aesthetic', *Callaloo*, 38 (1989), pp. 233–43; and Eric Lott's 'Response', pp. 244–6.

24 David Steele, 'Embarrassment to Just About Everyone', in *Iron Mike*, p. 295; Kristen Hunter Lattany, 'Off-Timing: Stepping to the Different Drummer', in *Lure and Loathing, Essays on Race, Identity, and the Ambivalence of Assimilation*, ed. Gerald Early (New York, 1993), p. 170.

25 Most noted (since televised) was the death of Duk Koo Kim following a lightweight fight with Ray Mancini in November 1982. George Lundberg, 'Boxing Should be Banned in Civilized Countries', *JAMA*, 249 (1983), p. 250. Since then, a broad international medical consensus calling for the abolition of boxing has emerged. For the British position, see BMA's *The Boxing Debate* (1993). After two bills to outlaw professional boxing were defeated in 1995, doctors were encouraged to withdraw their participation from the sport. Hugh Brayle, Lincoln Sargeant, and Carol Brayne, 'Could boxing be banned? A legal and epidemiological perspective', *BMJ*, 316 (1998), pp. 1813–15. For a comprehensive account of

the medical issues, see Friedrich Unterharnscheidt and Judith Taylor-Unterharnscheidt, *Boxing: Medical Aspects* (San Diego, 2003). New evidence of neurological damage emerges all the time. See, for example, H. Zetterberg et al. 'Neurochemical Aftermath of Amateur Boxing', *Archives of Neurology*, 63, no. 9 (September 2006), pp. 1277–80.

26   Women's amateur fights were first sanctioned in 1994 and the US Women's National Championships were held in 1997; the first Women's World Championships took place in 2001. In 2005, the IOC decided not to include women's boxing in the 2008 Olympics but have not ruled it out for 2012. See Edward R. Beauchamp, 'Boxing', in *International Encyclopedia of Women and Sports*, ed. Karen Christensen, Allen Guttmann and Gertrud Pfister (New York, 2001), vol. I, pp. 167–76; Jennifer Hargreaves, 'Bruising Peg to Boxerobics: Gendered Boxing – Images and Meaning', in *Boxer: An Anthology of Writings on Boxing and Visual Culture*, ed. David Chandler, John Gill, Tania Guha and Gilane Tawadros (London, 1996), pp. 120–31; Jennifer Hargreaves, 'Women's Boxing and Related Activities', *Body and Society*, 3 (1997), pp. 33–49.

27   Richard Hoffer, 'Gritty Woman', *Sports Illustrated*, 15 April 1996, pp. 56–62.

28   Emma Lindsey, 'She Stings Like a Butterfly', *The Independent on Sunday Review*, 2 July 2000, pp. 4–8.

29   David Usborne, 'Daughters Degrade the Ali–Frazier Legend', *Independent on Sunday*, 16 June 2001, p. 16; Ian Wooldridge, 'In the name of the father, these girls will drag boxing down even lower than Tyson', *Daily Mail*, 23 February 2000, p. 88.

30   Kate Sekules, *The Boxer's Heart: How I fell in love with the ring* (London, 2000), p. 76.

31   Harry Mullan, 'You can box, girl, but I can't watch', *Independent on Sunday*, 15 February, 1998, p. 6. Bert Sugar described the first officially sanctioned boxing match between a man and a woman in 1999 as 'an old carnival act updated'. Sam Howe Verhovek, 'Man–woman bout hammering bell of boxing world', *Arizona Republic*, 3 October 1999, Section A, p. 10.

32   Meg Ryan stars as 'sassy, brassy boxing manager Jackie Kallen' in 'true story' *Against the Ropes* (2004). Among the many documentaries about women in boxing, see also *On the Ropes* (1999), *Red Rain* (1999), *Shadow Boxers* (2000) and *The Lady and the Champ* (2002).

33   *Romy and Michelle's High School Reunion* (1997).

34   The male narrator of 'Tough People' cries when he sees his girlfriend get beaten. Then she leaves him for another man. Chris Offutt, *Out of the Woods* (New York, 2000), pp. 157–76.

35   Kate Sekules, 'Glove Story', *Guardian*, 20 March 2001, G2, p. 8. 'Do women subvert the ritual bullfight or do they create a different ritual?' asked Sarah Pink of women matadors. Sarah Pink, 'From Ritual Sacrifice to Media Commodity: Anthropological and Media Constructions of the Spanish Bullfight and the Rise of Women Performers', in *Ritual, Performance, Media*, ed. Felicia Hughes-Freeland (London, 1988), p. 125. On the 'variability of females' and males, see

Katherine Dunn, 'Just as Fierce', *Mother Jones* (November/December 1994), p. 39.

36   Sekules, *The Boxer's Heart*, p. 70; Leah Hager Cohen, *Without Apology: Girls, Women and the Desire to Fight* (New York, 2005), p. 225. Picket took up boxing to express anger at her cheating ex-husband. Lynn Snowden Picket, *Looking for a Fight* (New York, 2000), p. 7. The therapeutic benefit of boxing is also the theme of Laila Ali, with David Ritz, *Reach! Finding Strength, Spirit, and Personal Power* (New York, 2003).

37   See, for example, Peter Pasquale, *The Boxer's Workout: Fitness for the Civilized Man* (New York, 1988). The traditions of reforming Muscular Christianity are also maintained. In 2006 the Haringey Police Community Club in Tottenham, North London targeted 'kids in trouble' and in 2007 reformatory boxing became the subject of a reality TV show, *Amir Khan's Angry Young Men*. Daniel Herbert, 'Secrets of Haringey's success', *Boxing News*, 15 September 2006, pp. 38–9.

38   See Kasia Boddy, 'Franchising Fight Club', *Berliner Debatte Initial*, 12, 1 (2001), pp. 110–20.

39   On the bareknuckle revival of the nineties, see Bob Mee, *Bare Fists* (Woodstock, NY, 2001), ch. 15. Several bareknuckle fighters published authobiographies: Roy Shaw, *Pretty Boy* (London, 1999), Lenny McLean, *The Guv'nor* (London, 1998), and Jimmy Stockin, with Martin King and Martin Knight, *On the Cobbles: The Life of a Bare Knuckle Gypsy Warrior* (Edinburgh, 2001). McLean appeared in the film *Lock, Stock and Two Smoking Barrels* (1998).

40   Niraj Warikoo, 'Teen fight club stirs controversy', *Detroit Free Press*, 24 November 1999. See also 'Police Catch Local Teens Imitating "Fight Club"', *Chicago Sun-Times*, 11 November 1999; Andrew Gumbel, 'Blood runs at Mormon campus Fight Club', *Independent on Sunday*, 21 May 2000, p. 25.

41   George Pendle, 'Punching in pinstripes', *Times*, 30 August 2000, Supplement, p. 5.

42   Alex Wade, *Wrecking Machine: A Tale of Real Fights and White Collars* (London, 2005), p. 13. Wade likes boxing because the place it occupies 'outside' society is 'akin' to the 'psychological space' he occupies due to unresolved 'issues from my childhood'. *Wrecking Machine*, p. 321.

43   Alessandro Baricco, *City*, trans. Ann Goldstein (Harmondsworth, 2001), p. 152. The story of a boxer who agrees to throw a fight and then doesn't is just one of the pulp fictions that make up Quentin Tarantino's *Pulp Fiction* (1994). We don't see the fight itself (Tarantino suggests that we can take it as read), but join the boxer after he defies the set-up.

44   Baricco, *City*, p. 148. Boxing is often described as a reliable resource for writers who are 'desperate for material'. See, for example, Jonathan Ames, 'The Vanilla Thrilla', in *My Less Than Secret Life* (New York, 2002), p. 96.

45   For toddlers, see Allan Ahlberg and Janet Ahlberg, *Mr Biff the Boxer* (1980); for teenagers, Robert Lipsyte's *The Contender* (1967), and its sequels, *The Brave* (1991) and *The Chief* (1993). Pamela Longfellow's romance, *Chasing Women* (1993) has a boxing setting; Bruce Jay Friedman's 'The Night Boxing Ended' (1966) was included in *Arena: Sports sf*, ed. Edward L. Ferman and Barry N. Malzberg (New York, 1976), pp. 181–6. See also *Murder on the Ropes: Original Boxing*

*Mysteries*, ed. Otto Penzler (New York, 2001).

46 The poster encouraged critics to adopt its metaphor. 'Warhol TKO in 16 rounds', concluded the *New York Times*, quoted in Leonhard Emmerling, *Jean-Michel Basquiat* (Cologne, 2003), p. 71. The image drew on history of collaboration between the two artists and on Basquiat's self-portrait with Warhol, *Dos Cabezas* (1982). In 1985–6 they produced a series of paintings on punch bags, each including a head of Christ (by Warhol) and the word 'Judge' (by Basquiat). On the response of other black artists to this image, and to Warhol more generally, see Russell Ferguson, 'Tomato Cans', *Visual Arts and Culture*, 1 (1998), pp. 2–13. See also José Esteban Muñoz, 'Famous and Dandy like B. 'n' Andy: Race, Pop, and Basquiat', in *Pop Out: Queer Warhol*, ed. Jennifer Doyle, Jonathan Flately and José Esteban Muñoz (Durham, NC, 1996), pp. 144–79. In summer 2007 Pollock Fine Art staged an exhibition 'Warhol vs. Bansky'.

47 Charles Bukowski, 'Class', in *South of No North* (Los Angeles, 1973), pp. 65–9. See also Bukowski, 'The Loser', in *The Roominghouse Madrigals: Early Selected Poems, 1946–1966* (Los Angeles, 1988).

48 Max Apple, 'Inside Norman Mailer', in *The Oranging of America* (London, 1976), pp. 49–60.

49 Quoted in Larry McCaffery and Sinda Gregory, *Alive and Writing: Interviews with American Authors of the 1980s* (Urbana, IL, 1987), p. 30.

50 A. J. Liebling traced his 'rapport' with boxing's past 'through the laying-on of hands'. *The Sweet Science* (Harmondsworth, 1982), p. 1. Mailer is 'the man to beat for the men who punch out words', said Thomas Healey, *A Hurting Business* (London, 1996), p. 33. Another anxiety of influence is dramatized by Jonathan Ames in 'My Jewish Cousin, George Ames Plimpton', *My Less Than Secret Life*, pp. 104–11.

51 See Greg Johnson, *Invisible Writer: A Biography of Joyce Carol Oates* (New York, 1999).

52 Gerald Early, 'The Grace of Slaughter', *Iowa Review*, 18, 3 (Fall 1988), p. 181; Oates, *(Woman) Writer*, p. 303.

53 Reviewers often present Oates as a 'massive literary heavyweight' who is not allowed to compete. Helen Falconer, 'Wild Oates', *Guardian*, 27 October 2001, p. 10.

54 'A woman can rarely know the things that go on inside a man.' Norman Mailer, *The Deer Park* (New York, 1957), p. 88. 'She was a girl, after all, and could have no sense of who he was.' Leonard Gardner, *Fat City* (London, 1989), p. 89. Since Jack London's *The Game*, the woman investigator of boxing has become a recurrent fictional figure. In Harry Crews's *The Knockout Artist* (1988) a young hopeful is unhappy to discover that his girlfriend's PhD is based on him. The woman researcher in *Punch Drunk*, a 1992 BBC sit-com, is less sinister. She soon abandons her anti-boxing doctor boyfriend for the young contender.

55 Joyce Carol Oates, 'Selections from a Journal: January 1985–January 1988', in *Our Private Lives: Journals, Notebooks, and Diaries*, ed. Daniel Halpern (Hopewell, NJ, 1988), p. 335. See also Oates, *On Boxing* (London, 1988), p. 54. For a sympathetic reading of Mailer's fiction, see Oates, *New Heaven, New Earth: The Visionary Experience in Literature* (New York,

1974), pp. 177–203.

56 Oates usually presents gender in binary terms. In an essay on the Tyson rape case she argued that it was 'symbolically appropriate' that boxing and women's rights be contrasted since 'of all sports, boxing is the most aggressively masculine'. Rape, meanwhile, is the 'violent repudiation of the female', comparable to 'knocking out an opponent and standing over his fallen body'. Women boxers, therefore, can only be 'parody . . . cartoon . . . monstrous'. Oates, 'Rape and the Boxing Ring', *Newsweek*, 24 February 1992, p. 61; *On Boxing*, p. 73. This remark is often quoted in annoyance by women boxers. See Cohen, *Without Apology*, p. 17; Sekules, *The Boxer's Heart*, pp. 54–5.

57 Ted Gioia, *The History of Jazz* (Oxford, 1998), pp. 98, 278.

58 Seminole 'had a left hand like everybody else has a right hand'. Count Basie, as told to Albert Murray, *Good Morning Blues: The Autobiography of Count Basie* (New York, 1985), p. 9. On musical battles at Minton's Playhouse in Harlem, see Ralph Ellison, *Shadow and Act* (New York, 1964), pp. 204, 210. On 'bucolic cutting contests' between pastoral singers in Virgil's *Eclogues*, see John Henderson, *Writing Down Rome* (Oxford, 1994), p. 164.

59 Quoted in Jurgen E. Grandt, *Kinds of Blue: The Jazz Aesthetic in African American Narrative* (Columbus, OH, 2004), p. 91. Jack Kerouac mentions this 'wild bop record' in *On the Road* (Harmondsworth, 1999), p. 104, and *Visions of Cody* (Harmondsworth, 1993), p. 346.

60 Quoted in Burton W. Peritti, *The Creation of Jazz* (Urbana, IL, 1994), p. 114.

61 Duke Ellington, *Music is My Mistress* (Garden City, NY, 1973), pp. 464, 466.

62 Ralph Ellison, *Invisible Man* (New York, 1995), p. 8.

63 Ellison, *Shadow and Act*, p. 234. See also Mezzrow and Wolfe, quoted in Henry Louis Gates, *The Signifying Monkey* (Oxford, 1988), p. 70. Gates uses the Ellison quotation as an epigraph to his book.

64 Babs Gonzalez, 'Sugar Ray' (May 1952), on *Cool Whalin': Bepop Vocals* (Spotlight, 1979). See David Toop, *Rap Attack 3: African Jive to Global Hip Hop* (London, 2000), pp. 37–8.

65 *Antipop vs. Matthew Shipp* (Thirsty Ear, 2003). Matthew Shipp's poem 'Boxing and Jazz' provided the starting point for Patrick A. Gaucher's *Combinations*, a film which cuts between footage of boxers at Gleason's gym in New York and a performance of Shipp's trio. Matthew Shipp, 'Boxing and Jazz', http://www.matthewshipp.com/press/27boxingandjazz/boxing_and_jazz.html; Chris Chang, 'Sound and Vision: Black and Blue', *Film Comment*, 41, no. 1 (January–February 2005), p. 16.

66 'Famous rivalries have included Prince Buster vs. Derrick Morgan, Jazzbo vs. I Roy, and Beenie Man vs. Bounti Killer, to choose three periods.' Andrew Ross, *Real Love* (London, 1998), pp. 41, 218 n. 4. See Derrick Morgan, 'The Great Musical Battle', *Sucker Punch: Jamaican Boxing Tributes* (Trojan, 2004).

67 Beenie Man, *Back to Basics* (2004); *Undisputed* (2006).

68 Imani Perry, *Prophets of the Hood: Politics and Poetics in Hip Hop* (Durham, NC, 2004), p. 14; Michael Eric Dyson,

*Reflecting Black*, p. 9. See also Mimi Clark Melnick, '"I Can Peep Through Muddy Water and Spy Dry Land": Boasts in the Blues', in *Mother Wit from the Laughing Barrel*, ed. Alan Dundes (Jackson, MI, 1981), pp. 267–76.

69  Big Daddy Kane, 'Raw', *Long Live the Kane* (Warners, 1988). On the competitiveness of hip-hop culture, see Tricia Rose, *Black Noise: Rap Music and Black Culture in Contemporary America* (Hanover, NH, 1994), pp. 35–6.

70  Big Daddy Kane, 'Raw'; Coolio, 'Knockout Kings', *El Cool Magnifico* (Hot, 2002); Onyx, 'Slam', *Bacdafucup* (Universal/Def Jam, 1993); The Fugees, featuring Q-Tip and Busta Rhymes, 'Rumble in the Jungle', *When We Were Kings* (Polygram, 1996).

71  George Nelson, *Hip Hop America* (Harmondsworth, 1999), p. vii. Perry thinks the analogy inappropriate since, unlike hip hop, the boxing battles 'only engage the body, not the intellect or vocabulary'. *Prophets of the Hood*, p. 125. See also 'Hip Hop Rivalries', *Wikipedia Encyclopedia*.

72  Haruki Murakami, 'The Silence', trans. Alfred Birnbaum, in *The Elephant Vanishes* (London, 2003), p. 296.

73  Senam Okudzeto, Interview with Trevor Schoonmaker, *Freestyle*, exh. cat., Studio Museum in Harlem (New York, 2001), pp. 66–7.

74  John Updike, *Rabbit Redux* (1971) in *The Rabbit Omnibus* (London, 1990), p. 398. In *Rabbit, Run* (1960), Rabbit compliments Ruth, soon to be his lover, by telling her she's 'just a welterweight'. *The Rabbit Omnibus*, p. 41. Compare the description of Riggie Hines in Saul Bellow, *The Dean's December* (Harmondsworth, 1998), p. 44.

75  Her non-fiction is similarly concerned with 'shadow selves'. For a description of 'two young welterweight boxers so evenly matched they might be twins', see *On Boxing*, pp. 1, 12. For an image of identical twins battling it out in the womb, see Oates, *(Woman) Writer*, p. 265.

76  'The contours of [her] soul so resemble my own', she remarked of Enid. Oates, *(Woman) Writer*, pp. 379–80. *You Must Remember This* was the second in a series of novels set in Eden County, a fictional version of Erie County, New York (where Oates grew up) and a kind of Northern version of Faulkner's Yoknapatawpha. Greg Johnson, *Joyce Carol Oates: A Study of the Short Fiction* (Boston, 1994), p. 16.

77  Joyce Carol Oates, *You Must Remember This* (New York, 1988), pp. 36, 132.

78  Ibid., p. 233, 168, 181.

79  Ibid., p. 118. In 'The Boyfriend', a woman allows herself to be picked up in a bar by a man who then takes her to a boxing match. When she refuses to sleep with him, he kicks her in the stomach. She wonders if the kick has somehow enacted her former boyfriend's threat of revenge and remembers the defeated boxer lying on the floor with 'blood leaking from his nose and mouth'. Joyce Carol Oates, *Heat and Other Stories* (New York, 1992), pp. 69–81. In another novel littered with boxing similes, a slap on the face by a woman gives Corky Corcoran 'permission' to hit her. He's a 'skinny lightweight with a good jab', but soon 'all his fury is in his cock' and they have sex. Joyce Carol Oates, *What I Lived For* (New York, 1995), pp. 90–91.

80  Oates, *You Must Remember This*, p. 386. The equation of the self with the body is as disturbing for women as it is for boxers, for it means being 'identified with a certain weight'. Oates, *On Boxing*, p. 5. 'In Memoriam' links a photograph of the South Korean boxer, Duk Koo Kim, taken on the night he was 'doomed' to die in the ring with the narrator's memory of the image of her fourteen year old self 'dreaming in Woolworth's / window': 'she didn't know was it / her body she wanted to starve into submission, / or her soul. Which angered her most.' Joyce Carol Oates, *The Time Traveller* (New York, 1989), p. 13. On Oates's anorexia, see Johnson, *Invisible Writer*, pp. 172, 175. On her philosophy of 'tragic pain', see David B. Morris, *The Culture of Pain* (Berkeley, CA, 1991), pp. 256–63.

81  A similar contest is staged in 'Golden Gloves', in which childbirth and boxing are directly compared. While the fighter gives up, unable to confront his fear of pain and death, his pregnant wife 'means to be equal to it'. Joyce Carol Oates, *Raven's Wing* (London, 1987), pp. 50–69. See also Oates, *On Boxing*, pp. 72–3. Mailer also claimed that 'the fighter goes through experiences in the ring which are . . . incommunicable except to fighters who have been as good, or to women who have gone though every minute of an anguish-filled birth'. *Existential Errands* (New York, 1972), p. 17. The protagonist of another novel is told by her doctor to have a baby because her body suffers monthly menstruation like 'a battered boxer, staggering back from its corner into the ring'. Lorrie Moore, *Anagrams* (London, 1987), p. 21.

82  The narrator of *Bruiser* is jealous when his lover comes home from the gym because he recognizes that 'the beatings are sex, sex of a kind'. Richard House, *Bruiser* (London, 1987), p. 30. On parallel adventures in the 'sweet science of bruising' and the 'sick science of cruising', see Ames, *My Less Than Secret Life*, p. 113. See also David Wojnarowicz, *Memories That Smell Like Gasoline* (San Francisco, 1992), p. 41; and Tennessee Williams's story of a one-armed, ex-champ hustler who looks like a 'broken statue of Apollo', 'One Arm', in *Collected Stories* (New York, 1985), pp. 175–88. The 2003 film *Cock and Bull Story* advertised with the tag, 'Wannabe boxing champ has a secret – he gets a hard-on in the clinch'.

83  Rita Mae Brown, *Southern Discomfort* (London, 1983), p. 18. Haring compared his sculptures to children's toys. David Galloway, 'A Quest for Immortality', in *Keith Haring*, ed. Germano Celant (Munich, 1992), pp. 23, 26.

84  Judith Halberstam, *Female Masculinity* (Durham, NC, 1998), p. 276.

85  Tony Kushner, *Angels in America, Part 2: Perestroika* (New York, 1994), p. 37. See also Max Apple, *Zip: A Novel of the Left and Right* (1978).

86  Quoted in Edmund White, *Genet* (London, 1993), pp. 225–6. In 1996 the *Gay Times* Erotic Video Award went to a film of boxers in the locker rooms of Bethnal Green's York Hall, *Angels with Dirty Faces*. David Bret, *Morrissey* (London, 2004), p. 215.

87  Alan Hollinghurst, *The Swimming-Pool Library* (London, 1998), pp. 3, 242.

88 One of the novel's many inter-texts is E. M. Forster's *Maurice*. After being thrown over by his lover, Maurice becomes a stockbroker and spends Wednesday evenings teaching 'arithmetic and boxing' to the 'youths of the College Settlement in South London'. *Maurice* (Harmondsworth, 1972), pp. 126–7.

89 Hollinghurst, *The Swimming-Pool Library*, pp. 78, 135–9, 172.

90 Ibid., pp. 31, 38, 284. See also pp. 144–5.

91 Douglas Oliver, *Three Variations on the Theme of Harm: Selected Poetry and Prose* (London, 1990), pp. 70–74. See also pp. 60–64.

92 Julio Cortázar, 'Some Aspects of the Short Story', trans. Naomi Lindstrom, *Review of Contemporary Fiction*, 3 (1983), p. 28.

93 See *R. B. Kitaj: A Retrospective*, ed. Richard Morphet, exh. cat., Tate Gallery, London (London, 1994), pp. 168–9. See also Alan Woods, 'Paintings with Banging Doors: Art and Allusion in Kitaj and Hockney', *The Cambridge Quarterly*, 24, no. 4 (1995), pp. 315–39.

94 John Ruskin, *Works*, ed. E. T. Cooke and Alexander Wedderburn (London, 1903–12), vol. XXIX, p. 158.

95 Quoted in Andrew Merrifield, *Guy Debord* (London, 2005), p. 21. See also Guy Debord and Gil J. Wolman, 'Methods of Detournement', in *Situationist International Anthology*, ed. Ken Knabb (Berkeley, CA, 1981), p. 9.

96 Allyson Field, 'Hurlements en faveur de Sade: The Negation and Surpassing of "Discrepant Cinema"', *SubStance*, 28, no. 3 (1999), p. 96.

97 Wolfgang Becker, 'Le sport est-il un art?', in *Art et Sport*, exh. cat., Musée des Beaux-Arts de Mons (Mons, 1984), pp. 42–3. The poster advertising the event is reproduced in *Art et Sport*, p. 40. In 1997, 'during a three-day-and-night-long blockade' of Belgrade's main square, the Serbian performance artist Tanja Ostojic tried to repeat this performance. When no policeman accepted her offer of gloves, she undertook a 'promotional match in front of cordon with a friend': http://www.kultur.at/howl/tanja/set01/text01.htm.

98 Beuys's performance was filmed by Gerry Schum. A still of *Box Felt* is reproduced in *Art et Sport*, p. 107.

99 Claes Oldenburg boxed with dealer Pontus Hulten as part of his Venetian performance *Il Corse del Coletello* in 1985. In 1999 novelist Jonathan Ames (The Herring Wonder) and performance artist David Leslie (The Impact Addict) staged a 'Box Opera' at the Angel Orensanz Foundation in New York. Ames, 'The Vanilla Thrilla', p. 100. The Dutch artist Iepe Rubingh invented 'chess boxing' in 2003 (six rounds of chess alternating with five rounds of boxing). See Stephen Moss, 'Wanna piece of this?', *The Guardian*, 9 November 2005, pp. 8–11.

100 Philip Roth, *Patrimony* (London, 1999), p. 203. On trips to Laurel Garden, see also Philip Roth, *The Plot Against America* (London, 2004), pp. 293–4. The narrator's cousin manages the lightweight contender Allie Stolz. Stolz, like many of the characters in the novel, was a real person and his biography can be found on p. 384. Roth's bibliography includes Allen Broder's *When Boxing was a Jewish Sport* (Westport, CT, 1997), which contains more information on Stolz.

101 Philip Roth, *The Facts* (New York, 1997), p. 28.

102 Philip Roth, *Portnoy's Complaint* (London, 1969), pp. 166, 178–9, 234–5. Portnoy and his girlfriend Mary Jane also have a couple of 'rounds' with a prostitute in Rome. *Portnoy's Complaint*, p. 139.

103 Philip Roth, *The Counterlife* (Harmondsworth, 1988), p. 320.

104 Philip Roth, *Operation Shylock* (New York, 1993), p. 334.

105 Philip Roth, *The Ghost Writer* (Harmondsworth, 1980), pp. 84–5.

106 Charles McGrath, 'Zuckerman's Alter Brain: An Interview with Philip Roth', *New York Times Book Review*, 7 May 2000, p. 8.

107 Philip Roth, *American Pastoral* (London, 1998), pp. 4, 10; *I Married a Communist* (London, 1999), p. 18.

108 Roth, *I Married a Communist*, p. 54.

109 Fight imagery occurs throughout. Ira complains that he's only allowed one 'punch' a week on his radio show; Zuckerman imagines him hiding from the FBI in 'one of those austere training camps . . . where heavyweights used to go . . . before the big fight'; Eve's denunciation of Ira as a communist is the 'strongest punch she can throw'. Roth, *I Married a Communist*, pp. 25, 187, 212, 267.

110 Roth, *I Married a Communist*, p. 15; Max Schmeling, *An Autobiography*, trans. George B. von der Lippe (Chicago, 1998), p. 82.

111 Roth, *I Married a Communist*, pp. 27, 28, 32, 84, 263–4.

112 Ibid., p. 217. Roth is also reviving a common classical comparison of teachers with athletic trainers. Jason König, *Athletics and Literature in the Roman Empire* (Cambridge, 2006), p. 136. Carlo Rotella updates the comparison, although he is as much concerned with the 'lessons to be learned at ringside' as in the gym. *Cut Time: An Education at the Fights* (Boston, 2003).

113 Roth, *I Married a Communist*, p. 218.

114 O'Day's gear always included a 'light punching bag'. Roth, *I Married a Communist*, pp. 35, 37, 228, 318.

115 Ibid., pp. 314–5. *Macbeth*, IV.iii.219–21.

116 Philip Roth, *The Human Stain* (London, 2001), pp. 238, 280.

117 Roth, *I Married a Communist*, p. 106; *The Human Stain*, pp. 10, 204.

118 Roth, *I Married a Communist*, p. 49. Passing as a Jew, Silk pretends his name is derived from Silberzweig; that is, silver twig. *The Human Stain*, p. 130. Roth may also be alluding to Michael Silk, also a Professor of Greek and the author of a study of Coleman's favourite book, the *Iliad*. Thanks to Professor Silk for discussing this with me and for suggesting another allusion, to Coleman Hawkins. See Michael Silk, *Homer: The Iliad* (Cambridge, 1987), particularly pp. 103–4.

119 One of Portnoy's many names for his penis is 'the silky monster'. *Portnoy's Complaint*, p. 127.

120 Mervyn Rothstein, 'From Philip Roth, "The Facts" as He Remembers Them', *New York Times*, 6 September 1988.

121 Roth, *The Human Stain*, pp. 108, 342.

122 Ibid., pp. 90, 100; *The Counterlife*, p. 324.

123 Ibid., p. 343.

124 Roth, *I Married a Communist*, pp. 77–8; *The Human Stain*, pp. 25, 210.

125 Roth, *The Human Stain*, pp. 5, 13, 232. Faunia is also a 'contender'; all Coleman's relationships with women are imagined in boxing terms. See pp. 114, 121, 134. Coleman's nemesis, Delphine Roux, has a crush on Milan Kundera whose 'poetically prizefighterish looks' are 'an outward sign of everything colliding within.'

126 For a convincing reading of *The Human Stain* as a 'meditation' on Ralph Ellison's career, see Timothy L. Parrish, 'Ralph Ellison: The Invisible Man in Philip Roth's *The Human Stain*', *Contemporary Literature*, 45, no. 3 (2004), pp. 421–59.

127 Roth, *The Human Stain*, p. 337. Roth began *Everyman* the day after Saul Bellow's burial. Charles McGrath, 'Roth, Haunted by Illness, Feels Fine', *New York Times*, 25 April 2006.

128 Roth, *The Human Stain*, p. 316.

129 Ibid., p. 209.

130 Walter Benjamin, 'The Work of Art in the Age of Mechanical Reproduction', *Illuminations*, trans. Harry Zohn (London, 1970), p. 225.

131 Don DeLillo, *White Noise* (London, 1986), p. 67.

132 Don DeLillo, *Underworld* (London, 1998), pp. 15–16.

133 Paul Pfeiffer, *The Long Count*, exh. cat., MIT LIST Visual Arts Center (Cambridge, MA, 2001).

134 Twan Mac, 'Microphone Knockout', *Survival Tactics* (Bangin Beats Entertainment, 2004); Big Daddy Kane, 'Niggaz Never Learn', *Looks Like a Job For* (Cold Chillin' Records, 1993). On the controversy surrounding the *Rocky* statue, see Danielle Rice, 'The "Rocky" Dilemma', in *Critical Issues in Public Art*, ed. Harriet F. Senie and Sally Webster (Washington, DC, 1992), pp. 228–36. On the attempt to create a museum and 'Rocky Marciano Trail' in Brockton, MA, see Carlo Rotella, *Good with Their Hands* (Berkeley, CA, 2002), ch. 4.

135 Histories of rap usually mention Ali as one of its precursors. Houston A. Baker, Jr., *Black Studies, Rap and the Academy* (Chicago, 1993), p. 9; William Eric Perkins, 'The Rap Attack: An Introduction', in *Droppin' Science: Critical Essays on Rap Music and Hip Hop Culture* (Philadelphia, 1995), p. 5; Kevin Powell, 'The Word Movement', in *Step into a Word: A Global Anthology of the New Black Literature*, ed. Powell (New York, 2000), p. 4; Toop, *Rap Attack 3*, p. 19; Perry, *Prophets of the Hood*, p. 58. In 2006 George Lois compiled a book of quotations and photographs entitled *Ali Rap: Muhammad Ali, the First Heavyweight Champion of Rap*.

136 See, for example, LL Cool J, featuring James T. Smith, *G.O.A.T.* (Def Jam, 2001); Public Enemy, 'Timebomb', on *Yo Bum Rush the Show* (Def Jam, 1987); EPMD, 'You're a Customer', on *Strictly Business* (Priority, 1991); CC Crew, 'CC Crew Rap', on *The Big Break Rapper Party: Sounds of New York*, USA, *vol. 1* (Traffic, 2006).

137 Heltah Skeltah, 'The Grate Unknown', on *Nocturnal* (Priority, 1996); Das EFX, 'Wontu', on *Straight Up Sewaside* (East/West Records, 1993). See Perry, *Prophets of the Hood*, ch. 3.

138 Dyson, *Between God and Gangsta Rap*, p. 165. Chuck D, with Yusaf Jah, *Fight the Power, Rap, Race and Reality* (Edinburgh, 1997), pp. 1–3, 98–9.

139 Nelson, *Hip Hop America*, p. 53. Perry labels the 'in-your-face . . . black masculinity and excess' of rap as 'Jack Johnsonism' or 'Shine-ism'. *Prophets of the Hood*, pp. 29, 128. For a direct engagement with Johnson, see Mos Def, 'Blue Black Jack' and 'Zimzallabim', on *The New Danger* (Geffen, 2004). The album features the band *Black Jack Johnson*.

140 LL Cool J, 'I'm Bad', on *Bigger and Deffer* (Def Jam, 1987); DJ Jazzy Jeff and The Fresh Prince, 'I Think I Can Beat Mike Tyson', on *And In This Corner . . .* (Jive, 1989).

141 Tyson's fights were usually no longer than the average music video. Ian Probert, *Rope Burns* (London, 1999), p. 30. In 1987, Nintendo released 'Mike Tyson's Punch-Out!'. HBO tried to capitalize on boxing's popularity with hip hop fans with a short-lived show called *KO Nation*. See Charles P. Pierce, 'Let's Get Ready to Rumble, Yo', *Esquire*, February 2001, pp. 48–51; Rotella, *Cut Time*, pp. 159–60.

142 David Thompson, 'Banging Big with Mike Tyson', *Sight and Sound*, 9, no. 2 (February 1999), pp. 24–7. In 1995, the elderly British philosopher A. J. Ayer famously defended model Naomi Campbell from Tyson's advances at a New York party. To Tyson's declaration that he was the heavyweight champion of the world, Ayer reputedly replied 'And I am the former Wykeham Professor of Logic. We are both pre-eminent in our field; I suggest that we talk about this like rational men.' Ben Rogers, *A. J. Ayer: A Life* (London, 1999), p. 344.

143 Nelson, *Hip Hop America*, p. 54. Tyson often used Tupac tracks for his ring walks. Holyfield was later associated with West Coast rappers MC Hammer (who became his manager) and Snoop Doggy Dogg who boasted of 'breakin niggaz down like Evander Holyfield'. Snoop Doggy Dogg, 'The Shiznit', on *Doggystyle* (Columbia, 1987); MC Hammer with Tha Dogg Pound, 'Sleepin on a Master Plan', on *The Funky Headhunter* (Warner, 1994).

144 Canibus, featuring Mike Tyson, 'Second Round K.O.', on *Lyrical Warfare* (Group Home, 1998); LL Cool J, 'The Ripper Strikes Back', on *Survival of the Illest* (1998), vol. 1; Motion Man, featuring KutMasta, 'Winner Takes All (Knockout Kings 2002)', on *Clearing the Field* (Threshold, 2002). In 'Mama Said Knock You Out' (Def Jam, 1990), an attack on Kool Moe Dee, LL Cool J compared his rage to Ali's when 'they called him Cassius'.

145 Roy Jones, Jr, 'Who Wanna Get Knocked Out', on *Round One: The Album* (Body Head, 2002). See also *Body Head Bangerz: Volume One* (Body Head, 2004). In 1999, the American Association of Boxing Writers voted Jones 'Fighter of the Decade'. See Hauser, *Chaos, Corruption, Courage and Glory*, pp. 3–11.

146 Spike Lee, as told to Kaleem Aftab, *That's My Story and I'm Sticking to It* (London, 2005), p. 57.

147 Like Lee's earlier films, *Do the Right Thing* is framed by memorializing litanies. The film is dedicated to the families of recent victims of police brutality and ends with a roll call of black musicians by radio DJ Love Daddy.

148 *Do the Right Thing* prompted much critical debate. Andrew Ross described it as a 'complex late eighties version of the "fire next time"'. 'Ballots, bullets, or Batmen: can cultural studies do the right thing?', *Screen*, 31, no. 1 (Spring 1990),

p. 37. Complaints that the film would incite racial violence drew comparisons to the Johnson fight films. Ed Guerrero, *Do the Right Thing* (London, 2001), pp. 18–20. 'What, finally, is at issue are matters of style far more than substance', said Houston A. Baker, 'Spike Lee and the Commerce of Culture', *Black American Literature Forum*, 25, no. 2 (Summer 1991), pp. 237–52. Along the same lines, see Wahneema Lubiano, '"But Compared to What?": Reading Realism, Representation, and Essentialism in *School Daze*, *Do the Right Thing*, and the Spike Lee Discourse', in *Representing Black Men*, ed. Marcellus Blount and George P. Cunningham (New York, 1996), pp. 173–204.

149 These were intended as a homage to the tattooed knuckles of psychotic preacher in *The Night of the Hunter* (1955). Spike Lee and Lisa Jones, *Do the Right Thing* (New York 1989), p. 78.

150 On Lee's Brechtianism, see Douglas Kellner, 'Aesthetics, Ethics, and Politics in the Films of Spike Lee', in *Spike Lee's Do the Right Thing*, ed. Mark A. Reid (Cambridge, 1997), pp. 73–106.

151 W.J.T. Mitchell, 'The Violence of Public Art: Do the Right Thing', in *Spike Lee's Do the Right Thing*, ed. Reid, pp. 107–28.

152 Lee, *That's My Story*, pp. 83–4.

153 In 1991, Lee made a documentary *Iron Mike Tyson* for HBO. At one point, Tyson tells him that they're both 'just two black guys for the ghetto'. See Phil Berger, *Blood Season: Mike Tyson and the World of Boxing* (London, 1996), p. 295. Lee and Tyson are also compared in *That's My Story*, pp. 26, 49. Lee supported the boxer during his rape trial, and sent him a copy of Arthur Ashe's *Days of Grace* in jail. Tyson later tattooed an image of Ashe on his arm. Charlie Rose, 'Interview with Spike Lee', in *Spike Lee: Interviews*, ed. Cynthia Fuchs (Jackson, MI, 2002), pp. 87–8; Peter Hamill, 'The Education of Mike Tyson', in *Iron Mike*, p. 172.

154 Lee describes *Raging Bull* as the 'best sports film ever'. *That's My Story*, p. 231.

155 Cashmore, *Tyson*, p. 150. On Tina as 'a latter-day Josephine Baker', see Michele Wallace, *Invisibility Blues* (London, 1990), p. 108. See also Chuck D, *Fight the Power*, pp. 217–22; bell hooks, *Yearning: Race, Gender and Cultural Politics* (Boston, 1990), p. 179.

156 Ross, 'Ballots, bullets, or Batmen', p. 40. Ed Guerrero notes a sustained *Godfather* parody. *Do the Right Thing*, p. 75.

157 Henry Louis Gates, 'Final Cut: Conversation with Spike Lee', *Transition*, 52 (1991), p. 199. On Lee's capitalism, see Jerome Christensen, 'Spike Lee, Corporate Populist', *Critical Inquiry*, 17, no. 3 (Spring 1991), pp. 582–95, and W.J.T. Mitchell's response, 'Seeing "Do the Right Thing"', pp. 596–608.

158 *That's My Story and I'm Sticking to It*, pp. 259, 271, 297.

159 The portraits of Louis and John Henry used in *She Hate Me* are by Sandor Szenassy.

160 Boxers remain a popular subject for what has variously been termed folk, self-taught or outsider art. See, for example, Sam Doyle, *Joe Louis* (1980), in *Pictured in My Mind: Contemporary American Self-Taught Art from the Collection of Dr Kurt Gitter and Alice Rae Yelen*, exh. cat., Birmingham Museum of Art (Birmingham, AL, 1995), p. 60; Sam Doyle, *Abe Kane*, in *Black Folk Art in America, 1930–1980*, exh. cat., Corcoran Gallery, Washington, DC (Washington, DC, 1982), p. 6; Elijah Pierce, *Louis vs. Braddock*, in *Self-Taught Artists of the Twentieth-Century: An American Anthology*, exh. cat., Museum of American Folk Art, New York (New York, 1998). Five self-taught artists featured in *Low Brow Gods: The Art of Boxing*, Center for the Arts, San Francisco, 1997.

161 Emma Amos, introducing her work at the Flomenhaft Gallery: http://www.flomenhaftgallery.com/exhibitions/emma_amos_intro.htm.

162 Amos includes Ali, along with Joe Louis, in several works that tell stories about her own life, that of her family, and that of the black American twentieth century; works such as *A Reading at Bessie Smith's Grave* (1985), *My Mothers My Sisters* (1992) and *Freedom March* in the 1988 series, *Odyssey*. See *Emma Amos: Paintings and Prints, 1982–92*, exh. cat., The College of Wooster Art Museum (Wooster, OH, 1993); Al Murray, 'Interview with Emma Amos', October 1968, Smithsonian Archives of American Art, http://www.aaa.si.edu/collections/oralhistories/transcripts/amos.68.htm.

163 Donna Graves, 'Representing the Race: Detroit's *Monument to Joe Louis*', in *Critical Issues in Public Art*, ed. Senie and Webster, pp. 215–27. See also Ferguson, 'Tomato Cans', p. 12. Graham may have been drawing on Richard Avedon's portrait, 'Joe Louis, fighter', a photograph of his clenched fist with the thumb on top. Avedon, with James Baldwin, *Nothing Personal* (New York, 1964).

164 Hal Foster discusses the 'traumatic realism' of Warhol's series in *The Return of the Real* (Cambridge, MA, 1996), pp. 130–38. Ferguson notes the connection between *Buster Douglas* and Warhol's 1964 *Most Wanted Men* series in 'Tomato Cans', p. 11.

165 Others have simply dismissed his work as a kind of primitivist slumming. For a balanced account of critical responses to Basquiat, see Alison Pearlman, *Unpackaging Art of the 1980s* (Chicago, 2003), ch. 3.

166 Thelma Golden, 'My Brother', *Black Male: Representations of Masculinity in Contemporary American Art*, exh. cat., Whitney Museum of American Art, New York (New York, 1994), pp. 39–40. Golden locates this idea in James Baldwin's assertion that 'African-Americans need to reclaim their (lost) crowns and wear them'. Another possible source might have been Gary Byrd and Stevie Wonder's *The Crown* (1979) which asserts that 'Everybody in the world has a Crown' and includes the lines 'If you gonna fight don't do it free / Make 'em pay to see just like Ali'. See Toop, *Rap Attack 3*, p. 46.

167 Greg Tate, *Flyboy in the Buttermilk: Essays on Contemporary America* (New York, 1992), p. 238. Along with the crown, the raised arm (perhaps a Black Power salute) is one of Basquiat's most often-repeated symbols. See also bell hooks, *Outlaw Culture: Resisting Representation* (New York, 1994), p. 20.

168 Most of these paintings are reproduced in *Jean-Michel Basquiat*, exh. cat., Whitney Museum, New York (New York, 1992) and *Basquiat*, exh. cat., Brooklyn Museum, New York (New York, 2005). *St Joe Louis Surrounded by Snakes*, a recognizable portrait of the boxer accompanied by a hook-nosed

caricature of Mike Jacobs, is based on an Irving Penn photograph from 1948. See Milly Heyd, *Mutual Reflections: Jews and Blacks in American Art* (New Brunswick, NJ, 1999), pp. 186–93. Greg Tate and Leonhard Emmerling argue convincingly for the influence of hip hop, and its battles on Basquiat's work. *Jean-Michel Basquiat*, p. 88. Incidental images or references to boxers can be found in other works too numerous to discuss here. See also Kevin Young's collection of poems based on Basquiat paintings (many about boxers), *To Repel Ghosts: Five Sides in B Minor* (South Royalton, VT, 2001).

169 Benjamin H. D. Buchloch, '1984a', in *Art Since 1900* (London, 2004), p. 590.

170 On the difficulty in distinguishing '*critics* of the reification and fragmentation of the sign and *connoisseurs* of the same process', see Foster, *The Return of the Real*, p. 96.

171 Hal Foster, '1993c', in *Art since 1900*, p. 644. Roderick Buchanan, *Players*, exh. cat., Dundee Contemporary Arts (Dundee, 2000). *Deadweight* (and many of the other works discussed here) was included in *The Squared Circle: Boxing in Contemporary Art.*, exh. cat., Walker Art Center, Minneapolis (Minneapolis, MN, 2003). *Rumble, Young Man, Rumble* became part of a larger installation called *Skin Tight*. See Glenn Ligon, 'Skin Tight', in *Boxer: An Anthology*, ed. Chandler, Gill, Guha and Tawadros, pp. 58–69; Golden, 'My Brother', p. 41; Richard J. Powell, *Black Art and Culture in the 20th Century* (London, 1997), p. 190.

172 Paul-Felix Montez, personal correspondence, 11 September 2006. A model of *The Gloves* featured in his exhibition 'The 21st Century Las Vegas Monuments', Las Vegas Museum Library and City Hall Museum, 19 September–30 October 2006. See also Tim Dahlberg, *Fight Town: Las Vegas – The Boxing Capital of the World* (Las Vegas, 2004).

173 Ralph Rugoff, 'David Hammons: Public Nuisance, Rabble Rouser, Hometown Artist,' in *David Hammons in the Hood*, exh. cat., Illinois State Museum (Springfield, IL, 1993), p. 19. See also *Saint Louis* (1988), a white glove puppet supporting a cardboard torso of Louis in boxing pose; two fingers become his legs. *David Hammons: Raising the Rubble*, exh. cat., The Institute for Contemporary Art, P.S.1 Museum (New York, 1991), p. 60. Tyson and Holyfield are the subjects of *Ear of Corn* (1997), but neither man is depicted directly. Instead Hammons puns on their encounter with a sculpture consisting of a pair of boxing gloves which enclose a bitten ear of corn. Boxing has become a 'corny' phallic spectacle. Manthia Diawara, 'Make It Funky: The Art of David Hammons', *Artforum*, 36, no. 9 (May 1998), pp. 120–27.

174 See also Ian Geraghty's golden-sequined gloves, *Bright Lights, Cameras, Bloody Action and Flashes of Brilliance* (1996), in *Boxer: An Anthology*, p. 11.

175 See Keith Piper, 'Four Corners, A Contest of Opposites,' in *Boxer: An Anthology*, pp. 70–79; *Step into the Arena: Notes on Black Masculinity and the Contest of Territory* (Rochdale, 1992). *Four Corners* and *A Grey Area*, discussed below, were commissioned by the Institute of International Visual Arts for the touring exhibition *Boxer*, curated by John Gill at the Walsall Museum and Art Gallery. In the accompanying catalogue, David Chandler acknowledged the 'inspirational role'

of Oates's *On Boxing. Boxer: An Anthology*, p. 19. Curator Olukemi Ilesanmi made a similar tribute in *The Squared Circle*, p. 1.

176 Some of these are in the Tate along with a section of the woodcut parquet floor. See *Thomas Kilpper: The Ring*, exh. cat., South London Gallery Projects (London, 2000).

177 See *Boxer: An Anthology*, p. 22.

178 James Westcott, 'Sport at the Socrates Sculpture Park', *New York Arts Magazine* (September–October 2005).

179 Golden, 'My Brother', p. 41. Ferguson describes Simmons's allusion to Warhol's 162 dance diagram painting as a 'critique . . . of the whole Abstract Expressionist idea of painting as performance'. 'Tomato Cans', p. 11. A photograph of David Bowie in sparring gloves next to a dance diagram appeared on the cover of *Let's Dance* (1983). Bowie famously performed in boxing gloves during the 1974 *Diamond Dogs* tour.

180 A similar tension informs Jim Campbell's *Fight* (2000), part of a series entitled Ambiguous Icons. Campbell translates a colour video of a boxing match into a low resolution grid; it is only by identifying the colours provided by the boxers' bodies and their gloves that the viewer can see the image as a boxing match. Glenn Kurtz, 'Jim Campbell at Hosfelt Gallery', *Artweek*, 31, no. 6 (June 2000), pp. 15–16.

181 For Rosalind E. Krauss, the 'representational plane of the sporting event' is 'displaced' by the power of the rhythm. 'Pulse', in Yve-Alain Bois and Rosalind E. Krauss, *Formless: A User's Guide* (New York, 1997), pp. 161–5; '1993a', in *Art Since 1900*, pp. 631–3. See also Foster, *The Return of the Real*, pp. 42–3. Benjamin H. D. Buchloch argues the opposite – that because of its interest in history *Box (ahhareturnabout)* 'signals a major departure from American post-minimalist aesthetics'. 'Memory Lessons and History Tableaux', in *James Coleman*, ed. George Baker (Cambridge, MA, 2003), p. 97.

182 Anne Rorimer, 'James Coleman, 1970–1985' in *James Coleman*, p. 9; Lynne Cooke, 'A Tempered Agnosia', in *James Coleman*, p. 130.

183 Jean Fisher, 'The Place of the Spectator in the Work of James Coleman', in *James Coleman*, p. 25; 'The Enigma of the Hero in the Work of James Coleman', in *James Coleman*, p. 41. See also Fisher, 'James Coleman's *Box (Ahhareturnabout)*', in *Boxer: An Anthology*, pp. 54–7. Fisher describes Tunney as an Irishman, but although his parents were Irish, he was born in New York and certainly thought of himself as American.

184 Morrissey, 'Boxers' (1995). The track was first released on an EP with a picture of Billy Conn on the UK cover; then collected in *The World of Morrissey* (Reprise, 1995), the cover of which featured Cornelius Carr. Kenny Lane's picture appeared on the cover of *Southpaw Grammar* (Reprise, 1995). 'Sunny', possibly partly about Sonny Liston ('you punched and fell / And then you felt embarrassed') is included in *Suedehead: The Best of Morrissey* (Parlophone, 1997). See Bret, *Morrissey*, p. 148; Nabeel Zuberi, *Sounds English: Transnational Popular Music* (Urbana, IL, 2001), pp. 60-64.

185 Richard Ford's *The Ultimate Good Luck* (1981) begins with a boxing match whose narrative is determined by an unseen

punch. This foreshadows the novel's own narrative development. The 'essence of the modern predicament', the protagonist thinks, lies in recognizing that 'the guy who had it in for you was the guy you'd never seen.' Ford, *The Ultimate Good Luck* (New York, 1986), pp. 7. 35.

186 Steven A. Riess, 'Professional Sports as an Avenue of Social Mobility in America: Some Myths and Realities', in *Essays on Sport History and Sport Mythology*, ed. Donald G. Kyle and Gary D. Stark (College Station, TX, 1990), p. 90.

187 Rotella, *Cut Time*, p. 183.

188 Thom Jones, *The Pugilist at Rest* (London, 1994), p. 21.

189 Bert Randolph Sugar, 'Boxing Gyms: A Brief History', in *Shadow Boxers*, ed. Gattuso, p. 24. Katherine Dunn, 'School of Hard Knocks', in *Shadow Boxers*, p. 37. See also Cohen, *Without Apology*, p. 50. An abandoned baby is brought up in a gym by a 70-year-old ex-prizefighter in Harry Crews's *The Gypsy's Curse* (1974). When the protagonist of Gus Lee's *China Boy* is told by his father to decide whether he's Chinese or American, he instead 'picks YMCA' and an alternative father who teaches him to spar. Lee, *China Boy* (New York, 1991), pp. 212–13. Loïc Wacquant describes the work of the boxing trainer as 'virile mothering'. *Body and Soul: Notebooks of an Apprentice Boxer* (Oxford, 2004), p. 7. Two very different views of gym culture can be found in the films *Broken Noses* (1987) and *On the Ropes* (1999).

190 Sekules, *The Boxer's Heart*, p. 51. 'Boxing was my way into the ghetto,' she quipped. Nancy Hass, 'When Women Step into the Ring', *New York Times*, 1 October 2000, pp. 1, 7. Hass notes that Gleason's, which first admitted women in 1986, had 116 (that is 15 per cent) women members in 2000. *The Gleason's Gym Total Body Workout for Women* was published in 2006. After going to a 'proper' gym, Leah Hager Cohen found the pink hand wraps and wicker baskets offered by a 'spiffy' women's health club unsatisfying. *Without Apology*, p. 222.

191 The film was based on F. X. Toole's short story of the same title. *Rope Burns* (London, 2000), pp. 61–101. See also Toole's posthumously published novel, *Pound for Pound* (London, 2006).

192 Thom Jones, *Sonny Liston was a Friend of Mine* (London, 1999), pp. 13, 32.

193 Snowden Picket notes that the walk to Brooklyn's Gleason's Gym from the subway station that brought her from Manhattan is 'down a long hill'. She has to 'will' herself 'to descend'. *Looking for a Fight*, pp. 67, 142.

194 A similar soundscape accompanies Ana Busto's photographic series, *La Escuela Cubana de Boxeo* and, Busto with Sandra Seymour, *Night Fight*.

195 Arlene Shulman, *The Prizefighters* (London, 1995), pp. 36–9. Snowden Picket begins her memoir of Gleason's with a description of its smells. *Looking for a Fight*, p. 1. On Gleason's, see also Hauser, *The Black Lights*, pp. 129–30. Eric Trethewey's 'The Gym on Tchoupitoulas Street' is a eulogy to boxers who 'had fight in them like shit has stink'. *Perfect in Their Art*, ed. Hedin and Waters, pp. 197–8.

196 Robert Anasi, *The Gloves: A Boxing Chronicle* (Edinburgh, 2004), p. 34.

197 Pete Hamill, in *The Times Square Gym*, photographs by John Goodman (New York, 1996), pp. 1–2; Pete Hamill, *Flesh and Blood* (New York, 1978), pp. 7–8. On boxing as manual work, see Rotella, *Good with Their Hands*. Joe Rein describes the boxing gym as an 'endangered species' in need of preservation: 'Save the Tiger', in *Shadow Boxers*, ed. Gattuso, p. 157. See also Wiley, 'Kronk', in *Serenity*; Bud Collins, 'Boxing Grieves Loss of 5th Street Gym', in *The Best American Sportswriting 1994*, ed. Tom Boswell (Boston, 1994), pp. 84–6. Arcadia Publishing has recently brought out a series of books of photographs celebrating the 'boxing heritage' of American cities such as Cleveland, Philadelphia, Detroit, Boston and San Francisco.

198 Craig Raine, *Rich* (London, 1984), pp. 92–4. See also 'A Silver Plate', p. 46.

199 Toole, 'Frozen Water', in *Rope Burns*, p. 142.

200 On Howson's earlier boxing paintings, see Robert Heller, *Peter Howson* (Edinburgh, 1993).

201 Rotella, *Cut Time*, p. 8.

202 Anasi, *The Gloves*, pp. 62, 331; Wade, *Wrecking Machine*, p. 317.

203 Snowden Picket, *Looking for a Fight*, pp. 51–4.

204 Breece D'J Pancake, 'The Scrapper', in *The Stories of Breece D'J Pancake* (Boston, 1983), pp. 101–14. Also set in West Virginia, Pinckney Benedict's 1994 novel *Dogs of God* seems to take 'The Scrapper' as a starting point. In Pete Dexter's *Flesh and Blood* an imprisoned boxer rejects the sexual advances of his Black Muslim cell-mate by biting off his nose. See pp. 36–7.

205 Luis Alberto Urrea, *In Search of Snow* (New York, 1995), p. 70.

206 Foster, *The Return of the Real*, p. 149.

207 Wiley, *Serenity*, p. 227; Anasi, *The Gloves*, p. 315 fn.; Rotella, *Cut Time*, p. 103; Tom Boswell, 'Pain', in *The Best American Sports Writing of the Century*, ed. David Halberstam (Boston, 1999), pp. 455–60. The theatricality of professional wrestling is often evoked as the opposite of boxing. See Roland Barthes, 'The World of Wrestling', *Mythologies*, trans. Annette Lavers (New York, 2000), pp. 15–25.

208 Rotella, *Cut Time*, pp. 13, 207.

209 Rotella, *Cut Time*, p. 14. As well as 'hitting', naturalists also prefer to talk of 'fights' rather than use sanitizing words such as 'bouts' or 'contests'. Richard Ford disagrees. 'Hitting in the face,' he writes, 'is finally not particularly interesting, inasmuch as it lacks even the smallest grain of optimism.' 'In the Face', in *The Fights: Photographs by Charles Hoff*, ed. Ford (San Francisco, 1996), p. 10.

210 Quoted on the cover of Larry Fink, *Boxing: Photographs* (Zurich, 1997). On Sherman's own sparring experience, see Betsy Berne, 'Cindy Sherman: Studio Visit', *Tate Arts and Culture*, 5 (May/June 2003), pp. 37–41.

211 Oates views metaphor as the sign, as well as the tool, of the 'writerly' and thus claims to banish it from *On Boxing*, a work that strives to recapture, as well as document, the 'vanished world' of her working-class childhood. The book nevertheless remains anxiously figurative throughout. See *On Boxing*, pp. 4, 61, 93, 112; 'My Father, My Fiction', *New*

*York Times Magazine*, 16 March 1989, p. 45; George Vecsy, 'A Heavyweight Look at Boxing', in *Conversations with Joyce Carol Oates*, ed. Lee Milazzo (Jackson, MI, 1989), p. 149. Loïc Wacquant spent a year as 'Busy' Louie training for the Chicago Golden Gloves as an attempt to 'restitute [the] carnal dimension of existence' into a sociology 'riddled with false concepts' such as the 'underclass'. The 'social agent', he writes, 'is before anything else a being of flesh, nerves and senses'. *Body and Soul*, pp. vii, ix. The layout of the book – including courier typeface and photographs with visible sprocket holes – also signals authenticity. See note 22 above.

212 Claude Lévi-Strauss, *The Elementary Structures of Kinship*, trans. J. H. Bell, J. R. von Sturmer, R. Needham (Boston, 1969), p. xix.

# Select Bibliography

Adams, Neal, and Danny O'Neil, *Superman vs. Muhammad Ali*, DC Comics, no. C–56 (1978)

Algren , Nelson, *The Devil's Stocking* (New York, 1983)

——, *The Neon Wilderness* (New York, 1986)

——, *Never Come Morning* (New York, 1987)

——, *Notes from a Sea Diary: Hemingway All the Way* (New York, 1966)

——, *Nonconformity* (New York, 1996)

——, *Chicago: City on the Make* (New York, 1951)

——, *Who Lost an American?* (London, 1963)

Ali , Muhammad, with Richard Durham, *The Greatest: My Own Story* (London, 1976)

Allen, David Rayvern, ed., *Punches on the Page* (Edinburgh, 1998)

*American Fighters: A Century of Boxing in Art*, exh. cat., Frances Lehman Loeb Art Center, Vassar College, 1996

Ames, Jonathan, *My Less Than Secret Life* (New York, 2002)

*Emma Amos: Paintings and Prints, 1982–92*, exhib. cat, The College of Wooster Art Museum, 1993

Anasi, Robert, *The Gloves: A Boxing Chronicle* (Edinburgh, 2004)

Anderson, Sherwood, *A Story Teller's Story* (New York, 1924)

——, *Death in the Woods and Other Stories* (New York, 1961)

——, *No Swank* (Philadelphia, 1934)

——, *Selected Letters*, ed. Charles Modlin (Knoxville, TN, 1984)

Angelou, Maya, *I Know Why the Caged Bird Sings* (London, 1984)

——, *The Heart of a Woman* (London, 1986)

——, *All God's Children Need Travelling Shoes* (London, 1991)

Anstey, Christopher, *The Patriot* (Cambridge, 1767)

——, *Memoirs of the Noted Buckhorse, Wherein That Celebrated Hero is Carried into High Life*, 2 vols (London, 1756)

Antheil, George, *Bad Boy of Music* (Hollywood, 1990)

Apollinaire, Guillaume, *Le Guetteur mélancolique suivi de Poèmes Retrouvés* (Paris, 1970)

Apollonius, *Jason and the Golden Fleece (The Argonautica)*, trans. Richard Hunter (Oxford, 1993)

Apple, Max, *The Oranging of America* (London, 1976)

——, *Zip: A Novel of the Left and Right* (New York, 1978)

Archer-Straw, Petrine, *Negrophilia* (London, 2000)

Armstrong, Tim, *Modernism, Technology and the Body* (Cambridge, 1998)

Arp, Jean, *Collected French Writings*, trans. Joachim Neugroschel and ed. Marcel Jean (London, 2001)

Arroyo, Eduardo, *Panama Al Brown* (Paris, 1998)

*Art et Sport*, exh. cat., Musée des Beaux-Arts de Mons, 1984

*The Art of Boxing: The J. Terry Bender Collection*, exh. cat., The Emily Lowe Gallery, Hofstra University, 1978

*The Artist at Ringside*, exh. cat., The Butler Institute of American Art, 1992

Asbury, Herbert, *The Gangs of New York* (London, 2002)

Ashe, Arthur R., Jr, *A Hard Road to Glory*, 3 vols (New York, 1993)

Avedon, Richard, *Nothing Personal*, with an essay by James Baldwin (New York, 1964)

Bacchylides, *Epinician Odes and Dithyrambs*, trans. David R. Slavitt (Philadelphia, 1998)

Badcock, Jonathan, *Selections from The Fancy: or True Sportsman's Guide by an Operator* (Barre, MA, 1972)

Baden-Powell, Robert, *Scouting for Boys* (Oxford, 2005)

Bak, Richard, *Joe Louis, The Great Black Hope* (Cambridge, MA, 1998)

Baker, Aaron, and Todd Boyd, eds, *Out of Bounds: Sports, Media, and The Politics of Identity* (Bloomington, 1997)

Baker, Aaron, *Contesting Identities: Sports in American Film* (Urbana, IL, 2003)

Baker, George, ed., *James Coleman* (Cambridge, MA, 2003)

Baldwin, James, *Nobody Knows My Name* (New York, 1961)

——, *The Fire Next Time* (Harmondsworth, 1964)

——, *James Baldwin & Nikki Giovanni, A Dialogue* (London, 1975)

——, *The Price of the Ticket: Collected Non-fiction, 1948–1985* (London, 1985)

Baricco, Alessandro, *City*, trans. Ann Goldstein (Harmondsworth, 2001)

Barnes, Djuna, *I Could Never Be Lonely Without a Husband* (London, 1987)

——, *New York*, ed. Alyce Barry (Los Angeles, 1989)

——, *Nightwood* (London, 2001)

Barthes, Roland, *Mythologies*, trans. Annette Lavers (New York, 2000)

*Jean-Michel Basquiat*, exh. cat., Whitney Museum, 1992

*Basquiat*, exh. cat., Brooklyn Museum, 2005

Batchelor, Denzil, *Jack Johnson and His Times* (London, 1956)

Bathrick, David, 'Max Schmeling on the Canvas: Boxing as an Icon of Weimar Culture', *New German Critique*, 51 (Autumn 1990), pp. 113–36

Beauchamp, Edward R., 'Boxing', in Karen Christensen, Allen

Guttmann and Gertrud Pfister, eds, *International Encyclopaedia of Women and Sports*, vol. 1 (New York, 2001), pp. 167–76

Becker, George J., ed. and trans., *Documents of Modern Literary Realism* (Princeton, 1963)

Bell, Madison Smartt, *Save Me, Joe Louis* (Harmondsworth, 1993)

Bellows, Emma S., *George Bellows: His Lithographs* (New York, 1927)

Benjamin, Walter, *Illuminations*, trans. Harry Zohn (London, 1970)

Bennett, Lerone, Jr., 'Jack Johnson and the Great White Hope', *Ebony* (October 1976), pp. 72–81

Benedict, Pinckney, *Dogs of God* (New York, 1994)

Benson, Peter, *Battling Siki* (Fayetteville, AR, 2006)

Bergan, Ronald, *Sports in the Movies* (New York, 1982)

Berger, Klaus, *Géricault and His Work*, trans. Winslow Ames (New York, 1978)

Berger, Martin A., *Man Made: Thomas Eakins and the Construction of Gilded Age Manhood* (Berkeley, CA, 2000)

Berger, Phil, *Blood Season: Tyson and the World of Boxing* (London, 1990)

Berghaus, Günter, ed., *International Futurism in Art and Literature* (Berlin, 2000)

Berkowitz, Michael, *The Jewish Self-Image: American and British Perspectives, 1881–1930* (London, 2000)

Berkowitz, Michael, and Ruti Ungar, eds, *Fighting Back? Jewish and Black Boxers in Britain* (London, 2007)

Berry, Mary Frances, and John W. Blassingame, *Long Memory: The Black Experience in America* (Oxford, 1982)

Berry, Ron, *So Long, Hector Bebb* (Cardigan, 2006)

Berzmozgis, David, *Natasha and Other Stories* (London, 2004)

Besant, Walter, *East London* (London, 1901)

——, *All Sorts and Conditions of Men* (Oxford, 1997)

Bingham, Howard L. and Max Wallace, *Muhammad Ali's Greatest Fight: Cassius Clay vs. the United States of America* (New York, 2000)

Birley, Derek, *Sport and the Making of Britain* (Manchester, 1993)

*Black Folk Art in America, 1930–1980*, exh. cat., Corcoran Gallery, 1982

*Black Male: Representations of Masculinity in Contemporary American Art*, exh. cat., Whitney Museum of American Art, 1994

Blady, Ken, *The Jewish Boxers' Hall of Fame* (New York, 1988)

Blauner, Peter, *Casino Moon* (London, 1994)

Bloom, Matt, *Blue Paradise* (New York, 1998)

Bockris, Victor, *Muhammad Ali in Fighter's Heaven* (London, 2000)

Bodner, Allen, *When Boxing was a Jewish Sport* (Westport, CT, 1997)

Bontemps, Arna, *Famous Negro Athletes* (New York, 1964)

Borràs, Maria Lluïsa, *Arthur Cravan: Une stratégie du scandale* (Paris, 1996)

Borrow, George, *Lavengro* (Oxford, 1982)

——, *The Romany Rye* (Oxford, 1906)

Boswell, James, *Boswell's London Journal, 1762–1763*, ed. Frederick A. Pottle (New Haven, 1950)

Boyd, Brain, *Vladimir Nabokov: The Russian Years* (Princeton, 1990)

Boyd, Herb, with Ray Robinson II, *Pound for Pound: A Biography of Sugar Ray Robinson* (New York, 2005)

Brady, Jim, *Boxing Confidential* (Lytham, 2002)

Brady, William A., *The Fighting Man* (Indianapolis, 1916)

——, *Showman* (New York, 1937)

Brailsford, Dennis, *Bareknuckles: A Social History of Prize-fighting* (Cambridge, 1988)

Brayle, Hugh, Lincoln Sargeant and Carol Brayne, 'Could boxing be banned? A legal and epidemiological perspective', *British Medical Journal*, 316 (1998), pp. 1813–15

Brecht, Bertolt, *Diaries 1920–1922*, trans. John Willett, (London, 1979)

——, *Poems, 1913–1956*, ed. John Willettt, and Ralph Manheim (New York, 1987)

——, *In the Jungle of Cities*, trans. Gerhard Nellhaus, ed. John Willett and Ralph Manheim (London, 1970)

——, *Collected Plays: Two*, ed. John Willett and Ralph Manheim (London, 1994)

——, *Collected Short Stories*, ed. John Willett and Ralph Manheim (London, 1992)

Brontë, Patrick Branwell, *The Works of Patrick Branwell Brontë*, ed. Victor Neufeldt (New York, 1997), vol. 1

——, *Brother in the Shadow: Stories and Sketches by Patrick Branwell Brontë*, ed. Mary Butterfield (Bradford, 1988)

Brookeman, Christopher, 'Float Like a Butterfly, Sting Like a Bee: Mythologies of Representation in Selected Writings on Boxing by Norman Mailer', in William Blazek and Michael K. Glenday, eds, *American Mythologies* (Liverpool, 2005), pp. 47–62

Brooks, Chris, 'Burying Tom Sayers: Heroism, Class and the Victorian Cemetery', *The Victorian Society Annual* (1989), pp. 4–20.

Brooks, Gwendolyn, *Black Steel: Joe Frazier and Muhammad Ali* (Detroit, 1971)

Brown, James, with Bruce Tucker, *James Brown: The Godfather of Soul* (Fontana, 1988)

Brown, Lloyd L., *Iron City* (New York, 1951)

Brown, Sterling, *The Collected Poems*, ed. Michael S. Harper (New York, 1980)

Broyard, Anatole, 'The Romance of a Left Hook', *New York Times Book Review*, 15 March 1987, p. 8

Bryden, Bill, *Benny Lynch: Scenes from a Short Life* (Edinburgh, 1975)

Buchanan, Roderick, *Players*, exh. cat., Dundee Contemporary Arts, 2000

Buhle, Paul, and Dave Wagner, *Blacklisted* (London, 2003)

Bukowski, Charles, *South of No North* (Los Angeles, 1973)

——, *The Roominghouse Madrigals: Early Selected Poems, 1946–1966* (Los Angeles, 1988)

Burke, Kenneth, *The Philosophy of Literary Form* (New York, 1941)

——, *A Grammar of Motives* (Berkeley, CA, 1969)

——, *Language as Symbolic Action* (Berkeley, CA, 1966)

——, *Counter-Statement* (Berkeley, CA, 1968)

——, *Permanence and Change* (Berkeley, CA, 1984)

Burke, Peter, *Popular Culture in Early Modern Europe* (London, 1978)

Burroughs, Edgar Rice, *The Mucker* (New York, 1974)

Burrowes, John, *Benny: The Life and Times of a Fighting Legend* (Edinburgh, 1982)

Bush, W. Stephen, 'Arguments of Fight Films', *The Moving Picture World*, 15 May 1915, pp. 1049–50

Butler, Frank, *A History of Boxing in Britain* (London, 1972)

Byron, *Complete Poetical Works*, ed. Frederick Page (Oxford, 1970)

——, *Selected Letters and Journals*, ed. Peter Gunn

(Harmondsworth, 1972)

Cahan, Abraham, *The Imported Bridegroom and Other Stories* (New York, 1996)

Cain, James M., *Double Indemnity* (London, 2002)

Callahan, John F., ed., *Ralph Ellison's Invisible Man: A Casebook* (Oxford, 2004)

Callahan, Morley, *That Summer in Paris* (New York, 1963)

Callahan, Tom, 'Boxing's Allure', *Time*, 27 June 1988, pp. 66–71

Cantu, Robert C., ed., *Boxing and Medicine* (Champaign, IL, 1995)

Carey, John, *The Violent Effigy* (London, 1973)

Carpentier, Georges, *Carpentier by Himself*, trans. Edward Fitzgerald (London, 1958)

——, *My Methods, or Boxing as a Fine Art*, trans. F. Hurdman-Lucus (London, n.d.).

Carter, Rubin, *The Sixteenth Round: From Number One Contender to #45472* (New York, 1974)

Cashmore, Ellis, *Tyson: Nurture of the Beast* (London, 2005)

Cavanaugh, Jack, *Tunney* (New York, 2006)

Cavell, Benjamin, *Rumble, Young Man, Rumble: Stories* (New York, 2004)

Cendrars, Blaise, *Le Lotissement du ciel* (Paris, 1996)

Century, Douglas, *Barney Ross* (New York, 2006)

Chaiton, Sam, and Terry Swinton, *Lazarus and The Hurricane* (New York, 1991)

Chandler, David, John Gill, Tania Guha and Gilane Tawadros, eds, *Boxer: An Anthology of Writings on Boxing and Visual Culture* (London, 1996)

Chandler, Raymond, *The Chandler Collection*, vol. 1 (London, 1983)

——, *Selected Letters of Raymond Chandler*, ed. Frank MacShane (London, 1981)

Chaplin, Charles, *My Autobiography* (Harmondsworth, 1996)

Chapman, Abraham, ed., *Black Voices* (New York, 1968)

——, ed., *New Black Voices* (New York, 1972)

Chase, Stuart, *Men and Machines* (London, 1929)

Chemin, Michel, *La Roi du ring* (Paris, 1992)

Chion, Michel, *Audio-Vision*, trans. Claudia Gorbman (New York, 1994)

Chisholm, Anne, *Nancy Cunard* (Harmondsworth, 1979)

Christie, Ian, and David Thompson, eds, *Scorsese on Scorsese* (London, 2003)

Chudacoff, Howard P., *The Age of the Bachelor: Creating an American Subculture* (Princeton, 1999)

Clare, John, *Autobiographical Writings*, ed. Eric Robinson (Oxford, 1983)

Clark, Tom, *The World of Damon Runyon* (New York, 1978)

Clay, Charles E., 'A Bout with the Gloves', *Outing*, 9 (1887), pp. 359–67

Cleaver, Eldridge, *Soul on Ice* (London, 1968)

Clurman, Harold, *The Fervent Yeats: The Story of the Group Theatre and the Thirties* (New York, 1957)

Cobbett, William, 'In Defence of Boxing' (1805), in *Cobbett's England*, ed. John Derry (London, 1968), pp. 172–80

Cohen, Leah Hager, *Without Apology: Girls, Women and the Desire to Fight* (New York, 2005)

Conover, Roger et al., eds, *Four Dada Suicides* (London, 1995)

Colette, *Chéri*, trans. Roger Senhouse (London, 2001)

——, *The Last of Chéri*, trans. Roger Senhouse (London, 2001)

——, *Contes des Mille et Un Matins* (Paris, 1970)

*The Collages of Benny Andrews*, exh. cat., Studio Museum in Harlem (1988)

Colley, Linda, *Britons: Forging the Nation, 1707–1837* (London, 2003)

Cone, James H., *Martin and Malcolm and America* (Maryknoll, NY, 1991)

Cooper, Henry, *An Autobiography* (London, 1974)

Corbett, James J., *The Roar of the Crowd* (New York, 1925)

Corey, Mary F., *The World Through a Monocle: The New Yorker at Midcentury* (Cambridge, MA, 1999)

Corn, Wanda, *The Great American Thing: Modern Art and National Identity, 1915–1935* (Berkeley, CA, 1999)

Cowley, Malcolm, *Exile's Return* (Harmondsworth, 1994)

Cox, William D., ed., *Boxing in Art and Literature* (New York, 1935)

Cravan, Arthur, *Oeuvres*, ed. Jean-Pierre Begot (Paris, 1992)

*Arthur Cravan: Poète et Boxeur*, exh. cat., Galerie 1900/2000, Paris, 1992

Crews, Harry, *The Knockout Artist* (New York, 1988)

Crone, Rainer, *Stanley Kubrick: Dreams and Shadows, Photographs 1945–1950* (London, 2005)

Crouch, Stanley, *The All-American Skin Game* (Vintage Books, 1997)

Cunard, Nancy, ed., *Negro: An Anthology* (New York, 2002)

Chuck D, with Yusaf Jah, *Fight the Power: Rap, Race and Reality* (Edinburgh, 1997)

Dahlberg, Tim, *Fight Town: Las Vegas – The Boxing Capital of the World* (Las Vegas, 2004)

Danly, Susan, and Cheryl Leibold, *Eakins and the Photograph* (Philadelphia, 1994)

Davis, Miles, *The Autobiography*, with Quincy Troupe (London, 1990)

Davis, Robert C., *The War of the Fists* (Oxford, 1994)

Dearborn, Mary V., *Mailer* (Boston, 1999)

*The Works of Thomas De Quincey*, vols 5–7, ed. David Groves et al. (London, 2000)

Deghy, Guy, *Noble and Manly: The History of the National Sporting Club* (London, 1956)

DeLillo, Don, *White Noise* (London, 1986)

——, *Underworld* (London, 1998)

Dempsey, Jack, with Jack Cuddy, *Championship Fighting* (London, 1950)

——, *How to Fight Tough* (Boulder, CO, 2002)

Denning, Michael, *The Cultural Front* (London, 1997)

Dexter, Pete, *Brotherly Love* (Harmondsworth, 1991)

Dickens, Charles, *Bleak House* (Harmondsworth, 1996)

——, *David Copperfield* (Harmondsworth, 1996)

——, *Dombey and Son* (Harmondsworth, 2002)

——, *Great Expectations* (Harmondsworth, 1996)

——, *Hard Times* (Harmondsworth, 1985)

——, *Martin Chuzzlewit* (Oxford, 1982)

——, *The Mystery of Edwin Drood* (London, 1996)

——, *Nicholas Nickleby* (Oxford, 1990)

——, *Oliver Twist* (Harmondsworth, 2002)

——, *The Old Curiosity Shop* (Harmondsworth, 2000)

——, *The Pickwick Papers* (Oxford, 1986)

——, *Speeches*, ed. K. J. Fielding (London, 1988)

——, *Sketches by Boz* (Harmondsworth, 1995)

——, *The Uncommercial Traveller and other Papers, 1859–70*, vol. 4 of

*The Dent Uniform Edition of Dickens' Journalism*, ed. Michael Slater and John Drew (London, 2000)

*Dio Chrysostom*, vol. 5, trans. J. W. Cohoon (London, 1939)

Disraeli, Benjamin, *Sybil* (Harmondsworth, 1980)

Dos Passos, John, *USA* (London, 1950)

——, *The Fourteenth Chronicle: Letters and Diaries of John Dos Passos*, ed. Townsend Ludington (London, 1974)

Doezema, Marianne, *George Bellows and Urban America* (New Haven, 1992)

Douglas, Ann, *Terrible Honesty: Mongrel Manhattan in the 1920s* (London, 1991)

Douglass, Frederick, *Narrative of the Life of Frederick Douglass* (Oxford, 1999)

——, *My Bondage and My Freedom* (New York, 1969)

——, *The Frederick Douglass Papers*, Series 1, *Speeches, Debates and Interviews*, ed. John W. Blassinghame and John R. McKivigan, vols 3 5 (New Haven, 1991)

——, *Life and Times* (Cleveland, OH, 2005)

Conan Doyle, Arthur, *The Exploits of Brigadier Gerard* (London, 1903)

——, *The Green Flag* (London, 1905)

——, *The Last Galley* (London, 1911)

——, *Rodney Stone* (London, 1912)

——, *Songs of the Road* (London, 1911)

——, *The Penguin Complete Sherlock Holmes* (Harmondsworth, 1981)

Drake, St Clair, and Horace R. Cayton, *Black Metropolis*, vol. II (New York, 1962)

Dreiser, Theodore, *A Book about Myself* (London, 1929)

——, *Fulfilment and Other Tales of Women and Men*, ed. T. D. Nostwich (Santa Rosa, CA, 1992)

——, *Sister Carrie* (Harmondsworth, 1981)

Drew, Bettina, *Nelson Algren: A Walk on the Wild Side* (London, 1990)

Dryden, John, *The Poems*, ed. James Kinsley (Oxford, 1958)

Duncan, John, *In the Red Corner: A Journey into Cuban Boxing* (London, 2000)

Duberman, Martin, *Paul Robeson: A Biography* (New York, 1988)

Du Bois, W.E.B., *The Souls of Black Folk* (New York, 1995)

——, *Writings* (New York, 1986)

——, *W.E.B Du Bois on Sociology and the Black Community*, ed. Dan S. Green and Edwin D. Driver (Chicago, 1978)

Dugaw, Dianne, *Warrior Women and Popular Balladry, 1650–1850* (Cambridge, 1989)

Duis, Perry R., *The Saloon: Public Drinking in Chicago and Boston, 1880–1920* (Urbana, IL, 1983)

Du Maurier, George, *Trilby* (Oxford, 1995)

Dunbar, Paul Laurence, *The Sport of the Gods* (New York, 1981)

Dundes, Alan, ed., *Mother Wit from the Laughing Barrel* (Jackson, MI, 1981)

Early, Gerald L., 'The Grace of Slaughter', *Iowa Review*, 18, no. 3, (Fall 1988), pp. 173–86

——, *Tuxedo Junction* (Hopewell, NJ, 1989)

——, 'Three Notes Toward a Cultural Definition of The Harlem Renaissance', *Callaloo*, 14, no. 1 (1991), pp. 136–49

——, ed., *Speech and Power*, vol. 1. (Hopewell, NJ, 1992)

——, *The Culture of Bruising* (Hopewell, NJ, 1994)

——, 'Ali's Rumble', *Sight and Sound*, 7, 5 (May 1997),

pp. 10–12

——, 'Leaving Home', in Gerald Early, ed., *Body Language: Writers on Sport* (Saint Paul, MI, 1998), pp. 113–43.

—— 'Jack Johnson: A Man Out of Time', in Michael MacCambridge, ed., *ESPN SportsCentury* (New York, 1999), pp. 32–49.

——, ed., *I'm A Little Special: A Muhammad Ali Reader* (London, 1999)

——, 'The Art of the Muscle: Miles Davis as American Knight and American Knave', in Early, ed., *Miles Davis and American Culture* (St Louis, 2001), pp. 3–23

——, 'Muhammad Ali as Third World Hero', in *This is Where I Came In: Black America in the 1960s* (Lincoln, NE, 2003), pp. 1–35

Edwards, Harry, *The Revolt of the Black Athlete* (New York, 1969)

Edwards, Paul, *Wyndham Lewis: Painter and Writer* (New Haven, 2000)

Egan, Pierce, *Boxiana; or Sketches of Ancient and Modern Pugilism, From the Days of the Renowned Broughton and Slack, to the Championship of Crib*, 2 vols (London, 1818)

——, *Life in London. Or the Day and Night Scenes of Jerry Hawthorn Esq. and his elegant friend Corinthian Tom accompanied by Bob Logic, The Oxonian, in their Rambles and Sprees Through the Metropolis* (London, 1821)

——, *Boxiana: A Selection*, ed. John Ford (London, 1976)

Eisenstein, Sergei, *Film Form* (New York, 1949)

——, *Selected Works, vol. 1: Writings, 1922–34*, ed. Richard Taylor (London, 1988)

Eitner, Lorenz E. A., *Géricault: His Life and Work* (London, 1983)

Elias, Norbert and Eric Dunning, eds, *Quest for Excitement: Sport and Leisure in the Civilising Process* (Oxford, 1986)

Eliot, George, *Middlemarch* (Harmondsworth, 1994)

——, *Adam Bede* (Harmondsworth, 1980)

——, *The Mill on the Floss* (Harmondsworth, 1985)

Eliot, T. S., *The Complete Poems and Plays* (London, 1969)

——, *The Waste Land: A Facsimile and Transcript of the Original*, ed. Valerie Eliot (London, 1971)

Ellison, Ralph, *Invisible Man* (New York, 1995)

——, *The Collected Essays*, ed. John F. Callahan (New York, 1995)

——, *Shadow and Act* (New York, 1972)

——, *Flying Home and Other Stories*, ed. John F. Callahan (Harmondsworth, 1998)

——, 'Negro Prize Fighter', *New Masses*, 17 December 1940, pp. 26–7

——, *Juneteenth* (Harmondsworth, 2000)

Ellmann, Richard, *James Joyce* (Oxford, 1982)

Ellroy, James, *The Black Dahlia* (London, 1987)

——, *The Six Cold Thousand* (London, 2001)

——, *Destination: Morgue!* (London, 2005)

Emmerling, Leonhard, *Jean-Michel Basquiat* (Cologne, 2003)

Endelman, Todd M., *The Jews of Georgian England, 1714–1830* (Ann Arbor, MI, 1999)

*Envisioning America: Prints, Drawings and Photographs by George Grosz and his Contemporaries, 1915–1933*, exh. cat., Busch-Reisinger Museum, Harvard University, 1990

Erenberg, Lewis A., *The Greatest Fight of Our Generation: Louis vs. Schmeling* (Oxford, 2006)

Fabre, Michel, 'The Ring and the Stage: African Americans in

Parisian Public and Imaginary Space before World War I', in *Space in America: Theory History Culture*, ed. Klaus Benesch and Kerstin Schmidt (Amsterdam, 2005), pp. 521–28.

——, *The Unfinished Quest of Richard Wright*, trans. Isabel Barzun (Urbana, IL, 1993)

Fanon, Franz, *The Wretched of the Earth*, trans. Constance Farrington (New York, 1963)

——, *Black Skin, White Masks*, trans. Charles Lam Markmann (London, 1986)

Farber, Manny, *Negative Space* (New York, 1971)

Farington, Joseph, *The Diary of Joseph Farington*, vol. 9, ed. Kathryn Cave (New Haven, CT, 1982)

Farr, Finis, *Black Champion: The Life and Times of Jack Johnson* (New York, 1965)

Farred, Grant, 'Feasting on Foreman: *When We Were Kings* as Hagiography,' *Camera Obscura*, 39 (September 1996), pp. 52–77

——, *What's My Name: Black Vernacular Intellectuals* (Minneapolis, 2003)

Farrell, James T., *Studs Lonigan* (New York, 1977)

——, *Literary Essays, 1954–1974*, ed. Jack Alan Robbins (Port Washington, NY, 1976)

——, *The Short Stories of James T. Farrell* (New York, 1962)

Faulkner, William, *Absalom, Absalom!* (Penguin, 1971)

——, *Go Down, Moses* (Harmondsworth, 1960)

——, *The Sound and The Fury* (Harmondsworth, 1964)

Fergusson, Robert, *The Poems of Robert Fergusson*, ed. Matthew P. McDiarmid (Edinburgh, 1954–6)

Ferguson, Russell, 'Tomato Cans', *Visual Arts and Culture*, 1 (1998), pp. 2–13

Fielding, Henry, *Tom Jones* (Oxford, 1996)

——, *Joseph Andrews*, ed. Homer Goldberg (New York, 1987)

Fine, Elsa Honig, *The Afro-American Artist* (New York, 1982)

Fink, Larry, *Boxing: Photographs*, with an essay by Bert Randolph Sugar (Zurich, 1997)

Fisher, Philip, *Hard Facts: Setting and Form in the American Novel* (Oxford, 1986)

Fitch, Noel Riley, *Sylvia Beach and the Lost Generation: A History of Literary Paris in the Twenties and Thirties* (Harmondsworth, 1983)

Fitzgerald, F. Scott, *The Great Gatsby* (Harmondsworth, 1990)

——, *Tender is the Night* (Harmondsworth, 1986)

——, *The Crack-Up* (Harmondsworth, 1965)

Fitzgerald, Zelda, *The Collected Writings*, ed. Matthew J. Bruccoli (London, 1993)

Fleischer, Nat, *Leonard the Magnificent* (Norwalk, CT, 1947)

——, *John L. Sullivan* (London, 1952)

Fleischer, Nat, and Sam Andre, *A Pictorial History of Boxing* (London, 1959)

Ford, John, *Prizefighting: The Age of Regency Boximania* (Newton Abbot, 1971)

Ford, Richard, *The Ultimate Good Luck* (New York, 1986)

——, ed., *The Fights: Photographs by Charles Hoff* (San Francisco, 1996)

Foster, Hal, *The Return of the Real* (Cambridge, MA, 1996)

Foster, Hal, Rosalind E. Krauss, Yves-Alain Bois and Benjamin H. D. Buchloch, *Art Since 1900* (London, 2004)

Franck, Elisabeth, 'The Pugilistic Professor', *Lingua Franca*, July/August 2001, pp. 19–20

Fraser, George MacDonald, *Black Ajax* (London, 1997)

Frazier, E. Franklin, *Negro Youth at the Crossways* (New York, 1967)

Frost, Robert, *Complete Poems* (London, 1951)

Fryer, Peter, *Staying Power: The History of Black People in Britain* (London, 1984)

Fulford, Tim, *Romanticism and Masculinity* (London, 1999)

Gaines, Ernest J., *A Lesson Before Dying* (New York, 1994)

——, *The Autobiography of Miss Jane Pittman* (New York, 1971)

Gallico, Paul, *The Golden People* (New York, 1965)

——, *Farewell to Sport* (London, 1988)

——, *Matilda* (London, 1972)

Gardner, Leonard, *Fat City* (London, 1989)

Gates, Henry Louis, Jr, *Colored People* (New York, 1995)

—— and Nellie Y. McKay, eds, *The Norton Anthology of African American Literature* (New York, 1997)

Gattuso, John, ed., *Shadow Boxers* (Milford, NJ, 2005)

Gayle, Addison, Jr., ed., *The Black Aesthetic* (New York, 1970)

Gee, Tony, *Up to Scratch: Bareknuckle Fighting and Heroes of the Prize-ring* (Harpenden, 1998)

——, 'From Stage-fighting Fame to the Gallows at Tyburn: James Field – Pugilist and Criminal', in Barry J. Hugman, ed., *The British Board of Boxing Control Yearbook 2006* (Harpenden, 2005), pp. 55–8

Geertz, Clifford, *The Interpretation of Cultures* (London, 1993)

Gerould, Katherine Fullerton, *Ringside Seats* (New York, 1937)

Gibson, Truman K., Jr, *Knocking Down Barriers: My Fight for Black America* (Chicago, 2005)

Gilman, Sander, *The Jew's Body* (New York, 1991)

——, *Making the Body Beautiful* (Princeton, 1999)

——, *Jewish Self-Hate: Anti-Semitism and the Hidden Language of the Jews* (Baltimore, 1986)

Gilmore, Al-Tony, *Bad Nigger! The National Impact of Jack Johnson* (Port Washington, NY, 1975)

——, 'The Myth, Legend and Folklore of Joe Louis: The Impression of Sport on Society', *South Atlantic Quarterly* 82 (1983), pp. 256–68

Gilroy, Paul, *The Black Atlantic: Modernity and Double Consciousness* (London, 1993)

——, *Against Race* (Cambridge, MA, 2000)

Gioia, Ted, *The History of Jazz* (Oxford, 1998)

Giovanni, Nikki, *Re: Creation* (Detroit, 1970)

Girard, René, *Violence and the Sacred*, trans. P. Gregory (Baltimore, 1977)

Girgus, Sam B., *America on Film* (Cambridge, 2002)

Gittings, Robert, *John Keats* (Harmondsworth, 1971)

——, ed., *Letters of John Keats: A Selection* (Oxford, 1970)

Godfrey, John, *Treatise upon the Useful Science of Defence* (London, 1747)

Golden, Mark, *Sport and Society in Ancient Greece* (Cambridge, 1998)

Golding, Louis, *Magnolia Street* (Nottingham, 2006)

Goodman, John, with an essay by Pete Hamill, *The Times Square Gym* (New York, 1996)

Goodrich, Lloyd, *Thomas Eakins*, 2 vols (Cambridge, MA, 1982)

Gorn, Elliott J., *The Manly Art: Bare-Knuckle Prize-fighting in America*

(Ithaca, NY, 1986)

——, 'The Manassa Mauler and the Fighting Marine: An Interpretation of the Dempsey-Tunney Fights', *Journal of American Studies* (1985), 19, no. 1, pp. 27–45

——, ed., *Muhammad Ali, The People's Champ* (Urbana, IL, 1995)

Graham, Barry, *The Champion's New Clothes* (London, 1991)

Grandt, Jurgen E., *Kinds of Blue: The Jazz Aesthetic in African American Narrative* (Columbus, OH, 2004)

Graziano, Rocky, with Roland Barber, *Somebody Up There Likes Me* (New York, 1956)

Green, Benny, *Shaw's Champions* (London, 1978)

Green, Harvey, *Fit for America: Health, Fitness, Sport and American Society* (New York, 1986)

Greenberg, Martin H., *In the Ring: A Treasury of Boxing Stories* (New York, 1986)

Grieveson, Lee, *Policing Cinema: Movies and Censorship in Early Twentieth-Century America* (Berkeley, CA, 2004)

Griffin, Peter, *Along with Youth: Hemingway, the Early Years* (Oxford, 1985)

Griffiths, Leon, *Dinner at the Sporting Club* (London, 1978)

Grindon, Leger, 'Body and Soul: The Structure of Meaning in the Boxing Film Genre', *Cinema Journal*, 35, no. 4 (Summer 1996), pp. 54–69

Grosley, Pierre Jean, *A tour to London, or, New observations on England and its inhabitants*, trans. Thomas Nugent, 3 vols (Dublin, 1772)

Grosz, George, *An Autobiography*, trans. Nora Hodges (Berkeley, CA, 1997)

Guillén, Nicolás, *Man-Making Words: Selected Poems*, trans. and ed. by Robert Marquez and David Arthur McMurray (Havana, 1975)

Gumbrecht, Hans Ulrich, *In Praise of Athletic Beauty* (Cambridge, MA, 2006)

Guttmann, Allen, 'Out of the Ghetto and on to the Field: Jewish Writers and the Theme of Sport', *American Jewish History*, 74 (1985), pp. 274–86

——, *Sports Spectators* (New York, 1986)

——, *The Erotic in Sports* (New York, 1996)

Halberstam, David, ed., *The Best American Sports Writing of the Century* (Boston, 1999)

Halberstam, Judith, *Female Masculinity* (Durham, NC, 1998)

Haley, Alex, *Roots* (London, 1977)

Hall, Donald E., ed., *Muscular Christianity: Embodying the Victorian Age* (Cambridge, 1994)

Hamill, Pete, *Flesh and Blood* (New York, 1978)

Hammett, Dashiell, *Red Harvest* (London, 1974)

*David Hammons: Raising the Rubble*, exh. cat., The Institute for Contemporary Art, P.S.1 Museum, 1991

*David Hammons in the Hood*, exh. cat., Illinois State Museum, 1993

Hampton, Henry, and Steve Fayer, *Voices of Freedom: An Oral History of the Civil Rights Movement* (New York, 1991)

Hansen, Miriam, *Babel and Babylon: Spectatorship in American Silent Film* (Cambridge, MA, 1991)

Harding, John, with Jack Berg, *The Whitechapel Windmill* (London, 1987)

Harrington, Oliver, *Bootsie and Others* (New York, 1958)

——, *Why I Left America* (Jackson, MI, 1993)

Harris, H. A., *Sport in Greece and Rome* (London, 1972)

Hartley, R. A., *History and Bibliography of Boxing Books* (Alton, Hants, 1988)

——, *More Boxing Books* (Wembley Park, 1995)

Hauser, Thomas, *The Black Lights: Inside the World of Professional Boxing* (New York, 1991)

——, *Muhammad Ali: His Life and Times* (London, 1997)

——, *Brutal Artistry* (London, 2002)

——, *Chaos, Corruption, Courage and Glory: A Year in Boxing* (Toronto, 2005)

——, *The Lost Legacy of Muhammad Ali* (Toronto, 2005)

Harvey, Adrian, *The Beginnings of a Commercial Sporting Culture in Britain, 1793–1850* (London, 2004)

Hayden, Robert, *Poems* (New York, 1975)

Haydon, Benjamin, *The Diary of Benjamin Robert Haydon*, ed. Willard Bissell Pope (Cambridge, MA, 1960)

Hayes, Kevin J., ed., *Martin Scorsese's Raging Bull* (Cambridge, 2005)

Hazlitt, William, *Lectures on the English Poets and The Spirit of the Age* (London, 1910)

——, *Liber Amoris* (London, 1957)

——, *The Fight and Other Writings*, ed. Tom Paulin and David Chandler (Harmondsworth, 2000)

——, *The Selected Writings of William Hazlitt*, vol. 6, *Table Talk*, ed. Duncan Wu (London, 1998)

Healy, Thomas, *A Hurting Business* (London, 1996)

Hedin, Robert, and Michael Waters, eds, *Perfect in Their Art: Poems on Boxing from Homer to Ali* (Carbondale, IL, 2003)

Heinz, W. C., ed., *The Fireside Book of Boxing* (New York, 1961)

——, *The Professional* (Boston, 2001)

Heller, Peter, *In This Corner* (New York, 1994)

Hemingway, Ernest, *In Our Time* (New York, 1986)

——, *Men Without Women* (New York, 1986)

——, *A Moveable Feast* (London, 1984)

——, *Selected Letters, 1917–1961*, ed. Carlos Baker (London, 1985)

——, *The Sun Also Rises* (London, 1976)

——, *Winner Take Nothing* (London, 1977)

Henderson, William, *King of the Gorbals* (London, 1973)

O. Henry, *The Four Million* (London, 1947)

——, *Options* (London, 1933)

Hicks, Granville, et al., *Proletarian Literature in the United States: An Anthology* (London, 1935)

Hietala, Thomas R., *The Fight of the Century: Jack Johnson, Joe Louis, and the Struggle for Racial Equality* (Armonk, NY, 2002)

Himes, Chester, *If He Hollers Let Him Go* (London, 1986)

Hirsch, James S., *Hurricane* (London, 2000)

Hitler, Adolf, *Mein Kampf*, trans. Ralph Manheim (Boston, 1971)

Hoberman, John M., *Sport and Political Ideology* (London, 1984)

——, *Darwin's Athletes: How Sport Has Damaged Black America and Preserved the Myth of Race* (Boston, 1997)

Hogarth, William, *The Analysis of Beauty*, ed. Ronald Paulson (New Haven, 1997)

Holiday, Billie, with William Dufty, *Lady Sings the Blues* (New York, 1976)

Hollinghurst, Alan, *The Swimming-Pool Library* (London, 1998)

Homer, *The Odyssey*, trans. Richmond Lattimore (New York, 1991)

——, *The Iliad*, trans. Martin Hammond (Harmondsworth, 1987)

Horace, *Satires, Epistles and Ars Poetica*, trans. H. Rushton Fairclough (London, 1929)

House, Richard, *Bruiser* (London, 1987)

Howard, Robert E., *Boxing Stories*, ed. Chris Gruber (Lincoln, NE,
2005)

Howard, Seymour, 'Boxing Broadsides', in Elizabeth Adan, ed.,
*Popular Art: Essays on Urban Imagery* (Berkeley, CA, 1992),
pp. 18–19

——, 'Some Eighteenth-Century "Restored" Boxers', *Journal of the
Warburg and Courtauld Institutes* 56 (1993), pp. 238–55

Howe, Irving, *World of Our Fathers* (New York, 1976)

——, *A World More Attractive* (New York, 1963)

Hughes, Bill, and Patrick King, eds, *Come Out Writing: A
Boxing Anthology* (London, 1991)

Hughes, Langston, *Fine Clothes to the Jew* (New York, 1927)

——, 'To Be Somebody', *Phylon*, 11, no. 4 (1950), p. 311

——, *The Big Sea: An Autobiography* (New York, 1993)

——, *Selected Poems* (London, 1999)

Hughes, Thomas, *Tom Brown's Schooldays* (Oxford, 1999)

——, *Tom Brown at Oxford*, 3 vols (London, 1861)

Huntington-Whitely, James, *The Book of British Sporting Heroes*
(London, 1998)

Hurley, Jon, *Tom Spring* (Stroud, 2002)

Illingworth, Montieth, *Mike Tyson* (London, 1992)

Isenberg, Michael T., *John L. Sullivan and His Times* (London, 1988)

James, Henry, *The American* (Harmondsworth, 1991)

——, *The Bostonians* (1886) (Harmondsworth, 1976)

Jensen, Erik, 'Crowd Control: Boxing Spectatorship and
Social Order in Weimar Germany', in Rudy Koshar, ed.,
*Histories of Leisure* (Oxford, 2002)

Johnson, Christopher, 'Anti-Pugilism: Violence and Justice in
Scott's 'The Two Drovers', *Scottish Literary Journal*, 22, no. 1
(May 1995), pp. 46–60.

——, '"British Championism": Early Pugilism and the Works of
Fielding', *Review of English Studies* 47 (August 1996), pp. 331–51

Johnson, Jack, *In the Ring and Out* (New York, 1977)

Johnson, James Weldon, *Along This Way* (New York, 1935)

——, *The Autobiography of an Ex-Colored Man* (Penguin, 1990)

——, *Black Manhattan* (New York, 1991)

——, ed., *The Book of American Negro Poetry* (New York, 1931)

——, *God's Trombone* (New York, 1927)

——, *The Selected Writings, vol. 1: The New York Age Editorials
(1914–1923)*, ed. Sandra Kathryn Wilson (Oxford, 1995)

Jones, James, *From Here to Eternity* (New York, 1953)

Jones, LeRoi, *The Dead Lecturer* (New York 1964)

——, *Home: Social Essays* (New York, 1966)

——, *The Fiction of LeRoi Jones/Amiri Baraka* (Chicago, 2000)

——, *The LeRoi Jones/Amiri Baraka Reader*, ed. William J. Harris
(New York, 1991)

Jones, LeRoi, and Larry Neal, eds, *Black Fire: An Anthology of Afro-
American Writing* (New York, 1968)

Jones, Thom, *The Pugilist at Rest* (London, 1994)

——, *Cold Snap* (London, 1996)

——, *Sonny Liston was a Friend of Mine* (London, 1999)

Joyce, James, *Stephen Hero* (London, 1966)

——, *Ulysses* (Harmondsworth, 1992)

——, *Finnegans Wake* (Harmondsworth, 1992)

——, and Stuart Gilbert, *Letters of James Joyce* (London, 1957)

Joyce, Stanislaus, *My Brother's Keeper* (London, 1958)

Jules-Rosette, Bennetta, *Black Paris: The African Writers' Landscape*
(Urbana, IL, 1998)

Junghanns, Wolf-Dietrich, 'Öffentlichkeiten: Boxen, Theater und
Politik', *The Brecht Yearbook*, 23 (1998), pp. 56–9

Kaes, Anton, Martin Jay and Edward Dimendberg, eds, *The Weimar
Republic Sourcebook* (Berkeley, CA, 1994)

Kahn, Roger, *A Flame of Pure Fire: Jack Dempsey and the
Roaring '20s* (New York, 1999)

Kaye, Andrew M., *The Pussycat of Prizefighting: Tiger Flowers and the
Politics of Black Celebrity* (Athens, GA, 2004)

Kellmann, Steven, ed., *Perspectives on Raging Bull* (Boston, 1994)

King, Martin Luther, *Why We Can't Wait* (New York, 1963)

——, *A Call to Conscience: The Landmark Speeches of Dr Martin
Luther King, Jr.*, ed. Clayborne Crason and Kris Shepard
(New York, 2001)

*Thomas Kilpper: The Ring*, exh. cat., South London Gallery
Projects, 2000

*R. B. Kitaj: A Retrospective*, ed. Richard Morphet, exh. cat., Tate
1994

Klemperer, Victor, *The Language of the Third Reich*, trans. Martin
Brady (New York, 2002)

Knebworth, Viscount, *Boxing*, The Lonsdale Library, vol. 10
(London, 1931)

König, Jason, *Athletics and Literature in the Roman Empire*
(Cambridge, 2005)

Kram, Mark, *Ghosts of Manila* (New York, 2001)

Kuenzli, Rudolf E., ed., *New York Dada* (New York, 1986)

Kühnst, Peter, *Sport: A Cultural History in the Mirror of Art*, trans.
Allen Guttmann (Dresden, 1996)

*Kunst, Sport und Körper: 1926–2002*, exh. cat., Stadstsmuseum,
Düsseldorf, 2003

Kyle, Donald G. and Gary D. Stark, eds, *Essays on Sport
History and Sport Mythology* (College Station, TX, 1990)

Lardner, John, *White Hopes and Other Tigers* (New York, 1951)

Lardner, Ring, *The Best Short Stories of Ring Lardner* (New York, 1957)

——, *Some Champions*, ed. Matthew J. Bruccoli and Richard
Layman (New York, 1992)

Laubreaux, Alin, *Mulatto Johnny*, trans. Coley Taylor (London, 1931)

La Motta, Jake, with Joseph Carter and Peter Savage, *Raging Bull:
My Story* (New York, 1997)

Lee, Gus, *China Boy* (New York, 1991)

Lee, Spike, and Lisa Jones, *Do the Right Thing* (New York 1989)

Lehmann, Rosamund, *The Weather in the Streets* (London, 1981)

Lemert, Charles, *Muhammad Ali: Trickster in the Culture of Irony*
(London, 2003)

Levi, Primo, *The Truce* (1963), trans. Stuart Woolf (London, 1987)

Lévi-Strauss, Claude, *The Elementary Structures of Kinship*, trans.
James Harte Bell et al. (Boston, 1969)

Levine, Peter, *Ellis Island to Ebbets Field: Sport and the American
Jewish Experience* (Oxford, 1992)

Lewis, David Levering, ed., *The Portable Harlem Renaissance*
(Harmondsworth, 1994)

Lewis, Frederick Allen, *Only Yesterday* (New York, 1964)

——, *Since Yesterday: The 1930s in America* (New York, 1986)

Lewis, Wyndham, *The Wild Body* (London, 1927)

——, *Time and Western Man* (London, 1927)

——, *The Art of Being Ruled* (New York, 1926)

——, *Tarr* (Harmondsworth, 1982)

——, *Blasting and Bombardiering* (London, 1967)

Liebling, A. J., *The Sweet Science* (Harmondsworth, 1982)

——, *A Neutral Corner*, ed. Fred Warner and James Barbour (New York, 1990)

Lindsay, Vachel, *Collected Poems* (New York, 1925)

——, *The Art of the Moving Picture* (New York, 2000)

Lloyd, Alan, *The Great Prize Fight* (London, 1977)

Locke, Alain, ed., *The New Negro: An Interpretation* (New York, 1997)

Loeb, Harold, *The Way It Was* (New York, 1959)

Logue, Antonia, *Shadow Box* (London, 1999)

Lois, George, *Covering the '60s: The Esquire Era* (New York, 1996)

——, *Ali Rap: Muhammad Ali, the First Heavyweight Champion of Rap* (2006)

London, Jack, *The Abysmal Brute* (Lincoln, NE, 2000)

——, *Before Adam* (London, 1929)

——, *The Call of the Wild and The Game* (London, 1972)

——, *The Call of the Wild, White Fang and Other Stories* (Oxford, 1990)

——, *A Daughter of the Snows* (New York, 1902)

——, *The Game* (Lincoln, NE, 2001)

——, *The Human Drift* (New York, 1917)

——, *Jack London Reports*, ed. King Hendricks and Irving Shepard (New York, 1970)

——, *John Barleycorn* (Oxford, 1989)

——, *Martin Eden* (Harmondsworth, 1967)

——, *Moon-Face and Other Stories* (New York, 1906)

——, *No Mentor but Myself*, ed. Dale L. Walker and Jeanne Campbell Reesman (Stanford, CA, 1999)

——, *Novels and Stories* (New York, 1982)

——, *The Portable Jack London*, ed. Earle Labor (Harmondsworth, 1994)

——, *Revolution and Other Essays* (London, 1910)

Lonsdale, Roger, ed., *The New Oxford Book of Eighteenth Century Verse* (Oxford, 1984)

Louis, Joe, with Edna Rust and Art Rust, *My Life* (Boston, 1997)

Louvish, Simon, *Monkey Business: The Lives and Legends of the Marx Brothers* (London, 1999)

Lowenthal, Leo, *Literature, Popular Culture, and Society* (Palo Alto, CA, 1968)

Loy, Mina, *The Last Lunar Baedeker*, ed. Roger L. Conover (Manchester, 1997)

Lundberg, George, 'Boxing Should be Banned in Civilized Countries', *Journal of the American Medical Studies*, p. 249 (1983), p. 250

Mailer, Norman, *The Deer Park* (New York, 1957)

——, *An American Dream* (London, 1965)

——, *The Armies of the Night* (Harmondsworth, 1968)

——, *Cannibals and Christians* (London, 1969)

——, *The Prisoner of Sex* (New York, 1971)

——, *Existential Errands* (New York, 1973)

——, *The Presidential Papers* (London, 1964)

——, *The Fight* (London, 1976)

——, *Advertisements for Myself* (London, 1985)

——, *Pieces and Pontifications* (London, 1985)

——, *The Time Of Our Time* (New York, 1998)

Malcolm, James Peller, *Anecdotes of the Manners and Customs of London during the Eighteenth Century* (London, 1808)

Mandela, Nelson, *Long Walk to Freedom* (London, 1995)

Marable, Manning, *Race, Reform and Rebellion: The Second Reconstruction in Black America, 1945–1990* (London, 1991)

March, Joseph Moncure, *The Wild Party and The Set-Up* (Garden City, NJ, 1931)

Margolick, David, *Beyond Glory: Max Schmeling vs. Joe Louis, and a World on the Brink* (London, 2005)

Marquesee, Mike, *Redemption Song: Muhammad Ali and The Spirit of the Sixties* (London, 1999)

Martland, Harrison S., 'Punch Drunk', *Journal of the American Medical Association*, 91, 13 October 1928, pp. 1103–7

Maxwell, William J., *New Negro, Old Left: African-American Writing and Communism Between the Wars* (New York, 1999)

Mayer, Oliver, *Blade to the Heat* (New York, 1996)

McIlvanney, Hugh, *McIlvanney on Boxing*

McIlvanney, William, *The Big Man* (London, 1985)

McKay, Claude, *Harlem Shadow* (New York, 1922)

——, *The Negroes in America*, trans. Robert J. Winter., ed. Alan L. McLeod (Port Washington, NY, 1979)

——, *Home to Harlem* (Boston, 1987)

McKernan, Luke, 'Sport and the First Films', in Christopher Williams, *Cinema: the Beginnings and the Future* (London, 1996), pp. 107–16

McRae, Donald, *Dark Trade: Lost in Boxing* (Edinburgh, 1996)

——, *White and Black: The Untold Story of Joe Louis and Jesse Owens* (New York, 2002)

Mead, Chris, *Champion: Joe Louis Black Hero in White America* (New York, 1985)

Meade, Marion, *Buster Keaton: Cut to the Chase* (New York, 1995)

Mee, Bob, *Bare Fists* (Woodstock, NY, 2001)

Melville, Herman, *Moby-Dick, or, The Whale* (Harmondsworth 1972)

——, *Typee* (London, 1993)

Mendoza, Daniel, *The Art of Boxing* (London, 1789)

——, *The Memoirs of the Life of Daniel Mendoza*, ed. Paul Magriel (London, 1951)

Meriwether, Louise, *Daddy was a Number Runner* (London, 1986)

Meunier, Claude, *Ring Noir* (Paris, 1992)

Messenger, Christian K., 'Jack London and Boxing in *The Game*', *Jack London Newsletter*, 9 (1976), pp. 67–72

——, 'Tom Buchanan and the Demise of the Ivy League Athletic Hero', *Journal of Popular Culture*, 8, no. 2 (Fall 1974), pp. 402–10

——, 'Norman Mailer: Boxing and the Art of His Narrative', *Modern Fiction Studies*, 33, 1 (Spring 1987), pp. 85–104

——, *Sport and the Spirit of Play in Contemporary American Fiction* (New York, 1990)

Miles, H. D., *Pugilistica: A History of British Boxing*, 3 vols (Edinburgh, 1906)

——, *Tom Sayers, Sometime Champion of England, His Life and Pugilistic Career* (London, 1866)

Miller, Davis, *The Zen of Muhammad Ali* (London, 2002)

Miletich, Leo N., *Dan Stuart's Fistic Carnival* (College Station, TX, 1994)

Miller, Stephen G., *Arete: Greek Sports from Ancient Sources* (Berkeley,

CA, 1991)

——, *Ancient Greek Athletics* (New Haven, CT, 2004)

Misson, Henri, *M. Misson's memoirs and observations in his travels*, trans. John Ozell (London, 1719)

Moder, Joseph, *The Adventures of Timothy Twig*, 2 vols (London, 1794)

*Modernism: Designing a New World, 1914–1939*, exh. cat., Victoria and Albert Museum, 2006

Monson, William, and Murray McLean, *On the Ropes* (New York, 1970)

Moore, Thomas, *The Poetical Works of Thomas Moore* (London, 1891)

——, *Tom Moore's Diary: A Selection*, ed. J. B. Priestley (Cambridge, 1925)

Morgan, Johnny, *The Square Circle* (London, 1965)

Morrison, Arthur, *A Child of the Jago* (London, 1996)

——, *Cunning Murrell* (London, 1900)

——, *Tales of Mean Streets* (London, 1927)

Moses, Wilson Jeremiah, *Black Messiahs and Uncle Toms* (Philadelphia, 1993)

Motherwell, Robert, ed., *The Dada Painters and Poets* (Cambridge, MA, 1989)

Mrozek, Donald J., *Sport and the American Mentality, 1880–1910* (Knoxville, TN, 1983)

Mullan, Harry, *Boxing: Inside the Game* (Cambridge, 1998)

Murray, Albert and John F. Callahan, eds, *Trading Twelves: The Selected Letters of Ralph Ellison and Albert Murray* (New York, 2000)

Murray, Yxta Maya, *What It Takes to Get to Vegas* (New York, 1999)

Musil, Robert, *The Man without Qualities*, trans. Sophie Wilkins, 2 vols (London, 1995)

——, *The Confusions of Young Törless*, trans. Shaun Whiteside (Harmondsworth, 2001)

Musser, Charles, *The Emergence of Cinema: The American Screen to 1907* (New York, 1990)

Myler, Patrick, *The Fighting Irish* (Dingle, 1987)

——, *Gentleman Jim Corbett* (London, 1998)

——, *Ring of Hate: The Brown Bomber and Hitler's Hero* (Edinburgh, 2005)

Nabokov, Vladimir, *Glory*, trans. Dmitri Nabokov (Harmondsworth, 1974)

——, *The Annotated Lolita* (Harmondsworth, 1995)

——, *The Stories of Vladimir Nabokov* (New York, 1997)

Nagler, Barney, *James Norris and the Decline of Boxing* (New York, 1964)

Nathan, Daniel A., 'Sugar Ray Robinson, the Sweet Science, and the Politics of Meaning', *Journal of Sport History*, 26, no. 1 (Spring 1999), pp. 163–74

Neal, Larry, *Visions of a Liberated Future: Black Arts Movement Writings*, ed. Michael Schwartz (New York, 1989)

Negri, Antonello, *Aligi Sassu*, trans. Susan Scott (Lugano, 1998)

Newby, Zahra, *Greek Athletics in the Roman World* (Oxford, 2005)

Newton, A. J., *Boxing* (London, 2005)

Norris, Frank, *The Apprenticeship Writings of Frank Norris*, ed. Joseph R. McElrath, Jr. and Douglas K. Burgess, vol. 1 (Philadelphia, 1996)

——, *The Literary Criticism of Frank Norris*, ed. Donald Pizer (Austin, TX, 1964)

——, *McTeague* (New York, 1977)

——, *Moran of the Lady Letty* (New York, 1898)

——, *The Responsibilities of the Novelist and Other Literary Essays* (London, 1903)

Nelson, George, *Hip Hop America* (Harmondsworth, 1999)

O'Connor, Daniel, ed., *Iron Mike: A Mike Tyson Reader* (New York, 2002)

Oates, Joyce Carol, *On Boxing* (London, 1988)

——, *(Woman) Writer: Occasions and Opportunities* (New York, 1988)

——, *Raven's Wing* (London, 1987)

——, *What I Lived For* (New York, 1995)

——, *Where I've Been, And Where I'm Going: Essays, Reviews, and Prose* (New York, 1999)

——, 'Selections from a Journal: January 1985–January 1988', in Daniel Halpern, ed., *Our Private Lives: Journals, Notebooks, and Diaries* (Hopewell, NJ, 1988)

——, 'Rape and the Boxing Ring', *Newsweek*, 24 February 1992, p. 60–61

——, *You Must Remember This* (New York, 1988)

——, *Heat and Other Stories* (New York, 1992)

——, *The Time Traveller* (New York, 1989)

Odd, Gilbert E., *Ring Battles of the Century* (London, 1948)

——, *The Woman in the Corner* (London, 1978)

Odets, Clifford, *Golden Boy and Other Plays* (Harmondsworth, 1963)

Offutt, Chris, *Out of the Woods* (New York, 2000)

Oliver, Douglas, *Three Variations on the Theme of Harm: Selected Poetry and Prose* (London, 1990)

Olsen, Jack, *Cassius Clay: A Biography* (London, 1967)

Oriard, Michael, *Sporting with the Gods: The Rhetoric of Play and Game in American Culture* (Cambridge, 1991)

Orwell, George, *Shooting an Elephant and Other Essays* (Harmondsworth, 2003)

——, *The Collected Essays, Journalism and Letters: Volume 4*, ed. Sonia Orwell and Ian Angus (Harmondsworth, 1970)

Oxberry, William, *Pancratia, or a History of Pugilism* (London, 1812)

Pacheco, Ferdie, *Fight Doctor* (London, 1977)

Pancake, Breece D'J, *The Stories of Breece D'J Pancake* (Boston, 1983)

Pater, Walter, *Greek Studies* (London, 1910)

——, *The Renaissance* (Oxford, 1989)

Paton, W. R., ed. and trans., *The Greek Anthology* (London, 1918)

Patterson, Floyd, *Victory Over Myself* (New York, 1962)

Patton, Sharon F., *African-American Art* (Oxford, 1998)

Paulin, Tom, *The Day-Star of Liberty: William Hazlitt's Radical Style* (London, 1998)

Paulson, Ronald, *Hogarth*, 3 vols (Cambridge, 1991)

Pausanias, *Guide to Greece*, trans. Peter Levi, 2 vols (Harmondsworth, 1971)

Pearlman, Alison, *Unpackagaing Art of the 1980s* (Chicago, 2003)

Pearson, John, *The Profession of Violence: The Rise and Fall of the Kray Twins* (London, 1984)

Penzler, Otto, ed., *Murder on the Ropes: Original Boxing Mysteries* (New York, 2001)

Pepys, Samuel, *The Diary of Samuel Pepys*, ed. John Warrington, 3 vols (London, 1953)

Perry, Imani, *Prophets of the Hood: Politics and Poetics in Hip Hop* (Durham, NC, 2004)

Pettavino, Paula J., and Geralyn Pye, *Sport in Cuba* (Pittsburgh, 1994)

Philonenko, Alexis, *Histoires de la Boxe* (Paris, 1991)

Picket, Lynn Snowden, *Looking for a Fight* (New York, 2000)

*Pictured in My Mind: Contemporary American Self-Taught Art from the Collection of Dr Kurt Gitter and Alice Rae Yelen*, exh. cat., Birmingham Museum of Art, 1995

Pigolf, James, and Robin H. Dunitz, *Walls of Heritage, Walls of Pride: African American Murals* (San Francisco, 2000)

Pindar, *The Odes* (Harmondsworth, 1969)

Piper, Keith, *Step into the Arena: Notes on Black Masculinity and the Contest of Territory* (Rochdale, 1992)

Piozzi, Hester Lynch, *Anecdotes of the late Samuel Johnson, LL.D. during the last twenty years of his life*, ed. S. C. Roberts (Cambridge, 1925)

Plato, *The Laws*, trans. Trevor J. Saunders (Harmondsworth, 1975)

——, *The Republic*, trans. Desmond Lee (Harmondsworth, 1974)

Plimpton, George, *Shadow Box* (London, 1989)

Poliakoff, Michael, *Combat Sports in the Ancient World* (New Haven, 1987)

Pope, S. W., *Patriotic Games: Sporting Traditions in the American Imagination, 1876–1926* (Oxford, 1997)

——, ed., *The New American Sport History* (Urbana, IL, 1997)

Potts, Alex, *Flesh and the Ideal* (New Haven, 1994)

Pound, Ezra, *ABC of Reading* (London, 1951)

——, *Selected Prose 1909–1965*, ed. William Cookson (New York, 1973)

——, *Literary Essays*, ed. T. S. Eliot (London, 1954)

——, *The Pisan Cantos*, ed. Richard Sieburth (New York, 2003)

——, *The Selected Letters of Ezra Pound, 1907–1941*, ed. D. D. Paige (London, 1950)

Powell, Richard J., *Black Art and Culture in the 20th Century* (London, 1997)

Probert, Ian, *Rope Burns* (London, 1999)

Proust, Marcel, *A la recherche du temps perdu*, vols 2 and 3 (Paris, 1987)

The Tenth Marquess of Queensberry, *The Sporting Queensberrys* (London, 1942)

Rabinbach, Anson, *The Human Motor: Energy, Fatigue and the Origins of Modernity* (Berkeley, CA, 1990)

Rader, Benjamin, *In Its Own Image: How Television Transformed Sports* (New York, 1984)

Radford, Peter, *The Celebrated Captain Barclay: Sport, Money and Fame in Regency Britain* (London, 2001)

——, 'Lifting the Spirits of the Nation: British Boxers and the Emergence of the National Sporting Hero at the Time of the Napoleonic Wars', *Identities: Global Studies in Culture and Power*, 12, no. 2 (April–June 2005), pp. 249–70

Raine, Craig, *Rich* (London, 1984)

Ramsaye, Terry, *A Million and One Nights: History of the Motion Picture Through 1925* (New York, 1986)

Reed, Ishmael, *Chattanooga* (New York, 1973)

——, *Shrovetide in Old New Orleans* (New York, 1978)

——, *Conjure: Selected Poems, 1963–1970* (Amherst, MA, 1972)

——, *God Made Alaska for the Indians* (New York, 1982)

——, *Writin' Is Fightin'* (New York, 1988)

——, *New and Collected Poems* (New York, 2006)

Reid, J. C., *Bucks and Bruisers: Pierce Egan and Regency England* (London, 1971)

Reiss, Steven A., *City Games: The Evolution of American Urban Society and the Rise of Sports* (Urbana, IL, 1989)

——, *Sport in Industrial America, 1850–1920* (Wheeling, IL, 1995)

——, ed., *Major Problems in American Sport History* (Boston, 1997)

Recchia, Edward, 'Setting as Narrative Convention: Locales in the Boxing Film', in Paul Loukides and Kinda K. Fuller, eds, *Locales in American Popular Film* (Bowling Green, OH, 1993), pp. 183–203

Reed, J. S., 'Ritualism Rampant in East London – Anglo-Catholicism and the Urban Poor', *Victorian Studies*, 31, 3 (1988), pp. 375–403

Relic, Peter, 'Knockout! The Potent Presence of boxing in the life and music of Miles Davis', *Stop Smiling*, no. 20 (2005), pp. 32–7

Reemtsma, Jan Phillip, *More Than A Champion: The Style of Muhammad Ali*, trans. John E. Woods (New York, 1999)

Remnick, David, *King of the World: Muhammad Ali and the Rise of an American Hero* (London 1999)

Reynolds, John Hamilton, *The Fancy: A Selection from the Poetical Remains of the Late Peter Corcoran* (1820), with notes by John Masefield and illustrations by Jack B. Yeats (London, 1905)

*The Ring and The Glove*, exh. cat., Museum of the City of New York (1947)

Riordan, James, *Sport in Soviet Society* (Cambridge, 1980)

Rippey, Theodore, 'Schmeling, Sharkey, and the Transatlantic Significance of a Low Blow', in Angela Teja et al., eds, *Sport and Cultures: Proceedings of the 9th International Congress of the European Committee for Sport History* (Calopezzati, 2005), pp. 129–37

——, 'Athletics, Aesthetics, and Politics in the Weimar Press', *German Studies Review*, 28, no. 1 (2005), pp. 85–106

Roberts, John W., *From Trickster to Badman: The Black Folk Hero in Slavery and Freedom* (Philadelphia, 1989)

Roberts, Randy, *Jack Dempsey, The Manassa Mauler* (Baton Rouge, LA, 1979)

——, *Papa Jack: Jack Johnson and the Era of White Hopes* (London, 1986)

Roberts, Randy and J. Gregory Garrison, *Heavy Justice: The Trial of Mike Tyson* (Fayetteville, LA, 2000)

Rogin, Michael, *Blackface, White Noise: Jewish Immigrants in the Hollywood Melting Pot* (Berkeley, CA, 1996)

Romano, Frederick V., *The Boxing Filmography: American Features, 1920–2003* (Jefferson, NC, 2004)

*Romantics and Revolutionaries*, exh. cat., National Portait Gallery (2002)

Roosevelt, Theodore, *An Autobiography* (New York, 1985)

——, *The Works of Theodore Roosevelt* (New York, 1926)

——, 'Recent Prize-Fight', *Outlook*, 16 July 1910, pp. 550–51

Rose, Tricia, *Black Noise: Rap Music and Black Culture in Contemporary America* (Hanover, NH, 1994)

Ross, Barney, and Martin Abramson, *No Man Stands Alone* (London, 1959)

Rotella, Carlo, *October Cities: The Redevelopment of Urban Literature* (Berkeley, CA, 1998)

——, *Good with Their Hands: Boxers, Bluesmen, and Other Characters from the Rust Belt* (Berkeley, CA, 2002)

——, *Cut Time: An Education at the Fights* (Boston, 2003)

Roth, Philip, *Portnoy's Complaint* (London, 1969)

——, *The Ghost Writer* (Harmondsworth, 1980)

——, *The Counterlife* (Harmondsworth, 1988)

——, *The Facts* (New York, 1997)

——, *American Pastoral* (London, 1998)

——, *The Human Stain* (London, 2001)

——, *Patrimony* (London, 1999)

——, *I Married a Communist* (London, 1999)

——, *The Plot Against America* (London, 2004)

Rozen, Wayne A., *America on the Ropes: A Pictorial History of the Johnson–Jeffries Fight* (Binghamton, NY, 2005)

Ruffini, Franco, *Teatro e Boxe* (Bologna, 1994)

Runyon, Damon, *More Guys and Dolls* (Garden City, NY, 1951)

——, *On Broadway* (Harmondsworth, 1990)

Rutman, Leo, *Thy Father's Son* (New York, 2002)

Sackler, Howard, *The Great White Hope* (London, 1971)

Sammons, Jeffrey T., *Beyond the Ring* (Urbana, IL, 1980)

——, 'Boxing as a Reflection of Society: The Southern Reaction to Joe Louis', *Journal of Popular Culture*, 16, no. 4 (Spring 1983), pp. 23–33

Sanchez, Sonia, *We a BaddDDD People* (Detroit, 1970)

Sánchez, Yvette, 'Un round de littérature française et la boxe', *Versant*, 40 (2001), pp. 159–71

Sandow, Eugen, *Sandow on Physical Training: A Study in the Perfect Type of the Human Form* (London, 1894)

——, *Strength and How to Obtain It* (London, 1900)

Scanlon, Thomas F., 'Boxing Gloves and the Games of Gallienus', *The American Journal of Philology*, 107, no. 1 (Spring 1986), pp. 110–14

——, *Eros and Greek Athletics* (Oxford, 2002)

Scarry, Elaine, *The Body in Pain* (Oxford, 1985)

——, ed., *Literature and the Body* (Baltimore, 1988)

Schaap, Jeremy, *Cinderella Man* (Boston, 2005)

Schmeling, Max, *An Autobiography*, trans. George B. von der Lippe (Chicago, 1998)

Schrader, Bärbel, and Jürgen Schebera, *The 'Golden' Twenties: Art and Literature in the Weimar Republic* (New Haven, CT, 1980)

Schulberg, Budd, *The Harder They Fall* (New York, 1947)

——, *Some Faces in the Crowd* (London, 1953)

——, *Loser and Still Champion: Muhammad Ali* (London, 1972)

——, *On the Waterfront* (London, 1992)

——, 'The Great Benny Leonard', *Ring Magazine* (May 1980), pp. 32–7

Schwarz, Arturo, *The Complete Works of Marcel Duchamp*, vol. 1 (London, 1997)

Scott, Walter, *Two Stories* (Edinburgh, 2002)

Sekules, Kate, *The Boxer's Heart: How I fell in love with the ring* (London, 2000)

*Self-Taught Artists of the Twentieth-Century: An American Anthology*, exh. cat., Museum of American Folk Art, 1998

Seltzer, Mark, *Bodies and Machines* (New York, 1992)

Senie, Harriet F., and Sally Webster, eds, *Critical Issues in Public Art* (Washington, DC, 1992)

Serling, Rod, *Requiem for a Heavyweight* (London, 1962)

Shange, Ntozake, *Float Like a Butterfly*, with illustrations by Edel Rodriguez (New York, 2002)

Shulman, Arlene, *The Prizefighters* (London, 1995)

Shaw, George Bernard, *Cashel Byron's Profession* (London, 1925)

Shaw, Irwin, *Sailor Off the Bremen* (New York, 1939)

Shay, Art, *Nelson Algren's Chicago: Photographs* (Urbana, IL, 1988)

T. B. Shepherd, ed., *The Noble Art* (London, 1950)

Shipley, Stan, 'Tom Causer of Bermondsey – A Boxer Hero of the 1890s', *History Workshop*, 15 (1983), pp. 28–59

——, 'Boxing', in David Levinson and Karen Christensen, *Encyclopedia of World Sport*, vol. 1 (Santa Barbara, CA, 1996), pp. 147–53

Sinclair, Upton, *The Jungle* (New York, 1960)

Sklar, Robert, *City Boys: Cagney, Bogart, Garfield* (Princeton, 1992)

Smith, Gene and Jayne Barry, eds, *The Police Gazette* (New York, 1972)

Southey, Robert, *Letters from England*, ed. Jack Simmons (London, 1951)

Soyinka, Wole, *Mandela's Earth* (New York, 1990)

Spivey, Donald, ed., *Sport in America* (Westport, CT, 1985)

*The Squared Circle: Boxing in Contemporary Art.*, exh. cat., Walker Art Center, 2003

Steffens, Lincoln, *The World of Lincoln Steffens*, ed. Ella Winter and Herbert Shapiro (New York, 1962)

Steinbeck, John, *Of Mice and Men* (Harmondsworth, 1949)

——, *Of Men and Their Making: The Selected Non-Fiction of John Steinbeck*, ed. Susan Shillinglaw and Jackson J. Benson (London, 2002)

——, *John Steinbeck: A Life in Letters*, ed. Elaine Steinbeck and Robert Wallsten (London, 1975)

Steinberg, Paul, *Speak You Also*, trans. Linda Coverdale with Bill Ford (Harmondsworth, 2001)

Steiner, Jesse Frederick, *Americans at Play: Recent Trends in Recreation and Leisure Time Activities* (New York, 1933)

Stewart-Smith, Elizabeth, *Byron's Screen* (Mansfield, 1995)

Stott, Richard B., *Workers in the Metropolis: Class, Ethnicity, and Youth in Antebellum New York City* (Ithaca, NY, 1990)

Stovall, Tyler, *Paris Noir: African Americans in the City of Light* (Boston, 1996)

Streible, Dan, 'A History of the Boxing Film, 1894–1915: Social Reform and Social Control in the Progressive Era', *Film History*, 3 (1989), pp. 235–57

——, 'Race and the Reception of Jack Johnson Fight Films', in Daniel Bernardi, ed., *The Birth of Whiteness* (New Brunswick, NJ, 1996), pp. 170–200

——, 'Fake Fight Films', in Claire Dupré La Tour, André Gaudreault and Roberta Pearson, *Le cinéma au tourant du siècle* (Québec, 1999), pp. 63–79

Strickland, Edward, 'Boxer Byron: A Clare Obsession', *The Byron Journal*, 17 (1989), pp. 57–76

Sutcliffe, Thomas, 'The Punch', *Watching: Reflections on the Movies* (London, 2000), pp. 33–66.

Sweet, Waldo E., *Sport and Recreation in Ancient Greece: A Sourcebook with Translations* (Oxford 1987)

Suetonius, *The Twelve Caesars*, trans. Robert Graves (London, 1962)

Sullivan, Russell, *Rocky Marciano: The Rock of His Times* (Urbana, IL, 2005)

Tate, Greg, *Flyboy in the Buttermilk: Essays on Contemporary America* (New York, 1992)

Taylor, Frederick Winslow, *The Principles of Scientific Management* (London, 1993)

Taylor, Richard and Ian Christie, eds, *The Film Factory: Russian and Soviet Cinema in Documents, 1896–1939* (London, 1988)

Terry, Wallace, 'Bringing the War Home', *Black Scholar*, 2, no. 3 (1970) pp. 6–18

——, *Bloods: An Oral History of the Vietnam War* (New York, 1984)

Thackeray, William Makepeace, *Vanity Fair* (Oxford, 1983)

——, *Barry Lyndon* (Oxford, 1984)

——, *Roundabout Papers*, ed. John Edwin Wells (New York, 1925)

——, *The Fitz-Boodle Papers* and *Men's Wives* (London, 1857)

'Theatre and Sport', a special issue of *Mime Journal* (1996)

Theocritus, *Idylls*, trans. Anthony Verity (Oxford, 2002)

Theroux, Marcel, *A Blow to the Heart* (London, 2006)

Thomas, Donald, *The Victorian Underworld* (New York, 1998)

Thurman, Wallace, *Infants of the Spring* (New York, 1999)

Toulmin, Vanessa, *A Fair Fight: An Illustrated Review of Boxing on British Fairgrounds* (Oldham, 1999)

Toole, F. X., *Rope Burns* (London, 2000)

——, *Pound for Pound* (London, 2006)

Toomer, Jean, *Cane* (New York, 1988)

Toop, David, *Rap Attack 3: African Jive to Global Hip Hop* (London, 2000)

Torres, José, *Sting Like a Bee* (London, 1971)

Tosches, Nick, *Night Train: The Sonny Liston Story* (Harmondsworth, 2001)

*Transition and Conflict: Images of a Turbulent Decade, 1963–1973*, exh. cat., Studio Museum in Harlem (1985)

Trowbridge, W.R.H., *The White Hope* (London, 1913)

Tully, Jim, *The Bruiser* (New York, 1937)

Tunney, Jay, 'The Playwright and the Prizefighter: Bernard Shaw and Gene Tunney', *SHAW: The Annual of Bernard Shaw Studies*, 23 (2003), pp. 149–54

——, '*Cashel Byron's Profession*: A Catalyst to Friendship – Life Imitates Art', *SHAW: The Annual of Bernard Shaw Studies*, 25 (2005), pp. 52–58

Tzara, Tristan, *Seven Dada Manifestos and Lampisteries*, trans. Barbara Wright (London, 1992)

Uglow, Jenny, *Hogarth* (London, 1997)

Umphlett, Wiley Lee, *The Sporting Myth and the American Experience* (Cranbury, NJ, 1975)

Unterharnscheidt, Friedrich, and Judith Taylor-Unterharnscheidt, *Boxing: Medical Aspects* (San Diego, 2003)

Updike, John, *The Rabbit Omnibus* (London, 1990)

Urrea, Luis Alberto, *In Search of Snow* (New York, 1995)

Vance, Norman, *The Sinews of the Spirit* (Cambridge, 1985)

Van Deburg, William L., *New Day in Babylon: The Black Power Movement and American Culture, 1965–1975* (Chicago, 1992)

Van Loan, Charles E., *Taking the Count: Prize Ring Stories* (New York, 1915)

Veblen, Thorstein, *The Theory of the Leisure Class* (New York, 1953)

Vergani, Orio, *Poor Nigger*, trans. W. W. Hobson (London, 1930)

Virgil, *The Aeneid*, trans. David West (Harmondsworth, 1990)

——, *The Georgics*, trans. L. P. Wilkinson (Harmondsworth, 1982)

Wacquant, Loïc, *Body and Soul: Notebooks of an Apprentice Boxer* (Oxford, 2004)

Wade, Alex, *Wrecking Machine: A Tale of Real Fights and White Collars* (London, 2005)

Ward, Geoffrey C., *Unforgivable Blackness: The Rise and Fall of Jack Johnson* (New York, 2004)

Washington, Booker T., *Frederick Douglass* (New York, 1969)

——, *Up from Slavery* (New York, 1996)

——, *The Booker T. Washington Papers*, vol. 10, ed. Louis R. Harlan and Raymond W. Smock (Urbana, IL, 1981)

——, *The Booker T. Washington Papers*, vol. 12, ed. Louis R. Harlan and Raymond W. Smock (Urbana, IL, 1982),

Weatherby, W. J., *Squaring-Off: Mailer v. Baldwin* (London, 1977)

Weinberg, S. Kirson and Henry Arond, 'The Occupational Culture of the Boxer', *American Journal of Sociology*, 57, no. 5 (March 1952), pp. 460–69

West, Mae, *The Constant Sinner* (London 1995)

——, *Goodness Had Nothing to Do with It* (London, 1996)

Whitfield, Christopher, ed., *Robert Dover and the Cotswold Games: Annalia Dubrensia* (Evesham, 1962)

Whitman, Walt, *Leaves of Grass* (Oxford, 1990)

——, *I Sit and Look Out: Editorials from the Brooklyn Daily Times*, ed. Emory Holloway and Vernolian Schwarz (New York, 1932)

Wideman, John Edgar, *Sent For You Yesterday* (London, 1986)

Wiggens, David K., 'Good Times on the Old Plantation', *Journal of Sport History*, 4, no. 3 (1977), pp. 260–84

——, 'From Plantation to Playing Field', *Research Quarterly for Exercise and Sport*, 57, no. 2 (1986), pp. 101–16

——, 'Peter Jackson and the Elusive Heavyweight Championship: A Black Athlete's Struggle Against the Late Nineteenth Century Color-Line', in Ernestine Jenkins and Darlene Clark Hine, eds, *A Question of Manhood: A Reader in US Black Men's History and Masculinity*, vol. 2 (Bloomington, IN, 2001), pp. 283–308

Wiggens, William H., 'Jack Johnson as Bad Nigger: The Folklore of His Life', *Black Scholar* (January 1971), pp. 4–19.

——, 'Boxing's Sambo Twins: Racial Stereotypes in Jack Johnson and Joe Louis Newspaper Cartoons, 1908–1938', *Journal of Sport History*, 15, no. 3 (Winter 1988), pp. 242–54

Wiley, Ralph, *Serenity* (Lincoln, NE, 2000)

Willett, John, *The New Sobriety, 1917–1933: Art and Politics in the Weimar Period* (London, 1978)

Williams, Tennessee, *Collected Stories* (New York, 1985)

Wilson, Sondra Kathryn, ed. *The Messenger Reader* (New York, 2000)

Winckelmann, Johann, *Writings on Art*, ed. David Irwin (London, 1972)

Winmerding, John, *American Views: Essays on American Art* (Princeton, 1991)

Wodehouse, P. G., 'The Pugilist in Fiction', *The Independent Shavian*, 30, nos 1–2 (1992), pp. 12–14

——, 'The Debut of Battling Billson', in *He Rather Enjoyed It* (London, 1924)

——, *Bachelors Anonymous* (Harmondsworth, 1973)

——, *Psmith Journalist* (Harmondsworth, 1970)

Wolfe, Tom, *Radical Chic and Mau-Mauing the Flak Catchers* (New York, 1971)

Wolfe, Tom, and E. W. Johnson, eds, *The New Journalism: An Anthology* (London, 1975)

Woods, Alan, 'James J. Corbett: Theatrical Star', *Journal of Sport History* (Summer 1976), pp. 162–75

Wright, Richard, *Black Boy* (Longman, 1970)

——, *Uncle Tom's Children* (New York, 1993)

——, *Native Son* (1940) (Harmondsworth, 1972)

——, 'Joe Louis Uncovers Dynamite', *New Masses*, 17 (8 October 1935), pp. 18–19

——, *Lawd Today* (London, 1969)

Virgil, *The Aeneid*, trans. David West (Harmondsworth, 1990)

X, Malcolm, with Alex Haley, *The Autobiography of Malcolm X* (London, 1965)

——, *Malcolm X on Afro-American History* (New York, 1967)

——, *Malcolm X: Speeches at Harvard*, ed. Archie Epps (New York, 1968)

——, *By Any Means Necessary* (New York, 1970)

——, *Malcolm X talks to Young People*, ed. Steve Clark (New York, 1991)

Zangwill, Israel, *The Children of the Ghetto* (London, 1998)

Zinberg, Len, *Walk Hard – Talk Loud* (New York, 1950)

# Filmography

*Against the Ropes*, dir. Charles S. Dutton, 2004
*Ali*, dir. Michael Mann, 2001
*Battling Butler*, dir. Buster Keaton, 1926
*The Bells of St Mary's*, dir. Leo McCarey, 1945
*The Big Punch*, dir. Sherry Shourds, 1948
*Black and White*, dir. James Toback, 1999
*Body and Soul*, dir. Robert Rossen, 1947
*The Boxer*, dir. Jim Sheridan, 1997
*Die Boxerbraut*, dir. Johannes Guter, 1926
*Broken Noses*, dir. Bruce Weber, 1987
*Cain and Mabel*, dir. Lloyd Bacon, 1936
*The Calcium Kid*, dir. Alex De Rakoff, 2004
*The Champ*, dir. King Vidor, 1931
*Champion*, dir. Mark Robson, 1949
*Cinderella Man*, dir. Ron Howard, 2005
*City for Conquest*, dir. Anatole Litvak, 1940
*City Lights*, dir. Charlie Chaplin, 1931
*Combinations*, dir. Patrick A. Gaucher, 2005
*The Crowd Roars*, dir. Richard Thorpe, 1938
*Day of the Fight*, dir. Stanley Kubrick, 1951
*Do the Right Thing*, dir. Spike Lee, 1989
*Fallen Champ*, dir. Barbara Kopple, 1993
*Far and Away*, dir. Ron Howard, 1992
*Fat City*, dir. John Huston, 1972
*From Here to Eternity*, dir. Fred Zinnemann, 1953
*Gentleman Jim*, dir. Raoul Walsh, 1942
*Girlfight*, dir. Karyn Kusama, 2000
*Golden Boy*, dir. Rouben Mamoulian, 1939
*The Great John L.*, dir. Frank Tuttle, 1945
*The Great White Hope*, dir. Martin Ritt, 1970
*The Great White Hype*, dir. Reginald Hudlin, 1996
*The Greatest*, dir. Tom Gries, 1977

*The Harder They Fall*, dir. Mark Robson, 1956
*The Hurricane*, dir. Norman Jewison, 1999
*The Irish in Us*, dir. Lloyd Bacon, 1935
*It's Always Fair Weather*, dir. Stanley Donan and Gene Kelly, 1955
*The Joe Louis Story*, dir. Robert Gordon, 1953
*The Kid from Brooklyn*, dir. Norman Z. McLeod, 1946
*Kid Galahad*, dir. Michael Curtiz, 1937
*Kid Galahad*, dir. Phil Karlson, 1962
*The Killers*, dir. Robert Siodmak, 1946
*Killer's Kiss*, dir. Stanley Kubrick, 1955
*The Leather Saint*, dir. Alvin Ganzer, 1955
*The Life of Jimmy Dolan*, dir. Archie Mayo, 1933
*The Milky Way*, dir. Leo McCarey, 1936
*Million Dollar Baby*, dir. Clint Eastwood, 2004
*Monkey on My Back*, dir. Andre de Toth, 1957
*Muhammad Ali, The Greatest*, dir. William Klein, 1974
*My Life as a Dog*, dir. Lasse Hallström, 1985
*The Negro Soldier*, dir. William Wyler, 1944
*Night After Night*, dir. Archie Mayo, 1932
*On the Ropes*, dir. Nanette Burstein and Brett Morgen, 1999
*On the Waterfront*, dir. Elia Kazan, 1954
*Palooka*, dir. Benjamin Stoloff, 1934
*Pat and Mike*, dir. George Cukor, 1952
*The Prizefighter and the Lady*, dir. W. S. Van Dyke, 1933
*The Power of One*, dir. John G. Avildsen, 1992
*Pulp Fiction*, dir. Quentin Tarantino, 1994
*Raging Bull*, dir. Martin Scorsese, 1980
*Red Rain*, dir. Laura Plotkin, 1999
*The Roaring Twenties*, dir. Raoul Walsh, 1939
*Rocky*, dir. John G. Avildsen, 1976
*Rocky V*, dir. John G. Avildsen, 1990
*Rocky Balboa*, dir. Sylvester Stallone, 2006
*Romy and Michelle's High School Reunion* dir. David Mirkin, 1997
*School Daze*, dir. Spike Lee, 1988
*The Set-Up*, dir. Robert Wise, 1949
*Shadow Boxers*, dir. Katya Bankowsky, 2000
*She Hate Me*, dir. Spike Lee, 2004
*Snake Eyes*, dir. Brian De Palma, 1998
*Somebody Up There Likes Me*, dir. Robert Wise, 1956
*Spirit of Youth*, dir. Harry Fraser, 1938
*The Super Fight*, dir. Murray Woroner, 1970
*They Made Me a Criminal*, dir. Busby Berkeley, 1939
*Undisputed*, dir. Walter Hill, 2002
*When We Were Kings*, dir. Leon Gast, 1996
*Winner Take All*, dir. Roy Del Ruth, 1932

# Discography

*Antipop vs. Matthew Shipp* (Thirsty Ear, 2003)
*Battle of the Blues*, vols 1–4 (King, 1959)
Beenie Man, *Undisputed* (Virgin, 2006)
*The Big Break Rapper Party: Sounds of New York, USA, vol. 1* (Traffic, 2006)
*Blues Ladies, 1934–1941* (Document, 1996)
Canibus, *Lyrical Warfare* (Group Home, 1998)
Cassius Clay, *I Am The Greatest!* (Columbia, 1963)

Coolio, *El Cool Magnifico* (Hot, 2002)

*Cool Whalin': Bepop Vocals* (Spotlight, 1979)

Miles Davis, *Conception* (Prestige, 1951)

——, *A Tribute to Jack Johnson* (Columbia, 1971)

——, *The Complete Jack Johnson Sessions* (Columbia, 2003)

Mos Def, *The New Danger* (Geffen, 2004)

Snoop Doggy Dogg, *Doggystyle* (Columbia, 1987)

Bob Dylan, *The Bootleg Series, 1961–1991* (Sony, 1991)

——, *Another Side of Bob Dylan* (Columbia, 1964)

——, *Self Portrait* (Columbia, 1970)

——, *Desire* (Columbia, 1975)

Das EFX, *Straight Up Sewaside* (East/West Records, 1993)

EPMD, *Strictly Business* (Priority, 1991)

Faithless, *Outrospective* (Cheeky, 2001)

MC Hammer, *The Funky Headhunter* (Warner, 1994)

*Hits and Misses: Muhammad Ali and the Ultimate Sound of Fistfighting* (Trikont, 2003)

DJ Jazzy Jeff and The Fresh Prince, *And In This Corner . . .* (Jive, 1989)

Big Daddy Kane, *Long Live the Kane* (Warners, 1988)

——, *Looks Like a Job For* (Cold Chillin' Records, 1993)

Constant Lambert, *Orchestral Works*, BBC Concert Orchestra (ASV, 1999)

*Joe Louis: An American Hero* (Sony, 2001)

Roy Jones Jr, *Round One: The Album* (Body Head, 2002)

——, *Body Head Bangerz: Volume One* (Body Head, 2004)

LL Cool J, *Bigger and Deffer* (Def Jam, 1987)

——, *Mother Said Knock You Out* (Def Jam, 1990)

——, *Survival of the Illest*, vol. 1 (Def Jam, 1998)

——, *G.O.A.T.* (Def Jam, 2001)

Wynton Marsalis, *Unforgivable Blackness* (Blue Note, 2004)

Twan Mac, *Survival Tactics* (Bangin Beats Entertainment, 2004)

Ewan MacColl, with Peggy Seeger, *The Fight Game: A Radio-Ballad About Boxers* (Topic, 1999)

Memphis Minnie, *Queen of the Blues* (Columbia, 1997)

Motion Man, *Clearing the Field* (Threshold, 2002)

Morrissey, *The World of Morrissey* (Reprise, 1995)

——, *Southpaw Grammar* (Reprise, 1995)

Parliament, *Chocolate City* (Casablanca, 1975)

Phil Ochs, *The Early Years* (Vanguard, 2000)

Onyx, *Bacdafucup* (Universal/Def Jam, 1993)

Public Enemy, *Yo Bum Rush the Show* (Def Jam, 1987)

Richard Pryor, *An Anthology, 1968–1992* (Warner, 2001)

Simon and Garfunkel, *Bridge Over Troubled Water* (Columbia, 1970)

Heltah Skeltah, *Nocturnal* (Priority, 1996)

*Sucker Punch: Jamaican Boxing Tributes* (Trojan, 2004)

Johnny Wakelin, *Reggae, Soul and Rock 'n' Roll* (Astor, 1976)

Warren Zevron, *Sentimental Hygiene* (Virgin, 1987)

*When We Were Kings* (Polygram, 1996)

# Acknowledgements

The pictures in this book were made possible by generous grants from the British Academy, the Chambers Fund, Department of English, University College London, and the Dean's Fund of the Faculty of Arts, UCL, whose support I warmly acknowledge. I would also like to thank the many archivists and librarians with whom I have worked, and especially the staff of the UCL Media Resources Department, and everyone at Reaktion.

In the years I've been writing this book, almost everyone I know or have met has helped in some way: suggesting things to read, watch or listen to, lending and giving me books, tracking down obscure references, videoing movies, scanning pictures, translating poems, inviting me to give papers, writing references, reading and improving my writing, buying lunch and keeping me well, clothed and happy. I am particularly grateful for substantial help in all these matters to: Rosemary Ashton, Matthew Beaumont, Kiki Benzon, Michael Berkowitz, José Luis Bermúdez, Ada and Andrew Boddy, Janet Boddy, Tracy Bohan, Rachel Bowlby, Richard Brown, David Brauner, Christina Büchmann, Ardis Butterfield, Melissa Calaresu, Eoin Cannon, Jean Chothia, Jim Clemens, William W. Cooke, Valentine Cunningham, Greg Dart, Paul Davis, Jim Endersby, Silvia Frenk, David and Tanya Frisby, Tony Gee, Paul Giles, Heather Glen, Richard Gray, Fiona Green, Phil Horne, Luke Hughes-Davies, Erik Jensen, Wolf-Dietrich Junghanns, Danny Karlin, Thomas Karshan, Patrick, Gabriel and Oscar Kennedy, Simon Kövesi, Robin and Tad Krauze, Leya Landau, Alison Light, Tim Mathews, Sam Matthews, Andrew McDonald, Tôbi Megchild, Kathy Metzenthin, Charlotte Mitchell, Brian Moore, Edwin Morgan, Gary Moser, Michael Newton, Pete Nicholls, Lida Oskinova, Ian Ralston, David Robb, Carlo Rotella, Joan-Pau Rubiés, Steven Rushforth, Helen Russell, Elaine Showalter, Michael Silk, Ali Smith, Hugh Stevens, John Sutherland, Pete Swaab, Pam Thurschwell, Jay and Kelly Tunney, Ruti Ungar, Val Williamson, Sarah Wood, Henry Woudhuysen, and Yo Zushi. I would also like to thank the students at Dartmouth College, Dundee University and University College London with whom I discussed some of this material.

I am particularly grateful to those who read, and improved, parts of this book: Jaś Elsner, Geoff Gilbert, Lee Grieveson, Ali Smith, Pam Thurschwell and Mark Whalan, and especially, for their generosity and stamina to the bitter end, Andrew Boddy and David Trotter.

If I thanked David Trotter for everything I should, these acknowledgements would be longer than the book itself.

# Photo Acknowledgements

The author and publishers wish to express their thanks to the below sources of illustrative material and/or permission to reproduce it. (Locations of artworks not in private hands are also given below.)

Photo Acme Newspictures: 101; Addison Gallery of American Art, Phillips Academy, Andover, MA: 38; Altonaer Museum, Hamburg: 62; photo courtesy of the artist (Emma Amos), © 1998: 130; The Art Institute of Chicago: 24; photo author: 151; Berlinische Galerie Landesmuseum für Moderne Kunst, Fotografie und Architektur (photo courtesy of VG Bild-Kunst): 96; Beinecke Rare Book and Manuscript Library, Yale University (Yale Collection of American Literature): 99; The British Library, London (photo British Library Reproductions): 8; British Museum, London (photos © The Trustees of the British Museum): 2 (Vases C 334), 4 (Vases B 124), 5 (D84 and D85), 11, 14; photo courtesy of Cambridge and County Folk Museum: 51; The Cleveland Museum of Art: 40 (Hinman B. Hurlbut Collection); Delaware Art Museum, Wilmington, DE: 39 (Sloan Collection), donated to Detroit Institute of Arts (photo Paul Mastrogiacomo): 152; photo courtesy of the artist (Godfried Donkor): 125; from Christos Doumas, *The Wall Paintings of Thera* (Athens: The Thera Foundation, 1992): 43; Ecole Nationale Supérieure des Beaux-Arts, Paris (photo ENSB-AP): 23; Fondazione Aligi Sassu e Helenita Olivares, Città di Lugano: 61 (photo FASE-HOL); photo from the archive of the Glasgow *Evening Times*: 102; Hampton University Museum, Hampton, VA: 77; photo courtesy of the artist (Peter Howson) and Flowers East Gallery, London: 110; Hugh Lane Gallery, Dublin: 41 (reproduced with the permission of Michael Yeats); courtesy of the Huntingdon Library, San Marino, CA: 73; photo courtesy of the Huntingdon Library, San Marino, CA: 42; The Jewish Museum, London: 44, 74; photos courtesy of the John Murray Archive, London: 18, 19; photo by permission of Landov Galleries: 150; photos courtesy of the Lewis Walpole Library, Yale University: 10, 45; Library of Congress, Washington, DC (Prints and Photographs Division): 13 (British Cartoon Collection; LC-USZ62-132988), 30 (Brady Civil War Photograph Collection; LC-DIG-cwpb-02637, LC-DIG-cwpb-02638), 46 (British Cartoon Prints Collection; LC-USZC4-6765), 50 (LC-USZ4-7692); photo Mary Evans Picture Library: 59; photo courtesy of the Michael Hoppen Gallery, London: 70; from H. D. Miles, *Pugilistica* (Edinburgh, 1906): 3; photo courtesy of the artist (Paul-Felix Montez): 132; Museo Nazionale Romano: 7; Museum of the City of New York: 94; photos courtesy of the Museum of the City of New York: 37 (Byron Collection), 94; Collection Museum of Contemporary Art San Diego (photo Philipp Scholtz Ritterman): 124; photo courtesy of the NAACP: 105; photo courtesy of the National Art Museum of Sport, Indianapolis: 147; National Gallery of Art, Washington, DC: 31, 82 (Chester Dale Collection); National Portrait Gallery, London: 15, 16; National Portrait Gallery, Washington, DC: 88, 114 (photo © The Andy Warhol Foundation for the Visual Arts, Inc./ARS, NY and DACS, London); photo courtesy of the New York Public Library for the Performing Arts (Astor, Lenox and Tilden Collection; Billy Rose Theatre Collection): 81; Newstead Abbey, Nottinghamshire: 18, 19; The Gallery, Petworth House, Sussex (photo courtesy of The National Trust Photographic Library, London): 22; drawing reproduced from Ernst Pfuhl, *Malerei und Zeichnung der Griechen* (Munich, 1923): 6; photo courtesy of the Pennsylvania Academy of the Fine Arts, Philadelphia: 66; Philadelphia Museum of Art: 52; private collections: 20, 97 (photo courtesy of the Galerie St Etienne, New York), 111 (photo courtesy of the Michael Rosenfeld Gallery, LLC, New York); Social and Public Art Resource Center, Los Angeles (photo courtesy of the SPARCLA, © SPARC www.sparcmurals.org): 118; photo courtesy of the Sterling and Francine Clark Art Institute, Williamstown, MA: 65; Tate, London (photo © Tate, London 2008): 17; photo United Studios: 100; Victoria and Albert Museum, London (photo V&A Images/Victoria & Albert Museum, London): 98; photo courtesy of the Vonderbank Art Galleries, Berlin: 123; The Walter O. Evans Collection of African American Art, Savannah, GA: 55 (photo courtesy of Linda J. Evans and the Walter O. Evans Collection of African American Art), 144; Whitney Museum of American Art, New York: 87; The Whitworth Art Gallery, University of Manchester: 1.

# Index

474

478